BY HARRISON KINNEY

Dear Katharine and Andy

We have been as busy as a turkey fancier since we got home 2 weeks ago, looking for a place to live. etc. Found it — Woodbury, a dream, a poem of a house with all facilities, one of the nicest places we had taken it, I noticed lots of Ohio book and I had rented the place from the widow Columbus man, friend of my father. Honey is dog book illustrating EBW's Hopes here. We gotta see Diving to Columbus in October No trace of Althea

Love

# The THURBER LETTERS

## THE WIT, WISDOM, AND SURPRISING LIFE
## OF JAMES THURBER

**HARRISON KINNEY**, *editor*

*with Rosemary A. Thurber*

SIMON & SCHUSTER

*New York   London   Toronto   Sydney   Singapore*

SIMON & SCHUSTER
Rockefeller Center
1230 Avenue of the Americas
New York, NY 10020

The cartoon on page 145 is through the kind permission of *The New Yorker.*

For information regarding special discounts for bulk purchases,
please contact Simon & Schuster Special Sales at
1-800-456-6798 or business@simonandschuster.com

Designed by Jeanette Olender
Manufactured in the United States of America

3   5   7   9   10   8   6   4   2

Library of Congress Cataloging-in-Publication Data
Thurber, James, 1894–1961.
[Correspondence. Selections]
The Thurber letters : the wit, wisdom, and surprising life of
James Thurber / Harrison Kinney, editor, with Rosemary A. Thurber.
p.   cm.
1. Thurber, James, 1984–1961—Correspondence.
2. Humorists, American—20th century—Correspondence.
3. Cartoonists—United States—Correspondence.
I. Kinney, Harrison.   II. Thurber, Rosemary A.   III. Title.
PS3539.H94Z48 2003          818'.5209—dc21
[B]       2003045718
ISBN 0-7432-2343-8

# ACKNOWLEDGMENTS

Thurber rarely made carbon copies of his typewritten correspondence and it is our good luck that Helen, his second wife, whom he married in June 1935, saw to it that duplicates were made from then on. It is our greater good luck that a number of recipients of his earlier letters saved them for personal reasons, long before their importance to literary history could have been evident. Most of such correspondence has come to rest in the Thurber Collection of the Rare Books and Manuscripts department of Ohio State University, carefully but generously monitored by Geoffrey Smith, the curator, and his ever-considerate assistant, Elva Griffith. My Columbus friend, Julie McGuckin, assisted me in the lengthy perusal of the hundreds of letters there.

Thurber might well consider it his poor luck that the women he courted by pen and typewriter hoarded his romantic, wild and theatrical overtures, lectures, scoldings and pleadings. In 1981 Ann Honeycutt wrote to E. B. White: "I have a big stack of Thurber letters I would like to put under lock and key for the next ten years. . . . I have lied to Jim's biographers, family, et al over the years, claiming I have no letters. . . ." But within two years, needing money, "Honey" sold the letters to a patron of Cornell University, where they reside in the Carl A. Kroch Library. Thurber's letters to "Andy" and Katharine White are also at Cornell in the Rare and Manuscript Collection. Others addressed to Katharine are in the archives of the Bryn Mawr College Library.

Dr. Lewis Branscomb, former O.S.U. Professor Emeritus of Thurber Studies, tracked down both Minnette Fritts, in Washington State, and Eva Prout, in Florida, and persuaded them to send their Thurber letters to the O.S.U. collection. Years before, the night before Minnette's first child was born, she believed she was going to die and had thrown in the furnace all of Thurber's early letters to her from Washington and Paris, to her later regret. He resumed writing her in 1928; those letters she kept.

Thurber sometimes wrote Eva Prout as often as two or three times a day in 1920. When she and her husband moved to Florida in the 1930s she stored most of Thurber's letters in the basement of a friend's home in Cincinnati, to be sent for later. A pipe burst in the basement and the Thurber letters were lost in the flood, except for "a special few" she had taken with her.

In Columbus, The Thurber House, a unique repository of Thurber memorabilia and Thurber-related literary activity, was helpful in publicizing my search for Thurber letters, enabling me to obtain several from such loyal Thurber buffs as Stuart Hample of New York City and Judy Hahn of Dallas, Texas.

A good friend, Janet Stone Hall, of Newport, Rhode Island, prowling the more literary web sites, spotted the notice of a Thurber letter owned by Julie Chitwood of Gilbert, Arizona. The long, entertaining letter, written in 1919 to three Red Cross girls who shared Thurber's Parisian pension and were being transferred to "Roumania," had been stored in a box of World War I correspondence for eighty years. One of the Red Cross addressees was Mrs. Chitwood's great-aunt, who knew when a letter was worth keeping.

In 1984 *The New Yorker* magazine contributed its archives, dating to 1924, to the New York Public Library. The library staff has been years in the sorting, the enormous quantity of the files measured in linear feet. With the kind help of Mimi Bowling, Curator of Manuscripts, and the efficient staff of the library's Manuscripts and Archives Division, I found a number of Thurber's inter-office written communications, heretofore unknown. John O'Hara's daughter, Wylie, kindly loaned me the Thurber cartoon of her father.

Thurber donated the written products of his huge research for his book, "The Years with Ross," to the Beinecke Library at Yale University, whose staff was cordially cooperative on all of my visits there.

Rosemary Thurber has been steadfast in her support of this project, sending from her Michigan home hundreds of photocopies from her extensive literary inheritance. Her daughter, Sara Sauers, was vital to the search for letters and pictures. Rosemary's agent, Barbara Hogenson, has brought to the book's process a sure competence honed by her years of experience in getting Thurber books published.

Thomas Kunkel, the skilled editor of a volume of Harold Ross's letters, was kind enough to warn me: "Your biggest problem will be in deciding what to leave out." It came as no surprise to discover that he knew what he was talking about. As a lifelong Thurber admirer who continues to wish his memory and his readers the best, I can only hope that my decisions were the right ones.

To Sandra Blanton

# CONTENTS

# The THURBER LETTERS

# INTRODUCTION

James Thurber, 1894–1961, continues to be recognized fondly as one of the predominant and finest American humorists of the twentieth century. Thanks to the thousands of Thurber devotees the world over, most of his many drawings, stories, fables, memoirs, and essays remain available in print, in a dozen languages, on audiotapes, and adapted to movies and the stage. He continues not only as a literary legend. The late William Shawn, editor of *The New Yorker* magazine, extolled Thurber's role in helping set that new and struggling magazine of the twenties on its successful course. "Certainly," Shawn wrote, "there will never be an issue of *The New Yorker* of which Thurber is not a part."

Thurber was a first-rate mimic of others, and funnier than most stand-up comics at parties, but—to quote from the definitive biography of Thurber *(James Thurber: His Life and Times)*—"his life was beset by the childhood loss of an eye, a frustrating first marriage, disappointments in love, medical problems and the blindness that not only ended his drawing but necessitated an irritating dependence on others."

Though Thurber often made comic use of himself in most of his writing, he rarely intended it as literal autobiography. Like any good humorist, he skillfully and effectively employed exaggeration and cheerful, unmeant self-deprecation, as much for his own entertainment as that of the reader. Very little of his personal life, with its moments of pain, anger, affection, protest, triumph, sacrifice, and bravery, can be surmised from what he wrote for publication. It is his letters—to family; to friends in Ohio, Europe, Bermuda, in book publishing, theater, and film; to *New Yorker* colleagues; and to women with whom he was, usually hopelessly, in love—that comprise a reliable and fascinating portrait of Thurber, the man and artist, and offer a vivid understanding of what largely motivated his remarkable prose and art. Some of his most quotable letters are to strangers, for he generously answered the dozens of letters he received from admirers, aspiring writers, and friends of friends who continually sent him plays, articles, and fiction for his comment.

Thurber delighted in the malapropisms of foreign-born handymen and semi-literate maids. Like most white Americans of his day, he was slow to recognize the sad sociology that conditioned the language of blacks that he could so accurately imitate in recitation and writing. Long before he came to recognize it, however, his personal relations with those who worked for the Thurbers over the years had always been marked by mutual respect and affection. Eventually his compassionate liberal and political stances were sufficient to earn him a place on the "Americans to be watched" list of the FBI during the lamentable McCarthy "Age of Suspicion."

The legacy of this inveterate letter-writer includes a treasure of neat handwritten and cleanly typed letters from his early days, many of them masterpieces of wit, story-telling, and intellectual insight. When, in his mid-forties, eye operations put an end to his typing, he at first resorted to penciling large-sized words on yellow copy paper in letters to personal friends, but soon was dictating all his letters and manuscripts to a secretary. This enriched the Thurber literary heritage, for in dictation he was no longer limited by the mechanics of hand- or typewriting, nor, in his blindness, distracted by his surroundings. Blindness freed him to roam and report the interior landscape of his ever-original mind. His blurred distinctions between dreams and reality are often the fruitful sources of his art, and they permeate his letters. His proprietary love of language is frequently reflected in his responses to letters from his readers. He never allowed language to stand still; he reveled in it not only as a means of ingenious creative expression but as a playground, in which he found the potential for wordplay irresistible.

Though what he wrote for publication was tightly disciplined, his letters to friends are often filled with puns and deliberate violations of grammar in the interests of entertaining. This has sometimes made the editing of his letters challenging, even a guessing game. The goal here has been to correct Thurber's unmeant typographical errors while preserving the idiosyncratic mannerisms that have long been referred to helplessly as "simply Thurber." Another of his tendencies was to sign his letters and then go on writing quite as if there had been no complimentary close. The absence of a signature usually means that Thurber signed, in scrawled pencil, the original, mailed letter. In summary,

I would describe editing certain Thurber letters as similar to trying to herd cats. Still, the patient proofreading of Rosemary Thurber and her daughter, Sara, has reinforced my belief that there has been no betrayal of Thurber's letter-writing personality herein.

Important to tracking his career are the early, chatty letters he wrote his family, especially to his younger brother, Robert, in Columbus, Ohio. Though in later life Thurber suffered an emotional collapse after undergoing five unsuccessful eye operations, he rallied to continue both his work and a warm, courageous correspondence with Dr. Gordon Bruce, the surgeon. He often kept the doctor entertainingly informed as to the status of his fading eyesight.

Thurber's letters trace, in wondrous fashion, his progress from immature, lovesick college boy to youthful code clerk with the American embassy in Paris; his days of reporting for *The Columbus Dispatch;* his infatuations with a co-ed at Ohio State University and, later, a star of stage and screen, a grade-school classmate he had worshipped from boyhood; his introduction to play-writing through a college theater group; his marriage to another co-ed, Althea Adams; their time in Paris in the mid-twenties; their falling-out and reunion in New York; his job on *The New York Post;* the first "Thurber dog"; getting hired by *The New Yorker;* co-authoring a bestseller with E. B. White; the gradual souring of his long-standing relationship with the Whites; his frenetic pursuit of Ann Honeycutt; his marriage to Helen Wismer; his publishing adventures; co-authoring a play, *The Male Animal,* with Elliott Nugent; his infatuation with Jane Williams of Bermuda; his developing, affectionate interest in his young daughter, Rosemary; his stormy dealings with *The New Yorker;* his close friendship with Peter De Vries; his cooling friendship with the Whites over *The Years with Ross;* his Broadway appearance in his own revue, *A Thurber Carnival;* the draining efforts to get the revue staged in London; his tragic last days. The comments in his personal letters on all these events, the majority of them never before made public, contribute to an entertaining, informal form of autobiography.

Thurber's surviving letters begin in 1918, when he was twenty-three, and are presented here in somewhat chronological order by date, unless a lingering issue makes a brief concentration of letters more comprehensible. Thurber seemed unable to write a letter that lacked some form of humor, insight, amiable instruction, or general interest of value to us all. Among the warmest, most affectionate, and funniest were those he wrote to his daughter from her early teens until his death. I view her consent to the release of these and all of her father's available correspondence for selection, editing, and publication as a gratifying enrichment of the world of literary humor.

Harrison Kinney

# THE THURBER YEARS

James Grover Thurber was born in Columbus, Ohio, on December 8, 1894, to Charles and Mary A. Fisher Thurber, the second of three sons. Charles was a hardworking, underpaid civil servant most of his life. Mary, or "Mame," given to mischievous pranks and tall stories, is credited with setting the wild examples for dealing with the world that Thurber would follow as a literary humorist. At age seven he lost his left eye when playing a bow-and-arrow game with his brother, leaving him less active athletically as a boy and more of a reader. Popular with his classmates, he was elected president of his high school senior class. His first published short story appeared in his high school quarterly, *The X-Rays,* in 1913, as did a sentimental ode to the family pets, Scotty and Rex, an early indication of a lifelong affinity with dogs.

At Ohio State University, Thurber became friends with the accomplished former child actor Elliott Nugent, whose helpful interest in Thurber led to the latter's transformation from a withdrawn bookworm into an outgoing, witty and well-liked fraternity brother. Professor Joseph Taylor introduced Thurber to the works of Henry James, who became a lifetime literary idol of Thurber's. He was a co-editor of the campus newspaper, *The Lantern,* and wrote and drew for the school's humor magazine, *The Sun-Dial,* eventually becoming its editor.

With America at war, Thurber left college in 1918, without graduating, to become a code-clerk trainee with the State Department in Washington, D.C. During his four months there Thurber wrote his first personal letters—long, lovesick, and surprisingly adolescent ones—to Nugent, mostly about his infatuations with O.S.U. classmate Minnette Fritts and a former grade-school classmate, Eva Prout, now a professional singer and actress. He arrived in France November 13, 1918, working the next fifteen months as a code clerk at the American embassy in Paris. He wrote long letters home—principally to his brother Robert—and to Nugent and Eva. In Paris his emotional reaction to his first sexual experience seems to have led to his not writing letters at all for a time, causing concern among family and friends.

Back in Columbus by February 1920, Thurber courted Eva with impassioned letters and visits to her home in Zanesville, Ohio, to Mame's disapproval. The romance didn't survive the year. He soon became interested in O.S.U.'s dramatic group, The Scarlet Mask, for which he would write the book and lyrics of several productions. In August he was hired as a reporter by *The Columbus Dispatch*. Ted Gardiner, a local businessman, John McNulty, a reporter with the *Ohio State Journal,* and Herman Miller, a graduate student and, later, an English instructor at O.S.U., became his lifelong friends in this period and beneficiaries of Thurber's prized letters. In 1921 he met Althea Adams, an O.S.U. sophomore; they were married the next year.

In 1923, Thurber was given a weekly half-page of the *Dispatch*'s Sunday edition to fill with bits of comic commentary and cultural notes of local interest. Called "Credos and Curios," the feature was cancelled after six months. Disappointed, he quit the paper and, with Althea, spent the summer of 1924 in a friend's cottage in Jay, New York, unsuccessfully trying to freelance. Returning to Columbus that fall they both worked on Scarlet Mask productions and at part-time theater and public relations jobs.

In May 1925 they traveled to France, where Thurber tried writing a novel and then took work with the Paris edition of *The Chicago Tribune*. In the fall they moved to Nice where Thurber co-edited the Riviera edition of the "Trib." The following June, out of work, discouraged and plagued financially, he returned to New York, sending for Althea later with borrowed money. They spent the summer of 1926 in Gloversville, New York, at a friend's summer residence, another failed attempt at freelancing. Thurber took a job that fall with *The New York Post*.

In 1927 he made his first sale—a short humorous piece—to *The New Yorker*. He had briefly met E. B. White, already a staff writer with the magazine, at the apartment of mutual friends. White introduced him to Harold Ross, the editor, who hired him as an unlikely "managing editor" in February 1927. That uneasy arrangement lasted for six months, after which Thurber processed nonfiction copy for publication and finally was given the Talk of the Town department to edit and rewrite. Working on his own time he continued to contribute to the magazine the personal comic essays known as "casuals," which became his literary trademark and, to a greater extent, that of *The New Yorker*.

Thurber and White shared a small office where White, intrigued by Thurber's "doodling," recognized and promoted Thurber's talent as an artist to Ross and to the book publisher, Harper & Bros. Thurber and White collaborated on *Is Sex Necessary?*, a spoof of the current self-help books. It became a bestseller, featuring Thurber's first published drawings. White, who married Katharine Angell at the end of 1929, remained a literary inspiration of Thurber's for most of his life, though Thurber's persistent evidences of misogyny, increasingly aimed at Katharine, gradually drove the men apart socially.

Beginning in 1926, Thurber and Althea, both disappointed with their marriage, underwent several brief separations. In 1927 Thurber met Ann Honeycutt, who became the object of his obsessive fascination for nearly seven years, largely recorded in the passionate, pleading letters he wrote her. She enjoyed his company but refused his repeated offers of marriage. In 1929, after a temporary reconciliation, the Thurbers moved to a country home in Connecticut where Althea raised show dogs. Their daughter, Rosemary, was born in New York City on October 7, 1931. The decade of the 1930s was Thurber's best; his prolific output included a large majority of the stories and drawings for which he is best remembered.

In 1935, Althea divorced Thurber. When he heard that Honeycutt was to wed St. Clair McKelway, a prominent writer and editor at *The New Yorker*, Thurber promptly married Helen Wismer, a pulp-magazine editor.

Thurber left the *New Yorker* staff shortly after his marriage, though remaining a regular contributor. On a trip to Bermuda in 1936, the Thurbers became fast friends and eventual frequent correspondents with Jane and Ronald Williams, publisher of *The Bermudian*. Thurber was soon contributing essays to Williams's struggling little publication at no charge. In 1936, also, Thurber was expressing his negative views of the Thirties' political, literary left in long letters to Malcolm Cowley, as well as in book reviews and satiric essays.

In May 1937, the Thurbers began an eleven-month tour of England, France and Italy, followed by a four-month stay on the Riviera. Most of his letters from abroad were to the Whites, though he also stayed in touch with the Williamses, Nugent, Robert Coates, McNulty, Honeycutt, and McKelway.

In September 1938, the Thurbers rented a house in Woodbury, Connecticut, the first of such rentals before they settled on the purchase of "The Great Good Place," a large, old colonial in West Cornwall. The next year, 1939, was an unusually productive one for Thurber, during which he wrote his *Fables for*

*Our Time, The Last Flower,* and "The Secret Life of Walter Mitty." It was also the year that he and Helen traveled to Los Angeles where Thurber and Nugent collaborated on a play, *The Male Animal,* and the year in which his good eye began to fade seriously.

*The Male Animal* opened in New York on January 9, 1940, to favorable reviews, providing Thurber with his first substantial income. That year he underwent five eye operations by Dr. Gordon Bruce that did little to inhibit the onset of near-blindness. Despite Thurber's disappointment and a postoperative nervous collapse the summer of 1941, he remained an admiring correspondent of Bruce's. He gamely wrote a column for the newspaper *PM* that year and continued to contribute to *The Bermudian.* No longer able to see to type, he tried handwriting in pencil on yellow copy paper for a time but gradually turned to dictating his letters and manuscripts to a secretary. The flow of books of his collected casuals and drawings continued. Through exhausting concentration and the aid of a Zeiss Loop, or jeweler's glass, Thurber continued to draw intermittently until 1951.

The war having interrupted their Bermuda trips, the Thurbers spent their fall vacations at The Homestead in Hot Springs, Virginia. When the shortage of gasoline made commuting by car to the city from West Cornwall difficult, they rented an apartment in Manhattan. Agreeing to speak at a fund-raising event for *Poetry Magazine* in 1944, Thurber met Peter De Vries, its editor and an admirer of Thurber's work. The two men would remain loyal friends and correspondents. Thurber submitted De Vries's writing to Harold Ross who hired him as poetry editor and "Notes and Comment" writer. De Vries would become best known as a writer of comic novels.

In 1945, the best of Thurber's work to that point was published in *The Thurber Carnival,* a bestseller that greatly increased the number of his readers. He refused an election to the National Institute of Arts and Letters because his personal icon, E. B. White, had not been invited to join. When Samuel Goldwyn purchased the film rights to "The Secret Life of Walter Mitty," Thurber was retained to work with the regular scriptwriter in adapting the short story to the screen. His suggestions, which filled a number of letters to the West Coast, were all rejected. His dislike of the eventual movie was inevitable.

Learning that O.S.U. was changing the name of Thurber's beloved *Sun-Dial,* Thurber wrote to the university's president in fervent protest, getting the title restored. Blindness had led to Thurber's listening to the radio a great deal, and in 1947 he became interested in researching the radio soap-opera industry for a series of *New Yorker* articles. He also began examining his family's past for what would become *The Thurber Album*. His treatment of his father in that family history created a storm of angry letters between him and his brother Robert.

The excesses of Congress's Un-American Activities Committee began to attract his worried attention. Meanwhile his teen-age daughter, Rosemary, was visiting him frequently and receiving his entertaining letters at school. Fritzi Von Kuegelgen became his West Cornwall secretary in 1948 and the principal transcriber of Thurber's dictation until nearly the end of his life.

By 1950, Thurber was a frequent guest on radio and television programs. His work now included children's books along with the continued collections of his casuals and drawings. His fables and stories were being adapted to music and stage. He announced in 1951 that the self-portrait he drew for *Time* magazine's cover story about him would be his last drawing. He refused an honorary degree from O.S.U. to protest its practice of screening campus lecturers for any hints of "un-American" ideology, but he received honorary doctorates from Kenyon, Williams, and Yale.

In the spring of 1952, Thurber became afflicted with a hyperthyroid condition, wrongly diagnosed and treated, which lasted nearly two years. At times he couldn't tolerate alcohol or even tie his shoes, and, wild with frustration, was irritable with everyone, a condition that led to acid but often funny replies to letters from people seeking his help or advice. In February 1953, he attended Rosemary's marriage to Frederick Sauers in Philadelphia. His letters to the newlyweds were frequent and often hilarious.

After Ross's death in December 1951, Thurber steadily cooled toward *The New Yorker*'s content and its editors and they toward him. He more frequently sold his work to other publications. He was also preoccupied with writing a play about Ross and *The New Yorker* (never produced) and further plagued by what Helen described to their agent, Jap Gude, as mental aberrations, or "The Thurbs." It was an especially difficult time for Thurber. In 1953, Helen, his "seeing-eye wife," suffered a detached retina, and Thurber's frantic efforts to track down his eye surgeon attracted international press attention.

The Thurbers spent the summer and fall of 1955 in Europe. Temporarily reconciled to *The New Yorker* and its fiction editor, Gus Lobrano, Thurber resumed his contributions. Then Lobrano died, and Thurber argued with his next editor, William Maxwell, over the editing of Thurber's *The Wonderful O*. It was finally rejected, further alienating Thurber from the magazine.

In November 1957, his "The Years with Ross" articles began to run in *The Atlantic Monthly*. Preparation for the series, which resulted in a bestselling book, generated more Thurber correspondence than even that of *The Thurber Album*. Old *New Yorker* associates and friends sent him long letters of reminiscences, to which he replied in kind. But a number of Ross's former colleagues and contributors resented the book as a put-down of the founding editor. Thurber's disillusionment with *The New Yorker* editorially was augmented by his belief that he was never adequately compensated for his contributions to it, the subject of a number of his letters to the magazine's administration.

In 1960, some of Thurber's prose and drawings were put together as a musical revue that made it to Broadway. Later he joined the cast, playing himself. The next year the Thurbers traveled to England to promote the revue's British production. When no commitments could be found for staging the show, the Thurbers returned home dejected and worn out. Small strokes, undiagnosed, were resulting in Thurber's increasingly erratic behavior, evidenced in his final letters. He collapsed from a massive brain hemorrhage in his room at the Algonquin Hotel in October 1961, and died a month later, his obituary appearing on the front page of newspapers across the country.

# the

## EMERGING YEARS

*Except for accompanying his father on a business trip to Cleveland when in his teens, Thurber had not ventured far from Columbus until 1918 when, at age twenty-three, he entrained for Washington, D.C., as a State Department code-clerk trainee. He at once began writing his close friend and fraternity brother, Elliott Nugent. Nugent, already planning a career as actor and playwright, probably kept Thurber's adolescent outpourings as stage material. Nugent and his father did write a play,* The Poor Nut, *a few years later, whose principal, a bewildered and comic college student, was based on Thurber.*

*Throughout his life Thurber rarely found lasting satisfaction in his relations with women, almost, it seems, by design. He was handicapped by a prolonged and naïve incomprehension of his own sexual emotions, and imprisoned by an unrealistic, romantic "story book" view of the opposite sex. As he acknowledges, he preferred the chase to the quarry, the excitement of courtship to that of conquest. His strange variety of misogyny left him unable to fully accept or reject the often-baffled women who interested him. Here his headlong fascinations swing between Eva Prout, film and stage performer, and Minnette Fritts, an O.S.U. classmate. "Pomerene" was an under-secretary of state.*

## To Elliott Nugent

*THE NEW EBBITT*
*Army & Navy Headquarters, Washington, D.C.*
*Friday, June 28, 1918*

Mr. Elliott J. Nugent
Dover, Ohio

My dear old confrere, Nugey:

   Time has not yet served to efface your blonde handsomeness from my retentive memory, old keed. I have been in the capitol of our lil old nation just one week today, and every now and then I spare a moment for reminiscence on the college days etc. Sounds like the mournful words of one bidding adieu to his youth, doesn't it? Well, not youth exactly, Elliott, but certain of the haunts and pastimes and ways of things connected with youth, such as the "keen, bitter-sweet' days, blazoned against the night." For there you are in the navy, and there everyone else is in the navy except the misguided few who are trench food. And here I am in Washington intent on vying with the whole darn enlisted bunch in the matter of ultimate distance from Ohio State attained. When I think of the old institution with its rich gallery of imperishable pictures by Memory, I can see now only a drab chromo of the well-known Duke of Medina [Virgil "Duke" Damon], studying in a far corner, a solitary figure in the old Phi Psi Castle. That is my vision of next year.

I am not going back, Nugey.

If you have tears of joy or regret or whatnot, prepare to shed them.

Nugget, old fella, I am promised a place with an American Embassy, told that I can begin preliminary work in the State Dept here in a few days—to last a week or 10 days—and then go over. Furthermore and best surprise yet, it is almost a certainty that I will be assigned to Berne, Switzerland, where the well known Bernie Williamson is.

We came here with some good letters, especially 2 personal notes to Pomerene's secretary from some mutual friends of his and my dad's—newspaper fellows with a drag. We were then sent to the office of the 3d assistant Sec'y. of State where a dream of a brunette, just my type and not over 27, quietly informed us that she had charge of those appointments, that there was an opening and that I could have it, after my papers had gone thru the necessary channels. The Hague was the place. Then I mentioned about Bernie, whereupon she gave me another smile (there were several) and said she would very gladly shift the 6 or 8 fellows who were listed for Berne over to other places, and give that to me. It was all so quick and miraculously easy that I am dazed yet. The only ways I can account for the speed and certainty of her words is (if you'll pardon me and likewise God save the mark) that the lady was impressed with me. Pomerene's Secretary told us we could be certain of a place but might have to wait 6 months or a year as Pomerene himself had 4 recommendations in ahead of mine. . . .

That about covers my present status and my prospectus, I guess. As far as things else go—in Washington—the phrase "historical interest" describes my daily life in a nut-shell. I have seen more "here lies," more "This was builts", more "in the original handwritings" and that sort of stuff here than I imagined existed. But my dear fellow much of it is really interesting with a punch. And one can trust the relics in the Library of Congress to be authentic. It is only when one discovers, after adding up on his fingers the various individual ones he has seen—that Booth wore six spurs on his right boot the night he shot Lincoln, that one loses some zest. That is more or less a fanciful illustration, however. In the Congressional Library we saw the original draft of the Gettysburg Address. It contains on the first page 6 or 8 changes—additions or erasures. One line is like this, if I can remember it: "as ~~the~~ a final resting place ~~of~~ for those who here etc." You see even the wonderful grammarian Abe had to moil and toil a bit with his Mss. Also the original draft of the Second Inaugural, with the famous words staring up at you in Lincoln's own pen-script "With malice towards none, with charity for all." . . .

. . . Dad goes back tomorrow and I will be like a painted ship upon a painted ocean. Another phrase from that same poem will fit here too. "Water, water everywhere—" Washington is bone dry. The only thing I've seen in the way of liquor here is the law. Papa asks me to add his best regards and luck. . . .

Now, please, old rounder pal o'me' yout', *Write me quick*. I want to know how much more time you get before they sink you etc.

     Yours in Phi Psi

     Jim

&#x219d;   &#x219d;   &#x219d;

*1301 E St. N.W., c/o Post Cafe,*
*Washington, D.C.*
*July 16, 1918*

Dear old Pythias:

So a pair of Brown Eyes has wooed you away from old John Typewriter and allowed me to pine and waste away worrying about just what sector of the sea had embraced your sunken form. No, my dear Nugey, in all our many lil talks over the W.K. Omars; you never told me a word about the love that came but once, and then perhaps too soon. . . . The Romance of me life is, too, just such an affair as our well-meaning parents laugh to scorn, only I was not quite so precocious as to play Lothario at the callow age of knee high to a duck. Mine was one of the legended "school boy and girl" affairs. I played 15 opposite her 14 in the drama "The Seventh Grade," and ten years have passed, friend of me college days, and I love her yet. . . . I once wrote this wonderful girl a letter, 7 years after we parted back in the grammar grades—or three years ago. I was lifted aloft to places where cherubim twitters by a 12 page answer from Colorado Springs asking me to write again which I did in a way that set me back 8 cents for postage of the Rellum, addressed, as she requested, care of her sister 203 Underwood St., Zanesville, Ohio. No response. And, quite like the lackadaisical Thurber, I let it ride from thence to nownce. . . . But her voice, Nugey, her voice! . . . Hence, the stage for her. But she had ruined John voice when young. Thence, the movies. Thence, vaudeville. Now, Lord only knows. Ask your dad if ever in his theatrical circles he saw or heard of a certain little Dream named Eva Prout.

But, Nugums, I rave—where is the Blasety of yesterday! And now I'm going to tell you how I lost my mind. You remember The Minnette? Right, oh. . . . Of course, as you know, I at one time—and still—was rather attracted by the Fritts. . . . The Phi Psi Xmas dance was my first and only date. Until a week before I left.

Columbus, that week, heaved a huge Win-the-War parade. Thousands thronged the main travelled marts. In this vast crowd I upheld the basis of all O. Henry stories, by meeting Minnette. A date was inevitable. We saw Marguerite Clarke in "Prunella", which, by the way, I liked very much—hope you saw it. Took her in old John K. Reo, eats at Marzettis, 1.15 a.m. Date two nights later. Karl Finn, Tom Meek out of luck. Moonlight, Reoings along the Scioto; in brief, all the old paraphernalia and stage drops. And, deus ex machina, the Thurberian damn temperament or lack of balance. Oh, well, hell, Nugget, it's gone pretty damn far and I only wish I could hope for a repetition of the Minnette engagement history. But a little hunch informs me I'm in, that's all. . . . At any rate, I'll never be able to get back home with the suitcase I brought here, on account of Minnette's loving letters taking up so darn much space. And, Nugey, like a damn fool, I can't retrench or nothin! I haven't the heart to appear less amourous than I was during the moonlight madness of those few dates. I like Minnette very much, more than any girl at school by far, as you are aware; she used all her tricks them nights—and, there you are—or, rather, old thing, theah I am, don't you gathah? I think that we are engaged. Go ahead, you blonde Don Juan, and laugh your head off! Now I could learn to love the kid, and I'm sure that as married couples go, we would be domestically out there. But, Nugey, the blow that cools James is the Hope that Spouts eternal about the One Girl. Someday, somewhere I'll find her. I've quite an O'Henry philosophy and Faith. Oh, quite. I'm positive that me and the Eva are

Hero and Leonidas, or Heroine and Alexander or whoever it was, those eternal destined lovers, that swam the Halcyon. "Two shall be born" etc. The drift is yourn, I presume. . . .

But Time and Change now whet their rapiers and run the rest of the cast into separate wings where the forgetting is good, and, I hope, the suitability of affection is rife. For, dearest old Fellow, I have formally been appointed to the American legation at Berne and have accepted. Got the official letter here Friday, and am awaiting draft release and required Birth Certificate so that I can begin my "several weeks" course of instruction in the State Dep't here. The appointment is "duration of the war." . . . I expect to be here "in training" at least 2 weeks, maybe 3, possibly 4. Then home for 5 days or a week. That means Columbus about the middle or 3rd week of August—and you may be called the first, or thereabouts.[1] . . . I hope, my dear Nugey, that you do not take merely a poet's desire for a lyric in your case with the old love. I might wish for your philandering to cease, except, that I want us both to be free to fling a few twosome parties when this man's war is over, without having to dodge friend wife to arrange them. Marriage is all right in its place and time, but the Paldomain of Men must not be jeopardized for a mere—a mere quibbling of matrimony. I demur. Sounds like Isle d'Amour. But please be good and sincere with Brown Eyes, thus not emulating me. . . .

I really should shoot myself at sunrise, but moonlight and Minnette and 15 gals of gas leads the way that madness lies. I wouldn't dare show you the answers I send to her letters, simply because I believe I have compromised myself so that I can't get out of it, without being of the genus mucker or cad. . . . She is really a fine girl, and of all the kisses I have ever kissed none can compare to the peculiar quality of hers. . . . Gawd help me. I either want to be saved, or— garçon, a love potion, queek!

I guess your alert intellect now feels my predicament. I welcome your satire. Shoot! . . .

It's now 1.17 so good night, laddie, and when you write, you old DonjuanlothariapythiasRomeoCyranodebergerackberrygatherer—give me from the store of your experience and knowledge of sex problems and 5 part movies, some advice. But for God's sake keep my confessions to your ain self—Love towards you, Nugey,

Jim in old Phi Psi forever.

*James G. Thurber, 330 East Gay St.,*
*Columbus, Ohio*

*The Raleigh, Washington, D.C.*
*August 25, 1918*

Dear Nugums:

Pardong the delightful eyes rest I have given you, but you will come to know that atrocities in correspondence are always begun by me and reprisal is a weapon for my friends. . . .

However, something has happened to make further delay in weeping on your shoulder impossible. You will recall the status of the Minnette affair. . . .

Minnette kept on writing—and still does—about two to my one, and more loving each time. And like a damn fool—quite in character—I haven't the heart to register coolness. I tried it once and it was misconstrued resulting in a binding confession of the old undying stuff from Minnette. Really I do like her very, very much, because she is to me, I am positive, what she has never been to any of the other luckless lads, I mean she has done with trifling, jipping et al and she's mine for life. Don't think me a credulous, blind fish. She's been writing for 2 months and I know. She told Mullie that she had only known one man she would marry—I'm elected. The paradox is nice: I'm elected, but I refuse the nomination. There it is in a Chestertonian nutshell. But now for the worst:

3 weeks ago I wrote to the little girl of my schooldays and heart, taking a wild chance of reaching her. I wrote one regular Thurberian masterpiece, almost spraining my medulla, pen finger and eyes in composing the thing. Consider the artistic impulse, the pure font of inspiration. Madly in love with her at 14. She leaves her schooldays' sweetheart for a stage career. Five years after, he sees her name in a Los Angeles paper as playing out there and writes. She answers very delightfully and at length from Colorado Springs. After an interval I am set back 6¢ in stamps for another letter. This four years ago. No response. I believe she doesn't want to play any more, is engaged—married— thinks I'm a funny sort of curiosity—or boresome—and so I get peeved, sad, bitter and so forth and light a cigarette. Four years drift, and fate flings Minnette into my unanxious arms. In one of my last Sun-Dials appeared this poem by the erratic editor:

> I held her in my arms,
> This one at present dear,

And there came from out the past
Your vision clear.

The human touch is strong,
but close and warm as faith—
clings the memory of you,
My sweetheart wraith.

Words to that effect, a trifle more sand-papered, but no less insignificant. At that time Minnette was no more to me than a part of my memories of the Christmas Phi Psi dance—but still as you know, a name to conjecture about. You will remember my nutty infatuation as displayed to you in Dover, and also your nice damping down of old John damper. Now Minnette couldn't have held my thoughts for ten seconds then, if it had not been that I had absolutely reasoned my one and only love was gone for good. I imagined her laughing at my last letter—4 years ago—and giving it to her maid to read. Ten years away from me and a gay life en stage. You follow me in my figuring myself s.o.l. with her, don't you? Hence my forced attraction to the M.F.

One night Mullie and I had a M. date together. Afterwards a cigarette at Mullie's, and a confession from me as to my one and only, including the statement that Mullie was safe, as I couldn't fall in love with M. if I sprained 106 bones in the effort. Mullie, tickled to death, confides this in M. the next day. . . .

So I told Minnette "nuts to the Eva", and I lied and said I kidded Mullie to relieve his fears about me. What else could I do—she had got by that time a tentative line of "I'm for you, Minnie" from me. . . .

Yesterday I got two letters. One from M. ended with her jubilant over the fact that Mullie was wrong about my "grammar school" girl. The other, of course, from Eva. Wonderful letter—must have taken her 2 hours to write. Wants me to come to Zanesville (O.) where she lives and see her before I go to Berne. In my letter I expressed a craftily-worded desire of the kind. She repeats her wish to see me. . . .

Someway or other I'll square things with Minnette, like a gent. It was awful, but Lord knows it happened and it has to stop. I really believe Minnette is the kind who really can't be hit beyond repair. Heavens knows also I'd rather face a firing squad composed of Beta dentists rather than go back and see her, but once I get out of this deep town I'll get a shot of Old Something and prepare for the Scene. . . .

I know I have your sympathy, satire and best hopes, same as old John Always. There'll be more to tell and perhaps more satire and sympathy from you next time I write. . . .

I hope you have a trick of saving letters you get.

I leave the figuring out of that to you, my dear Watson.

> Always your
> philandering Don Juan of a
> luckless Lothario
> Jim

&. &. &.

*1301 E St N.W., Washington D.C.*
*Sunday, Sept. 15, 1918*

Dear Bringer of Wistaria into Waste places:

. . . The well-meaning folks o'mine did not forward your letter till yesterday, since they have been expecting me home every day, and since I have been expecting the same thing and so advised them even two weeks ago to be wary of sending important advices and missives to me here. Six weeks is the average stay of one in my position of trust and responsibility in this lovely, languorous war capital, and I am now in my ninth week. However, no definite visit here is stipulated and length of dolce far niente in this tranquil, dreaming world-conflict burg depends on many things, such as tall ships that sail amain, forinstance. . . .

. . . I realize what an iconoclastic thing a girl's voice is and how simple it is for the mere curve of a girl's cheek to smash the philosophy of a young lifetime. . . . The average girl is alway either an actress off stage or a girl "made up", or a mixture or vice-versa or what not. Only she never says which, leaves it to you to find out whether you have dashed into a movie scene or otherwise. Possibly she doesn't know herself.

All of which is an introduction to the present stage-setting of "The Minnette."—quotations for the comedy, plain Minnette, if it is real. . . . I wrote her what, under the circumstances, could not but seem a crude, smashing letter, rather contradictory, somewhat disconnected and certainly all the proof she needed to serve as a basis for insincerity on my part. Her answer was one of the most wonderful letters I ever got. Chuck full of winsomeness, cleverness, charm, naiveté, wistfulness, truth, sincerity and whimsicality. In the 3 months of letters from her I have really come to care greatly for Minnette. Perhaps she understands just how to "play" me, perhaps she really does care very lots. Certain facts make me believe the latter. At any rate she is a girl of whom I would not tire for, oh, ever so long, and a wife whom I could not fail to learn to love. She would be a wonderful pal, an understanding companion and all one might look for, if one were looking for things. Many men do. I could, if I made my mind up to it. But I would have to shut up a certain part of me for life, reconstruct a few eccentric ideas and forget many things in order to chime with Minnette. And those things are the things that to me mean what we're here for. In the case of Eva, the only girl, there is a fire and a crazy, *unreasoning* desire, and things Shelleyan and similar unpractical junk that eclipse all the things that are Minnettes. Minnette may be just the medicine for my ills, Eva merely an irritant—but the ills are mine and what's mine is me, and why try to be an electrical engineer, even tho' you could, if you'd rather starve in a garret. Tolerance of Luxury vs a penchant for penny. Something of the damfool sort.

Of course I still have Eva to see, to hear and to observe. Time often raises hell. Young dreams may be mirages. Romance may pall. I may be disillusioned or merely out of luck. Anything. Hence my last chapter is yet to be added. Please withhold the rubber stamps marked "life" "love" "comedy" "novice-stuff" until I advise further, let us hope in your room in Castle Phi Psi very very soon. . . .

> Here's to the Prettiest one.
> Your chattel for aye,
> Jim

Regards n' everything to whoever of the lads are there, if any. Don't even know when State opens this year; if it opens. Afraid to learn of prospects.

> O tempora, O moses, o hell

> Jim

❦  ❦  ❦

> *J.G. Thurber, 1301 E St N.W.,*
> *Washington D.C.*
> *October 15, 1918*

Dear Nugey:

At first blush, yes, it does look as if I had accepted a position of great trust and responsibility with John S. Wheat Co., and had been supplied with a handsome quire of paper, really "out of sight," hence quire invisible. However, uh huh. These are potential menus that never will become kinetic, the property of one George P. Martin, an Ohioan, owner of The Post Restaurant here and a Prince of Good Fellows. I struck up an acquaintance with him in June when I first came to Washington, an acquaintance which has become a very pleasurable friendship. We room at the same place and I spend much of my leisure at the Post Cafe—the "Cafe" part of the name being a rusty relic of the good old days. Quite Bohemian, too, me boy, since it takes its name from the Post newspaper whose reporters yahs and yahs ago held forth above its tables and above its wines, rolling Bull Durham and discussing the cherchez la femme of the Big Lead Pipe Murder Story. "George," as I call him invariably, albeit he is 59, supervises his place of business until 1 A.M. or later, and since I work from 4.30 PM till midnight, I always run down to the Post, smoke one of George's Murads or give him one of my Omars, order a cup of finely brewed coffee from a buxom waitress whom I chuck under ums 'ittle chin—and occasionally write a letter. Tonight the supply of paper I had is exempt, I mean extinct, and a frenzied search revealed only this rococo stuff. After this lengthy explanation I feel you will overlook this letter, I mean this paper.

. . . I admit I was in the deeps for a spell after your letter telling all about hells' bells bonging on the campus where sweet chimes were wont to ching, but shortly after dispatching my grayer letter back at you, I rose like the Phoeninix or Sphinix from the ashes and lo, I am once again not low. So, if you should meet me on the street and say " 'Lo, Jimmy," I'd say "hi, Nugget." The question of altitude is, I trust, settled.

However, the World is not laughing with me. I have a bet with a bird here that the next bit of Hell to take place will be the entire destruction of that region west of the Mississippi by floods—he bets the next thing will be the spread of painters colic among all the little babies of the world. But it was two days ago that I made the bet and now I feel I should have said the next holocaust, cataclysm and hellsbelling would be the entire disappearance of water from the world or the unputdownable uprising of maniacs, or yet the conquest of Ohio by the Bolsheviki. What is your pet hunch? There ain't no use dodging the mournful truth that times ain't what they used to be. However, being by nature an oculist, I mean optimist, I see the faint flush of the dawn of a newdick, I mean a new day, thru' the blackness of the pit from pole to slav, I mean from pole to pole. You mentioned Mary Flu in your letter,—(I refuse to call it John) Well, here's hoping Dover doesn't get in bed with it as badly and thoroly as Washington. All one sees here is nurses & hearses and all he hears is curses and worse. And such a heroic thing to pass out with—Influenza! dying of influenza in these times of brave, poetical deaths. Allan Seeger was a lucky bird. I imagine him writing:

"I have a tryst with influenza, at daybreak in some pest-house ward". I'd just as soon go with house-maid's knee. However, fear no fears for the J.G.T. I am in chipper condition with the correct psychological attitude of chestnuts and base-balls towards all flu. The influx of Enza will have to select a clever rapier and twist an adroit wrist to pink me, altho' I am in the pink of condition. To get my mind off the measured tramp of jazzless bands here, to forget the persistent odor of floral wreaths, to hear not the thud and scrape of the spade and to shut my ears to belated eulogies over Yoricks, I am writing a noval. No, not a regular one. My novel is very novel. It is called "The Wine Seller" and is similar in style to a piece of junk I wrote two years ago for a great pal of mine with lit'ry leanings albeit he has a wife and two marriagable datters. That venture was "The Salt Seller", so this present "book" is the second in the list of the six best sellers. To write a novel of this sort, one begins with no plot at all, and gradually loses the thread of the plot as he goes along. Settings are subject to change with or without notice. Slang and puns are allowed, character limning is banned, Billy Graves gets gray hairs, Joe Myers swallows a stogie and all is ready for the reviewer. Briefly the lack of plot of this famous novel is this:

Chap I

The king is bitten by a beetle. The royal ankle swells and gets all kind o' green sort of. This worries the queen, because she dislikes green. As she tells the King in one of the book's most charming passages:

"Lookit, green may rime with queen, but it doesn't chyme with my propensities anent colors befitting the wallpapers of royal bedchambers. You must sleep, therefore, with the seneschal."

"Royal robertchambers!" howls the King; forgetting for the nonce that Robert Chambers wasn't born yet. (The scene is laid in 1603.—There is a ghost in it, too, but that isn't laid till 1605. No cornerstones are laid.)

The Chamberlain, the Premier and the Duke of Mixture are called in, the latter rolls in wealth, has a powerful drag, and his job is a pipe. The King holds a star-chamber session with them in the sun-room. It is night and there is a moon. The Chamberlain suggests calling the Royal Doctor. The King says he's called him all the names he knows already. The Premier suggests shooting the beetle at sun-rise to which the King offers three objections: 1. there is in the whole realm no handkerchief small enough to bind the beetle's eyes, 2. this especial beetle has no eyes, 3. immediately upon biting the king, the beetle made good his escape. The Duke then puts in his oar and suggests that the King try abdication. (The Duke is next in line for the throne). The King whispers in the Chamberlains ear to get a medical dictionary and see what "abdication" is, but in order not to show his ignorance to the duke he receives his suggestion very kindly, says it may be just the thing and promises to think it over. The Duke twirls a satisfied mustache end. In this chapter there is also a duel between two courtiers who get into an argument as to which is correct, "bit by a beetle" or "bit with a beetle". The Royal grammarian endeavors to prevent the duel by telling them they are both right in a way, but that the generally accepted form is, "bitten at the hands of a beetle". "What do you think it is, a clock?", demands one courtier, and the duel goes on, the weapons vases at twenty paces.

This is as far as I have developed the wonderful thing yet, but in the next chapter, the royal palace is besieged by the noted bandit leader, Purple Jake and his wild band. Purple Jake's lieutenant is the profligate and evil Earl of Pongee and Madras, a former court favorite, whose banishment had taken place 6 months before at the behest of the queen who complained to the King that the Earl had up and hit her with a croquet ball, during what she supposed was going to be a friendly game in the Palace Gardens. The Earl, eager for revenge, eggs Purple Jake to the attack on the palace, telling him he knows the secret panel where the royal jewels are concealed.

There is a wonderful heroine, and of course a wonderful hero, yet to appear, the latter none other than the Wine-Seller—altho' events finally show he really isn't a mere wine-seller at all. You can see at a glance that I have written the Great Armenian novel. But enough of the plot has been told to put you in a position to steal the thing and win an unjust fame, so I will try to get your mind off of it.

There is one sure way: only girls—nothing else. . . . So like the persistent spider I fashioned an October world for the Eva and me. October burning on the far hills at daybreak, October flaming all the ways at noon, October smoldering in the purple vales at twilight, October ashes red beneath the moon at night. Blooey, is the song of the Brick as it nears my frail October world, faster and faster.*

* Thurber alludes to a current comic strip, "Krazy Kat," which featured a cat continually being hit by a brick, thrown by a mouse.

But one of these worlds will outlive the strong arm of old Percy Mike Fate, and one of these days, one of these days!

I see her mostly in blue, dark blue, with just the right dash of real red. . . . I have always had an almost irresistible desire to hug every pretty girl who has dark brown hair and wears one of those neat dark, navy blue suits. I'm afraid in this case it will really be irresistible. I imagine I will have to do something crazy and sudden, anyway, for time will be brief, too damn brief. Boy, can't you see the lil golden shield, the greatest pin in the world, gleaming richly and austerely and yet debonairly from the folds of that Blue? . . .

I have received the news of the death of my grandfather—mother's father—Tuesday. The end was long expected so comes as no shock. He has lingered near death for over two years.

My dad also enclosed a cut of the dear Minnette from the Ohio State Journal, which says she received her call for Red Cross training last week and leaves this week. It fails to say for what place she leaves. The letters of Minnette and I have dragged horribly—as to oftenness—in the last month—but when we do write we are as deep friends as ever—much more than friends. My folks are very strong for her, indeed I received some weeks ago a very remarkable letter from my father full of mellow advice, including the injunction that I do or say nothing to jeopardize my relations with Minnette and be not too sure of the felicity of things Eva. Letters forwarded via home drew from me a partial statement of feminine entanglements. The folks of course remember very clearly my terrible schooldays case on Eva, and it seems the fact that Eva's past and present are more uncertain than Minnette's calls up maternal fears. I have reassured home of my luck in handling the situation so far. . . .

Heavens alone, I believe, know when, if ever, I shall leave here. I am totally resigned to permanency. Eventually, is all I can say. It may be months. I have no hunch now that it will be before November. And I am even building a December world for two already. The cold information via Journal type about Minnette's going and the lack of word from her, altho' she knew it 10 days ago, not only hurts a bit, but makes me realize I like Minnette. So we'll close with her name instead of Eva's. Minnette . . .

Immutably Thyne,

Jim

*James G. Thurber, 5 Rue de Chaillot,*
*Paris, France*

*American Embassy, Paris*
*March 20, 1919*

My dear old Nugey:

. . . March 20th probably means nothing in your young life. But to a true Parisian it is a date. The famous maronnier blooms in the Jardin Tuilleries today. That is, it is scheduled to. My guide book fails to state how many years in succession it has kept its Rendezvous with Life—but it says it's famous—so I guess it blooms today all right. If it failed to bloom once, even once, on the 20th of March—it would surely become infamous. Such things are portentous to the emotional French nature. (Right here I should stop for half-a day). However, I'll give her a little more gas, and stick awhile.

A maronnier is a chestnut tree. The reason I have devoted so many pages of this diary, so many feuilles roses, to this particular chestnut tree—is because the thing appeals to me. Imagine running across such a thing in a guide book, all stiff and starched in statistics. The Maronnier of the Tuilleries Garden that blooms on the 20th of every March belongs in a sheaf of songs.

(Editor's note: the famous marronier should not be confused with the ancient mariner.) Ils ne sont pas le mème chose.

My pension rears its square bulk on the Avenue President Wilson, formerly the Avenue Trocadero (important point). I have read in Edith Wharton and 10 or 12 others of pale poets, of little seamstresses, of American students living in pensions in Paris. There was always a bit of fascination in the thing. And now I have been living in one for four months. Some of the pensions of Paris are famous—Gambetta and François Coppu and a host of other noted Francaises lived chez les pensions. My pension bids fair never to turn me out famous. My pension is a mess—I think all Paris pensions are. Of course there is a certain charm in the dark, old stairways—the high French windows. But gradually inconvenience and discomfort overcast fascination and charm. And there is no charm—even in the first week—of carrots 3 times le semaine. Nor in the utter absence of running water.

Half a square back of my pension curves the Seine. I can stand on the little iron balcony of my room and see, through a wide screen of tall old sycamores lining the parapet, fast little tugs steaming upstream, heavy, dirty barges crawling by. Just over the river, the Eiffel tower—like a giants' toy, plunges the tiny French tri-color on its peak almost into the clouds. Across streams in the other direction—the vast esplanade of the Invalides and the dome that rises above the porphyry vault that encloses the dust of Napoleon, sleeping, as he asked to sleep, "on the banks of the Seine, in the midst of the French people he loved so well."

There is a little café on a corner of the quai—"Aux Trois Maronniers"—and three craggy, little chestnut trees stand in its impossibly narrow little terrace.

Five minutes walk up Avenue Marceau just opposite, to the Arch of Triumph. And from it, the amazing perspective down the famous Avenue des Champs Elysees to where the obelisk from Thebes points the center of the Place de la Concorde. Stand on one of the little stone rectangles—islands of safety in a swirling sea of traffic—that mark official crossings—(it costs you beaucoup francs if you are injured while crossing the Boulevards at random places). Standing there you are in the direct "milieu" of the most cosmopolitan city in the world. Officers and soldiers of 10 nations weave lines of many colors in the moving pattern of the crowds on either side. The sky—blue and brilliant red of French officers' uniforms—or the dark, close-fitting blue of the Blue-Devils—the sedate-cane-swinging English—immaculate, posers—figures in a revere ensemble—the hideous yellowish-green cloaks and red fezes of bedraggled Algerians, puffing forlorn cigarettes—the stocky, colorless Polonaise, distinguished by their square, four-cornered hats—the graceful Italians with their high round caps—their superfluity of cape, flung with studied carelessness about them—debonair, attractive chaps, part cavalier-part troubador, with the music of Italy in their usually fine eyes.

*March 22*

. . . On re-reading the pages of yesterday I see the necessity of some foot-notes. . . .

. . . Perhaps you wonder why I cling to a pension, and infest not one of the famous hotels—or rather live chez la chambre and chercher toujours some of the even more famous restaurants. "C'est la paix". (pronounced "pay.") However, do not surmise that I have not enjoyed the cuisine, wines and filets of the more noted restaurants which education I am still pursuing—when francs accumulate a bit. Living is steep in Paris. La vie chère is a topic of moment. So that even my millionaire's ducat supply of $2250 (God's coin) or about 1000 francs per month (French money) doesn't call for the erection of a lead-walled compartment in my room in which to shovel lucre from a mobile derrick. To the noted Voisin's I have been twice (once with a pretty, clever little

Red Cross Girl from Columbus, Ohio),—and to the Café de la Paix, the Café de Paris (of Castle's fame) quite now and then. But a history of café nights would fill a monograph all by itself.

I sure do pine sometimes for the Nugent's engaging and inspiring presence here amongst all that is Paris. What I lack more than anything else here is a kindred spirit—it's a lack that detracts from the enjoyment and appreciation of almost everything. Still I can't kick too much—for I had a few days with Roland Hunter—a few more with Carson Blair—and just a week or so ago 3 days with one of my friends of grammar school days, Ed Morris, 1st lieutenant and erstwhile Chi Phi. I wrote you about the visits of Roland and Carson, I believe, altho' it's impossible to remember very much for certain out of the endless stuff I have written home—and to 10th Ave., Zanesville and other places. One could devote every hour of every day to letters—and then get occasionally inquiries from neglected aunts or 3d cousins.

I wander up Montmarte way quite frequently. Montmarte, the once famous, then notorious—now rather colorless and hectic, but Montmarte of a thousand legends and a hundred noted cabarets and cafes that contain them. They sing pretty French ballads in The Black Cat and serve vile beer. The April Moon has a catchy, tuneful revue. But most of the others haven't yet revived from the war. The Moulin Rouge is battered and rusty. I think it's closed for good. I wanted a night at the Moulin Rouge. And the Dead Rat is sure life-less. Not a creature is stirring—not even—however—

Notre-Dame always lures. I have been there five or six times—once with each of my Ohio State visitors, of course. Notre Dame is the first pilgrimage of all sightseers. Seemingly nine tenths of these sight-seers are Americans—the boys in the khaki and the gobs. You see them everywhere—they throng the boulevards—they crowd the restaurants—you can find them down the remotest rues—in the most secluded squares. Rushing about trying to cover the itinerary of "Paris in a Week" in their 3 day leaves—trailing guide books and maps, besieged by the army of post-card and souvenir hawkers. The "Y" conducts countless tours for them. I have never been in Notre Dame that the "gothic coolness" of it was not warmed by the speeding platoon of Americans in the wake of their Y guide who trolls an endless chant of dates, figures and statistics. And so it is in the Pantheon, the Tuilleries and Luxembourg gardens—at the Arch, the Madeleine—everywhere. An American army of occupation has certainly taken Paris. And they fling the festive franc with a gay abandon that startles the Parisian, and warms the cockles of the bourgeois shop keeper's heart—and causes his palm to itch—and his prices to mount. . . .

*  *  *

. . . I went to Reims by way of Chateau Thierry. I didn't stop off at this monument to America, because I intend to make a special trip up there soon. In Reims I saw the cathedral first of course—and took a walk about the city—rather the shambles that were a city. And then out to the trenches. I didn't reach the Hindenburg line, but I clambered into and out of trenches about 2 miles from the city which the Germans evidently took from the French. I ruined one shoe and one trouser leg scaling, descending, hurdling and floundering over and thru the world's greatest supply of barbed wire. And incidentally set off a hand-grenade, evidently attached to a strand of wire to form the fiendish hun contraption known as a "booby trap". Fortunately I didn't step on the primed wire very close to the grenade—it went blooey about 50 feet away. There wasn't much of an explosion—a sharp report like a pistol—and no pieces of the stuff fell very near. I think the thing was sort o' dead from the constant rain and mud. But I'm admitting herewith quite frankly that I was scared bad. With the guerre fini there is no glory in becoming mort pour la patrie on some dead, abandoned battlefield. Furthermore, I wasn't in the least worked up that moment into a careless over-the-top spirit of go-get-'em.

*March 29*

Another one of those weeks that will slip away with nothing much accomplished, lots of resolutions made, and 3 million more letters owed.

We'll have to abandon the Reims narration for a time. Day before yesterday I got a most wonderful letter from Zanesville, enclosing the most wonderful picture you ever saw—well, at least, that I ever saw. . . .

However, there is no use to rave. . . . I can only say that June will probably see me in Zanesville. I can't, I believe, possibly stay here any longer than the last of May. As much as I would like to, in many ways. It's a wonderful place to study in. And you don't have to go to the Sorbonne or the Ecole des Beaux Arts. Every one is a school. Every museum a college—and the whole of Paris a vast university of Art, Literature and Music. So that it is worth anyone's while to dally here for years. Paris is a seminar, a post-graduate course in Everything.

But, Nugget, old guy—the thing is simply this: All such stuff is dead compared to her picture. Paris is a swirl of dead leaves and she is a garden new in bloom. Paris is a comical laugh, she is the music of angels' songs. Paris is a steady gaze of sagacity—a penetrating look of analysis—her eyes are the eyes of youth. Hell, that's idiotic! Anyway, Paris is a cloyed Roué, charming, learned, gifted, if you will, but a Roué whose youth is dead at the roots. Paris is also a Pierrot—and that means youth and gaiety and love. But the Pierrot of Paris is a bit too sophisticated, a bit too satiated with life—the world is too much with him. Call Paris wonderful, amazing, charming—the capital of the world, the center of Art. It is all that. But it's too wise, too old in many ways. And even in its youthful, reckless moods, it lacks the clear vision, the true joy of love and life that is American. That's the big failure of Paris. Paris doesn't whistle ragtime, Paris doesn't walk with her eyes in the sky—and a dreaming gaze of hope and faith. Worst of all, Paris has a horrible sense of values. She is pagan—with a pagan love of beauty—but with a pagan "love" of women also. I have been calling Paris "her". It should be "him". French morals—rather Parisian morals—are to Americans impossible. In a recent Collier's, Mark Sullivan, in an article opposing entangling ourselves with Europe, and advocating the sending of the boys back home at once, says, "send them back before they acquire the European attitude toward women". Thank the Lord, I can say with an absolute conviction that it is true—the European attitude towards women will never be acquired by Americans. There are sporadic cases of the acquisition—no doubt about that. There are those who compare French and American girls. There has been a voice or two suggesting that American girls are too reserved—have a little too much of the Puritanical in them. But these are scattering voices in a vast multitude.

The A.E.F. in France has learned to respect American womanhood, to revere—to worship the clean, fine morals of American womanhood, to idealize American girls—and to worship them with a fire that burns brighter and steadier than ever before—and that will never die down. Things they have seen and heard and felt here, these American boys, have not added fuel to any base fire, or kindled any new and regrettable flame. And they never will.

Boy, it makes you love America and Americans, to see them here, in immediate contrast to 13 other nations' people! They are younger, they are happier, they are more hopeful, more confident, more full of the keen zest of life, than any others. And best of all, they are cleaner, finer than any others. Of course many of them have slipped. And there is much woe in many a sector. Physical. Morally and mentally, still American and always will be.

\* \* \*

. . . Please write a hell of a lot, old guy, and tell me everything. You know what I want. Things Ohio State and Phi Psi. Who's back in school—especially who's back at the house? Give my deepest and best to 'em all. Next to about one or two other calls—the call of Phi Psi and the Lads is sure most luring. . . .

I am almost sure I will go back to State next fall. I want to take Cooper's drama course—and a few others I have decided on. . . .

Let me hear all about yourself and the One.

Minnette writes she let you read a typewritten letter I sent her.

(Please observe following line closely.) I still am highly in favor of Minnette. She regrets that a Chi Phi dance prevented her from holding a dope-session with you. I understand you and she are taking Joey's novel course. Minnette doesn't say much about Joey [Professor Joseph Taylor]. Doesn't she like his line? That wouldn't do at all. You know my sentiments along the Joey line.

Need I point out to you how utterly superfluous it would be for you to let Minnette read this letter—unless of course it were merely the lines referring to Zanesville.

One thing is sure sure. I gotta get back pretty soon, and make a few decisions, or I'll be quite thoroly S.O.L.

Meet me in June Somewhere.

For always,

Jim

&a  &a  &a

*James G. Thurber, American Embassy,*
*Paris, France*

> *American Embassy, Paris*
> ***The Greatest City in John World***
> *June 11, 1919*

Dear old Nuggett:

. . . Heavens only knows where this missive will find you, for by the time it reaches the only shore you will be through forever . . . that is as far as burning the midnight cigarettes goes . . . with Ohio State. . . . You know, without my elaborating on the theme that I would sure have admired to have been back on the campus with you for the final fling. . . .

. . . I appreciated and liked very much your poem "The Two", as I suggested, or made a veiled allusion to in the preamble of this melange of words and ideas, mostly words. I have showed it to quite a few persons who have been enchanted, may I not say? One of these was a Red Cross girl whom you do not know, but who has a penchant for Browning and poetry in general; and she pronounced the last line of the last verse as very fine. . . . Charmé [Seeds] . . . liked your poem, too, and she showed me one she had written after tramping around the scarred slopes of battered hills north of Verdun, with the accent on Fort Douamnont, which I also visited longtemps ago. She is having a great time over here, having seen quite a bit of the front and being turned back by soldiers and station agents and generals and things on her way into Germany and Switzerland and a few other defendu spots . . . however, in some cases, the generals and other whatnots did not turn her back . . . she has a smile and a way, is it not?

. . . I think that I will stay in Paris as long as they let me, that is, up until the first of next November, and sh.h . . h . . h possibly longer if I can get to stay, which I can't, I am pretty sure. In that case I will apply to be transferred to some other post over here, say Warsaw or Bukarest or Berne or wherever they will use me, even Afghanistan if necessary. For a time, of course, I was all set on getting home this summer, but now I have it all doped out differently. I may be wrong about it, of course, and I doubtlessly am. But thus is it doped out, and therefore thus am I going to do, unless some tide in the affairs of me seizes me at the flood or the nape of the neck. The way I reason . . . or think . . . is that it is a long way back and this is in all probability the only trip I will ever make this way. So why not see all there is to see while, as we say in America, the seeing is trays beans. I thought at first that when my time in the Paris Embassy was up I would have enough money saved up to flit a quick flit about Europe and then beat it Home, but besides not having the money, the well known passports and visas are tres difficile pour obtenir maintenant, and that method of seeing Europe seems to have ended in a cul de sac.

Of course I may change my mind and get home by the first or middle of August yet, or at least in time to re-enter State and graduate. . . .

* * *

. . . The chap that sailed with [me] from Hoboken, a very fine lad named Corcoran from Brown and the Harvard Law School, is reveniring aux Etats Unis on July Fifth, and there is quite an urge to join him, and there is still the possibility that I may, but there is the greater possibility that I won't. I really must admit that I don't exactly and absolutely know what I want to do, either now or in the near future. I have arrived, or have been arrived, at that point in one's life which is extremely disturbing and full of hopes and fears and doubts and one thing anothers in wild profusion, I have a deep and sneaking feeling that I should return and finish school for the purpose of wearing the initials after my name and a few other reasons, and I guess that is the sensible thing to do, so the chances are that I won't do it at all . . . unless someone comes out for me, as H. J. [Henry James] always says for coming over.

I must admit that Paris is going to be a very hard place to leave. It is all that dear old Henry said of it, just as wonderful just as charming. There is surely no other place in the world where there is such a variety of things that interest or amuse or instruct or enthrall. Why, it is going to be hard just to leave the concerts in the Tuilleries garden where a symphony orchestra plays beneath the acacias, plays Madame Butterfly and Thais, all the prettiest songs from the finest operas . . . where the moon comes up over the Louvre that reaches its old gray arms towards you invitingly and a bit menacingly, like all old Paris buildings. And in the intervals, the plash of the fountain in the wide purple tarn, the witching glow of the near rose garden in the moonlight. I took Charmé there last night. And we had a real nice time, I aim to state. Dauphine terrace in the Bois de Boulogne with almost equally as good music and exactly as fine a moon, and chestnut trees as tall and whispering as the acacias . . . and ice cream or citronnade or biere or port, as your inclination may be. I don't think that some of these things would ever tire, and yet of course one must snap out of them eventually and the sooner the better in many respects I know. And yet, it's a long life, and one can really not get too much Paris if he only stays away a year. . . .

On the other hand, I have to get back and get at something. It is impossible to get a perspective or a determination over here. All that is Paris militates against determinations and decisions, and for that reason it isn't any too good for one in a sense. . . .

. . . Another element that may enter into the scheme and play the deus ex machina and the heavy lead etc is the fact that things are rapidly closing up over here, work is subsiding mightily and the chances are very great that all but one or two of the older men will be sent back, and I am not one of the older hommes.

I suppose I will have decided it for certain one way or another by the time I get your answer deciding it another way for me; anyhow I want that answer, and the best way to get it is to ship this letter. Hence, (not being a German) I will sign.

> Forever & Forver & frever,
> Yours, Nugget, yours,
> Jimmy

ٹ    ٹ    ٹ

*American Embassy, Paris*
*September 24, 1919*

Dear old Laurel-wreathed Elliott:

I should have answered your wonderful letter many days ago, as it has been in my hands for quite a lil space, but it required two or three readings and since in reading it I liked to linger above each phine phrase and satisfying sentence, two or three readings passes beaucoup time away very easily. It is the best letter I have ever received, in more ways than one or two.

Of course I knew that you were headed for the stage-game—we decided that many moons ago—but I never in my hopefullest dreams for you imagined that you would pounce on New York so quickly and grab her by the scruff of the neck at the same time getting a foot hold on fame as a writer. It is all very wonderful and fine, and, believe me, old youth, there is no one who is happier over your first few successful steps up old John Ladder than I am. You seem to have managed everything just right for the best possible start, even to getting Pathéd for winning the century dash, and I dare say that by the time I reach the shores again you will be standing on the top rung walking the ladder whither you wishest. . . .

So far no crafty ideas have come to me for a world beater along the dramatic line, although I am feverishly trying to develop a few stray ideas into material to upholster a one-act play or so. I am afraid that my range doesn't naturally reach beyond the skit sort of thing, and that if it ever does emerge above that level, it will have to be pushed with strenuous efforts. As a matter of real fact, Paris has shown me that I may have known considerable of the tricks of the writer's craft as an omniscient student of the OSU college, but that when you drift beyond the confines of old John Campus you find that there is considerable expanding has to be done. What I mean is, I am a bit shaken in old Samuel Confidence which is the most totally destructive thing imaginable. A few of the mirages melt, you know. . . . Air castles must be torn down, those mushrooms of a minute's dream, and a slow and labored foundation begun on the old site. I am also considerably uncertain as just what line to devote the old efforts to, and it is altogether a quite worrisome problem, this business of regarding the world and its chances from a point of view in Paris. Now and then I admit I sort of quail for the time being and them are the dark moments—moments which I have had to fight against all my life, mostly to myself, all alone. For I have never had a natural invisible supply of supreme confidence or even of transcendental courage, and it keeps me concentrating and gritting the molars every now and then to keep the manufacturing plant going. But eventually I always see the light, widen the slit in the dungeon walls, and let in a real ray.

Your natural bent for the drama and your turning all your efforts towards that branch of the literary field is the best possible concentration for the development of ability and ideas, and in some ways I hope they send you a rejection slip for your sporadic poems, although the arts are twins and I have a hunch that it won't retard old dramaturgic art to toy with the lyric now and then. And I have another hunch that they won't keep on sending rejection slips very long for the verse you may do, if it is as good as the "Two" thing you shipped over here.

I am also dipping occasional pens into poetic ink, or at least putting down sequences of words that rhyme now and then. (Have you ever tried rhyming "now" and "then"?) It all depends on the accent. . . .

I have made several trips around about France, especially up into Normandy. She of the chimes, the tears, and the apple blossoms you know. For Norma has always had a great attraction for me. And verily it is a wonderful and a charming country. I arrived too late for the apple blossoms, but the chimes are always chiming in Normandy, and, fortunately, if Joan looks down any longer from the skies she won't be able to detect any tears. If one likes to wander about September landscapes that are flawlessly beautiful, seemingly sculptured by the hand of a poetic giant, Normandy is the place for the wanderings; and if one, in his meanderings through September landscapes, likes to come upon mossey old manses, gray stoned old castles, crumbling old abbeys, ancient cathedrals, and the curious old gabled houses of the fourteenth century and earlier, to say nothing of occasional Roman ruins, Normandy is still the place. I leaned on the parapet along the Seine above Caudebec and watched the moon light dancing in the water like a million golden daggers, and across the stream chimes, the sweet old chimes of Normandy sounded. It was just one corner of old Normandy, and just a few minutes there, but there is nothing quite like it. And nothing quite like nosing about an old moss and ivy covered abbey, such as the one in the beautiful little town of St. Wandrille, the abbey which Monsieur Maeterlinck leased before the war because, I suppose, it seemed the most likely place in the world in which to conjure up pretty ideas and charming fancies.

Every thing in Normandy is old, richly old, many things are fairly palpitat-

ing still with the throb of history, for every one who ever amounted to anything from Vercingetorix through the day of Dick of the Lionlike Heart up to
the time of Jeanne of the Arc trespassed on Normandy. The Field of the Cloth
of Gold, which you may remember dimly from some old history reading
hour, is there, and many a castle and pile and stretch of ground that Fame
played in, or where Hate raged or Pageant parade or Glory shone. I wandered
several days in and around Rouen, for Rouen is crowded to the gates with interesting and historic and beautiful things. One hot afternoon I climbed into
one of the tired old carriages that are drawn about by tired old horses and driven by tired old cochers in dirty, semishining white hats, and told him to take
me to the church of Saint Gervais, for my guide book promised under that ed-
ifice the oldest crypt in France, and whereas I am not a collector of crypts as it
were, I rather liked the prospect of descending out of the heat into a coolness
1700 or more years old. There was no one in the aisles of the church but an old
woman who sat very quiet before a alter, praying. My footsteps, though I unconsciously tip-toed, rang very loud in my ears, like the sound of sabots in a
silent street. Candles burned whitely in dim spaces, their tips of light flitting
and darting gracefully above the black wicks as if balanced and juggled by
some invisible spirits. And then suddenly the sacristan appeared, in long
white robe and round black cap. He fitted eminently. His eyes were grey and
kind and they matched the stones of the church perfectly, and his voice was
very gentle as if he were used to talking only at times and places where talking
must be done in low tones. I brought up my best French, which isn't best in
any sense, and "demanded", which is merely "requested" in French, to see the
oldest crypt in France. He said "ah, oui" in a quiet voice and disappeared in a
gloomy room to return all lit up—pardon the idea, what happened was only
that he came back carrying a candle. And then he led me about the aisles a
space until we came to the choir and there with a deft movement he opened a
panel, carefully concealed, and the light from our candle lit the first two steps
that lead down into the darkest as well as the oldest crypt in France. Also the
chilliest, and in some ways the uncanniest, although I guess they are all bad
enough in those respects. The place was singularly bare at first round of in-
spection, but then M. le sacristan began to point out the things of interest, the
tombs, out into the side walls, of ancient abbots of the land, the spot in the
ceiling above which William the Conqueror lay on his death bed, the stones in
the wall that were put there by Roman hands, and lastly four skulls in a row,
grinning of course. Skulls of the troisieme siecle perhaps, or even earlier, or
perhaps not very old at all, only as far back as the douzieme siecle, peut-etre. I

cared not to lift one and murmur alases and poor Yoricks over its smooth dome, and very probably if I had picked the thing up it would have one-horse chaised with admirable suddenness. There was just a narrow line of pale light entering the crypt from the outer world, and when the sacristan held his candle behind him, the dirty daylight that filtered through the antique cob-webbed window gave the place an eerie look not conducive to desires to spend the night there below.

And then in the greater and more famous church of St. Ouen another sacristan, more voluble, gave me another candle and let me find my way up the narrow winding stairs, so narrow and so rapidly winding that had I started to run up them I would surely have been inextricably fixed there, like a vine that has woven itself in and out of the palings of an old fence. So I wandered about old thin galleries and feasted my eyes on the wonderful stained glass of the 14th and 15th centuries, and watched the old ladies kneeling like medieval wood carvings upon their prayer-stools, and watched the tips of the myriad candles like large flakes of dancing snow in the purple corners of little chapels. And then I climbed outside along the gargoyle parapets from where the view of the old houses and the tall spires of Rouen revealed so little of familiar things and so much of the stuff of sophomore history courses and the engravings in dog eared, out-of-print books, that it was no trick to imagine oneself back in the middle ages, and I stared with some surprise at the people passing below in modern mufti, whereas I half expected to see feathered, drooping cavalier hats on swaggering blades, and the cleft mitres of gloomy bishops stalking in the gardens of the church below.

From Rouen, I went to Havre for the purpose of looking at ships on the sea and also for the purpose of taking the famous boat ride from that sea-port up the Seine to Rouen. The very finest boat ride I have ever taken. The landscape is faultless on both sides the river, again with the suggestion of having been wrought by some beauty loving giant, tall trees, smooth rolling green mead-ows, high wooded hills, all spotted here and there with new chateaux, old cas-tles, mouldering abbeys, and the fine forms of Gothic cathedrals.

At another time I went through Normandy to the far end of the promon-tory where Cherbourg is, again to see ships on the water and to watch the lights on the far end of piers winking blue and red at night. And I am all in fa-vor of Normandy. I would like to own a new chateau or an old castle, prefer-ably one with hidden passages, in Normandy.

As yet I haven't made up my mind as to what I am going to do but there is so very much to see and study and be impressed with over here that it would seem sort of a sacrilege to give it all up until I have to, providing, of course, that that time isn't too late for getting the well known start back home. Whatever I decide to do I will let you know right away and I will cable you the date of my arrival in New York, as you suggest, for there must be no more missing of the N and T connections, if it can be helped.

Paris is, by the way, a very wonderful place for the study of the French theater, providing one had enough French to be able to gather the general drift, which is just about all I have, despite the fact that I have been over here so long, almost a year now. You see it would be much easier to pick up the language if there weren't so many Americans around that it is only occasionally, after all, that one has the opportunity of talking with French people.

I went to a very charmingly presented production of The Tales of Hoffman the other night, and tomorrow night there is "Carmen" and the night after that "Louise." It's a great life, in many ways, a great life, this Paris affair, so utterly darn different from American ways of going at things and getting places that it completely baffles attempts at perspective at times.

Be sure and find time toot sweet to answer this letter and if it is not asking too much write about the same number of wonderful pages that you did last time. Meanwhile the best of all in the world towards you, and much of it.

> Toujours and longer,
> Yours,
> Jim

## To The Thurber Family

*American Embassy, Paris*
*March 18, 1919*

Dear Old Thurber [Robert]:

I am awaiting further clippings—and also a letter from you and dear Old Bill. I am addressing this letter to you because I want to send you the enclosed check for 10 beans. I understand you are about to have six or eight more cuttings [operations] to add to your collection. As a ball player, you are quite a patient. But I sure hope you will be all fixed up when this arrives—and for Heaven's sake sign the pledge never to get anything else the matter with you. Of course you couldn't possibly get anything new but stick away from relapses and lay off of setbacks. Decline to go into declines—and refuse to be flung amongst the refuse. . . .

Don't infer that I mean for you to use the $10 for to pay any bills with. It won't go very far but fling yourself a little party, and write me a letter, using the remnants of the 10 seeds to buy a stamp with. William is able to work and you ain't just yet—so you can probably use the few bones.

I would ship you more now, but living is terrible high here now—and furthermore I feel I just gotta see Paris and that does take the money. Also I have made three trips to northern France—Reims, Soissons and Verdun—and R.R. fare is steep—but boy, oh, boy it was worth it. I seen things. I am writing accounts of my trips and will mail them home soon as they are finished.

Picked up a few souvenirs—no helmets altho' I saw beaucoup. There'll be more helmets back in America after all the boys get home than will be left in North France and Germany and Belgium together. The few things I picked up are more interesting than mere helmets, which at best are chunks of heavy iron. At Fort Douamont—5 miles from Verdun—I bought a pretty vase hammered by hand out of a French 75 shell case. I picked up some Allied propaganda—in German—from the wreckage of a plane near Soissons. I got near this place an Algerian soldier's service record with two bullet holes through it.

When I get home I'll have you all draw up around the fire in a semi-circle to listen tensely to my tales of action at the Front. Speaking of *Home*—I can't say yet when it will be. Probably not till August however—but certain and sure it won't be any later. . . .

Mamma's first letter telling about "Our dog" must have been de-railed. First I heard about him was her last letter telling me the names you were considering and asking me to suggest some. What brand of animal is he? Collie, bull, Florida wire/Spaniel, Iceland Seal terrier, or what? Anyway, he'll probably always consider me as an intruder when I get back. Show him my picture, let him sniff an old suit of mine and tell him the story of my life. . . .

Keep the Home Fires Burning.

Always

Your Bro, Jamie . . .

&a   &a   &a

*April 9, 1919*

Dear Old Bob:

The past three days have been quite crowded with joy, for your very wonderful letter-newspaper-history-dissertation-drama and comedy arrived. . . . The whole thing certainly furnished me with beaucoup pleasure, entertainment and information. . . .

The news clippings were all interesting, as all of them were new. . . .

It looks like all the boys were getting back, back there. . . .

As to myself, if I care to stay I could probably be here till Fall, maybe later. Again, if I wish to go back, I could no doubt leave here most any time. . . .

Opposed to this slant, however, is Home and the U.S.A.—and the boys—*and* the girls. Every now and then these factors swing uppermost in my mind, and I think I have seen enough of Paris. Because, on final analysis, there are more things to go back for, than to stay for. My heart is in Ohio. And there's no use trying to make-believe I am, or could be perfectly satisfied to stay here very much longer. I guess you all know back there how greatly the A.E.F. wants to go home. And I've naturally absorbed the A.E.F. spirit. All they talk about is the Statue of Liberty. You hear, on all sides, "My Alabama", "Me for old Illinois", "oh you lil old New York." And the most popular songs are "Homeward Bound" (which is sure class) and "When Are We going Home?" a song written by an Ensign over here.

Doubtless you have read of the A.E.F. unit shows, written, staged and acted by soldiers, and touring the various camp-cities and concentration camps of France. There are scores of these shows, and many of them very clever. I saw one in Verdun, and one last night here. . . .

I have heard but very few of the songs contained in the March Victor list you sent. "Beautiful Ohio" sounds wonderful, as a title. But I don't know the words or tune. I think the only two I recognized were "Ah, Oui, Marie" which is raging here—and "I'm always chasing Rainbows"—which was out before I left America. "Smiles" is still good here. You see the songs are slow in coming over. . . .

I am enclosing three small camera pictures, which will be of some interest, I dare say. They were taken by a chap named Cooper who accompanied me on my trips to Verdun and Soissons. . . .

The Cemetery of American Marines is at the corner of two roads between Vierzy and Verdun. Vierzy is about 12 miles from Soissons. We walked from Vierzy into Soissons, one of the most interesting jaunts I ever took, along the path of Foch's smash that drove 'em back over the Chemin de Dames last July. (I should say, as I was corrected by an Alabama Sgt. at Soissons, "Foch *AND* the Americans.") 208 Marines are buried in this little place, and it is a beautiful little cemetery, fenced in with birch boughs. A little American flag whips in the breeze in the far corner, but can scarcely be made out in the picture. It was quiet and sunshiny when we were there, and a hundred birds were singing. I cannot forget nor describe that place.

The other picture was taken from a landing half way up a ruined monastery in Soissons; the building was simply pounded to powder. It was rather a hazardous climb up that monastery, but the view over the city was worth it. We went up into the building by means of a slim, spiral-stone stair-case, and actually the steps and the wall were in many places shelled into a stuff as fine as talcum powder. . . .

Now for a piece of good news, especially for Mamma; yesterday afternoon I received a long, official envelope from the Army authorities at Hoboken Piers. MY SUITCASE IS TROUVE! And it is now nearing Brest, aboard the U.S.S. Agamemnon, and will be forwarded, by official orders, right up to the door of the Embassy. Six cheers! Bonheur! C'est joli! And one big worry is vanished.

Received papa's letter, one from Mamma, William's also, as I mentioned before, and one from Mrs. Botimer. I realize how busy papa is, and tell him not to feel at all that I do not understand it. Ca ne fait rien, to use a famous French phrase. I know he would like to write more, but Lord knows he has enough other things to keep him busy. . . .

. . . I am writing this at old John Embassy and gotta stop now. Thanks again for the History of Columbus, Ohio, and come again. Tell William to encore aussi. . . .

     Always
     Jamie

&#10087; &#10087; &#10087;

May 31, 1919.

Dear old Bro Robert;

I should have written to thank you long ere this for your series of histories of Columbus and Her folk. . . .

Mamma writes that papa is still an earnest advocate of putting his family to bed early, doubtlessly tucking them in securely also, and so I assume that you are getting your rest, which ought to help you recuperate in good shape.

Your very clever dialogue of the O.M. [old man] learning to crank the machine, since he might as well learn then, was one of the funniest things I have had the good luck to have come over to cheer me up, your final touch about the use of the brush to calm the Thurberian temperament was true to life, all right. I suppose by this time he has tried, tried again, and is now one of the world's swiftest and surest, if not indeed, fanciest, crankers of machines. . . .

Mamma mentioned that you still play old Sam Mandolin and I am anxious to get home and hear you play again some of the old time melodies, and better than that, some of the new ones that you tell me about, but that I don't know from Adam's first yodel. I think I told you that I bought a second hand mandolin over here, got it up in the famous Montmarte district. I play it occasionally and have got so that I can use all the necessary fingers to finger with. . . . Now I'll try to give you a little idea of how things are going with me in gay and festive old Paree. It still continues to be a very interesting place, and it would continue to be so if one stayed here for ten years, because Paris is easily the most wonderful city in all Jake world, with about as many different phases as can be crammed into the rues and boulevards of the old town, and there are beaucoup square inches here to crowd things into. I haven't seen one tenth of the things one could see, I suppose, and yet I have seen one big lot, also.

There are the most beautiful parks in the world to wander around in here, one of them, Parc Monceau only about three minutes walk from my hotel, which is a pension—hotel sort of place on the carrefour Haussmann—which means (carrefour) a place where several streets run in together, "square" we call them back home. The Boulevard Haussmann is one of the newest of the many boulevards of the famous berg. Stopping at this hotel are two other fellows from the Embassy, and four Red Cross girls, with whom one can have a real nice time. They are mighty nice girls and typically American, all right. You can sure tell an American lass from all the other races over here in half a glance, although not all of them are representative of the best looking girls we have back home. Still some of them are real nice to gaze upon; two of the four at my hotel are darn good lookers, and one of these two is very darn good looking. Funny coincidence, her name is . . . Bessie May Fisher. She doesn't, though, look a bit like our Bessie Fisher of the Kurt connection. Still queerer coincidence, her mother's name by marriage is Mary Fisher, so we naturally get along fine—not like brother and sister exactly, because that generally means not getting along without frequent arguments, pulling of hair and hitting with bricks. You remember the famous ballad, "Never strike your sister avec une Cobblestone", I daresay, which is a companion piece of that other very noted song, "Be wary of Hammering Friend Cousin with a Mallet". Bessie and I have chased around together quite a bit, the last few weeks going out to the pretty little suburb towns of Paris, where there are wonderful chateaus and grounds along the Seine, and lilacs are in bloom and wistaria, and roses, and all is sure pretty and nice to roam around amongst with a jeune fille. We were out to St. Germain not long ago, where the Austrian delegates are getting theirs handed to them, you know. There is a wonderful terrace out there from where you can see Paris in all its ancient splendor, but principally the Eiffel tower standing high above everything else, and the white spires of the Sacred Heart Church marking the top of Montmarte.

We are going to chase out to Fontainbleu before very long. I certainly don't want to miss that, as it is famous for its chateau and forest. However, our chasing together will soon be fini, for the Bessie is going to be sent in the Red Cross service to Bucharest pretty soon, in about ten days, and our little parties will be all over.

The most recent piece of news with me, however, happened today. The little French garcon who guards the Embassy door, that is the porte to that inner sanctum known as the code room, came in and informed me that une demoiselle Americaine wished to see me. I couldn't imagine who, but I hurried out all eager to see. An extremely pretty and bright looking American girl was standing there, in the well known trim gray uniform of the Rouge Croix. I recognized her face at once but couldn't place her, and she had to tell me that she was Charmé Seeds and that she had heard I was at the Embassy and had also heard a word or two about me in State, and thought she ought to come up and pass the time of day and one thing another. I had never met her, but of course had seen her quite a bit, as she is very famous at State, and was one of the most popular girls in the whole doggone campus in her day, and is yet for all of that. So I grabbed the afternoon off and we buzzed out to her place, a Red Cross Hotel in the Latin Quarter, and there we had tea in a very pretty garden, and cakes and marmalade and a long talk about people at State and things back on the old campus in general. She is certainly a dandy girl to know, and I am glad that she presented herself. . . .

I got a letter from Martha Pbetz today in the same mail with mamma's. She enclosed six or eight sticks of gum, the famous Spearmint and the equally renowned, if somewhat differently flavored Juicy Fruit. First I had seen, let alone chewed in a long temps, and I was very glad to get it.

Yesterday I went out to the cemetery of Suresnes, about six miles out of Paris, where a great many American boys are buried, and where one of the finest services was held. It was surely a thing not to be missed. There were oceans of flowers, and a very impressive honor guard of American and French soldiers, drawn up for no less a personage than the President of the United States who delivered a fine address, not a word of which I could hear however, since the closest I could get to him was jammed up on a hill at his back among about nine million doughboys and two thirds of the rest of the American war workers in France. French and American bands played the Star Spangled Banner and the Marseilleise, (spelled very uniquely I think) and then Chopin's Marche Funébre, and ending up with about as fine and touching a note as music is capable of, the sweetly sad tones of Taps floating across the flower shrouded wooden crosses; the bugle call was played by a fine looking American bugler, and somehow it left an impression that will always stick. . . .

Thanks again for all that you have sent, old boy. . . .

> forever,
>
> yours,
>
> Jamie

     ॐ  ॐ  ॐ

Wednesday June 25, 1919

Dear Brothers Bob and Bill:

 . . . The Games opened Sunday with beaucoup fanfare and waving of gonfalons, and I suppose the papers back there carry full accounts of the proceedings. . . . I have to work Sunday afternoons, but I don't mind it so much because by so doing I get all of Tuesday off. And therefore Tuesday, yesterday, was my first day at the games. . . .

Yesterday was a perfect day for the events, with a bright sun, pretty warm air, but not too chaude, and no clouds of any kind to obscure the brilliance of the affair. I have never seen the Yale Bowl, as I need not tell you, but I imagine this darn thing out near Paris comes about as close to it as any other stadium there is. It is, anyhow, one vast circle of concrete, sitting on one side of which places you in a position where you have to strain a neck and an eye in order to make out the people distinctly, on the other side. The space in the center, in other words, the field itself, is divided up into all the cinder tracks and dirt spaces and jumping bars that Ohio Field has on the occasion of Le Grand Six. . . .

There is a regularly arranged forest of flag staffs around the circular track that forms the periphery of the field and on which the hurdles and long runs are staged, as at O. Field and all other such places. And huge silk new flags of all the allied nations whip the air into a scrambled rainbow effect. Around the back of the stadium another series of gonfalons are nailed, and the flags alone would add enough color to the scene, let alone the dozen different uniforms that dash and prance and hop and swirl about . . . the different colored trunks of the prize fighters and wrestlers, the flagrant flare of the loudly striped sweaters of the seconds and trainers . . . orange and white . . . red and blue . . . and all sorts of startling combinations. Then the attire of the soccer teams, the splashes of national colors on the chests of the runners . . . and last but not least the brilliant array of uniforms in the stands and boxes. So that the stadium is like a huge kettle into which some Giantess of a witch with a savage's appetite for bright colors, had dumped twenty different kinds of material and fifty different dyes, stirred them up in the middle and then tossed them with a big stick around the field, onto the flag staffs, into the stands 'n' everywhere. . . .

. . . I have about as much interest in [soccer games] as a Russian Wolf Hound evinces in the V shaped motor of the Cadillac engine. In the afternoon, however, I had to sit through two of the things, each consisting of two halves of 45 minutes duration the half. . . .

. . . France defeated Roumania in what one or two of the papers called a brilliant game of soccer. Might just as fittingly speak of a dashing iceman or a soggy desert.

. . . The Arabian sabre combat was very wonderful as far as cleverness in flailing a sharp weapong right in a brother's face without clipping off a nose or a cheek, but it was so darn funny in the various dances a la Al Jolson and "no news for the news man" which they would suddenly waft into, away from each other, just when the give and take was at its roughest. The Americans in the stands were tickled to death and cheered and applauded, so that the Arabians thought they were getting by wonderfully, whereas the Americans, and most of the other onlookers for that matter, were overlooking the marvelous hand and arm work because the la dee da Pavlowa accessories were so killing, so to speak. The camel race was picturesque all right with true sons of the desert riding real ships of the desert, but the old boys weren't much at taking a curve on high, being content just to keep on going, across lots, toward the exit. Finally two of them ended up with a fairly close finish, a pacin' fool defeating a trottin' bird. . . .

Well, this day is drawing to a fini, and it is already the second that I have put in on this story of the games and one thing another, so I will not go any further.

> Hoping you will do the same, I am always
> Jamie

*Three Red Cross girls who also lived at Thurber's pension at 80 Boulevard Hausmann were to depart for duty in "Roumania."*

## TO BESSIE FISHER, ESTELLE FOSTER
## AND ROSALIE O'DONNELL

*The Greatest City in the World (Paris)*
*[June 1919]*

Dear Departeds:

I can see you now as the train pulled out of the Gare, standing on the rear platform of the caboose (that is, you, not the train), of the caboose, I repeat, that was carrying you away from me forever, or at least, he amended cheerfully, for quite a spell————carrying you away, I repeat, into what is undoubtedly the world's most barren stretch of country, or at any rate, he conceded generously, into what is indubitably not one of the brightest garden spots of the world. . . .

I am too modest to go into the story of my long and brilliant career of study to become the peerless and wonderful authority on Roumania that I am today, and it must suffice to say that one day I was feeling particularly gloomy, despondent and depressed, and my mind naturally running, therefore, in like channels, I dwelt on Roumania in a morbid sort of way, and gradually became the world's champion authority, as I have mentioned elsewhere in this letter someplace. (Editor's note: you will observe that in the sentence above, I say "dwelt *on*" Roumania, not "dwelt *in*". You must immediately realize that knowing as much as I do about the place I naturally get enough sense to stick away from it.) . . .

Roumania, then, is situated in the most unprepossessing spot in all Europe. It is hounded on one side by Bulgaria, a country overrun with desperadoes, banditti, highwaymen, garotteers and huge burly bearded men, affecting long stiletoes, whose chief pastime and ambition in life, is the midnight foray, consisting of a fell swoop down from their lairs and dens in the mountains, upon the defenceless women of Roumania. Bucharest is their favorite swooping place. And strangely enough, these fierce and wicked men have a fetish, not to say a propensity for foreign women sojourning in those parts, in preference to the buxom and laughing native lasses. This may be due, in large part, to the fact that their midnight forays have been going on for so many years now, that the available supply of buxom and laughing native lasses has been pretty thoroughly carried away, kidnapped and held for ransom. In the matter of ransom, it might be well to mention here, that it is purely virtual, so to speak, and extremely volatile, as it were, amounting almost to the protean. That is to say, the bandit chief—him with the green eyes and the purple breath—will set a price of 45,000 Jupazurkas as the amount that must be forthcoming for the release of a girl, and then, after her friends and family have worked for years and years, wearing their fingers to the bone, to raise this amount, and when they have finally succeeded and take the 45,000 Jupazurkas in six great camions to the headquarters of the bandit chief, they find greatly to their dismay, and to the further retention of the girl, that the price has jumped 3456 jupazurkas during the last fiscal year, or that the rate of exchange has advanced nine Kulks to the spiniffus or something else equally crafty and financial, and back to the village and vineyard the friends and family must go, to work for years and years more and wear their finger bones to the marrow. In this way a young and vivacious maiden is frequently kept bound and gagged in the wine cellar of the Pirates' Cave, until, as you may imagine, her youthful bloom is somewhat paled and her tinkling laughter tinkles not so tinklingly as of old, and her limbs become terribly cramped, and being gagged, she can't even chew gum or swear for relief, and being bound, she can't even kick about life in general. Things then come to a pretty pass, or, as my grandfather used so vividly to put it—Quote, There sure is hell to pay. End quote.

Statistics at hand, compiled during the years 1914–1918 show some interesting facts. I quote a few below:

## ROUMANIAN RESIDENTS CARRIED OFF
## BY BOLD BULGARIAN BANDITTI
### (During the years 1914–1918)
#### COMPILED BY THE CHEESE OF POLICE OF BUCHAREST IN CO-OPERATION
#### WITH THE MINISTER FOR PLUMBING AND GAS FITTING

Number of Native Roumanian girls abducted ................... 32
Number of Roumanian girls left ............................. 6
Reason they are left. . . . . Three of them hid during the forays
and the other three concealed themselves.

Number of foreign young ladies arriving
in Bucharest since 1914 ................................... 798
Number of foreign young ladies partieing from
Bucharest since 1914 ..................................... 798
Reason for their having partied .............................
Carried off by wild men from Bulgaria

As will be seen by even a cursory glance at the appended statistics, very few of the foreign young ladies who went to Bucharest were not carried away . . . in point of fact, all of them were, and it is worthy of note that they were not carried away by the scenery.

The leader of this gang of lawless girl snatchers is known throughout mitteleuropa as Gogettem Pedro. He is a bad man. It has often been said of him by his cutthroat admirers that he couldn't jump across a brook without becoming a pirate on the way over. Unfortunately for the young ladies going to Bucharest, however, he never took to a sea-faring life, but decided to lurk and prowl about the crags and cliffs and tarns and crannies and whatnots overlooking Roumania for his life work. In Pedro's crew are fifty six (cinquante six) desperadoes and outlaws, all of the same ilk and religion, which latter is the worship of blood and rough-housing. Each and every one of these bold bad men is hard boiled and each and every one of them, in a recent straw vote, went on record as being in favor of American Red Cross girls as opposed to all other nationalities and kinds. This fact, it seems to us, is well worth your attention.

It might also be of some interest to you to mention the nicknames of some of Pedro's wicked band. Hence, we mention some of them. Pink Eyed Paul, Sawtooth Sam, Knock 'em Dead Eddie, Bustalong Bill, Aloysius the Agony Producer, Charley the Choaker and Mean Mose Mulligan—to name just a few of the more fastidious and gentle of the well-known organization. Hack 'Em to Pieces Hank is Pedro's first lieutenant and right hand man, and oh boy, he's an unamiable individual, to describe him gingerly.

These men were simply born hard as nails and mean as life, and in a way they are not responsible, but that doesn't help the situation much of course. In closing this phase of my brief summary of the present situation in Roumania, I might say that of the 45 Red Cross girls carried off from Bucharest by this notorious and absurdly impolite gang, a total of 45 are now reposing bound and gagged in the bandit's cave, awaiting ransom, which, in all probability, will limp in a poor second to Judgment Day.

Roumania is hounded on another side by Russia, that is, to be more definite, Bolshevik Russia, or to be more definite still, by the most bolshevik of all bolshevik Russia. These bolsheviks that border and prey on Bulgaria are similar in many ways to the Bulgarian Buccaneers of the other side, that is, they are wild, untidy, mean and hard to get along with. Almost any one of them would shuffle a fellow man off this mortal coil for two Badrimbas, which is a

bolshevist coin amounting to about one-tenth of a sou. Their special characteristic and pastime is throwing things, mostly bombs. They overthrow lots of
things, too, mostly kingdoms. There is one tribe of these pagan and uncul-
tured bolshevists known as Mugwimpuses, which is easily the most fearful
and warlike of them all. This especial tribe inhabits a range of hills overhang-
ing Bucharest. Let us hope, girls, that wherever you go in Roumania, you steer
clear of Bucharest. The darn place is simply beset on every side by tribes, fac-
tions, armies and gangs of burly intruders, who take things and throw things
and make themselves in every other way very impertinent and disagreeable.
Well, anyway, this congregation of Mugwimpuses is about the worst division
the whole red army of the world sports, it is indeed, the last word in IWW, oh,
yes, it is even, forsooth, le dernier cri in the New and Dishonorable Order of
Chaos Champions. Unlike the Bulgarian Pedroites, the Mugwimpuses do not
conduct raids into Bucharest. This is because there is great rivalry between the
two bunches of roughnecks, which culminated one night in a free for all in the
streets of the Roumanian capital, when as chance and the leaders of the two
gangs would have it, they conducted synchronous midnight forays and
bumped square into each other right in the middle of the Place de Repulsive
in the center of Bucharest. One of the birds of the Mugwimpus outfit happened to take a fancy to a Red Cross girl (American) whom a prominent Pe-
droite claimed for his own, and a fight for all comers ensued. The result was
complete victory for the Bulgarian arms, and the utter rout of the forces of
Mugwimp, who beat it back to their mountain homes and have stayed there
ever since, content merely to fling bombs and other explosives into Bucharest
from time to time. This hurling of infernal machines reaches its highest point
generally at the apex of a Pedro foray, when the Mugwimpuses not only become excited by the noise and screams and shrieks and coarse laughter in the
city below, but when they also become perfectly angry at the recollection of
how Pedro's mob beat them up that time, and so they just dump every darn
bomb and bullet and rock and heavy object they have on hand into the city.
Many a cowardly and unworthy fiend has met a just reward when a rock
crowned his Sub-Prince of Hades or an explosive tore him limb from limb,
blew him to pieces, bombed the stuffin out of him, and otherwise injured him
in a vital spot, mortally wounding him, resulting in his death, and, in the end,
killing him, thus bringing about his demise. But alas, alas, alas, and a-lack-a-
day, and woe is me, many a beau—ti—ful Red Cross girl of the American per-
suasion, from the United States, has met an untimely and unmerited end

through the same agency and by the same means, not to say as a result of the same happening, that is, to-wit, viz., as follows: either by bomb, explosive, infernal machine, rock, boulder, piece of cement, hunk of scantling or other heavy, blunt object flung from the haunts of the naughty Mugwimpuses and alighting on her person with a dull, sickening thud. Woe! C'est terrible, ca!

But let us go on————from bad to even worse, for are you blissfully unaware that Roumania is hounded on yet another side by the world's most terrifying, disgusting, germ-inhabited and destructive body of water? This awful place is none other than the Black Sea. The last census disclosed the presence in that body of aqueous fluid of 6,789 sea serpents of the most poisonous nature, the most noxious coloring, the most baneful temperament, and the most wicked bite known to deep sea students. These quaint and interesting sea-going fish are of the sort that prowl around the land by night. They swim in the sea all day long, from the time they get up in the morning until approximately 8:46 P.M. in round numbers, thinking up devilish and low down tricks and antics to pull off when they get shore leave. Then promptly at 8:46 they sneak up to the shores, crawl on their stomachs onto the beach, steal silently over the banks and make for the largest city, which in this case is Bucharest. Once within sight of the city, they deploy under the leadership of the eldest and toughest and longest fanged snake in the crowd, and at a pre-arranged signal suddenly descent upon the defenceless inhabitants of the capital city, armed to the teeth, so to speak, and shouting loudly in the most terrifying and forlorn and menacing tone of voice one can imagine. First they make for the bar rooms where they proceed to get roundly liquored up, much to the discomfiture of the various cafe proprietors, and then, even more vicious and unruly and mean than ever, they get about to raise a general rumpus with the peaceful inhabitants of the place. By a strange and unsolved mental process, they take a fancy to plaguing and deviling and biting the young girls of the city, and even stranger still, there seems to be something about the uniform of the Red Cross (American) that lures and maddens them like the legended red flag does the storied bull. Many a time and oft have they pursued these particular girls for miles around the town, chasing them down alleys and over garden walls and onto house roofs and where not. This has come to be very annoying to the girls, and several of them have left the city on account of it, but sad to relate, they have but jumped from the F. P. into the F. for no sooner had they fled the city and shaken the dust of its avenues off of their neatly fitted shoes, than they have been set upon by sentinels, scouts, outriders, or reconnoiterers of one of the above mentioned bands of bandits, and carried away forthwith to a dark, gloomy cave to be bound and gagged and held for ransom that never comes, or if it does come, that proves insufficient, as we have related at length somewhere else in these columns.

So, then, the situation resolves itself into merely taking one's choice between being bound and gagged for life, or being bitten and choked to death by some muscular and unscrupulous sea serpent. It is said that the well-known phrase, "It's a hard life" originated in Bucharest, and is there anyone in this assembly tonight who will deny that it seems very plausible that this city must indeed be the home town of that expression? . . .

There is still another side on which Roumania is hounded, and that is to the west where Austria Hungary lies—and lies—and lies. As is well known, the former Hapsburg realm is made up of a number of races or elements or whatever one wishes to call them. Quite a few of these are peaceful peoples, or at least comparatively so, but there is one tribe, known as the woofelites . . . so called from the singular way they have of barking like a dog or a walrus . . . that is certainly a distinctly reprehensible bunch. As luck or fate will have it this tribe is the border tribe. That is to say, they live along the border between Austria Hungary and Roumania. Their characteristics are quite different from those of the Mugwimpuses or Pedroites; for one thing they do not throw things. Their special habit and pastime is to band together at night and bay the moon, thousands of them at once, in stentorian and sepulchral tones, and the effect is exactly like ten thousand Newfoundland dogs barking and baying and howling at once, only it's lots worse, because no self-respecting Newfoundland or any other breed of dog would or could make such an ungodly dissonance, discord and cacaphony as this gang of brutes does. Why, girls, it is something fearful. Good Heavens, it's impossible! And the worst feature of it all is that the sound penetrates very easily and clearly as far as Bucharest, and unless one is totally deaf, like the knob of a door or the roof of a shed or the cover of a rosewood snuffbox, or something, or unless, perchance, he can sleep during a battle or in a stock exchange at 2 p.m. on the day a war is declared, he will certainly lose a lot of needed rest and in all probability will either go crazy or into a decline. Statistics, of which I am fond of quoting, show that 7,890 foreigners who have sojourned in Bucharest, have gone either the one or the other after a stay of from five days to six weeks in the place. . . .

In looking over my comprehensive and discouraging volume on Roumania, which I have at hand here on my desk, I find that there are some Forty-five Thousand other jottings and inklings that I would like for you to know, but space forbids, and so I will just jot down briefly a score or so of the more important.

(1) In the early fall of each year there is an epidemic of the Black Plague in the city, due to the proximity of the Black Sea and the exposure to which the people are subjected by the visits of all the Johns and Elizas Sea Serpent.

(2) Malaria is not so bad in Bucharest . . . what I mean is it is not so bad as smallpox is, but there is more of it.

(3) The houses of Bucharest are so old that the cement has all worked out from between the bricks and if a whole side of a house doesn't fall in on you, you are reasonably sure of being nicked on the knob by a falling chimney.

(4) A railroad strike is threatening there now, and once a person gets into the place, the chances are he won't ever get out.

(5) And that isn't altogether due to the impending strike, either.

(6) Mosquitoes in Bucharest measure six inches from wing tip to wing tip.

(7) Three weeks out of the year it doesn't rain.

(8) The weather isn't much during these three weeks, tho.

(9) Sugar costs 456 francs a dish, tea 69 francs a cup, small cakes 27 dollars a dozen. But it is not felt that these low prices will continue.

(10) All femmes du chambre in Bucharest take things.

(11) One is not safe on the streets after sun down. Three are not safe either. But then, cheer up, there is nothing to see on the streets either before, after or during sundown.

(12) Some of the little children in the city are very pretty, but they all chew or smoke cigars.

(13) There are several movies in town, but they haven't had any new reels since Kalem's "The Midnight Diamond Robbery" which has been shown 456,679 times since 1903, thus establishing the world's greatest run for a theatrical attractive. Now, however, the reel has become so worn out that no one can tell what it's about. In fact one gentleman who forced himself to sit through it, said to a reporter for the Bucharest Trumpetzxksky that it put him in mind of animated Persian heiroglyphics portraying Charlie Chaplin in the role of Desdemona prepared for the films by W. J. Bryan and directed by the maiden aunt of Jesse James. This sounds to me more like a description of the city itself, but then I have never seen the picture.

(14) Bucharest occupies the former site of Nineveh and part of Tyre . . . the rim, I think.

(15) The death rate in Bucharest is four to the square yard per diem. The birth rate, 45 francs for an upper and 85 for a lower, Via Trieste, meals not included.

(16) My personal opinion is that a train taking an American Red Cross girl to Bucharest is carrying a good thing too far.

(17) The worst part about it is that you are leaving behind not only the greatest city in the world, but also me. Tomorrow I am going out to Fontainebleau with its wonderful castle and its famous and beautiful forest, and from there, after loitering around under the cool of the trees, I will take the cute lil tram to Barbizon, and get some vin rouge and real nice dejeuner on the white spread terrace of some secluded and quiet little cafe, presided over by a charming and polite red-cheeked waitress, and then I will walk around the famous little town of the painters, and see the homes of Millet and Rousseau and then I will come back to Paris in the gathering twilight, back to the gay boulevards and the white ways and the theaters and the parks and the quaint rues, and the color and the hum and the panorama 'n everything, and oh boy, won't it be fine! And you . . . . . . well, I have already tried to give you some idea, from my vast knowledge of the subject, what you will be doing. . . .

But even with all the various diversions of Paris to distract me, I am very sure that one of the finest and nicest of all the attractions will be gone in the persons of three of the dandiest and Americanest girls I have ever known. . . .

And at tea time I am sure I will sally up the steps light-heartedly to numero trent quatre, happily for the moment believing your bright faces and lithsome figures and airy graces and beautiful spirits and cheerful words will be there to greet me, only to find the room barren and deserted, the golden bowl broken. . . .

Still, let us look on the bright side of things, even if we are quite positive there is no such thing, and let us imagine a silver lining where none really is. Let us promise ourselves that bientot you will all come back, despite Bucharest, and that if even for only a day, we will all make merry once more, setting the welking to ringing with our happy laughter and the ancient rues of old Paris to resounding with the sounds of our reunited joy and the whole pension to tinkling with the jingle of our tea things, and all our ten fingers to being gooey with the stuffing and icing of little wonderful expensive cakes such as only Parisian boulangeries set in their windows to entice the unwary Red Crosser, and delight the soul, via the stomach, of the quatre of us.

And even if you do not come this way again, or if when you do, I shall have gone into that land from whose bourne no traveller will surely ever care to set forth again . . . the United States of America—even if we do not meet again on this side the wide, wide pond, someday, oh magic someday, we will all be sure that we will have tea together again, either in old St. Louis, or Old Columbus (O.) or old someplace else. . . .

And so even if I reach the next to the last step and they are not there, I am happy in the conviction that on the topmost step our tea things will be all arrayed, sparkling and gleaming and laughing with us, and all will be happy ever after.

> Good-bye, Good Luck, God bless you.
> (Jimmy)

*By Thurber's return to Columbus, Minnette Fritts had married. He was still shaken up by his first sexual encounter in Paris.*

## To Elliott Nugent

> *James Thurber, 330 East Gay St.,*
> *Columbus, Ohio*
> *Friday, March 25, 1920*

Dear old Guy o' mon coeur:

. . . First of all, concerning myself, I wish to speak of plans, or such plans as I have, for my future. Naturally I am still a bit unsettled and uncertain yet, and things are somewhat nebulous and a trifle worrisome. You see I am not in tres excellent condition, having had a very bad time of it with nerves in Paris—which is a hint of the silence story—untold yet by the way—but out of that life into a new routine altogether I am picking up wonderfully. The ocean trip in itself was a wonder worker, and home and the way spring comes up Ohio ways, are keeping up the good work, ably assisted by Fellow's hypophosphites and new mental orientation. . . .

Your second letter shows me that you believe I am in school, but I ain't. I got back too late for one thing and I didn't feel up to it for another, and there are also family complications—the sickness of my younger brother and things financial. However, all is a bit rosier than when I hit home, and I believe everything will turn out fine and bien tranquil.

As to plans, I don't yet know, I am certain that very soon I will start out as you have on the old road of life, which in my case can mean but one thing, writing. It must mean that, win or lose, fail or prosper. But I intend to hit it hard and consistently and go in for the big things, slowly, perhaps, but surely.

I have of course no assurance of success, even of ability beyond the outer rim of mediocrity, but I have the urge, the sense of what it is and means, and a certain vague confidence which will grow, I believe, as I grow and work.

I was, as you know, low in spirits and confidence over there at times, but I broke that and the victory was sweet. I grew up, at least, and became a man, oh, much more of a man than ever your erratic and youthful but willing dreamer of a Jamie ever was. I'm not saying I'm anything fine. I'm not. It's still a fight to down certain weaknesses, but an easier fight. I am more sure of myself, older, wiser and I've felt the bumps out there beyond the border of the campus, in the center of the cruel old world, damn her, sweet and beautiful always, too!

But the course is yet incompleted. I've much to learn, much steadiness and stability to gain. The wise Mrs. Proctor [Minnette Fritts] said I still need stability, but that she saw at once great improvement. Certainly I am not the ineffectual boy of Washington days. It's hard to recall them, but I was just a boy then. Minnette is next to you a wonder at understanding. I don't believe you know how good at it she is. If not, believe me, she has a quick sense for values and a sure finger for the right spot, be it strength or weakness. . . .

In our second talk we walked about the campus. The dialogue was good. Nugey, it isn't easy to let convention and Oscar [Minnette's husband] take such a dolly dialoguer out of one's life. . . .

. . . She counts me her Great Friend—of my sex—I count her my Great Friend of her sex. She said suddenly "Jim, you'll be coming to talk with me when we're sixty!" A lot of it is in that sudden sentence. . . .

Anyway, I'll never know the right answer to sex and marriage, sense and mirage. Will you, old dear?

And so, naturally, to Eva. . . .

Eva, the Girl of Dreams . . . The Girl heroine of movie stories, and "Prince Chap" plays and pipe-dreams, the girl one's heart yearns for and the devil take Joey Taylor's neat philosophy and H. James' cool churches! The girl of Browning gondolas, of Lee Robert's songs, of Douglas Fairbanks fifth reels and of Harold McGrath's novels. The one, after all, we marry.

. . . I can deal with her fairly, too. Letters and thoughts since seeing her have done wonders. I love her, always have, always will. I loved her when I saw her. There were the "rapid heart-beats" and all. I sat and stared at her as I never sat and stared at anyone. I didn't give one damn at first about talking. I didn't know what I said or what she said. . . .

I don't know what it is, or was to begin with, but there was the same sensation after eleven years that I had when, as a kid, I told her good-bye, pulled my cap to pieces, and felt an ache and an urge in my heart too old for my years, but too eternal and atavistically strong ever to be classed as "puppy love" or any other thing. She was the One Girl. And I felt it again, that unexplainable thing. When sitting opposite her, after dinner in her home, we were for the first time solidly alone. I wanted her. That's all. . . . And, god help her, she likes me in person! Now what do you think of that? Why darn it all, the finest letter she wrote to me in all of the time was one she sent after she had seen a recent picture of me. . . .

She is coming here a week from to-day for the Follies—and as she put it in today's letter—"to see you and the Follies". Step down, brother Ziegfeld! . . .

. . . I'll speak now of plans.

Very greatly I want to go back one more year to school, for the express purpose of amassing knowledge on certain courses, and with the determined intention of letting much of the rest of the campus world ride past.

After that—well, it will then be square up to me to say, finally, "hello, world." Meanwhile, I am going to rent a nice Underwood and try out a few things, while I am getting over the remnants of nerve-fog and physical near-wreck. After that I will have to take on something inconsequential but with money in it for the summer, and maybe, if the Purple Gods rule or if Saturn is in Taurus—or what ever does it—maybe for longer with the necessity also of giving up graduation—which of course I can do with no terrible blow to me or my career.

Somehow I can't accomplish much here at home, since never have my folks understood me, altho' they have always sympathized and helped wonderfully. . . .

Well, Nugums, there's a lot more to write, but I have many things to accomplish to-day, so I'll call this a letter, with the promise to do another one soon again.

Let me know how everything comes along, constantly.

Unshakably yours,

Jim

&. &. &.

*James G. Thurber, 330 East Gay St.,*

*Columbus, Ohio*

*April fourth, 1920*

My dear Old, better 'old, gold Nugget:

... The old atmosphere of our days in school and at the Phi Psi house together still comes back to me when I get up North of 12 53, like a vagrant
haunting sniff of O. Henry's mignonette. ...

Have I mentioned to you that Henry James has now become my greatest
enthusiasm along lines literary? He always was a big card with me, especially
in Joe Taylor days, but I cultivated him extensively in Paris, becoming possibly
the world's greatest authority on "The Ambassadors" which I bought over
there for $5 in the N.Y. Edition and perused many times with increased inter-
est, since I was right amongst his places and in the atmosphere, and no one
can enjoy it to the farthest ultimate who does not know Notre Dame, Le Tour
D'Argent and the Boulevard Malsherbes. Perhaps it is my deep interest in him
and his art and his philosophy and his orientation which makes the M.Y.F.P.
[Minnette] attraction never the less, for she not only can talk him with me but
she has always appealed to me as having many of the elements of his ladies,
tho' I quite concur in your earlier statement that she is not a Madame de
Vionnet and never will be. Still I can't help but know that she has a—what I
might call—"depth of charm" and a scope of manner and a princess quality of
bearing and a poise and reserve in dialogue which is so far above the average
American girl of these twelve cylinder, jazzomarimba days that it is refreshing
like the drift of May roses across a base-ball field. (If anyone should ever wish
to compile my letters after I am famously dead, and should call upon you to
furnish the most of them and of me, I fear you would have to censor and ex-
purgate with a free wrist movement.) ...

The day before Spring Vacation began I called Minnette and we met at
Lazurus where she went shopping, and there was a most interesting two hours
in the nice lil Tea Room on the Fifth. There was between us, besides the fine
understanding, a flat cut glass dish of sweet peas, my favorite flowers. The orchestra was playing things from a few of my favorite operas "Manon", "Boheme" and "Lakme." It was really nice. Then we walked up to Long and High
to get a car and one not being there we kept on walking. When we next looked
up, we were ten steps from Hennicks and I was in two street car tickets. She
left the next day for Chicago and Hubby. ...

Friday, three days after Minnette left, Eve o' Zanesville came down for the

Follies avec sa famille, and I had her and her wondrously good looking mamma out to my home, where she met the family of Thurber. Eve and I had but a very few minutes together this second time, not enough to make any progress towards knowing each other than before. It will take so many visits to establish a basis. . . . I have found this out that Eve never in her life bumped up against or associated with a personality just like mine or with a man of my interests and enthusiasms and my change of gait. I know that she is a bit puzzled, vastly interested, in a way fascinated and most of all half-eager and half-afraid about her own ability to find my plane. It is, as I say, a new field altogether for her, for she never went to college, has no idea then of that life, and about all we have at the start in common is I believe a mutual interest from some unknown source and a common playground in an affection for things of the stage. She still yearns for the stage a bit, but the call of home and happiness is strong too. She is balancing between the little comforts of folks in Zanesville and the call of the New York existence. That she has talent I am positive—in fact I have told you that she got as far as a principal at the Winter Garden five years ago and the offer of a contract with Roscoe Arbuckle in the movies, and that she left everything then at its peak and went to Zanesville to recuperate from nerves and has been there ever since. I forgot to tell you that in her book of autographs there is one written by your father—or I guess I did tell you that.

Another thing, she is evidently not very strong, and her nerves seem to be mated with mine in many ways, which is a discomforting reflection. I have fine reason to believe that she hates the idea of marriage because she and her mother have decided it wouldn't do for her to have babies—that is, an uncanny seventh sense of mine tells me that—but I am sure that she loves the lil things, les cheres enfants—just as I do; but you see I myself had arrived at the determination never to bring any children into this old vale to inherit the Thurber nervousness which is sure constitutional if anything ever was, the three of us brothers having had a double heritage of it, and before I believed Eva felt that way I had decided that I would never marry either, if the girl did want children; so I suppose after all this phase is what you might call "everything coming out all right"—I suppose you might, but it seems a form of hard lines or something like that.

However, here I am living in the cottage and everything and we may never get that far at all. In fact I met a girl at Wurlitzer's Victrola store to-day who hasn't faded yet, but may to-morrow morning, and then I ran into Marion Poppen on Broad Street to-day, she all bodiced up with a corsage of sweet peas. You never knew I long had a silent case on her, did you, in days when she seemed to be engaged to a w.k. ChiPhi?

There is no use in denying that, after all, this Eva girl is *not* the girl of all my dreams, that I really did manage through the years to build up a glittering image based upon a pretty little bob-haired girl, an image which was so wonderful that she couldn't, I suppose, live up to it. And since she couldn't, there is still what Henry J. would call a "drop", something big has gone out of my life. Maybe after a while something bigger will take its place, but the little princess of mine who played about willow trees on Yarrow is still there. I have never found her, I never will. There's something in this story of mine that would have delighted old Henry [James] who loved to play with psychological and social and imaginative difficulties. And he would have seen in it as you do something higher than emotionalism and stronger than fancy and sincerer than sentimentalism, something rather wonderful and big. He was a connoisseur of special cases—the things that happen to most of his "poor, sensitive gentlemen" could not have happened to more than one in a million—take his collection including "The Jolly Corner" "The Friends of the Friends" "The Altar of the Dead" the "Beast in the Jungle"—frail, too greatly attenuated too impossible the average person would say in some disgust, but of a pure type with mine, in uniqueness of experience and quality of thought. I won't let it take up all of my life or warp my perspectives, but it must always be bigger to me than most things, I am formed not to be able to let career or business become more to me than friendship and love. I am, I am proud and at once miserable to say, a follower after the great God James. I mean Henry James. Funny, before him, before I knew him my greatest most personal interest was in Edith Wharton who is admittedly a sitter at his feet and is nearest like him than any other writer alive or dead and gone. It was a great discovery to me that she was not the ultimate that I still had before me the exquisite pleasure of the Master. Joe Taylor and I when I saw him at his home had quite a James talk fest, for he is also more for H.J. than for any of the rest. . . .

\* \* \*

Carson Blair was in Columbus over Easter and trys to get me to go into advertising work in Detroit where Mully and he are both in that line, with different firms; Carson is making very good with Burroughs. I am still unsettled. I want to go back to State and intend to, if possible, but I have to do something pretty toot de sweet in order to finance things. I don't know what it will be. I have got this typewriter for a month and expect to do something along the Beloved Literary Line in that time—and it helps oil the works to write to you.

Ha, Watson, also I have another great interest in life which I cultivated in Paris: music, good music—I mean listening to it, not playing a flute or singing a wicked tenor. The family is already being made the more or less unhappy victim of my research for the records of songs I learned to love over there away from Jazz. I never quite got into the spirit of the thing here . . . but in Paris I became an opera hound and a concert spaniel. While the world goes along trolling Dardanella and The Sky Blues and Shanghai Mary Sings Dixie Like Mother Macree in Far Off Brazil I hum snatches from famous things. The Dream from Manon, the Musetta Waltz from Boheme, He Will Come Again from Madame Butterfly are a few of 'em, but boy, oh, they can never take the place of Sing Me to Sleep Rose in the Bud and Slumber Boat of the Eva O' Long Ago. . . .

And now about you. Your play opened up yesterday I believe you said. I am all anxiously primed to hear how she is going and how you like it and what your part is and all. . . .

*  *  *

Before I forget it, I hadn't been here long till I heard from several sources that one E.J. Nugent stepped out quite colorfully in Chicago. That you did or din't makes no damn difference. I just bring it in to pave the way to telling you that such things have a trick of getting around from which I was spared with my one or two affaires d'amour in Paris. I lasted a little over 12 long months in the gayest city in the world. I now have a picture of Ninette, the most wonderful dancer in the world, and memories of my first step aside, the pretty Remonde of Provins. The whirl when once it whirled went whirling so fast that I saw it as a reason for whirling home. Ninette told me once in the privacy of her cute Montmarte appartement, "Jeemy, at zee step which you step, you must last about two weeks." "Ah, non, ma cherie," I returned, lighting a Pall Mall from a huge red box of them which I had given her, and offering my glass for some more of her fine Porto, "Ah, non, vous vous trompez, you are very wrong, at this pace I will last all of ten days." Voila. . . .

I have no regrets, fortunately, but I will say that I can't see it except as a passing experience once in—or twice in—a life-time, providing there is no One Girl. I mean if there isn't One Girl, why then say six or eight passing experiences or nine or ten or . . . hell. The genus known as Gash Hound intrigues me not. Nor does it suffocate you with enthusiasm, either. But what have you to say as to how long your pace would have lasted? Come to think of it I never had your statement that you hadn't hunted forbidden berries long ago, but I at least imagined you hadn't. I don't believe I ever told you I got as far as Paris all right, either. It seems to have been a thing which we naturally didn't consider worth the time for discussing. And God knows it isn't.

\* \* \*

Some of the things in literary lines I am working on are: a book for next year's Scarlet Maskeraders—possibly—; an original sort of Washington Square thing called "The Fourth Mrs. Bluebeard"—the other wife who gypped the Homme de barbe bleu, you know, but who was never written about—she beat him by modern feminine craft. "The Call" which is powerful in my mind, but which will no doubt fail—a Henry James sort of thing with another special trick of mine as the basis, namely a gift I have at long but awfully vivid intervals of receiving mental telepathy messages from friends or family in trouble. Don't believe I ever told you that trick. It has really worked but five times in my life, one of which I will never tell but which is the most beautiful and complicated of all—and which, damn it, is the basis for my story, so I guess I'll have to do it under a nom de plume. Oddly enough, two of the five instances happened here since I returned, and of them had nothing to do with trouble at all, it was just a freak working. My mother has had the same thing several times. Then I am working on a comedy about a French wife with a new twist—(ps-s-t the story has the twist) an article along the line of "France and America, Last and First Impressions," which no American magazine would print, probably, since my status is about 67 to 33 favor France. And there are minor poems and things.

Your lil poem "Dead Roses" I like very much, but Nugey it is not as good as the unrevised thing—it may be a bit better technic, but what was matter with the technic of the other one? If you must revise the other one, darn you, do it over again. This one has the air of a wild rose bush jerked up and planted in a green-house by three expert florists. I like the first immensely.

When you have time write me again, lots, and don't forget I'm longing for to see you, old heart.

Always,

*Eva Prout and her mother stayed at the Thurber home overnight while in Columbus to attend the Follies.*

## TO EVA PROUT

*James Grover Thurber*
*April 6 [1920]*

My dear Eve:

. . . First of all it sure was terribly nice to have had you here. It had seemed to me always so impossible. I mean I never really believed it could happen—like Aladdin's lamp. Reminds me of a poem I read in Paris . . .

> "Never your steps where mine have trod,
>     Never my words to you;—
> And it all would have been so easy for God—
>     So simple a thing to do."

Well, it wasn't so hard after all. I am always discovering molehills and saying "oh, lookit the mountains!" And God slipped one over again on our friends the enemy—the Purple Gods. Life is very nice. . . .

. . . can I come up to see you a week from Sunday? . . .

I ask so long in advance because I don't want to ruin another date of anyone else. I refuse flatly to cause any poor love-lorn kid [Ernest Geiger] to lie awake nights. Tell him I'm a fatherly old soul whose interest in you is like the interest of Whitcomb Riley in roses or at the most like the avidity of Omar Khayam for jugs. Tell him I had a bet that I would meet you someday, is all. And he'll "get over it", as you said. . . .

The reason I want to come up is because I am determined to leave lil ol' Columbus before long. . . .

It's mental death to stay here where there is nothing progressive to do—at least until school opens. I feel I must get my degree. I will probably go to Detroit. One of my friends [Carson Blair] came all the way down here Saturday to talk Detroit to me. It has its pluses. At least I can try it.

We are both talking of going back to Paris for a year or so in journalistic work, if we can line up a few [news]papers etc. And once there we aim to look over the really vast field for American enterprise, with a possible view to working together there if it seems as big as I believe it is. . . .

You should see Paris someday. . . . I mean *my* Paris. . . . I would like to be there when you arrive to show you my Paris. Here's a tentative program for a few days—say in June, 19—?

First Day

1. Morning. A walk down the Champs Elysees, with a half-hour's rest under the flowering chestnut trees of the Elysee's Gardens. A half hour in the Spring Salon. Then over the Seine along the Quai D'orsay to the Eiffel Tower, taking in Napoleon's tomb. Then up past the Embassy and my hotel to the Arch. Luncheon at one of the open air . . . restaurants in the wonderful gardens of the Champs Elysees. Say we make it Ledoyen's, on the right side. Their hors d'oeuvre are really good and they have the best omelettes in Paris.

2. Afternoon. A taxi along the Seine to the Ile de Cité. An hour in Notre Dame. It's worth it. Then a taxi to the Luxembourg Gardens, taking in Rodin's Museum. After that a little walk down some crooked rues of the Latin Quarter. Dinner at the Café de Paris, with its plush lounge-seats, its lights, its beautiful service and some Chateau-Lafitte, 1904.

3. Night. A walk from the Café de Paris down the Rue Royal and up the Boulevards to the Opera. And there, happily, Thais or Aida.

Second Day

1. Morning. A walk in the Bois de Boulogne, the dream park of the world. Till ten o'clock. Then a taxi ride to Montmartre to get the vistas of Sacre Coeur and a view of that wonderful region by daylight. Then an aperitif—you can have a grenadine—or a Vermouth-Cassis is mild—on the terrace of the famed Café de La Paix, the center of the world. Luncheon at the same Café.

2. Afternoon. The jewelry shops and Modeste shops of the Rue de la Paix, right near, and over to the Rue de Rivoli and the afternoon concert in the Tuilleries—say we stay for the selections from "Lakmé" and the Nocturne of Chopin's. Tea at Rumplemayer's across the way. Then an hour at the Louvre, time enough to see the Mona Lisa, Venus de Milo, Winged Victory and a certain frieze of Botticelli's.

3. Night. Dinner at L'Abbaye's restaurant in Montmarte, with a dance or two. They have "le cuisine exquise." Coffee, gateaux, afterwards—you can have just a little chartreuse to see what it looks like anyway. And during the dinner a silver bucket holding ice and a bottle of Moet and Chaudone. A few minutes in the Black Cat . . . and the Lune Rousse, ending with a view of Paris from the Church of the Sacred Heart.

Third Day

1. Morning. A walk in Park Monceau, my one favorite spot of all. Here we will sit on a bench by the Lilac Lane and watch the beautiful Paris kiddies at

play, looked after by prim "bonnes" or maids. From there a few nearby pretty places, including a museum and old Gothic church or two. And at noon we'll run over to the left bank for lunch at Le Tour D'Argent.

2. Afternoon. Out to Versailles—the palace, the grounds and the Trianons. Tea and cakes at a place I know where big elm trees touch the sky. Dinner at the prettiest and most expensive and "chicest" place of all, the world's finest restaurant, D'Armenonville in the Fairy depths of the Bois du Boulogne. Then the concert under the [unclear] trees of the Restaurant Dauphine—real pretty music, including, of course, "Smiles" and the song which always will take me to Paris in spirit wherever my body is—"Some Day He'll Come" from Madame Butterfly. And there, under the moon-stained trees, while we eat their nice panache ice cream, I'll bribe the orchestra to play these songs: "Slumber Boat" and "Sing Me to Sleep." After which I won't have to be sung to sleep.

Oh, Eve, I've been in Paris all the time I was writing that. And you were there, too. Gee it was real! . . .

Time now . . . to quit dreaming and go to bed. But many of my dreams have come true—and over the hills and far away isn't so far away after all.

> Goo' night, Eve,
> dreamingly
> Jim

❧  ❧  ❧

> *Hotel Rogge, Zanesville, O.*
> *April 22, 1920*

Dear Eve:

The very competent, tho' somewhat irrascible, lady behind the grilled window of the Ohio Electric said she didn't have the faintest idea whether the car would run or not tonight. They are having power trouble. I decided it probably wouldn't go. And being fidgetty I came over here. I would rather wait three hours here than one hour in the O. E. station. Wouldn't you? And besides with you to write to—sweet mamma—the three hours are tulip time. It is, besides, my favorite writing hours. All the best writers write at queer hours. Lincoln wrote his Gettysburg Address on a train. Theodore Dreiser writes in the wee 'sma' hours. Booth Tarkington has regular hours, maybe, but he always uses a pencil—he has six or eight and when the point wears just a bit he gets a new one. He can afford it. They say he was cruel to his wife. They say Al Jolson was, too.

Kipling can write only when he's in the mood. Shakespeare had the worst trick of all—he picked out the 16th century to write in. Think of it! No one can do that now. Which shows he was in a class by himself.

I wonder how the name of this hotel is pronounced? "Rogge"?

> *POEM:*
> The cat, as every kiddie knows,
> Thinks the night was made to prowl in.
> And underneath the midnight moon
> Is the dog's pet time to howl in;
> And who, calling 'round at two a.m.,
> Ever found the owl in?
> The fish now is a wiser fowl
> Then is the cat or dog or owl
> When eight bells out at sea has rung
> Up in his hammock fishy's swung.
> Now take the husband of the hen—
> He thinks he beats a big Big Ben—
> He bothers his wife at ungodly times
> To sound his early morning chimes.
> His wife will cackle "You can't sing"—
> But do you think that hubby gives a ding?
> He used to think there'd be no light
> Unless he crowed to end the night
> And so he never got much sleep—
> He'd waken at the slightest "cheep"—
> He thought that if he slept too late
> The sun would stick at the Golden Gate.
> —But once he slept till half past nine
> And woke and saw the sun did shine!
> My oh, it was a cruel surprise
> To find *he* didn't make it rise.
> But you can read the story, dear,
> In Edmond Rostand's "Chantecler."

(Urgent note: the "dear" is poetic license or something. I had to get a rhyme you know. Mais, je ne regrette rien que j'ecrive a toi; quand m'eme.) . . .

The guinea pig's a funny hoggy
(Twelve thirty-one in the hotel Rogge)
He's awful fat and short and podgy
(Twelve thirty two in the hotel Rogge)
Of course, he's not a sure nuf hog
(Twelve thirty three in the hotel Rogge)
His wife is a thrifty little drudge—
We once had two named "Kewp" and "Budge"—
(Twelve thirty four in the hotel Rogge)
We kept 'em in a cave we dug
(Twelve thirty five in the hotel Rogge)
And after half a year or so
You should have seen the family grow
They had thirty children then, I know.
And hubby walked the ground at night
—Forty children, if I am right—
And his wife thought they were awful nifty—
These forty—or was it really fifty—
But she could sleep, land sakes alive—
And hubby up with all sixty-five—
Yet still he loved his little matey—
And him with the care of all them eighty!
He died at last one morn at light—
going on at such a sleepless rate
the funeral was very fine—
He left a wife and ninety nine.


The cuckoo clock's the worst of all
He's up at all hours in the hall;
He's scared of burgu-lars I bet
Or else he gets a bad night sweat.
He can't sing like a lark or Sinnet
But he keeps fine time—right to the minute—
I guess he thinks he's got a lot
Or else the clock gets too darn hot;
To feed him place a little sand
From an hour glass on the minute hand.
I think the cuckoo clock's just dear!

But he doesn't sleep enough, I fear,
And counting hours year after year
He often gets run down I fear
Which never happens to chanteclear.
Yet he may become a nervous wreck
But he'll not get an axe laid on his neck.

The barnacle, too, is a sleepless soul
He sleeps on ships and when they roll
They keep him up—altho he's down
Where the water turns the keel all brown.
He likes to sleep on the post of a dock
—Which is quite unlike the cookoo clock— . . .
The ostrich is a quaint fish, too,
He never sleeps like me or you.
His pillow's two feet under ground
And still he sleepeth very sound.
Green sod above, lie light, lie light
Or else the ostrich won't sleep tight.

   (. . . this may go on like this for several pages yet. Oh, I'm not either—I'm just thinkin' 'em up 's go along.)

Consider now the frail peacock—
He is a funny lizard—
He sleeps not like the cuckoo clock—
His head rests near his gizzard.
And never once the whole night long
Does he burst forth to sing a song . . .

*[Visiting Nugent in Dover, Ohio]*

*May Ninth, 1920*

Dear Eve:
   . . . I am wondern what you are doing now the weather up here is right smart nicer than what it was how is your ma Zeb Gibbs lost his wife last Saturday night but she found her way back and Zebs still out of luck He says hes goin t drop her in the Crick nex time the parsnip crop is tolerable this yere but we aint lookin much for no snortin barley harvest. . . .

Please, Eve, aren't you well and strong and husky now and going to our dance? I won't have you miss it for anything and I won't have you go unless you are feeling fully up to the effort.

Elliott is going to the dance whether his girl does or not, because for one thing he is anxious to see this Eve person. . . . He will only be home a week or two longer before he sets sail for Indianapolis and stock [theater] with Stuart Walker. We have certainly had a wonderful time of it so far talking over all the things we had to talk about. But I expect to leave here not later than Wednesday, so I want you to send me a letter nice and fast to Dover that I may know your plans, your condition, and for whom you are giving surprise parties now. . . .

Nugey wanted to make Akron this afternoon for to fuss with his girlie but mamma Nugent is jealous and I guess she loves him most and I bet he loves her most and anyway it's Mother's Day. God bless all mammas.

Please be sweet to me, Misseveprout, and tell me quick that you are feeling powerful as a turbine and will sure get to go. . . .

I think quite a lot of you.

> Always,
> Jim

*Eve accepted Thurber's invitation to a fraternity dance at the Columbus Country Club. Between dances Thurber found Elliott Nugent and Eve on the terrace looking at "a green star" in the sky. Says Eve: "Jim didn't like it at all that I saw green stars with Elliott."*

*Monday Evening [Probably May 1920]*

Dear Eve:

Well, thank Goodness, I have recovered quite from the "low" spell which I had just after I left you on that perfectly horrible old train. I haven't yet decided which is hardest to do—to see you go or to kill in myself the absolutely tremendous desire to hold you, just before you go.

(I can't imagine why I am so nervous to-day—would you look at this writing, but maybe it is the reflex action caused by surpressed desire.)

I do so hope, Eve, that the trip home didn't leave you just a wreck, and that we didn't misuse you so much here that you lapsed back into a need for more convalescing. . . .

Ol' Eddie [Morris] felt my depression worse than it was. I really didn't want to talk to him going home in his car, I just wanted to think of you. Eve, god knows how it could happen, but I *fell* in love with you when you were here—I mean it became stronger and yet simpler and so darn wonderful. I can't explain that. I can't see what happens, but something did happen.

I realize how you mean everything to me, what a marvelous thing it would be to have you always near, and how the light goes from all things when you go. . . .

Anyway—or rather "therefore"—I just can't be as I was in Paris or as I was at any time before. I can't help but be a little jealous and very selfish, I suppose. All I can do is to promise to try very hard not to "make you mad" and I will honestly try to be just "friendly."

. . . I probably won't be able to get up to Zanesville for maybe even such a long time as two weeks, because I gotta and wanta plunge headlong into giving dad's idea of syndicate-newspaper writing a real chance. We have talked it over today and he feels so confident of his ability to get the necessary contracts for me—and I am so confident of my own ability to make it go, if I get the chance, that it seems the thing right now to try and to try hard.

So, before starting things, I am going to reach Zanesville Tuesday—(today)—and probably worry mamma Barks to distraction the way I'm always popping up when relatives are arriving and when church surprise parties are being done.

Just remember that I am this way:—when I call up, if you want me to, say "g'on home'—can't see y' today." Please do that, if necessary, since I desire not to get in bad at 431. And it seems like I am there so darn often, in a way, and so doggone seldom, in another way.

> I'm awfully badly in love with you, Eva.
> Always,
> Jim

≈  ≈  ≈

Saturday Night

Dear Eve:

So my letter [never located] was sarcastic? Just a little bit too much so, wasn't it? It hurt just a little bit, because you really mind what I write, but care nothing, one way or another, for what I say. That's because you didn't or won't ever identify me with the hand and the heart of certain letters—mere dreams I wrote in idle or pensive hours, meaning nothing or almost nothing. I am two men to you. One of them you love just a bit, the other you care for only because, after all, he wrote the letters and you can't change that.

Why shouldn't I be sarcastic if I wish? Do you think it is a simple matter to give one's whole heart away, his whole being, his entire self—to a girl who may be a little amused, somewhat pleased, and only on occasions seriously realizing what she has had given to her?

I intend to revolt against you every darn week, or oftener, until you *LOVE ME*—so that if you never do I can say, well I had a good time, you didn't seal my heart up and toss all joy away with it.

A woman is often a wonderful thing. And you are. But in you, as in all of them, is the indifference of Carmen, the joy in cruelty of Cleopatra, the tyrannical marble-heartedness of Katherine De Medici, and the cold glitter of all the passionless despots of men's warm souls since sex first originated—since Eve broke the heart of humanity forever and laughed with sadistic joy at Adam sweating blood on the rack she made for him.

All those things are most in you now. They are always predominant in a woman who is passionately loved but who loves not at all herself. Women like that are greatly interested in the lover's sufferings, but to her they are a spectacle, a Roman holiday—a pageant of exciting emotions, nothing else.

Green stars mean, seriously, nothing to me or to you except a nice little incident—a cute reference to our Friendships. But deep down in your heart you appreciate what such a symbol *would* mean to me if I had cause for jealousy— how I would really suffer and how you would be untouched by anything but a sort of pride in your power to hurt me. . . .

I'm not blaming you. I'm blaming the age of women gone before you who handed such legacies down—blaming the radiant and sparkling and fidgety ladies of history who kissed in a moment of coquetry and saw men die, kings dethroned and nations fight in blood because of that careless caress. Men are fools, weak, wine-blooded, deeply-devoted darn fools. What have women done for them half so intent and potent as what they have done *to* them?

Or not always a kiss. Just a pair of laughing blue eyes, or a note passed in school. You know your monarchy over me. You know, too, what a power it is. But not caring for me, it means nothing. Supposing you loved me and I didn't love you? I would, unconsciously, gloat over my power—and I wouldn't realize how, sometimes, a little thing like a green star might, just by imagining the men and other stars, be the end of hope or the crash of years of dreams, or the embittering of the best stuff in a person's soul. A man's real and only love is a sensitive thing. It curdles easily, and when it does, it spoils all good and all everything.

That green star affair was like a word in fun which calls up a tragedy. It made me imagine what might be—what may happen yet. There are many men and other stars which you may yet see. Elliott I fully forgot. He represents but some shadowy person who may someday with a glance do what I never may be able to do with every act I know, for you.

Nothing is so near to tears as laughter is.

That's all my sarcasm meant.

Shouldn't I naturally, despite myself, want to hurt you if you never care for me? Whom the gods destroy they first make madly in love with a girl. . . .

Many a man who loves spiritually is a weakling—a professor. Many a one who loves physically is a brute. But when the two are mixed, he loves with all the fire and passion of a poet and a cave-man.

I am anything but "cold." I am ten times the affectionate nature you are. That frightens me. To be my wife a girl would have to want to be loved—lots and very terribly. If I ever kiss you you'll know that—and you'll know what a wonderful thing my love is. Kissing seems not a great matter, in a way. And yet in one way it speaks the million things which words can't—to kiss, for the first time, a girl whom one loves and has always loved is a thing too great for words to tell. . . .

I kissed this girl I told you about the other night. A real girl doesn't care to be kissed, much, unless real love goes with it. I won't explain anything else, except that, in certain moods, a man can be *impersonally* affectionate, and like it. I hope this makes you mad at me. I haven't kissed anyone for a long time and I wanted to, so I did, especially since she was young and pretty and started it anyway. I kissed her many times. . . .

Well, your desire came out all right—and I'm glad for you I couldn't come up. But gladder for me, because it's perfectly horrible to have been so near you, just after I leave you. You see I love you better each time and I want you worse each time, and I bruise more heart strings each new time I go away, until finally you'll just have to realize my life means you always near, and I can't be nice and unsarcastic and happy when you aren't near. . . .

When I sometimes think that someday you may be married to someone else and I may be lying awake at night when it's dark and still and deep and thinking of you, I wonder how I can stand to realize your blue eyes belong to someone else and that I can't even have so much as the touch of your hand. . . .

You see dark deep silent nights would be awful things to live through.

Nights when a green star would leer at me through a window all alone, the same green star which you and someone else would be—oh, you know. . . .

Please don't be mad at me, Eve, and like me more than a little bit. Please, please, please, please, Eve.

>With all my love for Always,
>Jim

&. &. &.

*Fourth O' May, 1920*

Dear "Just Eve":

. . . I didn't tell you that yesterday morning I met Minnette quite by accident on Long Street where she and other Kappa girls were having a rummage sale to get $ for the very selfish but nice purpose of throwing a house party at Buckeye Lake. I had Minnette home for lunch and it was the first time she was ever here. She was very disappointed that I had no picture of you. When are you going to send me a great big picture—one of those you sent to New York? Ever or never?

I helped the girls with their sale, managing the "men's shirt department."

Last night I had acute memories of you when I attended a dinner dance at the Country Club—quiet lil affair for a girl guest of Ed [Morris]'s sister. I saw no stars either green or gold. . . .

. . . I intend to come to say good-bye before I depart to work hard far away from Yarrow—which is Zanesville. I'll write you every day and let you know how things go.

I hope I am happier this time next year than I am now.

After all the thing which gives a man most content and comfort is his work, and success in it and growth of it, and a hold on the future. . . .

I don't want to *write* mean things again, and I promise after this to be the sweet child of my other letters—the wistful, kind-hearted James. . . .

I could "get there" without you. All rivers lead to the sea, all roads to Rome— and eventually all ways to the End. But, oh, lady, lady, how sweet the lilacs bloom along a certain path and how cruel are the stones set in another trail. . . .

. . . I am going to stop over in Zanesville either tomorrow or Thursday. I'll call you up from the station, and maybe you'll let me come out for an hour and a half—I promise not to stay longer, just to show you how I can do difficult things. I feel very happy today, Just Eve, because you have given me a waiting chance and I did fear that you might not be able to give me any. But being just, Eve, you couldn't have turned out the stars and blown out the moon, could you?

The enclosed "Nocturne" was written by me in the Ohio State Sun-Dial for May, 1918. Oh, yes, you are the person in mind—the "too much love" in it is just imagination. One often has to distort facts for art's sake, you know. . . .

As I promised, I promise again, I will never, if I can help it, say again that

I love you,
Always
Jamie

I held her in my arms,
This one at present dear,
And there came from out the past
Your vision clear.

The human touch is strong,
But clear and warm as faith
Clings the memory of you,
My sweetheart wraith.

᪥ ᪥ ᪥

*Tuesday, May Eighteen, 1920*

Dear Spangles:

. . . I am glad that Ernest was merciful about his date and really he seems to be either getting resigned to it or to be growing older (or perhaps not). I leave him to you, you know. . . .

Really, Eve, I am not, as you seem to believe, disappointed in your so-called lack of "enthusiasm." I hate enthusiastic girls or women. I know you had a rather pleasant time, and I didn't mean to say that you didn't show it sufficiently or any rot as that. You cared for no one here as I did. I loved several with all my heart. Naturally I had to be enthusiastic even if it made you believe I am "funny." Besides I am an enthusiastic being, which has its own punishments. I give my heart and soul completely away. Only men do that. The occasion was not brilliant or scintillating—I am also not a youth who is still eager about "parties." But it remains the most wonderful time of my life, and I really don't care whether anyone understands that or not. Goo'bye—or so long, I mean.

Always—Jimmy

᪥ ᪥ ᪥

*Neil House, Columbus, Ohio Sunday*
*[Possibly May 30, 1920]*

Dear Eve:

. . . I have been for a week or two writing most mournful "pomes" about things. Nugey likes one or two of them, particularly one called "October" which is just a dream and isn't sad at all. If all my other sins don't queer me maybe these will:

> *October*
> October's burning on the hills
> And rainbow leaves are falling,
> And your blue eyes are in my dreams
> And your dear voice is calling.
>
> June has charms of wide array,
> And May can still a lover's ills—
> But every pathway leads to you
> When October walks the hills
>
> For Once October called me up,
> Through rainbow leaves a-drifting,
> And gave me you to love until
> The years of time cease sifting.

I have always loved October—and you. What will October do to me this year, I wonder?

Here's one a little more tragic:

> *When Dawn Will Come*
> There will be an afternoon of careless meeting
> And we shall pass like ships pass in the night—
> It will be just one, like any other greeting—
> Yet your eyes will come back with next morning's light,
> And never after shall I lose them from my sight.
>
> I have seen in afternoons of idle hours
> A thousand eyes whose dead ashes never glow

I have forgot long years of women
            as one forgets the flowers
In gardens seen but once. But I will go
Back to you as unerring and as
            happily as rivers to the ocean flow.
There will be a night of magic air
Whose alchemy will change mere
            clinking dreams to gold
And I will find the very fragrance of your hair
A chain that will never loose me from its hold—
Then dawn will come and I will
            look into your laugh and find
                  myself grown gray and old.

That's not so nice. This one is even less nicer:

*Last Roses*
If past the poor new grave of youth's dead dreams
We two shall pass at unguessed hours in afteryears,
May God give me the carelessness to smile for them
And you the sweet remembrance which shuns not tears.

Where once the brave high heart of first love wrote in gold
The shimm'ring splendor of a soul lost in its song—
Here where the leaves of my last roses drift to earth,
May you not stand too lightly or I too long.

There is a tiny flame of fear that this is all;
So let me pray above this place that when we're old
You then may be no more than love which lacks a form,
And I no less than one who wrote your name in gold.

Oh, I've got a few more but that's enough to show that Jim's choice lies between a "Paris life" of futile pomes and a real "American life" of real human
happiness. Please, please do something, Eve. But nothing too darn final, if you
are "mad at" me.
        Always,
        Jim

# TO ELLIOTT NUGENT

*June 23, 1920*

Dear old Nugums:

. . . I went to Akron and was there 3 days, finding out finally that the loss of the old left eye was a barrier with Goodrich. So I'm back and figuring some more. I may give my pet Ohio syndicate idea a fling, but I'm uncertain of the next move as yet, even uncertain as to returning to State, altho' I believe I will.

I got your trysting telegram and was all busted up because I couldn't be there at the hour, but I had to leave early that very a.m. for Akron and Neorpheus held a previous date with me.

On my 2 trips to Akron I saw Katherine both times for long talks. The first date was just a few days after your Saturday trip to Akron at her request. The second time was just after your roses and your note reached her. So you see I probably know much you didn't suspect about the latest chapter in your idyll.

The Garvers treated me wonderfully. The first trip, Mrs. G. took me to luncheon at the Portage and the last time I was at their home for lunch. It wasn't such a difficult situation as I feared at first because of being the Nugent's Great Friend.

Katherine and I talked much. She was very frank with me and told me "all." Your roses hurt a bit and your note more. That is, when you came that Saturday evidentally things were again left forever secured, so that altho' in my estimation your note was fine and well-meant, it struck her as just a third severing cut. You must understand the single-track mind of a girl who has loved, *who still loves,* and who was engaged two years. Sensing her situation, I could read into her conception of your note all that she did, and all that was left for me was to sort of agree with her. My situation was hard. One can't insinuate to a girl that she isn't lovable, once she *was* loved. One must pretend to search for faults in *you.* All of which wouldn't have been necessary if I was not assured that she still loves you, would be for a time positive she could never take you back the same, but would finally, if you came, because she told me she will always care for you and will never care for anyone else in the same way. Her mother is "disappointed" in you. She "thought you were different." I was silent. Then she was big enough to say that she guessed a man has as much right as a girl to "change his mind." Katharine couldn't meet your note and your roses on the basis you set in your letter, you old nut, simply because it isn't a case of a mutual return to friendship. She still loves you. And, oh, the difference in that. You must realize her position, and figure out just how you and she can unite again. It is a hard thing. She holds the idea that if she hadn't so readily fallen in with your talk that "fatal" night about marriage, she could have—shall I say—kept you "interested." She feels she seemed too quiescent, too much "yourn." And so she set me to wondering if old human nature really did play a part. I wonder, I mean, what your attitude would be now had she, that night, set you down gently, as a nice lover, but as one whom she was, when face to face with marriage, not so damn sure of. . . .

And now, concerning Me.

Three weeks ago Eve wrote me a letter which hurt bad. I tore it up, even . . . The gist was that she likes Ernest muchly and that "there was just One man who could have made her forget him and she never saw him again." She said she felt it would be nice for her to love me, but she "probably will end by loving the wrong man." And much more like that. I went up two days after her letter—two weeks ago tomorrow. We fought a bit—rather I "bawled her out." I told her I was going to Akron and could only see her on Sundays. Well, in her letter and in her Saturday talk she held firmly to not letting me come even on Sundays, since Ernest was given a standing Sunday date. Do you blame me for being just damn mad and quite disappointed? I went to Akron, came home, and haven't written or heard from her since—or for two weeks. The old interest is a bit dimmed, and the old dreams a bit bruised. . . .

. . . Perhaps Eve is teasing me—only I think not. My last waking thots are not of Eve, but of someday coming home to a happy little home in a cool valley of dreams and finding in its doorway, the girl of my College Romance, and since that will never be, and since I spoiled it myself largely, write for me when I am dead, "Here lies one who died of dreams."

And write to me, alive—much letters.

All success and Everything, Elliott,

  Always and Longer,

  Jimmy

     *❧ ❧ ❧*

*Saturday, July 17, 1920*

Dear Nugey,

. . . I've got the idea that something is not so good with you in the Jimmy relationship at present. One gets "feelings" every now and then and mine seldom prove foolish. Perhaps you are sort of disappointed in me because I am as yet "nowhere" in particular, or perhaps Milt's old accustomed but well meant opinion of me has disillusioned you. Or perhaps my letter in regard to Katherine struck you as uncalled for or something. If that's the point, I can only say what the hell.

As a friend I make my mistakes and have my faults—and my friends sure do need a "graveyard for my faults," and often I know I don't seem up to much, and I expect before I die to lose 'em all, but the loss would be quite gigantic because my friends are wonderful folk and I myself am *some* friend, too.

. . . If I am wrong, tell me what the matter is.

. . . Hope you are making out fine and that this summer's doings may put you across on Broadway next winter, or something grand like that.

. . . My own plans have been bumped about by chance and family ties as well as by sickness on my part (the 'ol stomach) for most a week. But the horizon looks clear, despite certain gloomy forebodings I have that 1920 means me no good, and that a lot of my luck and happiness is behind me, youth as I be. Wurra-wurra!

There are quite a lot of things I want you to know, but write me for God's nice sake and get off your good old heart and strong old shoulders the grievance or whatever it be that I feel. . . .

 always, Jim

    &#10086; &#10086; &#10086;

*Monday [August 9, 1920]*

Dear ol' Nugey:

Soon after getting your damn wonderful letter, I lost most ground gained at Magnetic Springs, and until today have been rather out o' life again. Do you know, old keed, what I need is work, all right, but before that, I should use about six months out of doors in some fine climate. . . .

However I'll probably work for a month or so at something practical here and my plans to get away may not get going till next year.

I am convinced that for a time I was so low physically and all the ways, from innocuous desuetude, flatulant ennui and God damn head over tailism, that my reasoning was akin to movie cogitation. But I have got a hell of a lot to worry about, and I'm one efficient worrier.

Boy, it is good to hear of you knocking off a lead like that Merwin Henry one, and I bet me you now have a good clinch on Indy [Indianapolis] critics and may be said to have taken two rungs upward at one mount. . . .

But, cheers, me lad, I've given over funk and folly and fol-de-rol about people, girls especially, in fact with the accent on women. My mind is getting single-tracked for health, success and money. . . .

When I get out of these doldrums you won't be petrified by any more old-maidish fears and such.

Meanwhile, act up, Nugey, and up, and up—as Chris Colombo said. And also remember, "the play's the thing." . . .

>Sincerely, always
>Jim

*In August 1920, Thurber was hired as a reporter for The Columbus Dispatch and was soon writing for O.S.U.'s male musical comedy group, The Scarlet Mask.*

>*thurber*
>*Columbus January 22 [1921]*

Dearest ol' dear, darn you anyway:

I am enclosing [*Dispatch* critic] Cherry's very fine review of our Scarlet Mask play and [O.S.U. professor] Billy Graves's unusually unrestrained praise of it. I might add others of similar tone . . . I would say that "Oh, My Omar!" is probably the biggest and best thing Ohio State has ever done outside of football. . . .

Our music was great, our costumes great, our cast very good, our settings nifty, our chorus classy, our specialty artists crafty and all very neat indeed. As to my BOOK—to you I shall say that I like it, too. I honestly believe that I have succeeded in putting over a plot in a musical comedy which tells an interesting, original story, holds the attention, grows funnier and funnier and AT THE SAME TIME (which required all I got) which moves with the snap and variety and specialty tempo etc. of a revue. Not a bad feat, huh, especially when it had to be done rapid at that. I labored most on direction of the principals. With the exception of writing in many new lines, the play stands, scene for scene, situation for situation, as I wrote it in a total of 16 hours, ten on the first act and six (in two settings) on the second.

. . . Starting Feb. 3 we play seven or eight Ohio towns, including Akron, Cincinnati, Toledo, Painesville, Lima, Dayton, Sandusky, Norwalk and Elyria. . . . We have already showed at Cleveland, Youngstown and Springfield with great success. . . .

I really got a vast amount of fun and instruction and everything else out of my work with the Scarlet maskers, and have evidently won the lasting friendship of many another fine Ohio State boy. Pat insists that their admiration is also mine, he having declared that certain chorus "girls" and cast members of the lower classes think "the sun rises and sets in a certain portion of my person". Phi Psi enthusiasm. But it was a lot o' fun. I never worked with a better bunch of fellows. I have a special liking for every one of them. They are a bunch of Princes.

. . . Five days after I was put on City Hall I attended my second council session at 7 p.m. Wed. Jan. 12. At 8 p.m. the building burned up, or rather down. The fire started in the cupola, got a terrific headway before it was discovered and raised unholy hell with the ramskackle old building. I remained in the ol' hall ten minutes after the councilmen and prominent city officials and local residents attending the session had beat it. I found out all about the fire by so doing. Inside dope, so to speak. I was the last person out of the now swiftly burning joint. Before I sauntered out, with lots of time to spare, comparatively, at that, I gazed about the abandoned council chamber and decided I'd save something or bust. All that was there to save were three huge blueprints which were being used in street-car extension discussions and two letters to council from railway presidents. I put 'em under my arm and got out. Naturally I didn't take a hell of a lot of time in doing all this, even though the general assembly of nuts and notables had abandoned the ship while I was on the smoke-clouded third floor gathering dope and choking a bit. It appears that Fire Chief Daniels rushed into the structure and told 'em all to get the hell out of there before the roof should cave in. They got, but as I say, I was upstairs, and when I came down the council room doors had been shut and fastened to prevent draft. My coat and hat were inside, so I bust 'em open, got said apparel and the letters and blueprints and made an easy escape although the whole roof was by this time burning like a match and within half an hour the interior was a furnace.

. . . Phones functioning futiley I went to the Dispatch, lit the lights and managed to reach the managing editor. Then the telegraph editor came in, said he guessed we could do nothing, wherupon I said nuts I got th' story, so he said write it, and I did. Well, to make a short story shorter I wrote the story and we shot out an extra, beating the city—meaning Citizen and Journal. We got on the street at 9:30, an hour and a half after the fire alarm and one hour after I wrote the story. I was complimented by both Editor-in-Chief and managing editor for my story, and all in all it was a gala night for James. I am now drawing 35 per week. I started at 25. Bin here six months. Just what happened to the Journal and Citizen reporters who were in the hall with me but who beat it quick I can't say. I have had the delicacy not to ask them. It was my Big Story—one of the cub fiction stories one reads about and which never happen. I dashed off my extra in twenty minutes and it was set up 2 column, 20 point I guess, and outside of the headlines it was all mine. Let us finish by quoting the telegraph editor who is an old newspaperman, a bit acrid, seldom enthusiastic, never effusive. He says to me says he, "That's a damn fine story." It was scarcely edited at all.

. . . I expect to stick with the Dispatch for two years, that is to say until July 1923. During this interval I shall have got onto every hook and crook of the newspaper game, shall have tried my hand at every angle of reporting and shall have learned the game fully, unless I suddenly lose my mind or strength. In my plethora of off-hours—comprising almost every afternoon and evening I am going to concentrate on free-lancing. Hey, hey—that just reminds me of your Smart Set story. A hundred congrats, old keed. Perhaps you do not know that many a good writer of the present day has failed to land even his fiftieth attempt with them. . . . So you beat me to the first sale after all?? Well, lay on, McNugent, and poverty-stricken be he who first shouts "back to plumbing." I am now looking for other sales to follow and very shortly and more especially the gleam of lights along Broadway spelling the Name of Your great American play.

. . . In my spare hours, then, I am going to turn out stories, trying first for the Smart Set, too, since I have a mindful of stuff with "nuance" and "esoteric" and "chartreuse" in it, admirable material for the . . . S.S.

Then I am going to try my Big Fling at the Century or Scribners or some other of the sort. I want at least to land three or four stories in the two years.

Then starting in July after leaving the Dispatch I expect to line up a few Ohio papers for a weekly Sunday article, including the revered Dispatch; several trade journals for monthly articles; a paper in some Eastern city for a weekly dramatic story; a semi-contract with some movie magazine and other kinds of publications for occasional articles—and then—then I hies me to Paris, France, whence I shall ship many a glowing story of affairs European, French, English and etc.

Free-lancing over there is soft—few newspapermen in peace time go into it—few want to—fewer can—fewer yet know anything about it—and me, well, I gotta big drag with Embassy and other officials there, know the ropes and should get over big. In the interim between contracts for stories, I shall write many bits of inconsequent verse, short stories, and my great American novel, of course.

Yet one other thing. In the two years between Now-and-Then, I want to find The Girl. I have little or no desire to traipse back to France, much as I love Her, without the Girl. Just who she will be depends on Fate and the nice Gods and everything. I see few prospects right now. But I crave a Sweetheart, and must, in fine, have one before long. I am, I find, cut from the stuff which demands a Lady in the Case. I believe—as I have told you—that I lost the Only One after all, to Chicago—but Youth's heart is resilient, I must have someone, and there may be one or two who are very good girls at that. I have already written M. [Minnette] asking her to suggest someone. She would know. She knows every plan, specification, desire, inclination, pulse-throb and heart-beat o' mine. She will be here in May for a visit.

Well, it's getting late and I'm getting either morose or sentimental, I couldn't say which, so I'll let 'er ride. Please answer, old sweetie, at your earliest convenience and do it quick. I crave as much of a continual flow of Nugentiana as I can get. Let me know all about the new show and everything. Love to you and yourn—ever-ever—Jim

ॐ  ॐ  ॐ

Columbus<br>July 10 [1921]

Dear old Nugey:

This will apprise you that, incredible as it may seem, I am not dead. Death, it appears to me, would be the only valid and acceptable reason for my long desertion of the great Nugent. As a matter of fact, it has been increasingly difficult for me to get down to writing letters this summer. . . .

Just at present Moi-meme, which is almost French for Me, am at work on what appears to stand a half way chance of being a successful local movie venture. I have already turned out a 3-reel comedy drama for the starter of the thing which hereafter will confine itself to news reels, features, etc and with which organization I will not be identified. My Picture, if any, will be an ad scheme, and will involve a local popularity contest in selecting the leads. . . .

In addition to that I am still turning out a lot of helpful and uplifting news for the [Columbus] Disp. The work has by no means begun to pall on me and I consider that it has been the most valuable training I have ever got, in school or out, for a life of literary crime in the future, if any.

As to the Girls, God bless them, topic. Well, perhaps it is the position of the planet Neptune in relation to Venus or Iphigenia or something. At any rate, I have had quite a melange and compote of romance—or call it philandering—since you left. I believe philandering would more closely apply. I shall describe things at length when you arrive. The most important item in this connection is probably the fact that the great Minnette and I no longer write, as per agreement suggested by her when she left. That is the usual involved and sentimentish and damned unsatisfactory story.

I, as I grow older, seem to enter deeper and deeper into the spirit of this "age of discretion" thing. Discretion, my boy, is the practise of reasoning coolly while being hotly kissed. Woe unto the young man, Solomon might have said, who allows his breath to be taken away by a woman's words, who loses his head because of his heart, or has his feet swept from under him because of her legs.

I may say, however, that I might well have heeded that maxim six weeks ago. Still, when my faculties fail me, there is always the consolation of Lincoln's beautiful and truthful metaphor; the silent artillery of time. May it batter down all your troubles and miss all your dearest memories. Yours for an immediate answer full of good words,

Jim

*Nugent married actress Norma Lee in October 1921. Thurber traveled to New York to be best man at the wedding. In the spring of 1922 he became engaged to Althea Adams, in her junior year at O.S.U.*

*Saturday [March 19, 1922]*

Dear Nugey:

You know, dam it, that you were to pass thru here at your usual genial hour of 2 a.m. and whistle to me on your way to Chicago—I waited and there came no trill. Meanwhile your letter was mislaid and I had no idea of where to reach you—but I learn by the Chi sheets that Dulcy is fulminating and corruscating at the Cort. . . .

. . . Fanny Arms wrote Ray Lee that you were doing wonderfully in your part and had got a lot of praise. Wish I could drop up and look it over—and is there any chance of a stopover here on its way New Yorkward?

. . . A short story I am now working on . . . "The Bones of Bill Dadd" is a dice-shooting tale which I am striving to work up into shape. However, my most enthusiastic, ambitious and best effort now in more or less lackadaisical construction is a one-act play in two scenes, called "Riot"—and dealing with race-troubles. It could of course have no stage presentation unless they did it in Green'ich with Gilpin gallopin' as my bronze lead—and no paper would carry it unless the revered but irreverent S.S. [Smart Set] took it on. I got the idea during my special assignment a week ago in Springfield where for three days I kept the wires hot with stories on the race-rioting there which bust forth after a rape and a shot last Friday night. I was hauled out of bed at 12.25 and machined to Springfield towards dawn. I went 44 hours without sleep, but I beat the A.P. to the Saturday afternoon lead, shot in pictures in time for our noon edition even and generally had a great experience. My stories were spread all over the front page and the old name was set up in 12 point black face directly under the head and over the stories. . . .

Yourn as for the usuality which is until everafter,

Jim

*In the spring of 1922, Nugent, his sister, and their father opened in Boston in* Kempy, *a play written by the Nugents with Russel Crouse.*

*James G. Thurber,*
*The Columbus Dispatch, Columbus, Ohio*
*[Postmark April 4, 1922]*

Dear Old Neglectee:

I have neglected all my best correspondents and they are not many and of them you stand first, old love. Your vague notion that I might be peeved or something got a color of conviction from my horrible silence, but append this to your notes on Thurber, as I Knew Him: he was a man of singular affection and of love and faith, whose friend could do no wrong or say no evil, who loved and asked to be loved by a few and cared not much what was else. Here let him lie, then, having lived a lovely life. Requiescat in Roses.

Excuses for such neglect as mine can't be made. But I have unaccountable doldrums of the fancy and the will to write. Maybe there's something a tiny bit Freudian in it. I know damn well that's rot, but one must mention Freud. Work, much work which has left me worn at night and in idle hours has been the chief reason. . . .

By this time you will be tickling the Bostonian ribs, I fancy. I suppose you will run six or eight weeks there. . . . I am eager to know what plans you have for the summer. . . . I should love to have us four meet. . . . Althea has heard more of you than of any other living American she has not met, and of the charming Elliottess much also. Recently Strollers were given a dinner in the Barn, Columbus' newest and most unique restaurant, to which Althea and I came as the only invitees of the alumni of the gang. Such is our popularity, as who should say. A picture of the group was taken showing me very handsome with the somewhat prettier lady at my side. I wish for the two of you to see the pose and will send a print as soon as I get one made.

Pardon this diversion, but at a banquet given by members of the three Columbus newspapers, Althea was accounted by most the most strikingly beautiful lady in the 60 or more present, which I set down to let you know the Thurber is a nice judge of many things. Thurber, in other words, is the berries, says Thurber. Which is the very latest campus expression. Not only beautiful is she but ravishingly intelligent with characteristics so much like mine in many directions you would of course find her fetching. But this night she was more beautiful than new snow with the light of stars upon it, or than cool flowers in the soft of dawning—ah, one raves. A new sheet, Watson.

So pretty was she that my managing editor a man of few words and of less commendation wended to my desk the next morning to tell me I should be proud indeed, whereupon a nice girl reporter seated near and hearing, observed the Lady Althea was easily the prettiest girl in the room. Watson, this must be the same sheet.

How goes the old married life, youngsters? Papa would crave words relating the beauty of it all, the magic and the wizardry of two lives bound in a single plait. Ah, speak not that it has its bad hours. I firmly believe each moment must be enchantment. Watson, the disillusioner, quick.

She and I are set to kick off the single coils and face a ministerial barrage of nice-sounding phrases in October. . . . Money has not flowed in fast enough to warrant a setting nearer of the date yet. But prospects look good. Two weeks ago I got the Columbus correspondence for the justly great Christian Science Monitor of your whilom city. It means a lot in possible prestige and not a little in money since they pay the wonderful rate of 37 and one half cents the inch, or about 8 to 10 dollars a column, and since they use much academic, literary and educational stuff I plot many articles of length. Also, I am set to handle occasional telegraph stories for the Cleveland News Leader, and I have a press agent job for a concert operator who brings Farrar, Rachmaninoff and others to this God forsaken place to cudgel what passes for the artistic sense of the benighted heathen. That will mean 300 rocks for little effort over a period of two or three moons. I am, as usual, also, planning writing free-lance stories whenever I get set to it. Many droll stories, rich in the salt of American existence and bright in the coloring of our little scene, crowd the chancel rail of the mind asking for holy water and once I set my writing mitre on straight and dip my fingers I shall throw it. Look for me in the Century or the Smart Set or the Housemaid's Annual. I am toying with a story of university and Columbus life introducing a mooncalf of a sort, the thing to be a neat, if possible, parody, but written with every evidence of intense sincerity. Such a one as critics years to come will seek to find the true motive in and the actual purpose, a rather hard task since perhaps it will develop neither.

Last night Althea and I went to Newark in the cute little Ford coupe the lady of my choice has recently obtained. Her mother is head of the university domestic science school for teachers and supervisors, with a nice income, for two at least, and she decided a Ford should be the starter. They need one.

We visited Curly and his wife, Curly the Davis you know. He married Beatrice Sherwood, a Kappa and Althea's special chum. We had quite a nice evening, or rather night, with little sleep, playing cards till late and afterwards engaging in a spontaneously invented pastime in which one twirls the lids of milk bottles, the paper stoppers, as I believe they are technically called, at a receptacle, the object being to see who could toss in the greatest number. . . . I got to work half an hour late and ran plump into "Man Loses life In Storm, Leaving Widow and Nine Children." It was my task to worm from a heavy-minded and wide-breasted widow, her eyes rimmed with the redness of much crying, the thin story of their lives, and to line up all nine youngsters in various states of excitement and happiness, for it was all like a circus to them, that the photographer might shoot a flash at them. The raising of the flash above his head, precipitated a riot and it took a new half hour to drape them about the family horsehair sofa again. It's a hard, but interesting life, working for the zest of pathos craving readers. . . .

Ludwig Lewisohn, whom perhaps you knew better than I, has issued a new book called Up Stream, an autobiographical thing in which he takes up Columbus, under a name not that, and the university and subjects the whole scene to a searching north light, revealing with deft satire, much bitter pinking with swords and not a little hurtful truth, the ways of people and things as he saw them here. It is a smashing indictment of what he pleases to call the mental and intellectual vacuity of the region. I have read only quotations in reviews and news stories so far, but suggest we both get the book and chuckle as we see his Menckenian lunges leap past us at everybody else whoever went to school here. . . .

Minnette is now in Rochester Minn. Do not touch that bush, Watson, the leaves fall easily. . . .

Ray Jackson is coaching this year's play, Mrs. Bumpstead Leigh, the Fiske success of a decade past. . . . Al Callen, Ray and I and the rest of the studio hounds often touch on you. Althea is a great favorite of studio hours.

My Scarlet Mask play "Many Moons" as I called it went over very well, being called by Billy Graves and others the best yet. It netted me $350. I agree. I was not without a light moment or two when the lines went easily.

With my very best love to you and the lovely and well-remembered Norma, I promise once again never to do it again. Shrive me this once and make your own delinquency the penalty of a second offense. Then indeed would the lights descend.

   Hell—all is happiness.

   Yours for ever and what they call aye,

   Jim

ɕ ɕ ɕ

*May 18, 1922 E.N., Thursday*

Dear Elliott and J.C. [Nugent] and Ruth:

Bless God, the world is yours!

I have just recently, within the afternoon now fading into one of the most triumphant twilights of my life, read Heywood Broun's review. It is a quart of old champagne which has left me reeling gloriously about the rooms of my home and the streets of my town. Yesterday, after haunting early morning newsstands I clapped trembling paws and nervous eyes on Woollcott's write-up and on the Herald panegyric. They were enough, but along comes Heywood, entirely surrounded by lofty nouns and soaring adjectives, spouting praise like spray from a busted 34-inch trunk line water main, and I understand that Percy Hammond, love his life, has also conformed to the uniformity of high commendation. Good Heavens above, it surpasses my wildest dreams. Never could I have got drunk enough, were I a drinking man, which I were, but ain't, to have woven in fancy a finer victory. One of the best plays of the season! Comparison with "The First Year" in almost every review! Awarded the Broun derby and the glass slipper! The Nugents robbing Lotus of her legended power to win men with a taste and relegating her with Grant Mitchell to an "also in the cast"! As authors and actors supreme! Please send me one pair of cast iron pincers that I may gouge my arm to see if I sleep.

I have spent the whole day darn near, and me with a million pre-nuptial things to do, riding a mad machine over wet streets carrying the word to friends of your and to perfect strangers. I have called up everyone you ever nodded to, spreading the news. I have pooh-poohed the Dumas father and son, I have tut-tutted Frank Craven, I have scooped up the Barrymores in a scup and scooped them out of the window, I have trotted out long unused phrases and praises and halleluias and glory to Gods. I have completely forgot my wedding almost, and it only two days off! Greater love and excitement hath no man than this.

Enclosed is a news story which was printed today in the Dispatch, written by your press agent [Thurber]. It is even better than the several paragraphs I wrote on different occasions after coming home from NY about you, and which I (damn it) never sent to you. But in those early paragraphs I predicted confidently the rise of the Nugent star. Little did I reck, however, that it would go spang thru old John Zenith, canopy and all. . . .

Now to inform you that I shall see your darned old play, concerning which New York critics of the drama have alluded in terms of hashish and white clover blossoms, next Thursday night, unless you jerk it off the boards to hold for next season. Althea and I leave here Saturday aft. for Washington to remain thru Wednesday, then running up to NY for a day or two. I will contrive to have a few minutes with you, famous though you be. Please leave word with all sub-assistant secretaries that J.G. Thurber, a friend of your lowly, only by comparison, days, is to be allowed the freedom of all your town houses, your five cars, your Long Island estates and your personal theaters—the Nugent theater, the Eliott, the J.C. and the Ruth Roof, also the Grace Garden. Expect then, on Thursday or Friday, a word with me and Mrs. James G. Thurber.

Elliott, in closing let me say that Broun's wonderful write-up for you leaves me glowing like an acetelyn torch. I am happier about it than anyone but you could realize. But you must know. Lord love you all, sez I.

     Always,
     Jim

*Nugent and his father next wrote the play* A Clean Town, *a spoof on Prohibition, which tried out in Washington, D.C., in October 1922, starring Nugent's*

*wife, Norma. Thurber was offered a role in it but, luckily, didn't accept. The play
soon closed.*

*J.G. Thurber, The Columbus Dispatch,*
*Columbus, Ohio*
*[Postmark: Sept 1922]*

Dear Old Nugie:

Your letter, which was waiting in my box for me when I got back to the office from a very drab round of city offices this morning, was like the whispered promise of a shot of Chambertin 1904. It revived me. Columbus is a rutty place, whatever you say, and it takes a jolt to shake up the ambition in me. Such jolts you provide in those rare occasions when you cease doffing a constant hat to your public and curry your Corona. . . .

I am more than sorry that I can't be in Washington on the twenty two of October, but my heart will be in the audience and backstage beating loudly for your continued success. I am glad to hear that Norma is to have the ingenue part. Too bad you all can't be in this play, too. Washington is full of pretty men so have a care of your girl-wife as the newspapers say of them. "Beautiful girl wife" is the exact phrase, I believe.

If the weather has been as bad in NY as here recently it would serve to melt the plot considerably. But better days are in store with October in the offing— the finest month of them all. Too bad you can't be here to whiff the football air and to see the Stadium dedicated. It is nearly completed now, a wonderful structure, set down in the pastoral back eighty of the OSU like a modernized Greek temple or a Roman coliseum born of mirage. Michigan plays here on Oct. 21, dedication day, just before your own play goes around right end for a touchdown.

On football, I wonder if you have heard of the truly sad condition of Chic Harley. He has been in a bad way since last winter and is variously reported as hopeless, his case being diagnosed as dementia precox by a number of examiners, although the Harley mind, unless known of old, might bother any medical man. At any rate he has dropped out of life, and is now in a Dayton sanitarium. There is food for deep reflection in his case. Perhaps the most striking figure this town has ever known in point of popularity, and now, at 25 or so, it is all ended. I used often to wonder what would ever come of him after football days were over. It seemed to me that his last game must mark the end of him, but little did I think it would be such a pitiable end. Some middle western Henry James might "do" Chic in a really great story. The only immortal piece written about him so far is my own epic poem in three eight-line plunges, called "When Chic Harley Got Away" and having as its refrain "Like the glory of the going when Chic Harley got away." . . .

Now as to my own plans other than this I have an idea for a play which I think I will tryout on Strollers next Spring if I get it written. It will be an honest but probably unsuccessful attempt to enunciate Columbus, to pull the curtain upon the average middle class family which makes up this university city—a town by the way as typical of America outside of New York as any other city in the United States. It has often appeared to me that the cities of this size have been lost sight of in the dramatization of the small town folks and foibles. It seems to me there is a rich mine of stuff here. It is of this stuff that the second novel I mentioned would be made—a chronicling of people in this thoroughly Middle Western town, largely autobiographical as we are told all good novels are and written from a University-Paris-Newspaper chronology of events, impressions and developments. It would be quite melancholy since the longer you live the more you see that life is a melancholy thing, don't you think. Nothing to get morose about, for there are many pleasures and lots of fun, if one has a sense of humor, to keep one going, but what a welter of futility, commonness, unenlightenment, frailty and insignificance life is made by the average person. Out of living here I get only an increasing conviction that America has no cultural or intellectual or even intelligent future. The signs of it are everywhere. It is all stocks and bonds, automobiles, real estate, super movies, business deals, pettinesses and other junk, with one person out of 10,000 who seems inspired by any outside light at all. When you think about it it is amazing. Columbus is reading avidly Ludwig Lewisohn's "Upstream" which I believe I told you to get. It is I found on reading it a few weeks ago after waiting weeks to get it from a library, one of the most remarkable documents ever written in this country. If only for the beauty of the man's literary style, it is worth the reading. But to an Ohio Stater the book is indispensable for its pictures of people in the university and in Columbus. He has caught the city and the university with cruel truthfullness, exaggerated here and there by the marks of animus and bitterness, but in the main marvellously right. You will find in it Doc Thompson, rather terribly maligned in spots, Jim Light, in passing, the Sun Dial, the Sansculotte, the co-ed, the men students, the class room, the faculty and the faculty's wives. Don't miss it. It is a book worth buying and I most urgently advise you to get it.

I don't get as much time for reading as I would like to, for it would take a long time each day to read the things one ought to keep up on. But I do manage to skip through all the more important periodicals and to read, after a fashion, the more important books.

Meanwhile, every so often, favor my recluse state with such another letter as today's. I appreciate your crowded hours, but the continuation of this correspondence we owe to our country, or something, and one must make these sacrifices in the interest of a coming generation which is already jeopardized by a paucity of belles lettres. How would "Hells Belles Lettres" be for a book of essays?

My deep devotions towards you and Norma and the same from Althea.

Always,

Jim

*In 1925, Thurber, with Althea, sailed to Europe to try his luck as a freelance writer. Williamson was a Columbus friend and a former State Department code clerk.*

## To Ben Williamson

*Berne, Schweiz,*

*192fünf*

Dear Benny:

Dropped in at number 4, Berna Strasse this morning and looked over your old coding ground. All is, I presume, the same. I met the keeper of the reception room who said he had been there ten years and so I named you, and he said ach jah, oui yes, I should say, how is this Williamson? Before I could relate all your successes et al and submit dossier with a view to this and that . . . a secretary led me away.

I am doing a series of articles on embassies and ministers with lots of personal items and whatnots, and it occurs to me that your long experience at the legation might serve me some purpose. Wish you were here to tell me about them over a Müncher, at some Beer Halle. What I want is anything you might think would fit into a sort of rambling essay account of the Berne legation, its doings, its specialties, its this and that. Of course I interview each minister and ambassador and the rest serves as sort of background, but sometimes the background is very important.

Being a newspaper man you will get the drift of what I am after even though I don't make it specifically clear. Do you know any hidden crannies in the legation—did they use to watch the fairies dance at mid-day, was the by-word "Down with Poland?" or etc.? Do all ministers here get the goitre—do they all become iodine fiends or what? Any little interesting item that my clamoring readers would crave. I leave it to you.

Only I must have a hell of a sight more rapid action than you are accustomed to give, as a correspondent. The last letter I wrote you was in 1919 and it is still unanswered. Damn near long enough. I want to write all my yarns up this summer, in the next eight weeks and hence please shoot what you can to me now. . . .

We have been in Europe more than a month—three weeks in Paris, then a trip around the southern circuit, through Tours, Carcassonne, Marseilles and Nice, staying a week at Villefranche, just out of Nice where we swam and swam and got all red and peeled like the church bells molly o zed o george.

Then we tripped to Milan, had three beers, a Cinzano, coffee, an expensive room and a look at the cathedral and went on to Berne. Naturally it was the loveliest trip of all and me and the wife are crazy about the well known Schweizcapetenhallenfussenfaher, which is, I think, the German name for Swiss capital—at any rate it's close enough. After smelling so many French and Italian towns it is wonderful to find one that doesn't smell. Nothing can smell like a French and Italian town. Whereas Berneschweizsuisse is the cleanest place in god's world. We go on to Paris tomorrow and then perhaps to Brussels and London. Maybe up into the North this summer. After that, Jenny say quoi-quoi. Et puis et puis alors alors. . . .

Well, toot de sweet with an answer, now, or as the Swiss would say fuhngerhaltensprachetnbargenfunf.

Sincerely,
James Thurber

*My address is*
*The Guaranty Trust Co.,*
*1 Rue des Italiens,*
*Paris, France*

## TO TED AND JULIA GARDINER

*Aug. 27*
*Grousseey, pres de Correlles-Bourg, par*
*Jullonville-Bouvillon, Manche, Normandie, France*
*(The place made famous in the remark, "knock you*
*so far it'll cost $10 to send you a post card")*

Dear Ted and Julia,

The postman brought a packet of letters today, vis: a bill from Dunlap's shoe store, an announcement of an increase in pew rent at the Second Baptist Church, an appeal for funds to build a new wing on the Eagles' home, a bill from Dunn-Taft, a schedule of interest rates from the Buckeye Bldg. and Loan, a postcard from Joe Zilch, the Journal for July 9th, and a letter from you. It's an ill wind that blows no one good—but you might have written a few more pages. I can already recite the 387 words you wrote. We read it every hour and twice after meals.

The news of the gold rush in Florida set us to packing at once. We sail on the Leviathan (famous tea and coal boat) Sept. 15. But I am holding no great hopes since Land Value Casto is on the ground—such of it as is left. I had a hunch the California quakes moved from Florida—The Bankrupts' Paradise. Whammee! We have speculated a little in real estate over here—I having bought a piece of land in Brittany which was recently visited—after I bought it, but we had to wait 12 hours to see it, the tide being in when we arrived.

Your letter came like a breath of fuchsia from the wide open spaces. We were glad to note that the authorities allowed those Buckeye Lake cards to go through. They give a new light on Byron, I think.

Well, sir, we got to Europe all right. We had another fine day for it. The Leviathan is one of the biggest ships I ever crossed in, measuring 1,172 feet, from bowsprit to capstan bar, drawing 727,000 tons of bilge water at the bunker holes, carrying a midriff shippage of 110,762 port feet and a super-structure tenancy, between keel and scuppers, of 7,261,431 ampoles. Our desti-nation, Cherbourg, was reached in good time. We had another fine day for it. The authorities allowed Althea to debark without question, and I got by after a thorough search. The trip was without incident, save when one of the Gross-man passengers, sleeping in the engine room, thought he heard burglars in the night and threw a shoe into the machinery.

We were 15 days in Paris before we saw a Frenchman. But you could ask

anyone you met for a match, in English, and get it. Most of the quaint and picturesque natives one sees are from Kansas City or Peoria. You needn't study up
French when you finally pay for your bale of tea on the old ship.

After two drunken weeks in Paris visiting Napoleon's tomb, the Folies Bergere and the Eiffel tower we slunk out of town for the South. Contrary to custom, however, I went South with my own wife. You can be arrested for less
over here, you know.

We visited quaint Touraine, with its picturesque chateaux, quaint old Carcassonne, with its picturesque old walled city, and then went on to the picturesque Mediterranean, with its quaint red towns. By this time we had $107
left and had been here a month. So we went into seclusion at Villefranche, a
quaint old sea port on the Medit, built on a hill, and stayed there a week for $7,
leaving us just $100 of 11,726,203 francs. It costs just 75 francs a week to live
over here, and when I say live I mean enjoy life. Fancy beer for 4 cents a pail
and Benedictine, wine, Chartreuse, Champagne—Althea, open the closet
door so I can read the rest of names on our stock!

Villefranche was quaint, but smelled. We have no sewers, but lots of sewage.
Set me down blindfolded in any part of the South and I can tell you where we
are. It is worthy of note that no soldier in the Great War who hailed from the
South suffered from gas. Just as they claim Brazil stayed out of the war because her nuts would be shell-shocked.* We had some lovely bathing at Villefranche, and once I nearly drowned, which isn't as funny as you make out. The
buoyancy of the water and not of my spirits kept me up, but I am proud to say
that when a trawler man with a wooden leg named Raoul pulled me out, I
asked him to save the women and children first thing after he got me out.
Most of the women need saving too.

We next set out for Italy. We had a good day for it. I speak almost flawless
Italian, but the natives indulge in a queer bastard sort of Italian and couldn't
get me. I even went so far as to tell one Italian that he spoke a bastard tongue,
but it seems he had sold peanuts in New York and he right back and called me
a son-of-a-bitch. The fight was on. We had a good day for it. In Italy we visited
Milan Cathedral, the grave of Robert Browning, three cafes, the tomb of
Washington Irving and a house in Genoa where Pershing spent the night. I
laid a wreath on the lintel, in the name of the Swedish State Railways and was
presented with a key to the city.

After that, Switzerland! They have quaint little "stations" or "depots" where

*Far fetched.

one buys "tickets" entitling him to a seat in the quaint "railroad trains," as they are called. Switzerland lies largely in the mountains, or "Alps," as they are known. We had a chance to hear the famous Swiss yodelers, coming down one mountain side. Their quaint song is "Yoy, yoy, yoy, yoy, Musselltoff". It was *picturesque,* my dear! At our hotel in Berne was a very wealthy, and picturesque, Hindoo Prince, the Whammee of Punchjob. We thought of Ted, not on account of his being rich, tho. By this time we had $67 left. The chief attraction of Berne was a beautiful beer garden up above the city where we drank Munchner, listened to "Parsifal" and watched the city light up. We lighted up a little too.

In Paris once more we visited Napoleon's tomb, the Folies Bergere, the grave of Washington Irving, a hotel where Pershing spent the night. We laid a wreath on the doorstep, in the name of Lafayette. Some French people asked us what we were doing, in the name of God.

Then 5 weeks ago we came here, a little Normandy coast town, quaint and picturesque, where we live in a farmhouse right amongst the French, cook our own meals, bathe at a wonderful beach and enjoy a beautiful Countryside full of quaint old houses, ivy-clad walls, gigots*, presales#, sheep, moutons (3), and wool bearers. We will be in N. Y. Sept. 20. Hope to see you there for a little party, at your expense. For at this time their money had got down to $21. But they had a good day for it.

> Lovingly,
> Jim & Althea

*sheep # sheep (3) sheep

*After working for the Paris edition of the* Chicago Tribune, *in Paris and Nice, Thurber, broke again, sailed for New York. Joel Sayre was a Columbus friend and newspaperman who, while attending Oxford, visited the Thurbers in Paris.*

## TO JOEL SAYRE

*[Excerpt from missing letter written aboard the* Leviathan, *possibly May 10, 1926]*

Dear Joe:

... What are gaiety and vodka in the old sleigh, when that thing bumping your elbow is a wolf. ...

. . . I write mostly soi-disant humor since I haven't brains enough to write more solid articles and wouldn't if I could. I often worry about my future since I am no doctor and at best but a mean scrivener, but out of all the things one does, from pipe fitting to testing seamless leather belting and from ceramics to statesmanship, I can do only one thing, even passably, and that is make words and space them between punctuation points. . . .

## To Elliott Nugent

*New York*
*May 20, 1926*

Dear Old Nugent:

It's me.

Don't drop dead—if you remember me. If you don't, I used to go to school with you: Ohiostatebillygravesphipsidrthompsonjackwilcechickharleyetcetc. But maybe you have forgot to remember, as they sing in America. I have just come from where Rose Marie is new.

I dropped into the Lamb's club and asked after you and JC and they told me that you were in Philly. . . .

Who, me? Well, I'll pluck you by the sleeve, wedding guest. I been in France ten years. Althea is still there. We're very happy, though. I mean together. I came over for just as long as it takes me to do what I want to do and get back. That may be two weeks. Again it may be a month. It won't be longer. I should admire to see you and Norma and the Annabelle, but suppose no. I'm used not to seeing people. I'm used to lots of things you ain't used to. But I'm still young, though thinner. By still young I mean the glistening star is up there yet. I may be even hungrier when I get to it, and quite tired, but what the hell. . . . Walking is good for the character.

. . . I'm here to try and influence Putnams Syndicate to let me do a regular bit of junk that will bring in a little silver—I mean by regular, money once a week, so one—I mean two—can eat three times or twice a day. Conrad said something about beefsteak being his inspiration. He said a mouthful.

Hard times and good, and all in all a great experience. With a few conquerings, such as they were, thrown in. I scooped the world on a couple of stories, if that means anything. . . . I come so back to New York and can still act Prussian to the caviare. One has the illusions of Brummel's last hours—one imagines one's cockade is still gay, at least, I hope, until 40. I sign off not before forty. But I'm in no signing off mood. If you last through the Year of the Big Snow, you last.

I wish I could send you herein and forthwith the money I still owe you, old kid, but I can't.

. . . My best love to you and Norma. I'll be for a week at 147 West 13th street.

Toujours toujours,

Jim*

*g. Thurber

# *the*
# WANDERING YEARS

*In the fall of 1926, reunited with Althea, Thurber joined the* New York Evening
Post.

## To the Thurber Family

*Gotham,*
*Feb. 6, 1927*

Dear Father, Mother, Brother and Airedale:

You will be interested to know that I have just come into possession of
seventy-five volumes of the late Harry Houdini's famous library. I was sent on
an assignment to Sing Sing prison a few days ago and with my usual good luck
on assignments got there the same hour that Mrs. Houdini did. She was taking Houdini's set of old books on crime and penology to Warden Lewis E.
Lawes, an old friend of the magician. On the way back to New York I found
myself on the same train with Mrs. H and asked her for some more information about the books. She proved to be a very sweet and charming lady and
certainly interesting to talk with. The warden, by the way, is a fine chap,
strangely unlike a Sing Sing warden should be—very quiet and gentle and
courteous soul. Before I left Mrs. H, in the Grand Central, she asked me if I
would like to come up and pick out some of the Houdini books for myself. I
said YES. I went up twice to her house, the second time with Althea. Houdini
left a library on dramatic and theatrical literature valued at $500,000. His li-
brary on magic, an extremely valuable collection, went to the Library of Congress, and his psychic books to the American Society for Psychical Research.
The family and a few friends shared the rest, his miscellaneous books. I was
certainly lucky to be one of the "friends".

She gave me a rare Latin book on magic, dated 1648 to start with. One of my prizes is a book presented to Houdini by Harry Kellar, the great magician, containing Houdini's signature and an inscription by Kellar. That book is doubtlessly valuable. There are also three first editions of James Russell Lowell's works, two volumes in German on German cities, with the bookplate of David Belasco on the inside front cover, one of them having a sentence in Belasco's writing on the fly leaf. Many of the volumes are more than a hundred years old and deal with all sorts of subjects. I think one collection is of thirty-two paper-backed . . . American song books, some of them printed as early as 1845 and all together . . . contain probably all of the American songs from Yankee Doodle to The Sidewalks of New York. One of the song books is "The Harrison Log Cabin Song Book", published by A.H. Smythe Columbus Ohio, in 1888 and edited by O.C. Hooper. Its full title is "The Harrison Log Cabin Song Book of 1840 revised for the Campaign of 1888 with Numerous New Songs to Patriotic Airs". Many of the songs deal with old Allen Thurman. Originally sold for about 25 cents, its cover is marked 75 cents—the price Houdini paid for it some years ago, due to its comparative rarity. . . .

A very rare book is one called "The Life and Death of John Wilkes Booth", published in Memphis. Houdini is said to have bought up almost every copy of this book to make it rare. I have the only copy outside his family.

Then look at this: an old pamphlet, published in Cambridge, Mass in 1883 by Abner C. Goodell Jr., called "The Trial and Execution of Mark and Phillis, Slaves of Captain John Codman". Of this pamphlet only 200 copies in all were printed. AND THIS ONE BEARS ON THE OUTSIDE COVER THE AUTHOR'S own inscription as follows:

"Rev. Edward Everett Hale, with the compliments of A.C. Goodell Jr., Boston, October 9, 1883."

I have no idea as yet what our total collection is worth, but several of the books have sentences written in them by Houdini, such as "I got this book in Paris, March 18, 1919" etc. and they have a value in themselves, I dare say.

You would be interested in another rare pamphlet called DeWitt's Special Report of the Trial of the Hon. Daniel E. Sickles for shooting Philip Barton Key, U.S. District Attorney of Washington D.C., February 27, 1859. It is illustrated with quaint old pictures of the shooting and of the house on Fifteenth street where Key met Mrs. Sickles etc. There is also a pamphlet on the Richardson-McFarland tragedy of 1870, whatever that was.

I have no doubt but that our collection will someday, if indeed not now, be worth upwards of a thousand dollars, maybe more.

Mrs. Houdini told us a lot of interesting yarns about him, his relations with

Conan Doyle, their arguments about psychic phenomena, her friendship with Anna Eva Fay who wrote her recently "I used to bring spirits to others but I have tried in vain for 18 years to get a message for myself." Remember Anna Eva Fay?

Mrs. Houdini believes all mediums fakes and none of them has yet come close to getting the message from Houdini that he arranged to send her. He tried for years to get a certain word from his mother but never did. . . . I got a $5 bonus for the Sing Sing books story, since it was a beat. I've collected several such bonuses, including one on trench mouth being epidemic here. Funny thing, I had a slight recurrence of the trouble the day after I wrote the story and I went to the specialist whom I had quoted and he treated me for nothing and gave me medicine to use.

. . . I have just completed a survey of the NY water situation from the standpoint of metering the city, and will have three stories in the Post on the subject. . . . The editor in chief took my word for it that the city should be metered after I conducted my "survey" and the stories are written from that viewpoint. I found Columbus was 100 percent metered and that seemed a good argument. The NY water supply system being the greatest in the world is an interesting thing to study up and my city hall training in Columbus helped me to know how to go about the thing.

> Greetings to the gang,
> Jamie

*Later that February, Thurber was hired by Harold Ross, editor of* The New Yorker *magazine. That summer his friend and office-mate, E. B. White, invited the Thurbers to a Fourth-of-July weekend at Amawalk, New York, where Thurber met and fell in love with Ann Honeycutt, who worked for the CBS radio network as an assistant program director. In this 1932 letter to her, Thurber describes that first meeting, thinly disguising "Honey" as "Estelle Darlington," or "Darling." By the end of 1927, though still sharing an apartment, Thurber and Althea were leading independent social lives.*

## TO ANN HONEYCUTT

Chapter I

The first time I ever saw Estelle was one Summer evening about nine o'clock in a summer cottage which was really an ice house made over into a summer cottage. It was dusky in the room because it was lighted only by coal oil lamps.

I saw her in a corner of the dark room and somebody introduced her. "This is Estelle Darlington," somebody said. "She's called Darling." My first impression was of her smile, which was nice, and of her figure, which was nice, too, but, I thought, a trifle buxom. This may have been due to the bad light and to the fact that I do not see very well, having lost one eye, a disability which sometimes causes me to look like a distraught bird and militates, at such times, against any girl really looking upon me as a romantic figure. I only hazard this as a guess because, of course, no girl would mention such a thing to a man, although she might to a friend. I can not too early make the point that I view myself as a romantic figure and should like to be looked upon as a romantic figure, for this feeling of mine greatly enters into the story of myself and Miss Darlington, whom I shall hereinafter allude to as Darling.

My next recollection of Darling is meeting her some hours later by chance in the moonlight outside the Ice House, as we called it, and telling her that I intended to marry her on the 19th of the following June. I did not say this so much to startle her as because I really felt that I would like to marry her, a curious feeling when it is understood that, at the time, I was already married. Darling made the usual smiling and witty responses to my remark, turning the edge of its sincerity and making of it just a "line" that a drunken man (for I was a drunken man at the moment) would "hand" any pretty girl suddenly encountered in the moonlight at a gay party. I remember wanting to take her in my arms and kiss her and say those throatily sincere and eloquent things which, on such occasions, I always want to say but which die in my throat and are succeeded by the more or less humorous and fantastic remarks of a facetious nature which it has been my custom to employ when I am rebuffed or think I am rebuffed or think I am about to be. My nearsightedness and lack of handsomeness, together with the fact that I am some thirty pounds under weight, always restrains me from going through with the mad, dashing, he-man tactics which I should greatly love to employ with what somebody has referred to as "my girls".

Thus the little moment became not one fraught with prophetic significance and that kind of startling intensity which we are lead to believe in novels and plays some men can convey to some women on first meeting them, but degenerated into a kind of mockery and a kind of light-hearted and, God bless us all, sophisticated playfullness which, to a great degree, set the tone for our future relationship and never once, for more than a stray moment here and there (which I shall go into later) completely departed from that relationship.

I had then, which was five years ago, to a greater degree than I have now—for I was not greatly mature at the time—a horror of being placed in a ridiculous or ludicrous light and therefore I did not press my admittedly abrupt and unexpected suit for Darling's hand. Since she chose—as indeed almost any modern girl would—to treat the incident lightly I took my cue from that and sought refuge from the ridiculous and the ludicrous in a playful, light-hearted mockery of the incident. It must be understood here that, in such attitudes, I am really quite amusing, so amusing, in fact, that most girls—as well as men—not only prefer that attitude of mockery and fun to my more serious and sincere moods but actually encourage it. Once in a while I am beguiled by this flattering attention, this tacit praise of my ability at being amusing, into becoming a downright clown, a state into which I most unfortunately allowed myself to descend on this night of my first meeting with Darling. Having laughed a great deal and enjoyed the little moonlit incident, Darling wandered away from me to show a rather definitely admiring attention to a friend of mine at the party named E. B. Brown [White], who at that time was a surly, almost morose man with a disposition to draw apart from the general gaiety and observe with a fascinating and sour detachment the antics and idiocies of foolish mortals at their play. Such men and such attitudes invariably attract women because they lead women to wonder whether or not they (the women) could, if they tried, interest such men and break down such attitudes.

Thus before long I observed Darling and Brown, drawn apart from the main group and sitting talking quietly on the stoop of another summer cottage which we called the God Head. The effect of this sight on me was to make me both jealous and sad. My stomach twitches oddly at such times and it twitched then, a rather perilous thing since I had gone considerably farther in my cups than I should have. I determined to go over to the couple and try to win Darling away from Brown by another display of the light banter with which I had turned off my first serious words to her and which she had apparently taken a whole hearted and genuine pleasure in. Thus am I often reduced to trying to win the attention of women, not by the strong, silent disdain which I so greatly admire in men, but by the rather idle and futile fireworks of wit and humor. And I should put down here, for those who may seek guidance in these matters, that it is fatal to make a woman laugh at you before she has been made to look at you with sombre eyes. The first laugh may lead to complete fatty degeneration of the sentimental and amorous instinct in a woman. No woman wants a man at whose brighter remarks she can not smile, at whose expert mimicry she cannot laugh outright, but every woman wants to look back upon a first impression of a man which is an impression having to do with his stability, his power, his strength, and his sober qualities. After that let the quips fall where they may, there is always the first impression.

But such philosophical reflections did not deter me from wandering drunkenly toward where Darling and Brown were seated. In so doing the most ghastly thing that has ever happened in my life—next to the time I bowled over a dinner companion's hand and knocked a fruit salad fifteen feet straight down the fairway of a banquet table—happened to me there in the dark. I have already said I do not see very well—indeed I have but two fifths normal vision—so in walking toward Darling and her companion I stumbled over one of those outdoor stoves constructed of rocks and a piece of sheet iron. I fell sprawling awkwardly. I was not grievously hurt, although I was hurt some, for a sharp blow on the shins is always painful, so I scrambled up and continued on my way amid a veritable uproar of laughter from Darling and Brown. Instantly I became a victim of my admitted egotistical desire for applause and instead of dismissing the episode of the fall and launching firmly and seriously into some discussion which would have established the high quality of my graver mental powers, I let go completely, fell over several more stoves, on purpose, and ended up by being put to bed by a disgruntled wife and several friends, only to get up out of bed several times to return to the scene of what, being drunk, I actually believed to be my triumph. Finally I did stay in bed and went to sleep with the laughter and jeers of Darling still ringing—and as god is my judge, pleasantly—in my ears.

Of course the next morning, a little reflection, a little reconstruction of the night before, sickened me. I realized that what had begun as perhaps the most romantic episode, and one of the most serious in my life, had degenerated into common, knockabout clowning. Being extremely sensitive at heart, and extremely romantic by nature, I was inordinately depressed by my remembrance of what had taken place and I tried to keep it out of my mind but couldn't.

When I saw Darling for the first time that day, which was a beautiful day, she laughed aloud as soon as she looked at me and said something about I certainly was a scream. I need not emphasize the disconsolate effect that this had upon me. I realized more and more that this woman was going to play a big part in my life and I realized that, at the very outset of this important affair, I had set up the almost insurmountable handicap of making myself, to her, essentially a crackpot and clown. Years later her memories of me, her first impression, were to pop up with a burst of laughter in the midst of my most intense moments. And it was partly to offset this deplorable recurrence that my usually genial nature began slowly to turn to a nature out of which I could summon up the most biting, cruel, and uncalled for remarks and actions, to prove that I was not a clown. Better to go to the other extreme, I thought, and be a horrible brute than endure, in the eyes of a loved one, the stigma of funny-looking clownishness. Of course therein did not lie the full reason for my turning, at times, bitter, nasty, and mean—the further reasons I shall take up in due course, in the chapters devoted to sex analysis, but therein did lie some of the reasons.

The next time I saw Darling was on another occasion, a week or two later, at the same summer place. My heart leaped up when, in looking out of the door of the ice house one morning I beheld her sitting in a chair in the doorway of the God Head wearing an enchanting sweater and reading a book. I wondered if by any possible chance her knowledge that I was at the Ice House that weekend had caused her to come back again. Later I was to find out that it had. She said she simply *had* to come back and see me because I was the funniest person she had ever known in her life.
Chapter II
The Emergence of the Sensual Element
[Signature indistinguishable]

*In early 1928, Althea was in Greece, and Thurber invited his brother Robert to stay with him at their Horatio Street apartment. News that Robert's dog, Muggs, was fatally ill took him back to Columbus prematurely.*

## To Robert Thurber

*[March or April 1928]*

Dear Robert:

You must think I am a coo-coo, as the French say, not to have written you, but several things have had me down: first the hemorrhoids, known to the Sioux tribes as Flame-in-the-Bowels (which would be my tribal name, if I am ever made President like Coolidge) and then a slight attack of dysentery, crick, naushy, spring sickness and a recurrence of the old Black Plague. This added to the fact that I have to get out a little work to hold my position kept me floundering, but I seem to be okay now. I sent off your slippers, terribly late, because the maid had placed them on top of the highboy, or old Chippendale garmentoire, where she wanted to see if I could find them without being told, a sort of game she plays because she lives in Jersey and gets such little fun. For days this went on, me missing her when she came here, so that she couldn't even help by saying "cold" or "warm" when I searched. Finally I found them and mailed them. . . . Thus I have your stamps which I will send back so that you will be reminded to write. If you don't want them send them back and we will keep them going back and forth for ever so long until finally we get a piece in the papers about it:

## THURBERS KEEP TWO-CENT STAMPS
## GOING FOR TEN MONTHS.
Columbus Boy and former Columbus Boy Believed To have Set
New World's Record Exchanging Little Bunch of Stamps

.    .    .

LOTS OF FUN, SAY BROTHERS, WHEN INTERVIEWED. . . .

I certainly felt badly about Muggs, on account of you and the rest, and the old dog himself. I know what it would mean to me if Jeannie passed out and we've only had her little over a year. When I lost her in Columbus I was nearly nuts. That's the hell of having a dog. I still feel bad about Rex and often dream of him. They can't live long, and ten years is a long time for a dog. Why can't we have alligators as pets, which live to be 1500 years old, or crows which live to be ninety? Seems strange that God would pick such cumbersome and morose animals and birds to live that long and give a dog the bad break of a handful of moments, as the years go. Still, our family has been lucky about deaths and we got to buck up against them because the years are going on and people die and what the hell, a person simply must build up a philosophy that will endure it all. I have, because my imagination is forever running on ahead of the present and I know that the blows are set to come and a person has got to set himself to meet them. It won't save anyone from grief but it will set up a reserve power finally to meet grief and stand it. It's a strange life, and so far I don't seem to see where anyone has figured it out, but sometimes it seems to me that time goes by like a flash of rain and that's all we amount to in this world. Some of the rain is clear and pretty and some is muddy and bounces off of rainspouts and down into the mud and our family seems sometimes to have been selected to play the part of the rain drops that do most of the bouncing, but my idea is that in the end we seep into the ground somewhere and help a hyacinth to grow or something like that, or maybe seep farther than that and spatter on some hot gentleman or lady in Hades. There ought to be some point to it all and I live in the hopes that the adventure of death is something equal to the adventure of life which is pretty colorful and interesting even if hard. It would seem strange to me if God made such a complicated world and such complicated people and then had no more to offer than blankness at the end, so I live in the curiosity and the hope and the excitement of what there may be afterwards and thus I have got myself to believe that those who pass on perhaps pass on to something as interesting, but lovelier and more happy, than this life. I may be wrong but I have persuaded myself that I'm not and so I don't have the terror of things that some do. None of it helps blunt the edge of grief, though, and no one will ever discover a way of doing that, but as time goes on what once was grief becomes easier to bear if you believe that it all isn't plain useless and silly. At any rate a hell of a lot of people have gone on and I have heard no complaints from them, that's one thing. . . . Maybe Muggs will have Christy Mathewson with whom to scamper across the porphyry and chrysophase fields. Jeannie will be excellent company for someone like that too and I expect any day to find that she has wandered off and got lost upstate or been killed. . . . One day our dog, left here to her own devices too long—both of us were gone from eleven in the morning until eight at night—got fed up on having nothing to do and dragged down, or out, or up, everything we had practically. The house looked like twenty-seven burglars had organized and gone through it hunting for money. Hats, coats, pans, rugs, spools, needles, cigarettes, clocks, overcoats, suitcases, pillows, pillowslips, bedspreads, letters, bills, manuscripts, books, magazines, lamps, dish cloths, curtains and ties were strewn from one end of the house to the other. Many things were chewed but a lot were not. She had specialized on the cigarettes the match boxes and the bag that held Althea's sewing things, especially chewing the spools of silk thread. Only one book was gnawed and that was one we had borrowed from a lady and it was autographed by the author—the one book of our six or eight hundred that she should not have got hold of. Althea corrects her but when I come home alone and find the dog has got things out I always say, "For God's sake, dog, let's hurry and straighten up here or there'll be hell to pay." She is wise enough to know that I will not beat her (which I should). When Althea and I come in together and she has been chewing, she crawls under the bed. Althea says in a firm contralto voice, "Come here, Jeannie". Jeannie bats her tail once. Finally, she comes out for punishment and gets it. She seldom yelps, no matter how hard you spank her, but she yelps if you step on her. When I come home alone and she has been up to something she doesn't crawl under the bed but takes to running up and down the apartment like a race horse, thus interfering with me putting the spools, coats, hats, bedclothes and matches back where she got them. This is to show her pleasure at getting away with murder. She knows she will get licked for raising hell but she does it because she is willing to stand the gaff—you can tell that by the way she comes out for it. She used to sleep on the bed and we spanked her, so that when she heard us coming she would get down and crawl under the bed, and then come out slowly looking sleepy and surprised. But she neglected to pat the pillows and smooth out the bedspread where she had been laying. This is a trick she has never learned but if I come in on her someday patting the pillows into shape I'll call the police, or a minister.

Althea will not be home before the 15th of April I think. She is scheduled to sail [from Greece] on the 8th. It is too bad you had to leave here just as it got fine weather. . . . I wish you could get back and stay till Althea comes, because it gets pretty lonely here. I don't like to stay alone at nights, even in an apartment house and on such nights as I see a mystery play or read a mystery story, I leave the light on in the bathroom.

. . . I wrote a story for Talk of the Town, on the O. Henry region, which appears in next week's issue and I put through a check for $20 for you, and had it made out to me. I explained that the story was yours (we always pay for tips and the dope, and then write the story ourself which is what makes my job pretty complicated, as few people can write the stuff just the peculiar way we want it, or short enough, or whatnot, so if we get a good story we either rewrite it, or send it back and pay for the idea. Someone just turned in one about a toy railroad a mile and a half long some guy built here, a musician, but the story was not right, so we paid the woman for the idea and White went up and looked at the railroad and will write the story. Thus the O. Henry idea was absolutely yours as we never would have thought of it if you hadn't brought on the book. Too bad that you couldn't have gone with me the rest of the places because, just a few feet from the house at 55 Irving Place I found the "Old Munich", the place where he wrote "The Halberdier of the Little Rheinschloss". At first I was disappointed when I came on the Third Avenue entrance which I recognized from the picture in the Mentor, for the place was vacated and the room bare and dusty. Then I found there was an entrance around on the other street—Seventeenth street—and inside was the fine old beer hall just as it was, rafters, white-clothed tables, a big fire place and steins and tankards all around. The son of the manager was there and he had been there when O. Henry was and showed us (I went with Charmé Seeds) the table O. Henry ate at, right before the fireplace, and mentioned that his favorite drink was Scotch. . . . So I wrote a piece about it, which I will send you when it comes out next Wednesday. I wish you could in some way get more idea checks from us, but naturally it isn't every day that such a yarn comes up. I had to hold the story to about 800 words, because our space is limited. . . .

. . . I wish you could get back here—maybe if you could scrape up the money, we could dope out some way for you to make expenses here, so it wouldn't really cost anything. There are hundreds of ways to make money in this burg.

>Love to all,
>Jamie

*In 1924, Eva Prout married Thurber's former rival, Ernest Geiger, who became her piano accompanist and dancing partner in vaudeville. In May 1928, Thurber read that they were playing on Broadway and routinely visited them at their hotel after the show. Their "act" was next booked in Toronto, where Thurber writes them.*

## TO EVA AND ERNEST GEIGER

Dear Act:

I took your key back to the old Flemish Hotel and felt very sad. The room clerk and I had a good cry together. "They'll never come back," I said. "Jesus, I hope not," he said. It was very affecting.

I suppose you are full of Canada Wet by this time and how true it is that you should quit drinking. You will think better and dance weller. I should say it would be better to cut it down to a little sugar in a spoonful of rum once a day. I imagine the cherry trees are in bloom up there, but again maybe they are not. Canadian cherry trees are funny. Sometimes they bloom and sometimes they sulk until the Royal Secretary for His Majesty's Colonial Trees speaks to them about it, for $15,000 a year. Then they bloom, if they feel like it. Wait for the apple tree, though, it blooms loveliest.

The weather here is fine, Alice and the twins are here, your uncle fell and broke his foot, your Aunt Emma is blinder than usual and lost her crutch, the top is gone off the percolator again, the cat is poorly—it's her liver—the last she got from the butcher's was spoiled, but we gave it to the colored maid who said she would cook it in vinegar and it would be all right, there's a hole in the front room curtains, the dog's been on the body Brussells again and spotted it, I found George's cuff links, your cousin Arthur has the prickly heat, their child isn't going to be smart, I guess, he's two now but hasn't said anything since he was born, he gets it from your grandfather, who didn't say anything to the day he died except "How is McKinley now" (that was a year after McKinley was shot). The dog's front paws are all funny, he's got into the tar and tarred up every room in the house, bananas have gone up but sugar's a little cheaper, the subways make more noise than usual, a cop shot a man yesterday named Reilly, the cop's name was Abraham Cohen (really true)—Abie's Irish foes. And so it goes, and we are all getting along in years.

Althea went to the country and so did I and we brought our dog back. Jeannie looks wonderful, has gained ten pounds and went accommodatingly into heat the day we got there, so Althea is taking her to a professional dog husband at Hempstead L.I. today so she can become a mother. She would have become a mother before we got there but her friend, Teddy, the big sheep dog didn't seem to be able to do anything about that, because Jeannie's legs are only four and a half inches off the ground and she won't stand on a top step of the porch long enough.

Althea likes the records I divided up with the waiter her favorite being "Blue River" or whatever it is, by the Revellers.

That's all. Write to me.

I'm well, and sunburned. I played deck tennis yesterday at which I turn out to be pretty good but it has made my joints all stiff. I'm not as young as Ernie used to be, I guess.

I'll send you that picture of me.

My love to Jimsy, Jean, Gladys, Buzz, the electrician, Roy Cummings, Mrs. Fox and Manager Whoozis, of the Pantages theatre. If this reaches you.

> As ever
> Jamie

*Thurber's short story, "Menaces in May," based on his reunion with the Geigers, was published in* The New Yorker *May 26, 1928. Thurber eventually turned against the story, and it was only collected for book publication posthumously.*

## TO ANN HONEYCUTT

*[Undated, probably May 1928]*

Dear Miss Honeycutt:

I am sending you a copy of the NYer containing the piece called "Menaces in May". I hope you like it. The Julia, the Joe, and the Lydia of the piece are mostly, as an author so frequently has to point out, imaginary characters. Art must be the twisting of characters and of motives to suit one's purposes and one's mood. Even so, I lost the Julia [Eva] I think, because of this story— maybe not. The Lydia [Althea] took it for what it was. The Joe [Geiger] didn't no what it was all about. The "man" [Thurber] believes, even now, almost two years later, that this lil story, originally intended to bear the sub-caption "Notes for a chapter in a book," is the best thing he has done, and an earnest example of the book he sometime expects to do—all things being equal, which they ain't ever. However, perhaps inequality of all things is better than an even break. My novels, if any, will deal with menace. And God knows the menace of George is greater than the menace of Joe, who was a kindly fellow, save when in his cups. The essential merit of this story, to me (who ought to know) is its consistent holding of a certain minor note—I got hold of a mood and kept hold of it, didn't I?—and also its absolute sincerity. It could have fallen with a tremendous bang if I had been "arty". It's really as real as hell. Just between me and you, I think that it should have been included in the best short stories of 1928. I got to get around to doing the things that somehow I really believe this small and casual piece shows I can do. I hope, really, that you think it shows it. If you don't, it's okay. I am a swell dart thrower.

    Jim

&#10086; &#10086; &#10086;

*[1928]*

Dear Miss Honeycutt:

The editor of the New Yorker has asked me to write to see whether you can help us out in a matter which troubles us greatly. Our Mr. Thurber, whom we understand you are familiar with, has not been himself for several days. Of course when he is himself it's rather bad, but now it's worse. Discreet inquiry has elicited only the vague statement from him that he is going to have dinner with a young woman Wednesday evening. Whenever he mentions this, which is frequently, he acts so exaggeratedly overjoyed and ecstatic that we can only believe he is not, at the moment, mentally "right." Our Mr. White tells us that you are the young lady with whom he is having dinner. If it is not asking too much, would you mind letting us know how he acts? We feel that perhaps some action should be taken before it is too late. Also Mr. Ross thinks you should be advised to treat him a little distantly on the ground that, if he acts the way he does over a mere dinner with a woman, how would he act if she touched knees with him under the table. While we have no disposition to interfere in what must be a truly delightful companionship, we nevertheless feel that you should know that Mr. Thurber's heart is already strained to the utmost at the mere prospect of seeing you at dinner. Obviously if you should be overly kind or gentle to him—if you should walk with him down a fairly dark street even—his heart might burst. Mr. Thurber has a great deal of work to do and is perhaps not the strongest man in the world anyway, and we trust that you will do nothing to excite him. We all think that if you could manage to calm him down a little and get him on some safe middle road between this silly excitement over a dinner and his occasional moments of depression when he throws things out of windows, it would be an excellent thing for all of us. You must know how it is in an office like ours, since we understand you also have a great number of crazy men around your office and things are bad enough here when Mr. White and Mr. Thurber are normal, but when they have their "streaks" as we call them, that is, long months of worry and fretting over a woman, the place is just barely liveable. We all think a great deal of Mr. Thurber, although God knows none of us women would engage to cast in our lot with his—we have too much to do here to give as much time to love as he seems to consider necessary. We feel that Mr. Thurber dwells on love overly much—in a nice, wistful sort of way, of course—but dwells. We often find him all alone in an unused room, dwelling. It might be a good idea if you arranged to let him pat your hair now and then, as I am told that a person ceases to dwell, as soon as he can, as you might say, practise. From all we can gather he is in no immediate danger of having fits, but we all feel that the sooner you take him in hand, seriously—if you can keep a straight face long enough to do that—the better.

I trust you will accept this letter in the spirit in which it is written. Here's Mr. Thurber, now, so we must all quit.

Sincerely
Grace L. McTush,
Secretary

❧  ❧  ❧

*sunday*

Dear Honey: I came to the office to work today, but appear to be too restless and melancholy. A restless and melancholy tall man. I get that way when I become convinced you will never marry me. It amounts to a conviction today. I'll never succeed in being "close" to you. Yet when I feel that way, I have a strange sensation in the pit of my stomach. I feel like a kid who has got lost from his nurse at the State Fair. I'm afraid you'll never quite understand that feeling. I can be independent of anyone, and quite detached, and I could go for weeks and months without showing that I was anything but self-sufficient, but behind that is an almost panicky feeling of disaster and waste and deterioration without you. I'm too crazy, volatile, and impetuous—mentally—to be allowed to work out my own salvation. I'll only feel secure and certain of myself when I know that what I do and how I am and what I write is of importance to you. I have lots of reasons for loving you. Yesterday I walked down Fifth Avenue in an effort to convince myself that I would see from ten to a hundred women whose appearance would persuade me that, after all, what I want is merely some girl, any girl. I ended with the feeling of being on a desert island again. There wasn't one woman out of the thousands who has the effect on the Thurber heart and mind that you have. I also ran over the list of ladies who have been so sweet as to show some interest in me. There isn't one whom I could marry with the feeling of hope and eagerness and security that I get out of knowing you are alive.

I saw "Journey's End" last night. It is a splendid and affecting thing. Far superior to "Street Scene" and anything else I have seen since "What Price Glory?". The first act seemed inordinately slow and groping, but even so was well written, and the whole piece is marvellously acted, isn't it? It didn't come to life and grip me thoroughly until that moment when Osborne laid his pipe on the table and said something about "I hate to leave a pipe when it has that nice hot glow on top." . . . Nevertheless, "Journey's End" does not have the magnificent rhythm of "What Price Glory?", none of its incredibly consistent truth—there wasn't to me a moment in the American play when I thought of lights or stage directions. Of course I am one who believes that "Glory" is the finest thing ever produced in the literature of the United States (hoo—ray!), the finest drama and the greatest poetry we have yet turned out. Except Ross and myself most of the New Yorker people were somewhat disappointed in "Journey's End." . . . White felt the English play was a bit syrupy, which is ridiculous. I'd personally love to have the English air about me if I were in the trenches. . . . Of course had I been in the trenches very long I would have gone crazy and retreated. . . . My courage is the desperate sort that wouldn't mind the raiding parties half so much as the quiet hours, and I would go all to pieces during the ticking of a watch eight minutes off from the zero hour. I would have run from any bayonet attack, no matter how charmingly it might have been conducted at me. At the same time I would have a sentimental lift in a pistol duel. The great dread I had during the play last night was the dread of injuries and pain rather than death. Osborne's passing out was a relief to me, Raleigh's caused me to break all the knuckules on one hand. A bullet in the heart is somehow an intimation that there might be a God, a bullet in the intestines is a pretty sure proof that there ain't none. In this connection it might amuse you to know that I was the quite innocent prospective target of a gent with an automatic the other day. I wasn't home, but he came to get me, or scare me. . . . For a joke, someone had led him to believe that his girl was stopping the night with me (Ed. Note: No girl has been allowed to stop the night with me for so long that I can't remember now whether it would even be desirable or not). He phoned me one Saturday morning and asked if I knew where she was. I thought he was crazy, or that it was someone else kidding me, and thought nothing of it. Later I learned he did come to the apartment with an automatic and the swell idea in mind of shooting off the lock of the door in case no one answered his knock. After that I suppose he was going to shoot me or the girl or both, or all three. Ah, well, I'm pretty used to a hard life by now, but I'm damned if I'm going to be bumped off by any gun before I have got some things done which I have in mind.

This is a fairly silly and aimless letter.

I hope you haven't been stabbed.

I want to be shot for you, just you, and nobody else but you.

Is that all right?

Jamie

&. &. &.

Dear bewildered and thoughtless Honey:

One of the tragedies of life for an intelligent person is the knowledge that reason and resolve are not always stronger than human nature. After a terribly bad afternoon I have given in to my human instincts despite hell. Every now and then I have an almost uncontrollable desire to take some young lady to dinner, and to some show, or to ride with her on a ferry boat, or to do any-thing. I have known more charming girls than any ten men in this town. Since I was 17 I have cultivated them. They have liked me. I built up a greater desire to be with some girl than with some men, or at least as great a desire, alternat-ing between the two. Since my separation I had nobody but Althea, and that was a little strained, and a little sad. Then she went away. She will be away vir-tually always from now on. She was a swell person to be with, at a concert or a theatre or any place, but that is out. In the past six weeks or so I have killed that natural desire in me to have a girl, and it has nearly killed me. You, with all your troubles, my dear, must not overlook the fact that you do have a man, of whom you are fond. That's nine-tenths of life. I spend long cheerless evenings alone, writing, reading, playing dice—games of my own invention, very elaborate. I have never in my life been in that state before. My great desire and need for you of all girls is what has kept me from getting some girl friend, and made my life pretty blank and cheerless. Occasionally you don't seem to show that you appreciate exactly what I am going through. I think if you did, old dear, you could never have managed our luncheon today as badly as you did. It was thoughtless, and that's all, but it hurt. Thoughtlessness, an indica-tion that a friend has not taken the trouble clearly to see that his friend is in a bad way, is worse than intentional hurting, much worse. I had asked you yes-terday to go with me to a certain place and you had not said you wouldn't go. You hadn't said you were going to a movie with our pal, you hadn't taken the trouble to make anything easier for me at all. Strictly speaking, you have no right to do that even to a casual aquaintance, much less to someone who should count a little. . . . When you tried to slip away at Mark's, when you in-sisted on going instantly to the nearest subway, when you arranged lunch to-day so that it would be at a place convenient for meeting George on time, when you didn't try to soften the blow of my thinking you could dally for an hour or so longer—after not seeing you for two weeks—you acted in a way, dear befuddled child, that no nice lady ever does to any nice man. You're like Katherine Angell [soon to be Mrs. E.B. White], another swell person, willing to take all that James can give, emotionally, too thoughtless to stop and say, "See here, woman, this man is alive, and normal, and has been fairly decent to me. I wonder if I shouldn't make some little effort to give him a happy hour? He must have a hell of a dull life, with nobody doing anything for him, but everybody saying, "Oh, don't *you* abandon *me*." Maybe it would be worth while to even go so far as to lie to someone someday just to spend a few hours with him and cheer him up, give him some reason to believe that all his faith and effort have not been wasted in vain on an unseeing, careless and thoughtless person."

It's 7 p.m. of another dreadful day. Mind you, I am going home to a blank and sad apartment, which has certain hurting memories, from which I should be saved. . . . Please remember again that you see, all the time, a person who is crazy about you, an important factor, and of whom you are fonder than you are of any other man. Is that unhappy, compared to me, who am going home to a sad bleak apartment to stay there all alone? I wonder if, when the friends to whom I have been devoted, decide finally to be devoted to me, it could mean so very much? . . . And I have the oh so sad sad feeling that, after reading this, you will simply hate me, and be hurt, and think somehow, in a tangled sort of way I didn't understand etc etc etc.

> With all my sincerest devotion,
>
> James

*In this undated 1929 love letter to Honeycutt, Thurber pretends to write as his psychiatrist responding to Honey's.*

Dear Dr. Gilpie:

I have at hand your chart-graph of Case history 45 . . . with your request that I suggest a suitable Rationalizing Mate from case histories of my own. No. 45 of course presents, as you know, an unusually difficult problem, what with its evident potentialities for immediate Sublimation or Frigidizing trends, unless properly rationalized. I have a young man, aged 34, who has certain requisites but would seem utterly unsuitable because of certain equally significan't Militancies. His Tenderness graph shows a gratifying complementary High—94.5—and his Appreciation and Sympathy chart reveals correspondingly excellent trends. Furthermore he reacts with satisfactory Understanding units in his Feministic Urges—insofar as they present merely a spiritual comprehension of the problem with which we have to deal. This young man, however rates extremely low in the Musical Paternity field—.34—and gave a definite minus reaction in the Prayer Paternity field—about 4.3 below the usual norm. His Pleasure-Love readings over a period of eight months have averaged 99.8, with a somewhat alarming tendency in the vernal and equinoctial seasons to verge upon an Ecstasy-Love Urge. . . . What we are met with, therefore, is the curious situation of a young man, whose worship-fervor amounts almost to the early Christian, transferring it bodily, you might say, to a finite female entity, but undergoing none of the usual Sublimation changes. Rather than the Pedestal approach, he definitely has the Four-poster approach—both as to love and as to paternity. . . . Thus whatever else we should have in the mating of these two cases . . . we could look for nothing but disaster in the field of the various Love Urges. I need not emphasize to you the certitude that a low reading and a high reading subject have almost never arrived at a tenable compromise of life. Nor . . . do I feel as if I should care to risk the present Happiness (71.8) of my case in the apparently careless and incomprehensible (to my case) hands of your case 45. His Ecstasy-Love urge, as I have indicated, transmutes very badly and I see only deterioration for him in any attempt to transform his Four-poster fixation into a Pedestal fixation, despite his Worship and Goddess readings.

 Dr. C. B. Chumley

Dear Gilpie:

 My case 54 says no. Has a definite black and white pajama complex which naturally militates against complete, or sheer, devotion reaction. . . . Has a clearly defined Clinging Ideal, if given a chance, but clings better to shoulders or waist than to stars or dreams. Can cling to both without difficulty. . . . Has an almost puppy-like desire for warm places, which would seem to explain the Snuggling phenomenon which we have given so much space despite the fact that I seriously question its importance in the field of academic research. Personally, I never snuggle, my Urge being the Lets-Get-At-This type. 54 would appear to be satisfied merely to be quite close to 45 . . . a desire so beautifully transcribed in music in the French song "Aupres de ma blonde (qu'il fait bon dormir)." . . . He is however, inclined to believe, oh, so very sadly, that all they, as two, will get out of this is the remembrance of having missed the road that leads by the waterfall in favor of taking the safer road that leads through town . . . [Incompleted]

 SUPPLEMENTARY REPORT.

Dear Gilpie:

 The young case history of which I wrote you and which, as I so reluctantly stated, would not appear to be the proper complement for your 45, is nevertheless not exactly proper for any other case I have yet studied on his behalf.

With this in view, I am wondering if you may not have a suitable feminine case in your graph files—unless of course you insist on bringing him into touch with 45. Yet, alas, in the very word touch, we have definite Trouble Reactions as regards 45 and my case, No. 54 (just the reverse of your number, significan'tly enough). This young man (54) has been tentatively tried out in association with several cases (34, 56, 471, 87, 82, 3, 78, 107, 24 etc.) with no better results than a few affirmative-devotion-readings, all highly variable, without integration of any sort, and representing no norm that I personally have ever heard of. His range of association reactions runs over a higher scale than anyone I have yet tested . . . with absolutely no point of orientation. While lacking a constitutional Promiscuity Trend (volition minus-5, initiative minus-3) he nevertheless has a distressing Snuggle Urge, registering 178, or higher than any other tested-case on our records. Pure definition of the nature and boundaries of this Snuggle Urge proves beyond the power of any instrument of measurement we possess over here. It seems to incorporate both the *dormir* and the *coucher* tendencies (subject takes 10 to 12 hours sleep). His Casanova readings are nothing to write a book about, yet he has a definite Don Juan latency—checked by several of our young women recorders, and restrained only by a persistent wistful Devotion complex amounting almost to an Ideal Fixation.

Strong masculine depredation-emotions are balanced by equally strong feministic affection-emotions, resulting often in sleeplessness, lack of ambition, lack of hope, and lack of giving a god-damn. Case 54 obviously demands that difficult balance in this day and age: the Maternal-Lover Response. Has tried both the pure-maternal and the absolute-lover experiences without any visible integration. Even now has two Maternals looking after his interests—seeing that he has a clean handkerchief, buttoning up his overcoat, giving him money for lunch, finding his hat—but seems to develop an inertia amounting to melancholy because of the definite absence in these Maternals of any actual practice of Normal maternal contact, doctor, if you know what I mean. Is distinctly a Direct-Kiss man as opposed to a Love-Pat man, thus showing a greater lean toward the Lover impulse than the Maternal impulse, yet in the case of the Absolute-Lover suddenly develops a Love-Pat tendency which overcomes the Direct-Kiss impetus. At times we lose track, and three of our lady recorders have resigned, on the ground that psychology is no longer a science. Has curious minor-fetiches, such as an extravagant and apparently unvarying Necessity Trend toward knees. Definite affection range covering ears-to-diaphraghm field, and knees to feet. This seems normal manifestation of Snuggle urge, probably atavistic in the case of the upper register, but shadowy as to lower register origin, perhaps proving contention of Origin of Species. I might say in connection with your 45, who you advised me has a three-months-of-the-year love range, my 54 has a 12 months range, at the rate of 16 to 24 hours per diem. This wears us all out, and is silly.

54 appears to get more work done in a condition of emotional hopefulness. Goes slack, sometimes comes to complete stop when he intellectually abandons all love urges, as he has been doing lately. Definitely not a Casual, but a permanent lover, and has unhappy reactions and readings in trying to apply permanent strategy and tactics to casual affairs. . . . Seems likely to become entangled with a Casual-Permanent Case, thus resulting in loss of virtually everything. Have you got anyone who can do anything about this? . . . When questioned on this subject maunders some about an evening in a room over a garden with the Chase National Bank or something of the sort. Practically impossible case.

L.B.C.

Dear Doctor Chumley:

I have carefully sounded out my 45 in regard to the necessities of your 54. Things look pretty bad. I see no immediate hope of a lot of little numbers, 45 to 54, running around the home. My 45 has a definite Swoon Reaction when approached, no matter how deftly. . . . Has thorough going Scream and Frenzy readings at times, mere thought of case 54 in his underwear or nighty bringing on these attacks. She has, as you apparently are unaware, had relations with 54 at lunch, or claims to have had. When it was pointed out to her that relations, in the broader meaning of the word, are practically impossible at lunch, showed a definite Incredulity reaction, which caused me to abandon the subject. Obviously believes danger of sudden maternity lurks in having lunch with case 54 except in restaurants where no music is played. Refuses to dance with him later than 10.30 on same ground. Also, doctor, it appears that 45 has gained a definite Aversion Impulse from an unfortunate contact with 54's knees during a dance one evening. Has an ungovernable suspicion that he might try to take off her shoes, should she see him alone and has thus developed one of the completest cases of Outdoor Association Impulses I have ever observed. Does your case have shoe-removing tendencies? Strongly suspect from what you say of his Snuggle Urge that he might have a definite Lingerie

Excitation Impulse. This, as you know, often leads to uncontrollable desires to remove ribbons, especially blue or pink, from bodice garments, leading to unfortunate culminations. 45 submits that she can dress and undress herself, but since first association with 54 has developed Disrobing Phobia and now sleeps fully clothed. Would this be undesirable to your 54, if carried to extremes? I should think if he has such high Snuggle readings, he would compromise on the removal of hats only—45 seems to have no aversion to removing hat. 54 would have to agree not to remove shoes—his own or hers. Economic arguments might of course soften 45's feeling in this regard, as obviously 54 could not afford replacement of clothing, both bed and street, every few weeks. Some say 54's clothes look pretty well slept in anyway. Reports that he does not know what to do with his hands at night and thus keeps them suspended above him like a seal's flippers, most of the night.

I would suggest that the possible union of these cases be definitely abandoned. I have never known Bed and Victrola antonyms to be reconciled. This is hard on the Victrola and the husband both. 45 reacts [as] 98.7 New England, with no Latin tendencies whatever. Definitely opposed to snuggling, with or without hat or shoes, and largely unaware of the obsessions which characterize the reactions of your 54. At present rate of Pedestalism and Musical Paternity, or Maternity, or both . . . could not attain motherdom before August, 1936.

As for Love as such, apart from purposefulness, has strong Vestalism feelings. Would have to have 57 children in order to keep husband from being restless. Can't your case satisfy his devotion by mere contemplation of delights of her existence, whether near or far, and devote himself singly to the old-fashioned Aucassin and Abelard approach?

Gilpie

---

*Honeycutt was sharing her apartment with Antoinette Price, known as "Pricey" to Thurber. Althea, in Sandy Hook, Connecticut, was breeding Scottish terriers and French poodles. "Jeannie" and "Tessa" were Scotties.*

Dear Honey:
Dear Pricey:
The day that I so extraordinarily ran into you in West 44th Street this city, you said that things would be worse than they were then. This turned out to be so.

After Althea's aunt was killed at Fort Dodge—the troops from which place did not, as they usually do, arrive in time—Jeannie ran away and was gone four days. I hunted for her for two days and she was finally extraordinarily saved from a car which was taking her to New York, when the driver and Jeannie got out at a filling station to whose attendant I had complained of the Scotchwoman's disappearance. He wrested the small bitch away from the automobilist and returned her to me. The next day she and Tessa went down to the first house on the right and killed two pet crows belonging to a neighbor whom we had hoped to meet in a pleasant way. Instead she called up and said, "You'll be glad to know that your little sluts have killed the two black crows." I supposed she was joking and said I wished to the hell it had been Amos and Andy or Mr. and Mrs. Rudy Vallee (the former Fay Webb). Well, that ended that friendship ere it was begun.

Last night I was dreaming about kissing Norma Shearer or some woman who looked a lot like Norma Shearer (we were wrassling), when an apple tree fell down in the aged orchard behind the house, startling the sheep so that they all awoke and gave me the raspberry, or bird, as only a lot of sheep can. Before that, however, Tessa gave birth to four puppies under the corn crib . . . and also under a big log under the corn crib. When we got them out we found at a glance that their father was not a respectable Scotchman but a plasterer, smart aleck young dog that worked in a kennel near the Norwalk Tire factory. Three of the dogs have sport shirts of a cheap material and the fourth a brown suit which he evidently bought in a walk-up store on Seventh Avenue, thus saving half.

Then my mother wired me and wrote me three letters to the effect that . . . Isabelle, now in Columbus, is ruining my young brother (aged 34). "Save," wrote my mother, "save your good brother from that woman." She says Isabelle is going to marry Robert and inasmuch as she got just as excited when I married Isabelle (although the marriage was annulled, as you know) I told her I would take no action until Isabelle married my older brother, William, and my father, Charlie. We got to have evidence, I told her. You can't go off half-cocked and sue a woman for marrying one brother, or even two. Any woman who would want to marry one Thurber is crazy; one that would want to marry all the Thurbers is a god damn fool.

I have reproved the Fall River boat people for their nasty dirty actions in annoying Pricie, although I knew some years ago they were planning it, because of her having got away with so much as regards ship people generally, particularly officers ("At what a price!"). You can't monkey with ship people and not get into trouble and I say she is lucky not to have been found washing up and down in the surf at Long Beach amongst the grape fruit rinds, as one girl did who annoyed ships' officers.

My chair ticked last night like a clock, and I ignored it until I thought I would scream, then I found there was a black hard bug under the seat, ticking. I had ignored it because I knew that a chair cannot tick. Been funny, seeing I was wrong, if the sunofabitch had blown up.

I feel very very badly, Miss H.

I do trust the rain has scrammed, but it has rained four days and nights in the woods where I live. Doubtless God is weeping for his lost children, of which you are, I sometimes think, even loster than me. Then sometimes I think you are not. My analyst said to me yestiddy "what do *you* think is wrong with you Thurman?" I told him passion. "Passion has got me, doctor," I said, "that's what has me—passion." He then asked me what had *you*. I said you had the lethargy. He said that where passion weds with lethargy and the union is blessed with an issue, it ticks like a clock but does not move.

> Love and peace on your house.
> And on my house too.
> jamie

❧ ❧ ❧

*[Undated, probably spring 1930]*

Dear Annie:

At night I dream about cats, as a rule, or catastrophes, rarely about women, and when I dream about women they are not sexual dreams but anxiety dreams: six women are going to go with me, separately, to the same show on the same evening. I wake up in a perspiration (not sweat; finer than sweat) and am glad to be alone. Dreams of panty-pants, breasts, etc. I no longer have; never any more does Mary Pickford sneak into my room and ring her breasts above me as if they were little pink bells—those were the absurd longings of a long-gone youth; the fantasies of an undisciplined adolescence, the evasive wish-fulfillments of a pallid and incidentless yesterday.

Over my coffee in the morning, I think clean colorful thoughts of creative work, I plan stories, I think of plots, I make little lines. Up until noon I am at my best, I get things done. At noon I exchange ideas and thoughts with my friends and if, among them, there be a woman, I content myself with a casual and faintly interested examination of her wit and her intellect. If she be rather more witty and superficial than intellectual and weighty, I like it better. Light badinage, merry banter is the stuff for lunch.

About 3:30 in the afternoon, Sex begins to creep in. It knocks at my door, it rears its ugly head from behind the radiator, it calls on the phone, it whistles in the wind. I drink water, sharpen pencils and write, but Sex comes between me and the page. I fight off erotic revery, a natural phenomenon, but very futile and rather mentally weakening. Erotic revery, as the psychoanalysts know it, is usually reminiscence on departed scenes, memories of certain amorous moments, certain exciting gestures, certain yielding words, certain astounding and indefensible actions. With me, it is scarcely revery, because instead of thinking back on women I have "been with", as my mother says, I think forward on women I want to be with; thus the whole thing comes under the general heading of "Planning" rather than of "reminiscing." . . .

At 8 p.m. after a few drinks, there forms in my mind one crystallized desire, one intention: to get some individual woman around to the theatres and speakeasies as fast as possible in order to get her home and to bed before my wit and my strength and my finesse are so atrophied by liquor and carousing that I begin to get mean rather than loving. I have never yet met a woman who would rather go quietly home with me, at a decent hour, such as 11 o'clock, even for the purpose of talking, or communing. Always, she wants to sit in Tony's till she has had her glut of liquor and of seeing people and of wild talk and of being seen. By this time it is a quarter to four and everybody feels like a 1908 Newfoundland dog rug. All inspiration, all beauty, all freshness is gone. Everybody has had his belly filled with glut, the glut of our modern New York nights. Lips begin to ooze out over faces, hair gets wrassled, eyes grow dim and wavy, finer sensibilities are drowned. This is no time for love, but if you're going to get love this is when you're going to get it. You're going to get it and like it, even though by this time you can take it, so to speak, but you can't dish it out. The whole thing is rather unlovely, and just around the edge of the next hour (for by the time you get the girl to her apartment or hotel it is 4:30) lies the damp gray face of morning, morning the charwoman, morning the street-cleaner, morning the house-maid, clearing up yesterday's dirty glasses and cigarette stubs, sweeping away last evening's blithe hopes and happy dreams and wistful desires. Love, under such handicaps, becomes a mockery, a routine.

That, in a word, is my day, has been my day. In books and in plays we see, and flutter to, romantic affairs, even though they sometimes carry with them the suggestion of tactual situations, are ordered more sweetly. There is a time for love, or should be—a nice time. Me, I have never found it; me, I have never been offered it. The only times I have ever called on a girl, at her home, in the decent early hours of the evening, has been when she was sick in bed from being in the gutters the night before. Speculations upon this modern arrangement naturally, at times, cause me to become morose, and now and again to break glasses, slap ladies down, and sit glumly in taxicabs while doors are slammed on me. Of course, if girls want to go to Tony's I'll show 'em how to go to Tony's.

I haven't time, really, for this, and it serves no purpose, except I owed you a letter.

Love, Jamie

Please save this. I may want to use part of it in a book. Don't you use it in your book, too, or they'll know we've been up to something. Who makes me dream all day? [From the lyrics of the song "Who," a favorite of Thurber's]

*Hastily Dashed Off Idea, Inspired*
*By Walking In the Rain After Short Phone*
*Conversation with A.H.*

When I go walking in the rain
It doesn't ease life's fevered pain;
I try to think of rain as swords
Cutting off my worries' gourds,
But rain does not come down in spears—
It softly falls like ladies' tears,
Provoking not a thought of war
But just a gal that I adore.

I count the raindrops as they fall
But even that won't work at all;
Whate'er I try to think or do,
I'm walking in the rain with you.

jt

*In early 1929, the Thurbers had declared a "friendly" separation. Althea remained at their rented farmhouse in Silvermine, Connecticut, Thurber at the*

*Algonquin Hotel, occasionally visiting Althea on weekends. Made lonely by memories of past infatuations, he sent a lovesick letter to Minnette Fritts Proctor, by then married with children in Seattle, asking if he could visit her. The letter did not go over well with Proctor, and Minnette's scolding included Thurber's signing his name by typewriter rather than by hand. (Is Sex Necessary?, by Thurber and E. B. White, was published November 7, 1929.)*

## To Minnette Fritts Proctor

*11-11-29*

Dear Minnette:

You're such a little idiot that I ought not to write to you. But, after thinking it over for eight months, I have decided not to let you have the last word. . . . If I want to hurt someone I hurt 'em—in big round words, usually uncalled for and always unmeant. I did not know until you told me that I had signed the letter on the typewriter. Then, of course, I realized I probably had since I always do—or used to. Your reaction has made me change. Trouble is, I *never* have ink in my office—they don't allow me to because I used to spill it on manuscripts, visitors, suits etc. If I signed this longhand, I'd have to sign it in pencil, which blurs, because I use soft pencils. So, damn it, I'm going to sign it on the typewriter.

Perhaps you have been so happy, or so lucky, or something since you cut me off, and how, that you won't want to risk writing me again. I can promise that I have grown very sane and mature, though, and will never write childish letters again—if that's any inducement. Nor ever talk of love, tangles, life etc.—if *that's* any inducement.

I don't know whether this will reach you or not, since I have lost your address (I lose all addresses, so don't think I threw yours away, or am deliberately pretending I don't know it.) . . .

I have written a book with another guy. I'll send you one, and write in it, if you want me to. Elliott is in the movies for two years or more on contract; . . . Althea is raising poodles (big black French), Siamese cats and Scotties; I lost fifteen Dollars on the Yale-Dartmouth game; and I'll tell you more if you want me to. . . .

Affectionately and with every sincere apology and every contrite expression of sorrow, and wrong doing, and nasty humor (now passed)—and all—except I *won't* sign this other than the way I really, after all, should, because pencil blurs and finally disappears, which I never shall, ink blots and covers things up forever, but

Jim

goes on forever.

and you know how I "go on"!

Jim

and on and on!

Jim

and on

Jamie

and

Jimmy

and

James Thurber

Take one, or all, of me!

I should think you'd like to make up without having to kiss!

*ખ   ખ   ખ*

*[Undated, probably November 1929]*

Dear Minnette:

Your charming letter just came, and made me glad.

No, my mamma didn't write me that she had heard from, or written you. I suspect her of writing people—she writes Eva's mother—and one has to know my mother to see through her. Pay little attention to what she says. She can so awfully misrepresent me—God knows why!

. . . I simply had to write her when I felt it was ripe to. My letter was a beautiful defense of Althea against those silly and baseless suspicions, charges and dislikes which a boy's mother has for the girl he marries. . . . You see she has the old 1900 viewpoint of love and marriage. But we're . . . straightened out now—even though she may be a bit confused as to just what makes me tick.

. . . The Post, my old paper here, did a swell charcoal portrait of me. I'm sending some reviews of the book [*Is Sex Necessary?*] and of me!—and I'm also sending you one of the books. I don't know how it will sell but it has been a considerable success d'estime. Perfectly marvelous reviews. And I am all set up by being, suddenly, a really important figure about town! I'm not so sure I enjoy it though. I realize how easy it is—like becoming editor of the Sun Dial, although Althea stoutly maintains it isn't that easy.

She is still hard at it raising lovely doggies. Ours is a relationship at once charming, fine, and hurting. I get a great pain in the heart at times. But doesn't everyone somehow in life have a great pain, make a great misstep, go along with a big regret? No sensitive person, no human being, can avoid that, can he? It seems to me everyone I like has some such dark moods in his life. Maybe it's a sign of something good rather than bad—anyway it gives one a real reason to be courageous—and more and more I see courage as one of the finest virtues. But how hard it is, my god how hard, sometimes!

. . . As you say, so much cannot be written in a letter. Generally, I am pretty well confused, but also I have got discipline. I am the captain of my soul—but do you know the famous remark a man who said that, made? "But," he added, "I had more fun when I was cabin boy!"

Something goes, doesn't it, when one nears thirty-five? And something takes its place. Since what takes its place has more solidity and firmness and gives one surety and poise, one should not be truly sorry the other has gone. The apple is more satisfying than the blossom, but oh, my dear!

In the place of indulgences, I have got dedications. They are harder, and not so exciting. . . . I live in dread only of hurting, in the hope only of helping. I really don't think of myself enough. I have had to make so many compromises. But now I rather like the man who has come out of them. He really has some of the splendidness now that once he merely thought he had! And yet, also, lest you worry that I have changed too much, he has some of those terrible old weaknesses and irresponsibilities still—enough so that should you ever meet him again, you need not be *too* proud—proud I mean to the awful extent of fearing he just might never hesitate again on the shadow line between right and wrong. He still does. He still would.

Jim

And he still has, in the event of a great crisis, your telephone number!

☙ ☙ ☙

*[Undated, January or February 1930]*

Dear Minnette:

I've been in the throes of everything this year, promising myself the release of burdening you about it . . . but I get tired. I'm going to Columbus next week for the Golden Jubilee of the Phi Kappa Psi. . . . I really was quite touched to be told that most of the men of my years in school asked whether

I would be there. . . . So I'm going. Elliott and I are included in the 10 or 12 "distinguished alumni" of the old frat's 50 years—there doesn't seem to have been any "distinguished" Phi Psis since our day. . . .

. . . It ought to be impressive to see the boys I used to know, now the baldish dads of familys.

Elliott won't be there—his mother died here about three weeks ago, with only poor Ruth in town—one of the few times the Nugents have ever been separated. . . . She was buried in Dover—Elliott and J.C. going there by plane I think. . . .

Althea's lovely French poodle won first prize in the Westminster Dog Show here—a triumph which unsettled her so she almost cried when the judges handed her the blue ribbon. I was as thrilled as the day I made Sphinx! It's a great impetus to a Kennel, when you win a Westminster ribbon. . . .

Last Wednesday I broadcast over a coast-to-coast network but didn't know it was coast-to-coast till I read about it in the Columbus papers which gave me far too much space for the crazy talk I made. I would have let you know just to see if you could have got me on your radio if I had known it was going so far. I'll talk again sometime and will let you know. My family heard me clearly on a small set Robert has.

The book (which, by the way, your Seattle Town Topics calls "E.B. White's new book") is still going great guns, and after being third or fourth on the best seller list is now first, much to our surprise—and delight. It has sold around 40,000 copies, which is very good, but not enough to make me wealthy as everyone seems to think, although I'm going to go to Europe this summer and expect this time to have enough resources not to have to worry where I'm going to eat next—as I did when I was young.

The trip to Europe may be a turning point. Just for your eyes, I may be married again—although I'm not divorced yet—to the Louisiana girl I think I have mentioned once or twice; she is really exactly right for me—or shall I say, nearly so. What is exactly right for me would take too long to explain. I am really so tangled up that I don't know what to do—I mean in every way. I spend most of my time wondering, fretting, and planning, and coming back to where I started, but I do know that I was never cut out to be a bachelor and to live a sort of house-to-house life. If it were not so rather pathetic sometimes, it would interest me—my story. It does interest me—but against a background of discontent, uncertainty, and, I could almost say, heart-break. About which there is no reason why I should worry you. You won't like me to be married again, will you? I wouldn't like you to be married again. I think I'd have a feeling of distrust about the man—as you will have about the girl. She is reminiscent of you—quite a lot—the contour of her face, her voice, and the way she moves about. Perhaps you don't want to know any more than that—perhaps not even that.

I'm past the stage of being especially thrilled by anything. It's funny how that goes, isn't it? I can watch myself, somewhat impassively and as from a front row seat, doing things, saying things. I compare the man I see with the boy I was, and it amuses me, in a sad sort of way. It's hard to settle on what I want this man to do, hard even to settle on what I want him to believe, and to live by. It can't be religion, or social service, for me—it must be creative writing—partly at least, but one doesn't live by writing alone. I mention religion etc. because one gets the desire for a dedication of some kind—when I was younger a dedication to some woman seemed enough. It isn't. Women find out sooner than we do, that a dedication to one person will not serve. It doesn't finally cover all the edges of our desires and our longings; our feet of clay stick out from under the covers and get cold, or else our shoulders do. I spend a great deal of time sorting over my past—some of my emotions are as disturbing as some of the pieces I did for the Sun Dial, when I come cross them. What a child I was: And yet some of them I'd like to have again. I'd love to recapture, frankly, some of that ancient tremendous urge I had about love; it's terrible to be able, as I now am, to consider, never to lose my head, to analyze a kiss, to ponder on the individual psychology of the person being kissed, to study the whole thing out, as I might the notes for a chapter in a book. I don't like that, in one way—but I do in another. The writing part of me enjoys an ability to see things clearly, for what they are worth, and to feel that his emotions can not so distort a thing that he is unable to present it truly; but the ancient Jim in me longs for the desire and the power to lose himself, to believe that this kiss, this love is all—that of such is the kingdom of heaven. . . . The one illusion I have about girls is that I could so lose myself with you—yet, in spite of the years. It is an illusion better left untested—isn't it? You, I suppose, would be frightened of me. Why I keep this childish feeling about you, I don't know. A somewhat similar illusion about Eva crumbled in my hands, but that was because the illusion was built out of the sentimentality of my teens—actually, though, I tried to keep that whole; I couldn't, and it hurt. The one about you is built on more solid things and yet its basis is a very simple one: I feel that if I kissed you, now, or anytime hereafter, I would still find that magnificent, impossible land which as a sophomore—or was it a junior?—I so ardently had to have to live. In sorting over my kisses, I still find, on top, as exciting as ever, and as lovely, the time I kissed you one night in June. . . .

Althea still plays a great part in my life. She is still, except for her dogs, unanchored. I wish she were not. We have some moments that tear me to pieces—for this after all was my undertaking, this girl. I have done more to her life, actually, than to anyone else's and I feel responsible about it. You see, one can't go back, one must go ahead on what he has built. And I live so much in what is past—the realized past and the unrealized, but we live by what we have been through, in accordance with the life of the person to whom we have given our mature years—that is those years when we were growing into final maturity. There is no getting away from that; there is no real starting over again; there are the shadows and the monuments of the past always. Naturally, my going away to Europe would be an effort to escape, to start over, to found a new happiness. I know that I could do that only partially. Sometime in France I would turn a corner that she and I turned, under such different conditions, five years ago. The emotions of that day would come back, and I would be that man for I don't know how long, just as surely as, when I go to Ohio State next week, I will be the man I was when I was getting out the Lantern, when first you appeared before my desk—I'll be that man and no other. I wish I did not do things like that, but I do.

This grave-eyed girl from Louisiana, where old abandoned manors still stand, over-run with mosses, sees my problem, and my complexity, quite clearly. If she didn't it would be impossible. She has had her past and has her present entanglements too. Her room looks out over Washington Square, a room in one of the oldest and nicest houses in town. Sometimes under a street lamp she sees the imagined shadow of a man whose heart is hers and from whose impossible dedication she tries to escape, too. We feel that we are miles apart from each other, sometimes; but we have this clear comprehension of each other, because our problems have been so much the same. Our friends—those few who know me best—are for her, because they know she understands me, because they know she appreciates what I need, what I ought to do (intellectually anyway); because she is the only girl I know here whose tranquil understanding seems to me a sort of harbor into which I can go when storms come up. . . .

This shows me pretty clearly, doesn't it—for here I am making love, or something, to three separate girls—especially, I think, you, against which I

fight—or is it that?—by excursions into other harbors—perhaps trying, a little plaintively—to make you either happy or unhappy about it. That sentence
shows my entanglement. It reminds me of a line from a show I saw last night.
A man says to a young chap who comes to New York to live "Don't let that girl
entangle you." "Aw, no girl can untangle me!" says the youngster.

No girl can untangle me,

   ever,

   Jim


. . . My drawings are now coming into a strange sort of acclaim. The New
Yorker is going to run a series of my animal pictures ["The Pet Department"],
and a concern wants me to do ads for it! Imagine!

My best work is an amazingly naturalistic capturing of the primary motives
with a hint of the Unequal Struggle of the soul against them. I'm enclosing a
few, which you can throw away. They'll alarm you.

   J.


    ßå ßå ßå

        *[Undated, probably spring 1930]*

Dear Minnette:

. . . Either you are opposing my coming to the great Northwest, or you are
favoring it—just a windlestraw are you—windlestraw to my spindrift—and a
hell of a lot of decision *they* would arrive at. I doubt if I would ever have the
courage to round a corner and see you standing on a porch, or come into a
room and see you there. Consider the complications—the comedy and the
drama of it; the possibilities; I still go off at a tangent, leaving my resolutions
and my better sense behind, if a certain color, or a curve of the cheek, or a distant church clock takes part in the proceedings as it almost invariably does.
Perhaps it might even be that, in the midst of all my solemn integrity, a Seattle
breeze might reveal the charming roundness of your knee—something as
simple as all that.

I don't know what I'm going to do—I might do anything almost at any
minute. I certainly will if I ever get economically free of responsibilities, which
sometime soon I may. Me released from an . . . anchorage would be a menace.
Sometimes I want to see you because I want to see what you're like; sometimes
because I want to see what you think I am like; sometimes because I want to
enjoy the situation—as a critic of situations; sometimes (and mostly) because

(and you know it damn well too) I want to make love to you. That couldn't be. Neither safe nor sensible, however lovely, however desirable—however necessary, even. . . .

. . . What surgeon wants the author of a flippant book on sex to drop in on his wife; or even to think that he might drop in? No surgeon.

We're too far apart; I'd change my mind in Utah; or you'd change yours. . . .

. . . We'll always blow hot and cold about our life, about what might have been, even about what might be.

(At this point the editor came in with a suggestion for a change in a story I wrote about a man who deals in old used gin and scotch bottles—always being brought back to earth.) That—to take it out of the parentheses for a moral—is a perfect instance of what happens. In the midst of moonlight on Jericho, a woman gets a pain in her stomach at City Hospital, or one of Althea's puppies gets a pain in its stomach. One is snapped back into his greatest reality—the reality of a long marriage—the solidest reality we know, whether or not. . . . Dismissing all and any arguments for seeing you is as ridiculous as building up the arguments. We're always in the squirrel cage, going round and round, theorizing and knowing that theory is nothing. Thus we'll just let it go on until the force of life, or the inertia of it, does something to us, or doesn't do anything.

Isn't that so, Garfield 7844, and are you still home Mondays?

Jim

*Thurber's drawings first appeared in* The New Yorker *February 22, 1930, in "The Pet Department" series.*

                                          *[Undated, probably summer 1930]*
Dear Minnette:

The long delay has been due to new, and bigger, complications. In February, my cousin Isabelle descended on New York, half-ill, separated from her husband, wanting to work here, and suffering from a delusion of grandeur about me. It's been indescribably difficult. The Althea situation is as complicated as ever. The next man hasn't showed up for her. I'm standing by, bolstering, cheering, comforting. She's quite wonderful, but at times lonely, herself against the world, on a Connecticut farm. The Louisiana [Honeycutt] situation has deepened into something infinitely nice, altogether non-sinful, quite psychologically intricate. Then, three weeks ago, along came Paula.

You once wrote me there'd always be a dream girl—whoever else there was. I guess you're right. I don't know whether it's a fault, or a necessity, or what. Now I have several dream girls. The Paula thing is quite romantic—and my reactions a proof I'm still me. She is quite famous here—Paula Trueman, an actress of, as the Herald-Tribune critic said, "an infinite charm." Sweet, pretty in a misty, loveable way, intelligent, witty, greatly gifted, five feet one inch tall, petite, with an entrancing figure. I've long liked her intensely from orchestra seats. Many times in the past year I've told Althea "I have the oddest desire to look up Paula Trueman." "Well, look her up," said Mrs. Thurber. Three weeks ago I got in my office mail a letter with the name Paula Trueman on the back. It was a simple little note, asking if I had ever seen her, telling me what kind of things she did—as if anybody in N.Y didn't know!—and asking if I would write a skit for her to use in a big Broadway revue soon to go into rehearsal. She said she took the liberty of introducing herself to me because she had long admired my "delightful sketches" in the New Yorker! Now I ask you, Minnette!

She lives at 61 West 12, I at 65 West 11. I can see her front windows from my back ones—never knew she lived near.

I went down one May night and rang her bell (by appointment) (Incidentally, 3 people had told me she looks like Honey, the Louisiana girl.) I was quite excited—as when I phoned you one December night. She lives in a top floor apt. with a big sky-light and a little cat. I knew when I saw her standing there that it was going to be just too bad. It was. In 3 weeks we've got really far—too far, perhaps, but how lovely! (Nothing sinful—don't you love that word?). There's a man, named Thorton Delehanty, a movie critic, nice fellow. Been living with him two years or more. I met him one midnight—called her up because I couldn't sleep unless I saw her. She has a lovely voice. They had been on the roof watching the Zeppelin fly over. "Delehanty says come on down and have a drink" she said. I went. . . . It was a swell night.

Then ten nights ago we went to [a hotel] roof in Brooklyn, which has the loveliest view of any place in America I have ever seen, a view of the harbor and the New York sky line, lighted entrancingly. There was nice music. I fell horribly in love, awfully, madly. We stayed for hours. We got charmingly involved. I'll always hear her voice saying "oh, Jim!"—that was in the taxi, crossing Brooklyn Bridge, with the lights of ships moving mistfully below, through the soft June night. She kisses as only one other lady I know, whose identity I beg you to be discreet in guessing, can kiss. If, in being lifted out of myself, there was still that lurking, damnable detachment which permits my aging and critical mind to examine, scientifically, the workings of my heart in action, and to point out where ecstasy begins and ends, it was nevertheless, for a moment, supremely lovely. And what is there, after all, with finding in the world, but lovely moments?

\* \* \*

All this was, now, a week ago. It is rainy and a little cold. A chill, slight but disturbing, has fallen on my moment. I am restless and again discontented. Oh, my discontent! What is it slips away from me? What is it I can't hold? Something terribly important, essential, but impossible to keep. I whistle to keep my mind off its going.

She is still enchanting, but now we have our feet more firmly on earth. . . . Put this down: there is something in a man which hates attainment even of the thing he most wants to have. You, who have something of that same quality, know what I mean.

But Honey was wonderful. I told her, not quite directly, but nearly so, of my desertion—of my infatuation, anyway—which is what I called it. She said nothing I did would change her opinion of me. I asked what if I married, or lived with, someone else. "I shall expect to see you all the rest of my life, whenever I have to," she said. I explained that this other girl's warmth, her quick response—which Honey has never quite given (but is capable of) had overcome me, because it is so much what I need. And I said I didn't think she, Honey, really loved me. "I have," she said, "a deep and fundamental love for you." And few sentences have ever touched me so profoundly, because she meant that. It seemed, and is, so Big.

Honey has been uppermost these last few days. She is so deep, so tranquil, so understanding, and she does care so very much. And so do I. I can't get away from that. She is afraid, oddly enough—or maybe not oddly at all—not of Paula, but of Althea.

Honey and I week-ended with Andy White and his wife last week. We came back Sunday night, at the Katonah station, as the train whistled down the track, she said to Andy "Who are you for, me or Paula?" "Oh," he said, "It's Tilden and Cochet [tennis players]—I'll read about it in the papers some day." They love Honey, the Whites, but they are afraid of a lack of emotion between us. In two years, of much being alone, nothing has happened beyond a few cautious extravagances in caresses. That, in its way, fascinates me. We have so much to build up to. We wouldn't start too high, and fall slowly to a colorless level. But you can see the oddity of me in such a situation so long a time. The oddity of it, and the charm. Isn't it just what I want, too—the non-attainment of the desireable? Is that why I am writing to you? If it is, why then is Althea so important? Do I want both—something I can have and something I can't? Then I won't ever "get anywhere", will I?

Said Honey one day, "When you are over your affair with Paula, I know the place where I want you to take me—a lovely inn at the end of Long Island." "You would just submit," I said, "you wouldn't really want to." "I would go with a great deal of pleasure and abandon," she said—using two nouns which stand for qualities I once said she did not enjoy. She has a lovely wit. Her case history is interesting, but long. I won't tell it. She has known submission—from an impulse of generosity—and disgust—which naturally follows. A lady can never give herself for any reason other than real desire, and come out of it unscarred. . . .

Sunday night, when we got to Grand Central, we were tired. I got into a taxi with her—and our bags—and automatically gave my address. She said nothing. After ten blocks, I realized I had made a mistake, and said so. "I was ready to go with you," she said, "because, after all, I have my brushes and a nightgown. But I'm afraid I wouldn't be very interesting—I'm so tired." So I took her to her house and went on home. It was a nice happening. Thus we go on. . . .

Always 'n' Ever
Jim

&. &. &.

*Sept. 1930*

Dear Minnette:

Lots has happened to me since last I wrote you, and it seems like a year since the 4th of July, a gala three-day holiday, during the course of which, at a great drinking joust, up in Westchester county, I definitely went to pieces. Some of the people at the office bought me a ticket and shanghaied me to Canada where, in two weeks, I got on my feet, saw how silly I had been to let New York get me down, gained four pounds—no, six—and recovered my appetite and my sense of humor.

One of the results of the glorious fourth was the mutual discovery of Honey and myself that we were not in love, so now we are friends—a condition at which, you know, I always arrive. Friends with you, friends with Althea, friends with Honey, even friends with Paula, I think. I am beginning to evolve a theory, a serious theory, about me, and I want you, who really knows, to tell me if it isn't true. I figure myself as a man who is, in a certain subtle sense, rather more feministic (not feminine) than masculine, a quality in me which women sooner or later detect, but which is usually lost on men. As a result of this, I always become, in the minds (not in the hearts) of women—the four or five women—a symbol rather than a person; they discern a great capacity for understanding, sympathy, and entertainment in me, but in so doing they lose the unreasoning headlong affection which they have for the man they are in love with. I have never had such an affection—no woman has ever felt, I blush to say, a definite and authentic passion for me. I have just realized that. Yet all the women I have known intimately have been the kind who have wanted, needed, and eventually got the proper object for a really demonstrative love. The kind that cools, yes, but which, while it lasts, may sometimes be worth everything else in life. The kind which I have always wistfully longed for and, now I see, never had—because of this damnable quality in me. I analyze too much, I talk too much, I am never the strong, silent man who puts this or that lovely lady to bed and causes her to remember the incident the rest of her life, or at least for the duration of the current month. Seeing in me the makings of an interesting and dependable friend, women always set out to bring us to that basis as shortly as possible. They show, finally, as much interest, almost as much passion—if that were possible—in and for my friendship as they show for whatever man it is, or was, in whom they are, or have been, amorously interested. Often a friendship for me outlasts their love interest in someone else; sometimes it is, or seems to be, more important even. Take Honey. She has said in so many words that she hasn't any emotional feeling for me, but qualifies this by adding that whoever she married would have to understand that she expected to see me three fourths of the time the rest of her life. That's the only necessity in a woman for which I can ever hope. It is rather nice, too, knowing that some lady just has to see you and brightens when you appear, but since I am 100 percent male, despite this strange feministic aura of mine—this ruin of mine—it is also melancholy to realize that it is never because the lady wants to be kissed, fondled, mauled or anything else. She wants to sit and talk, she wants to listen; she goes forth satisfied and contented by the experience of a kinship of spirits, etc. etc. Then she may be tortured by other desires, by other necessities, by other fears, and pains, and hopes—usually, however, for some man who is less kind to her, who understands her not at all, who is often not even interesting—but who has that strange, indefinable something I haven't got—perhaps a sort of cave-man something or other.

I'm not asking for advice, for advice wouldn't help. I just have a great desire for you to help me crystallize this theory of mine into a definite basis for my future actions, by telling me that you, too, never could have imagined me as a lover. I want the truth about that. I want to have the courage to face my destiny, and the sense to understand myself, which I never have had before, because I have proceeded on the wrong basis. I want, finally, after much prayer and suffering, to be able to endure my fate. It's going to be hard for me to realize that I'm just God's friendship-gift to women, and to bring myself to accept that as a very wonderful, beautiful thing, and to give up hoping for anything more, but I'm mature enough to go through with it.

I understand William called on you. That must have been rather confusing. William is a strange boy. What have you been doing? How is everybody? And wouldn't you, too, like to see me because I don't know why it is, Jim, but I don't love you, and never could, and yet I would rather see you than anyone else I know.

Honey even said that the only thing in life which could upset her would be my death or my going away for a long, long time. Even in the throes of a love affair, that would upset her—for a time, I suppose, for a month or a year.

Well, I'll never marry, or even have an affair with someone, who doesn't want me in some other way. I'm really tired of this business of being the school girl chum of girls, their confidante, the sharer of their candy and their joys and their sorrows, the receptacle of the story of their heart-breaks, the guide and the mentor, the big brother, the beacon, the helping hand, the understanding soul, the pal, the best friend.

> Your old school girl chum,
> Jim

I'm sorry to seem so depressed, but I am depressed. I have a dull pain in my forehead and, somehow, the feeling that it's all futile and silly this life, and that girls aren't much. You see I don't really think they are much as friends. If it were simply friendship, and someone asked me what five persons I wanted to take to a desert island as friends, I'd take five men. Oh, when a girl is in love with you, that is more important than friendship, but it saddens me to know that their attitude toward me is rather short-sighted and selfish: not one of them has one tenth as much to give me, on that basis, as I give them. I get almost nothing out of it, really. I wish I could, but what gives me this headache is the realization that, if it's just to be friendship, and nothing else, there isn't any girl I consider important, interesting, inspiring, or anything else. Some of them are faintly witty, some of them are fairly well-read, some of them are good sports, but their great qualities, their great gifts, are those which they keep for someone else, not me. And when a girl is simply trying to be a friend, a pal, a sport, she is, God help me and God help her, an almost total loss, a sad, annoying thing.

*In 1930, Thurber purchased a 20-acre farm in Sandy Hook, Connecticut, where Althea continued to raise dogs. Their only child, Rosemary, was born in October 1931. Herman Miller, on the O.S.U. faculty, had become a close friend of Thurber's. The "Monroe" stories ran in* The New Yorker *in 1929.*

## To Herman and Dorothy Miller

*Sept. 22, 1931*

Dear Herman and Dorothy:

Sitting on my porch this warm night, with a small breeze and four dogs wandering across, I got to thinking for no reason that our correspondence has been terrible. . . .

Of course I've been leading a mixed-up and fretful life, with the heat, approaching fatherhood (although Althea is unquestionably the world's most patient and finest mother-expectant), office work, meditation upon the probability that I shall never write anything really as good as I should like to . . . the thoughts of a man of thirty-six. Anyway, here I am now at my country estate, having a few weeks' vacation (Althea's mother is here, which is a kind of sanctuary) and sitting for hours at a typewriter thinking muddled thoughts and putting down absolutely no words that are interesting or novel. I did write the first chapter of a novel to be called Rain before Seven, but I am afraid all of my novels would be complete in one chapter, from force of habit in writing short pieces and also from a natural incapability of what Billy Graves would call "larger flight"—which is a veritable Banshee wail, anyway. So I try to write and don't and then I read something, now and again dropping a pencil or rattling some papers so that Althea, reading in the next room and thinking the softly confused, half ethereal, half economical thoughts of approaching motherhood, will not know that my mind has become a blank and my creative talent, such as it was, gone. I have read Evelyn Waugh's two books, which are my favorite two books, Crime and Punishment, and the letters of Frances Newman and her first novel. Kind of a mixed lot. I don't suppose it

has helped my thought processes any. Meanwhile, outside, there is the inter-
mittent fall of apples from my apple trees, and the curiously unnerving raspberry which my neighbor's sheep hand me, and the sounds of my five female
dogs, two of them in heat (I inadvertently let Jeannie loose one day and she
didn't show up till next morning, with seven of the finest specimens of manhood among the shepherd dogs of this county following her, each trying to
outdo the other in order of attention). I have twenty acres, and a house a hundred and twenty five years old, when Washington was seducing the Mount
Vernon chambermaids. I also have arranged a series of croquet wickets so that
they make a golf course running completely around the house. Every few
hours I get out and struggle trying to make the course under twenty-three
which is my record so far. It is maddening to me, my wife, her mother, the
cook, and the dogs. But nothing so completely holds me as competitive en-
deavor. Nothing except sleep and, I suppose, sitting in a speakeasy on a rainy
evening with somebody else's wife. I really like that. I sometimes wonder at
just what age I will get over my, until now, secret desire for and belief in fairly
clandestine monkey-business. Of course I justify my numerous loyalties in a
number of ways which, if I could only put them down as beautifully as I feel
them, would make a wise and lovely piece of writing. Ah, well. That will be for
a time when all the wheels are run down and the beauty of it all is not so fresh
and vibrant as to make literary tinkering with a kind of hollow and painful
desecration. I suppose even I will one day reach a quiet place where I can view
tranquilly and, please God, with more humor than I have ever been able to
thus far, the sad, sweet, mixed-up pulsing of sex and beauty and drink and unfair kisses. . . . There should be some fine novel of a not despicable but also
not admirable person, whose pleasant habits and even noble dedications in
one chapter are seen with their hair in their eyes and an utterly unexcused
desire on their lips in the next—and so on. . . . Any novel by and of me, however, would be so flagrantly historical as to be embarrassing. The Monroe stories were transcripts, one or two of them varying less than an inch from the
actual happenings. Of course I could never do a novel seriously; it would
slowly begin to kid itself, and God knows what it would turn out to be like. . . .

As to my fame: I received last week a letter from Homer St. Gaudens, son of
old Augustus, and head of the Department of Fine Arts of the Carnegie Institute at Pittsburgh, saying that the Institute was giving a luncheon for the three
foreign judges for its thirtieth annual International Exhibition and that one of
them, Paul Nash, "the leader of the new idea in British art" had expressed a
real desire to meet me. I had been, in fine, one of the three or four people in

America he had asked to see. I went to the luncheon and met him—in the midst of such people as Jonas Lie and Blackens and Hopper and twenty other dignified gentlemen of the old school. He was immediately interested in me to the exclusion of almost everybody and incredibly nice. He had many words of praise for The Owl in the Attic (he has never seen "Is Sex") and in the end we arranged to see each other when the exhibition is over. He had previously written an article in the London Week-end Review, on Modern American Humorous Draughtsmen (get the draughtsmen) in which he mentioned Seven: Milt Gross, Walt Disney, the Katzenjammer man, Arno, Soglow, John Held Jr. and me. (I was coupled between the same commas with Matisse!

My dear people, you should be here for the fun!! There were place cards at the luncheon and I was placed next to Nash. I must see you some day soon to tell you, in greater detail, how Alice in Wonderland it all was.

Love, Jim

*Thurber's marital misery, for which he took most of the blame, combined with speakeasy booze, self-pity, and a jealous preoccupation with Honeycutt, led occasionally to his uncontrolled behavior outside the office. On one such occasion he trashed Honey's apartment. These outbursts were always followed by abject contrition on Thurber's part and desperately sincere pledges to do better.*

*Antoinette (Pricey) Price was a roommate of Honey's.*

## To Ann Honeycutt

*[Undated, probably 1931]*

Dear Madam:

Last night my husband and I were about to retire when a tall, unkempt man, obviously a gentleman but not well, rang our bell and asked for someone named Price. Our name is McCalliper and there has never been a Price in the apartment—45 Barrow street—to my knowledge. The man forced his way in, however, and began to cry. He mentioned you and said that you censored him for bragging simply because he had stayed with every girl in the city. He put in a number of phone calls, asking people over, so we had to get dressed and mix some drinks. A man named [Scudder] Middleton, a French sculptor named Gotch and a Mr. Glibbs [Gibbs] finally came. Mr. Middleton was very sweet and so was the foreigner, but this other man lay down on the bed with his coat and hat on and said that he had once been lovely but was not lovely now. At this the tall man—Huber [Thurber], I believe is his name—accused my husband of never having suffered, at all, although he was suffering right then. Glibbs had a flask and they all drank. Later they phoned other people, a Mrs. Demson [Sally Benson], a Mr and Mrs. Coates (long distance) and a Miss Boogan [Louise Bogan]. They all came but the Coates, and Mr. Huber began to talk about you. He spoke very highly of you, saying that although he had struck you several times you had never hit him back but once, when you kicked him in the stomach after you had kicked the glass out of a door. He said that he loved you very much but that you were a cold and cruel little pussy cat and that you could have saved him if you had accepted his offer of marriage—he said he had the license and all, but you walked out saying that you didn't know. He said that Gladys Lee was a finer woman than you, but that he loved you, and that you were a beacon to him which is why he goes around staying with girls and drinking. He said all that he was, both good and bad, was your doing. The Coates arrived shortly after 3, and phoned a Miss Truesdale [Paula Trueman], asking her to come down and take Mr. Huber away. She came with a lame man. Glibbs got out some dice and he and your husband played for ten dollar bills. Glibbs kept sweeping his left hand over the carpet and said he was surrounded by heath hens, although I did not see any. Glibbs said he was right about you, and that you would not even stay the night with God. Huber said he thought of you every time he did something awful, and that if it hadn't been for you he would be the same as he was when he first met you (in a stove, somewhere, he said). He spoke very highly of you until almost dawn, when he began to scream the awfulest words and say awful things about everybody but this Price. He said Price was his idea of somebody, and that you simply were a killer. Glibbs cried through all this. Mr. Middleton went home with a bottle of our rye. They all left about six. I thought you might want to know. Mr. Huber tried to get me to spend the night with him, because he said he didn't care what he did, now, having lost you, but I was not flattered. I think that you should be kinder to him. I felt that he was deeply shocked by your kicking the glass out of the door that time. He said he would have bled to death that night if it had not been for Mrs. Price, whose husband was in Detroit.

Sincerely,
Mrs. Charles Allan McCalliper

฿ ฿ ฿

Dear Honey:

Out of the shambles one bright consolation looms up: I did not throw the three pound box of assorted chocolates. I remember having the tendency to throw it—it attracted me more than anything else in the room, including the wooden Russian people, the dog, the tumblers, and Coates. But, crazy as I was, I knew that if I threw that candy, the last spark of manhood in me would be gone. It was bad enough to revile my friends, traduce my wife, and compromise the neighborhood, but it would have been unsupportable to have thrown the candy. Picture to yourself, a gallant arriving at 8 p.m. with a ribboned box of sweets, bending over the charming girl. Picture, then, this same swain several hours later, she slapped down on a couch, he going around like a mad plumber, wrenching off fixtures, plucking out pipes, screaming fuck. Alack, a day! When *I* was a girl, they didn't do such things, my dear! It was impossible, in the old days, to produce so great a change of pace—to step from a sweet little picture, innocent enough to serve as a Lowney's ad in the Atlantic Monthly, to a scene comparable to a gang shooting in Brooklyn—and done by the same cast!

We will now sing, She Broke My Heart so I Broke Her Jaw.

With love and curses,

Jamie

*Through Honey, Thurber had met John "Jap" Gude, then her fellow employee at CBS, who became a firm Thurber friend and the lifetime agent for E. B. White and Thurber, handling the subsidiary rights to their work.*

Dear Honey:

I am sending you along with these few words Mr. Hergesheimer's "Swords and Roses" which I hope you will be reading in the hospital for several days yet. I don't want to hear of you sneaking out past the nurses; Mino's can wait, although it is not the same without you and me. You can't go there because you're at St. Antoinette's and I can't because I owe them $5, and it seems silly to pay for drinks of which the effect has worn away.

The first chapter of Swords and Roses is largely military and outside of a few lovely descriptions of the flora of the deep South, you may not want to read it: although if you are papa's sweetheart you should like the manoeuvres of the Civil War. I understand that one of the Honeycutts lost his head at the battle of Chicamauga. . . .

I had lunch at the Algonquin today with Helen Wismer, who is a nice and calm girl. It is easier to have lunch with her than with most anybody else because she works at the corner of 44th and sixth, which is as far as I can get nowadays. I wrote two casuals yesterday and drew seven pictures, which finished me off last night, but it is the first solid work I have done for so long that it reminded me of old times when I was a hard-working, serious-minded man and as safe around a woman as anyone you'd want to meet. Now of course I'm just a bragging old spaniel who comes back from the settlement with tales of his conquests.

Jap is having me and my wife—a tall dark woman of the highest character—over to his house Saturday for a kind of farewell roughhouse.

He has asked me to prepare a little talk on the subject of Nobody Ever Did Anything for Me, in which I am to touch on the career of my wife as a dog fancier, the Whites, Gibbs, Paula, the apartment on 12th street, Jack Delaney's handling of broken glass, guts, Pricey's courage, the simplicity of love and how it is complicated by women, the fact that I am the greatest writer in the world, the things I have done for people and what have I got in return etc? . . .

One of the pictures I drew today—or last nite—shows a large woman talking to a doctor and saying, "We might as well have it understood right at the start, doctor, that I wouldn't even let my own father put me under ether." A shop on 45th street is showing photographs of the different parts of the two women that Winnie Ruth Judd cut up and put into a trunk.

Joe Sayre has been paid a $1000 for an option on movie rights to his story Rackety Rax. Does old Mark Prentiss sell Valentine cards, Nettie? If you don't stay there long enough for me to send you white roses—that's for love of the Highest Order, no pawing—I shall be very heartsick. Heartsick is a flower that grows in Connecticut. I have a bed of heartsick, fever-sore, megrims, falling arches, baby's yell, love-in-a-slip, vagina, Cancerbury bells, hangovers, pain-in-the-ass, and vericose.

I wrote a swell casual in which I suggested that presidents of banks should go down with the bank, the way ship's captains go down with the ship. I'll tell you about it in detail, with much bragging, when I see you. I'll bring you a bunch of heartburn and rudies of the vallee, too.

Please accept the sincerest expression of my deepest affection and the assurance that my wishes are entirely dedicated to the most sanguine hopes for your earliest recovery.

Jamie

Dear Honey:

The New Yorker has got to worrying about this picture now. Ross, worried, was asking a group of Middletons, Gibbs, etc, what they thought that thing looked like, or if it looked like anything. They said it was absurd to think it looked like anything except what it was drawn for. They asked me, I studied it, and says, says I "Why, they're crazy, anybody can see it's a penis; what do people take it for: a diploma or something?"

Haha ha.

"Was he handsome, was I drunk, did my mamma give me hell."
—The Follies

*"Turn around—show Aunt Sophie!"*

The New Yorker, June 6, 1931

Things have been hot and bad here; I have written checks for $1100 in the past ten days—farm, auto, baby, life insurance, blackmail, hush money, woman keeping, etc. etc. You know the responsibilities of a husband and a land owner.

I trust, really, that you have forgotten, if not forgiven—which you have no right to take the attitude you could do—my $15 conversation with you at Old Mountain House, old Stop Gap, Pa. Never before has my indignation run into more money. Had I stayed at Mino's and spent it on thomas collinses I would, by 5.30, have lost track of what I was broken up about, and would have began screaming fuck and pee and that I am a greater writer than White.

Everything is for Best & Co.

> Yours truly, as always your devoted friend, even though you are
> either a fallen woman now or you are not, and I'm not asking
> you is you aint I'm asking you aint you is. And I'd never believe
> what you said, but if you have a baby it will be proved; if you
> start to hear one, please don't kill yourself, just whisper in my
> ear and, blushing, I will tell you how to get out of it for $125
> (my money, on a loan basis).
> Jamie

*In February 1932, the Thurbers, with Rosemary, sailed from New York to Miami to vacation with Morris Markey, a* New Yorker *colleague, and his wife. Thurber's heart wasn't in it but with Honeycutt.*

*Monday*

Dear Baby:

The boat docks in the morning. . . . I am not a seaman, although I didn't get sick. The sea afflicts me with a kind of melancholy, a sort of subdued and delicate sense of terror. Also it isolates me so that I become a prey to my sins, which follow the ship like gulls. My sins have graceful dark brown wings, faintly edged with white. In the midst of them flies a rose cockatoo, which is, I suspect, my guilty love for you. They flap at me and make little mewing . . . sounds. Once the second officer surprised me staggering along a corridor fighting off imaginary winged creatures. "Owls?" he asked. "No," I said, "chickens come home to roost." . . .

Professional gamblers were as thick as cockroaches. Slick, evil-eyed gents, with an affable manner and a truly remarkable gift for acting. One approached me directly—one whom I had spotted a few hours out. It is amusing to try and pick them out, and usually easy, although now and then, I suppose, a person does a great injustice to some professor botany travelling for his health, or to study flars. . . .

The Deep South is lovely! What would you and Louisiana be like! Oh, God, too sweet for this world with its meagre gifts to tall hopeful men!

I'm wondering all about you. Will you write and tell me, when I send my address, as yet unknown?

> Love and Everything,
> Eternellement,
> Jim

*Thursday Feb 3rd*

Dear Honey:

I'm sending you the story of Suslova and Dostoyevsky not because I think you haven't got anything to read, but because I think it's a grand story. It reminds me of everything. It also reminds me vaguely of myself and of you, although I don't see just why. It's rather sad and also gay to think that so much passion and trouble, so many fits and protestations, so much dilly-dally and sex, went on in the Paris summer of 1863, almost seventy years ago, with nothing left to show for it but some marks on paper. It all comes down to words, finally. Life is just words. The flesh goes, the spirit goes, Pauline and Fyador go, Grant, Lee, Jackson, Forrest, Stuart go, hopes, visits to Italy, fits in attics, embracing of your knees go, but words go on for ever. I don't see, although the author of this piece insists it was all in the particular romantic manner of the time, that it is much different from the manner of today. There is so little difference—except for the words that survive—between Paris and Charles Street, Italy and Amawalk. I can see that old Fyador, as great a man as he was, still enjoyed emotional scenes as much as I do, and had as hard a time telling sincerity from illusion, right from wrong, life from fiction, as we all do. It is also clear that individuals understand each other just as little now as they did then, and will not improve any in that respect during the next seventy years. Love was just the same, mixed-up, indecisive, glamorous, exaggerated, lovely. Nobody really got anywhere. The days in Baden-Baden were as confused and unsatisfactory as the days in South Norwalk [Connecticut], or in Miami. And even so great a writer as Dostoyevsky had to use dots when his wife's eyes gave him a look! That is immensely sad somehow. I wonder whether all flights to Italy would come out the same. I become overwhelmed with trying to figure out what should be done about life: you can't just let it carry you along; you got to aspire to some Italy and to some Suslova and to some change. I'll let you figure it out.

I keep being slightly morbid down here; I am a fish, I'm afraid, whose waters are New York. Here I am, stranded on a sunny beach, wondering how goes everything in the cool speakeasies, which are one's undoing and one's solace. Everything reaches its highest and its lowest point in a New York speakeasy. One wallows in his despair and rambles through his castles in Italy, right there at a table. That is living one's life vicariously—loving, divorcing, marrying, writing, planning—without ever turning a wheel really. Thus it is very bad and very good. Other people would be satisfied with a fair country and a sunny beach all their lives; and my companions here speak very high and mightily of how they never hope to set foot in Tim's or Mino's again, to which I say nothing, since I hope to. There is, of course, something in a broad expanse of blue water over which clouds and flamingos aimlessly drift, but there is also something to a stuffy room and a damp bar and a seventy-five cent drink of mediocre rye, and a companion who is pleasantly cocked.

We went to the jai-alai games last night—pron.hi-li—in which husky Spaniards wearing long narrow baskets on their right arm slam a hard ball at a concrete wall, sixty feet high, and bounce it back at terrific speed upon a concrete floor 180 feet long. Like handball in a train shed. They catch it in the basket again, and slam it again. They also have dog races here, and a Marathon dance which has been going on since the 17th of December. It's reminiscent of the playgrounds of hell, in a way. You bet on everything, it's the bettingest place ever I see. I haven't got much done, in fact nothing except a letter or two to you. I keep thinking of you, and have decided, since Sunday, that you are to me what you said you weren't to anyone—indispensable. You are unquestionably indispensable to me. Just what to do with this indispensability I don't know. A. diagnozes my morbidity as brain fag and recommends lying on the beach and speaking to the birds. "Hello, birds," I say, morbidly.

I wonder what would happen if you and I went off to Italy. I also wonder what would happen if we didn't. This wonderment always leads me into a confused analysis of what is right, what is wrong, what is the difference between sacrifice and realization, between commitment and desire, between courage and meekness. Who in the hell will inherit the earth, anyway? The meek, or the brave? And what will they do with it? Of course, I would have thought that Suslova and Dosty might have found their way out easier than you and me, because they weren't after all born in Louisiana and Ohio. Yet it doesn't seem to have helped them any. Apparently every country was Ohio in the 1860s. I am anxious to read the second installment of their life in the Tribune this coming Sunday, judge, to see how it came out, although I could write it myself. It's all in that five days in Baden-Baden when he gambled and assumed gaiety, and she sat in the hotel room writing, and he got tired of being her fatherly confessor and made a pass at her skirts and she felt very sorry for him, but wouldn't sleep with him, so he became gay again—and yet they had gone off to Italy together. Both worried by the memory of a guy she thought she loved, but who didn't love her, and who didn't amount to a good-god damn and who, in the days when she first adored Dosty, wouldn't have made any impression on her! Maybe I shouldn't let this prey on my mind, and yet it is so perfect a retelling of perhaps everybody's story. Two people who wanted to and could have got together and yet when they did get together, found a lot of silly barriers in their way, a change of sentiment, and everything else. Life is a flux, don't you think? Flux, flux, flux, all winter long, Judge.

I note that the novels which recently have come out all seem to be concerned with restless people, led by "Weep No More", in which a group of Southern ladies and gentlemen go merrily to hell. In all the reviews of the recent books I've read, nobody seems to be having a good solid happy time, or even a fair to middling contented time, but to be moosing and smurzing and skikling through life, got down by something or somebody. The lower animals, realizing that life is merely a day in which you hunt for food and seek shelter and sleep, never allow themselves to get mixed-up by desires for things outside this routine. No tiger in India ever woke up in the morning with the sudden realization that a lady tiger in North Africa was his only way out. No bullfinch ever breaks his heart over a caged canary. They never want things to be just opposite from what they are. We, being dissatisfied with virtually everything that nature and chance and our own management give us, are always wondering how to get out of them. I should write a piece about a Canadian bear that ran away to Italy with a snow tigress from Tibet.

This has been more or less in the nature of a lecture or something. Still, you don't want to hear about the coconut trees.

Give me regards to Jap and Helen [Gude] and all others that you see. Tell them I am fine.

James

## TO CARSON BLAIR

Dear Carson:

Last night I had an amusing and unaccountable dream about you, and this afternoon I got a letter from my brother Bob enclosing your picture from the paper—the 283d of a series of Columbus Presidents. I lay the whole thing, therefore, to thought transference. He was probably cutting the picture out, while I was asleep.

I dreamed that I was living at home with my family again in Columbus, when a messenger brought me a note from the Chief of Police. It was a simple official document and said merely that a policeman would call the next morning at 8 o'clock to shoot me. Some violation of the law. I took the matter up with my father and he said he'd go uptown and see what he could do to fix it up with the mayor. He came back about midnight and, naturally quite nervous, I asked him how he'd come out. It transpired that the matter had slipped his mind entirely. He had had a soda, bowled a little, and forgot the execution completely.

Well, I moved out—packed a suitcase and went to the Neil House. The next morning I got up at 6, thinking to get the hell out of Columbus before the cop got me. There at the door of the hotel, however, just inside the lobby, you sat, tilted back on a chair, your hand in your overcoat pocket. As I tried to slip out, you rose and handed me your card—Carson Blair, Shooting Cop, it read. "If you'll just step down the alley," you said, "We can get this business over with." "Now, see here, Carson," I said. "I haven't the slightest idea of doing that. In the first place, it's all a mistake." Whereupon I walked out the door into High Street. You followed me, your hand still ominously in your pocket. I walked right out to the traffic cop at Broad and High and told him that you were annoying me. You were in plain clothes, and he apparently didn't know you were a cop. He asked me who I was, and, with a really smart idea, I handed him your card. "I'm Carson Blair, the Shooting Cop," I said. The cop gave you a look. "All right, you," he said, "Get along." So you got along and I went up and took a train for New York.

The psychoanalysts can work on that one.

I'm down here in Miami, Florida, trying to rest up and write at the same time. My wife's at the races today, and the baby is crying, but I've learned to work right along. I got to wondering, after that crazy dream, whether you were still at 390, and was glad to find out that you haven't gone back to France or someplace else, to become a beachcomber or something. If you do go, drop me a wire, and I'll come along, for I always enjoyed the adventures we had on the boulevards with the ladies who were crazy about Zhack, le sailor. I often think of the one who wished to weep on your shoulder. Those days, those tears, alas, are gone forever. You look as handsome (barring the sailor's suit) and as happy as ever. Do you ever get to NY? I know all the nice speakeasies, if you do. If you have any explanation for hounding me with a gun, please let me know.

    Yourn,

    Jim Thurber

*8521 East Dixie Highway,*

*Little River, MIAMI, FLA.*

*While still in Little River, Florida, one of Thurber's best-known cartoons, The Seal in the Bedroom, appeared in* The New Yorker *January 30, 1932. Robert Benchley wrote editor Harold Ross that it was the funniest caption he had ever seen and hoped to have the original cartoon. Ross sent Benchley's note to Thurber.*

## To Robert Benchley

Dear Bob:

    Ross dropped me a note saying you would like to have the seal drawing. Well, even though I promised it to someone else, you can have it. After all I only promised it to a girl. And she never sent me a petit bleu, such as is a much greater prize than the seal anyway. I am sure you will see that the bed, in the drawing, could not be slept in. Certain critics pointed that out to me, just as others remarked that there is no way for a seal to get into a bedroom. Ross himself once said that nobody could sleep with Thurber's women. "His men could," said Connelly. The actual fact is that they are all kewpies from the hips down but mentally oversexed.

    I think that the drawing is tucked, with a bunch of others, between the pages of a November issue of Liberty on Bob Coates' desk in my office. I'm writing Ralph, in the office, to get it out and send it to you.

Ross said something about how much did I want for the drawing? Well, a month or so ago, me and some other frontrank American artists were asked to send a drawing each to an exhibition of important American art to be held in Vienna. The artists were asked to name the price they wanted for their pictures, and also the insurance they wanted put on them. I marked "Not for sale. No insurance." I got three French poodles and two Scotties for sale, however, but if you held out long enough you could have them, too.

This is a very romantic city. The other day a married lady was sitting on her screened-in porch with her little eight year old boy. Her lover, a middle-aged carpenter, called around 5 o'clock in the afternoon. He gave her a silver sweet greeting, but her feet were killing her or something and she refused to open the screen door, which was latched, and let him in. He picked up a half-brick and began whamming at the door. The lady dispatched her son for a pistol and he brought it, just as the importunate lover knocked the door loose and entered. He whammed her with the brick and she shot him twice. It seems that the affair will be straightened out—for everybody except the lady's husband, anyway, who I imagine keeps turning the thing over in his mind. The lady told police that the carpenter was simply an old friend, and the old friend chivalrously said that he had got tangled up in the gun—it was caught between his feet some way—and it went off a couple of times. The police, who appear to be quite sensitive, do not seem to have asked any questions about the brick.

Also today's paper announces the arrest of a gentleman who will always be my favorite character. His name is Dutch Futch.

Thanks again for that petit bleu—I told Ross before I left to tell you how much I appreciated it. He probably didn't. I was going to come over but I had to get a wife and child and a nurse and an automobile and thirteen pieces of baggage on the boat.

    Jim Thurber


## TO ANN HONEYCUTT

Dearest Buddy:

A reporter interviewed me and asked me what I thought was the loveliest thing I had seen in Florida. "The business-size air-mail envelopes," I said. "What are you doing down here?" he asked. "Oh," I said, "worrying and writing letters to Ann Honeycutt." "What do you worry about?" he asked. "Oh," I said, "the traps and pitfalls of life and my considerate indecision in matters affecting the welfare of myself." I got your limpid little letter, written in that clear and amusing manner for which, if you weren't so tahd, you could become notable. In the matter of the undignified and funny posture of the couples you allude to, I would say that a great deal of happiness sometimes results from the undignified and funny. Look at my undignified and funny drawings. Eating, of course, is undignified and funny, when you contemplate it. So is breathing, especially if one breathes deeply, and says "mee, mee, mee, mee, mee." Then again, consider the dignified and serious things of life: bank presidents, church services, the Constitution of the United States, probate courts, hymn singing, annual reports, funerals. What did you think of my bloodhound pictures? I hope you liked the bloodhound, for after all he is a big dog—they weigh as much as ninety pounds, and are dignified but funny, or a sort of cross between an annual report and fornicatory gestures, in a way. I have got what you might almost call the Thundering Melancholia down here; there's no doubt but what that's what I got. That's what *that* is. I am sure I could never successfully be away from you for more than two months. It affects my appetite, my heart, the expression around my gills, my temper, and my work, which last has gone completely to the bloodhounds. I was accused last night of "pining", which, come to think of it, is what it is. I pine noticeably, although I don't tan much. I strive to be gay and to whistle and even sing a few notes, but it is a considerable effort. I sleep as much as I can, and dream about being shot by policemen. If Gladys knew about it she'd say, theh he is, pinin' his haht away for me dowan theh in Flahda. Wa, Ann, the man is quiv'rin' for me, quivrin his fool haht away, and theh he is the youngest and tallest of 11 brothers all over seven feet tall. Each one of em has a fountain in his yard a hundred feet high, and they all carry their mothah in to lunch. It's the sweetest thing I eveh saw. . . .

The Everglades swamps down here have been burning ever since I got here ("There's a little bit of muck still burning and yearning, down in my swamp for you"—remember? Ah God, the old songs was best!) The swamps are composed largely of muck, with a few alligators and trees, all of which are burning. The off-shore wind brings a fog of smoke which smells, as King Lear said, like some god damn municipal incinerator (King Lear. Act II.Sc.4). The morning's paper quotes a swamp farmer as saying that eleven of his cows are burning now. Florida, which has no money to put out the fire, has appealed to Hoover and to Congresswoman Ruth Bryan Owen to put it out. I have appealed to William G. McAdoo and Mrs. George Benholtz Heinz. There are also spiders down here, house spiders, which measure 6 inches from feet to feet.

It is interesting to recall how the female breast has long been, to man, the symbol of loveliness and desire, while at the same time it performs one of the most utilitarian of all purposes. No one ever caught a bull inscribing verses to his heifer sweetheart's udders, which shows that animals have a saner and sounder viewpoint than we have but that they lack those fragile and charming illusions which make life for the higher animals so bearable and confused.

I am afraid that you don't quite know Jimmy [James] Cabell well enough to keep from being pleasantly hornswoggled by him. There has never been a man more completely dedicated to the utter necessity and the great beauty of love affairs. His books, as cynical and sad and disillusioned as they are, nevertheless contain intimations of an amorous romanticism in James which outruns that of most mortals. He himself is married to a large, amiable, woman and has been for many years. He is too much of a Virginia gentleman to be caught fondling strange breasts or pinching illegal thighs, or even wistfully contemplating the sweet curves of the neighbor's eighteen year old daughter's legs. Nevertheless he has to do something about it, so he writes these books of the adventures of man with woman, of desire with reality, of beauty with sex, etc. It also depends entirely upon the love affair, whether or not one gets into the mood for turning a gracious and careful phrase or not. It is also true that Mr. Cabell spends a leetle bit too much time turning phrases, so that his works always have the careful look of a pin with the Lord's prayer on its head. Nevertheless I am for him, but never believe anything he says outright. I think he might be a bad influence for you and I am glad that when he was in NY for the broadcast he did not meet you and thus become a person who began to think up excuses for getting away from Richmond. "My darling," he would say, "I must run up to NY for another broadcasting. I'll be at the Commodore."

Yesterday was one of my very bad days. My spirits were at 14 below zero all day. I finally got out Volume TRI to ZYR of the encyclopedia here, and read in it all afternoon, until it got dark and twilighty. I read sitting on the edge of a straight back chair with the book held between my calves, a stiff and awkward position which I somehow got into. Elbert could have dropped me onto the floor with a feather, the way I sat. I read the pieces in the encyc. about Woodrow Wilson, Queen Victoria, the United States, Uric Acid, (which is principally found in boa constrictor's pee), White Lead, St. Vitus dance, Verlain, Vespasian, Vampire Bat, and the World War. I read all about the messages between Wilson and the Imperial German Empire. I thought for a time that the United States was *never* going to get into the war. They finally did, however. It was full of suspense and terribly exciting. Germany was defeated in the end.

Cabell knows that a wistful man, with a great sense of the beauty of love in his heart, is usually married to a woman he doesn't want to sleep with, but who wants to sleep with him, and that he wants to sleep with a woman who doesn't especially want to sleep with anybody. We all need sleep. You must get your rest, as my father used to say. He quit sleeping with mamma when he was 39, I think, whereas mamma comes from a long line of people who slept with other people until they were a hundred. You see, everywhere you turn there is this confusion and complexity about the simplest thing that two people can do together. Target shooting, skiing, figure skating, lunching, dressing, dominoes, theatre-going, crap shooting—all are more difficult in every way than fairing de l'amour, as the French say, yet people accomplish them easily in their stride. Almost nobody makes a practise of having lunch with somebody they don't want to have lunch with, while somebody they do want to have lunch with is having lunch with somebody that doesn't want to have lunch with them. It's so mixed up. It reminds me of the story about the brother and sister who were sleeping together. "I'd rather sleep with you than with mother," the boy told her. "That's what father says," she replied. Life is that way, I suppose.

I really had a terrible day about you yesterday. Your lovely image, your gay laughter, your charming wit, your quick understanding, your refusals to see me any longer, or have anything to do with me, your comments that there are a thousand reasons why you should let me ride, kept coming between my eyes and the articles on Woodrow Wilson and Uric Acid. As a matter of fact, there are not a thousand reasons. I went over them last night, and there are only 46, of which you don't know anything about eleven.

Your constant admirer, the apple of your eye,

James.

&. &. &.

Nettie [Ann Honeycutt]

This drawing illustrates the modern trend in self-expression of the child, made possible by a total lack of parental discipline. The father, in this particular scene, has just said to the mother (who is in the next room) 'Dear, you better put little Marcia to B-E-D'. With what result the reader well knows.

This type of frank, accurate representation of American family life became known, in the late thirties, as Thurber's 'Middle Style'. It wasn't until 1941, however, that any magazine dared to print the artist's excellent and valuable portraits of contemporary American scenes. In that year the weekly called "FUCK" was published—by the sons of the former editor of "PUCK". As one of the sons, Elbert, said "We simply knocked the 'p' out of PUCK".

Today is better. I am coming home long about March 31, leaving my wife and child here for two weeks. That will enable you and Pricey to get many a meal for me at night in exchange for me making you fried eggs in the morning. I ought to be able to fry seventy or eighty eggs in two weeks, without attracting undue attention, as I would if I fried them all in one morning.

## EDITOR CHARGED WITH FRYING EIGHTY EGGS
### Police Arrest 'Hen Fiend' In Charles Street Love Nest.
#### NO REASON ASSIGNED FOR THE DEED.

*Two Village characters arrested As City Thunders Welcome.*

NEW YORK, April 6 (AP)–Police yesterday arrested James Thurbid, alleged egg-fryer, in a Charles Street love nest, on complaint of neighbors who had not been able to buy any eggs in the vicinity for three days. Detective Charles Crupper broke down the door of the elaborately furnished apartment, which was protected against raids by two locks and a crowbar. He found Thurbid sitting on the toilet seat frying eggs on a small toilet stove. Lolling on a luxurious chaise-longue in the one room of the lush apartment, which was redolent of illicit love and eggs, Crupper discovered two Village women, clad only in pajamas of an extravagant and voluptuous design. The women had plates of fried eggs, and others were 'coming up' from the 'kitchen' from time to time. Crupper counted more than seven dozen eggs, in and out of shells, in the nest. No reason could be assigned for the deed. Crupper also reported that no reason could be assigned for the lease, since one of the women said she was going into a nunnery in June and the other talked vaguely of suicide with Thurbid's gun, which was not found. One of the women admitted she was a village character—known as old Annie—but defended this on the ground that somebody had to have character, since the egg-fryer had none. Crupper did not take his prisoners immediately to jail, but lay in wait for other members of the gang, who showed up at odd hours during the day and night and were placed under arrest. These included Nick Dawson, the underworld character, Big Jess Honey-cutt, wanted in Pennsylvania, Gil ('Box Car') Gillespie, the notorious letter writer, Johnny the Horse Parker, Monty Schuyler, known as the terror of Amawalk, Robert M (Red) Coates, a muscle man, Willie the Card Shark Cole-man, a gambler, Elbert or 'Doc', a nudist, Aristide Mianne, a desperate looking French cutthroat, and J.G. (Jap) Gude, a quiet looking man who police say is the most dangerous of the lot.

From words that one of the women, who gave her name as Antoninette (Tony) Price, let drop, Crupper got the idea that she might have had something to do with the kidnapping of the Lindberg baby. She kept asking where the baby was, Crupper said.

I got to go to the postoffice now.
Thurbird

"You know what you can K-I-Double-S, too."

≈  ≈  ≈

Dear Honey:

Here it is five thirty and I just phoned Wi-2-2000 [CBS], thinking to ask for Jap [Gude] and then ask him casually if you were there, mentioning that of course you don't want to see me and that I don't give a good god damn and that he can tell you, if you happen to mention me, that that's what I said; when I remembered that you were at St. Antoinette's, the patron saint of doctors and people with dirigibles they haven't got any place to anchor. Did I ever tell you about the time that the doctor and I were having a stag party at my apartment and you and St. Antoinette came in, having promised you wouldn't, and I didn't have a stitch on? I guess what I am is an Interior Desecrator gone wrong. I take off the loveliest wall brackets, or did before I reformed. I came here from Ohio when I was 27, although I had the mind of a child of 17, and became a candy-thrower and also monkeyed around at figurine-breaking, but it didn't pay, so I got a job following glaziers around taking out the defective door glass they put in. I then became a liar-caller after which I joined the firm of Bragg and Boast, specializing in a lack of women's ware. I am on call for Fourth of July parties, New Year Eve celebrations, and the like. I can give you a lot of disreputable references, including members of some of the oldest families, such as the Schuylers, Mr. and Mrs. Mathew Josephson and son, Eric, Mr. and Mrs Malcom Cowley and party of three—Mr. Cowley's girl and Mr. and Mrs. Peter Bloom, their house guests—Mr. and Mrs. Robert M. Coates and dog, Mr. and Mrs. Aristide Miass, Mr. and Mrs. Reynolds Benson and Gibbs, Mr. and Mrs. J.G. Gude. etc. The report that goes around about me plaguing girls and women is entirely false and is based on an inferiority complex, due to an unreasonable fear that, even if the lady surrenders, how can you gracefully get her things off so that she won't laugh and cause the whole thing to crack up? Few people realize that this inordinate fear of mine has spoiled what would have been otherwise a most adventurous career. There are, of course, several ways to manage the removal of a lady's things, none of them really successful. You can come right out, after she has yielded to your embraces, and ask her, with boyish gaiety, if she will now remove her clothes. This has to be done just right, however, and usually in the heat of things, the gentleman gets so wrought up, what with this and what with that, that he fairly barks it at her, thus either making her mad, hurting her feelings, or shocking her sensibilities. Another method is to say to the lady, "Now I'm going to get rid of some of these crazy things we wear," and start taking off her shoes. No matter how expert you are, however, or how much you practice on department store window models, you are likely to get into trouble anywhere from the shoe buckles to the brassiere. Tearing things off is a system some people use but you usually have to replace, or think you have to replace, the things you tear off, particularly if you begin with a new evening gown. I have known few men, however, who could remove the panty-waist and those things worn around the middle successfully. To do it successfully, you have to whisk them off quickly and adroitly, or the girl's mind will get on something else. If you try to whisk and the panty-waist holds, this is likely to lead to a grim and determined effort, in which the gentleman goes about the process much as if he were trying to fix a gasoline engine. He will mutter and swear and say, "How the hell does this dam thing fasten?"—which is fatal. The old theory that you really don't have to take off many things is fatal, too, because nobody looks quite so funny as a person, nor two persons, with practically everything on except pants and skirt. Each one is afraid to get up first for fear he—or she—will look comical. So someone says "Now close your eyes" and then he gets up, closing his eyes too, with the result that he is likely to forget that his trousers are around his knees, and be thrown with great violence. I think the best way is to say "I'm going into the next room for a minute" and then go into the next room, leaving the girl to undress. In the next room you undress, always tortured by the fear that when you get back, she will not have touched a stitch but will be sitting quietly in a chair reading a book. This so worries a certain type of man that he gets himself into a frightful state wondering just what clothes, if any, he should wear when he goes back. I think the best thing to wear is shirt and trunks for if the girl is really reading when you re-enter the room where you left her, you can trot around, jump over canes, and pretend that you got undressed simply to go through some exercises. I know of one man who favored the idea of turning out all the lights and then suggesting that they undress in the same room together. In this man's case, the idea was a mistake for he always takes off his glasses when he undresses and without them he can't see a thing, so there he was, stark raving naked, as his mother used to say, and unable to get successfully to the place where the girl lay giggling. "Where am I, dear?" he asked her, as he stumbled into a table filled with books and vases.

There has been an ominous silence about the pictures [cartoons] I handed in today and about the casual I wrote yesterday, so I am beginning to get my usual six p.m. depression. It would be a good time now to go to Tim's with Jap, but Jap has gone from his wife. He is a nice boy and I wish I were he. He has a pretty wife named Helen, and a lovely baby named Joe. He was married before to Katherine White but divorced her because of a scene at Amawalk when she went away with Mark Prentiss, the former Mrs. Taylor. Taylor was the brother of a well known painter named Remington Scuyler who was disowned by his family during the war for marrying a German woman named Elsa. Her father, old Herr Coates, objected and caused the marriage of her chauffeur, Cecil Crawford, an Englishman, to be annulled, proving that Crawford had been joy-riding with Mrs. Vera Brown, wife of Slater Burke, the killer. Burke, a confederate of Malcolm (Two-Gun) Cowley, was later captured at 49 Charles Street after a terrific battle in which the police finally resorted to tear-gas bombs and [Wolcott] gibbs. The situation was straightened out when Tony (52nd Street) Price offerred to share her children among the disputants. Of these, Thurber got the prize, a four months old girl named Annette, descendant of a long line of love children, known as the Love Brothers, and discovered in 1923 by an oil-driller named Pepper, now a member of the St. Louis Cardinal baseball team.

I have to go down to Charmé Seeds for dinner tonight and only wish that you were well and that you and I were having dinner at some little hotel in France with the chimes of a Normandy clock sounding across the orchards filled with white apple blossoms. I'll tell you another impossible story. . . .

> as always,
> James

*As assistant program producer at the Columbia Broadcasting System, Honey was plagued with strange radio proposals from the listening public. Thurber sends her his own suggestions.*

Dear Gentlemen:

I am a lady of eighty-seven years but I can still read without glasses and my ears are as sharp as a girl's. You will make out from my typing of this lether that my hand is just as steadfy as ever, two? For many years I have enjoyed the pograms that we have from the Columbia and it means a great deal to me and to my bed ridden daughter and my bed ridden father and my bed ridden sister to have this form of amusement and entrainment night after night, day in and day out, hour upon hour, until I think sometimes I will go crazy. I often ask myself, Ella, I ask myself, what would you do if it wasn't for the Columbia?

In all these years whilst I have not always liked some of the pograms that came in over the Columbia nevertheless I haveenjoyed the most of them even the sports and have never found anything to take exception to as regards decency and morals until the other nitht when a pogram had on it a Victrolar record of a popular song called "I am Walking A Baby Back Home." My ears being as quick as a girl's although I am eighty-eight (it has takenme a year to git this far) I was able to detect the use of the word "fuck" in one place in the lyric. You could have knocked me down with a fender. I wisht you would trace this up and discharge the person who said it as it was a great shock to my bed ridden daughter.

> Respy,
> Mrs. Madge Blue

> *Queens Road, Queens Were Ridden,*
> *Queens Were Bed Ridden. Queens*

❧   ❧   ❧

*[1932]*

Dear System:

   I am just a woman and I don't claim a man's perogative which is to be executives for large organizations, but a woman's hand in the "home life" which is back of all organizations would certainly be a godsend to some organizations I could name you. I am not going to name names however for my husband happens to be an executive of a certain large concern, or I wouldn't be wrong even if I said "unconcern" because when somebody waits for him a couple of hours and sends in the girl to say he's waiting my husband says "A P after the L" in a game he plays and that is that. But when they all go home, or rather away from the office is when the "hell" starts and I could tell you stories that would make the hair stand up on end of prominent members walking on couches and women being put to bed. Where do you suppose their mothers think they are at such an hour? All of them gather together with employes and drink whisky sour and about midnight are having whoopy I can tell you, if I wanted to make trouble.

> Sincerely,
> Mrs. Joe Knicple
> Imperial Arms,
> Queens

There is an "outsider" who eggs people on and makes trouble.

🐝 🐝 🐝

Dear System:

I have a little daughter aged seven who is a marvel on the violin and would appreciate it if she can begin playing for you on some "hour", starting next week; we would prefer having her on the best hour you have, such as Lucky Strike hour, with Ted Husing as her announcer if he is possible. Do you think he is possible? If she can play for you would be able to accompany her myself although I am not a professional accompanyist still I am her mother and unless I am in room when she plays she becomes frightened and can not control her kidneys; this was very painful to us all at the First Methodist Church social last month when I could not be there to quiet her.

If Mr. Husing is impossible, I should like to know at once.

    Sincerely,

    Mrs. Gertie P. Quickly

*6574 Queens road, Queens, Queens.*

My little girl heard Mr. Husing give the Broadway Derby race in Kentucky a few weeks ago and was so excited she wet herself but would be more careful next time.

🐝 🐝 🐝

Dear System:

I feel there should be Bible texts on the "air" and would suggest broadcasting texts every day on some "hour"; there is too much music from these loud bands and should be spaced out more with Bible texts; this could do no harm and might do some good as you have lots of "listerners" who would be pleased to hear Bible texts; the "hour" before going to bed would be nice for the Bible texts and they wouldn't have to take up much time since you could just give a short text like telling what time it is from the Bible or could be put at the end of each and every program a Bible text and could go through a whole chapter of the New Testicles in one day this way.

This idea just came to me one night and I would like to send in other ideas from time to time, as they come to me quite often. I am told that you pay for "ideas" for "hours" and would like to be paid if this is exceptable to you. Also my husband's cousin, Bert Blosser, is a perfectly wonderful singer and everybody says he is much better singer than most of the singers on the "air" now, so could he start singing on some "hour" for you beginning in June as he is working now at nights for a gypsum company and would prefer to sing at nights. How much will he get for this?

Respectively yours,

Ida Blosser Pee

(Mrs. Otto Pee)

*1567 Peeridge road, Bethany, Pa.*

🙚 🙚 🙚

*5675 2345th Street, Queens,*

*Columbia Broadcasting System,*
*484 Lexington avenue, City*

Dear System:

I am a great radio "fan" and have the radio going all day so I feel I know what is wanted. I would like to give you an idea or rather sell you this idea which is for a Musical journey around the World. The first week—or "hour"—would be from England, then Belgium, and so on, giving an "hour" for each different country and playing the famous songs of these counrtries, ending up with America by playing the Star Spangled Banner. All my friends think this is a fine idea for you and is greatly appreciated.

If you like this idea and pay for it I could send you lots of other ideas as ideas come to me from time to time but I thought you got up all your own ideas till somebody told me you get ideas from other people also. So I thought I would send this idea for an "hour" in and could send others from time to time as they come to me. I could use the "money" too right now for my husband is not well and has been out of work in the plastering trade for some time with stomach ulcers and trouble with the kidneys which keeps him from doing the plastering work. He is not good at anything else not having any ideas. Will you please let me know when this hour starts, as I should like to "listen in".

Very truly yours,

Nettie Gooch Filpins

(Mrs. H.R. Filpins)

*Joel Sayre had written an article for* The American Mercury *about* The New Yorker. *Thurber sends his comments to Sayre who is on his honeymoon in Bermuda. The first of Thurber's comic casuals about his family's life in Columbus, referred to here as his "autobiography," was about to run in* The New Yorker.

## To Joel Sayre

[Undated, probably June 1933]

Dear Joe:

Now you quit fussing about the New Yorker and Ross, and go on to more elevating things. White, Gibbs, Mosher, and me are all claiming that you meant each of us separately in that crack about manicuresses. There is a lot of abba-dabba in every honeymoon, and once you get off on the subject of what this and that periodical really is like, you won't have time for anything else. You stop playing with that nasty [George Jean] Nathan boy, and that snooty Cabell boy, who thinks he's smart just because he lives in the white house with pillars up on the hill. Bob Coates thinks the crack about men trying to do the right thing is aimed at a piece he printed here three years ago. Sally Benson has phoned to complain that she never wrote a monologue about Tony's [a speakeasy], Mrs. [Dorothy] Parker is sore about the one about Negro maids, and Louise Bogan has wired a rather incoherent cable from Italy, which we can't make out what she is offended by. Everybody is keeping the article from Ross, on account of him not being very strong. And that Singer Sewing machine agent, gentlemen, was Alexander Woollcott!

Let me send you, by freight, a huge book which will get your mind off of dooba-dabba: Sherman, Prophet of War, by Lloyd Lewis. What a book! You'll like the anecdotes of Ohioans (probably Columbusites) in the war, especially one about how Colonel Appler, of an Ohio regiment, seeing the Johnnies coming streaming across a field at Shiloh, went and lay down on his back behind a tree and shouted, "Oh God, here they come, here they *come!*" He then arose, shouted "Save yourselves!" and plunged through the woods toward Ohio, never to be seen in the fighting zone again.

My autobiography is about to start running in this dooba, but Ross says now that he wisht it was more like "Cabbages and Kings".

> There's so much dabb in the worst of us
> And so much doob in the best of us
> That it's hardly like Hoover for any of us
> To talk about the rest of us.

Jamie.

*The popularity of Thurber's cartoons and his comic memoirs,* My Life and Hard Times, *had made Thurber a literary star by 1934. Ross had begun to query*

*him about his writing plans. In 1933 Thurber had given up a salary for a "draw-*
*ing account"—regular weekly compensation against which payments for his*
*writings for the magazine were subtracted. Thurber was soon in arrears. In*
*1934, after a particularly difficult day and night of rewriting Talk, Thurber de-*
*cided to state his case to Ross for getting off a drawing account and, as an "out-*
*side" contributor, spending more time on his writing and drawing. Ross agreed.*

## To Harold Ross

*[Undated, probably 1934]*

Mr. Ross:

You have always wanted to know, and have consistently asked, whether I wanted to do Talk, whether I was going to, what my plans about it were, etc. Well, here, in these 3 pieces I have rewritten, together with comments attached to them, is my answer. Here, also, is the soundest and completest criticism of Talk of the Town ever put into writing. I have been fair, comprehensive, and sincere about it; I cite examples, I give proof, I name instances. This, I repeat, is the story of Talk, and of my feeling about Talk. In a way it's my history of Talk, and I have written it for eight years or more. It will only take you twenty minutes to read what I have written in my comments. Please read them in the order in which they are marked—that is, (1), (2) etc.

Thurber

I sat up all night to do this.

2 of these 3 rewrites are ready to go.

Dear Ross:

I suppose this piece will serve as good as any for an example of why, after all, I prefer writing casuals to doing Talk. It's a good piece, interesting, but, like almost all Mss that have ever come to me for re-write, it has its uncertainties, its omissions. I have marked on my rewrite the first one (1): Wickware does not say whether, if you are denied your permit, they keep your finger prints. Naturally, being an old detail reporter, I thought of that. It haunted me during my three re-writes of this piece. I have left it, as you will see, so that you can either cross out the words "are kept just the same" or "are destroyed". I took three hours on this thing because of things like that popping up after I had already done the thing once. Now, in writing casuals, my mind is my own checking department, I am my own reporter, my fantasies (as against Talk facts) are bound to be accurate. It is altogether a pleasant, and a comparatively easy, task. I am not worried, uncertain, plagued. I hate uncertainty. The fact of the finger prints will have to be checked. I doubt the police department would tear up any prints it ever took. Yet it has no right to the prints of a man who merely asked for a gun permit. Or has it? These things absorb me, as well as try me.

The last sentence in this piece I made up and it must also be checked. Wickware does not say who, or what, got the 60 licenses for tear-gas bombs. I imagine I am right. But again it must be checked.

I put in that some permits may be granted for very special reasons, but he makes no mention of any, nor says whether he asked about any special cases. . . . I doubt if the police would have told, but I don't know. . . .

Don't let it all get you down, as it did me. Life is too short. It's one of those pieces that we may as well toss off glibly, with "as far as we knows" and "if we remembers"—as we might while talking to Jed Harris at Adele Lovett's, for instance. A guy could spend his life mulling over this thing, holding it up for one reason or another, putting it down, trying to write it first one way and then another as I have been all evening. Now it is 1 a.m. and I'm damn sorry I didn't write another casual (for $300) or draw forty pictures for $4,000. You see my point? And is it a partial answer to your oft-repeated question: do you intend to do any Talk? Do you really want to do some work—meaning not casuals or drawings?

> Yours, for explanations,
> Thurber

. . . I never was a re-write man, and I suppose as a leg-man who got and wrote his own stuff, I am just naturally opposed to doing a piece from another man's notes. I get mad, and helpless, and I scream. If I got my own notes, I'd make only $100 a week and never have time for casuals or drawings. The situation is one that consistently floors me.

> jt

Mr. Ross:

Now, as opposed to the gun license piece, take this one. It took me only two hours to write, as against three, and it was fun. Here were all the facts, a bit scattered, of course, as in all our Talk Ms (from [Eugene] Kinkead to [Stanley]

Walker, I had to go) but in half an hour one could digest the dossier. I write, you know, rather slowly, and especially Talk pieces of 600 words. Greater men than I have said it took longer to write a short piece than a long one (I wrote the piece about the derringers and the game calls, in the B Issue in something like an hour and ten minutes) (Some of my casuals take days, but not all).

Now, the chief difficulty in doing a good job on this Costello man, is that the main thing, next to the amazing fact, is getting the atmosphere of the style to fit. A little awe, complete sincerity, a note of O. Henry romance. It takes a while to stir those things up, longer than to make a Manhattan, about as long as to make a Martini. Atmosphere in a Talk Piece is sometimes as difficult to get as a piece of tail in the back seat of an Austin. Requires skill, patience, prayer, effort, and several re-writes. (Nothing that is not written over at least 3 times was, or ever will be, any goddam good at all). You have asked me so many times why I don't do Talk, why I don't want to do it, that it occurred to me I might give you a pretty clear picture of me as a Talk writer, and of Talk, as both a pleasure and a task and a torture, in a few prefaces and comments on each separate piece as I finish them. Well, we don't often get pieces as good, as interesting as this. Most Talk pieces are just so much tedious, tedious crap, out of which [E. B.] White and I have been supposed to get (and to want to get) a light and breezy piece of 600 words. Take the piece I am sending back, un-rewritten, about the sizes of liquor bottles. Jesus, what a horrible, headachy, sonofabitch THAT is! I'd just as lief tackle a description of my Uncle Jake Fisher's stomach (he had three-fifths of it removed because of ulcers). After all, I've served my apprenticeship in such pieces. I have put wheels under, and given wings to, a hell of a lot of heavy, dull stories. So has White. Neither of us has the stomach for it again. It's like going to war and digging latrines. Now, with [Russell] Maloney to do the toughies—because he hasn't been at it so long—and someone to help him, and with me getting the sweet, soft, but really worth-while and interesting pieces to do (like this baby) we all might get some where.

Are you beginning to see my point?

Thurber

This piece runs to 650 words. Don't let it fool you on account of the three pages. I've given it a two-inch margin and I'm using big type. It is worth all I've given it.

jt

Mr. Ross:

Now here's this piece on liquor bottles. You will say, first off, well, for Christ's sake, don't bother with such pieces. Well, says I right back, such pieces represent, if you can do them, fifty or sixty dollars, especially when you have given your evening over to Talk and have the strength left for one more (and no strength, or inspiration, left for a casual or a drawing). I never throw away fifty or sixty dollars. But, in this case, I do without a whimper or a sigh.

I give you, first of all, Mr. [Eugene] Kinkead's opening sentence: "The question of the size of liquor bottles is a subject that might easily drive you crazy." Well, I grant you that! Only he means you, or him, not me. My day for that, my day for dying on the barricades of two pounds of crap like this is gone (why, with Clarence Day outselling me 20 books to 1 on the open market, would I plough through this—when I have notes down for 12 $400 casuals, and ideas for ten more?)

I have marked for you, with a big X, the point beyond which I could not read. I will wager you my wife [Althea] against yours that you can't either. Feel the weight of this dossier in your hands, strain your eyes merely glancing at it, and realize that this kind of MS has been coming to me, fairly steadily for eight years. I marvel at that. I don't believe it can be, but here it is, whether you or Walker or Maloney or [Ralph] Ingersoll or [Geoffrey] Hellmann are running the department, here it is and here it always has been, the customary one piece out of three. That's really fair and true. Now, I deem it a wonder unmixed that this still goes on in a civilized world and on a smart magazine, made up, largely now, of expert, keen, trained newspapermen, who realize the value of conciseness, who, working on any newspaper, would throw this junk in the wastebasket the moment it was placed on their desks (as I am throwing it now). Just look thru the myriad and amazing pages of this thing and realize the effort, the time, the money, the space that might have been given to other stories, that was wasted here! It will sober you, my friend, and it will be item number three in my treatise on why I don't like to do Talk, why it slows me, worries me, bothers me, makes me yell.

I imagine, although I haven't read it, that the idea was to find out why there are "fifths" as well as quarts. Well, I could have gone out and got that story and put it down in 1000 words of notes, and it is absolutely silly to think all this junk has to be assembled about such a dull and minor thing. Who gives a good god damn, anyway? It's an extremely minor idea. I would have tossed it out instantly. One story on a subway guard who translates Latin is worth eighty of these.

It would be an imposition, cruel and unusual punishment, to ask Maloney or anyone else to even read this s—t, let alone try to write a 500 word piece about it. The thing to do is instantly to can this stuff which would eat up one whole day of Maloney's, or mine, or anyone's time. Better yet, to have some supervising system which would prevent this tumorous growth as soon as it started and release the 12 men who must have worked on it a week, to do other, simpler, and better things.

Thurber

General Comment:

Why is it that, in the four pieces I am turning back to you, none of them was written by our best reporters, Mr. and Mrs. Cooke? Here are three Kinkeads and one Wickware, whoever in god's name he is. I know absolutely that Cooke and his wife are better than these two men. I have always expressed a preference for their pieces. Why don't I get them, then? What has happened that I get these four pieces in a clump, with no Cookes?

I don't want to get anyone hired, or anyone fired. We've had enough of both. But, in all honesty, since I am doing my history of Talk, who's looking to the hiring and the firing of Talk reporters, and who is supervising their work? I don't know. Once it was Hellmann (who was pretty good—he at least saved me from a lot of things which he had come to find out I hated, and he gave me some things he had learned that I enjoyed rewriting). I have the feeling, without any basis for it, that you and Walker and Maloney are all trying to do Talk together. I have the conviction that Walker could do it alone, if he was given free rein and not hampered by having to do eleven other things. In this whole bunch of stuff, naturally enough, the best story was the tip and notes he sent you on the subway guard. . . .

I am here not judging anybody, but putting down my feelings after one whole night of mulling over four pieces that Maloney handed me. I am also trying to answer, in all these, your various questions about my feelings and attitude and intentions. You have to take the bad with the good, in what I say.

I have had just this one story by Wickware. I would say, basing my feelings on that one, that he is not a first rate reporter. I had, I believe, four questions on his notes—all interesting, all important, to the story. As a reporter who really never went out on a story without draining the essentials dry, it is hard for me to be lenient to a man who leaves the rewrite man fuming and cursing and asking for facts. As a writer who has got somewhere, in a minor way, I am not going to go back to being a second assistant city editor and do this kind of thing consistently. I'd starve and make no money. Just the fact of giving up this night to all this, probably means I'll have to borrow money for Christmas. I'd rather write casuals, and God knows I can, than monkey with Talk when the former would allow me to give my wife a bracelet and the latter, for all my feeling for you and the magazine, would allow me only to give her a dozen oranges. I'll do Talk for you at a slight loss, but not a complete one. If you like my rewrites of it, it ought to be made as easy as possible for me to do it, since I get only one sixth as much for a Talk piece as for a casual.

Kinkead seems to me never to have got any better. He is a nice boy and a hard worker, but so is Senator Victor Donahey of Ohio, whom you will never meet in my house, as much as I admire his ardor, his intensity, and some of his principles. I can't railroad Kinkead out. He works hard, almost too hard. I ask for a 1000 words of notes and he gives me the history, not only of liquor bottles, but, by God, of all bottles and of Jack and Charlie [Proprietors of "21"] and all their bottles. . . . He has no feeling for values or for words. He simply works his heart out and gives you everything he's ever found out. I admire that but I can't rewrite it. I don't want him fired. He's on the verge of being good, and concise, and knowing what's wanted. What he needs is supervision, direction, editing; a sane, knowing hand to direct him. Let's give him that.

Meanwhile, where are the Cookes? If anybody at all has told you they are no good, that person is wrong.

On final thought, I'm willing to do these notes on every piece and every occasion, if they are any help to you and God knows they ought to be. But that will put me back on a salary basis again.

Thurber


ADD:

. . . I've only been writing, man and reporter, twenty years, but I know enough to know that leg-work, pondering, making notes, writing them out etc. must have kept Kinkead out of anything else for a week. Is his absence on this piece the reason we have a man named Wickware doing pieces? Good God, with every reporter assigned pieces like this, it would take a staff of twenty to give me enough good ones to do every week!

JT

I'd burn this, give Kinkead $50 for his work, and send him out to find out whether Captain Becker's widow still lives in the house in the Bronx, and if not, who does? And who lives in the Elwell house, and are the three girls still living in the West End Avenue apartment in which Two-Gun Crowley held off the police? and do they still rent out the room in the Park Central in which Rothstein was shot? It's that kind of stuff our readers want. Who could possibly care about what kind of bottles liquor comes in? The point is what kind of liquor comes in those bottles.

     T

There are probably no good reporters left since I quit the New York Evening Post, in March 1926.

*By the early 1930s, Thurber had become disturbed by the growing prominence of the literary left. Malcolm Cowley was the editor of* The New Republic.

## To Malcolm Cowley

*[1934]*

Dear Malcolm:

I am writing this to you as a friend of mine and not as an editor. . . . The idea of writing it came to me tonight when I was sitting alone in the Algonquin lobby reading the current New Republic and, in particular, your article on [Joseph Wood] Krutch's new book. . . .

In the past few years, certainly the past year, a great many things concerned with economics, communism, writing, proletarianism, life, happiness, love, and whatnot, have bothered me as much as they have bothered anybody. I am not so tied up in my own interests and in the peculiar field of my own thought and writing that I have not observed that Great Changes have taken place and are taking place. My essential weakness, in this regard, is that I am not, in certain subjects, well enough read to be able, conscientiously, to set myself up as a spokesman, a student, a protagonist, or even a sound and well-documented opponent of many of the great and important factors that now enter into national and international life from the standpoint of government politics and economics. I find myself, when such subjects come up, at a loss, but being me, not at so great a loss that I don't put my oar in and argue. I have argued, even fought, with certain literary people who espouse Marxism, Communism, etc.

and I admit that they have usually, technically speaking, won the arguments, but they have never won me. If I have resorted to invective and silly talking etc and have been unable to point out exactly what I want and what I don't want, it seems to me that they have also been unable to point out exactly what they want and don't want.

I refer, I think, especially to my unhappy and, in some ways, deplorable set-to with Michael Gold [a communist writer] some months ago at a party to which I wasn't even asked. Even Bob Coates, who took me there, was disgusted with me and as tolerant and generous as he has always been with me, in my cups and my moods, he told me, out in the street afterwards, that I had made a horse's ass of myself and he disappeared into that New York night he loves so well, leaving me to get home as best I could in a taxi, having only thirty or forty dollars on me. After every such scene I always wake up to remorse and regret and real anguish. I am always willing to face the real facts about what I am, think, and do, insofar as anyone can face and untangle and identify them. So many elements go into what a man is, thinks, and does that this is not always easy. There is no one of us who can be absolutely sure that his arguments last night came purely out of his dispassionate beliefs about politics or writing or whatever and were not, in some way, influenced by his emotional nature, something his wife said before the party, something that happened years ago and was grazed in his consciousness by a stray bullet that night, some subtle, hard to recognize beast in the jungle of his experience, his past, his desires, suppressed, thwarted, or (what is even more important) satisfied. . . .

I have been accused by several persons, as the result of arguments or diatribes on this or that, of being unintelligent. If that were true, it would end this letter. The unfortunate fact is that I am not unintelligent. I have my distortions, my special leanings, my highly specialized ambitions and feelings, my silly and curious desires and hopes, lusts and vagaries, but I am not unintelligent. I have acted unintelligently at times, as you yourself know, but then who hasn't?

A great many things have happened to me since the night of the Gold argument to worry me. . . .

One of my arguments was that I dislike "literary communists". I did then and I still do. I regard Mike Gold as a literary communist. He and various others like him are enough to make me turn against the whole idea of communism, the worker, Russia, proletarianism. I think that what communism needs is communists, more communists and fewer writers. Maybe Communism has them, but where are they? I am bewildered now, in a genuine desire to know about communism and what it is and what it wants and where it stands, by the most tremendous whirlpool of literary writing that has befogged the horizon since all the boys jumped in and fought, with equal bewilderment and eloquence, about the New Humanism and, later, Technocracy. . . . If I did go back, to the files of the New Republic, the New Masses, the Saturday Review of Literature, I would find the same final, glib, thundering articles, the same warnings, threats, and ominous announcements and prophesies, wouldn't I, that I find now in the same journals about proletarianism? . . .

Humanism, essentially a moral and religious idea and ideal, was turned into a literary idea and ideal by writers; Technocracy, essentially an economic thing, was turned into a literary thing; isn't it true that proletarianism, essentially a governmental and political thing, is being turned—has been turned—into a sheer literary exercise? . . .

It seems to me that every article I pick up on the subject has been written by a man who is essentially a literary man. These men give their own ideas, I have never yet seen one of them quote, directly, a worker or a leader of workers. . . . I have read Gold himself on the subject of Ring Lardner and on the subject of Thornton Wilder. Am I to believe that before Communism can get anywhere all writers must cease to write anything that isn't proletarian? . . . or are these literary men, merely for their own amusement, doing nothing at all about their real cause and simply showing off what they know about writing in America, bad or good? . . .

. . . There must be in this country hundreds of persons like me, intelligent, groping, not, in the field of economics and politics, well read—because we have largely let the world go to pieces around us, thinking it would all blow over like the Civil War and take its little place in history. We know now it won't. We know that the structure, the fabric, the destination, the purpose of everything has changed. We are caught with our mental pants down. We don't know where to turn for the facts, for the drawn lines of battle. . . . It is our own fault that we have thus been caught out of life, fishing in our little stream, nursing our own baby, planning our vacations, making love to a girl, writing silly little pieces about timid men afraid of the night that comes with sundown, oblivious of the night that comes with revolution. But there we are! What books, what few articles, what leaders' statements, what rules and by-laws, what statements of purpose are we to turn to out of all the million-word welter of fine writing? . . . And that brings me to one of the things which caused me to raise such a fuss when talking with Gold. It seems to me that the literary communists have almost got to the point where they believe that motherhood and passion and love and all that belong solely to the communists. That you must be a communist to make even your private life important. . . . I remember that when Gold and I were arguing—and by the way he started it by saying to me (whom he didn't know then, even by name) that the New Yorker was edited by "College punks". Again the tendency to make of everybody except a communist a punk or something equally low. Of course I called him a non-college son-of-a-bitch, matching fighting words with fighting words. Instantly he took the sweet martyred attitude that all Bourgeois people want to fight, to use bad words, because, as he said, they are all inferiority complex people. Two other men who came up later both used, separately of each other, the words "inferiority complex". That struck me as odd and as significan't and as revelatory. . . . What Gold emphasized was that if I understood Marxism I would do better and truer and more important stories and, yes, even pictures. For, it seems I deal, in my stories and pictures, only with this strange amorphous indescribable group known as the Bourgeoisie. I thought I had an opening there and I plugged at it. It was my contention . . . that my stories and my pictures were about relationships between men and women which are entirely apart from any consideration of economics, politics or anything of the sort. I asked him if he was married and he said yes. I asked him if he was happy and he dodged that. Later he came up to me, alone, and said that he hadn't answered that question because, as a matter of fact, he had not been happy with his wife for five years. I asked him if it were any different being unhappy with your wife when you were a communist. I asked if bedroom familiarities and intimacies, morning before-coffee irritabilities, evening grouchinesses were any different. He smiled his patronizing smile, as much as to say certainly, they were. That is the seed of a dangerous illusion, that is the little weed in the cranny that can, finally, break down a castle. It is there, for one place, that proletarianism, having been taken over by the writers and not the workers, goes off the track and causes people who still hold on to Capitalism, or still ignore the present world situation, or still blindly keep to themselves and their little private lives, to become afraid of this great plan for a new world because they see in it . . . a partly unconscious envy of, and hatred for, and incipient desire to destroy not only the economic regime of the capitalistic people but the personal culture and the individual destiny and happiness of those people. . . . When mobs break in they don't only arrest Louis and Antoinette, they take a special joy in hacking to pieces fine paintings and in pissing on royal beds.

. . . I don't see how anybody could fail to see, in [Gold's] writings on Wilder and on Lardner and in his talk to me—a viewpoint which a dozen of his colleagues have endorsed—a desire to subject the individual to the political body, to the economic structure, to put the artist in a uniform so like the uniform of the subway conductor that nobody would be able to tell the difference. It is this desire to regiment and discipline art—the art of writing and the art of living—that some of us are afraid of, that some of us seem to see a greater menace in than the critics do. . . . We need someone to say, listen, you sons of bitches, hands off—keep your noses in your economic and political dishes or we'll knock them off! . . .

I have admitted that I am largely ignorant about Marx and about Communism—as an economic and governmental matter. I should like to know more about it. I have tried Marx. I have tried the dozens of explanations of Marx. I can't go it. Any more than I can go Racine or the Greek tragedies. I think I do know a little about literary proletarianism and I know that I don't like it and that I feel it should be as consistently attacked as it is consistently advocated and fought for. . . .

Have you ever noticed: a man writes a book on a subject of great importance. It is reviewed by a brilliantly writing critic. Sometimes the critic barely mentions the book in hand; usually, at least, he doesn't get around to the book for three or four hundred words—being busy writing a little essay of his own, showing to begin with how much he knows about this and kindred subjects. Then comes a few quibbles about wrong dates, misspelled words, things left out that should be in, and finally, maybe, a word or two of praise for the really good points that the man makes (only isn't it too bad that the points are not the ones he should have made!) Then the author sits down and writes an answer which it takes him a whole night of rewriting to get down to six hundred cold calm words, explaining that the critic has missed his point entirely, that he hasn't understood a God damn thing, that the author did not say Pareto on page 217, he said Proust. This is printed in the magazine which printed the original criticism and it is followed by the critic's answer to the author's answer, in which the critic says that the author's answer shows that he is just as far off the subject as he was to begin with only more so. And the careful, struggling reader of the whole business, looking for a little light, puts the whole works down and goes out and gets cock-eyed at Tim's bar and asks Tim, an old Ballyharness man, what he thinks of things. "It's all balls," says Tim, and the reader goes home to bed, sure of only that one thing.

Somebody in the New Masses a month or two ago took the annual crack at the New Yorker. Overlooking the fact that the New Yorker is a business enterprise which would fail if we all began to write like the Masses, the writer descended to such silly and unimportant work as to seriously analyze and show up the fact that we writers here are not "living in this world" because we don't write about the worker. The Wilder-Lardner thing all over again. We all inhabit a Lost Atlantis, we drink our old-fashioneds to the last drop careless of the fact that the world is crumbling around us. In short, we don't attack communism but we don't go for it, head over heels. Therefore, the inference is, what we write—no matter how funny or well done or, in its way, right—should be stopped. If these men, who write such attacks, should ever get in control, do you think there wouldn't be a commissar of literature who would be appointed and commissioned to stop it, who would set us at work writing either poems in praise of the American Lenin or getting up time tables for work trains? If you do, you're missing a low, faint, distant rumbling. . . . What I want to know is, just what constitutes saving the working classes? I read about the woes and the perils of the present system, of Roosevelt's plans and ideals and fumblings, I read all kinds of threats and prophesies of disaster, but I have not put my eye yet on a succinct statement of just what it is that the communists, or the socialists, in this country want? . . . Our own lives must always be the subject for our writings, come what may. Why don't they see that? As I said to Gold, you have your [Robert] Cantwells and your [Albert] Halpers (My God, they now even have their Saroyan, and welcome to him!) Why not let the other alone? You can't live by bread alone, or by factories and foundries alone. Why is that such a difficult thing to see, I wonder—such a difficult thing to concede? . . .

I have been working for weeks on a Saroyan parody—I get so mad I spoil it and have to let it dry. It seems to me significan't that this man, who can not write and in admitting it really boasts that he can, should have caught whatever fancy it is that he has caught. Is he a proof and sign of the fact that if your writing deals with poor people out of work etc. it is now bound to sell, no matter how bad it is? Was it the consistent pounding of the critics about proletarian writing that put him over? I wonder. Naturally I sympathize with Hemingway's attack on him in Esquire. I thought it was just the way he should have been attacked, drunkenly, sloppily. I thought Hemingway's saying aw, what you need is a smack in the puss was precisely the right note. . . .

. . . Are the proletarian writers going to have the added advantage of writing sloppily and mushily just because whatever they have to say is so important it doesn't make any difference how they say it? I worry about things, too.

. . . I worry about the first time I ever saw my daughter look out of a window at night, a window in an old Connecticut farmhouse, and watch, with wide, wondering eyes, the first snow she ever saw, falling silently over the old orchard behind the house. That to me is as important as any of the things that happen to the people in "The 42nd Parallel" or "1919" (none of whose names I can remember). Must I explain this, to anyone except myself? Must I answer for it in a communist's literary court? . . .

One of my favorite characters in another Lost Atlantis was a mythical figure named Tristram. He was born in a land called Lyonesse which sank into the sea. There is no trace of that land now, no proof of it. There is no trace and proof of the men he fought with (with usually no social purpose in mind), no sign left that ever a woman named Iseult lived. Yet he was wont to say, and every now and then I hear him saying it, "I come from Lyonesse and a gentleman am I." I like to think of that; I get a kind of solace out of repeating a line never said by a man who never lived from a land that never existed.

It must be almost dawn.

Yours,

Jim Thurber

*In the summer of 1934, Thurber, Honey and Edward Angly of the* Herald Tribune *rented a cottage at Martha's Vineyard. Thurber soon returned to New York pleading work demands but actually in a sulk over the attention Honey was paying Angly.*

## TO ANN HONEYCUTT

*Hellward Bound, 5:30 pm—*
*Thursday*

Dear Honey:

. . . I want to go down to the sea again with a burn on my milk-white chest, I want to see the pretty stones on the beach and the sea-weed and the lily cups and the Crackerjack boxes and Walter the dog. . . .

I forgive you the scene you made the night of the party. Never hit a man when he's down, you little witch, you sea-sprite. . . . You're so . . . well-adjusted to your maladjustments you could charge admission. . . . I'm still red as Hell everywhere but my fanna and that, I daresay, will be tanned by some-one when I get back, to match the rest. . . .

The New Bedford gulls are coming out to meet us, wearing black and white hatbands, so we must be nearing dat ole davil mainland, the son of a bitch. . . .

But it is so nice there is a you, changeable, fixed, genuine, insincere, stout as a rock, shifting as the sands, with a heart of roses growing out of granite cran-nies. Old Cranny Honeycutt! . . . As they bury you I'll be there to say "Let 'em down gently, Ann!" The poor men! Keep them for pall-bearers, all of them that you know. But don't go Bride of the Church on me. . . .

    Jim

       🐚  🐚  🐚

*Hell*

*Friday*

*[Undated, summer 1934]*

The portage from the Naushen
to the Providence was accomplished
without the loss of a single suitcase . . .

Here's some strordinary, pathetic, and amusing news: Martin and Mino [former speakeasy proprietors] have taken over Alice Foote McDougall's Fierense restaurant on 46th just west of fifth avenue, the great big monasterial room whose gloom used to be lit by little candles which threw wavering high-lights upon hammered brass trays, yellow-flowered china and teakwood boxes and green mints. There they stand, happy as two kids in June, beaming at all the bewildered customers from 52 when they drop in. Gibbs says they opened up Thursday. Mino called him and said, "Dees ees Minno, We have just taken over Aleece Fuht McGonigles on 46th street. Please come over." Gibbs thought it was me, putting it on a bit thick, so he said, "Go screw your-self" or something to thees effect. But Mino called back and proved he was Mino with tears in his eyes. . . . They have some hope of keeping both the Mc-Dougal crowd of old ladies and little girls and the old 52 crowd, but as Gibbs said the former will leave and never come back the very first time one of the Columbia [CBS]-New Yorker crowd gets drunk and begins singing I Had a Dream, Dear. "Eet ees joos like a street in Italy," says Mino, pointing to the old

Italian walls, draped with old Italian batiks and hung with old Italian scimiters. "Eet is wonderful, no?" "No," said Gibbs, to himself.

The crème de la crème de la jest is that Mino and Martin told Gibbs they borrowed $250,000 from a bank to go ahead with dees. good goddamighty.

You're in my heart, you're in my eyes, you're in my dreams,
you're in my hair.
Jamie

Love to old Uncle Ed (Squirl Dawgs) Angly

ꙮ   ꙮ   ꙮ

*[Undated, summer 1934;*
*written from the Algonquin Hotel]*

Dear Honey:

It's *still* terrible down here and I earnestly advise you to stay where you are. . . .

One of those sulky twilights is falling over New York. Worn and pasty people are drinking Tom Collinses downstairs, waiters are staring damply into space, men are removing their collars and shoes and cursing, women are patting their sticky hair and wriggling moistly out of their damp pants, children are whining, radios are cackling insanely, automobile brakes are shrieking, and away off a swan is flying, wings outspread, into Hell, screaming like a cowardly condemned man. The whole broiling city is complaining: The dirty curtains at my window are blowing into my face; they smell like a closed up smoking car. A tired maid is knocking at my door. She has a husband and a sickly child in Hoboken, a leaning house on a broken street.

From across the Sound, out of the quiet sunset, a cool wind is stirring your hair. The fresh sea-food is on the porch table. The first fishing boats are coming in. Two lovely yachts lie in the bay. A sturdy Mayhew goes up the path and calls "good evening! I hazard it'll be fair tomorrow!"

Stay where you are, it's terrible down here.

All my old doubts and depressions are back. I found them in my unsent laundry and my unanswered mail, in [John] Mosher's facetious remarks, in [Wolcott] Gibbs' sharp comments, in Ross's swagger, in Mr. [Algonquin owner Frank] Case's glib "Welcome back! Welcome back to Hell!"

I sit and ponder your advice to stand on my own feet, matching it up with those other fragments of advice I've had from you during the years. They go together like green and blue. You zig-zag—and so do I—only I never become so smug as you do in my pronouncements—violent and adolescent, but not smug. You're a lovely little smug. But stay where you are, it's terrible down here. I can take it, but you stay up there and dish it out. You wouldn't last a month down here. . . . Eyes that can't stick to the type in a book up there would never do down here. . . .

Tell Ed to stay. . . . I'll stick it out here—you have all of life before you. You stay there and write me a few sharp admonitions about standing on my own feet. There's a great peace comes out of that. Man is born & dies alone. Why shouldn't he live alone? You tell 'em baby, you know the answers.

Love,

Jim

Nothing in this letter is to be construed as indicating I don't love you. I do. And even though I have the emotions of a rabbit and you those of a fish, it still goes. Most unions are too ordinary. One would be worth while trying in which the man gives up the peace and ecstasy of love, and the woman (just to be fair) gives up cigarettes, Riesling wine, and music.

J

❧  ❧  ❧

Dear Honey:

Not in justification, but perhaps in extenuation, of the way I acted (and I acted so badly I shall never let you ask me to your house again), I should like to quote here parts of a letter just received from my wonderful mother:

"William [Thurber] has no job and simply worries the life out of us because he hasn't—it has almost finished us the way he gets his spells and wants to turn a "machine gun" on all of us and relieve us of our "*misery*"— then end his own life. Last Sat.—week ago—he got one of his mean insane spells and tore around here raising his voice—and with no excuse for it—Just goes nite after nite without sleep and isn't really responsible for his actions— My heart aches for that boy who has so many fine qualities and when he is *making* money he is so good to us and everybody and happy, but even *then* is never well—has these awful thots constantly running thru his mind, as he puts it, and worst feature about it all is way he *laughs* to himself all nite— he has told me and I have slipped in and listened and he laughs so loud—it startled me—just like one would do in seeing a funny picture of Charlie Chaplin. It is not a case for a physician but a psycho analyst something must be got out of his subconscious mind. Well, any way—not to care to worry you but I feel you should know something of what is going on here in Thurber family—so I must tell you what happened last Friday Aug. 19th about ten o'clock in the A.M. William sleeps in front room, gets up about 9.30 or the like, gathers up his clothes, comes thru dining room to get to bathroom of course—well, he had a bad night worrying about all of our lives and inheritances way *back* as he puts it—in family—always begins about what our Ancestors handed down to my *two* afflicted sons—whatever he means God only knows.

(Ed. note: the 'two afflicted sons' is not supposed to include Jamie)

Well of course your father asked him to keep still, that he himself was worried to death also—that he wasn't well either etc.—Then the big fight was on—Wm. raised his voice and *raved* and declared he'd get a "machine gun" and put us *all* out of our misery—one word brot on another of course and I turning to quiet the bunch on acct of the neighbors here—and Robert getting so mad at Wm's actions told him to "shut up". Then Wm had a good chance to lay Robt. out—told him he was worse off physically than he was and that he should get out and work.

By this time the "fighting squad" had gotten into the narrow hall near the bathroom—not much room to fist fight, so I drove them best I could back into dining room—more space—It kept up until your father fell to the floor in sort of a faint afraid Wm would kill Bob—then such excitement—Bob and I thot he was dead he did look so white—I ran for Mr. Kinney—landlord—he came in and helped us get your father on sofa in the front room. And we got all remedies we could and finally got him to himself. Robt sure was frightened about his father and is so cool-headed at such a time—got pillows for under his head, rubbed his head and all while I was heating milk to get up a circulation—Then when Wm saw what he had caused he came to himself and begged for a doctor and how he cried and was sorry But we had to have it quiet so Mr. Kinney kept him back. Then Wm said to me "Mamma, let me help my poor father" and I wanted to frighten him for his crazy actions. So in a very *dramatic* way (Ed.note: You'd have to see this to know what Mrs. T. is like when she's very dramatic) I told Wm. it was "TOO LATE NOW". Then the unearthly yell he gave. Then Mr. Kinney told him his father would be okay. The woman below heard it all and ran across the street. It was the worst, Jamie, I ever knew in my life. (Ed.note: This is exaggerated—she has known worse). and I am so ashamed and mortified I don't know what to do for everyone seemed to think we were the "*cream*" of the building as I class them here as *trashy*—"Bootleggers" one tenant—and Elevator Man—other Blacksmith and one a shoemaker and other one a "Huckster" but good kind folks but now I feel we are the "*alley trash*"

You will remember, Miss. H., that I told you I hadn't been doing anything but laugh. I'm laughing now. The Thurber laughing has come on me. It can't be long now, I'm sure. Robt hasn't got the laughs yet but he is younger than me and has had flashes of laughing. I've heard Wm laugh the night out; sometimes he sings, too.

Of course I have to make the family believe that I'm the normal one, so don't let on. Also destroy this letter and keep its contents to yourself.

Ha ha ha ha ha ha ha ha ha ha ha ha ha ha ha ha ha ha ha ha ha ha ha haha h ha ha ha ha ha ha ha ha ha ha ha ahha hahhahhahhahhahh hhhahhahhahha hhahhahhahhahhahhahhahhahhahhahhahhahhahhahhahhah

HA HA HA HA HA HA HA HA HA HA HA HA HA AHA AHHAHHA HAHHAHHAHHAHHAHHAHHAHHAHHAHHAHHAHHAHHAHHA HHAHHAHHAHHAHHAHHA this is terrible.

   Amusedly yours,
   Jamie

The worst part about it is that I laugh about the way I acted that evening. I should feel sorry, and in a way I do—remorseful, repentant, etc. and ashamed—but in the midst of thinking of it I'll begin this laughing—go off into veritable gales of it, end up actually crying and weak.

When can I come down?

*a   a   a*

*Hotel Algonquin, 59 to 65 West Forty-fourth Street,*
*New York, Frank Case*
*[Undated, probably 1934]*

Dear Honey:

I didn't say that I couldn't have lunch with you, to be nasty. I wanted to say that I didn't believe, for your own good and mine, that we should see each other again. I know you believe that, too, but you are too generous and too really, at heart, appreciative of me to say so, finally. You have had only suffering with me not only lately, but always. It isn't your fault—or mine—but the fault of an impossible union. We have both known that, since Christmas Day. I haven't come to any quick conclusion, I have spent a week seeing clearly the impossibility of you and me as proved over seven years.

. . . We are bad for each other so long as I persist in insisting on a love interest which you never asked for, which at times you felt you could go through with, but which we both know you couldn't, finally.

I'm not so foolish . . . as to say I never want to see you again. You have been the one person I cared about most of anybody. Nobody with any mind or heart throws such a thing away completely. I hope to re-establish myself as an individual apart from what we've been through. It will be hard but not impossible. I'll do it. I know that we can both be happy apart, with somebody else, or nobody else, just living and being [with] each other. I know we couldn't together. . . . I'll be all right, too. I don't know how long it will take because I have identified myself with you and us for a long long time. It has made definite and great changes in me but not fundamental or permanent ones because we never got that close together. I need a new orientation, a new outlook, and a new set of plans. We have just had futile hopes, mutual despair about the situation, uncertainty of the future, inability to get anywhere in the present. We'd always be that way, afraid of each other as two people together. But as individuals, still somebody, each of us, too damn good to let anybody get us down, least of all ourselves. . . .

. . . I'll always, always hold the image of you, as you, and not as mine, in my heart.

I want you to remember, on your part, some of the nice things. There were some.

> Jim

&a    &a    &a

Dear Ann

If, however, at the end of a year, I have lived an admirable life, I should appreciate a small word from you saying so. I'll not be proud—if I must admit what isn't true—of my 'colorfulness' or my anything any more. I ought to know in three months whether it is going to work. If it doesn't I have figured on dying in my double-breasted suit I always look nice in it, I think, proudly, even when lying in the gutter or a field.

> awful

&a    &a    &a

*[Feb. 19, 1934]*

Dear Miss Honeycutt:

My patient, Mr. James Thurber, appeared at my office today for the first time in several years, with the usual complaint. He seems to be back where he was in 1929, which is, of course, more, in a way, than can be said for the most of us. Physical examination revealed a total absence of any reflexes even including batting of the eyelids when a lighted match was held in close proximity to the eyes. Impotence, remorse, oak poisoning, lover's itch, inability to stand upright without wavering, naushy, groaning, and capering regret were extremely noticeable. Mental examination revealed that you have left his board again and that this is the motivating causatory impulse which has put him back where he was.

Dr. Hughes Hawes, your analyst, refuses to conduct another co-operative cure along with me, on the ground that he is fed up on it. He seems persuaded that you are a Curable Unromantic but will not undergo treatment.

I was surprised to turn up, in examining Thurber, a possible contributory causation which hitherto he has never revealed to me, namely, the occasion in his youth when he was debauched by his Aunt Ida, a woman of fifty-four, who was stronger than he was. Thurber has the illusion that he was raped, but rape under such conditions is impossible. For a woman to be thrown and raped is one thing, but for a young boy in his teens to be thrown and raped is another. I trust we need not go into the biological determinatives in this regard. Thurber does not even seem to have kept a stiff upper lip during the struggle.

I have succeeded in co-relating my patient's attitude toward you, culminating recently in his sending you home from a dinner which he did not touch, with another gentleman, and the traumatic throwback of the Aunt Ida incident. Thurber, in a word, has a surpressed desire to be thrown by you. While I have never had the pleasure of meeting you, a thing I look forward to with patience, I gather that you are not what we call in my profession the throwing type. I daresay you have never torn a man's clothes off except in a spirit of pure fun, or deviltry. My patient seems to think that you take everything too lightly.

Thurber's inability to arouse what we call passion in you is, of course, regrettable. It does not, oddly enough, seem to have given him an inferiority complex, for he proclaims, in what I can only call braggadoccia, that he can and what's more has, aroused passion in practically every other woman he has ever seen or heard of except you. This of course I take with a grain of salt just as I do Thuber's remarkable statement that you said you had been kissed by two hundred men and knew more about kissing than any other woman in the country. If you really made that statement I urgently suggest that you return to Dr. Hawes for another going-over.

I have endeavored without success to gain the cooperation of the gentleman who was with you two at that deplorable dinner engagement, but I can find no Mr. John Mosha [Mosher] in the phone book. It may be, of course, that he was simply a figment of the imagination of you two, what we call the Imaginary Third Person, or Hallucinatory Triangle Cloture.

There are some elements of Mr. Thurber's case which I do not believe you thoroughly understand, for I feel that if you did you would play ball with us better. In the first place, he said nothing at that lamentable dinner engagement about you not being as good as Al Smith at making records of any kind whatsoever. I believe that you have never made a record, and Mr. Smith's records are, so far as I know, confined solely to reproductions of certain of his speeches. Mr. Thurber is, unfortunately, what we call in my profession a Bubby Idolizer, a phrase which, I realize, is scarcely of the nicey-nicey type which you prefer to these plain statements of fact. I myself sympathize with but do not understand this particular mania. He has, however, described your bodily graces with such fervor in between his denunciation of you as a woman who is not half so good at making records as Al Smith that I feel emboldened to have the sanguine hope that some small regard for you of an emotional nature still stirs somewhere in the depths of that great heart of his. For it is a great heart, and an unusual one. I believe that if you understood it more thoroughly, you would treat him with greater consideration and would not be so shocked and disturbed by the liberties he sometimes attempts to take, the reprehensible proposals he makes, and the so-called poison-tongued dinner talks with which he favors you. He is of course what we call in my profession a Nervous Talker, but deep down behind that golden tongue is one of the greatest and most remarkable hearts I have ever examined into. I am taking the liberty of enclosing a copy of my chart of his heart, for your information.

Of course, I don't give, as a man, a Good Goddam, as we say in my profession, whether you and Mr. Thurber get together or never get together. I think that perhaps you would be happier with this naked doctor at Bedford Hills with whom Thurber says you spend so many nights together in Miss Price's apartment. That is none of my business, but for that man to have told Thurber that he (the doctor) had had more trouble than Thurber ever had is, on the face of it, ridiculous. Thurber, in the first place, was stripped and the doctor, as I understand it, had thrown something around his (the doctor's) shoulders. I should think that Miss Price, lying there in the hallway, was having more trouble than any of the four of you. But for you to have opened the door to her for the purpose of allowing Thurber to see you and Dr. Bedford together, in a compromising situation, was a thing which it would have been far, far better for all of us had you left it undone. Did you do it to torture him, as he claims? He says it was a forthright strip-tease act, as we call it in the profession.

So far I have scan't hopes of getting Thurber into any better shape than he is in at the moment, lying here in my office on a couch, with his hat and overcoat on. I took him home, or to a place he said was his home, a church in Brooklyn where he said he had an apartment in the basement. Either we went to the wrong church or there is no such apartment, which I am inclined to believe.

At any rate, here is the chart of that great heart which, if I were you, I would hesitate to break again.

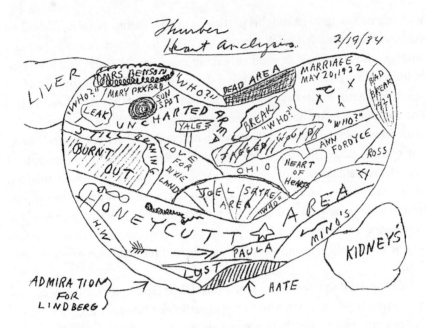

In March 1935, Thurber caved in to depression, insecurity, and a nervous anxiety brought on by his unrequited love for Honeycutt, news that Althea had filed for divorce, concern over whether he would see his child again, financial worries, work pressures, and the consequences of a self-destructive lifestyle. At Honey's insistence, he finally admitted himself to Dr. Fritz Foord's sanitarium at Kerhonkson, in the Catskill Mountains, then a popular drying-out place for New Yorker writers and editors.

[Undated, probably March 1935]

Dear 'Toots':

I'm sorry about that sharp tone in my [telephone] voice an hour ago. Now that I'm on my feet again, instead of yours, I'm ashamed to have depended so on you to get me here. . . . After this you will observe with awe my self-reliance. I need hold on to no woman's brassiere.

Now don't you fall down on me about coming here Saturday . . . my heart leaps up at the thought of seeing your wide blue eyes and golden hair again. I think of you as my "Blue and Gold Girl." You will find me calm and poised and altogether a charming, if slightly aloof and reserved, companion. The jitters have left me. My right hand is almost steady enough to hold peas on a knife. Not quite, yet, but almost. . . . The violin strings are slowly losing their tautness and the winds of life now set up in them a low murmurous tranquil sound in place of the high sharp whine that used to throw Tony's kitchen into a rage. See how evenly I write this line. . . . My countenance has resumed its wonted studious, determined look . . . and even my hair has quieted down. The turmoil that was sex now comes but faintly to these serene ears, like the far away sound of retreating artillery. I am almost ready for the World again. . . .

They have run my ass off up here but the discipline has been fine, my Creole beauty. I expect my Forties to be fine. What a name I shall leave behind for future ages to search for in vain! Fox tracks in the snow, but boldly made, my queenly dowager!

I anticipate with some misgivings the letter you said you were writing, for I suppose you will deny everything with a sweet despairing courage. *Live* alone, then, goddam it, and see if I cease to care! . . .

Who said I had no money. I make enugh for you to bathe in, you & ed and willie. . . .

. . . Look out for these quiet dreamers. You're safer with a man that talks it off. . . .

. . . God be with you, Ann Honeycutt, my tube rose!
      J.


P.S.

I have just been hosed and pummelled (one "l"; they beat the other one out of me). Every day for an hour I'm hosed and pummeled. Then I go to my room and read: Emerson, Plato, The Marhouse Murders, Wordsworth, Byron, Rab and his Friends, Swedenborg, Mr. Fortune Explains, the American Mercury, and your dear little note, my haughty minx! I would put that note under my pillow *every single night* only I forget about it. Not a word have I wanted to write for the NYer. . . .


Half the poems the poets used to write were to Ann, I find. Most of them bewail the coldness of these Anns. Here's one:

> *Snowdrop*
> When, full of warm and eager love,
>     I clasp you in my fond embrace,

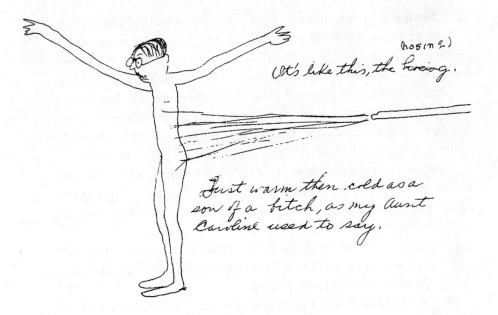

(nosing)

It's like this, the nosing.

Just warm then cold as a
son of a bitch, as my Aunt
Caroline used to say.

You gently push me back and say,
"Take care, my dear, you'll spoil my lace."

You kiss me just as you would kiss
    Some woman friend you chanced to see;
You call me "dearest,"—All love's forms
    Are yours, not its reality.

Oh, Annie! cry, and storm, and rave!
    Do everything with passion in it!
Hate me an hour, and then turn round
    And love me truly, just one minute.
        William Wetmore Story (1819–1895)

Well, he lived to be 76 in spite of her.
Here's hoping I don't do the same.
    Jamie

Dear Honey:

The first fowarding of mail from the Nyer arrived today, with 45 letters, some 23 days old, and the batch included the one I am enclosing. I read it over and it seems, in my present mood, a little impetuous and insane in spots, but I signed it again, okayed it, like a tired business man. I don't subscribe to it as much as when I wrote it (and never leave a hotel without a forwarding address, my dear) because of those true and accurate but nevertheless cruel remarks you make about how people can have freedom of expression since I am no longer [at] the party. I am no longer like that. You refer to a period which is past and gone. The mail also included several other depressing letters, so today is bad. Also I am in a rather depressing fix, as far as life goes, which does not seem to improve so much as it seems to worsen. It worsened the other night. God has seen fit to place me in the spot I'm in, and all I can do is accept, and try to be a good, fine Christian boy, hoping that the animus of people will fall off my back like a duck's water. The fix I refer to includes my associations with practically everybody in the world except the King of Italy. I seem to have managed it all very badly, as you know. I don't know anybody who has managed so badly. In my next letter however conditions will seem better. Keep on the wagon, no matter what Coates's dog says. Give my love to all, and say that I shall be happy in receipt of your obedient servant 21st ultimate in consideration your daily bank balance now below bill due please remit must have escaped your attention can't understand in hands of a lawyer for collection.

    Yourx,

    Jim

             ঌ  ঌ  ঌ

*[Undated, March or April 1935]*

Dear Honey: At Foord's.

You remind me of a husband with morning sickness. But seriously I'm worried about you. Dysentery, your ass. What does that naked cupid know? I think you should go to a specialist or something. My own private theory is that you need the bitter medicine of sex—plain god damn sane sexual regularity. Not a cross between prison and taxicab kissing. There is a technical word for ladies who have never borne children—something like eudolpholophiam or precalpsus, an ugly word but useful to medical men because so many maladies arise from continence when continence becomes stubborness and from childlessness when childlessness becomes an intellectual conviction. It is a matter of plain medical statistics that unmarried ladies have more troubles than married ones and of even grimmer statistics that childless women suffer more diseases and die younger than married women with children. Cancer is, I believe, the great bane of the childless woman. You haven't got that—what you have—and it is a wonder unmixed to me that no doctor seems to have told you—is a general basis for maladies growing solely out of your unique and unrealistic personal life at 33. I suppose that if doctors have asked you about your private life you have lied about it with that oda-lisque smile, that disarming charm, that apparent adjustment of yours. You have no more real adjustment than a caged rabbit. Unmarried rabbits always die. I raised rabbits. Nature . . . brooks no interference with, or distortion of, her simple rules. The eye was made for seeing. Mules that work in deep coal mines go blind. Arms carried in slings wither. There can be no exception no matter how firm the illusory mental or emotional compromise. . . .

. . . There can be no real or lasting value in an arbitrary rearrangement of those laws. There can be no beauty or peace in it, either. One can accomplish frigidity, virginity, even barrenness, but the adjustment is only apparent not real. . . . Something like 80 percent of so-called unamorous women become normally adjusted after child-birth. Behold this fact: the penis is no more unlovely than the nose, the vagina than the lips. All distinctions of the kind are arbitrary. Of the so-called erogenous areas, the lips (long sung by poets) are made of the same material as the glano and the vulva. Their contact, except for sentiment, tradition and convention, is identical. If Nature had so arranged it that pregnancy was possible by contact of the lips . . . you would never have kissed 200 men in taxicabs, you would have slept with 200 men in beds—and walked home.

Notes to this effect I have been taking for years to be enlarged some day for my book whose working title is "The American Woman." They are my own interpretations of indubitable facts. I expect the volume to be a monument to me and a boon to woman-kind. I will make it as simple and truthful and well-written as Emerson's essays on Nature and the Spirit. It is really my Work, based, finally, on 50 years of observation, experience, and reading. I am already ahead of Stekel, who had his hands on it and then let it go, by overlooking the romantic, the sentimental, and the traditional factors behind all forms of maladjustment. . . . Perhaps I shall go in for the practise of my own theories and set up an office. I would take only the cases of sensitive intelligent people with humor and imagination. They get into worse spots than most, but the way out, although difficult, is surer—under my care. I'll charge $3,000 a patient. At 50, with gray hair, I'd be a prepossessing consultant, radiating confidence . . . but I allowed myself to become patient rather than physician in your case. . . . It is odd that knowing as much as I do I should have let myself get into a state similar to those I like to examine. . . .

I have written you 2 letters already—unmailed. . . . I'll bring them to town. Your letter was here when I came back from my morning walk.

It is odd that I should be emotionally bound to my favorite patient, and yet probably a good idea as I can conceive of no one else who could carry out with you in practise the theories I have. . . . Everybody else has only been bad for you.

Your pondering the idea of marrying Willie [Coleman, *Herald Tribune* journalist] is just another step in the unconscious furtherance of your gentle determination to avoid reality. You think of separate rooms and separate lives. . . .

Keep in mind that you and I have avoided simplicity and courted complexity. We (especially you) insist on making simple things difficult. . . . Confusion is not a way out. See "Rain" and read the Bible (here & there). . . .

. . . I haven't written to anyone but you. . . . I think the line "after all's said and nothing's done" is wonderful. I am still saying too much but won't afterwards. The thing is to quit talking and do something. . . . I've gone back to the theory of laughs. . . . I have taken things too heavily. I'm going to be quieter & funnier. After I marry you, which I am pretty sure I will. I *won't* look upon it as an experiment, a peril, a task, or a doubtful enterprise, but as a simple thing, like moving out of the Algonquin. . . . I thought it was impossible to get out of there. It was easy. If we were the most miserable persons in the world we couldn't be half so miserable together as we have been apart. . . . I wouldn't make things difficult. After all, you have never been married to me. I would marry very nicely, surprisingly nicely, without ranting or anything. . . . I can't imagine living with anyone else. It's simply you, as you are—everything you are—that I want to be with. . . . You are the main person in my world. . . .

Who said you'd have to look after me? I didn't. Only about laundry and dentists' dates, not about work or life or fun or strength in sickness. . . . I don't really ever whine, I shout. That's better, but the shouting and the tumult will die. This place has helped me already to see things straight. I'm never again going to let lawyers & taxes & [John] McNulty & my family & Tony's & the Algonquin get me down. Even when they did I wrote & drew more stuff for the

NYer than anyone else. I'm a great big brave man and rather nice looking as you can see when I shut my mouth.

>With love and assurance,

>Jim

🐦 🐦 🐦

Wednesday<br>[Undated, spring 1935; from Foord's]

Dear Honey:

I have not only got away from New York but from writing, and it's bad to think I'll always have to get back to *that*, anyway. But I'll want to, finally. . . . Excuse the lack of that certain artificial style I usually use (in which I would never use "usually use" together) as I have let it go with everything up here.

It's nice here, the place, the people, the country. I have gained 2 pounds and feel better than I have since June-November, 1918, already. I do not accept that lank, sick, nervous man who for years wandered from the N. Yorker to the Algonquin to Tony's. I don't accept the things he said or did. I never want to see him again. I don't marvel that you & everybody else avoided him.

I go to sleep at 10:30 & up at 7.45. Long walks, lots to eat; and my mind is slowly getting back to where it belongs. I don't miss drinking at all—as if there had never been any such thing as drinking. My nervousness is wearing away, with slight reactions such as now when I try to make sense in writing, but that's natural. The state I was in, I can see, was not only awful but perilous. I'll be saved in the nick of time. I was writing & drawing on sheer nerve force or something. The humor was purely mechanical like a six-day rider sleeping as he rode. . . . I'll never stay so long in NY again. I dread coming back to the income tax, the [divorce] court judgments, the grind for money, but I'll be able to do it when I do.

. . . I'm a little drugged by the peace & quiet, the release from that hell down there where no one can, or has, lived a decent, motivated life of which he can be proud. Your "living from day to day" is not so good as I thot it was when you said it. It's another escape mechanism, another justification for a life without beauty, purpose, or meaning & I want you out of it, too.

. . . Don't tell me about any people except yourself. Keep well & sober. There's nothing in drinking & carrying on. There's a purpose in life.

Have faith in Ohio.

>As always (only better)

>Jim

❧  ❧  ❧

*[Undated, probably spring 1935;*
*handwritten from Foord's]*

Dear Honey: . . .

You'll love it (ah, but for a day!) up here. It's like a Longfellow Inn, only moderner and stone-&-stucco. The living room is 42 x 42 and its windows look out on a lovely sweep of valley now cut by a tumbling stream of melted snow . . . (If the mountains of Nebraska look like a woman's breasts it is unfortunately true that under certain lights the far Catskills look like monteo veneris shaved for an operation . . . ).

The food is excellent, the rooms bright and easy, the people easy; the woods and cascades and cliffs make you silent like stout Crotz (who would have run some of the fat off his adventurous ass up here). There is no vista in Tony's and where there is no vista the people perish.

. . . Perhaps no one ever gave a clearer insight into her strange and misty intentions than you did in the fading days of the old year when you told Ed you were going to marry me, but discussed a trip to Europe with Willie. And yet you could "break with" . . . Willie easier than Ed, and make up faster. Do you suppose I am finally getting a rounded picture of your nature? A person has to pick up clues about you, the way they do in mystery stories. Put mine all together and they do not make much sense. . . .

I have been studying philosophy here, as god is my judge, with books and encyclopedias and dictionaries all around me. . . . Hence your line about only egoists want to reproduce their kind annoyed me. Did you ever encounter an egotistical rabbit? . . .

How about the egoism of wanting to be the last of the mad Honeycutts? . . .

Real egoists want to live alone, and die alone. Like Shelley, they want their ashes cast away over the ocean when they are dead. I want to be, in death, just as much a part of the world as Wordsworth's Lucy when she died:

> No motion has she now, or force;
> She neither hears nor sees;
> Rolled round in earth's diurnal course,
> With rocks, and stones and trees . . .

But, for your contentment I'll say this: egoists are okay. What would we ever do without you?

Until Saturday, my
> Violet by a mossy stone,
> Half-hidden from the eye,
> Fair as a star when *only one*
> Is shining in the sky.

James . . .

      🙟  🙟  🙟

*[Undated, spring 1935; handwritten while at Foord's]*

Dear Honey,

The grand thing about this place is the discipline. Not strict or rigorous, but gently firm—the hours, the meals (including a quiet tea time), the walks, the baths, the massages. It makes the rusty wheels of my mind begin to turn in rhythm again—old thoughts and plans and ideas fall into line; I can think, already, straight again. Before, it was just a jumble out of which came all kinds of detached, unconnected stories and pictures. From the Japanese Navy piece to the Wanderer piece—and what a symptomatic, tight, egocentric, constipated piece that was! (But good, technically). I wonder at it and at its acceptance by editors instead of its rejection by doctors.

I'm not completely whole yet—but it takes time. I'll always have to fight to hold what I get up here, but I believe I will, even in the welter of obligations (which first cracked me up). You see, I'm still thinking about myself a lot but that will wear away, too, to normal, which is high for me. I can't ever be a strong, silent type—a banker or a truck driver (any more than you could be a banker's moll.) But I'll get my feet on my own ground, which, in its way, is solid ground. Such men take some looking after, but not enough to spoil them. I have thought about your dilemma (did you know you had a dilemma?) Your dilemma is that in every way except intellectually you need a banker. As you have said, you need someone to look after *you* (some banker) being in no shape to look after anyone else (some writer). But there you are, caught between the two. Your emotional nature, however, follows your intellect (which is bad for the happiness of the banker). . . . I think that the theoretically dangerous imminence of marriage to me a month ago set you to thinking (and hiding away). You don't like doors closing or arms opening. . . . This is the last time I will ever talk or write about us but after all I didn't answer your question and it keeps popping up in the idle hours.

The only test, for you and me . . . is one of time, and I mean time after I am divorced. . . . I think that within six months after my decree you will be married. (There was just a knock at the door. It was my masseur, walking companion, and pal, Mr. Reiderson, a Norwegian of perhaps fifty, ruddy, gentle, and a swell guy; also, I found, an extremely well read man with a good mind. He walked me 2 miles the afternoon I arrived. I had stayed up all night Saturday so as not to miss the train—it's a long, restless trip, with a change of trains. He thought I was a good walker—"with the build and practise of it" as he said. I think he had genuine admiration when I said I hadn't been to bed. The next morning at 9:30 we did five miles in snow. He doesn't seem to think I need anything but a return to regular hours. Physically, I amaze myself. Most of the wrecks that come here have to be built up slowly to five miles and they end exhausted. I have gone right in to ping-pong & deck tennis, till he stopped me. . . . I can't tell you of my present loathing & dread of New York. I feel as if I had escaped from Matteawan with its crazy inmates and dreadful nights. That isn't healthy, but it's presently good. In time I'll enjoy being in NY for a while at a time, but never more than a while. I'm not emotionally strong. I'm emotionally crazy, but that will be abated with mental and spiritual strength to help it. The mind rises and falls with emotional weather. Once I get them all to working together, I'll be fine. . . . You have never really had the jims. And I don't blame you for guarding against them.

A person who can be emotionally bad can also be emotionally strong. I've been through the worst case anybody has had. I don't believe I will ever get it again. After all, I'm forty. Emotion belongs to the youngsters, like measles and whooping cough. I will be satisfied with a plain, sane, ordinary life, no far reachings, no romantic illusions, no exaggerated protests. But, I do want the peace of mind and the calm foundation that, for me, can only come with someone with whom I can share my life. Life alone to me is a barren and selfish and pointless thing. The thought of it gags me. But that's me, not you. You are, in some ways—not all—the best aloner the world has ever known. . . . In eight months you will be married. I don't know who to. The situation has nearly wrecked us, maybe it has. You were dreaming of bees four years ago, bees that I let loose (but in the dream you were also hunting a house—in Bermuda).

. . . It is still my conviction that you will marry within a month after I am divorced. After all, you can be mildly irrational yourself—you can do crazy things in a moment. But you better decide not to do anything till October, no matter how drunk or panicky you get.

> After this, no more about you and . . .
> Jim

ᶥ⸙  ᶥ⸙  ᶥ⸙

*[Undated, spring 1935; probably while still at Foord's]*

Dear Honey:

My sainted mother wrote me a peremptory letter demanding the answer to 15 questions which she set down. . . . One question was as to my intentions about you, and the real situation that exists between us. . . .

I explained that the situation was just as puzzling and incredible to us as it would be to any outsider, maybe a little more, that anybody's guess was as good as ours; that whereas I have been quite happy in my time with other women I could not say that I have been happy with you, that, nevertheless, it is my solemn conviction that I am in love with you; that I really could not say whether you were in love with me or not. That I thought you were at times, and at other times were so fed up you became physically ill and on the verge of a decline, that we were always bright and cheerful and happy in the days just after we give each other up and do not see each other; that we are a little uncomfortable together and have the goddam best meetings; that you run out on operas, wine dinners, theatres, engagements; that you spend all your time with Willie and the Hunters; that you have not given Willie a definite answer yet but have nevertheless given him more encouragement since our "engagement" than you ever had before. That you may go to Europe with Willie if we become engaged again, and that you are almost certain to run away, kill yourself, or go into a coma in the weeks following my divorce. That I have never knocked any woman down but you and that we call each other terrible names of the most derogatory sort and that you once kicked me in the stomach simply because I had broken your door down. That you would not sleep with the Lord God Almighty. That Garrick says, with tears, that you are the goddam motherly marvel of the modern world and have been sweet and kind to everybody in the city, taking them baskets on Thanksgiving Day, wiping away their tears, holding their heads when they are ill, and so on. That this I have never seen. That it sounds a whole lot to me like Huey Long describing what wonders he has wrought in Louisiana. That you tell people in Tony's your father slept with colored girls and that you will give them a smack in the puss if they won't believe it. That you are an excellent cook and housekeeper. That your panties are made of metal. That you drink like a fish and smoke like a Honeycutt and that it is gradually offsetting the effect of the alligator pears you eat. That you used to live with an untamed nurse. That you were once engaged to Gibbs. That you have, on your own admission, kissed some 200 odd men and that you know more about kissing than anybody else in the world. That, nevertheless, you always kiss with your lips closed like the top of a zipper purse. And so on. I am sure she will be pleased and send her blessings. She has always wondered why I would rather be unhappy with you than happy with somebody else. So have I.

> Trusting you are the same,
> as ever,
> jamie

*By May 1935, Thurber knew he had lost out to McKelway. Following is probably the last letter he wrote Honey before both married others.*

Dear Honey:

After as much sober reflection as an habitual rye drinker can ever have, I have come to the conclusion that any luncheon date for us would not be much fun for either one of us, and I am sure you think so, too. You have already been told all my latest jokes, etc. by those colleagues of mine whom you see (I hope they give me credit for the gags that are mine—there's been a lot of stealing of gags in this city), and neither one of us wants to talk about *us* again, as the sweet child Jesus—as McNulty calls Him—well knows. Ten million words have already been shouted and moaned on that subject; only about seventeen of which ever got home with either of us. We are both emotional adolescents about love; I never grew up fully emotionally and your emotions were still-born. You get as much satisfaction reasoning with me as you would an eighteen-year-old college suitor, and I get as much reasoning with you as I would with my four-year-old daughter. All we had together was our rather cultivated sense of the better wisecracks (which is a damned important thing, too). Once I could tell you the latest McNulty cracks, but now Johnny Parker can do it better, and I could give you the latest New Yorker cracks, but you get them from newer sources. . . .

I have ranted and raved and had middle-aged man's rye hysterics when I was with you, and you have had spinster's booze-gloom and would tell me how you had the window up and almost jumped, how you have no feeling, and simply live from day to day, how you are incapable of happiness etc. We could both get that sort of companionship in a psychopathic ward. What you need is freedom and a number of men and you have darned interesting and attractive ones, too. What I have to be is head-man. . . .

. . . I suppose I should get married and that you should never get married.

... I wouldn't try to conceal from you the fact that the final realization that you didn't want me was the hardest thing I have ever had to bear. . . . But as Meredith said of one of his characters, "his heart is not made of the stuff that breaks." . . .

I could never go to the gutter or the dogs. . . . I am too proud of myself as a man and as artist (by which I mean, as you know, a writer who has talent but so far has not done with it the things he has the ability to do. I intend to get those things done). . . .

I expect to be married in due time. I'm not in any hurry. I'm getting along fine now, mentally and spiritually. . . .

. . . I would rather you didn't let people imagine you "threw me out", but that we mutually agreed, in all good humor and with the best of feeling for each other, not to go ahead with something which was not right for either of us. I hope when we meet at parties and here and there as we are bound to that you will say hello as cheerily as I will. You need never fear that I will put on any scenes again. That's as gone as my marriage. I wish for you in real sincerity happiness, even if you now insist you can't have it. It isn't so damned hard, really. I expect to get it—at least the peace of mind and sharing of fun and trouble that is as close as we ever get to happiness. Having some one person mean more to you than anyone else and meaning more to that person than anyone else is, I believe, the best of all arrangements. . . .

    Sincerely, Jim

One other thing . . . There is only one thing I have ever given you that I would like to have back and that's the decan'ter which I gave you at Christmas time. Everything else I would appreciate your always keeping but somehow, when I bought that, it was with the feeling that someday it would be both yours and mine and in our house we would pour drinks for our friends out of it, including McKelway (who can always have a drink in my home. . . .) I have visions of people picking that up and saying "This is very nice, where'd you get it?" and I don't want my name and the intimate associations of six years to fall into the pause that follows. This may seem silly to you, but it does mean something to me. It is only that one thing. . . . I'm going to Virginia with Markey May 2 for the reenactment of the battle of Chancellorsville, on which we are both experts. We'll probably get in the battle on opposite sides. . . .

    J

*Following Thurber's June 1935 marriage to Helen Wismer, the Thurbers vacationed on Martha's Vineyard, where his friend and agent Jap Gude had a summer home. Mame Thurber visited New York to see a doctor while Thurber was still in Martha's Vineyard. Ross wrote Thurber that he had invited her to meet his wife, Frances, and daughter, Patricia, adding, "If she shows up I shall ask her to stay to dinner and lead her into conversation on the Thurber family which still baffles me."*

## TO HAROLD ROSS

*[Undated, from Martha's Vineyard]*

Dear H.W.:

I am sending you under the same cover, a series of pretty pictures, representing a great deal of labor—I blacked-in the blacked-in ones with a fine pointed pen, not having any brush save a whistbroom. I think that this streak shows me at my best, probably. I am sure you will love the Poker Series—the first two are enclosed, but I may think of more. I got the idea when I played straight draw with my wife one night and she began by getting a full house on the deal and later filled an inside straight by drawing the two cards she was hoping for—a four and a six.

I hope there is a final art conference Tuesday. If not you better just go hog-wild and hay-wire and buy a few of these, as my eye-sight is not what it used to be and very likely I have nothing more to say. It's all said, what I had left to say, in the collection of drawings. (You should see me drive my V-8 at night. I go along like a bat through molasses, seeing little old men and young women and motorcycles on the road in front of me, which do not exist. Thus I often whirl off into fields or dells or bracken to avoid imaginary objects, thus upsetting the bride somewhat, as steely-cold as is her nerve and as great as is her faith in me.

> Hoping yours is the same,
> truly,
> Thurber

I want to thank you for having my mother over. She wrote the most ecstatic letter about you and Frances and Patsy (that's what she calls her, anyway). The greatest tribute my mother can pay to any woman is to say, as she said of both your wife and mine, "she looks and acts like an actress". Her theatre-going days, you see, were ante-Talullah, and I think she has in mind such actresses as the young Julia Marlowe and such plays as "Rosemary". Anyway, it's her highest tribute.

*Thurber submitted his drawings directly to Ross and his fiction to the fiction editor. Wolcott Gibbs was acting temporarily as Thurber's editor. The "casual" Thurber is submitting is "The Departure of Emma Inch."*

## To Wolcott Gibbs

### *[Undated, probably July 1935; from Martha's Vineyard]*

Dear Wolcott:

Here's a piece. In case the fan and running water seem familiar, it's a story I've told—about my mother—but never printed. We are settled, or almost, in a cottage in Menemsha, Marthas Vineyard, Mass.—that's the full address and would like to have you and Elinor [Gibbs] come up. Let us know when. We have three bedrooms. It's a sweet place with good food and nice bathing. The Gudes are nearby. The Coates are going to visit them around the 17th. Let us know if you can come up. We'll get roaring drunk. I need the money for this piece as soon as I can get it—if they take it. I wore myself out rewriting it.

It makes a fair summer casual.

We are very happy, my wife having selected the perfect person for her. He is full of gaiety and strength and is kind and considerate at all times. She is a very fine woman herself and the two of them get along beautifully. We can only wish for you one half of our happiness, my friend.

The weather is swell. It's cool, even cold, at night.

Get away from that goddam city!

jim

&a. &a. &a.

### *[Undated]*

Dear Wolcott:

We got cock-eyed after the check came and bought a Ford. You have to have a car to get around this island since it's 17 miles to the only place where they sell liquor. I got a 1933 V8 in swell shape, for 250 bucks. This is a French machine and there are no dollar signs on it, just é ˆ à ç etc. Snooty. I mean the typewriter.

I think I've fixed this enclosed piece all right. Ross can make her live anywhere he wants to in New York but just because he never walks is no reason Emma Inch can't. Has he heard of just a-inchin' along? If 78th street isn't far enough, make it somewhere else. Maids live on west 78th and thereabouts.

Both right about the guy giving her money—I meant to put that in but forgot. It's in now.

I've changed one Turner to Thurman to show Emma got my name wrong. I am unalterably opposed to using my own name—gives a story a kind of nusty-wutsy bolgarium tone, it seems to me, full of mahafitti and onduronce.

I be god dam if I have been able to title that show piece. I've thot and thot. Their Little Hour, or Plays with Diagrams or How to See a Bad Play. I can't think of anything. I can't.

I'll be sending in more remarkable pieces as the month draws to an end. Helen and I are going to Colebrook, Conn., on the 1st. Probably won't get to town till September 1. But I'll be in there working, my friend, and the magazine will brighten up.

Give my love to all the boys who're glad I'm married and all the girls who're sad.

> Best to you and Elinor from us,
> Jim

*In September 1935, the Thurbers were living in the summer home of Helen's parents, in Colebrook, Connecticut. Thurber's submission to Gibbs is "A Couple of Hamburgers." His promised "beautiful reminiscence" is "Doc Marlowe."*

**[Undated, fall 1935]**

Dear Wolcott:

Here is another casual and although it has motoring in it, it is mainly a husband-and-wife fight piece in which any background would do. I won't do any more motorists pieces after this. I am quite sure you will like it. I suppose I am rapidly breaking down marriage in this country, but it is all observation with me, not experience. Helen, as it happens, only likes cute diners and can't stand ones at an angle from the road, but we never get bitter about it, even when hungry. Nor about my humming and whistling and singing certain songs. . . .

> I'll be seeing you.
> Love, thurber

... I have finished, all but, another casual—a beautiful reminiscence of Columbus. My friend, I shall dispatch it to you by the next mail.

I hope that this one enclosed herein can be bought without sending it all the way to Japan for K.S.W. [Katherine White] to read. What is the hold that woman has on you fellas? Goddam it, I keep needing money. Will you ask Ralph [Paladino] for me, old timer, to put all checks in the bank for papa?

I love you, Gibbs.

> Respectfully yours,
>
> Jim

*ã ã ã*

*[Undated, fall 1935]*

Dear Wolcott:

(1) in the casual enclosed here called "Aisle Seats in the Mind" I may not have exactly right my quotation of the snatches from "For He's a Jolly Good Fellow". I quote them "as everybody knows, as everybody knows". The checking department, which is full of male quartets, will know.

(2) I have been concentrating night and day on casuals since the governments, both state and national, are going to distrain me again and it is now the 1st of the month, so I need money. Any expedition of these pieces would be appreciated.

(3) Me, and some of my intimates, believe that my drawing about the dog being stuffed is as funny as the seal in the bedroom. If the argument is that there would not be a stuffed dog in the window of a pet shop, all I can say is there would not be a seal on the head of a bed, either.

(4) My wife (and I) wonders why in the Reminder List in our book department my little book [The Middle-Aged Man On The Flying Trapeze] has been consistently left out although Walker's and Markey's are kept in from week to week. I somehow, in the mood I am in, see this omission as deliberate. Walker's and Markey's books are better, I know, but it has always been a courtesy on the part of the magazine to list all the books by its staff members. It's rather late for the New Yorker to be ashamed of pieces it once printed. I know there was some indignation because I did not put in the front of my book "reprinted by permission of the New Yorker". As I have explained several times, my failure to do that was not intentional. The book has got consistently good reviews.

(5) Some weeks ago a caption I wrote for a picture was thrown out and one

written by somebody else substituted. ("He looks a little like Thomas Wolfe and he certainly makes the most of it") That kind of preys on my mind because never before have I had a caption changed on me without my permission being asked or my at least being advised of the change. Is this a new policy of the art conference? If so, this is my solemn protest against it.

(6) Out of all these silly and minor little things I have got the notion that I was being gently eased out of everything more or less. I think that would be a mistake. Is the New Yorker going to keep on its staff only men who are gentlemen? Mencken once said that no real artist was a gentleman.

(7) Will you place this document in the hands of the proper authorities? Who looks after and mollifies abused writers and artists, anyway—Whedon? Hague? Miss Johnson? Miss Terry?

(8) Love to you,

Thurber

(9) The casual called "The Breaking Up of the Winships" is as good as "Smashup" only funnier. I hope that nobody wants to know the symbolization of the rabbit in the last paragraph. If they do, you tell 'em. As Joe Cook said of Alice in Wonderland, there are some good gags in it.

(10) I used "Ella Wheeler Woolsey" intentionally in the Mary Pickford story. If it doesn't seem rational it can be changed to Wilcox (which, however, is the name of the Columbus girl you met that time). "Do you want the monkeys mounted?" asked the taxidermist. "No," he said, "just shaking hands."

(11) "Essay on Dignity" the New Yorker will probably not want (it would if I hadn't turned in 3 at once). I have headed it up so that I can send it on to Harpers for their Lion's Mouth. If you'll turn it over to Miss Terry I'll call her and ask her to send it to Harpers for me, at 49 East 33d Street.

Whatta you hiffum a mob?

jt


## To Herman and Dorothy Miller

Aug. 1935

Dear Herman and Dorothy: . . .

Helen Thurber and I have just returned from dinner at the Elm Tree Inn in Farmington, some twenty miles from our little cot. It was such a trip as few have survived. I lost eight pounds. You see I can't see at night and this upset all the motorists in the state tonight, for I am blinded by headlights in addition to not being able to see, anyway. It took us two hours to come back, weaving and stumbling, stopping now and then, stopping always for every car that approached, stopping other times just to rest and bow my head on my arms and ask God to witness that this should not be.

Farmington's Inn was built in 1638 and is reputed to be the oldest inn in these United States. I tonight am the oldest man. You know my sight of old, perhaps. I once tried to feed a nut to a faucet, you know, thinking it was a squirrel and surely I told you about the time I ruined my first wife's tomato plants by riddling the white paper sacks she had put over them to keep off the frost. I thought they were chickens pecking up the garden and I let them have it with a barrage of stones. (The faucet was in the statehouse grounds). A further peril of the night road is that flecks of dust and streaks of bug blood on the windshield look to me often like old admirals in uniform, or crippled apple women, or the front end of barges and I whirl out of their way, thus going into ditches and fields and up on front lawns, endangering the life of authentic admirals and apple women who may be out on the roads for a breath of air before retiring.

This was the worst driving experience I have had in five or six years. When I was in the O S U and drove the family Reo to dances I once drove into a tulip bed and once again, taking a girl to Franklin park, I ran into a clump of trees, and once reached the edge of Goodale Park lake, thinking it was asphalt.

Five or six years ago, when I was visiting my former wife at Silvermine, she had left the car for me at South Norwalk and I was to drive to her house in it, some five miles away. Dinner was to be ready for me twenty minutes after I got into the car, but night fell swiftly and there I was again. Although I had been driven over that road 75 or 100 times, I had not driven it myself, and I got off onto a long steep narrow road which seemed to be paved with old typewriters. After a half hour of climbing, during which I passed only two farm boys with lanterns, the road petered out in a high woods. From far away came the mournful woof of a farm hound. That was all. There I was, surrounded by soughing trees, where no car had ever been before. I don't know how I got out. I backed up for miles, jerking on the hand brake every time we seemed to be falling. I was two hours late for dinner.

In every other way I am fine. I am very happy, when not driving at night. And my wife is very happy too, when not being driven by me at night. We are an ideal couple and have not had a harsh word in the seven weeks of our married life. Even when I grope along, honking and weaving and stopping and being honked at by long lines of cars behind me, she is patient and gentle and kind. Of course, she knows that in the daytime, I am a fearless and skilled driver, who can hold his own with anyone. It is only after nightfall that this change comes upon me. I have a curious desire to cry while driving at night, but so far have conquered that, save for a slight consistent whimpering that I keep up—a sound which, I am sure, is not calculated to put Helen at her ease.

Looking back on my hazardous adventures of this evening I can see that whereas I was anguished and sick at heart, Helen must have felt even worse for there were moments when, with several cars coming toward me, and two or three honking behind me, and a curved road ahead I would take my foot off of everything and wail "Where the hell *am* I?" That, I suppose, would strike a fear to a woman's heart equalled by almost nothing else. We have decided that I will not drive any more at night. Helen can drive but she has been out of practise for some years. However, she is going to get back into it again. She can see. She doesn't care to read, in the Winsted Evening Citizen, some such story as this:

"Police are striving to unravel the tangle of seven cars and a truck which suddenly took place last night at 9 o'clock where Route 44 is crossed by Harmer's lane and a wood road leading to the old Beckert estate. Although nobody seems to know exactly what happened, the automobile that the accident seemed to center about was a 1932 Ford V-8 operated by one James Thurberg. Thurberg, who was coming into Winsted at 8 miles an hour mistook the lights of Harry Freeman's hot-dog stand, at the corner of Harmer's lane and Route 44 for the headlight of a train. As he told the story later he swerved out to avoid the oncoming hotdog stand only to see an aged admiral in full dress uniform riding toward him, out of the old wood road, on a tricycle, which had no headlights. In trying to go in between the hotdog stand and the tricycle, Thurber somehow or other managed to get his car crosswise of all three roads, resulting in the cracking up of six other cars and the truck. Police have so far found no trace of the aged admiral and his tricycle. The hotdog stand came to a stop fifteen feet from Thurberg's car." . . .

When we get to Columbus we will all get cockeyed and I will drive you out after dinner some night to Rocky Rork. It ought to be an unparalleled experience for all of us and the police.

You'll like my wife and she already knows she will like you. She is as calm as ice when I am driving at night, or as cold anyway.

> Love again,
> Jim

ia ia ia

Dear Herman and Dorothy:

What, as an old girl of mine used to say in her notes to me, in the name of Jesus Christ has happened to *you?* Or do I owe you a letter? (This girl married not only a writer but a chap who was a manufacturer of contraceptives as well, a business which my old mother once thought of going into).

Look, we're coming to Columbus for Thanksgiving and want to set aside a rip-roaring night or two with youse. . . . Why does Henry James have to be dead? Goddam it, people are always crocking off at the wrong moment.

Speaking of Henry, I went down to my first wife's home and got the set of H.J. she once gave me for Christmas and I have been reading some of the 17 volumes I never had read (all I had read was the other 17). I had never, God bless my soul, read The Spoils of Poynton. What a nicely glowing point of honor he put upon two people for giving up Love for a principle! It seems so far away in this day when we give up principles for Love—and somehow the Love they gave up seems, God help us all, rather more worth the having, and the principles not so much. He would have been most unhappy now, I'm sure, in an age when the male sometimes doesn't even take off his hat or the woman her overcoat. (In bed, of course, I mean). There's an essay in it, my friends. Apropos of the present fun that pops up out of his faint far adorations, look at this from The American:

> She came in at last, after so long an interval that he wondered if she had been hesitating. She smiled at him, as usual, without constraint, and her great mild eyes, while she held out her hand, seemed to shine at him perhaps straighter than before. She then remarkably observed, without a tremor in her voice, that she was glad to see him and that she hoped he was well.

Their candles burnt at one end and they will last the night.

. . . Max Eastman's book called "Enjoyment of Laughter" comes out soon. Herald Tribune Books asked me to review it (I've become, you shall see, a reviewer). . . . He himself made you my English teacher, confusing you with Joey Taylor. (I didn't do the book for the H.T.) You must see the goddam thing. Every now and then he says I am a fine humorist and then, to prove it, quotes, by mistake, something of White's. All very lovely.

We went to Boston last week and saw all 9 Noel Coward plays and I wrote about them, and drew pictures, for Stage. We had dinner with Noel Coward, just the three of us, a lovely time, a swell fellow. I loved his plays too, and he dashed them all off this summer.

And, I just finished for the Saturday Review a piece on a book they sent me called "Be Glad You're Neurotic". I am doing—have done four chapters already and the Nyer has taken them, an inspirational book of my own, to be called "Let Your Mind Alone".... I've had to read the most incredible crap—dozens of books like "How to Worry Successfully"—but filled with such a walking into my spider trap as you wouldn't believe. Or maybe you would.

We have taken the most charming house in Litchfield, the loveliest of towns. I would God you two were the tender apple blossom and could be shipped here in a sachet bag. We have three bedrooms, three baths, three everything. Acres of elms and maples. Across the road is the house in which Henry Ward and Harriet Beecher were born. Down the road is the birthplace of Ethan Allen. Around the corner is a house built by a Colonel Talmage of Washington's staff. In it the colonel's great grand-daughter lives, now 96. It is all the most beautiful place! You'd love it. . . .

I've joined the men's forum and am known.

In driving back from Boston, 145 miles, night hit us 80 miles away. While I drive better at night than I used to, it is still me driving at night. We made what Helen thought was a wrong turn. She said back up so we can throw the lights on that signboard. I backed, blindly, into the blackness. We hit something. It took four men with two crowbars to pry us off a bank. You would have loved it. The dialogue for a while, there in the pitch dark, was better than Coward's will ever be. We got home, somehow.

Love to you both, and we'll be seeing you.

Jim and Helen

&. &. &.

*Winter 1935–36*

Dear Herman and Dorothy:

Your very fine letter was just brought in to me (the evening was at tea-time) and I read it with delight and astonishment. The astonishment came from the fact that you actually got it written and sent off. To be sure, it was addressed: "James Thurber, 25 West Indianola Avenue, New York City, Columbus, Ohio" but it reached me on time. The delight came not only from the content of the letter but from your promise of coming here. . . . You are not going to stay at the Woonsocket Hotel as you call it—I suppose you meant the Woodstock—but at No. 8 Fifth Avenue, in our apartment, in our huge spare bedroom with twin beds, soft mattresses, bath, toilet seat, shower, windows peeking out on Fifth Avenue and the Hotel Brevoort, the usual guest room books—"The Owl in the Attic", "The Seal in the Bedroom", "Is Sex Necessary?", "My Life and Hard Times," "The Middle-Aged Man", and two albums containing the better reviews which the books have received, as well as a portfolio of photographs of the author and fan-mail from women. We will in no wise consider any departure from this arrangement. You will be shot as soon as you enter the portals of the Woonsocket by my bodyguard and sensibilities-protector, a taxi driver named Charlie Rosenberg, who carries a short length of lead-pipe as well as a pistol.

We have been lonely in our apartment since Gertrude Sayre went away. We were just saying the other night that we wish you was here. You can stay up as late as you wish and go to bed as early. Our bedrooms are so far apart we have to phone each other or write, so that it really isn't like moving in with anyone, if you dread that. Just the other evening I practised throwing the javelin in the living room and, standing at my bedroom door, I could not quite spear the guest room door. I did 67 feet, 2 inches, though. . . .

You let us know instantly when you are going to arrive and you come right down to 8 Fifth Avenue, corner of Eighth street. You have to walk up three flights, since the Rhinelanders, who own the house, lost their elevator in the market crash. We'll be there. . . .

Thanks for your sweet words about the middle-aged man hurtling through the air towards his wife's unoutstretched hands. You say why didn't I choose "One is a Wanderer"—but I did, and I guess you maybe meant "Menaces in May"? If so, I read that over and after the years it seemed a little sugary and fuzzy. I do like "A Box to Hide In" myself, but I couldn't resist drawing that dog sniffing around the box. Mrs. [Dorothy] Parker once said I should keep my writing and my pictures separate and I guess I should, only I have so much fun drawing pictures. I'm glad you liked "The Evening's at Seven" because I like it myself and so far you are the only person who has mentioned it. I've got some nice reviews particularly from Soskin in the American who came out with the truth: namely, that the book is better than "Of Time and the River", "The Green Hills of Africa", and "It Can't Happen Here". Those lads have got a long way to go, but they have promise. It's kind of funny to see the favorites that some reviewers pick. Me, I've always been strangely fond of "The Black Magic of Barney Haller". What does that prove? . . .

as ever and ever,

Jim and Helen

*In late 1935, Malcolm Cowley, editor of* The New Republic, *asked Thurber to review* "Proletarian Literature in the United States," *edited by Granville Hicks. Along with Thurber's submitted review was a nine-page letter of commentary to Cowley.*

## To Malcolm Cowley

*[Undated, probably late 1935 or early 1936]*

Dear Malcolm:

I have written, I suppose, at least fifty thousand words in my fifteen or twenty rewrites of this piece. I have spent at least fifty solid hours of work on the mere writing, perhaps twenty on the reading. It came out to be a thing I had to do, and to do right. Here is the right way I had to do it. I am sorry it is so long. . . . I have been influenced by nothing except my own feelings, definitely my feelings as a writer, possibly my feelings as a bourgeois (a hell of a goddam loose word to apply to all Americans who are not proletarians. . . .

. . . What is the essential matter with "Proletarian Literature in the United States"? . . . Nobody, reading this book as carefully as I have, can fail to see that these people are, for the most part, essentially writers. You feel that, as such, they would, first of all, like to have this be a Utopian world, as quickly as possible, in which it would be all right to write for the New Yorker. But it isn't such a world. Therefore, they go over to writing about the proletariat (about whose actions, reactions, idioms, and gestures they betray a constant pathetic ignorance) and because they *have* to do this rather than *want* to do it there arises bitterness, anger, and, of all things, this curious wail and plaint against the sex life of the bourgeois. John McNulty, an old newspaper friend of mine, discussing here the other night the farmer and the city man said "Hell, for one thing the farmer knows the city man has better women than he has!" For one thing, I'm afraid, the proletariat writer and critic believe the bourgeois has lovelier and more passionate women. . . .

Now, I don't by any means go fully over to the side of the Freudians. They've missed a lot. But, just as you must, so do I know that dwelling on sex differences, hurling sudden sex challenges, is likely to be based not on intellectual opinion, not on ideology, not on dialectics, not on class feeling, but on plain personal intimate and private disturbances. It is, of course, a thing that none of us can really get at. I happen to know a lot of bourgeois people, and especially a lot of bourgeois writers, but I don't know how I'd go about finding out whether their sex life and ideology is really this or that. I don't think Freeman, not having my advantage of acquaintance and friendship, could come as close as I could. Well, then, he bases it on books? On things like O'Hara's "Butterfield 8"? I believe he does. But what, then, are you going to do about Chad Newsome and Madame de Vionnet in Henry James's "The Ambassadors"? What about Jean Stratton Porter's "The Harvester"? What, even, about "My Antonia" (dismiss it, and all the rest, except "A Lost Lady"?). The field is so wide, the writers, the characters, the regions, the feelings are so diverse: and the nasty taunt of the Freemans is so narrow and tight! And on what persons, what characters, what writers, does Freeman really base his challenge that *all* the bourgeoisie are merely lechers and Narcissists? Just what is the difference, sexually, spiritually, between him and me, since we are both writers? . . .

. . . I am not really worried or broken, as the boys would like to think. I have probably more fun than most people. I don't think the revolution is here or anywhere near here. I believe the only menace is the growing menace of fascism. I also firmly believe that it is the clumsy and whining and arrogant attitude of the proletarian writers which is making that menace bigger and bigger every day. They won't compromise, they won't debate, they won't listen, they just annoy and disturb people. They have made a god-awful mess of Scotsboro but, like the little boy who owned the baseball bat, they won't get out of the game. Communism, and literary proletarianism, lose friends every day. Why, in God's name, can't they have one or two likeable, genial, humorous, natural human beings to espouse their cause? Why is it that people like Cantwell and you and Coates just cannot fully bring yourselves to going over completely? Well, I'll tell you: Bob, being a sound and sober thinker, is no more sure than I am that fascism in this country would be any worse, if as bad as, Communism. Cantwell, being an admirer of and student of Henry James, knows he could not burn James's works for all of the Communist principles in the world. You, being a wise and philosophical man, know that leftism often means a mean, tawdry, and stupid viewpoint; you know that there can be no sharp line drawn between the worker and the bourgeois in this country—that often the bourgeois is right and the worker wrong; you know that, in friends, in home, in family, in parties, you have had more real and genuine fun with the non-proletarian writer or the partly proletarian writer than you can ever have with the Freemans and the Golds. You know, whether you say so or not, that Cantwell and Coates and even myself . . . are not only better company but sounder Americans than the ranting writers for whom you write a poem to go on the back cover.

Well, that's all this time.

> Love and kisses to you and
> the wife and the baby, and
> if they were only starving
> wouldn't that be realer and
> better?

## To the E. B. Whites

*[Undated, probably August 1935]*

Dear Katharine and Andy:

I suppose that was the first successful call ever put through from Winsted 334—Ring 5 to Sedgwick 30—Ring 3. No wonder we got cut off. Not since they shot McKinley had there been such a to-do over the phones as when I tried to resume connections. I talked with four operators, Miss Tynan (there had been an old abandoned call in from her), Manhattan operator No. 73, and a chap named Floyd Bullsware, who was trying to reach Old Orchard about a plane or something. Seems like a nice fella. I was a little nervous about the call and am still afraid I shut Katharine off. I was lying on a chaise-longue in my Japanese lounging suit at the time and let pencil, paper, and map fall behind it, so since I wanted to talk with you, too, I got all snarled up. . . .

. . . Helen and I have been having a lot of fun. We had to buy a car in Martha's Vineyard because you simply couldn't get around to the beach and places without one—you were marooned. Jap had an old Packard he bought at a rummage sale but we could hardly keep calling on them. Before we got the car we had to walk to their house, half a mile away. I picked up a Ford V-8—a 1933 they told me—but it turned out to be a 1932—the year that ate up the oil like a baby eats mashed bananas. It had only gone 23,000 miles, though, and in the 2500 I have driven it the engine has held up swell. I have to get oil every 100 miles but I get 15 miles on a gallon of gas. The engine has a lot of pep and pickup and is nice to operate. I drove it around the vineyard for three weeks and got back into my old easy driving style, reminiscent of the days when I was the terror of the roads in Ohio and my mother wouldn't drive with me because I went around the wrong side of streetcars and shouted at the motormen. I find that I am just as natural born a driver as Morris Markey, Public enemy of the Highways No. 1. We left the vineyard on the last day of July on a boat at 6 A.M.—got up in pitch darkness, groped down some coffee, and were off. We got off at Wood's Hole and drove to Colebrook, which is 175 miles from there. That was my first long trip ever (it ain't long to me now but it was then). I made it in six hours, and we had to drive through Providence and Hartford. Bob Coates had told me that Providence was the damndest city in the country to drive through, what with trick light signals, twisting streets, etc. I made it gracefully and calmly. Last week we drove over to Newport for the tennis there, and once again took Providence and Hartford in our stride, and came back that way, so I have no fears left. Didn't so much as collide with a bus full of school-children.

I got my license in Danbury, and having a license made me feel easier in my mind. I am an Ohio boy driving a car with Massachusetts license plates and a Connecticut driver's license, up to Maine, but I may be able to explain that if I am asked to. It does sound evasive or something.

. . . I have got two casuals done—one that you saw and one that was really good about a husband who is afraid to drive the car and then gets so he isn't afraid. It's called "Smash Up"—which has a symbolical connotation.

I weighed 164 pounds the last time I was weighed—which is six or eight more than I weighed before I was married and more than I ever weighed before. My lovely charming and noble wife has gained only one pound, but she is younger than I am. Did I tell you that I suggested calling our cottage at Martha's Vineyard "The Qualms" but Helen said she hadn't any and I said I hadn't either—and we haven't, either—so we just called it Break Inn, since once Mrs. Max Eastman came and stole half a bottle of rye and a honeydew melon.

The first two months of our wedded life has been serene and fine. It took me just forty years, six months and sixteen days to arrive where I should have been when I started. The hazards and honeycutts along the way were rather disturbing for a time, but all that is a faint mist far behind me as I roar along at fifty miles an hour, passing the mckelways and shouting at them to get over. It will amuse you to know that when we arrived at Matty's Vineyard, the only cottage available was the one Honey and Ed Angly and I had occupied last year, in a perfectly stainless (at least as far as I am concerned) but confusing (to the neighbors) way. I told Helen when we looked at it the quaint and tortuous story of its previous occupancy; but she took it like a good sport with a laugh—she always referred to it as the Old Honeycutt Place. (Ann Fordyce had stayed in it a little while too in those hectic days of 1934). But she liked it and I did, too, and we had a nice time there, without any ghosts from the past to haunt us. (We got a lovely note from Ann F. asking us to come up and have Sunday dinner with her at her new house in Southport some time).

Except for these private notes I am making, my past has long been decently and thoroly buried. Ahead of us stretches Route No. 1, clear and long and curving (I hate straight roads). There is the promise of elms and unexpected lakes and mountain coolness over the rise. You'll find us an agreeable couple. We hardly drink anything at all any more. The hold of 21 and Tony's has been broken, headlock though it was.

Jap had a hell of a time driving his Packard to the Vineyard. It is a sedan about five years old and it heated up on you so that hot water spurted out from the radiator cap and splattered the windshield. It took him 13 hours to drive to the island because he couldn't go more than 30 an hour. That got him to the Vineyard after dark and it is a mass of narrow faint country lanes, intertwisting, dying out, wandering off into dumps and sumac growths. . . . He had a hell of a time finding his own house. Joe McElliott was with him but he was no help because he had passed out from whisky. In the back seat was the baby's play pen. Jap had to hold that up off Joe with one hand and drive with the other. "Turn the light out whenya leave a room," Joe would growl whenever he did come to, and then go back to sleep again.

Welllllll-l-l, ten feet from the back door of the Gude cottage is a stone wall, about three feet high, the top of it flush with the backyard up onto which you drive. Jap went right on over that wall. There he was, finally at his own house after hours of struggle and cursing and sweating and despair, and he crashed within fifteen feet of the cool sheets of his beddy-bye. Jap got out and surveyed the damage. The two front gasket-heads had been shorn off like butter, the pan-drain and baffle-board were crushed in like berry-boxes, the universal joint had been driven completely through the bearing-discs and into the crank-case shaft. The borings were torn loose, one differential wheel had been snapped off, and a connecting rod had bent up in such a way that it pressed on the klaxon button and kept up a continuous shrieking. "Go sleep now. Shutta door now," said Joe and made himself more comfortable, at a list of 33 degrees. Jap sat down on the ground and cried. He actually did. You can't blame him.

And Jap is one of those calm men equipped with non-crying devices and tear-wipers.

I told him that it would have been worse had somebody emptied out the kerosene from the kitchen stove into a bucket and had the car caught fire and had he run into the kitchen, seized the bucket and, thinking it was water, doused it on the Packard. It did not cheer him up. His car was out of commission for ten days. They had to send to Detroit or someplace for gaskets, wheel-ratchets, and a new pan-drain. Some of the parts such as the screw-bevel on the differential shafting—which had been wrenched loose—had to be specially made, since there are no parts like that in stock any more for the 1930 Packards.

But I don't know why I am telling you everything I know when I am going to see you. I'll only tell it all over again. I hope you forget how it came out, then you won't be bored.

Love to all.

Jim and Helen

# the
# TRIUMPHANT YEARS

## To the E. B. Whites

*[Undated letter from Bermuda, probably April 1936]*

Dear Katharine and Andy:

It was fine to get the little woman's letter today which certainly contained a lot of news in two pages . . . we read it just before dinner. I wouldn't have been able to read it earlier because last night we started with Manhattans at our little cottage and then went dancing at the Bermudiana with Ronald and Jane Williams, two lovely youngsters I met when I visited the Sayres here. He edits the Bermudian magazine. Jane is one of the world's prettiest girls (Helen says I kept telling Jane last night she was the world's most beautiful girl.) We sat up all night and drank Scotch—the first time we have misbehaved really . . .

Helen has put on five pounds (she weighed almost nothing when we came here) and she looks better than ever I saw her. So do I. We are both tanned . . .

The Williamses—he's 28 and she 23—are the sought-after people down here. They usually have a writer in their home, which is tough, but they like it. Sinclair Lewis is one of their great admirers and we all went to dinner with him one night. Your dinner with him, my sweets, was nothing. Nothing. I'll tell you about it later. We decided, though, that he would be quite a swell guy sober. Maybe because he can, and did, recite most of the Owl in the Attic. The only drunken writer I ever met who said nothing about his own work and praised that of another writer present. He was poured onto the boat that took him home. He did one swell thing: he brought down here the 83 year old mother of his secretary, paid her way for two weeks in fine style. She was a wonderful old lady who had never been out of Rutland, Vt. before. Lewis went into a church with her, and knelt down when she did (and he brags about being the world's leading atheist). He was extremely fine with her and I liked him for it.

I wore my mess jacket last night and looked cute, my friends. I bought it a year ago and never wore it. My hair is turning as gray as an Ohio woman's past. Andy once said I looked like a third-rate British novelist in a dressing-gown when my hair was long. I don't know what he would think I looked like in my mess jacket. It didn't hike up in the back or anything, though. I weigh 165 now. . . .

. . . One woman, an admirer of my works, told us how she also enjoyed the Morris Markey reporter piece on the mountain girl [written by Thurber]. My life is like that, my beauties. Whereas I usually get from one to seven letters about every casual, I did not get a single letter about that piece. Maybe Markey did. I did get a nice note from of all people Dorothy Canfield Fisher, complimenting me on my "keen and penetrating" review of Proletarian Literature in the New Republic. She said she would have liked to be the author of it. She is an Ohio State woman, her father having been once president of the university. I got $35 for the proletarian review and spent weeks on it, but I enjoyed doing something different for a change. . . .

Ada has a tennis court, on which we played ten sets in two days, me cursing every second stroke, for I never played before. I got 5 games in the ten sets by some miscues . . .

Helen says I have used too many "my pals" etc. in this letter, so you can cut them out. She is always right.

I must tell you a lovely story about the Governor of Bermuda, Sir T. Astley Cubitt whose incumbency here just ended after 5 years. I ran into him first with Ronnie in the bar of the Yacht Club, an exclusive place in Hamilton. I was delighted with him because he is the perfect type of English military man. He is six feet four with great moustaches and beetling brows (you know, beetling brows—they say Waterloo was won on the beetling brows of Eton), straight as a ram-rod (how do you like my freshly turned similes) looking a little like Kitchener and a little like Pershing. No dogs are allowed in the Yacht Club, except his two dogs, which look like him and act like him . . . His wife once asked him to carry down from upstairs a priceless Ming vase (probably a Chung vase, but Ming is all I know). The old fellow limps slightly, from a war wound, and half-way down the steps, in the presence of his horrified wife, he slipped and came down feet first, but miraculously held the vase safely in his arms. Bumpity, bumpity, bang! down he came, twelve or fourteen steps, finally landing at his wife's feet, the vase clutched to his great chest, unharmed. "Mercy, Astley!," cried his wife, "You might have *broken* that *vase!*" Astley got to his feet, unaided, drew himself up to his full height and, without a word, *wham-bang!* he dashed the vase to the floor at his feet, bursting it into ten hundred million pieces. Isn't that beautiful? . . .

To revert to tennis a second . . . I am much better every time I play. Helen is really very good, although she hasn't played for ten years. She used to win cups and things. She trimmed the panties off papa, too. Once in a while I got in a fine forehand drive down the line. But in making a backhand I look and act like a woman up under whose skirts a bee has climbed. I will get over this. I must get over it.

I got the proofs of the Where [Are They Now?] stories, two of them, and will send them back with this first boat . . . I want to thank you for getting some action on those pieces. I was pretty gahdam low about it all when we came here, because I thought nothing would ever be done . . . I signed the piece . . . Jared L. Manley for no sane reason. There ought to be another name. I don't want mine used because as I have said I don't feel I have a right, or would want, to take full credit for pieces on which Kinkead and others have done so much work. Please see to it that Kinkead knows how fine I thought his reporting and writing of the last four pieces I got was. It was one of the best jobs ever done around there, and I want him and Ross to know that I appreciate it . . .

You need have no fear that I will keep the pieces going. I think I have showed I will. I enjoy doing them, especially now that I know they are going to be printed. Ross says he is going to pay Talk rewrite rates on them, and I suppose that is all right but I have spent on each of those stories from four to ten times as much work as I ever put in on a Talk piece . . . The thing is a very special job, and requires a very special way of doing. Maybe, in view of this, I should get $10 a piece extra, or something. It is not really Talk rewrite . . .

Give my best regards to everybody, and kiss Ross. He is, as my mother said, a mighty splendid man and, as his mother said, I hope some day he will become connected with the Saturday Evening Post. He deserves a future and I think he will go far.

> Special love to you both, from both of us.
> Jim & Helen

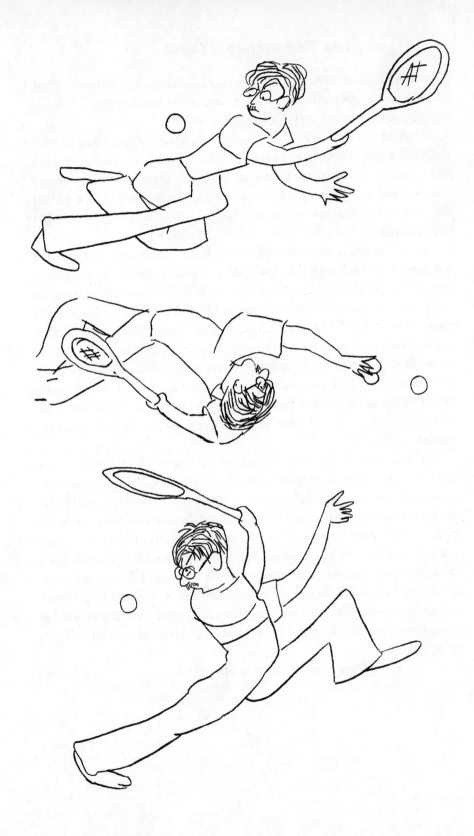

## TO WOLCOTT GIBBS

*[Undated, probably spring 1936, from Bermuda]*

Dear Wolcott:

I called this casual originally "The Cocktail Problem," which it can be changed back to, although I like this title. I realized that I was up against Ross's strange antipathy to anything about liquor, and I have accordingly and deliberately made it plain, for his benefit, that not all cocktail drinking is wild or prolonged. He once said to me "Eighty percent of the people I know are sound about liquor." I have never forgot that. Two things about it impressed me deeply, the utter conviction with which he spoke, and the complete untruth of the statement.

I really believe this piece should not disturb him. After all, it is based on an actual question-and-answer in the papers, thus coming under the Answers to Hard Questions thing.

I wish they would put it thru kinda fast for me, because I am running low on money.

This place is indescribably lovely, indescribably lovely.

> Yours,
> Jim

As for that drawing of the man and his wife in the bar and the two other women dressed identically, I don't know what it means exactly either. The hardest question I was ever asked was how could a seal get into a bedroom. I didn't know the answer to that either. Life, however, has a way of following my art. Seals keep people awake, a man shoots his wife in his sleep, both of which I had done. In a short while two women, dressed alike, will corner a man and his wife in a bar, probably Bleeck's, and the wife will be dressed like the other two women. I am minded at this point of something Mrs Parker wrote in her preface to the Seal in the Bedroom: "Mr. Thurber . . . deals solely in culminations. Beneath his pictures he sets only the final line. You may figure for yourself, and good luck to you, what under heaven could have gone before, that his sombre citizens find themselves in such remarkable situations." In my own preface to my next collection of pictures I am going to deal briefly with the age-old problem of how far, if at all, a picture has to be explicable. I think it is probably wrong to try first to figure out, next to laugh or not to laugh. Not just any jumble of characters in a unique situation is funny, but one of my men, plagued always by one wife, who finds himself, somehow, confronted with three, is funny to me. I'll admit that under the weight of examination, the first quick ridiculousness of the situation breaks down, as everything does under the weight of examination. I often wondered if they ever printed the picture about which Ross so soundly asked "Which elephant is talking?" I imagine they flung it out. Alice after all had the only answer when, having said they would talk only about things beginning with M, she was asked why, and said why not?

Well, see you soon. Keep sober, keep happy, keep going.

Jim

Or maybe it wasn't Alice.

## TO THE E. B. WHITES

*[Undated, July 1936, from Colebrook (Winsted), CT]*

Dear Andy:

Ain't heard from you yit but pears like you're busy in yer garden. The corms are gittin our thrips already, but none of the thisbies has yit bin torn from the zatches. The gelks are in the pokeberries agin, though, and grandma has lurbs in her hust. Look out for drebs.

We're going up to Vermont and Canada in a week, to call on Helen's sister and the quints [Dionne quintuplets].

Look, I couldn't agree with you all the way on the changes you made in my Howard Scott piece. I wish I could of talked it over with you. I knew Scott, too, and followed the business. I can't agree that people saw "death and destruction" in Technocracy. Of course, by that expression you intentionally exaggerated, as you did by saying the "multitudes were frightened and appalled". Everyone I have consulted with on the subject thinks the multitudes were perhaps a little worried, but mainly amused, after all. Actually, I don't believe the multitudes ever gave it much thought. I don't think it ever reached the importance generally that your slant on the lead gave to it, any more than Humanism did. From where we sat, in Scott's headquarters, it was hard to get the country-wide slant, but I saw Time's pieces on it and they played it amusingly down, as did several other magazines. It never reached serious critical attention in the standard magazines I saw. Scott was debunked so soon. Hence, without knowing who made the changes in the piece, I changed some of it right back, raising hell with Ross for keeping a story four months, then sending me the proofs the day before the office closed, marked Rush. Somebody probably meant to show it to me before, but, like so many things down there, it slipped up. I am a little touchy about these pieces because I have done them with a hell of a lot of thought, research, and care. I certainly don't object to your helping on them, but I object to Ross's not letting me know. I left in some of your lines, they were better than mine but I couldn't see the "death and destruction" even as hyperbole.

Anyway, let's hear from you.

Love to all.

Careful of grebs.

Yourn,

Jim

*Smith Hill Road, Winsted*

&a   &a   &a

*[Undated, summer 1936, from Winsted, CT]*

Dear Andy & Katharine:

Well, we made it. At 164th Street the radiator began to steam. It turned out water was getting into the oil, lots of water. I kept filling the radiator and changing the oil. I abandoned your carefully drawn route for the only one I feel at home on—via Hutchinson River parkway. I find out all drivers take a different route to reach the same place. Bob has one, Cowley has another, you have another. Bob says yours is not as good as his, you say mine is not as good as yours; I stick to mine, because the only sure way I have of reaching Ridgefield is to turn right, left, right, and left through New Canaan, coming out behind a car barn onto a road only I ever travel. In Greenwich (this was Sunday) I could sense bearings frying, but could find no mechanic—mechanics don't work on Sunday, there's too much to do. I put in the sixteenth quart of oil and the 20th gallon of water and we were off again. I reached the [Bob] Coates' house exactly six hours after we left 85th avenue, travelling mostly at 22 miles an hour to keep the water from boiling over and the gaskets from frying. Only a Ford could have made it. I took the car to Bob's favorite garage man who worked on it all Monday and Monday night till 10 changing an engine head, finally discovering the whole block was cracked. The block was cracked. This is what carried off Coolidge. They told me I couldn't run the junk pile to Winsted, 40 miles north of Bob's, but I did.

Took it to my garage man in Winsted Wednesday, another garage man you can trust. Traded it in for a 1935 Ford V8 Tudor Sedan, a sweet little car. Ran it all day Thursday, took it to Hartford this afternoon, Friday, and now have Conn. registration, license-plates P 976, and my renewed driver's license. . . .

I am planning a little piece, setting down all the ten or 12 best known parts of an auto and then giving the Sedentary Writer, or Thurber, definition of what he thinks they mean. Manifold is one of my favorites. The block crack ran right through the manifold, which is a triplicate sheet of asbestos between the engine and what the engine rests on to keep the chassis from scorching. I shall deal with transmission, differential, cam shaft, carburetor, etc. in the same way.

We are very happy and calm here in Colebrook. It is a truly lovely spot, for miles and miles and miles. My favorite part of the world. The place E.L. Marius was looking for but never found. (I'm glad he didn't). . . .

I hope you all got up there all right and that Katharine's throat is all cured by now, and all your other pains and ills and worries gone. . . .

Helen sends her best, and you have mine. Write me about your life.

    with love,

    Jim


The strange saga of James Grover still grows, however. . . .


*Thurber was covering tennis for the* New Yorker.


                                    *[Undated, probably August 1936, from Newport, RI]*

[To the Whites]

I made it all right.

Helen and I have had quite a two weeks. We been in Conn, N.Y., Vermont, New H., Maine, Mass., Canada, and Rhode Island. Had a big night with [Frank] Sullivan in Saratoga. Then drove up through the Adirondacks and ferried across Champlain and drove to Craftsbury Common, Vt., where we stayed a week at an inn, three miles from where Helen's sister and her husband have a camp for kids. Then a swell drive through N.H. to Quebec. I remember a drive with you and Jim Wright through Canada. From the border up it's all flat, dusty country, with sometimes 20 miles and no sign of a service station or anything. About four hours out of Quebec we came upon a car completely turned over and tossed up a hill at one side of the road. There were a dozen cars there but it was father Thurber who had to take two women and a girl of six to a French doctor in a French village two miles on. It's amazing how morbid and ugly the sight of people at an accident is. It was a miracle but nobody was more than shaken up, except the child had a bump the size of a baseball on her forehead. When I got to the Dr's house—a Dr. Brochu—he had left for the accident. There was only a French maid there. I swung into my French for the first time in a long while. It creaked but I got along.

There had been two men in the car, too. What happened was that one of them had surrendered the wheel to his wife, so he could rest up a bit. He rested just about 28 seconds. It's a tough road to drive because it's so straight, so dusty, and full of hard, quick jolts owing to a rough surface. I gripped the wheel so hard my fingers were calloused and stiff. (You know what I mean about a straight road being tough. Give me long slow curves any time, baby.) God knows what the woman did. All she would say to me was "I couldn't get it stopped." That was obvious. . . .

We stayed in Quebec three nights and then drove down to a place called Parlin House, about 25 miles inside the Maine border. A lodge for hunters and fishers on a lake. It was very nice. On the way we had seen a slick roadster with both back wheels wrenched off. My God, people are crazy. We've driven 1700 miles since Winsted without any trouble. It takes concentration. I think most people let go for a fifth of a second and whammy. . . .

We passed somewhere to the west of you. I wanted to make Boston before dark—it was 275 miles from Parlin House—and we got there at 7 p.m. Then we drove down here, a swell drive. We've had a lot of fun. Some time I'll tell you about St Anne de Beaupre. The tennis is next week here. Then we go over to Matty's Vineyard for three days and back to Boston for the doubles there; then Forest Hills and back to Winsted, unless I go to Hollywood. Sayre wrote he expected to come east this month, but Helen read in today's paper where he signed up to adapt a picture for Ann Shirley. Whenever I realize that George Kaufman beat me to a movie star's admiration I begin imagining what I could do. It's hard to imagine Kaufman taking his shoes off in a boudoir. He looks so permanently clothed. I got some kind of an offer from MGM but asked a thousand a week and haven't heard since. I don't care much. . . .

When I see you I will explain why I always put the wastebasket in the bathtub before we go out to dinner. I am sure I can make you do the same thing.

        Love to Katharine and all your menage.

        Jim

                     🙠  🙠  🙠

*[Undated, probably fall of 1936]*

Dear Katharine:

   I am working away at a series of pieces which I will outline here, in the far fear that someone else might be about to do the same thing. And also to clear up any misconception of repetition of my piece on Wake Up and Live. In that piece I simply had at one chapter in one book. Since then, I have had Putnam's send me a dozen or so of the flood of books that keep coming out on how to train the mind, how to succeed, how to improve the memory, how to this and that. They are deluging the country like the sex books Andy and I stopped (you remember how we stopped *that*). In the past 3 weeks I have written first and second drafts of four pieces, the longest 2000 words, the others around 1500. In each case I take apart the phoney soundness of the inspirational books. Mine are distinctly dispiriting pieces. I think you will all like them. Anyway, I will bring to town when we come next Monday the completed first two or three. I plan about seven or eight in all.

   We are excited about the house we have taken for the winter—October to May, in Litchfield. North Street in Litchfield I have always thought the loveliest street in the world. It's half a mile long, and its outer lawns run 90 feet from the fence to the street, and it is lined with elms 200 years old. . . . It's a beautiful place and only $75 a month. Never been rented before. From our lawn we can see, at the corner of Prospect and North, the old Henry Ward Beecher home. Litchfield is to me the old flower of American life. In one of the great old white colonial houses of North Street lives the great grand daughter of the man who built it, Colonel Talmage, who was aide-de-camp to Genl. Geo. Washington. On that street was the first law school in the continent, and there studied Aaron Burr and Noah Webster. In the house of a Miss Benton nearby a date is scratched on a stone of the fireplace, the date of the birth of Ethan Allen, another Litchfield boy. It's all very exciting to a schizo who lives partly in the past. I'm crazy to have people see the place and want you to come up.

        See you soon,

        Jim

ﺒ ﺒ ﺒ

[Undated, winter 1936]

Dear Andy:

Try to get aholt of a book called "Abinger Harvest" by E.M. Forster. . . . Especially I like the piece on one Howard Overing Sturgis, an English writer, American born, who lived between 1855 and 1920 and wrote three novels. Mainly he wrote to please his friends. Writes Forster, in all seriousness: "Sturgis . . . wrote to please his friends, and deterred by his failure to do so he gave up the practice of literature and devoted himself instead to embroidery, of which he had always been fond." It's a way out, all right.

Then, further on: "I once went to Sturgis' house myself—years ago . . . My host led me up to the fireplace, to show me a finished specimen of his embroidery. Unluckily there were two fabrics near the fireplace, and my eye hesitated for an instant between them. There was a demi-semi-quaver of a pause. Then graciously did he indicate which his embroidery was, and then did I see that the rival fabric was a cloth kettle-holder, which could only have been mistaken for embroidery by a lout. Simultaneously I received the impression that my novels contained me rather than I them. He was very kind and courteous, but we did not meet again."

In later years, when somebody confuses my books with the books of Chic Sale or Thorne Smith, I will not be perturbed, but let them mistake a kettle-holder for one of my embroideries and there will be a scene. It's a rather comfortable life to look forward to. . . .

There are dozens of other pieces in the book, . . . I came across this in his piece on Mickey Mouse:

"But is Mickey a mouse? Well, I am hard put to it at moments certainly, and have had to do some thinking back. Certainly one would not recognize him in a trap."

The guy is full of swell lines.

I like this, also about Mickey Mouse: "He is energetic without being elevating, and although assuredly he is one of the world's great lovers he must be placed at some distance from Charlie Chaplin or Sir Philip Sidney." And, in discussing Mickey and Minnie Mouse as a pair, he says: "It seems likely that they have married one another, since it is unlikely that they have married anyone else, since there is nobody else for them to marry."

Well, that's all for the nonce.

Jim

*Thurber was asked to comment on a poem submitted to the* New Yorker.

*[Undated, probably 1936]*

Dear Whites:

In connection with these phrases which can go either forward or back, I am reminded of the woman motorist who could go forward or turn right and left but could not go back. To me the word "caul" as used here must have been meant for "cause" or possibly "clause"—we speak, or used to on the old Atlantic, of a man being born with a caul, or in a caul, or even with a cause, but never I believe with a clause, since clauses come only after the child learns to talk. If the author means "cave" or "Claude" he should make it clearer. If in any piece of writing half the phrases go forward and half backward, the author is surely doing no more than holding his own which, in a poem, is scarcely getting anywhere. "Out calls the night from fined deeps" seems to me clearly fuzzy, yet powerful. Perhaps he means "found" or simply "fine". I should suggest rewriting the thing backwards if I were not half persuaded that it is backwards now. Final opinion: mousey but penetrating.

> Thurber

## To Wolcott Gibbs

*[Undated, September 1936]*

Dear Wolcott:

This charming little idyll, based on the lights and shadows of our recent return to Connecticut, represents two days and a night's work in the cool September air. I don't want you guys to get the notion that I just tear these off like my drawings, and reject them the way you do the drawings (of which "There's something in the air here tonight" is one of the best five I ever did). I happen to have hit a streak of casuals and it may die out any time, probably with the first snow. Gather ye, therefore, these rosebuds while ye may.

> With my severe love for all,
>
> Jim

Please expedite payment on this masterpiece and would you ask Ralph to deposit the check in the Guaranty Trust Co for me. I'd like to have it in there by Thursday. Thanks.

I'm finishing another one, not quite the classic this is, but okay, my friend, and will ship it down tomorrow. I have notes and beginnings and missing sheets for various other casuals that I've been thinking about and turning over in my mind these several months. They may come Upon you in a flock. They can be spread over several years, if they are too many, but I would like to have them bought.

We want you and Elinor to come down to our palatial Fifth Avenue apartment and be entertained by us snootily but well, in the best Rhinelander manner (they own the house. Kip's [Clifford Orr] old girl is our maid). The other night in Reuben's we bought caviar and pate de foie gras. It's what happens when you leave the Seymour Hotel and Morton Street and get married.

> J

## To Harold Ross

Dear Mr. R:

A year or so ago, a very amusing picture of mine depicting a man saying "Good morning, my feathered friends!" to a lot of unfriendly birds was rejected on the amusing ground that in 1931 Miss Hokinson had drawn a small picture of a woman addressing some goldfish.

Nevertheless, anyone apparently can do something exactly like what I have done. Mrs. J. G. Gude, Mrs. Thurber, and a man you don't know have all asked me how come the New Yorker bought Broun's almost identical version of my somewhat famous casual "Everything Is Wild". I am now asking you. The thing has appeared in anthologies and in "The Middle Aged Man." It is pretty well known. You should only do one piece on a grouchy poker player who hates variations of the game.

Mr. [Robert] Taylor hits just as exactly on a thing I had done in the magazine, once and for all. Max Eastman quotes it in his book on humor to be published in October. It is about a man who caught tree blight and had to be sprayed. Remember? No, you forgot. But one magazine should only do that once. His limerick, I feel, was a direct steal, only he substituted an elm blight for chestnut blight.

Once in a while I think of something pretty original. How about letting me keep the credit for it? Do you mind if I send in the man-and-parrots picture again, since you seem to have let the bars down?

> Yours for justice,
> Thurber

{a  {a  {a

*[Undated, probably 1936]*

Mr. Ross: My feelings grows stronger and stronger that the Art Conference has lost its interest in, appreciation of, and ability to judge my drawings. I feel that some of the weaker ones have been bought, slowly and cautiously, and that some of my better ones have been rejected. I don't want to hand in any more drawings to the Art Conference unless those selected and those rejected are shown before final action either way to either White, McKelway, or Alva Johnston.

My respect and esteem for the separate members of the Art Conference as individuals and as writers and editors etc has never faltered, but my faith in the present Art Conference to know what is fresh or funny, after so many years at it, simply does not any longer exist. Just one new, eager, untired, unjaded face at that Tuesday table would be fine.

Respectfully

James Thurber

*Unsolicited submissions to the magazine were often addressed to Thurber by people he didn't know. "Miss Terry" was office manager and secretary to the art conference. Margaret Thurlow was a New Yorker secretary who helped Terry handle Thurber's correspondence from readers and regarding reprint requests.*

## To Daise Terry

*[Handwritten, undated, probably 1936]*

Dear Miss T:

Here are some awful bits by sad people, sent to me the good Jesus only knows why, and now sent to the hard-hearted editors for brutal rejection. Say to the sad people that I died and that it is too bad.

There are also here three spots by me. I don't know whether they will be bought or not but I wish you would say to Ralph [Paladino] that I should like to give the N.Y'er only *half* the money for the drawings they buy instead of all, in payment of my $500 debt. He'll know. If the powers agree—and by god and by jesus they betta!

Kisses for you and Miss [Margaret] Thurlow

Otto Thurber

Kiss Ralph & Ross for me, too!

## TO HERMAN MILLER

[*Undated, probably December 1936*]

Dear Herman:

I think you should have saved yourself from so much trouble by telling Phil Adams you are too close to me and my drawings to be able to talk about them happily. I don't like to think of you having to bother about me and my art; but I can't think, on the other hand, of anyone I would rather have talk about me and my art. I only wish I could be there, in the front row, with my Sunday glass eye (the one that keeps on staring even when the other is closed).

(It isn't true I ever do drawings twenty times before I submit them). (Just what is true about what I do it is hard for me to say). I think it was in 1902, however, that I did my first drawings. My father was in politics—had been all his life and although his three sons grew up to hate politics, there was a time in our extreme youth when we were fascinated by the thought of some men being elected and others defeated. So, we used to draw pictures of men and take them around and ask family, friends, and strangers which one they wanted to vote for. Each of us would draw one man for President, you see, on a separate sheet of paper, and submit the three sheets to people. I was eight years old and my brother William nine. He was at that time considered the artist in the family. He used to copy, painstakingly, the Gibson pen and ink drawings. I remember nothing about the men I drew as my candidates, but William had a man named, for no reason at all, Mr. Sandusky. Mr. Sandusky was elected President almost always over the man I drew. Mr. Sandusky had a mustache, and after 34 years, I remember him well—out of hate and envy I guess. I'll show you what he looked like.

Mr Sandusky

Now, I don't remember my own men well at all, but I imagine they are like this:

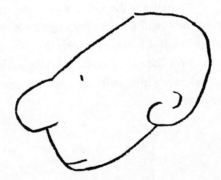

It is fairly easy to see why people chose to place the fate of the nation in the hands of Mr. Sandusky, rather than in the hands of my nameless candidate, a man obviously given to bewilderment, vacillation, uncertainty, and downright fear.

It is true, of course, as Ralph McCombs wrote in the Citizen—if it was the Citizen and if A Benvenuto is Ralph—that I used to draw in Caesar's Commentaries and also illustrated the Manual of Arms at Ohio State (usually with pictures of Mutt and Jeff). The divine urge rose no higher than that. I did pictures for the Sun-Dial when I was editor because all the artists went to war or camp and left me without any artists. I drew pictures rapidly and with few lines because I had to write most of the pieces, too, and couldn't monkey long with the drawings. . . . In those years, I was absolutely uninterested in the art, not only of myself, but of anybody else. . . .

I just made a sound which caused Helen to look up and say "That didn't sound like you; it sounded like a phone being dialed somewhere." I suppose that I am rapidly becoming, in her ears, like a phone being dialed somewhere, and I daresay that I am the only husband in the city who has been so characterized by his wife this night. It seems to me that she has enunciated as clear a definition of me and my art as anyone could think up. In "a phone being dialed somewhere" there is, I go so far as to say, the utter implication of everything I have done, and try to do.

You will see that I am not being of any help to you and that the suggestion of these things to your audience on Sunday might prove disconcerting.

Well, I had drawn pictures for years, after Ohio State, largely as a nervous gesture. The flop-eared dog grew, I am sure, out of a desire I had to baffle and annoy certain Columbus business men into whose offices I wandered. I used to fill up all the pages of all the memorandum pads on their desks with pictures of the dog. The big ears and the big muzzle filled up the pages faster, you see.

It was, to be sure, E.B. White, a man given to examining everything carefully, who first began to look at my drawings critically. Like the discovery of San Salvador and the discovery of pommes soufflé the discovery of my art was an accident. I reproduce on the next page the first drawing of mine ever submitted to the New Yorker—it was submitted by White. Naturally enough, it was rejected by an art board whose members thought they were being spoofed, if not, indeed, actually, chivvied. I got it back and promptly threw it away as I would throw away, for example, a notification from the Post Office that a package was being held there for me. That is, not exactly deliberately, but dreamily in the course of thinking about something else. In this manner a great many of my originals have been lost. On the other hand, more than eleven thousand originals of mine are on hand, in one place or another. Joel Sayre has a sequence of 34 or more called "American Marriage". I gave the Whites as a wedding present a series called "Mr. Prufrock and La Flamme." I gave my former wife thirty or forty drawings for Xmas one year (because I hadn't had time to buy her certain presents, or had forgot to). I am pleased to say that she found the present rather amusing, since every time she made a bed or opened a drawer or picked up a sofa cushion hundreds of drawings toppled out on the floor. With them, usually, was one of those old-fashioned green eyeshades, which city editors wear, or are supposed to. This eyeshade was always turning up in a clump of drawings and with it old razor blades, burnt matches, and a black dress tie. I had only the one green eyeshade but she, and the maid, finally got the idea that I had twenty or thirty. This does not give you much of a notion, really, Herman, about anything.

Now the seal drawing had been lost for some months (and with it the package at the post office) (but the green eyeshade kept turning up) when we submitted the MS of Is Sex Necessary? to Harpers and along with it the drawings. White put them on the floor in the office of the publisher and said "These are the illustrations". And thus I was first published, that is, my drawings, under the ancient and honorable and dignified seal of the House of Harper (who were so scared by their own intrepidity that they brought the book out practically without any advertising).

Well, the book took holt, as my aunt Margery used to say, and Ross began to think. He remembered the seal drawing and asked where it was. White reminded him that the art board had rejected it, along with the memo to me that "a seal's whiskers do not grow this way". "That," White said to Ross, "is the way a Thurber seal's whiskers grow". This impressed Ross so that from then on anything I drew was the way something I drew went, so it didn't make any difference. Ross denied that he had rejected the seal and the explorers. This little argument lasted for years. Well, anyway, I began drawing pictures and at first White submitted them for me, just as, at first, he went over my pencil lines in ink. It was two years before I began to draw straightaway in ink. I prefer pencil because you don't have to keep dipping it in ink or, as I sometimes do with a pen, in the ash tray, my glass of Scotch, or Helen's hand. Once, at the Algonquin, where I used to draw, I spilled a whole bottle of India ink all over the room and that very night, in going to the bathroom in the dark, I cut my forehead open, so that the room was also covered with blood. It was an indescribable shambles. I cut my forehead open on the edge of a door.

I had wished to send some other drawings to the Columbus Exhibit particularly, for its special interest, one drawn on yellow copy paper with a pencil. This one, called "Intelligent Woman" I had left half-finished and had thrown upon the floor where Rae Irvin picked it up. He liked it and gave it to me asking me to complete it. It had on it, plainly, the mark of a dusty rubber heel, where somebody had stepped on it. I did complete it, in a few minutes, and it was bought. and used. Three or four years ago I was asked to submit one picture to be hung at a show in Vienna of the work of comic artists of all nations. That was the picture they wanted. I sent it to them and it was shown in Vienna. I put on it, no value, no insurance—since there were spaces on a blank they gave me, for that purpose. It came back to me all right. . . . I had erased the heel mark with art gum.

. . . Just exactly what I feel about my Art, I can't say. I have refused to allow it to be used on sofa cushions or as ornaments for automobile radiator caps. On the other hand I have drawn a dozen pictures for the Vacuum Oil Co's advertising campaign for Bug-a-Boo (a thing like Flit) in the Saturday Evening Post. I have yet to meet anybody I have ever known, even casually, who hasn't got at least one of my drawings. It seems that at times I have drawn as many as thirty pictures for drunken ladies at drunken parties, drunken ladies whom I had never seen before but who now pop up here and there and remind me of our old intimacy.

The farther I go on, the more confusing this gets. To the hell with it, as Grandmother Fisher used to say.

Love to you and Dorothy, and write me that letter.

Jim

Helen sends love and the word that she wishes you would make a sound like someone stamping an envelope somewhere.

*Dr. "Duke" Damon, O.S.U. fraternity brother, was now the Park Avenue specialist in obstetrics and gynecology who delivered Rosemary Thurber in 1931.*

## To Virgil "Duke" Damon

*Litchfield, Conn.*
*February 11, 1937*

Dear Duke:

I wonder if you would have a moment, in between helping the increase of the population of a collapsing world, to suggest a really good eye man to me? He can be an expensive one, because I haven't got any disease that needs treatment. I haven't any million dollars to spend, but I have become a bit wary of

$10 or $15-an-examination men. Have you got anything around $50 or a hundred? I may have to have my glasses changed, and I may not. Oculists seem to disagree. I have just had three separate pairs of glasses made, none of which I seem to be able to stand wearing. You can imagine me with three pairs of new glasses and one old pair.

I can promise any eye man one of the remarkable clinical eyes of the country. All oculists have agreed on that. They start out by deciding I shouldn't be able to see anything but moving shapes, end up with me reading two lines below normal on the chart, and finally discover a tiny hole left on a lens which otherwise is covered with "organized exudation".

You see, I was shot in the left eye with an arrow when seven or eight years old, and lost that eye. Then infection set in in the other and they thought I would lose that. But it was saved somehow.

At forty-three, one naturally begins to wonder when he may have to give up the typewriter for the tin cup. And what would this world do without my drawings and writings? Save Thurber's Eye has become my motto.

I went to an eye man recently, but the fact that the lenses he thought were fine turned out not so good, and the fact that the lens I have worn for some years he thought was awful, whereas it seems to me fine, has kind of got me to worrying. . . .

. . . I thought maybe you would know the kind of eye man I mean.

. . . I would like to see you and I don't want to have to wait till I have a pregnancy before doing that. Can you drop me a brief note, giving me the name of a good eye doctor, if you know of one? I'll give you a ring when I get to the big city.

All my best, Duke,
Jim Thurber

*In the spring of 1937, Thurber covered a Noel Coward show in Boston, interviewing him for* Stage *magazine.*

## To the Herman Millers

**[Undated, probably April 1937]**

Dear Herman and Dorothy:

Why don't you answer my drawings? Here I keep sending you lovely pictures of myself and Vachel Lindsay that wonderful night at Dr. Berg's and no answer. Meanwhile, Helen and I have been going around with Noel Coward. . . . He lets people talk and is very attentive.

I am studying Colonial architecture now, and also music. The broken-pedimented round-headed sidelighted doorway, and the contra-bassoon. My dream is to sit in such a doorway, playing the contra-bassoon. God, what an instrument. Noel is studying German. I sent him a line from the chorale finale of Beethoven's fifth (or is it ninth?): So pocht das schichstal an der pforte, and the translation "Thus Fate knocks at the door". We must all study German. When Fate knocks in German, by God you hear it. . . . Certainly it is no pansy Fuller Brush man tapping. . . .

I am having a show of my drawings in London S.W.1, England during the coronation. Also one in Hollywood next month and in San Francisco in March. I have on hand enough drawings left to have several more. Do you want a show of mine? I have done, or am about to do, a picture called "Dr. Snook and Psyche" after the famous Cupid and Psyche painting.

The New Yorker gave me 100 shares of stock to keep me quiet, or shut my mouth, or something, and Helen and I may sell some of it and go to Europe in May for my show—and for other things; maybe not for the show. I went to one show of mine and that may be enough.

I sent to Bob Coates tonight a strange thing I wrote called "Toasted Susie is my Ice Cream," the god damndest thing you ever saw. . . .

> Love from Helen, and me,
> Jim

*A University of Chicago student wrote Thurber asking for his "theories or views of literature."*

## TO MR. MILLETT

*[Undated, probably spring 1937]*

Dear Mr. Millett:

No, there is no oil painting of me in existence and I wouldn't be surprised if there never will be. Max Eastman's wife started one once, in Martha's Vineyard, but nothing came of it. James Montgomery Flagg did a very good profile, in crayon, of me, but that's all. I don't think there's much about me in the usual books of reference, and, if there is, it's probably inexact. . . . No longer a member of the [New Yorker] staff, I still appear mostly in that magazine, although I have written for Harpers, the Forum, and other magazines.

My theories and views of literature vary with the lateness of the hour, the quality of my companions, and the quantity of liquor. I have a great affection for the works of Henry James and lug the 35 volumes of the definitive edition around with me wherever I go. I am interested in the writings of George Milburn, William March, Robert M. Coates, John O'Hara, Conrad Aiken, Hemingway, Fitzgerald, Edmund Wilson. I am opposed to every restriction, mould, pattern, and commandment for literature that is set up by the Marxist literary critics. A few of my special favorites in fiction are "The Great Gatsby", "Lady Into Fox", Cather's "My Antonia", "My Mortal Enemy" and "A Lost Lady", which will indicate that I like the perfectly done, the well-ordered, as against the sprawling chunk of life. I can't read Thomas Wolfe. I owe a great debt to the late Prof. Joseph Russell Taylor of Ohio State University, whose rich understanding of literature and life gave my urge to write a push and a direction. I also owe a debt to E.B. White of the New Yorker, whose perfect clarity of expression is it seems to me equaled by very few and surpassed by simply nobody. He writes the first page of the New Yorker. . . . I came to the New Yorker a writer of journalese and it was my study of White's writing, I think, that helped me to straighten out my prose so that people could see what it meant.

This is all very rapid and sketchy, and if I sat down to do it again tomorrow, it would come out very different, I suppose. . . .

Sincerely,

James Thurber

P.S. Just before Christmas I drew a picture of a solemn, frowning man sitting in a chair with his chin on his hand. A woman is saying to another "He doesn't know anything except facts." Your President Hutchins wired for it, and I sent it to him. He said in his wire that the man was "a composite of all his faculties." I'll tell him, if I ever see him, that *you* asked for my "theories or views."

## To Ronald and Jane Williams

*London, Hengland. July 11, 937,*
*(I lost a thousand years in there, somewhere).*

Dear Ronnie and Janie:

. . . We sailed from New York May 14. Who should arrive in that big city two days before, to see us off, but Joe Sayre? His first trip east in almost four years.

Gertrude followed him later, after we were gone. I understand he is now in Martha's Vineyard, care James Cagney, Chilmark, Martha's Vineyard, Mass., U.S.A., would reach him.

We've had a swell two months. Landed at Le Havre, drove ten days through Normandy and Brittany, then to Paris for three weeks, then to Calais and across to Dover, and drove to London, got lost in London, finally found our flat and have been here 18 days, having wonderful time.

We're going to Scotland in August and then back to the continent and probably to Germany, Italy, Austria, etc. We expect to be over here a year if everything goes all right back home—and over here. Wish you both were along. We've been everywhere in London and met everybody, having arrived here full of the best French wines, truffles, pate de foie gras, and brandies.

Went to Wimbledon three days—quarter finals, semi, and finals, and watched Budge knock 'em cold. . . . It cost the New Yorker 3 pounds a ticket for us. . . .

I've been writing for the London papers and a week ago I went to Alexandra Palace and did a television interview—drawing men and dogs and women with crayon on big sheets of paper. Television is far advanced here and very good—clear as a bell. I saw Budge and Parker play on a television screen— 8 x 10 inches, very interesting. My London show of pictures—which ran for three weeks—was a tremendous success, much greater than all my US shows put together. They sold 30 pictures, many of them for 18 guineas each! I was only counting on making a hundred dollars or so out of it but have already got a check for 130 pounds, with another of the same size to come. If you ever travel, have a show in London, and you can quit working for a while.

We had dinner with Charles Laughton and his wife one night and have met H.G. Wells, David Garnett, etc. and I was asked to do dialog for a Korda picture, but I turned it down. Lots of fun we've had.

> Yourn,
> Jim

## To the Ted Gardiners

*7, August, 1937*

Dear Ted & Julia:

We got to France May 20, motored thru Normandy & Brittany for two weeks, then to Paris where I drove round & round the Arch of Triumph unable to get out of 16 lines of cars. Crossed from Calais to Dover June 23, got lost for 3 hours in London. Had fine time here for 7 weeks. . . . Return to London in Sept. for week, then back to France, Italy, Germany, etc. & on Riviera I suspect . . .

> Love
> Jim & Helen

## To Daise Terry

*The drawing being questioned by the art conference, referred to in the letter below, was probably published in the* New Yorker, *October 16, 1937, captioned: "A subtle change has come over my wife, Doctor."*

*August 7, 1937*

Dear Miss Terry:

Here are two drawings. The one without a caption will probably be turned down but I don't think it really should be. However, somebody is sure to want to know what it means, etc. All I can say to that is that the wife, being in love, or having had an idea for a poem, or being pregnant, or reading a novel, or something, appears to her husband in the mysterious light we see her in here. It is, I believe, a characteristic scene in married life. The woman is not dead.

Look, I hope to God people are back to work there for everything has simply gone to hell for me. The last word I got as to deposits for me was for the first casual I did, more than two months ago. I have not heard of anything else save a deposit of $83 for tennis expenses, but no word as to how much, if any, was deposited for tennis stories, no word as to how much was deposited for second casual bought, no word of what was ever done with third casual submitted two months ago, no word as to whether drawings have been received, acted on, no nothing. Virtually no mail has arrived, except a casual from a Minna Slupshotz, which, return envelope and all, was sent on to me, since Minna has all year. Please tell them to whip into shape over there.

> With love,
> Mr. Thurber

Minna's casual is enclosed, unread. Also my Davis Cup, and final, tennis expense account.

If they don't buy these pictures, will you please have them mailed back to me . . . I've just sold $500 worth of rejects over here and the market seems endless. It's the New Yorker's fault if they won't buy em. They can hardly expect me to throw away pictures they reject with all these guineas lying around.

*◆ ◆ ◆*

*[Undated, probably October 1937, from London]*

Dear Miss Terry:

The old complainer is back again. My rejected pictures were returned with a piece of brown cardboard that didn't hold its color so that the top drawing arrived looking like a platter from which a cat had just eaten beef liver. If the magazine has laid in a supply of this liver cardboard, you will find the magazine sued by all artists who get rejections back . . . Some salesman unloaded on the purchasing. Old Miss Bendley in Purchasing knows better but she's blind now.

An idea drawing is enclosed and also a spot which you will note is inscribed to Chas Laughton, cause I drew it for him but thought maybe it'd make a spot first. In any case will you please mail it when used, or not used, to Charles Laughton, 34 Gordon Square, W.C.1, London?

The New Yorker for Sept 11 has a drawing about trains going to Litchfield which would not be terribly funny even if any trains did go to Litchfield. No trains do. I presume Connecticut's Litchfield was meant, at any rate it is the famous one. You see we-all lived there-all about 7 months and as McKelway knows we had to meet our guests either at Torrington, 6 miles away, New Milford, 19, or Waterbury, 17. It is an almost incredible circumstance that of all the famous towns in the United States, Litchfield is the only one to which trains no longer run. All the good folk there will now believe I never worked on the New Yorker like I said. I reckon the checking dept don't check captions, and anyway it isn't their fault. I want somebody to take blame down there besides checking dept. No artist ought to go batting off lines about eleven different kinds of trains going to a town which has none. The editors all knew about Litch. If the checking dept is to be blamed for this inconsiderable error, for God's sake don't tell anyone.

We go to Paris tomorrow from here after 3 months. Would have gone two days ago but lost our passport and had to go through red tape to get new one. Cost $15 and all new visas to be got. Two passports a day are lost by Yanks in London. I think ours was stolen.

. . . Kiss everybody for me.

Love,

Thurber

*ϗ ϗ ϗ*

*[Undated, probably October 1937]*

Dear Miss Terry:

Here's a spot and an idea drawing. The idea drawing, somewhat changed, was once submitted under another title, and rejected.

Mr. Thurber

Please do not let anybody paste any more butcher's wrapping paper over my captions. A hundred of my best drawings were ruined for exhibition and sale by this barbarous and needless practice. It arose out of the feeling that spies at the engravers were informing Life and Ballyhoo of our captions, in code, over the phone. This was never done. Arno etc. simply went around the night clubs blabbing ideas. Paste butcher's paper over the night clubs, or Arno. If they must cover up captions, let them erase, with art gum, the captions. Of numerous offenses we have committed against art and belles-lettres, this fiendish butcher's paper pasting was the most heinous.

T.

*ϗ ϗ ϗ*

*[Undated, probably October 1937]*

Dear Miss Terry:

Here are two drawings for the atcnfc [art conference].

One was suggested by Andy White and he should get proper fee. This is "Comb those woods!" "Comb the woods!' " was caption White suggested. I think "those" is better, but leave it up to him and the atcfn. The captions both got written in indelible pencil by mistake, but *under no circumstances are the usual pieces of vandals' wrapping paper to be pasted on them* . . . Please let the atcn know that they are not for sale if fiends wrapping paper is pasted on them. Story of this practise unbelieved in England but I keep telling it, insisting on it.

Love to all,
Thurber

## To Harold Ross

Dear H.W:

As a loving student and long practitioner of the English language, I must object to a recent manifestation of the hyper-precisionists on your magazine, including your distinguished self.

Now and then the magazine seems to go through a phase of finicky and meticulous queries on English, as the result of which some incredible changes in sentence structure are suggested. Since I never write, for publication, a single word or phrase that I have not consciously examined, sometimes numerous times, I should like to have the queriers on my pieces realize that there is no possibility of catching me up on an overlooked sloppiness. I think I can say this, without smugness, but with some fire. Because I see a tendency to regard my constructions as hastily batted out constructions. This feeling, I believe, led someone, without my permission or knowledge, to drop a comma into a sentence on page 24 of this week's issue, thus spoiling the sentence. I wrote the phrase "In this day when" and it came out "In this day, when". Now that is simply not English. For want of a better word I call that phrase an Integration, that is, it is as tight as a single word. All you have to do is to say it aloud to see that you can't say it with the comma in there. There can be no pause in that combination of words.

The New Yorkers should say sentences aloud when they are in doubt, as very often the rightness or wrongness comes out when you do that. Nobody has, fortunately, yet divorced the written line from the living spoken word, for in the living spoken word is all the color and strength and energy of the language. Mere precision according to rule of thumb is a dangerous thing, leading to prissiness, stiffness, artificiality and, worst of all, a faint violetness.

I recently wrote "This is what I can only call a paradise of errors." In the margin of my proof, it was suggested that I change it to "This is what I can call only a paradise of errors." You merely have to say that sentence out loud to see that it is not English, but sounds like the awkward sentence of a recently arrived foreigner. Again, the whole point of the thought was missed. I did not say that there is only one thing I can call this. I said that there is only one thing I can do at this moment: call it a paradise of errors. "What I can only call" is an integrated clause, abiding no possible change of words. It also has reality. It is what people say.

You recently queried a sentence of mine: "These things happen in a world of endless permutations," because it followed the citing of a single thing that had happened. The expression is, and must be, invariable in English. For instance: a man says to you "My wife had triplets today", and you say "Such things happen" or "These things happen." You do not say, "Such a thing happens". A foreigner would, but not you or myself or anyone else we know. "Things of that sort happen" would be impeccable even to the purists, even though you have "things", because "that sort" refers with a single demonstrative to the preceding incident. "These things" is a simpler and idiomatic way of saying "Things of that sort". "These" takes the place of "of that sort". Hence the structure is defensible even by a purist, granting the natural elisions, transferences, etc which are of the very blood and bone of English.

On one set of galleys of mine at least seven changes of this kind, all not only wrong, but ridiculous and bad, were suggested. Hence, having been implicitly accused of sloppiness I can only fire back that the sloppiness was on the other foot. Mrs. White thought that the sentence "None of them would be usable even if I could find them" was a plural use of "none". It's tricky, but the way you prove the singular usage here is to rephrase it this way: "None of them is usable even though I have found them."

Now, this is all very unimportant in a way, and anybody can make mistakes—and I have and will continue to make them—but to have six or seven sloppinesses found in a Ms that had none, but which proved sloppinesses in the readers, is something any writer must raise a small protest against. You see, it isn't myself you must be careful about down there, it is yourselves. It isn't the mistakes I am writing in manuscripts that will spot up the book, but the mistakes the New Yorkers will spot up the book with by changing my sentences. In other words, this phase of fine-tooth combing manuscripts seems to me likely to breed, not prevent, bad construction, indefensible English, and blotchy writing generally. You are about to be hoist by your own rhetoric down there. Fowler would have prevented the "only" transposition that was suggested. What's happened to everybody's Fowler? What's got into all of you that you can't read properly any longer? I don't want any more of this changing of my sentences without my knowing about it. (As a matter of fact, that comma is the only change ever made in a MS of mine without my knowing about it and maybe I didn't catch it in the proof, but if youse guys want to go around sticking in commas you know where you can stick them.)

> Your old pal,
> Thurber

*At the end of July 1937, Andy White quit* The New Yorker, *continuing only to edit "newsbreaks." He remained in Maine after an August vacation with Katharine and his son, Joel, explaining to her that he felt himself to be "in a rut," and that writing "Notes and Comment" was no longer fun for him. The departure from the staff of Thurber in May, his friend and office colleague for*

*nearly a decade, could not have helped Andy's mood of discouragement.*
*Katharine, the magazine's fiction editor, returned to New York with Joel. News*
*of White's departure and of his writing for other publications upset Thurber.*

## TO E. B. WHITE

*London, England*
*1937*

Dear Andy:

As far as I can make out, what you have is sheep blast. It comes from an admixture of Comment writing and whisk broom catchings. You look up under "blast" in the dictionary. It is really a flatulent condition of certain sheep, and this is unusual because sheep have almost no diseases. You couldn't give a sheep syphilis, for instance, or vent gleet. Sheep bleat, of course, is common enough, and I have it myself. It causes one to say, "Hello, George," to himself in the mirror of a morning. Over here everybody turns Catholic when anything is the matter, and perhaps you should try that. T. S. Eliot turned Catholic and so did Evelyn Waugh and they look fine.

Your letter was appreciated in this far land, for no *New Yorker* mail ever reaches us. I sent in a casual June 15 or so, where it was met with a stubborn silence, although I heard from a later casual and an earlier one. I'm sure they didn't buy it, but I'd like that it should be mentioned what happened, for you could hear a bomb drop I wait so quietly. Ross sent a note saying a check had been deposited for my last casual but Ralph Paladino is dead and I never hear from his estate as to what has been deposited.

Fortunately, I have been selling drawings over here and we live very nicely on that. *Night and Day*, the London imitation of *The New Yorker*, bought a flock of rejected drawings yesterday, which Miss Terry shipped me, and when they are printed there will be a hell of a kick from the Art Conference, which will not remember ever having seen them. The only drawings they remember vaguely are the ones I send in three or four times until they are bought to shut me up. *Night and Day* bought "The Patient" series, which I did in Bermuda and which you liked, but nobody else liked but me—nine drawings of a guy in bed. The Art Conf. dropped them like a mechanical match box. When I told *Night and Day* that you and I liked them, they said fine.

You are held in considerable awe over here for your Comment, Newsbreaks, verse, captions, and dizzy spells, but also because every piece ever printed about my drawings relates how you discovered them and stuffed them down the throats of [Gene] Saxton, Hartman and Ross, and me.

There's a very amusing guy writes for the *Express* here under the name of Beachcomber and he says ferret bite is responsible for most of the world's ills, so perhaps what you have is ferret bite . . . Beachcomber, I'm told, is a shy, tubby little man with no more aggressiveness than Frank Sullivan, but he leads an amazing little life of his own. There is, of course, something the matter with everyone who writes amusing pieces consistently, and some day I shall do a monograph on the subject and perhaps discover what the hell causes it all. Evelyn Waugh, you know, drinks other writers' sleeping potions, although I guess not so much any more now that he is a Catholic.

Helen and I got the car out for the first time since my memorable advent in London, and drove to a beauty spot in Hampshire sixty miles from London, on the old Southampton road, now the new Southampton road. Three or four couples who are painters, writers, editors, rented a great estate there with thirty rooms, tennis court, bowling green, *boule* court, etc., for $45 a month. We had a swell time, for they are all very nice people. Our contacts with the English have been very nice and maybe we've been lucky. We're going this weekend to a place near Kenilworth to visit a guy I went to Ohio State with, who assures me in a note that he hates the guts of all English. His letter came in the same mail with one from Miss Dawes, who used to be Ingersoll's secretary, asking me did I remember the time I threw an alarm clock out of Mac's window onto 45th Street. She lives in Bath or Flinders Bottom, or Horsey Rinse. I think she has ferret bite. . . .

The English don't drive as fast as the French but they take just as big chances, passing on curves, blind corners, up grades, etc., with only a tenth of a second to make it in. I think the American drivers are, on the average, better than any. It is our garage mechanics, men in their forties who have been unsuccessful in love and got drunk, and youths in their twenties who have been successful in love and got drunk, who crack into things back home, together with college professors eighty years old who forget they are driving, but over here everybody drives like that. If you haven't got your license yet in England your car bears a big red *L* for learner, but you can't tell the difference in the driving. I am really the cat's arm when it comes to driving, and going on the left you soon get onto, although it's a little bad having a left-hand drive in England. Most Continental countries drive our way . . .

Let me know more about whatever goes on. And be sure and get tested for sheep blast. Helen joins me in sending our love to you and Katharine and all the children, dogs, and turkeys. Look out for turkey wart, which catches you in the nerves and kidneys.

As ever,
Jim

&. &. &.

[Undated, but possibly October 6, 1937]

Dear Andy:

You may be a writer in farmer's clothing but you are still a writer . . . Every man must make his choice . . . This is not a time for writers to escape to their sailboats and their farms. What we need is writers who deal with the individual plight and who at the same time do not believe in Lippmann. It came to me today, walking in the rain to get Helen a glass of orange juice, that the world exists only in my consciousness (whether as a reality or as an illusion the evening papers do not say, but my guess is reality). The only possible way the world could be destroyed, it came to me, was through the destruction of my consciousness. This proves the superiority of the individual to any and all forms of collectivism. I could enlarge on that only I have what the French call 'rheumatism of the brain'—that is, the common cold. David Garnett has come out with the quiet announcement that I am the most original writer living, but I have no clean handkerchiefs and the linge is not due till tomorrow. I started to make a list of all the writers living but the names blurred on me. Of course, if you are no longer a living writer you don't belong in the list, which ought to cheer you up. Garnett goes on to say that in one miserable place I sound like Mark Twain talking from the grave, which ought to cheer you up, too. (This is where I say that I don't believe in scientists). He thinks I ought to give up ideas and institutions, which I have long suspected, as after a great deal of study of them I feel that I do not know anything at all about them. This leaves me with only the dog and the wood duck and my own short-sighted blundering into other people's apartments and tulip beds, to deal with. Which is just as well. Garnett points out that Twain ended up by telling everybody there is nothing at all in art and music, in the aesthetic in general, and I guess he feels I will end up by telling everybody there is nothing in science, whether natural, organic, inorganic, or Freudian. It's high time I shut my trap and was reminded of the time my father got locked in the men's room on his wedding night. Well, his warning came just in time (Garnett's) for I have been on the verge of saying there was nothing in collectivism or in Lippmann's denunciation of it, either, and one more step from there and you are in Twain's grave.

... Ted Shane ... called on the [Nunnally] Johnsons and wouldn't leave for three days. The Garnetts' toilets will not flush; Elliott Nugent directs Madeleine Carroll through dark glasses, and you hide away in Maine ... Here's McNulty pacing the floor and imitating Rosoff, Ann Honeycutt writing a book on dogs, Johnny Parker cutting great pieces of chaos out of the Third Avenue night, and my brother William losing one of his testicles at 43.

Helen has been in bed in our red room (everything in the room is red) for three days and I have established a remarkable relationship with a waiter at the Cafe de Flore on the corner. This cafe is one of the few places in France which makes orange juice the way Helen wants it: pressed out of fresh oranges, strained, served with ice. Last night I went there to explain in my unusual French that I wanted a glass of orange juice to take to my sick wife in the hotel Crystal just around the corner. The waiter wanted to sell me orange juice that comes in a bottle, but I said I had to have it in a glass. So everybody in the cafe got in on it and finally the patronne of the cafe said all right, if I paid a deposit of three francs on the glass. So I did that. Then next time I borrowed a glass from the hotel and, taking the cafe's glass back, explained that now they could keep their glass and give me the three francs and put the fresh orange juice in this, my own glass. Helen said I would never be able to work that, and she was right. There was a discussion in French, English, American, and gestures, about this, and although I got my idea over it was flatly rejected. All the waiters got in on it, as well as the patronne, the gerant, the patron, his sister, a dishwasher, and two Frenchmen who were sitting in a corner. It was decided that the orange juice should again be put in the cafe glass which I had brought back and that the hotel glass should be returned to me, which it was. I have made several trips since then, taking the cafe glass back and having it filled up again. I'm going to try to work in the hotel glass again in a few days when things quiet down and although I don't expect to get away with it, it is all very good practise in speaking French and in understanding the French people. Donald Moffat would have known right away that the business of substituting my own glass for the cafe glass wouldn't work. It is things like this, small, intense, unimportant, crucial, that make life in France a rich experience. There's no use in you or anyone else trying to get at the fundamental reason why I couldn't work in that hotel glass. These things are, au fond, beyond the comprehension of our simple and direct Western minds.

I haven't had a common cold since House and Wilson were friends but one threw me here: at 42 one's sentinels are asleep and the outer walls begin to crumble. You don't need any Trojan horse, you just walk in through the chinks in the wall. Everybody we know is cracking up. The loss of my brother's testicle will probably affect our trip, as my mother is frantic. I gather there is some talk of cancer, and I am pretty frantic, too. Life seems to close in. It's the personal and intimate that really affect one's life. All this concern about political forms is nonsense. I have arranged it so that when the bombs start to fall Helen will lean out the window and say, "Cut that out! My husband is trying to write a letter!" It is the attitude to cultivate. When the mobs form under my window, I shall simply say to Helen, "Throw 'em a book." Burning the book will keep them busy till I finish the letter. No government in the world is as big as a man's liver. Hitler is bellicose but he is also costive and I think it is the latter condition that will bring him to book and to bed. Individual physical idiosyncrasy is behind everything; the state of the nations is simply a symptom. It is comforting to know that when the bombs begin to fall, all I have to do is try to work in that hotel glass again to get my own mind and the whole neighborhood's off of the bombing.

I may do a piece on the hotel glass, which may well make Garnett believe that not only Twain but Whitman is speaking from his grave.

You are not the writer who should think that he is not a writer. Let [James Branch] Cabell do that. Why doesn't Cabell decide he is not a writer? Why does Hervey Allen go on thinking he is a writer? What makes [Bernard] De Voto put down so many words? H G Wells has got the idea he is three or four writers. Meanwhile the bacteria are working quietly away. The sheep tick in England has just about got sheep and man, too, where he wants it. And forty thousand of them don't have to drill with spades all at once, either. The sheep tick knows what he is doing. Up in Warsaw, owls attacked an old woman who was just walking along. Owls know what they are doing, too.

We may be back home soon; I don't know. We wanted to spend the winter in Southern France, or Corse, or somewhere. But I can't desert my family. My daughter will be six tomorrow, and I must see her soon. Elsa [Coates] says she looks like me now, poor child, but then it's possible for a girl to look like Ross or Sayre and still be lovely. This is one of God's great dispensations. This letter has not held together in any way, and does not form a logical statement of anything, or even make a pretty pattern, like a stone tossed in a brook. Ah, well.

as ever, Jim
love from us both to you-all

## To E. B. White

Dear Andy:

You could take an Italian ship—the Rex, say—which we saw in the harbor mantled with lights in the dark as we drove in tonight—get off at Nice and there we would be with Old "Non ho pius benzine" to meet you. At your age another New York winter would just about do you in. In a secluded study of the Villa Tamisier from which you can look out at the Isle Sainte Marguerite, you could write "Memoirs of a Master"—with the constant inspiration of our big genial Maria and her husband, the Russian gardener, a Mr. Smessof—as god, White, is my judge—a man much too slight and sad to carry such a name.

. . . We came down from Rome today over the old Hannibal route, a route I've always wanted to follow—like the Custer route in our West and the Andrews route in Markey's South. Janet is handling the Alps part of the Hannibal route—over by the little St. Bernard pass where the Gauls rolled rocks as big as freight cars down on Hannie and his 37 elephants and 9000 horses and 50,000 foot soldiers. It has always been a sad thing to me that after crossing the Pyrenees and the Alps with those goddam elephants, he lost all but one in his first battle—on the flats. He reminded me of Rex, my old bull terrier, who, as a pup, worked for three days trying to get a telephone pole in through our kitchen door, only to have it taken away from him, with some effort, by eight linemen who had been wondering where it was. . . .

In Rome I had the gas tank filled to the top—the gauge showed it and the guy that filled it said he could just get in the last litre, it was so full. Well, bowling along ten miles out of Naples I was non-plussed to observe that the gauge showed very little gas—a full tank should have taken me twice as far as I had come and then some. I figured the gauge had tricked me the way it did in the Lake Country one day when we ran out of gas while the gauge showed half-full. Well, she gave suddenly that "phaaf" sound when I pressed the accelerator—"phaaf—guh—phaa"—you know. And stopped. The luck of the Thurbers was with me—half a mile back was a gas station.

On the way back to it I thought as I walked along how bad off I was—stuck in Italy without knowing anything about Italian or anything about cars. Doubly stuck. But I had my little book with me—"Manual of Conversation for

Motorists" given me by the A.A.A. in N.Y. I found "I have run out of gas": "Non ho più benzina." This I said to a garage man who without a word went and found a man who spoke English. A boy on a bicycle carried 10 litres of gas to the car which was by this time surrounded by men afoot, on mules, on carts. They were very amiable; the air was full of suggestions in Italian. The engine wouldn't turn over. One man spoke a bastard English. He got me excitedly out of the car to look at a fender bump 2 years old, he said we gotta wipe off the bougies with a bandana (bougies is French for spark plugs). I was against wiping off the bougies with a bandana. So they pushed the car—backwards *and* forwards. Nothing doing. It started suddenly . . . but wouldn't pick up beyond 30 miles an hour most of the way in. Naples is 3 times as hard to drive in as Rome—which is the easiest town in the world to drive in—easier than N. Brooklin, Me. It got us to the hotel, though, past Vesuvius smouldering in the dark and past the lighted Rex in the harbor.

I know nothing about a motor (my mother knows less than nothing in that she believes you can run one without gasoline but that it is bad for it if you do). The trouble, though, I diagnose as both a clogging and a leakage in the tuyau d'alimentation, of Benzinaflussrohr—as the Germans say—alimentatore to the Italians—gas feed line to you, White. This is merely my whimsical guess. For all I know it may be a faulty kontaktschraube or trouble in la scattola di velocita, but I know nothing is wrong with the cinghia del ventilatore (fan belt). These, too, are okay: das hinterachogehause, der geschwindigkeitsmesser, l'amortizzatore, and le gicleur . . .

We'll be here for Christmas—brought our presents with us, each in his own hiding place, together with all the tissue paper, ribbon, stickers, cards, etc. Like Englishmen dressing for dinner in the desert, we will bravely carry out a Connecticut Christmas in the midst of these palms and olives and oranges . . .

Europe may cease to exist as it now is before many years—I give it four . . . In four years I too will have ceased to exist as I now am. I'll be as old as Benchley (it's cheering to know Benchley is four years older than me—he's so happy. He sing, he shout, he drink, he gay. Well, me too! . . .

Have you noticed that unconscious snobbishness about playwrights? A novelist, Comment-writer, casual writer, historian, or poet can do his work and at the same time get a lot else done, but playwrights think they must shut themselves away from the world and stop the business of living completely while writing a play. They go—often in pairs—to ruined farmhouses, abandoned islands, West Indies beaches, mountain cabins, yawls at sea. There seems to be some odd compulsion to make it all pretty hard to bear, you will notice. It turns up in the autobiographies of playwrights. One will say, "That was the year that Cyril and I rigged up a tent on an old flat car on a siding at Higgins' Beach and wrote 'The Moon Is Up.'" Or, "In January Bert Lagoon and I rented a slaughter house in Canarsie and with 3 pencils, a bag of booze, and a ream of paper went out there to write 'Love's Joke.'"

I think there is defense mechanism in it somewhere, for outside of a few touches which you can get Abbott or Connelly to do for you on the stage of the Hudson Theatre or in a room in the Algonquin, plays are easier to write I believe than anything since Livy's history of Rome. This is because to write a play you do not have to be a writer. Hence play *wright*—like wheelwright. It's that confusion in words that has caused people to believe a playwright is a writer. Plays do not have to have sentences in them—just scraps of phrases . . . Here I am travelling all over Europe, monkeying with a car in foreign strands, writing casuals, Talk, reporters, Onward & Upwards, drawing pictures, and keeping up a correspondence with *fourteen families* steadily—from 3 to 5 letters to each family so far—and about a dozen other letters a month in addition. Take it in my stride, too. I reckon I've written 75,000 words to friends and family—but I have gained 3 pounds and never miss my morning exercise or my after-dinner romp with the dog . . .

Well, Happy New Year!

Jim


## TO KATHARINE WHITE

*[Undated, from Paris]*

The French au quatrienne have gone to bed and I'm afraid to use the typewriter, but will try to be legible. (I got P. underscored in penmanship in the 2nd grade in 1901 and took my report card home crying). We have a funny room, with a tan wall and wine red carpets, upholstery, bedspreads, and curtains—curtains at door, window, and also curtaining off the bathroom! Only 45 francs a day, or about $1.50 at the rate of exchange. We're in my old St. Germain des Pres neighborhood, where I once lived with what's-her-name, ever so long ago. You know—the mother of Rosemary. I sent R. some hdkchfs & a toy, a lovely toy, for her birthday which was Oct. 7. Six years old and the loveliest girl child in the country, they tell me. . . .

❧  ❧  ❧

Dear Andy [White]:

I agree, as usual, with all your sound conclusions about things except the one about not being able to escape from beaten states, and like periods, by merely taking a boat and watching somebody balance a 20-gallon water jar on her head. That is, it seems to me, the only way to escape from such things. Grimly holding on, getting tangled in lampshades, getting so close to one's child and his school that you feel neither one nor the other can go on without you, can not possibly resolve anything. We Americans have a way of becoming an integral part of everything; we can't muse a little pace like Lancelot and say she has a lovely face: we are a part of the face, we drift down to Camelot on the goddam barge, clothed in white samite and looking a little silly. I felt I could not leave New York and my trips to Cambridge and my nervous overnight post looking toward Columbus where hell of one kind or another pops every few minutes, or did. But my daughter and I have established a new and strong tie; we engage in a fine and remarkable correspondence, notable for her ability to say everything that is necessary in two sentences without punctuation and my own surprising ability to write that hardest of all things, a letter to a girl six years old. My family seems to have taken on new courage and strength now that I am away; my mother's letters, while no funnier, are more cheerful, William is coming along all right, Robert has never been better, my father is doing all right. And nine months have gone by, all quite easily. I had worried a lot about being away a year, came close to abandoning the idea as being impossible, and then saw that because of, as well as in spite of my fussing about it, I'd have to go. You got to get away where you can see yourself and everybody else. I really believe you got to do that. A week at Foord's, quick trips to Maine, a month on the wagon, are no good.

Of course, I haven't got my child with me, and when I do have I'll be tied down by school, too. . . . The basic trouble, of course, is the astounding fact that the offspring of man have not developed the ability to become self-sustaining until their parents are practically worn down and in the grave. The guinea pig is on his own the second he is born—even has his eyes open, leaps from the womb to the nearest carrot or lettuce leaf. Dogs are raising families of their own before the first anniversary of their birth; and so it goes among all the known species of animal except man, whose young are practically no good at all until they have wobbled around the house for almost a quarter of a century! This is perhaps the most fantastic fact about human life, and I imagine the other animals never get over their astonishment at it. Have you never caught your dog giving you that straight, long puzzled look—friendly, of course, pitying, too, but puzzled? What the goddam hell, he seems to say? A man marries the nearest eligible female, or the one next to her, gets a job within walking distance of his home, raises children that will be underfoot until his arteries begin to harden, and devotes his life to the opening of envelopes containing pieces of paper with numbers written on them. That is the second most fantastic fact about human life. Our everyday lives become, right after college, as unworkable as a Ford in a vat of molasses. . . . A world in which there are millions of people, hundred of millions, can have no possible chance of working. If you get more than six people together in a room, it won't work. More than twenty is a loud, idiotic shambles. Nobody has really got anywhere in the study of that either. . . . I know there's nothing to laugh about. That is, consistently. Never has there been so much to laugh at off and on. Those of us who are able to do that must keep on doing it. . . . Not long ago in Paris Lillian Hellman told me that she would give up writing if she could ameliorate the condition of the world, or of only a few people in it. Hemingway is probably on that same path, and a drove of writers are following along, screaming and sweating and looking pretty strange and futile. This is one of the greatest menaces there is: people with intelligence deciding that the point is to become grimly gray and intense and unhappy and tiresome because the world and many of its people are in a bad way. . . .

Today I bought De Kruif's book called "Why Keep Them Alive?" and you really have to read it. After spending many years writing about the wonderful cures for ravaging diseases discovered by brave solitary geniuses he suddenly discovered a year or so ago that people are still dying like flies, with medicines, food, clothing on all sides of them. I share his indignation . . . "It was now clear to me that the whole human show wasn't decent," he says. This was clear to my old pal Cato the Elder exactly 2050 years ago and to certain wise guys in Babylon a thousand years before that. But everybody has to go suddenly nuts about it now.

. . . I think that maybe if women and children were in charge we would get somewhere. It is almost impossible to have any faith at all in the adult male in these days; he continues to boggle everything as he always has boggled it. But because he is doing this I see no reason to go to pieces personally. I see every reason not to. I don't think the barricades is an answer, nor giving up appreciation of and interest in such fine, pleasant, and funny things as may still be around. . . . Everybody wants to do something strange, and is. It remains for a few people to stand and watch them and report what it all looks like and sounds like. Among such persons there isn't anybody better qualified for the job than you. If you will quit sending pieces to the Saturday Evening Post. I have pondered all day about you sending the Memoirs of a Master there. What was the matter with that excellent weekly called the New Yorker? . . .

. . . I doubt very much that your 'year off' has been any less productive than mine—except that I got away where I could look at myself and people. The Memoirs of a Master, sight unseen, is unquestionably better than my pieces on Nice, Macbeth, Cato and Col. Johnstone, and the Michelin Guide. My output in nine months would discourage you if you were me. The thing is to keep your hand in. Nobody can write anything who doesn't. You say maybe you should write a piece called "What's So Funny?" and then add but you're sure you won't. . . . I want you to write that piece called "What's So Funny?" if only for Jamie, the boy artist.

Enough of this goddam lecturing or whatever it is.

The case of a swell guy like Don Marquis is enough to depress anybody. It makes you think of God as somebody like Max Baer. There must be some kind of strange law about disasters piling up on certain people. Take my brother Robert. He not only had goitre, but pleurisy, t.b., eye trouble, soft teeth, permanent rheum, and a dozen other things, including duodenal ulcer which he seems to have been born with; also he broke his right arm in two places, his left in three, sprung out the spool pins of one ankle, fell out of a bus on his head as a child, was run over by a milk wagon, and so on. I got shot in the eye at six years old and they called it a day. And even then it was the luckiest shot in the eye that medical science, optical branch, has probably ever known. Ten million men out of ten million and two would have lost the sight of both eyes as a result of what I stepped into. Oculists love my eye, since it is the only one they ever saw in which an unstoppable infection, having passed the sixth stage, stopped just so short of utter blindness that the naked eye can't figure out what mine sees with. Marquis goes blind playing pool, and for a strange reason. I see for an even stranger reason. This does not improve my argument about anything; but I often wonder what I would be like now if I had gone blind at the age of seven. I see myself as kind of fat, for some reason, and wandering about the grounds of a large asylum, plucking at leaves and chortling.

It was funny to get your letter and one from the Coates in the same mail, you talking about giving up your town house and life and moving to the country, they talking about selling their country place and moving to the city; both of you uncertain as to whether you can, or ought to. You two families ought to get together and compare notes. We are all against their selling their country place. They have got to the city after too long a time at a stretch in the country and have fallen under the city's spell—a pretty strong one at first— but in a year or so they would be exactly where you are, only they wouldn't have a home they own to go to. I think you should firmly argue them out of selling the country place. I am going to scream against it. The New York life will get them sooner or later, probably sooner, as it gets everybody. I don't mean "city life", I mean New York City life, two different things. There is nothing else in all the countries of the world like New York City life. It does more to people, it socks them harder, than life in Paris, London, or Rome, say, possibly could. Just why this is I have been very interested in pondering over here. I know it is a fact, but I am not sure just why it is. Perhaps Gibbs gets close to it in the comment of January 8th when he speaks, rather more easily and naturally than bitterly, of "our horrible bunch." He means, of course, their horrible life. And God knows it sometimes is. People have to run away from it, broken or screaming, at the loveliest times of year, on fete days, just before parties, on Christmas Eve. It has been interesting to see the perfect picture drawn in a few sentences in each letter we get, of New York life. "There has been a steady traffic to Foord's and back among the Gibbs McKelway and unstrung group." If I got out my letters from everybody else and put all such sentences together it would be an amazingly vivid and accurate picture of that city and its life. It rather scares me. I know I never want to live in it again for long at a time, just run down for a visit now and then. God knows it got me. I was the leader of those it got. This seems remarkable to me, now, from here. I can see that tall, wild-eyed son of a bitch, with hair in his eyes, and a glass in his hand, screaming and vilifying, and it's hard for me to recognize him. I know that I will never let him get on the loose again. I also know that a steady life in New York would do it. . . . New York is nothing but a peaceable Verdun, with music and the theatre—the only things that keep people as sane as they are. Liquor, of course, tends to keep people away from music and the theatre. Bleeck's, when you analyze it, is very much like a front line dug-out—the noise, the dogged courage of the men holding on till zero hour, the fits of hysteria, the sitting around in sullen gloom. The women are like the shattered trees of Verdun or the shells whistling overhead. A Place like Bleeck's would be impossible, I think, in Paris, Rome, London, Vienna. To see Villa Borghese, Berkeley Square, the Bois du Boulogne, is to realize that Central Park with its grim mall, its brave trees, its iron and cement closing in on all sides, is merely an extension of Bleeck's offering no liquor. A person can admire New York and so on, and all that, but I feel it is absolutely impossible to love the place. One more or less holds on there. It is an achievement to have lived there, not a pleasure to do so. It has to be seen now and again, visited, lived in for short periods, but I swear that all the laws of nature and of the constitution of man make it imperative not to live there. Not, at least, in our horrible bunch. Something, I suppose, could be done about the dreary, fatiguing, and maniac parties, although it is a little late. They could be given up completely for a while. Why is it that people go on the wagon instead of giving up all intercourse? It may be the intercourse rather than the liquor, although I think it is both. The cocktail parties at which it is obviously impossible to have any fun at all look very strange and wonderful from here. I keep telling people about them; nobody believes me. They no longer sound real to me as I tell them: everybody slugged or sick at a quarter to seven, holding on without dinner until 10.45, going home to sleep in a draught with one's hat on and a cold corner hamburger sandwich in one hand, rousing up at twelve to vomit and call somebody up and say you're sorry and to hear him shout at his wife to shut up, it's just Bert calling back. I say nobody believes it, and I am beginning to doubt it myself. And then back to bed, without quite getting your pants off, and the bell rings and it's Harry and Ella, he sick all over his Christmas scarf, she wanting to go on to Harlem. And wonderful stories of how Louise let everything burn or get cold so she and Jack didn't get any dinner at all, and how they left Merton asleep under the piano, and the whole crowd went over to Spitty's on Third Avenue for steaks but didn't eat them when they were brought. And Mike finally got Bill told off about his wife and she screamed that she loved Mike and Bill just sat down and cried, only on the overturned chair, so Mike stayed on and Greta made scrambled eggs for all three of them.

This thing is running on and on. I got to get to bed. I'm sorry as hell you are going to miss the sweet life that revolves around the little villa. It's terribly nice, my boy, with the rosemary in bloom and the fragrance of the mimosa trees coming in your room like rain when you open the windows, and sunsets such as nobody ever saw before, and Maria's chats about the political situation and life in general just before she leaves us for the night, after serving the coffee, and a great peace and quiet all over everything (and bottles of scotch and rye and brandy untouched upstairs for weeks, awaiting the arrival of Miss [Janet] Flanner and our bi-monthly party). . . .

> Well, let me hear from you,
> love to you all, from us both,
> Jim

PS

. . . I was asking Helen today how she liked having had nine months without winter and in the ensuing conversation she mentioned your fine paragraph about Maine. We both decided it made real American winters seem the best. But Helen also said, "Andy makes an idyll of it, but your feet get cold." If there were no women there wouldn't be any such brief, penetrating comments as that.

> Well, keep bundled up,
> Jim

&. &. &.

. . . We've been having a really wonderful time at the [Paris] Exposition and the art galleries. Fine weather, too. We'll be driving south about November 1 and plan to spend the winter on the French Riviera or the Italian, if all goes well. My brother William has had a testicle removed and my mother writes of a 'cancerous condition curable by X-rays'! I don't know yet what the hell it is. The Columbus situation is always worrisome . . .

I'll be sending casuals along, and drawings. Glad they took those three. Hold the other. I may think of something. Love to you all from us both.

> Jim

&. &. &.

*[Undated, from Paris, 1937]*

Dear Katharine:

. . . Think it's fine to have [Robert] Coates for Art and hope that's settled. Got to get him away from Ti-i-Time -ime-ime.

> Time in your brain
> And it cracks like a bell;
> Time out of mind
> And you're sure to get well.

I think maybe he was a little sad and a little hurt that the Nyer didn't save him from Time when he came to town. He was never a little boy who would grab for cookies. You have to say "Where's Bob?" and carry him cookies. I know, of course, there isn't always something to hand to people, suddenly. I hope it works out so he can do Art, or something.

Jim

*Thurber was submitting his "Let Your Mind Alone!" pieces to* The New Yorker.

*[Undated, 1937]*

Dear Katharine:

. . . I think Bob Coates feels he deserves a raise in his casual word rate. He says he was promised 10 cents a word a year or so ago and I remember him telling me he had got it, at that time. Well, it seems the last piece adds up to 9 cents a word, or appears to. You know how shy Bob is about these things. I think he mentioned it to me only because I am no longer an editor down there. I think he dreads taking anything up with "the office"—as he seems to think of it—officially; and that he dreads even more taking it up with anyone, even you, informally, feeling he oughtn't to bother you when you meet so- cially, and so on and so on. You know how he is as well as I do. I really dug at him when he mentioned something about word rates obliquely, because I felt he had something on his mind. He has appreciated an awful lot some notes you and Gibbs have written him about his casuals. Up there in the lonely wilds it must be pretty nice to get them. He also is proud of the fact that his casuals have been much better in the past two years or so than his first ones. He loves to get pieces in the magazine and I am glad that he cares so greatly about them. . . .

Now all this is just between you as Katharine and me as Jim. I just wanted you to know. I don't know a thing about his word-rate as compared to anyone else's, or what should be done, or shouldn't. I know you will know. But I do know this, that whereas the average writer puts up a request, or raises a fuss, or asks a question, or drops a hint, so that the magazine can keep track of, and be reminded of, his rate, Bob never does. Like the time he didn't know he had a pigeon-hole in our mail box at the office into which his mail was put and one day timidly told me he hadn't been getting his Talk check—and I asked Ralph and we all looked in the box and there were THREE CHECKS! In those days he had hardly any money, either. You know I sometimes think that Bob's stammer, as much as he ignores or even disowns it, is behind this excessive timidity. I know that one reason he didn't get a square deal at Macallays was because he would not go down there and talk to them, wouldn't even stick up for his 50-50 rights on the Literary Guild thing, and was handed 40-60, short end. Eventually, this apparently enters into one's whole attitude, so you can't even ask in writing, or anything. Well, there's that. Something else for you to deal with, who haven't got enough on your hands. He's not, by the way, sore or anything remotely like that, just wistfully wishing he might get a little more. The fact that you all tell him they are so good, his pieces, seems to be a component part of his hope and feeling he should get more.

Here it is midnight!

Sweet dreams,

Jim

Can you put the Bisch piece through soon? And thanks a million for buying those pictures! An unexpectedly early windfall.

🙋 🙋 🙋

Paris,
*November 8 [1937]*

Dear Katharine:

I have told my mother that, in view of the x-ray treatments, hospital bills, etc., brought about by my brother's trouble, I would try to get the New Yorker to advance me $500, to be made out to Mary A. Thurber and sent to her and charged to me. As security against this particular loan, the New Yorker can hold one of the fifty share blocks of stock of mine, which is already being held by Ralph. I left them with him when we left New York. I think I owe the magazine now only a little more than $500 and this is being steadily cut down by their taking off twenty percent of every casual and drawing. I am sure that, after this $500, I can handle the Columbus situation without trouble. I have been able to send them money each month and will be able to make these money payments each month out of my own checking account as I have for the past two months or so, from now on. But because of what has arisen out there I felt that a solid block of money would not only be a financial aid but a much needed morale support for them, with the cold weather and the years and disease closing in. This is a thing of very great importance to me. I have offered to come home if they needed me but so far they have assured me they don't. In the case of this special, and last, $500 advance, I have not told Helen about it, so that you can't very well send me a letter about it. If it is okay, just send a letter beginning 'Everything is all right, here.' If it isn't okay, I will manage things all right. This all sounds very silly and evasive and Thurber, I suppose, but it is the way I seem to have to do it this time. It isn't because H. doesn't always think anything I do about Columbus is fine. But she's way off in a far country over here and I wanted to keep as many of the worries to myself as I can. Women worry in far countries enough, anyway (although she is not the worrying kind). I keep up a bright face about Columbus and I know she would think this has me down worse than it has. Once in a while there are things between me and Columbus that have to be just between me and Columbus, for the mental ease of everybody.

I want the New Yorker to go on taking off 20 percent of all the things I send in until what I owe them at the moment of your getting this letter is cleared up. As for this $500, I'd like that to be held over, not added to the debt out of which 20 percent is taken, until I get back. I can easily settle it then. I will have my present debt there cleared up in a few months, or sooner, as I am really sending in a lot of things —drawings, casuals, and even Talk stories.

We are driving out of Paris tomorrow, the 9th of November, stay in Fontainebleau that night, then Dijon, and then Provence and Nice for a few days. We are going into Italy then for a while and after that we take a house for the winter in the French Riviera where I can settle down and get a lot of stuff done. . . .

All this in a hurry. I'll keep writing to you all. With lots of love,
Jim

## To the John McNultys

*The McNultys had sent a recording of Maxine Sullivan's "Loch Lomond" to the Thurbers.*

*Nice*

*Nov. 2, 1937*

Dear John and Donia:

Well, sir, had they brought us a wire-haired fox terrier (terrier *au poil dur*, as we French say) or a motor-boat we would not have been so surprised as when the records came in. We instantly went over to the apartment of a woman named, believe it or not, Solita Solano—whom I always call Venita Vanessa, as being a shade more reasonable and apt. "Be apt, boy," my grandfather Fisher used always to say. "Be apt, god dam it," whereupon my grandmother would say, "Son of a bitch talks to children like he'd been brought up in a whore house," and would give us bread and jelly to assuage the hurt of his ugly words.

We were nuts, and I mean nuts, about that gal, her own perfect, easy, no monkey-business style—as smooth and exciting, as easy and stirring as a bottle of Romanée-Conti; mostly we played Loch Lomond. What a sweet and rocking song! All the other three were fine, too, but Loch Lomond they can sing at me funeral—or she can. Honey writes us she is crazy about Burt Williams' records or is collecting them. Burt should have lived to marry this here singer you all saint to us ovah heah, boy. You know what she could do, with just that faint hint of modern swing in it?—why—In the Shade of the Old Apple Tree and a dozen others of around 1905. I say this because once, in the 5th grade at Sullivant School, Miss Ferrell, teacher, we had a Xmas concert and Eva Prout, my girl, sang "Slumber Boat" and "Sing Me to Sleep" and others sang similar songs;—"Silent Night," etc., got into it and in the end Miss Ferrell called on a tall [black] gal whose name I remember after all these 32 years was Almeda, and she asked Almeda to sing—so Almeda gave us In the Shade of the Old Apple Tree with something of that plaintive, sure, easy individuality that your gal has, and in it, that simple song, was therefore a touch of that black shining glory that never quite illumines the brow of the lowly white race. So I've never forgotten Almeda. . . .

Thanks again for the records.

We are in a hotel room that looks out on the Bay of Angels, that great curve of blue sea that lies in front of Nice. We drove out of Paris one dark day to Fontainebleau, next day to Dijon, next day to Valens, next day to Aix-en-Provence, by way of Avignon—so that in 72 hours we had shed our coats and I was fanning myself with a straw hat and Helen was running around in slacks. Then by way of Marseilles and Joulon, along the coast, high up among the red hills, we drove to Nice. It would take somebody with the colorful mixed metaphors of Snider ('the whole ball of wax is in apple pie order because the cat's out of the bag—bang! like a dream.' Etc.) to do justice to this blue, purple, warm, snowy melange of sea, mountains and valleys. God, what a place to drive a car in! You're always a mile high looking down at the sea, or on a valley floor looking up at a town a mile above you.

We're going to Italy a week from today, then back here to find a place for the winter where we can have a villa on the sea and I can write a play and some fitting memorial to Almeda.

Did I tell you that Helen, who was treated by a Harley Street doctor in London for a badly cut bridge of the nose, due to a fall in a bedroom, scaring me to death, was stretched out on an operating table in a doctor's office in Nice when we'd only been here two days? Well, one night she went out to the ladies' room just across from our bedroom door and there was this tinkle of glass. I ran out and here was Helen holding her left wrist which had a gash in it as deep as a well and as wide as a church door. She had knocked the glass out of the can door in some manner and cut herself to the bone. I screamed "That this should happen to me!" (I always go into the subjunctive when Helen gets hurt) but she was calm and brave. Seven stitches had to be taken and this made me a little sick but Helen was fine. She just lay there and let a French doctor sew her up like a torn mattress. . . .

She's healing like a baby, though, and I can only pray to be delivered from the menace of bedroom and bath in some quiet Italian hotel far from the slippery roadways, the swift traffic, and the rock slides. . . .

Love to you both,
Jim & Helen

## To the Elliott Nugents

*Le Sextius, Aix-en-Provence*
*November 15 1937 middle '30s*

Dear Elliott & Norma:

If you should take a map of France and draw a line from Calais in the far northwest to Aix-en-Provence in the far southeast you will trace the course of that phantom motorist, James Grover Thurber, and his bride. From the Pas de Calais to Languedoc, across the field of the cloth of gold, under the limes and chestnuts and plane trees, through the vineyards of Burgundy-Clos-Vougeot, Chambertin, Romanee, all the great good wines, up to your axle in Richebourg, up to your eyes in Pommard—down to the olive trees and the oranges of Provence. We did the Calais-Paris trip in September, stayed in Paris 6 weeks, for the Exposition and the great shows of paintings—Van Gogh, El Greco, Picasso, Matisse, Poussin, a lovely glut of paintings—and just as that cold unceasing northern rain was setting in, we're off for the South, stopping overnight at Fontainebleau, then at Dijon (the heart of the Burgundy country and the capital of good food), then at Valence, below Lyons, & then to Aix, via Avignon and its bridge and its surfeit of history. Down here you reach out and grab great handfuls of rich red history. Starting at Fontainebleau, on to Dijon in some field around which Julius Caesar defeated Vercingetorix, an exploit which I used to translate out of the commentaries for Daisy Hare, Latin teacher at East High, Columbus, as long ago, my young sir, as 1912! We've been in this storied land, Provence (meaning now, as in 70 B.C., Province of Rome) for 3 days, stumbling over Roman ruins, visiting the courts of love of the Troubadours, driving to Tarascon (of Tartarin), Arles with its arena, Les Baux, a ghostly, unbelievable ruins of a town on a lonely and strange hill-top. . . .

We could have had thrush tonight, only I don't eat warblers. I do a lot of things but I don't eat warblers. Four and twenty blackbirds, yes, but not warblers. Please pass the nightingale is something I shall never say. Help yourself to the lark, however, if you feel that way—live and let live, is what I believe. But someday you and I must have snails, with a white St. Peray, and wild boar with a Chambertin 1911. Then we'll have some 1887 Calvados with the coffee, and recite all of Aucassin and Nicolette.

Our love to you & Norma and the girls,
Jim & Helen

## To Wolcott Gibbs

*Gibbs and McKelway had recently spent time at Foord's sanitarium at Kerhonkson, New York.*

*November 25 '37*

Dear Wolcott:

Enclosed is a drawing and a beautiful colored what's-this of the Alpes Maritimes littoral, I mean Riviera. A pencil-drawn arrow, looking like a flying swordfish, points to the almost exact location of a villa which Helen and I have just about decided to take for the winter. It is on the Juan-les-Pins side of Cap d'Antibes, the promontory between Nice and Cannes. We were driving over there today and saw this sign saying for rent. It is a villa belonging to a French doctor who lives in Nice and specializes in maladies de l'estomac. It faces spang on the big blue bay, sits back in a long garden and has two floors, four bedrooms, living room, dining room, two baths. We are going to take it for from now to April first and all it costs for all that time is six thousand francs, or just about $200—that is about $50 a month! This is the way to live. Roses were in bloom in the garden when we were there today, and oranges ripening on a tree in front of the house.

We are going to go to Italy first, for about three weeks, so we'll miss that much time there, paid for time, but it's worth it, for this here is a bargain. . . . Swell sunny room to work in upstairs and all I need is something to write and draw about, which will no doubt come to me. I overhear funny remarks now and then and have perfectly killing little adventures, out of which I have made what I laughingly call a life work. . . .

Helen, who cut the bridge of her nose in London and was stretched out in a Harley Street doctor's office, cut a gash five inches long in her left wrist here in Nice. . . . Papa Thurber got to feeling a little funny in the stomach while it was being sewed up, but he, too, was brave and didn't faint. The doctor was French and his office is in a big musty building, dark and gloomy, like an abandoned railroad station; his office had all the heavy ornate charm and fusty fragrance of the ladies' room in a Denver whore house. He filled a big iron pan with alcohol and set it on fire, as if he were about to make crepes suzette; when this cooled he dropped a couple of needles in it, which he had had some trouble getting out of their containers. However, it all came out all right. . . . As I said in a letter to McNulty, we have driven along the edges of precipices a mile high, we took Devil's Elbow in Scotland on a rainy day, we wormed our way through Lisieux on a market day—the streets are 9 feet wide, traffic both ways, parking allowed, and they run up and down steep hills; we drove into Valence at night in a rain storm, not knowing where the hell we were, we've swirled around that hellish merry-go-round at the Place de la Concorde and at the Arc de Triomphe—where one is approximately as safe as your child would be practising with the Minnesota football team. We were lost in London with buses and trams on all sides, we did 60 miles an hour in Provence for twenty miles. But nothing ever happened. Then in a quiet bedroom in Fitzroy Square and in the ladies' room of a Nice hotel, Helen came face to face with old man Catastrophe. Verily, life is peculiar.

How's everything in Kerhonkson? Is the old Scandinavian trainer still there? And the Foords? How did McKelway like it? . . .

I hear Sally [Benson] is back in town sober and serious.

Let's hear from you, love to all,

Jim

*· · ·*

Dear Wolcott:

Here is that drawing of the animals on the wall. If the bizaarerie seems now rather more super-imposed than congenital, I shall be glad to do it over again with my brush (this brush stroke is known as the latest Thurber manner). (That is, in the ateliers and salons of Paris and London). Maybe it's all right this way. The art conference has, and always has had, different ideas from mine about going nuts. . . . The art conference should always bear in mind, like a lamp, Thurber's desire to keep his animals from being in the least like Doctor Seuss's animals. The uncles of this man George (who got the penguin somewhere, you may recall) are likely to go nuts simply because the animals they shot were smiling faintly when, after crashing through the underbrush, they finally fell. It is the faintly remarkable, rather than the utterly impossible, I believe, that finally unhinges the mind; but, as I say, the art conference and I have seldom seen eye to eye in these matters. That fate has jockeyed the conference into a position where it can change my animals and left me unable to change the conference's ideas about animals is one of the fundamental failures of our politico-social structure. It is basically immutable circumstances like these which make me believe that nothing will ever be different and that Dorothy Thompson is just wasting her time. What ever happened to Markey? What ever happened to Sally Benson? Helen and I are having dinner with Lillian Hellman day after tomorrow. Jim Lardner gave a housewarming last night that started at one in the morning, so we missed it; but we stayed up all one night, until 8:30 arguing about Russia, marriage, Bonnard, etc. with Bill Bird the Sun man here and Webb Miller. Miller had been sent by plane from London to cover a luncheon given for the Duke de Windsor, but he missed it, not waking up till 2.30 p.m. So he just took a plane back to London. That's what comes of running into old Bleeck people like Helen and me in Paris. We closed all the bars and cafes on the left bank and then closed Harry's bar and then closed all the joints in Montmartre . . .

> love to all, Jim

Watts' line about not knowing there was a war in Spain when you see that light comedy, very interesting. Of course, one would know there was a war in Spain to see the New York comedies: Having Wonderful War, Room Spanish, Bombs Can Take You with Them, etc.

Aristide Mian (Sally's Gadge, as TIME would say) was with us on the all night party, looking very much like a distinguished French painter with his now fully flowered beard. He couldn't get in a word all night long except that Bonnard was the greatest of living painters. This, being apropos of nothing, got nobody anywhere. Eugene Saxton, of Harpers, was in town, he comes over every year to talk to authors, and I had lunch with him one day at Prunier's, with Hamish Hamilton, my English publisher, also along. They both looked grayish because it turned out they had had a conference with Louis Bromfield the night before which started at the Ritz at 6 p.m. and ended in Montmartre at 6 a.m. Said Saxton: "There was a time at the Bal Tabarin when I would have welcomed the idea of withdrawing." He had to have dinner the night after with Maurois. A publisher's life is hell. My book has gone into a second edition in England. How is yours doing?

## To Katharine White

*[Undated, noted as November 24, 1937, from Nice]*

Dear Katharine:

First, thanks for your consistent stream of notes, (and word about pieces being bought, deposit slips, etc.). I envy you going to Hanover for a game. We have missed football, all right. . . .

Don't worry about having to edit my stuff—you have to, that's all. I'm not worrying about it.

I have got out of my brush-drawing mood, and you are probably right. It was a phase, though. Just finished a drawing which will be coming along, in pen and ink. . . .

We've been in Rome a week, and had a fine time although there have been four days of rain, and one night, having gone to a movie—two miles from the hotel, there came up a cloudburst and no cabs were available, so we had to walk at least a mile when we finally found a horse cab. We were soaked to the insides, having forgotten to take an umbrella and me without a hat even. . . . Mussolini yesterday gave out his announcement about withdrawing from the League but we stayed home on account of the rain—and my Nice story. We've been waiting for a fine morning to take in the Sistine chapel and the other rooms of painting and sculpture, of which there are enough, of course, to take up a dozen fine mornings. Our few fine days have been spent among the ruins—Roman ruins being one of my dishes, as you Americans say. We were driven out the Appian way in a horse cab and Sunday drove to Tivoli and wandered around the villa of Hadrian, on a perfect day. I took some artistic snapshots and when they're developed will send you some. An artist with the camera is what I really am. . . .

We had two fine days in Rapallo and two rather bad ones in Genoa and a frightful rainy time in Pisa, although it was clear when we walked up after night to see the leaning tower. An exciting thing to see at night, too. . . .

We have enjoyed Bob [Coates]'s pieces a lot. I'm glad he's doing art and think he is fine at it. . . .

We had Thanksgiving dinner at a nice restaurant in Nice: turkey, Corton red and Hermitage white, and the orchestra played "Trees", "The Star Spangled Banner", and "Pennies from Heaven."

A very very merry Christmas to you and Andy and Joe and all, from Helen and me, together with lots of love,

> Jim (and Helen)

Thanks a lot, my darling, for everything you do for me. You are a great and sweet lady.

## To the *New Yorker* Magazine Art Conference

*Rome*

*Dec 16, 1937*

Dear Conference:

The caption for the idea drawing is: "She's reading some novel that's breaking her heart, but we don't know where she hides it."

The shading, or shadow, in the lamp was an act of God—blot—but I guess it will pass: possibly it holds the composition together, like the trees in the background of Cezanne's Baigneuses. It could I suppose be Chinese-whited.

The spot shows, as Bob Coates will see at a glance, the influence of the Roman phase. Just what the allegory is, if there is any, I don't know. I call it "Hope after Hannibal", I think. I am very fond of lions, and of angels with wands—if this is a lion and an angel with a wand. I do not see how you can use it in the magazine, nor do I see why you can't.

I have an idea that Hokinson could use: two of her lovely plump fiftyish women touring abroad. I don't know just what they are doing but one says: "We must save some of our strength for the English lake country." Hokinson has been over here—she knows her backgrounds. If she wants them in the Roman Forum, picture of Roman Forum enclosed. . . .

Did I ever get paid, do your records show, for the idea I gave you for her: "She's not *really* quaint, she's a college graduate." My records do not show this, but you know my records. HAPPY NEW YEAR! . . .

Thurber

I just got another idea, for Arno . . . Full page. Two of Arno's military men, elderly, pompous, old South—one of them especially. This one is showing the other his room of large paintings of famous warriors—Caesar is there, Napoleon, lots of guys with beards, fierce eyes. They have come to a halt, however, in front of a certain immortal general. Of whom, says the speaker with great sonority:

"Hannibal, suh, the Joseph E. Johnston of the Punic wars!"

This is a wonderful idea, really, conference. Let no man say, in mah hearin', he ain't evah heard of Joseph E. Johnston. . . .

For the benefit of those who drowsed in their American history courses in the grammar grades, Jos. E. Johnston (not to be confused with Albert Sidney, who died at Shiloh—a battle from which one Colonel Apple of the 6th Ohio fled, shouting "I told you so!") was one of the 3 or 4 most eminent, able (as Time says) Southern generals, famed of course for opposing Sherman in Georgia (up to the time Joe was relieved of command and Pope was put in. If I should get Pope and Hood confused occasionally it's because I always have, a little. They're like birch and beech to me, in trees).

Main point of difference between Hannibal and Joe was that Joe fought a defensive war on his own soil, Hannibal carried an offensive war into the enemy's country and, I may say, how! Of southern invaders, Lee in Pennsylvania fails of sound comparison with Hannibal in Italy because Lee stayed a matter of weeks, Hannibal seventeen years. It was as hard to get Hannibal out of Italy as it is to get the boys out of Bleeck's at 4 a.m. . . . .

Of course if we went in for possible substitutions we would never stop: change Hannibal to Hasdrubal, Johnston to Jeb Stuart, etc.

I think I have made my case for Johnston.

> Love
> Thurber

Hannibal, I forgot to say, was the greatest than any general that ever lived. Like Sid Luckman of Columbia he played on the wrong team . . .

P.S. My wife doesn't think the average New Yorker reader ever heard of Johnston *or* Hannibal. Okay, then:

> "Lord Nelson, suh, the Marshall Goldberg of Her Majesty's Navy!"
> How the hell did we get started on this anyway?

## To John McNulty

*[Undated, spring 1938, from the Riviera]*

Dear John:

This is just a note to tell you that, with the coming of Spring, the rixe has taken the place of the bagarre on the Riviera. It's a little too warm now for the bagarre and there probably won't be anymore until September. There have been at least four rixes, however, in the past two weeks. The most important of these involved a taxi driver, two English sailors, and a stranger. A rixe does not involve, as a rule, more than four, or five persons. Not more than four, I'd say, really. Five would make it a lutte, I think, but I'll have to spend more time on my researches before I could say with absolute exactness. There are, you see, a number of other involvements: the querelle, melee, vacarme, and the emeute, which takes in even more people than a bagarre. The causes of an emeute you can always put your finger on and the thing is invariably marked by the presence of officers or soldiers on horseback, I should say. My researches would also have to give some attention to the braillement and the clabaudage (or clabaudement)—which are mainly noise—nobody much hurt—and the tapage, which is also mainly clamorous.

The papers refer variously to the rixe I have mentioned above as the Rixe of the Jardin Albert Premier and the Rixe of the Rue de la Croix Marbre (it seems to have covered considerable ground, having started in Villefranche and ended in Nice). The first reports said the sailors were American, which is natural because it is usually American sailors that get into rixes, but when it came out that the taxi driver won, by shooting one of the sailors, perhaps fatally, the papers knew without checking up that they couldn't be American sailors, who never lose a rixe. Turns out they were English. An American sailor who was done in by a French taxi driver would die of shame, not bullet wounds.

When I was in Nice before and the American squadron in European waters was in, the sailors were involved in constant rixes, vacarmes, and bagarres, and of course no end of tapages and clabaudages.

I have decided that in a lutte the weapons that are going to be used are pretty well defined, or guessed at, beforehand, whereas in a rixe you can never tell what they are going to turn out to be. A lutte is rather more confined, spatially, whereas a rixe can spread out over all hell and could, of course, grow into a bagarre. A lutte would, I think, more likely degenerate into a vacarme—more on the hubbub order.

I expect to hear from you any day now.

We got caught for parking on the pair side of a street on an impair day, in Cannes recently. The system of issuing a traffic ticket I haven't yet figured out, but am working on it. We had parked the car while at a movie. When we got out there it was, no ticket on it. We drove home, some six miles, to the villa and I put the car up, in a place not easy to find. Next day it was same as ever. But the third morning we found a ticket pasted on the outside of the windshield, a piece of paper about four by six inches, with the news that we had, on the 23 March, violated a regulation of the circulation de Cannes, etc. How it got there, and why at such a late date, we didn't know. We drove to Cannes and to the cop house where a cute agent with a moustache and full of garlic let us off but said the prochaine fois we would be in for a contravention (which is not as bad as a proces verbal, of course). I forgot to ask him how the hell they worked it: why they just didn't slap on the ticket when they found the car parked wrong, how in hell they found out where I lived, etc. Maria, our cook, thinks they quietly followed us home, on a motorcycle, and saw where we put the car, and then arranged to send the ticket pasters over the day after that, or rather two days after that. It's a wonderful country.

Love to you both,
Jim

## To Katharine White

*The piece Thurber refers to was published in* The New Yorker, *January 29, 1938, as A Reporter at Large, subtitled "La Grande Ville de Plaisir."*

*The casual mentioned in the following letter was published in the* New Yorker *as "A Ride with Olympy," April 30, 1938. "Philip Wedge" is a fictional character in an E. B. White casual.*

*January 15, 1938*

Dear Katharine:

Enclosed is, mainly, a casual. And two spots and an idea drawing. The casual I am very fond of and I hope you will like it. . . .

We are very content in our villa. It's really swell. I'm sitting between two fine wood fires (we have a huge bagful of pine cones for kindling, which burn with a fine fragrance) and Helen is in the kitchen getting dinner—it's Maria's night off. . . . We look out on the sea from our bedroom windows and also on a long garden and lawn filled with orange trees, roses, rosemary hedges, mimosa, and a lot of other bright and fragrant stuff. All this for about $50 a month and an additional twenty a month to Maria, who is large and jolly and intelligent—we go over the international situation and the present French political crise every day—and a most wonderful cook, turning out marvellous soups, vol au vents, cassoulets, omelettes, soufflets, etc. We have breakfast in front of the provencal fireplace every morning and the Paris Herald-Tribune and the great Eclaireur de Nice is on the table, and orange juice virtually from our front yard, and excellent French coffee for me and Maxwell House for Helen. I really like the French coffee best. . . .

We had one big adventure down here, which you have probably heard about from Bob [Coates], to whom I wrote the other day: going to the mansion of the great Maxine Elliott, who is queen of the social life of Cannes, with Jimmy Sheean. Quite a remarkable afternoon. I can't write anything for Talk about it, but I wish I could. . . . I thought Winston Churchill, whom we met at her house, was an old Pooh (but then he thinks I am a young Pooh). . . .

. . . Night & Day closed down, as you may have heard. . . . They managed to use up all my pictures, paid for all of them. The last one or two appeared in the very last issue. I felt rather sad about my patient in the patient series who was sick in bed in the magazine for nine weeks and got up only to have it close down.

The Christmas cards for which I did a drawing and which were made up in London and sent to us in Rome eight weeks ago never arrived. We don't know what the hell, but are trying to find out. If I ever find them I'll use them next Christmas, if there is one. . . .

I got a letter from [Clifton] Fadiman asking me to contribute a piece to a book called Living Philosophies, the other writers to be the Mahatma, Wells, Trotsky, Santayana, and a dozen other of us leading thinkers. Whee! Feeling as well and cocky as I do now, in this eternal sunshine, I'll probably do the piece, too.

> Love and kisses, from us both,
> Jim

ॐ  ॐ  ॐ

*Jan 22*

Dear Katharine:

. . . We've got a swell flood of mail in the past three days: you and Andy, the Coates, McNulty, both our families, all very fine, McKelway also, and nice note from Ross, too.

. . . Lord, you now have enough men to experiment with on the New Yorker. Lobrano, who was once described in Comment as the nicest man in the world, and Henderson, who is, of course, the Henderson of Bob [Coates]'s "Yesterday's Burdens"—I always felt he would show up on the magazine sooner or later. We had to have a man named Henderson the way music companies have to have a man named Schwartz and jewelers a watch-repairer named Schneider. And just as, in the larger boiler rooms, there is always a man named O'Shaughnessy. . . .

It's all right about the drawings. I didn't expect them to use the lion and angel, really. I do think the dog ones were good. But tot homines, tot sententiae, as Ross has often pointed out. I do feel bad that they thought the one picture turned on the man's having no hair. None of my men have hair. Hair on one of my figures denotes a woman. I have never yet gone in for that kind of humor, or whatever it is. The point was simply in the caption: the man could have had lots of hair. However.

I will try to do something about the Roosevelt caption and the other. Possibly combine them with "Why doesn't your precious Roosevelt do something about itty bitty Betsy?" Kincaid's idea seems good, too. . . .

It's awful funny about Gibbs not being revealed as the commenter, because his Comment is just as obviously his as if it were signed and also had a little inset photo of him, like Broun's in Broun's column. As I said to Andy, his referring to "our horrible bunch" was a give-away. Same page he also said "idiotic bulletin", and several other footprints were around. I don't see the need for secrecy. I doubt if a secret comment writer would be a good idea. But maybe I don't get the point.

I'm glad McNulty has been taken on and sure do hope he stays. I know he is crazy about it and will work very hard. Of course my rating of him is as one of the great people. What he knows about journalism, New York, Jews, Irish, cops, waiters, bartenders, city editors, Columbus, war, soldiers, social figures, bums, millionaires, is all there is to know. He's a fine reporter, the best mixer I know—he can get in with anyone anywhere—and has a sense of humor, a turn of wit, and a gift for phrase absolutely his own. I think that more and more he will be able to write what we want back there. But I don't want him to lose his marvelous original genius for phrases, sentences, and ideas. About a third of the things I like to remember when I lie awake are things John has said, found, or revealed.

In his latest letter he says he thinks it would be presumptuous of him to go to Foord's when he has been on the magazine so short a time.

Having been on the wagon almost two years, and having in the past 12 months associated with the horrible bunch, he is, I think, immune to liquor now. He never liked it anyway.

You've got me worried about your casual bank. I'll really do some casuals, and try not to make them all European. Your and Andy's analysis of what is in the New Yorker nowadays is pretty sound, but, from over here, one can see how marvelously well the thing holds up. You both overlooked, though, the great flood of casuals that begin like this:

1) It was snowing a little when Mr. Prentice set out for the drugstore.

2) When Mr. Birdseed took hold of the table runner, a tiny shower of sequins from his dead wife's party gown sifted to the floor.

3) Mr. Applegate walked out on the back porch, sniffed the first fine cold air of winter, and sighed. He walked on down to the drugstore, noticing, as he stopped for a moment in front of the Whitneys' gate, that the fine cold air was there, too. Vaguely uneasy, he. . . .

We've had an awful lot of the sad drifting little men, muddling gently through the most trivial and impalpable of situations, ending up on a faint and, to me, usually evasive little note of resignation to it all, whatever it all is. . . . Of course, Sally [Benson] does the other type of story frightfully well and Maxwell gives signs of doing it even better; but a lot of 'em get in so that the foreign pieces are a kind of relief. I'm glad Mr. Monroe and little Mrs. Monroe are dead. (Been dead these ten years!) (Don't let any of this get to Sally via Gibbs. I think what she does is usually swell, and want to go on the record simply as saying that). . . .

. . . We won't be back in time for a summer anywhere, but have planned, and rather arranged, with Helen's family, to take the Colebrook place for such part of the summer as we may have this year. Having been away so long we will want to be within driving distance of New York, there'll be so much to do, and we'll probably have to be there quite a lot. And there is Columbus, too.

Furthermore, you owe us a visit! We never did get you to Litchfield. We are terribly anxious to see you and want to know in more detail about your plans—for the cottage, for the chicken coop—is Andy going in for big scale chickenry and turkery? Are you making plans for a self-sustaining life in Maine, or what? . . .

Must get to work. Love to you all from us both,
Jim


. . . The Pepper for the Belgians piece brought in a fine, long letter from Rebecca West, about how Catholicism, as practised by the literati of England, is playing havoc with them. . . .

I still think, of course, that Andy should not give up comment for good. We all think that. He thinks it's tough to be a writer, but I am told old turkey raisers grow to believe their lot is a hard one, too.

🐝  🐝  🐝

*February 23, 1938*

Dear Katharine:

. . . There seem to be as many changes in the New Yorker as in the European situation, both of which may lead to war. I think it may be fine for you to get away but still stay in touch, with a certain amount of work; after all I have done that successfully—having done more since my jump to Bermuda and Litchfield and here than in the previous two or three years. Of course, from here, all you New Yorkers seem to make such extremist decisions. Andy quits, completely, for a whole year; you both are going to stay in Maine for a whole year; the Coateses want to give up Gaylordsville for good and stay in New York forever. There is always a certain perverse satisfaction in finality, I suppose: the clean break, the dawn of a new day, tomorrow is another life, etc. Living in Maine "the year around", though, doesn't seem to make any more realistic sense to me than my living in Litchfield the year around would have. We compromised on about three of Litchfield to one of New York, and I should think you would do that: both of you like New York and get so much out of it. Andy, I know, really loves the place; nobody who didn't could have written the piece he did for the Saturday Evening Post which said in effect that you couldn't make him stay in Maine the year around. . . .

It is pretty hard from a distance to figure out just what actuates you and Andy. When I am with you two I can always tell the fact from the supposition because you both have such bad poker faces. As bad as Bob Coates. Bob's eyes give him away but with you and Andy it is your pauses. You also throw lateral passes at each other that a blind end could break up. The health argument sounds okay, but somehow not okay enough. No decisions made by old New Yorker editors are ever as simple as all that. Retreating to Maine with a handful of newsbreaks, the untimely comment, and one third of an editorial job may work out all right, but it sounds a little temporary. Well, all you can do is try it and if it doesn't work out you won't have burned any bridges behind you, will you? Your Post-script in handwriting leaves me a little bewildered since it makes the New Yorker situation seem a little like that of Czechoslovakia. These things used to be cleared up by getting rid of Jim Cain. . . . It seems like that over here. I think now it is a good idea that we use so much foreign stuff, too, because not many things are more interesting or important. And there is still plenty of New York stuff in the magazine, a ton each week to hold down the franchise. I can remember when there was some small question as to whether my stories of Columbus life, all in a clump, were "New Yorker stuff"; that seems a long time ago in years and in policy. The stories were better than [Fillmore] Hyde's Ritz-Carlton's anyway and I doubt if any readers questioned the wrongness of mine or the rightness of his for a magazine called The New Yorker. I don't see why we have to hold to that too strongly— many of the foreign pieces, such as Emily [Hahn]'s piece on the stolen money and Janet [Flanner]'s on Weidman have been better than most local casuals and articles. I get more tired of Bronx and Jew stories than of foreign ones, really. The thing that marks us most, I think from here, is the pussy-cat quality of most of the males in most of the casuals. That's awfully deeply rooted now, I'm afraid, and I had more to do with it with Mr. Monroe than Andy did with

Philip Wedge, too. But who was to know that there would follow a Sally Benson, a [Richard] Lockridge, and, as good as he is, a William Maxwell, all members of the same school, all devoted in their separate ways to what Henry James called "poor sensitive gentlemen". Mr. Opal, that is—the One that was a Wanderer, too; oh, thousands upon thousands. And yet all around us roars and thunders the maleness of the characters of Hemingway, Cain, Horace McCoy, and others. We are up with the times in going in for foreign pieces, and I'm glad of it, but the male characters of our casuals live in Admiral Dewey's time. We got to give 'em pokers to bend, women to lay, guys to smack in the puss. What ever became of John O'Hara?

This health business is something that even I, once known as The Iron Man, may soon have to bother about. I been having night sweats and a new coldness has come to my extremities—paws and tootsies that once were as warm as a mouse in a muff now go cold on me. But I haven't lost weight, have the color of an old Burgundy, and feel all right. England feels all right, too, but her feet are cold. Heil! It looks as if your Joe [Joel White] would escape the next war and pass the buck to his own son.

I'm about to start a casual now about the wondrous trip I took in my Ford with my Russian gardener, whose name, I have just found out, is Olympe! Pronounced O-lym-pe, accent second syllable to be sure. I could never call a man Olympe, I simply call him Alors, or Dites, or Bon Jour. He wanted to learn to drive the Ford and it was a breathtaking mile and a half that we rode, mostly in low gear, bumping like a broncho, missing things and people by inches, finally coming to grief against a pole and losing the right front fender. He with his Russian French, me with my American French. The whole thing was thus one or two moves from reality.

Let me know the latest developments about everything.

    Love to you both from us,

    Jim

As to what will happen to the magazine with you gone, that remains to be seen. I don't see Maxwell being the fountain and the shrine that you were. Probably the New Yorker will have night sweats and get cold feet. Well, in another twenty years we would all have to give it up anyway, for a newer generation of Bryn Mawr, Cornell, and OSU girls and boys. I have never been able to picture us all at sixty getting out the New Yorker. It would be funny if you became a novelist. Will you become a novelist? . . .

P.S.

I have decided that the Little Man, the bewildered man, the nervous, beaten, wife-crossed man, is a realer and stronger thing in American life than the Cain men who lay Mexican women in churches or the Hemingway men that choke guys to death. American life being what it is, we couldn't leave the Little Man out of it. It has been interesting to notice the American ads over here, as against the French. The French picture-ads show the male dominant, the wife asking permission, etc. The American ads show a woman, full page, frowning, saying "I won't go a step with you till you shave!" and "If you think you can wear that messy shirt, you're crazy." . . .

Thurber.

## To Daise Terry

*Von Cramm was a well-known contemporary German professional tennis player.*

*Abraham Washingtine's Birthday, 1938 (apologies to F. Sullivan)*

Dear Miss Terry:

Thanks for all the slips of paper. I don't think I ever got deposit slips for two comments bought and used, although an item for one of them, apparently, turned up on my monthly balance sheet from the bank. It was a deposit of $54. I suppose it was for one of them. . . .

"She's being psychoanalyzed by her medium," I had thought of as a possible change in the caption of that one picture they are holding.

The dog in "That must be George coming, etc." is, of course, not my regular dog, who appears in the picture called "We think maybe his heart is broken." The same blood-line appears in the breed of most of the dogs I draw but now and then I draw one of different ancestry, outlook, political viewpoint, etc. The dog in the "That must be George" drawing is, to be sure, quite large. There is a dog lives near here just as large, but as light on his feet as a minnow, and he brooks no spirit-breaking.

It might interest the Art Conference to dwell on the subtle shades of infer-ence to be drawn, perhaps, from the fact that in every picture I have ever drawn mentioning George, George never appears in the drawing. "I don't know, George got it somewhere," "Yoo-hoo, George, I think I got it straight-ened out now," "Look, George chanteclear!" and some three, four others. This is known as the Figure in the Carpet and will perhaps interest more psychoanalysts than art critics. If anyone ever drops around wanting to do a biography of me in two volumes, specially boxed for the Christmas trade, you might mention this little fact to him about George. I daresay he will prick up his ears. . . .

> Heil Hitler!
> Vive Autriche!
> La guerre commence!
> Mr. Thurber

I expect to do pictures featuring the dog from time to time, and don't want to hear the Conference say "But he did a picture with the dog in it." He did a picture with the woman in it, too, and quite a few with the man in it, and God knows how many of the bridge lamp. They can space the dog pictures out if they want to. Agents report the dog is very popular, even more popular than the bridge lamp, and the painting of the sea that hangs on everybody's wall. I personally like the "That must be George coming" drawing better than most I have done. Matter of fact, I think it is very funny; but then I am amused by a lot of things the Art Conference simply stares at, and not amused by a lot of things which make them laugh like Roosevelt. . . .

> Mr. T

  🦐 🦐 🦐

*[Undated, 1938, from Nice]*

Dear Miss Terry:

We get the vague feeling over here that everybody has gone away forever, leaving Henderson in charge. Is it Anschluss Who's on Art now? I'm a little worried about the make-up of the Art. . . .

[Helen] Hokinson has done the two funniest pictures in a long while: the winking man one and *"I'm* the one that should be lying down." Who blunted the glory of that caption by adding "somewhere" to it? Did the Art Conference think that people would figure the lady wanted to lie down in the cage? . . .

One thing they might do for me: let me know what happens to Comment and Talk I send in. Three months ago I sent what I thought was a swell anecdote about Rome street vendors. Whether it was bought or rejected I have never been told. I suppose they rejected my Comment on the year 2000, but I don't know. I'd like to.

I had an arrangement in Bermuda that, on receipt of stuff from me, I instantly was sent a letter acknowledging this receipt. Otherwise I have to wait until a thing is bought or rejected before I know whether it got there. 11 days over and 11 days back (an average time) makes it over three weeks after I mail a thing before I can know it was received, even if acknowledgment is made at once. It makes me feel lonely and forgotten when no mention at all is made of things for months. I realize that things are pretty well messed up there during this period of transition when the Old Guard is departing and all the graduates of Amherst, class of '32, are taking over. I hope we don't give up Humor completely on behalf of a Fine Sensitivity. That would be fatal. Of course, 90 percent of my things have been handled with dispatch, care, and a lively interest—and I appreciate this—but tell 'em Thurber never forgets even the smallest anecdote he sends in and until the last tiny bedroom slipper is dropped on the floor above he can't sleep. I wish all departments kept me in such close and instantaneous touch with things as you do.

I close with an Imaginary Art Conference meeting, the subject being "Is the Caption of the Hokinson Winking Man Picture Right?"

A: She just says she wants to report a winking man. She doesn't say who he was winking at.

B: I agree. She is obviously too old and unattractive to have a man winking at her.

C: Yes, you're right. What about "I want to report a man I saw winking at a young lady."?

A: Much better.

B: Why just winking? How about "I want to report a man who has been annoying young women."? Takes in more territory, applies to more people. Many of our readers are young women who are annoyed.

A: Much better.

C: Shouldn't the woman in the drawing be this young woman? How about letting Garret Price do the thing over, with a pretty girl?

A: Much better.

B: No. I'd say have this same oldish woman drag the man she is talking about up to the officer and say "This man has been annoying my niece."

I think it was after some such conference as this that "somewhere" was added to the "I'm the one that should be lying down" picture.

Yours,

J. Thurber

&.  &.  &.

Dear Miss Terry:

Thanks for the slips. Three people there besides you have said they liked the ride ["A Ride With Olympy"] casual, and I am cheered by such generous applause. Thanks for your own kind words. . . .

Only two things worry me now: 1) what the Germans are doing to Von Cramm and 2) why a healthy, fattening man like me should have night sweats, or transpirations, as the French say. Could the checking department find out about this? (I haven't got a hectic flush or a hacking cough).

Yours,

Mr. T.

I'll do that "Well, Mrs. Bixby, welcome back to the old water hole" but I cannot say when.

One more thing: I'll try to get a caption for the analyzed lady. I don't want them to use any they make up that I don't see. I feel I have as much right to reject their captions as they have to reject mine. Most artists Can't Think of a Thing and are glad to have a staff of experts put captions on their drawings, but that does not go for me. There is a kind of figure in the carpet in what I draw and what the people in the drawings say (the second letters of the third word of every caption for the last 15 times spell "To the hell with it"). Most artists think the art conference captions are a Scream. This I do not always think. I am in the business myself and we all have our vanity and our stubbornness.

"What ever became of the Socialist Party?" was very funny, I thought, and I got a Laugh out of it, but since I had nothing to do with the caption, it gave me a Lonely feeling, made me feel funny. If people compliment me on something I not only didn't think of, but never would of, all I can say is "yeh" and look like a goat.

## To Robert Henderson

*Thurber wished to cover the Wimbledon tennis games for the* New Yorker *in 1938 but was told that the magazine had to pass up the event because of financial setbacks stemming from the 1937 recession.*

*March 26*

Dear Bob [Robert Henderson]:

It's okay about the tennis, only isn't this the only year we have passed it up? And with Mrs. [Helen Wills] Moody making her comeback, dearie me. If the thinness of the magazine keeps up, it will gross only $1,589,000 this year, I'm afraid.

I still ought to have that Western Union card, regardless. Can't tell when I might get the real lowdown on the Russian trials. Also, I might get drunk and want to send a long collect cable expressing my condolences over the loss of advertising. Well, pearls and furs get hit first in any recession and a magazine that depends on luxury ads never knows when the sheriff is going to come and take its yachts away. I remember the day we were so rich we could refuse Macy's ads. So it goes, here today and panhandling tomorrow.

     Regards,

     Jim

I'll be in London for the games and, if the magazine can dig up $75 and expenses for the finals, I might do them a piece. I realize that a magazine can't always put its hands on $100 or $150 when it wants to, but they might borrow some from Time. Time is doing fine, fatter than ever. Esquire hasn't lost any weight, either. I'm sure Luce or David Smart would be glad to come to our aid, the way Italy did to Austria's.

*John McNulty joined the* New Yorker *staff in early 1938 and was assigned to rewrite* Talk of the Town *pieces, Thurber's former job. He soon confided his uncertainties to Thurber.*

## TO JOHN McNULTY

Dear John:

You seem to be sitting in the same room, or one a whole lot like it, and thinking the same thoughts I used to when I was first on the magazine. My last letter, which crossed your rather depressed one, maybe didn't cover the main points of your depression (which was once also mine). Ross ran my stuff through his typewriter for months, threw it away by carloads, often rewrote the things so I didn't find a phrase of mine left. I would try to imitate his rewrites of my rewrites, keeping in mind what he always said: "limber it up, make it easy and off-hand, like table-talk." What came out often sounded like the table talk of Bindle stiffs. I was imitating the wrong man. Ross is a great editor but often writes with a hoe. "A man came in the room with a brown suit named Jones" is what he used to write, striving for the easy and off-hand. I listened too much to his descriptions of what Talk should be, too. Maybe it's just as well you haven't seen much of him. He's likely to fill you up with too many ideas and maxims and instructions. He could rattle off "Don't build it up, make it limber, we don't have to know too much, we want goddam it like table talk, interesting stuff, full of facts, to hell with the facts, we don't have to be experts, let yourself go, thousand interesting things in the city, for Christ's sake, etc. etc." I got bewildered. I finally figured what he wanted, in a way: "A man we know was telling us the other day about gaskets. Seems they are little funny kind of what's-its-names. Fellow named Pritch or Feep invents them, or imports them, or something of the sort. Otto H. Kahn has ninety-two and a Mrs. Bert Geefle of the Savoy Plaza seven. Nobody else has any, except Madame Curie who was presented with four thousand by the city of Nantes for telling the city what time it was one night when it called Meridian 1212 and got her by mistake." There you have an easy, off-hand statement, full of facts, presented with a nonchalant, almost insolent disregard for facts, highly informative but sounding like my mother on the subject of Einstein's theory. Talk thus has a style because Ross outlined a definite style that he wanted. You are not imitating Maloney if you write like that—or in any one of the half dozen other veins that fits the goddam thing—nor are you imitating White or me. Maloney probably went through the same half-depressed, half-angry period of wondering if he had to imitate me—just as I did about Andy. It's really the style you're imitating and to a certain extent have to imitate, but finally you get to putting in little phrases, little "explanatory openings", or something else, all your own, which fits the style, imitates nobody. Suddenly you find yourself writing the damn stuff without much effort (which is a big thing) and actually liking it. You are doing a hell of a sight better than I did at the start. Ross used to despair of my journalistic sloppiness, etc. Andy was the first guy that ever did perfect Talk pieces and nobody has ever surpassed him. Everybody has in a sense imitated him because it was obvious he had hit on the perfect formula for Talk. It is a formula, all right. No use worrying about that. John Steinbeck, Walt Whitman, Evelyn Waugh, and Shakespeare would all have to get the knack of it, if they got any stories printed. I can see Ross calmly running the copy of all of them through his typewriter, too. "A friend of ours has been telling us about a bank where the wild thyme grows. Claims a good deed shines no farther than the rays from a small candle, too." I can hear Ross saying of Will Shakespeare, as he edits his copy, "Son of a bitch falls into a kind of goddam sing-song only it don't rhyme." As far as Talk goes, he would be right, too.

Talk, though, is a thing apart. Talk and Comment. They both have to be written more or less in a formula vein. It's a million times freer than Time style, say, but it does stick to a general mould. If you want to do Comment, do it the way you have to do Talk, more or less in imitation of a style. It's not as tight as the sonnet formula (just seems so at first) and look at the world-wide diversity of sonnets! But don't feel you have to carry the Talk style over to reporters, casuals, or anything else. If there is a general similarity to them it isn't of style, but of form. Where nothing runs much over 2 or 3 thousand words—as in casuals—there is bound to be a similarity of form. But style doesn't come in to that—as you'll see by comparing the wide range of casuals with the short range of Talk stories. People sometimes speak of a New Yorker Style, but they are either thinking of Talk or of the form and shape of the casuals. It takes a knack to do things in from 1000 to 3000 words. They are bound to be different from short stories running to 5000 and 7500 words. But it is a knack of form, and not of the arrangement of words. I am sure anybody who has done as many casuals as I have learns to think unconsciously in the casual form. I find most of my stories, after I have typed them, run to 6 and a half or seven pages. I haven't tried for that. My brain has unconsciously formed that kind of mould for them. In a way this is bad, because everything I start—play, two-volume novel, or what not, finally rounds itself out into 6 or 7 pages—seems complete, too. The Saturday Review recently spoke of Gibbs' and my pieces as being of a special New Yorker form, neither essay nor short story but a little of each. It really is a form of its own, too. Slighter than the short story, stronger than the essay. They can probably never be great, but they certainly oughtn't ever to be stuffy. The greatest fault the form has is its likelihood of being thin, and we've had plenty of thin ones. "Casual" is a perfect name for them, for that's what they all really are. Too casual for anyone ever to be afraid of them. Sally Benson probably does, as far as the form goes, the perfect casual. You never confuse her stuff with a real short story. Bob Coates, on the other hand, has ingeniously managed to get short stories into the casual form. Fine short stories are better than fine casuals, taking the purest form of each one. A casual can never be great. It can be goddam good, though. A casual is just the right size to curl up with cleverness and look as cute as a pair of love birds on a mimosa bough. But if the black panther of Passion or of Drama climbed on the bough the thing would crack under it in a second. Once in a while the old cat has made it, of course, but I have always been sensible of its poising there a little dangerously, wishing to god it had more room. Toy panthers look better on the mimosa bough of a casual, and make Ross feel more comfortable, too. He has always said he wouldn't ever use a short story. I think he vaguely means by a short story something with more than four characters and at least three changes of scene. Sometimes he means something else, nobody knows just what. Of course, one good definition of a short story is that at the end you never feel like saying "So what happened then?" Most casuals seem to end in such a way that that question could well be put. Sad little husband wanders down to the drugstore, notes it is snowing, remembers once when it was snowing in years past, goes to store, selects tobacco his wife says is best for him, goes back home, enters. Wife calls down from upstairs, "That you, dear?" George looks upstairs. There the casual seems to end. We have invented, or perfected, something that is neither a happy ending nor an unhappy ending. It might be called the trailing off. "George heard someone on the porch. The door opened and it was Wesley. Well, Jesus Christ! said Wesley. He came forward in three long steps, his hand held out. George looked at him." We seem to find a high merit in leaving men on bases. We don't like to have a guy doubled off second on a line drive: too rough and abrupt. October mist is better than noon light. More gentlemanly, perhaps. I don't know. It's the ballet finish; rather than the third act tag or the black out. More people are left standing and looking in ballets and New Yorker casuals than in any other known art forms. I try to end a casual so that you know what the characters are going to do next. (This is not true of the drawings which end in a situation in which nobody could possibly do anything else: a kind of rigor vitae). I don't care what the fashion in casuals is, nor should you. I read very few of them. It is easy to get New Yorker glut, casual fag. Don't read the magazine too consistently. If you read it from cover to cover it's like eating a two pound box of candy. It needs beef steak medium, I think. Now that you have the hang of it, and know, as you say, that you 'can write the stuff', don't read so much of it that its little tricks of form and style keep running through your head. You'll probably want to stick to Talk and reporter pieces. If you get an idea for a casual, try it out, work it over, throw it away if you don't like it, and try another one, or to hell with them all. It seems to me now that casuals are easy as pie, and probably one day it will to you. Again it is something not to struggle and worry about. Writing for that magazine ought to be fun, in the main, anyway.

* * *

Reading this over the next morning, it does not seem very helpful. Maybe I should have done it in a few words, or maxims: "don't let the magazine new-yorker you, mcNulty the magazine." Etc. Get the New Yorker slant or attitude or whatever it is, but take nobody's style. Be a little egotistical, remembering that nobody in the world can tell a story better than you and that all of us experts in story tellers know that.

I have just read your Where Are They Now piece and it is absolutely okay and fine. You've got the whole idea. You're going great. There's nothing more you have to learn from the New Yorker—the rest is what it's got to learn from you.

A lot of this has been beside the point. Don't puzzle about any of it. Much of it may be crap. We old hands get to maundering. Let me hear how things go, all the time, and ask me anything you want. One of these days I'll bat off something to the point. Remember, anyway, it's all easier than it seems, not harder, it's better to relax than tighten up, it's better to laugh the problems off than worry about them.

Helen and I send our love to you both, as always.

Jim

*&a. &a. &a.*

March 8, 1938

Dear Stockin' Foot Pals [the McNultys]:

I was writing a novel tonight, but stopped a while ago to write letters to the following: Detective Inspector Alexander Dawson, of the Glasgow Police, Pelouze & Campbell, opticians, Camden, N.J., U.S.A., the Hon. Robert Frazer, Consul General of the United States at London, England, and the Manager of the Central Railway Station Hotel, Glasgow.

All this was called out on account of Mrs. Rogers' son, James McGregor Rogers, who was a hoist attendant at the C.R.S. Hotel, Glasgow, got to snooping into the rooms of nearsighted guests last August and taking things. Seems he got my passport among other articles, and a couple of empty billfolds once used to carry letters of credit into 'em, as the brakemen on the Pennsy used to say over at Taylor and Mt. Vernon avenyahs. "I got a blue suit with a red stripe into it," they'd say. Did you know I used to work behind the counter of a cigar store over there? There was a Pennsy calling station in the back of the store, run by a little gray-haired guy who wore gold collar buttons, front and back, but no collar. He'd phone Calloway and say "You're going out on Number 197, at 3.15." Then he'd phone Jennsen and say "You're firin' 197, at 3.15. Calloway drivin'." The place was usually full of firemen and engineers a-spinnin' yarns. One fireman was the roller skating champion of Port Clinton, Ohio, which had the highest syphilis rate in the state at the time. My Uncle Kirt got the syphilis there the first time. Kirt had all the known venereal diseases at one time, including a couple that the doctors only knew to nod to, from the farther Hebrides and the Western part of Cuba—and what my aunt Margery Albright when she was 80 used to call the 'blue boars', scaring me to death. That was when I was only 12 or 13 and had heard from a boy named Karl Yoakum that if a man made love to a girl he always got the 'collapse'. What with the collapse and the blue boars it is a god's wonder I did not retire to a monastery when I was in my teens. Kirt died of his unprecedented complications when he was only 38 or 40. Up to the last, my mother says he wouldn't let the surgeons take off his what's-its-name. 'That's my friend,' he told Dr. Wilcox. Dr. Wilcox replied that it was his worst enemy. 'But awful good company,' says Kirt, who had a dry humor. In his last years, Kirt used to sleep with the colored women at Smokey Hobbs, a fact my sainted grandmother died in blissful ignorance of. The Fisher boys were never what you could call choosy about their tail, as old Mrs. Albright once called it. Let's see, where were we?

Oh, yeh, the cigar store. Well, it was run by a man named Una Soderblom and I worked there after school when I was a senior in East High school in 1913. That was the year of Row, Row, Row and In My Harem, and I Lost The Sunshine and Roses and Shooky Colors and the Gaby Glide. I hadn't seen Una Soderblom, a little, small-footed blond guy, since 1913 until my brother and mother took me over to call on him last year. He lives out across from Douglas school and is dying from an incurable disease that eats up your bones and was braver about it than I would be with the mumps. He was just the same after 25 years, except that he was dying. We sat around and talked about it as if it were a poker game in which he held only a pair of treys. I had never liked the guy much when I worked for him. He once thought I stole pennies. But he was a fine fellow, after twenty-five years, and I liked him. I had mentioned his name once in a New Yorker story and his wife had seen it and somehow she knew my mother, because she clerks in the Women's Exchange and my mother sooner or later talks about me to everybody, particularly to women who have sons around my own age who my mother figures haven't done as well as I have, a fact which she feels called on to take up with these women, in a nice way. She tells them that there's everything in the way a boy's brought up and who his mother is. Mary-Tact, they call my mother in the neighborhood. *Now*, where were we? Oh yeh, Kirt.

Kirt was the youngest of the Fisher boys, all of whom were strange. Grant died of a knee disease when he was 48. Like Kirt, he was buried in a hard collar. Willie is the only survivor. He does nothing now, my mother tells me, except wind clocks. And lie down in the backyard on warmish days. Life has closed in on him, and has him against the wall with a clock key in his hands. My mother views this extraordinary narrowing down of Willie's activities with a scientific detachment. She never liked Willie much, and once threw a cup and saucer at him. This was the year that "Underneath the Stars" came out. Kirt could ride a bicycle with his head on the saddle and his feet in the air, a position that was not half as bad for him as when he was prone. He was prone everywhere from Front Street to Seventh Street most every night. We never liked Kirt when we were kids because he was severe, but we liked him as we grew older. I remember William and I once had lunch at his house and William put butter in his coffee cup (his own). "For God's sake, Bessie," says Kirt to Bessie, "Hide the eggs!" Bessie was his wife. She insisted on marrying him even after he said he was the clinical wonder of all the venereal specialists in the Middle West. "I don't care," she said. "I will throw myself over a cliff if you don't marry me." "Well, Jamie," says my mother. "She not only married him, she buried him." Bessie was a great gal. Kirt without sex was better than any other man with sex, to her. And so it goes. Now let's see, oh, yeh: those letters.

Well, this James McGregor Rogers, the hoist attendant, seems to have done a little burgling on the side and one of the rooms he got into last August was occupied by a Mr. and Mrs. James Thurber, of New York, American, as Detective Inspector Dawson calls it. He was arrested in January and when they searched his room there was our passport, which we hadn't missed until we got to London. I had long ago figured out it was stolen. I just sat and thought one day, and figured this out. If anything Helen has charge of can't be found, it's stolen. I began with that and ended with that. And comes out I was right. Well, sir, Dawson draws himself up a remarkable little report of the case, which he had figured out to a fine point, and this report is sent to the New

York police who turn it over to a Detective Connelly who one day brings to Miss Terry a couple of empty leather billfolds which Jamie McGregor Rogers had also taken with the passport, overlooking Helen's emeralds. These had once been used to hold letters of credit and it must have been a big shock to Jamie when he found nothing in them except what Detective Inspector Dawson calls "a list of correspondence." That description must have baffled the Chief Inspector of the Glasgow C.I.D. to whom Dawson sent his report, but he apparently let it ride. What it was was a list of correspondent banks used by the Guaranty Trust in Europe. So you'd know where to go and get your letter of credit cashed.

The passport, Dawson reports, was turned over to a Mr. Lillienthal, the American vice consul in Glasgow. But along with the empty billfolds was sent a pair of spectacles which Dawson also figured out to belong to this man Thurber, the American, on account the case the spectacles came in said Camden, N.J. on it. That's probably where a New Yorker would go to get his glasses, Dawson figured. So I have written these letters just to see what responses I get about the spectacles. The elephant laboring to bring forth a spectacle case that belongs to a Camden man seems to me amusing, too amusing just to let drop. I have written Dawson that, as far as the spectacles go, he is just where he was.

Your records were here on the table one day when we came back from Nice. But what to play them on we didn't know, until Maria, our wonderful cook, said she'd just go and apporter her phonograph, which she did. It's the size of a 1907 Corona and blats like a crow but we played all the records, over and over, they being, as you say, American. With the phonograph Maria brought a bunch of their own records, some of them very good: Chaliapin, music from Manon and Werther (two of Maria's favorites) and the most wonderful ancient rendering of Rose-Marie you ever heard. Sounds like it was played by motormen on pans and bottles. I want to bring it home to you. It's pre-swing, pre-jazz, practically pre-music. Otchi Tchornia is one of the records. Do you know that by that name? Well, it's "O Tes Yeux Noirs" in French. That is, "Don't Bat Dem Big Black Ahs at Me, Man" in English. But all it can ever be to me again is the song the Ritz brothers, especially the middle one, parodied, burlesqued, and tore to pieces in one of their movie musicals: the one in which Madeleine Carroll and Dick Powell were in love. "On the Avenya, to make it as simple as possible, my Stockin' Foot Pals."

From your report everybody is passing everybody on the high seas. We were sorry to hear about Katharine's father, but glad to know they were reconciled to it. Seems too bad she had to be in bed sick when he really died, after chasing all the way to Florida. She's had a hard time. . . .

That will be all for this time, Stockin' Foot Pals. Enclosed a few more pictures, with maybe notes on the back. Love from us both to you and Donia,

Jim

*In April 1938, McKelway, who managed nonfiction, discussed rejecting a Thurber "Comment" submission with executive editor Ik Shman: ". . . I thought it a good idea to stall rather than reject it to Thurber because rejections always drive him crazy and bring on a flood of letters; I thought he might forget about this, it being only a page long, but no. Now that it has to be rejected, I suggest a good way out would be for you to write, saying that it was rejected by Gibbs and myself, but that it hadn't been sent to either of us; it was routed somewhere else for rejection and got bogged down somewhere in the middle of the various absences this winter. Something on that order. If I have to reject it I'll have to tell him why and god knows where it will all end."*

*Unknown to Ross, the New Yorker management had subsidized the start-up of a rival magazine, Stage. When news of its ownership broke, Ross threatened to quit. Stage was soon terminated.*

## To Harold Ross

*[Undated, 1938, from Nice]*

Dear Harold:

Here finally are some drawings. The art conference must remember several things: 1) I am no Robert J. Day from whom one may expect six different versions of 14 drawings each Tuesday; 2) at 44 one is neither so gay nor so prolific as one was at 32 when one went to work on the New Yorker before the depression, the bombings, the birth of his and your children, the Roosevelt regime; back in the days in fact when there were tourists in Spain, the Angells were living together and White was a lone figure skater. Times change and one's spirit with them. John Jay Chapman says in his letters that he was no good between the ages of 40 and 45. A little research by me has shown that almost no man ever is, except maybe Tilden. All artists, writers, painters are at their worst from 40 to 45, publishers and editors, too. I have only a year and a half till I'm out of the woods and you must be darn near out now. The first half of the forties will probably kill White and Gibbs, though; I mean they will really die. If they worry as much as they do in their thirties, they will never survive the forties.

Now, as to the enclosed drawings: I have numbered each one in the upper left hand corner and will now take them up seriatim:

1) a redrawing of a very funny picture the Nyer turned down because the art conference had the audacity and the stupidity to think the point turned on the doctor having no hair. The fact that one sees no hair on my men does not mean they are bald. George Bellows' prize fighters had no faces, but that didn't mean they had no faces. I would never have made the point on the basis of baldness. Christ, but the art conference can be dumb!

2) New caption on picture rejected by art conference.

3) screamingly funny new picture, with as good faces as I ever drew. "Ooooo, guesties!" was my original title, and perhaps better. But you people like to have everything made so explicit.

4) New picture.

Love,

Thurber

PS. How are you, my boy?

Janet Flanner and I are thinking of starting a magazine in London called "Stage". Would Fleischmann be interested in putting in half a million dollars? J

## To the McKelways

[*Undated, spring 1938, from Nice*]

Dear Mac and Honey:

We got back from a long trip of a week to Carcassonne, Luchon (on the Spanish border, or a few miles from it) to find letters from the both of ye, as McNulty says. By the way, he has been longer than usual writing and was one of our Old Reliables. Tell me about him. When I see a guy named McCarty has been and done a job of work a guy named McNulty could have done, I wonder how many more guys you goin keep taking on. And whether John has been lost sight of in the mad rush of Henderson hiring and etc. As I keep saying, I think you got a good man in McNulty, if only the old curse of the magazine, just letting guys kind of drift around without a cheerful word or a soft-boiled egg, or a hint or a helping hand, hasn't set in again. That is the old curse of the magazine, or one of them. Another is working 2 years on a plan to save money by a system of word payment which will cost the magazine approximately $11,500 a year and result in so many 1200 word pieces from Parke Cummings and Alice Frankforter that you won't have filing room for 'em and will have no effect at all on the longer pieces that, after 10 years, people have fallen into an unbreakable mould of turning out. But as I told Katharine the new system is gay and strange and wonderful and I love it. . . . Well, it gives Ross something to do of the kind he is nuts about. How about 10 line sonnets getting a higher rate than the old 14 everybody is so sick of wading through? What we want is a snap to everything. Tell Ross if he runs out of systems, he might try seeing how many words he could cut out of Conrad's "Heart of Darkness" so that, at 10 cents a word for the first 5000, 12 1/2 for the next 2500, and 4¢ for the balance, he would still get within $10 of what he would have got under his old rate, for the whole works. It might become a parlor game. Ask people to cut "The Red Badge of Courage" so that it is worth "as much to the writer and to the magazine" as O. Henry's "Gift of the Magi". Economics and a fine taste in literary judgments both come in to this and make it a high class game for smart people. Who was it there, what Genius of Belles Lettres, who figured that after 1500 words a piece of writing is not worth any more to the author than the first 1500 words? Compare Conrad's "Youth" with "A Piece of String" and show why this is. Show how, if I had stopped my piece on Olympy just as the ride begins, it would have been worth more to me, in an artistic sense, than going ahead with a lot of words. Point out how the admitted space limitations of the New Yorker have changed the old permanent values of literary composition, for the better.

It is the goddamdest thing any set of editors ever thought up and if I am a little surprised at its stuffiness, a little shocked at a formal office announcement which has all the ring of the kind of thing we make newsbreaks of (or did in our heyday), and if I am a bit alarmed at the advent of a new regime whose masterpiece of thought seems worthy of the staff of the old Everybody's, I am still tickled to death at being handed one of the best laughs of the year. I keep getting that goddam announcement out and reading it over. I see traces of six or eight hands in it; it was obviously labored over; it runs like a doctored up 1904 Cadillac; it reeks of the old Cassaret ads in Pearson's. At its best it rates "How's That Again" department. If Andy were still the power there that he happily used to be, that's where it would have ended up too. The pitiful thing is it doesn't mean anything. It is just a portent of the end, a first faint smell of decay. It shows the editors have taken to hard collars, that a new set is in who belong to university clubs, who smoke cigars after dinner, who make desk memoranda about buying new garters, who are inclined toward croup, who have stuff put on their hair by barbers, who can explain life insurance, who know When They Have Had Enough to Drink, who go home from a party at 12.30, who rub Vick's salve on their chest on chilly nights, who believe in budgets and the Things that Count, who begin dictation at 9 in the morning, who contemplate the underwear of little girls on trains, who call people mister, who use words beginning with "im", such as improper, imprecise, who take tea at shoppes, who brush and shine their own shoes every morning, who carry little cloths in their billfolds to clean their glasses with, who have great albums of Red Seal records, who think Bert Williams was a sprinter, who think that sexual intercourse in the day time is decadent, and who send birthday greetings to their uncles. This is the way this looks to me. . . .

Honey's letter was fine. Yourn was okay, too, my boy, but not the classic you did on small red pieces of paper. Your wife could write casuals, as we all know, and when she has this dog book done, she ought to do some. Still keep her office. Swell place to write casuals. About the dog pictures, I will do them, but I think Birnbaum, the great dog artist, would be better. . . .

I shudder about this two-day drinking bout of Honey and Sally [Benson]. Honey said she had a fine time and if anybody can have a fine time with Sally on the second day of a bout with the cups, she (Honey) must have been coked to the gills. Personally, I think it can not be done, this having a fine time on that second day. As to What All Was Said, I imagine that God himself was a little surprised and said "Come heah and lissen, Gabriel—dey up to somethin' new in de way o' gassin' down yondah, them two women." I've never knew Honey not to be amusing when coked, but Sally B. usually goes in for disemboweling the reputations of all the people whom she calls Darling. Look out for a lady who disembowels Darlings. Sally undoubtedly has it all over town now that Honey had an affair with Elsa at the Half Moon Inn. Well, the bowels of Gibbs and me lie drying in the living rooms of a dozen Darlings. It's safer over here. But we aim to join in the drinkin' along in August. Keep us informed. . . . It occurs to me, le lendemain, that I make too much fuss, draw too wide conclusions, raise my voice too high, and etc. as in regards to this New System. I don't think the staff is really like what I say. I just draw a dark picture of it as I don't ever want to see it. With you in there it will be safe.

Love to you both,
Jim and Helen

## TO KATHARINE WHITE

*Katharine gave up her job as fiction editor at the end of June to join Andy at the Whites' salt-water farm in North Brooklin, Maine. She continued to be sent material to edit, but Gus Lobrano was hired as her office replacement.*

*Art Samuels was a former* New Yorker *managing editor.*

*Life* magazine *had just published an explicit photo essay on the birth of a child.*

*John Mosher was a veteran* New Yorker *editor and writer.*

*March 24, 1938*

Dear Katharine:

. . . We are staying here till May 1. I am sorry I missed the chance to see Vienna as Viennese and it's terrible to think of it in the hands of the worst bastards the history of the world has ever known. The worst of it is that the rank and file of young Germans are all little Hitlers. I think Hitler's claim that Fascism will last a thousand years is probably true. So many people think it can end over night, like the Whiskey Rebellion. The young Germans are half for Hitler and half for war. Wish there were no Czechoslovakia. That noble little country annoys me the way Ann Harding does, or the movie we saw called "Green Light". It would have to produce the noblest man, in Masaryk, the modern world has known, and it would have to be as brave as a tiny lion, so that France will have to hurl herself against Germany with about as much chance of winning as a 15 year old Ohio virgin in a West Fifty-eighth street night club. It's been pretty discouraging to watch England kissing all the bottoms in Europe, France squabbling like a bunch of neighbor women, Russia executing all their prominent men in a way that makes pulp stories seem like Atlantic essays, while Hitler goes in and does whatever he wants to. It's a wonder I don't lose patience with the wonderful freedom of democracies—the right of squabble, the right to have a to-hell-with-it attitude, the right to make fools of themselves—like a bunch of drunken bums in a barroom.

Let us know how everything is.

Jim

ᥣᥣ ᥣᥣ ᥣᥣ

April 19, 1938

Dear Katharine:

. . . We kept the villa, as I must have said, through April, but leave here, sadly, too, May 1, for northern Italy, Suisse, and so on, and England for a spell, then back to Paris, and sail in August if all goes as planned. . . .

Oh, yes, the Saturday Review wants me to do a piece on Andy! They sent me Gibbs' piece on O'Hara and another piece. They don't know how little Andy would care for a piece on himself, or how scared I would be to attempt it. Not that it isn't something I would enjoy doing, and it was a pleasure to be selected as the guy to do it, but somehow I can't yet see a piece by me that would please both me and the Saturday Review—and Andy. . . .

My family, happily, seem to be getting along fine. Althea hasn't let me know about Rosemary since Loch Ness, although she sent me a card at Xmas time.

Love to you both and to Joe, and keep your cache-nez wound tight. Spring is bad for colds in the head and hot flashes in the heart. We drove through poppies and lilacs and it was very fine. The car has held up wonderfully. The left front tire sighed and went flat—an hour after we reached the villa. It's a considerate car. I feel I ought to win an arm decoration or something, maybe crossed wheels embroidered over my heart, for my 10,000 miles of safe driving among the mad people of three countries. You got to watch the person five cars ahead of you and five cars behind all the time. Fortunately, there aren't a fiftieth as many cars, but we drove back 250 miles on Easter Sunday and they were all out. Their favorite hazard is passing a car that's passing a car. This is apparently considered great sport, like skiing. You have to learn a new traffic signal here, that is: waving your left arm and hand madly in a gesture meaning "Stay back there, you feeble-minded son of a bitch!" Only one person out of every 15 in any country should be allowed to drive, I find. Sometimes I think it is only one out of every 150. The death rate here and in England is appalling, I imagine that, for miles travelled per car, higher than ours. We have 12 and 1/2 times as many cars as France, but how much bigger we are in size I don't remember. This reminds me of the New Payment System. Who wins, writer or New Yorker, on a piece 2190 words long? At just what word-point is the payment exactly the same under both systems?

Keep letting us know about these things.
Love again,
Jim

ॐ  ॐ  ॐ

*April 30, 1938*

Dear Katharine:

I'm not sending the Character o' Catastrophe proof back because the one or two minor changes are okay with me. . . .

Got a very fine, very amusing letter from Andy yesterday which was greatly appreciated. The Nyer also came in today with his wonderful parody of the Birth of a Child. I keep reading it over and over. I am glad he is getting those books out. I have long thought he suffers mainly from Repression of Writing Instincts, which can be a much worse repression than that of sex. I think now that he is writing more he will find that street dizziness and the ear trouble vanishing. Like his fallen stomach and paratyphoid I believe they are merely symbols of Writer's Repression. Or do I mean symptoms?

Did you and he ever read Man the Unknown—it really, here and there, has some fine new stuff in it. This Carrel is quite a guy. He's on the right track. He knows that everybody from Marxists to New Dealers think of human beings as Units in a Scheme and not as Individuals who have to be understood and treated as such and not like marks on a graph or figures in a chart. You see clearly, after pondering his ideas, how the Marxist boys try to twist Man around to fit a Plan instead of making the plan fit Man. It reminded me of Malcolm Cowley's telling me that human nature would automatically change when communism became general. Sex jealousy would go, for instance. All the boys really seem to believe that; they are trying to twist man around the way they think would be nice to fit their schemes. Carrel knows the big problem is man and not the schemes. He thinks Marx and Freud have got things into a hell of a mess, and all the other guys, with One Way Out. He shows you that nobody at all is thinking about Man's tissues, for one thing. . . .

They haven't forgot about my piece on Olympy and the ride, have they? I keep looking for it a little wistfully, and finding Sylvia Townsend Warner.

In the last comment they bought—the one that was mislaid—I realize I never once used the word 'millennium' which belongs in there and I hope somebody puts it in where it belongs. When I talk about the year 2038 I am right when I say century, but when I refer to 2000, it's a new millennium. Or am I all twisted on this? Or does it matter?

Gibbs' first theatre piece was beautifully written. The boy is writing exceptionally fine stuff, I think. I wish I hadn't passed my prime for writing New

Yorker stuff. I feel one's thirties are the best for it and that we'll all have to give up at 45. I think I am going through a mental menopause, with my mind and intellect at its lowest, but maybe Paris will snap me out of it—we'll see Margaret Speaks there and her husband—and O'Hara and his new wife in London—just got a note from John. . . . Let us all try to hold on a little longer. I've got to see what Ross is doing about Arno and Fleischmann and all the little payment problems when he is 65. I got to see that. Please God let me see that.

Love to you both. I'll write Andy soon.

& & &

May 15 [1938]

Dear Katharine:

This marks the day that St. Anne Honeycutt loses a bet of $15,000 she made one day that we wouldn't stay away from NY a year, on account we sailed from NY a year ago yesterday.

We were shocked to hear about John Mosher and glad to read in the next sentence that his eye will be all right. Instead of setting fire to Fire Island, he might be happier taking virgins to the Virgin Islands, or sticking to manhattans on Manhattan Island. We got a letter from him just the other day and will answer it. Give him our love and sympathy.

Maybe we can visit you in October, if I am not in a state where I got to hide in Connecticut. We've been in a lot of Spain, politics, war, arguments and talks, since getting to Paris. People, including me, never seem to understand exactly where I stand on all this. Sheean wanted to take me to Spain with him and on 2 scotches I said fine, but on Maturer Reflection—which is as mixed up in my case as the Heat of Argument—I decided I would only get in Spain's way. I am somewhat convinced that Spain-politics-war, etc. is not Precisely My Field. Either writing about it or blundering around in it.

I will get around to casuals pretty soon, I guess. Drawings I don't seem to do many of nowadays and probably they'll run short of them first, rejecting as many as they do.

We go to London in three days and maybe I'll get something done over there—Paris right now is not the place for it. One reason we're getting out of it, though it's a mighty sweet city in May.

We'll be seeing you before very long now.

Love

Jim

## TO THE JOHN McNULTYS

*Russell Maloney, then editing "Talk" in the office Thurber once occupied, had
wallpapered over a Thurber drawing, McNulty reported.*

*2 Clarges St, London, Hingland*
*June 1, 1938*

Dear John:

McCulloch, who runs this bldg full of service flats, began talking hosses two
weeks ago when he came in to open the curtains, and the maid who laid the
fire told us ten days ago that Pasch would run their hoofs off. Cecil, who looks
like a cousin of Charles Butterworth or a small sized Sterling Holloway, and
who brings breakfast, was all for Scottish Union. Everybody in the house from
belowstairs to the man who has nightmares every night in top (that is, in the
top apartment) is horse nuts (as my old grandmother Thurber used to ex-
claim when she burned her hand on the stove). Everybody in England is
horse-wise and even the people on the dole wager. Everybody wagers, from
the blind pencil salesman to the Kinnig (the one here and the one over the
ocean). You see why the English Derby is the greatest of all races, why the Kentucky Derby is just a great big race. Everybody in these isles, even unto the
outer Hebrides, from infants to ladies of 107, had their money on and listened
in on the radio. We didn't get out to the actual runnin' although we hankered
to. Cyril, not Cecil, is this nice little waiter's name. He stutters. Over the phone
he can't say anything and for a long time was thought to be nuts. But McCulloch who knows hosses found out Cyril knows hosses, so his job was saved. He
hasn't been workin' here very long. . . . McCulloch and Cyril got up a house
pool days ago—there were twenty-two of us in it, including an aged, sad lady
school teacher who said "I've wagered a mite each year since the Queen died"
and a crotchety old Arno colonel of 78 who said "What? what? dammit, man,
what are you sputtering about? Out with it! Better still, be off! What? Oh, a
pool on the Darby? Dammit all, say so, man! Don't stand there going piddery-
jiddery!" Janet Flanner drew Boswell and won a handful of shillings. Helen
drew Pasch, me Flyon (and on and on and on for all I care). We wagered a
pound, also, on Scottish Union—Cyril or McCulloch place all bets for all ten-
ants and love it, but to win, not each way, so we lost all. . . .

Your line "An Irishman named Russell [Maloney] is the wrongest thing I
know of" has taken England by storm. We quote various things from your letters, giving you credit a great deal of the time.

Never you mind about that Russell coverin up the old sign. I'll do a better one and paste it over the son a bitch's wallpaper directly I git back.

Keep in there a swingin. . . .

. . . Yeah we know Dick Maney. Been through a lot with him. Been thrown out of his house by the Mrs. Great guy, but as you say hard to git along with.

We live in a nice flat just two steps off Piccadilly on Clarges, within three minutes walk of St James's, the Marble Arch, Hyde Park corners, Piccadilly Circus (if you walk fast), Selfridge's, the Mall, Pall Mall, Buckingham palace, Park Lane, Birdcage Walk, Berkeley Square, etc. Whores frequent this part of Mayfair and often six or eight are prowling up and down before the house. At 3 or 4 in the morning they play together, toss, catch, pig-in-a-poke, kitten-for-a-corner, you-chase-me, etc. also in front of the house. Their approach: "Would you like to talk with me?"

We have return passage booked and bought on Champlain sailing August 25 from Le Havre, arriving in NY Sept 1, 1938. See you then.

Dear Donia & John: This letter is also for you. Hahya, kids?

Love from us both,
Jim

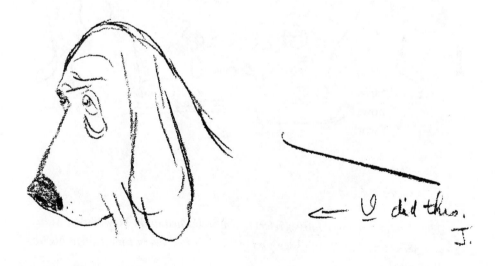

## To the E. B. Whites

*In 1938 Simon and Schuster published* How to Raise a Dog, *by Dr. James R. Kinney and Ann Honeycutt McKelway. Thurber agreed to illustrate it.*

*September 15, 1938*

Dear Katharine and Andy:

We have been as busy as a turkey fancier since we got home 2 weeks ago, looking for a place to live, etc. Found one yesterday near Woodbury, a dream, a poem of a house, 225 yrs. old but complete with all facilities, one of the nicest places in the world. . . .

Busy illustrating Honey's dog book & looking forward to EBW's Harper's [magazine] pieces. We gotta see you before long. Driving to Columbus in October in new Ford I just got. No trace of Althea & my daughter yet—she's gallivanting I guess. We're going to N.Y. tomorrow for a week.

Love to you all,<br>Jim & Helen

Honey's book is very fine.

## To Gus Lobrano

*The mislaid drawing Thurber refers to was published in the* New Yorker *March 5, 1938, captioned: "Don't keep saying 'God forbid' every time I mention Mr. Roosevelt!"*

*September 27, 1938*

Dear Gus:

I am enclosing three drawings with new captions. You will recognize these drawings. Two of them the New Yorker has been holding a long time for a new caption. The other one was a reject but I think is good with the new caption. I mean the one that was originally about Belle Lett (a caption I sent in for a joke and wistfully hoped might be bought, though). The new caption has no pun in it and the drawing has been added to to give a greater idea of books, writings etc around the house. The caption for this drawing is:

"There isn't room in this house for belles lettres and me both."

Can you cut that out and put it on the drawing? Please ask Miss Terry to see that nobody down there puts paper clips on my drawings. You will see what they do to the paper on the analyst drawing enclosed.

This is a funny drawing and I know it. Also I know the "Won't you put your burdens on me?" one is.

So is the third, but on this one the art conference and I seem to be at a Czecho-German pass. Anybody who would prefer the George Jean Nathan caption to mine (either the original or the new) has about as much sense of humor as a police lieutenant. You all know how hard it is for me to deal with an art conference that thinks it's a scream and no longer believes that I draw funny pictures. These three pictures are funny and for the love of Jesus give them a break. I still know more about what's funny than they think down there.

The New Yorker seems to find it difficult to buy very many of my pictures at a time, although the purchase of 30 or 40 Hokinsons or Steigs at a clip is easy. For this reason I never intend to send in more than three. Of the ones sent from Europe in a year and a half, seven were approved by the New Yorker as funny pictures, but they wanted new captions. Here are three of the seven. The others will be coming in next week. They are already to go now, after days of solid work on them, but I know goddam well half of 'em would be rejected if I sent them all this time. They'll all be bought if I string 'em out.

The magazine has somehow mislaid the picture which I had captioned "Why doesn't your precious Roosevelt etc." I didn't get it back.

I sent to Andy White, for him to keep against the day we write our history of the New Yorker, the two slips of paper which were attached to the George Jean Nathan caption on which, in fine pencil was timidly lettered the sentence "He'd never sue." This, as I told Andy, explains why differences exist between me and the art conference and always must. I could laugh about that if I didn't want to cry. It's one of the saddest things that ever happened to

Old Thurber

## To E. B. White

*In September 1938, a fierce hurricane struck eastern Long Island and southern New England.*

*[Undated, September 1938]*

Dear Andy:

. . . I enclose two little slips, a red and a yellow, found among more than one hundred and thirty such slips that were waiting for me at the office when I got home.

In a letter from Europe I had threatened to sue if the New Yorker ever used a caption on a picture of mine intimating that my people knew, sexually or otherwise, George Jean Nathan. The whole story of the present Art Conference and my differences with it seems to lie in those tiny pencilled notations on these enclosed slips.

(Maloney, of course, knows nothing about this—nor did I know the idea was his. I like Maloney and think he is doing okay.)

I feel pretty far away from the arms, the councils, and the understanding of the New Yorker. It's not the place I worked for years ago, when you and I removed Art Samuels' rugs and lamps in order to draw pictures and write lines for Is Sex Necessary. This is perhaps because I am an older man, with my youth definitely behind me and fifty around the corner. There is an air of college halls about the place; people bow to you; there is a faint precise ticking sound; an atmosphere of austere incoherence dwells there. (They sent me a caption, approved by the art conference, to put on a drawing. I did a drawing and put the caption on it. They advised me that they liked the drawing but they didn't like the caption. My anger is exhausted; I just get tired).

Except for dear and wonderful Miss Terry, I feel that I am looked upon as an outsider, possibly a has been. She sends out letters and packages for me, handles mail etc., but I feel nobody else thinks I really have any right to any such services. With my name no longer on the list of editorial folk and no room of my own to go to, this is only natural. . . . This may be a mood caused by wars and floods. I daresay I shall get over it, perhaps by being put back on the editorial list as art conference advisor at $1 a year. The aging humorist I suppose is bound to be a sad figure. They go in for the fleeting smile down there and the neatly pressed pants and I have the notion that they shake their heads politely over what I think is funny. Of course, I withdrew from the actual halls but I never considered myself as withdrawing from the magazine. If only one person had asked me what I thought of one idea in the dozen times I was around the place I would have felt less like a waiter in the Beta house. They didn't mention anything at all; they didn't even tell me to my face that I'd never sue.

I was a little disturbed about Rosemary and her mother but seems they started from North Conway in time to get to Cambridge before the storm broke. I'm to see Rosemary this Saturday at Sandy Hook, driving down from Joywalls, our house near Woodbury which we move into this weekend. The woman we rent from (a Columbus woman, it came out) is a bit balmy and told us that joy comes right out of the walls of the place, that in 225 years there had been nothing but joy within those walls. She is right out of a Sally Benson story, only she's in italics. . . .

I didn't reach Althea till two days ago. I have always had a feeling that nobody close to me is going to be ended by a flood or earthquake. This is a silly feeling but there it is. Fly-paper is something else. Althea says there is not going to be a war.

Out of 167 letters to answer, I picked yours first, but now I got to tear gloomily into the others. We'll let you know our new address on a postcard of Woodbury soon.

> Love,
> Jim

&a.  &a.  &a.

[Undated, late October 1938]

Dear Andy:

. . . We got back from New York a few hours ago, worn and a little depressed, the way I have never been otherwise . . . in getting back from New York. I can't take it calmly or slowly or happily down yonder. We slipped into town this time—four days ago—without letting anyone know, so as to get to bed and be ready for the dentist, oculist, and rectologist. But I came down from my room for some cigarettes and there in the lobby were Gibbs, McKelway, Alan and Dorothy [Parker] Campbell; so it goes. The next night there were Charmé [Seeds] and Mary Rennels and John Mosher and Bob Coates and all the others named above, to say nothing of Lois Long, her husband, Ursula Parrott, Howard Baldwin, and . . . that other man from above-stairs. You find yourself drinking. This is a practise I no longer care very much about but fall into, the way a man whittles or eats salted almonds or reads Life.

It is nice to be back under the 200-year-old maples and the apple trees. Cows from up the road get into the yard when I leave the gate open and their owner comes for them around one a.m. on a motorcycle. One morning (he having said the hell with it) I heard a cow eating apples under my bedroom window. It was 7 o'clock. After she had eaten 27, by actual count, I got up and chased her home in my nightgown. I figured she must have eaten a couple of hundred during the night; she is up and around, though, giving cider and apple jack, I suppose. . . .

My bottom doctor, Robin Hood, told me he had had a man in his office who was "almost exsanguinated". My favorite expression now for bleeding to death. Fellow had just let his rectum go for twenty years, taking a little iron and liver compound from time to time. Scared Ross into going back to Robin, I think. Ross bleeds. He claims he is getting smaller down there, is, in fact, slowly closing up. Asses to ashes, I said to him, dust to dust.

Mrs. Parker has solved it all now by not going to doctors or dentists, but just letting everything drop out or close up. My dentist says I will have my teeth for "quite a while". My opthalmologist says I won't need reading glasses for "a time". My rectologist says, well - - -.

Margaret, our cook, is rounding nicely into a casual. She says one of her sons works into the incinerating plant where they burn the refuge; has had the job since the Armitage. I'm going to have to combine her with another lady of the vicinity who pointed out a flock of fletchers on her lawn and who also told me of a young man who had passed his civil service eliminations. As far as real estate values goes she says there is great disparagement. You begin to feel insane after an hour or so of this. Margaret lost only one child, "a beautiful girl of 24." Margaret is very black and so is one living beautiful girl of hers we saw. I asked what had carried the other girl off and Margaret said "Tuberculosis. She got it from her teeth. Went all through her symptom." I'm hedged about my misnamed terrors. Much worse than old familiar terrors you can put your finger on. . . .

Honey has a new apartment at 9 East 63 so she can be near the park and hear the seals. Mac is staying at the Mansfield which the Connells left because they couldn't open their door when they wanted out. Mac lost his key the other night and they had to give him another room. They have no pass key or anything.

I am thinking of getting around to that play—the one that gave you an idea for a poem eight years ago or so.

Paula, Honey tells me, is not very happy in her married life any longer but can pay $30 for her hats, so is contented.

I was by no means satisfied with my piece [on White] for the Sat Review but was caught between all the mill-stones you get caught between writing a piece about a friend for the Sat Review. I don't really know them very well, you see. Your quality of thought is tempered by the magazine you sit down to write for, I think. The time of year, the year of life shape the contours, too. Bob [Coates] said it was "ornate". The Thursday before or the following Friday I would have been better. Everybody liked the piece, all right, but I am planning for my next book a piece called E.B.W.: Second State, which will be better. Little apt sentences come to you in the night, paragraphs reshape themselves, ideas take off their dancing shoes and sit down so you can see what they are. Meanwhile the piece has been locked in the forms and there you lie remaking the living room of the story, putting in a rock garden, selecting new bedroom wallpaper, and on and on. . . .

Did I tell you about seeing Rosemary? I helped move in here one Saturday, then drove to Sandy Hook and helped Althea move, then took a walk in the woods with Rosemary and helped her move fallen trees out of the path, a thing which it seems had to be done. I share her conscientious compulsions in these matters, which sets me off for her from all the other adults in the world, I guess. She has the most calm and poise of any child of seven I ever saw. But there's a lot of sparkle, too. I was overwhelmed by her. She came running out of the house and threw her arms around me, and I saw she wasn't a baby any longer. Always it used to be that I had to win her over, with skill and patience. She played me two pieces on the piano and read to me. She is inclined to think that Hitler will not be satisfied with what he has got. She pressed the bags out of the knees of my spirit and combed my spiritual hair.

We all loved both your pieces in Harpers. . . . Helen is very fond of the hens who can sit around singing and whoring. The Sat Review is right when it says you are among the great living essayists. . . .

Ross undertook to edit a sentence of mine, which needed editing because I had mentioned two different Washingtons without realizing it. It read, originally:

"Montana, the Dakotas, and Washington were admitted to the Union and Washington breathed more easily when Sitting Bull was shot dead."

Ross tried: Montana, the Dakotas, and the state of Washington were admitted to the Union and Washington D.C. breathed more easily etc.

I told him it would have to be: Montana, the Dakotas, and the *territory* of Washington, etc.

Finally, I showed him how to change the second Washington to "the government," and everything was all right, but it was fun when we got to the point of a parentheses explaining that a state is a territory until *after* it is admitted, etc. I said you can't "admit a guest" to your house if he just happens to drop by, because he isn't a guest until he is in the house. The question of whether he was a guest before he was admitted if he had received an invitation came up, ending in a sentence like this.

We still hope you will be able to come down for Thaxgiving. . . .

Love to you and Katharine from us both—and to Joe.

Jim

## To the Herman Millers

*Charles Thurber died on Easter 1939.*

Dear Herman and Dorothy:

We never did thank you for the flowers. My mother appreciated them a great deal. . . . Sometime soon we will have a long and quiet time together, with just ice water or milk so that Herman's blood pressure and my volubility will not go up.

Everybody in the East is sick.

My mother says everybody will be bad off till 1940 and then there will be a good year till 1941 when the war comes, as prophesied by Evangeline Adams.

We must make the most of 1940, my dears. Let's start planning it soon, that one year of brightness . . .

All our love,

Jim

## To Harold Ross

[*Undated, probably 1939, from Woodbury, CT*] *Thursday*

Dear Ross,

I . . . send back the John Silver-black patch break, with the comment that even you and your brilliant staff can get into a cul de sac of reasoning. Let me try to get you out of it.

The point of the news break is that a distinguished English novelist thought that John Silver, character in a distinguished English novel, wore an eye patch. Silver, of course, had only one leg, but both eyes. It is this amusing mistake which we seek to point out. How we point it out, by whatever reference or example, is beside the point. Your staff is noted for its ingenuity, but is often tricked into immobilizing it on the altar of fact-checking. Let's forget what pirates had eye patches. Try some line like this:

"Didn't wear a crutch, like old Pew, did he?"

That isn't it, but it ought to give you the idea. Just quit thinking about one-eyed pirates—the hell with them.

      Love,

      Jim

JT:HWT

2 enclosures.

## TO THE RICHARD CONNELLS

*[Undated, probably spring 1939]*

Dear Dick and Louise:

You will think that we are a pair of lice. But this is not exactly so. Trouble is: old man Middle-Age has finally caught up with me and he has called in his fiddlers three to play the tune for me to jig to. Characters in order of appearance:

    First Fiddler . . . . . . . . . . . . . . . . . . . . . Disease
    Second Fiddler . . . . . . . . . . . . . . . . . Symptoms
    Third Fiddler . . . . . . . . . . . . . . . . . . . Basal Metabolism
    Dancers, Groans, citizens, doctors, nurses, breathe deep,
    say ah, internes, luminol, let's see your tongue, etc.

All I've done since I seen youse has been to see doctors, and that's why we didn't see you when we were down the last time, which was for only a few days, all of which I spent on my back, or left side (I have to lie on my left side for Dr. Robin Hood, my rectal specialist). Well, sir, they found that I have a thyroid of 12 above and although Helen and her friends and family, all of whom have, or have had, thyroid readings of from 48 below to 65 above, say that this is a mere nothing, my doctor rubs his hands and says how would youse like to go under the knife to relieve that pressure? What pressure, says I, the financial? No, says he, the thyroidal. Nuts, says I, kiss me ass says he, and the fight was on.

It seems like this year is very bad for everybody. You have autonomous imbalance, Jimmy Sheean has a floating kidney, Martin Somers breaks out in yellow spots, Joe Sayre is in the Marburg clinic at Johns Hopkins having a general overhauling and Norma Nugent went over a cliff in an automobile . . .

. . . We will be in New York next week, probably Saturday, the twenty-fifth for a couple of days and this time I don't have to see any doctors, not even my dentist, who, last week, put in a new bridge with one of those things they use to tear up old asphalt with, and a sculptor's mallet. God, what I have been through with, and me such a delicate child, more on the spiritual than the physical side. They x-rayed me lungs, too, but the doctors were out when I first saw the pictures on his desk. There were dozens of little white spots between the ribs, and I had ordered a one-way ticket for Tucson when the doc called up and said the x-rays showed nothing at all. I guess the spots were just some ole embroidery floss I once inhaled, or something I picked up in France when I was a boy and didn't give a god damn.

Norma would never have gone over the cliff, if I had been well. Elliott and she were coming on last week and the week before to see me on account of a play we are mooning over, but I wired no, that I was on my back and they better wait and see if I was going to get up; it might be, I said, that I could never work again but would just have to be read to. So Norma takes her mother and Norma's two oldest children out for a ride along the cliffs of Cal. on one of those rare lovely days you have out there, and she stops the car on an observation point, and gets out with the children, leaving her mother in the back, the car headed for the cliff, and no brakes on. So the car starts sneaking toward the cliff, mamma screams, Norma jumps on the running board, madly turns off the radio, jerks out the cigaret lighter, and pulls out the choke, groping for the hand brake and lo, over the cliff they go. Providence, however, guided the hurtling car toward a projection of earth which had been muddied by recent rains so that when the car hit it the front wheels dug in and clung, and there they hung screaming and laughing and praying, 150 feet above the jagged concrete, broken glass, and hungry sharks below. They were both jiggled and jarred and got some nasty sprains, cuts and bruises but no broken bones or internal injuries, metabolism tests, or hyper-thyroids. Cost me lots of money long distance to find all this out. Winchell had shouted it over the radio scaring everybody to death. Helen and I, waiting for the Cal. connection, had already married Elliott off again to a woman of strong, fine character who could look after those three little girls. . . .

Love and embraces, from us both,

Jim

*The New Yorker began publishing Thurber's "Fables for Our Time" in January, 1939, and "Famous Poems Illustrated" that March. Gene Saxton was editor-in-chief at Harper & Bros., Thurber's publisher, which was just bringing out White's Quo Vadimus?*

## To Eugene Saxton

*February 17, 1939*

Dear Gene:

I am sorry that your letter about Andy's book caught us between places. . . . If it isn't too late—or even if it is—I'd love to see the proofs of Andy's book. I don't know whether or not he'd like to have me say anything about it—you know how strange he is about that. He doesn't want anybody's proofs sent to him, was pretty upset about getting Charles Cooke's How to Raise a Dog in the Circus, and wouldn't want his proofs sent to anyone. However, proofs have to be sent to people and White will just have to get used to it. I would love to read them and write something about them, but I'm afraid I'd have to ask him. Maybe not. We'll see.

Another matter for you to bother with: Simon & Schuster, the demon publishers, want to publish a small volume of the Fables I am running in the New Yorker, of which there will be about 25 in all. They seem very eager about this, anxious to pay a large advance and, apparently, a damned good royalty rate. I said I'd have to take it up with you. Everybody, I suppose, has a desire to let S & S do ONE book of his, just as everybody likes to try sliding down hill on skis once, or mixing kummel with sherry, or seeing what would happen if he made passes at Dorothy Thompson. Let me know your and Harpers stand on this little matter. . . .

As always,

Jim Thurber

*March 9, 1939*

Dear Gene:

Pardon this old . . . writing paper, but I use my type-writing paper to draw on and it goes fast and is gone.

It's all right about the Fables. Harpers is after all my publisher, but the triangle develops in work as in love. Now and again I get the idea that I am not a good business man and that everybody else is getting more money than me because they are tough or persuasive (or maybe sell more books). But we'll talk everything over and everything will be all right.

I haven't got enough fables done for a book yet and won't have for a while. They are hard to do, as simple as they look. One runs out of animals, or at least human motives for morals. They have had a remarkable success with all kinds of people, from the office boy to Mencken.

I want to get out another book of drawings. I will have seven years of them to draw from, including the War Between Men and Women, the Masculine Approach, the Patient (a series of nine drawings printed in Night and Day in London, and one of my own favorites), and Famous Poems Illustrated, of which I have done six already and will do four or five more (the first is printed this week). It ought to be a good book. I have some 150 one-panel, caption drawings to select from, too. The Seal was printed in 1932. Remember 1932? I know the book would go well in London and I might ask David Garnett to do a preface. Here I would like to have Benchley. I'll talk to him about it. Meanwhile I'll phone you when I get to town—next week sometime, I don't know when, maybe week after. We'll have lunch—maybe with White along too? . . .

    All best wishes,
    Jim Thurber

## TO THE E. B. WHITES

*[Undated, probably May 1939]*

Dear Andy and Katharine:

Last night I finished the drawings for Curfew Shall Not Ring, the 5th of the series I have finished, and tonight I am working, or going to, on the Secret Life of Walter Mitty. This noon Quo Vadimus arrived. I had it for an hour and then Helen took it; she still has it. I will take it to bed. . . . It is just as I expected it would be, as Leslie Howard said of Berkeley Square; a lovely and funny collection by my favorite author. I must do a piece on you some day, White, my boy. I am already planning a little essay on Style. Everybody, when he is in his mid-forties plans a little essay on Style. In his fifties he lectures at Sarah Lawrence, I think. In his sixties he goes blind and has to give up whisky at the same time. I hate the prospect of running my hands over my grandchildren's faces to see which side of the family they resemble. I had to have reading glasses a few weeks ago, and keep taking them off and putting them on. I have an idea I don't see as well or as far as before; I am teaching Helen to drive. It may be the mist in the air or the dirt on the windshield, but it is probably that Change.

I got this idea about a piece on style by opening for the first time Donald Culross Peattie's Book of Hours, which for some reason I bought for five dollars just after it was selected as the book of its year most likely to become a Classic. It is boxed and has cellophane for a jacket and unless somebody rewrites it, will not become a Classic, I do not believe. I haven't got past the second page, of course, and maybe it gets better. But it starts this way: On sleep's fringe, there is a tremulous, mirage-like realm, a long narrow kingdom like Egypt's land, with the shape of a scythe and the feel of a sea strand. It is neither the ocean of oblivion, nor the continent of waking. Here the small waves whisper and flash; the half-drowned swimmer lies beached, innocently, with his face in the warmth of sand, and the ebb of sleep lapping his tranquil nakedness. He knows that life is given him back, but is not sure that he does not regret the sweetness of death. And etc.

"Style is the thing that's always a bit phony, and at the same time you cannot write without style," says a character in Elizabeth Bowen's new book, which has a perfect style. "To write is always to rave a little . . . There are ways and ways of trumping a thing up: one gets more discriminating, not necessarily more honest." Donald Culross needs a little more discrimination, or something, maybe even honesty; perhaps he feels too well; I think he has a favorite chair and embroidered slippers and always has hot milk at exactly a quarter after ten every night. This leads to expressions like sleep's fringe and Egypt's land, and warmth of sand, instead of the fringe of sleep, Egypt, and the warm sand. He would have begun that lyric of Poe's "Ah, Helen" instead of just "Helen, thy beauty is to me." "Life is given him back" is a thing for which men should be hanged. You're bound to read it "giving" as you first hit it, then finally you get it, take off your reading glasses, put on your outdoors glasses, and go for a walk. Says Peattsie-weattsie: "That realm is neither of Ra nor of Dis. And the hour is not the butterfly's nor the moth's." There is no discrimination in that second "nor"; it sticks out like a doorknob. But who am I to talk, I in one of whose pieces the checking department found three "befores" in four consecutive sentences? I told them, in a marginal note, to let it stand because to change it I would have to take the whole piece apart like a clock and would probably end up by changing the title and the whole point. . . .

. . . I brood about your book coming so close to Book of the Month (or was it Literary Guild) and then not quite making it. The United States does not read the right books in large numbers, which may be what is the matter with the United States, and what is right about the books.

We spent a week in New York having me examined. I took a metabolism and came out 12 above and old Chick wanted me operated on right away . . . He x-rayed my lungs and found nothing at all, not even a lung, I suspect. . . . I suppose I will go to a thyroid man and breathe through that tube again, and see what he says. I am growing a little dubious about the clowns. Very likely all I have is Aspergillosis. It goes, in man, when April comes. . . .

We look forward to seeing you in New York in a few weeks. We are going down next week for a few days because Elliott Nugent is coming on. He intends to get this play done which I suggested he and I do together. . . .

I got to get at Walter Mitty now. Let us hear when you will arrive in New York. We will get roaring drunk and then make plans for the future. And what is all this about you looking for another job? It sounds silly to us. We got to know about it.

Love to you all, from us both,

Jim

*In May 1939, the Thurbers traveled to Hollywood, where Thurber worked with Nugent on the play* The Male Animal. *Earlier that year, Thurber's eye had begun to hurt and his vision to deteriorate.*

## To Dr. Gordon Bruce

*June 9*

Dear Dr. Bruce:

I guess you better give me the name of a good man out here who can get me some reading lenses. The old eye is the same as ever for distance but I'll be goddam if I can read—except—and this is funny —under a big umbrella outdoors in a bright sun; under those conditions I see to read even newspaper type exactly as well without my glasses as with my *distance* ones. (Not reading ones—or anyway, almost the same). If I use my right lens as a magnifying glass and pull it away I can see as clearly for a fifth of a second as I did in 1896. I can also do a lot of other tricks, but I am getting crosser and snappier and sadder every minute straining and struggling to type and to read and to draw (the latter is the easiest). I'd rather atrophy those muscles in two years than by god go through life like a blindfolded man looking for a black sock on a black carpet. If I use the old distance lenses and only have stronger ones for reading, wouldn't that even up on the atrophy problem? Couldn't I go without glasses when not reading, or something? Life is no good to me at all unless I can read, type, and draw. I would sell out for 13 cents. Seems to me the eye began to dim slightly on the third day at sea—anyway I had been able to read for two days and then it got slightly harder . . .

    Best regards,

    Jim Thurber


## TO GUS LOBRANO

*The submitted story, "The Man Who Hated Moonbaum," wasn't published in* The New Yorker *until March 1940.*


*July 5 [1939]*

Dear Gus:

    As always, just after I send off an irritable letter, I get a dozen deposit slips and a nice, well-written, cheerful letter from you. Eye strain gets on my nerves. Today has been a good day, though. The doc says that I will vary: will see better when I am feeling peart, not so good when I'm not.

    I hope you like Mr. Moonbaum: I did that over and over, which is harder for me now than it used to be. Fortunately I can see the keys on the keyboard fine because the letters are so big, but I don't see the type on the page as well; so overlook my spelling: I write boin for join and then for when and Fus for Gus, etc. People will have to get used to this.

    I knew Ross didn't want that dog cover: maybe he overlooks the fact that, if some of the dogs seem well drawn, my dog in the center stands out as kind of funny by comparison or so I thought. However, it's all right, turn it down; I'll do the other one. I have a 4th of July one to send to you, all done, ready to go. Will you have Terry send me two more cover boards marked out like the last two? I keep getting ideas for covers. If Ross rejects the dog cover he now holds

I'd like to have it sent to me for Dave Chasen. He gave a swell party for us on Helen's birthday, and I want to give him a drawing. I also have to sell him some. We like Dave's better than all the Brown Derbies put together, a swell place where you meet the New York crowd, seems more like New York than anyplace out here by twenty miles, swell food, good wine, fine service. . . .

The play is coming along fine. I think we have something.

Love,

I also want a few
envelopes big enuf
for the cover boards

Jim
This is the best
type for me

## TO HAROLD ROSS AND THE *NEW YORKER* STAFF

*June 26*

Dear Ross and employees:

I enjoyed that telephone talk with you, but didn't understand it—that is, who paid, and why we had to go into the steam room to talk. So many things amaze me out here, though, that a $45 phone call seems unimportant. There is more social life out here than in a rabbit warren during the rutting season, and it is this which may drive me crazy first. We have seen all the best patios, the largest swimming pools, and the more famous Glogauers. Jack Warner wanted to know yesterday if I was any relation to Edna Ferber—was I her husband? I spelled my name and then pronounced it. Zane Ferber? he said. Any relation to Zane Grey? Elliott Nugent patiently explained the whole thing and Warner nodded. On his way out of the party he stopped and shook hands. Good-bye, Ferber, he said. So long Baxter, I said. It's a great place.

For lunch yesterday we were asked to the Chaplins' and stayed for tennis and tea. He told us all about his dictator picture—which sounds swell—and gave a long talk at lunch on capitalism, culture, and the disappearance of the individual craftsmen with the coming of the machine age. There are weeds in the garden of his thought but he is a sincere little guy and a fine fellow—plays tennis left-handed but not like Johnny Doeg.

I had to make a little talk one day at an authors' club luncheon, which please god I didn't intend to. The guy who runs the Cocoanut Grove was there—with Paul Draper—and in his talk he said he had wired Harold Ross to suggest a description of Draper and Ross had wired back "Call him the Dancing Hamlet". This amused me for the rest of the afternoon and well into the night. I told about how a beggar had asked me for $500, but it did not get over; afterwards a guy said to me in all seriousness, "You'll be bothered by a lot of those guys. Just give 'em twenty bucks and go on."

Nobody has made any offers or passes at me, and you can expect me back there in the Fall. If I had been a relative of Ferber and Zane, I might have got a bid from Warner. . . .

Oh, yes, Chaplin started right off at our introduction by saying that he was a greater admirer of my work, particularly of one thing I wrote—and as far as he was concerned that was all I had to write. This one thing turned out to be Andy's description in Max Eastman's book of why he became a writer of humorous pieces. I usually disclaim these false honors but I was afraid to this time; I just stood there grinning and silent. He thinks I'm feeble-minded, I guess. Well, the two drawings of mine which Broun likes best were both done by Steig. I am used to these things.

You might send this on to Chaplin's favorite humorist [White]. I intend to write to the old farmer some time, if my eyes hold out. They have been having their ups and downs out here. Sometimes I see as clearly as a barefoot boy; at other times the atmosphere seems to be composed mainly of milk; today I can read a little but sometimes I can't read anything smaller than a quarantine sign.

Benchley was going to take me out to see three pretty girls at his studio, but he failed me, the dog. It seems that as he was about to start out for the Nugents' the day they gave a party for us, he mentioned it to three honey babies, Rosalind Russell, Vivien Leigh, and one other, who shall be nameless only because I can't remember who it was. Anyway, they all wanted to meet me, as you might guess, and Benchley says "Well, I'm bringing him to the studio tomorrow as a matter of fact." So he told me this tale and asked me not to let him down, but to come to the studio as he had promised I would: said he'd send a car for me at 11 the next morning. I was all pomaded and macassared up and wearing my velvet suit with the frilled cuffs when 11 o'clock came. The phone rang, and it was Benchley's secretary saying he "had to go out on location."

I got to go to the Fox studio now and have lunch with an author I know.

See you soon, but not soon enough.

Thurber

I suppose you've heard what really happened to Errol Flynn who was reported to have been badly injured in an automobile accident—seems he swerved his car to save the lives of two girl children and an aged woman. What happened was, if you haven't heard from your favorite columnist, that he was 3 hrs late at a party given for him and her, so she broke a glass and cut him in the puss with the jagged edge; then he broke her nose and knocked out two teeth. The host, a Mr. Blumenthal, ran screaming out of his own house.

Chaplin doesn't like dogs, likes cats; doesn't know the number of his own house, can't remember a name for five minutes—every time a new guest arrived the Nugents and Thurbers had to be introduced by someone else. He tried it a couple of times and gave up.

## To Daise Terry

*[Undated, probably July 1939, from Hollywood]*

Dear Terry:

What I got to have now is a picture of a beaver. All my beavers look like seals or dogs. Could someone sketch one out of a dictionary or something? Doesn't have to be good—-just a rough idea of how his head and legs and body look. I know about his tail. I need this as soon as I can get it so please send it back air mail.

Love,
James Thurber
The Boy Artist

🙙 🙙 🙙

August 23, 1939

Dear Terry:

This is to inform you that Mr. Ross bought the Autumn cover when he was here. He asked to see it and said "I'll take it. It's sold." Mrs. T. was a witness to the transaction. I expect to be paid for it at once, without any nonsense.

Two drawings enclosed, the last you'll get for a while since I'm illustrating my book now. Play is finished and being read by Connelly and Max Gordon. It's a good play.

  Love
  Thurber

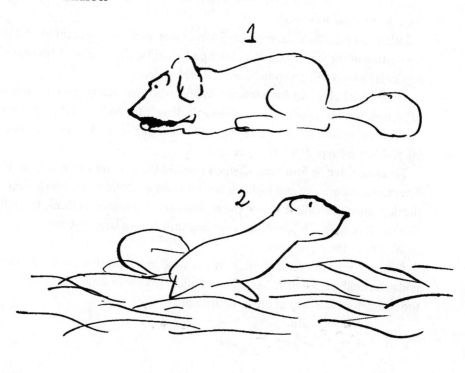

            *[Undated, 1939, from Hollywood]*

Dear Crew:

  Would any of you experts know how I could get hold of a copy of Vanzetti's letter to his child or children which he wrote just before his execution?

  Nobody out here knows how to get hold of anything. There is nothing out here to get hold of. Nobody here has ever got hold of anything, anyway.

  Ross arrived, in dark clothes, making him look thin and lost.

  My address is 261 South Crescent Drive, Beverly Hills.

    Best wishes,
    Jim Thurber

Ross got restless here in about 6 hours and is probably up in the mountains fishing.

ዼ ዼ ዼ

*[Undated, probably September 1939, from Hollywood] Monday*

Dear Terry: Dear Everybody:

Helen and I couldn't stand it here for even one more day, on account of it is the bottom of the world. So we are taking a Union Pacific train at 8 bells of the p m today which will get us in New York Friday. . . .

The play is being cast for a try-out. People who have read it are enthusiastic, actors, writers, producer. We believe we have a hit and a good play. I am even worrying as to whether Life with Father will beat us to the Pulitzer Prize. We hear from Sayre that it is a sure smash hit.

I enclose three or four fables, which I would like to have run pretty soon. They can leave one out and I will do two more for a second series. Maybe leave the dog one out. I leave that, and the arrangement up to them. I think, though that the illus. might be just of the man and unicorn—a largish space. . . .

We'll be at the Algonquin.

Give my love to one and all. It is 104 here today but the papers in this godawful hellhole proclaim "Angelenos Suffer No Discomfort." That would be too bad. I hope the sons of bitches burn up.

> See you soon,
> James Thurber

It would be nice if I took all but say $50 of the fables money. I may need that. I'll be working like a dog for the magazine and liking it.

## To Gus Lobrano

*[Undated, probably August 1939, from Hollywood]*

Dear Gus:

Here is Barbara Frietchie, the historic poem which started this crazy series. This is in eight drawings, or one more than Locksley Hall. Couldn't be done in less. The cutting of the poem and the arranging of the drawings were the hardest problem yet, but I think I got 'em all right. Tell Knowles to count on me as usual for extending drawings, etc., although I'll be goddam if I will draw another flag and fill in around those stars. Try that for a steady hand.

Lots of fables outlined but as I say, they can't be forced. I'll be getting some in in a week or ten days anyway.

     Love,

     Jim

The question of taste, if raised, is not involved here. This is a silly poem and I am showing how silly. Barbara waved no flag at Jackson. Jackson, a sensitive gentleman, a Christian soul, and a great soldier, would never have ordered anyone to shoot at the flag. The command "halt, fire!" given to an army corps in a city street is the highest point of nonsense ever reached. His "dies like a dog!" is almost as silly. He was a grave and solemn man. All she did, anyway, was wave a flag at the Northern troops when they drove out the rebs.

"Rebel Tread", I have always thought, would be a swell name for a tire made in the South. However, I'm always thinking of things. Six, seven years ago we had a Talk piece about a woman of 70 who had seen for 25 years every performance of the D'Oyly Carte company, here and abroad. I just thought it should have been titled There Was an Old Woman Who Lived in a Show. What good does this do now?

     J

*The Thurbers returned to New York from Hollywood in September 1939.*

## TO CHARLES DUFFY

*September 28, 1939*

Dear Mr. Duffy:

As an old Amembassy man (Paris) I should have answered you at once, at least this time. I believe you didn't give your address last time. You have coming to you a check for $15, which I trust you will find enclosed. I also hope that before long you will get another one, as I like the Heathcliff idea a lot. None of our editors, however, have ever read any books or seen any movies, so they may not know who Heathcliff was. Our editors do nothing but smoke cigars and go to baseball games. They are a tough and insensitive lot. . . .

Do they still use the old Green code? After twenty years I can still put up "United States Transport sailing recently New York carries French shipment."

I used to speak Green code quite fluently. They were just bringing in the AI code when I quit. The newest code we had when we got in the war was about

67 years old. So they set to work on one the Germans didn't have (even German children got onto the code). The AI code came out in August 1919, I think, long after the war was over, but in plenty of time for this one.

   Sincerely,

   James Thurber

## To the E. B. Whites

*[Undated, fall 1939]*

Dear Andy and Katharine:

I am about five pounds lighter than when I saw you, on account of the play and Harpers.

In addition to reversing cuts and leaving blank spaces in The Last Flower, Harpers has got out ads which sound as if they might have been written by some of the old ladies Mary Petty draws. I am sure they would stir Mrs William Tecumseh Sherman, or the late Mrs William McKinley.

They lead off at the top in black type with "The Book That Captured a Hundred Over Night" leaving you to guess what that means. I guessed it meant maybe people they had sent advance copies to (including Mrs Roosevelt, I see by Saxton's list—I once wrote a bitter parody of My Day when it wasn't as good as it is now). Then Harpers got into some kind of jam with LIFE which wanted to run a page of the drawings this week. It came out a double page spread, using 26 pictures, or practically the whole book, certainly the whole story, only probably cut to the bone and ruined—the cuts will be terribly reduced. I was not told about this till it was too late. Saxton demanded money for me, they offered $250, he asked $500, and today they called him back and bullied him into $350—only I will get into action on that. I am always buttoning Harpers pants and seeing that they have lunch money and a clean handerchief before they start out in the morning. Then they get lost in Central Park and I have to go out and find them. You can't turn your back on that ancient firm. Gene also wanted me to put the $500 LIFE money into a fund—with $500 of their own money for ads! I had a long talk with him today and said My God no. It's too bad that nice gentlemen like Harpers have to be so bad at publishing books or rather promoting them. . . .

You got to choose between gentlemen who know the nice places to eat and the guys who sell your books. I haven't much cared till now, but this book I want to see sell. (The Times Book Review ran an unsigned review under Children's Books—along with Patty, the Pacifist Penguin, etc.)

This light isn't good, so if I hit wrong keys, I won't be able to fix the words.

But there is good news, too. Elliott and I have spent ten days rewriting the play and last night read it—Elliott did—to Herman Shumlin. Took three hours. He had never had a play read to him before, but since Elliott had acted in it and it had been produced, he wanted to hear it. Warned us he would just listen and then take the script home and go over it by himself. But at the end of the reading and a short discussion of changes he wanted made, he said he would do the play. This is pretty near a record, I think. Selling a play in three hours to the producer who has the biggest record for successes in town and who can have his pick of the play crop. He gave us our first advance royalty check today. . . .

(By the way, the hundred who were captured overnight turned out to be secretaries, editors, Lee Hartman, printers, Rushmore, Mrs Rushmore, phone operators, engravers, Saxton etc. Well, your guess was as good as mine. I pointed out to dear Gene that when you run a big boast about a hundred copies on the same page with boasts by other publishers running into the 27th edition and the 234,000th copy, it's like saying "Fifty People Jam Carnegie Hall to Hear Gluck.") . . .

We both liked Shumlin a lot. . . . He counts on opening the play here New Year's Week, even that is rushing it a lot. We'd have to play Xmas week in a try-out city. I am confident that we have a swell play now, and that it will be a big hit. I think as big as Life with Father. . . . It was wildly received in San Diego, Santa Barbara and Los Angeles, even when it was full of dull spots and bad writing and some gags that creep in when your back is turned. The theatre would drive you nuts in a week, White. . . .

. . . [Marc] Connelly took it apart for us in a long speech but, as Charlie McArthur said to me the other night, "Marc is an instantaneous orator." He used the word "therapy" (Connelly did) several times as he lectured to us out there and I began to feel easier. Even easier than that when he mentioned Brahms fifth. (I think he only did four symphonies, anyway). . . . God knows you get all kinds of viewpoints. Everybody wants to change this or that or put in business or suggest lines. When I got out there the play had lines in it and business suggested by secretaries, cousins, mothers, bat boys, doormen, and little old women in shawls. . . .

Let me hear from you. We are now in two lovely rooms, each with bath, very quiet and comfortable, at the Grosvenor, 35 Fifth Avenue. I could throw a rock in any direction from my room and hit some old misery of mine. . . .

I go on Information Please next Tuesday night.

This is James Thurber saying—goooood nite!
James Thurber
the Boy Artist

## To the Ronald Williamses

*1939*

The first tournament staged at the Somerset Cricket, Lawn Tennis, and Croquet Club for the Padgham Cup ended yesterday in the three-set defeat of Ronald John Williams by Admiral J.S.C. Tittbury-Willets R.N., retired. Admiral Tittbury-Willets took the second set at love. Between the second and third sets the aged seadog, who is a hundred and four, was allowed to rest for half an hour in his wheel chair. He played the final set in shawl and tippet because of a fancied breeze which he claimed was stirring. Mr. Williams, who had been up for two nights singing and arguing at King's Point House and Les Revenants, never seemed to get the upperhand of his own racket, let alone of the old admiral. "Chap may have Welsh in him," muttered the admiral, after the match, "but he seemed full of Scotch to me." Whereupon he chuckled. Admiral Tittbury-Willets used the old underhanded between-the-thighs serve, which seemed to bother Williams. "Looks to me," he said at one point, "as if the old fellow was serving the ball underhand between his legs, but of course he couldn't be." He was, though, and took six straight games before Williams became aware that he was indeed up against the old crotch serve. Asked for a statement after the match Admiral Tittbury-Willets said, "Never even got up a sweat. My niece is in better all round trim than the young men of today. They don't drink enough, probably."

## To the Herman Millers

***March 19, 1940***

Dear Herman and Dorothy:

I don't know what you can think of us for not replying to what, believe it or not, comes to three separate communications from you: the telegram about the play, the letter before Christmas, and the letter about the two magazine boys. Whatever you think is wrong if it deals with neglect, lack of remembrance, cooling of love, the swell head from having had a lucky hit on the

Great White with Black Spots on the Edges Way, lack of appreciation of your swell letters, or lack of concern and interest as to what you are doing.

What happened was that Helen and I both went to pieces physically at once, nervously, and mentally, too, I guess. I have been until just a few days ago a shadow of my former self, a shell, a relic, and an old pooh-pooh. From about the time of your first letter I began to lose grip, what with rewriting the damn play, staying up too late arguing and fussing, smoking too early in the day and too often, and drinking too much. The try-outs in Princeton and Baltimore took a lot out of us and the New York opening more. We should have ducked right then but we tarried and had to submit to interviews and god knows what else every day for weeks; I also had to do most of the publicity drawings and stories. We didn't get a moment of rest or quiet and nobody heard from us at all. Every day I counted on being able to write, but I just wasn't. I figure we both lost about ten pounds—I was described in interviews as "emaciated", "painfully thin", "peaked", "moribund" and "washed up." Helen's collapse was fast and bad: she was taken to the hospital where she stayed two weeks with a blood count so low they were scared to death of leucoemia or leuchoemia or whatever it is. She only had six red corpuscles left and four white ones. They jabbed her full of liver extract and she gradually came up out of the vale. Meanwhile I was down in bed in the hotel, running a fever, seeing mice with boxing gloves on, and the like.

They finally bundled us on a ship for Bermuda and we are just now beginning to get some color in the cheeks and some flesh on the bones. And the strength and the spirit to be able to write a letter. We have rented through May a lovely old house down here on a turquoise bay with birds and flowers all about. The weather has just got fine and the light bright enough for me to see by—for my eyes took a header with the rest of me and for a while all I could see was the larger Neon signs and 45-point type. That also kept me from quill and typewriter.

. . . We were surprised and also delighted to know that you had given up that teaching job because we knew it was getting you down and because we always wanted you to get to writing. It would have to come when I was in no state to answer your letter with words of cheer. However, better late than never. . . .

The only ideas I have had down here haven't been much. I'm going to do a book of animal drawings for young and old, with text describing them: the bandicoot, the platypus, the coatimundi, Bosman's potto, the aardvark, and half a hundred others. The kind of easy and soothing idea that a broken down playwright gets. The only book I've read has been "Bernadette of Lourdes", the amazing and well written story of the little girl who saw the visions, done by a woman psychologist with no monkey business or shenanigans. It struck me there was a play in that. I wish you would read it.

Our play got good notices and happened to click fast—it's like tossing a coin, I guess. . . .

Our house is really called "Les Revenants," which my limited French tells me means ghosts. If you know of a more soothing translation, please let us know.

> With love and kisses and all best wishes,
> as ever and always,
> Jim and Helen

If you need any money for cheese and crackers until the checks begin coming in, there is no one you know who would more happily, or could more easily, thanks to Broadway, send it. *Don't forget that.*

> Jim

*The Whites were co-editing an anthology of American humor. Robert Thurber brought his mother to New York for skin-cancer treatment. News that Helen's father was dying brought the Thurbers from Bermuda to Newport, Rhode Island.*

## To the E. B. Whites

*Bermuda*
*March 10, 1940*

Dear Andy and Katharine:

This is a belated enough answer to Katharine's Valentine letter, but we have just really got settled and have just begun to feel better. Helen is gaining weight and looks fine, everybody comments on it. We stayed at Mrs. T's two weeks and then rented for March and April one of the nicest houses on the islands, a big one, on Mangrove Bay in Somerset, right on the turquoise water and with lovely grounds all around. I'll send you pictures later. It is well furnished, has a lot of good books. I've been reading Faust, Emerson, Voltaire, and Ring Lardner. The other boys date a lot but Ring's "Some Like Them Cold" is as fresh as ever, and "Golden Honeymoon." He wasn't as stuffy as Goethe, after all, or as glib as Voltaire, and he was too much of a re-alist to believe that Everything Is Going to be Just Dandy, the way Emerson did. I looked up the Emerson piece I mentioned on visiting Coleridge, Wordsworth, Carlyle, etc., and while it's amusing in spots (but not as amusing as I remembered it to be) it doesn't belong in your anthology, but it's worth reading (in "English Traits") if only because he tells how both Coleridge—who was wearing green spectacles—and Wordsworth recited their poems to him, Wordsworth rendering three sonnets without stop-ping. They were old men, of course, but I doubt if Andy, at 80, will button-hole visitors and recite to them that poem about how the young man (me) was going to write a play, but always at some other time of day. (P.S. the young man made it). I am much better than I was, too, but I wasn't anything as low as Helen. They were scared at Doc's Hospital, because in 48 hours her bloodcount dropped two-thirds of the way to the bottom, and I guess they were afraid we'd have to get out the lilies and the spade. But she recuperates fast.

Speaking of the spade, Althea had to have poor old Medve, the 13 year old poodle, destroyed. I know it was a blow to her and I worry about its effect on Rosemary. The poodle was in the house when she was born—more than eight years ago—and that's a long time to have a dog, and such a sweet dog. I knew she was dying when I saw her at Christmas time, but she lay there with that same quiet dignity, waiting for the angels as she would wait for dinner. Dogs are on to the fact that it's all a part of life, this dimming out, and is as necessary as the last movement in a symphony. My mother's family have never got on to this and for three hundred years have lived in the sublime belief that when everybody else was dead, they would still go on.

I think that my eyesight is improving and that it rises and falls with my state of health and my weight. At first I bumped into horses by day and houses by night but now I only hit the smaller objects, such as hassocks and sewer lids that are slightly ajar. . . .

The play seems very far away but it also seems to be doing well, even better than before, because one weekly check was as high as $750.

I am coming to New York for a few days arriving April 1, this to arrange a meeting between my mother and brother and Rosemary, who will assemble there. My mother hasn't seen Rosie since she was a little past two. The family will also see the show and it ought to be quite a busy week but I'll have the strength for it after six weeks down here.

I'd like to have you see the play again, as you mentioned, because I really believe people get more out of it the second time, and my best friends are less nervous, too.

Best of everything to you all from both of us,

As ever,

Jim

ᕦ  ᕦ  ᕦ

*[Undated, probably April 1940]*

Dear Katherine and Andy:

Miss Terry forwarded your letter up here to Newport and I take pen in hand to tell you not to worry about me. Denmark, yes, Norway, yes; me, no. I do A LOT of howling and fussing about nothing at all but I take the bigger things more quietly. As Dr. Bruce says, the operation for Cat [cataract], or Kitty, as I now call it, is as simple as tying a shoe lace. He says he could even go in there now and get it out, but it is better to wait. . . . Bruce sent me to Dunnington, who with Bruce is rated tops in New York, just to make assurance doubly sure and they both agreed that that's what I got. It is in a very early stage now and I can see to type and to read and could get around alone all right but Helen won't let me. They think it will form fast but I notice no change in the week we've been here.

Bruce will do two operations, instead of one as this is customary where the patient totes only one glim. The first in June maybe, the next in the fall. In between I will be able to see better. I will have to be in the hospital for five days, he says (probably means 7) but all that worries me is whether they will let me get up and go to the bathroom, as I do not care about using jugs and bowls, but I am a great hand at chaffing nurses and may learn to knit or make little pin trays and bread boards like McKelway. Almost everyone on the magazine is in a sanitarium now, some of them fishing with bent pins in washbowls, others coloring comic strip figures with penny crayons, still others tatting or simply playing Lotto.

<blockquote>
There was an old fellow named Ross<br>
Whose staff became covered with moss<br>
And lichens and splotches<br>
And soft fuzzy blotches<br>
And mouldy old green stuff, and floss.
</blockquote>

Helen's father, poor sweet soul, cannot live and it is a sad vigil we are holding here. He still can recognize us and since he has always been fond of me I think it is a good thing that I can be here. Helen and her sister are here, too. Mrs. Wismer is bearing up beautifully, with all the fortitude of her Scotch heritage. She is not very strong herself and we worry about her but she seems cheered by our being here. . . .

It is certainly fortunate that I did that play when I did, as it is nice to have the weekly checks coming in and I will get $15,000 a year for three years from the movie sale, so I can handle all these problems of mine with my left hand. We have bought government bonds with the first $4500 payment and Morris Ernst is handling things for me, together with the astute advice of Elliott Nugent, who is as good a business man as he is an actor.

I managed the week with Rosemary and my mother and Althea and Robert all right and everybody was satisfied, but it was a strain I was glad to get over. I took my mother to a specialist and while she has a skin cancer it is not by any means serious and can be excised, as the doctors (or clowns, as Robert still calls them) say. It does not need immediate operation, either, so I can space these things out. My main problem is to keep her away from quacks, crystal gazers, layers on of hands, salves, ointments, wall mottoes, radium water, snake oil doctors, swamis, etc. She and Robert listened to a lecture from me on quackery and next day looked up one Dr. Jutt in the west Fifties who cures all by making you eat meat three times a day. Robert had found and bought for a dime a pamphlet by the good doctor on the bargain counter of the book department of a drug store.

Rosemary is fine. I took her to the Central Park zoo, which she has always loved and we got there on the first warm day of the year when all the animals were cutting up, giving each other the hot foot, playing leap frog, and what not. The polar bears were wonderful, ducking each other in the water by getting hold of each other's ears, jumping in and pulling down. The seals were even better. Even the begal [Bengal] tiger came out and said well, well. (A begal tiger has long droopy ears.) I tossed a penny from a bridge among some people, so exciting Rosie that she swallowed her . . . gum. My mother brought her a little mother-of-pearl box containing a small diamond and sapphire ring which my mother had when she was 12, and a hundred year old silver bracelet. Althea is as strong as a female moose and looks fine. . . .

All my books are in this house and I have been looking them over. I think Emma Inch is as good a short story as any of mine, and maybe Tea at Mrs Armsby's from the Mrs Monroe stories which I like even after ten years for some reason. I don't like Menaces in May much any more.

I got a copy of Mosher's book with the fine Petty drawings. I wish all my crises with people, particularly women, could have been no larger than Mosher's, an unfortunate phrase at tea time, a page missing from a phone book, a moment of anxiety at Schraffts. No drunken lover trying to get his key in the lock while you frantically hunt for your other shoe and the girl can't open the window leading to the fire escape. He is, however, a minor Henry James—amazing sometimes the style—and a Forty-fifth street Proust whose bête noirs are no more fearsome than a sea horse. . . .

This is not the criticism that I am sending to John, to be sure, for he is a very sensitive artist and he was in such a dither when he held his first book in his arms—-I happened to be in the room—-that it was wonderful to watch. Exactly like a father with a baby. As the tired father of seven books—or is it eight?—I tested the binding roughly, criticized the blurbs, spoke pessimistically of low royalty rates, etc. before I was really aware of his condition. He almost had a seizure. Ruth, Helen's sister, first met John, she was telling us, when he came nervously into a large party we gave at 8 Fifth Avenue, was presented to her, bowed, sat down, and said to Helen, "I *must* have a lozenge." Ruth says Helen got him a lozenge.

The war I try not to think about. I have become, I think, an interventionist, because I cannot imagine living in a world with a Germanized France and a destroyed England. The American intention to live on a hemisphere instead of a planet seems to me a bit unworkable. I have an awful hunch the Allies can't win without something. I don't know whether we could help. I wish we could stay out, but I don't like the looks of things. Trouble is, I like France about as well as I do America. Pretzels and beer in those great restaurants is a picture I can't dwell on. Can't you just see a German captain drinking a bottle of Chambertin 1915 right down, out of the bottle, in one swig? . . .

One thing that has cheered me up is a line from one of Agatha Christie's books in which a character says, "The guilt lies between one of us." She hasn't had no schooling; should be *among* one of us.

In conclusion I call your attention to the heartening fact that

> The world is freer
> Of gonorrhea.

Love and kisses, to you all,
from us both,
Jim

I have put my poem aside for a while since it is not right yet. It is fun to have Ross, the Mark Van Doren of Forty-third Street, criticize poetry. He and Gus agreed that we had to excise the last stanza and what they would do to the triolet and other repetitive poetical forms would be worth watching. The old ballads would take a beating, too, and Ross could cut out two of those "half a leagues" and the charge would still make sense—move faster even. Ross was 37 before he had read any poetry except comic valentine verse, and I am thinking of giving a little dinner for him and Edna Millay and Muriel Rukeyser or whatever her name is.

I am thinking of copying out on yellow paper and handing in something by Swinburne or Coleridge, to see what they want excised before they print it. I have an idea Gus lives in constant dread of Ross and of disagreeing with him and I watch Gus every day for signs of sanitarium fever. The gentle, quiet type that never screams is likely to go out like a candle one day. The office, as you know, is filled with sad, slow-moving young men of twenty, older emotionally as hell itself, taciturn, laconic, who seldom speak. No more does anyone set fire to his waste basket or pour glyco thymoline into the envelopes of rejected newsbreaks. The younger generation is non-plussed and cautious and definitely alarmed. They stand staring at the headlines for hours on end, then move carefully away. They keep their overcoats and hats on, like men in a flooded area. They turn over for several minutes in their minds what you say and then murmur something politely. I find myself speaking slowly and loudly to them. They are all on the verge of weaving baskets. There is about them all the air of a man who has lost his wife and four children in an outboard motorboat accident. I don't know what has come over youth. You have probably not met Felsch and Wittman and Harberger. They turn ashes over with their paws and sigh. They chew gum, drink coca cola and sit facing the door, with their hats and overcoats on. I think they wear garters. They call me sir and give me lots of room. They have lost something that they never had. I suspect that they get up before dawn to lean carefully out on the sill and study the street. I suspect they are better prepared for this Thing they see coming than I am.

\* \* \*

I just reread your letter about the humor anthology and the S&S book and find I didn't answer it really. It is apparently impossible for me to remember stories, even my own, unless I have a book of them before me. To dispose of me first, Helen agrees on *Walter Mitty,* or *Emma Inch,* or *The Greatest Man in the World.* I may have others but I swear I can't remember them without looking them up. The same thing is true for me of Andy, Bob, O'Hara, Sally etc. What I get in my mind is a nice suffused sense of quality, without edges. Of course, Philip Wedge I remember of Andy's and the piece the Nyer let an English magazine print about the minister who went to sea. Others of Andy's, like mine, are casuals, essays, not short stories. I loved the *Flocks by Night,* of course. You just practically have to go through the New Yorker writers' albums, I guess.

It seems to me that anything is a short story in which a character does something, such as cutting his face with a razor and trying to deal with a dachshund and a ewe. I will look through Andy's book and see what I like best! It takes time, thought, and special moods to pick out what you like in your own or anyone's work. Ordinarily, you just kinda swing in a sense of the whole style and content of a man's stories being swell. We've all written so many, too, making it twice as hard as picking out one of Conrad's novels. Sally has surely written 1100 pieces, O'Hara, 750. Things of Andy's come to me in the night, or when I'm bathing, or at the tobacconist's but I can't just sit down and conjure them up. The part of your mind that remembers things you liked doesn't work when you push a button or pound on the table. You got to let it reveal things in its own way.

Let's exchange some more reflections on this subject.

J

Good old Helen Wismer, one of the women from whom the verb to wismer or to wismerize is derived. There were only three Wismer women ("thank God", as undisciplined husbands who were afraid of having their affairs put straight, used to say). These three, however, could put a house to rights three times as fast and three times as competently as all the birds and animals in Snow White. If a man should bring into the house a brass cap from the rear axle hub of a dismounted 1907 Chevrolet, to use for a cigarette tray, a Wismer woman would, even through sleet and snow or fire and heat, carry it back to the stable and replace it on the wheel where it belonged. . . .

## To Dr. Gordon Bruce

Dear Dr. Bruce:

I wonder whether you know about Hints on the Care of the Eye for Young Ladies as outlined by De Quincey a hundred years ago. "The depth and subtlety of the eyes varies exceedingly with the state of the stomach, and, if young ladies were aware of the magical transformations which can be wrought in the depth and sweetness of the eye by a few weeks' exercise, I fancy we should see their habits in this point altered greatly for the better." That's all he had to say.

I don't know about depth and sweetness, but what I allude to laughingly as the "power" of my eye seems to be about what it was when I saw you. I probably see as well as the water buffalo, reputedly the blindest of all large jungle animals. It is interesting to note that the water buffalo can lick a tiger in spite of his opacities and indifferent, if not, indeed, detached retina.

My opacities, or spaniel hair, as I like to call them, give me lots more annoyance than my buffalo sight. Since I can't see very far beyond them, I sometimes just sit and look at them. I am familiar with all the new shifts they make and could draw an accurate map of the whole dirty brown constellation. (If I actually did, the Bermudians might think it was a map of the islands and put me in the military jail).

. . . There are more things in my eye than were dreamed of in Horatio's day, anyway, or maybe Hamlet had opacities and thought they were ghosts. This would also explain Macbeth's looking at nothing at all in the banquet scene and shouting "Take any other form than that!" I think I know how he felt, if it was opacities he saw and not Banquo.

We get back June 6th and I'll get in touch with you right away . . .

    All best wishes

    James Thurber

*Throughout the war Thurber's letters to the Williamses often included references to Captain Blandish, a fictional figure who Thurber credited with every military mistake that turned up in the news. "Drax" is the Williamses' son.*

## TO THE RONALD WILLIAMSES

### INTELLIGENCE REPORT OF AGENT 4R FOR BERMUDA

*May 4, 1940*

Dear Intelligence Department,

London W.C.1, England.

There isn't a great lot to report today, I am sorry to say. We all woke to dripping skies and a bit of a blow and vowed as the day wore on we had never seen a more tiresome May 4.

I have my eye on one of the greengrocers in Hamilton who chivvies one about a bit and seems far too unconcerned about England at war, far too unconcerned. Chap name of Smythe or Frith or some such name.

The James Thurbers flew back after a mysterious five weeks in New York. I shall quiz them discreetly when we meet.

The German soldiers whom one supposed one would find in that whale were not there, really. It was a most authentic whale and smell.

Blandish became lost in a cloud bank the other day on what he calls tiffin patrol—he refuses to go up at dawn—and our searchers have not yet found him.

No outright conspiracy against the welfare of His Majesty has yet come to view.

I am soddy there is no more news.

> Respectfully yours,
> 4R
> Somerset, Bermuda
> Station 75W

P.S. The jolly sun came out at 4.22 p.m. today.

*Dr. Bruce's first of five operations, a "preliminary iridectomy," enabled Thurber to read and write during the summer of 1940, but by the middle of September it was no longer safe for him to walk alone outdoors. He had sold* The Saturday Evening Post *his short story "You Could Look It Up." Thurber was on the board of Ronnie's* The Bermudian.

### The last of August and who cares (1940)

Dear Janey and Ronnie:

I wish we were sitting out in front of the slave quarters in the moonlight telling riddles, matching pennies, drinking rum, and running down the right people.

It was very nice to hear from little Janey and to know that her one letter a year went this time to us. Most American girls would rather lose their front teeth than write letters, but science does not know why this is.

I have not had a very good summer in my mind, it being full of dark gibbering figures dressed in black bombazine with lamb's blood on it, whilst in the background scamper the gray wet bodies of dozens of little cheeping wail-

wice and grunting uoolowfing chudhubs and small round mailbacked cree-
blies whose scales come off in your hand and stick to you like wet onion
skin.

Helen just reread me both your letters, Ronnie's going as far back as June
20. It is almost time for me to go back to Hospy-wospy for more monkey business. I can't see any better but I don't see much worse and can write on the
typewriter with ease, having just finished and sold a 7500 word story to the Sat
Eve Post, a baseball story, which won't be printed until next year because I got
it in too late. Ross wrote me when he found this out that for two months he
has been going around in his stocking feet shushing everybody and talking
sadly about how I couldn't see anything smaller than the sign made of flowers
and reading ELYRIA to guide the airmen flying over that Ohio town. Now, he
says, I find you are writing serials for the Saturday Evening Post. He wants me
to get to work on that Bermuda story, the dope on which was turned over to
me a few days after I got home from Janey's Vineyard. I think I will send it on
to you, as it is interesting, and you can send it back, and I hope the censors
don't get it but if they do I'll just say, "Ross, the censors got it." Got what? he'll
say. The piece on Bermuda, I'll tell him. I don't know what you are talking
about, he will then complain, for he no longer remembers anything for more
than five, six weeks.

Of course I get into some trouble on account of not seeing too good. Do
you raise them? I said to a lady on a bus. Raise what? she says. Those chickens
like the one you have in your lap, I said. She pulled the emergency cord and
brought the bus to a halt and got off at the corner of Mobray and Pineberry
Street in Jersey City. What she had on her lap was a white handbag. I may be
put away any day now by the authorities.

We went to Martha's Vineyard for a week and felt fine, since we had to get
up for breakfast at 8.30 every a.m. hangover or no hangover.

Let us hear from you again soon, my frans, and let us all pray for the speedy
downfall of the apes who are striving for control of the world. When they shot
that old Jew for shaking a stick at them, we should have got in the war, but we
will wait until they take Baltimore. The most remarkable and typical thing
about this country is that it can run like a startled fawn when the news comes
that the Martians are here, but it goes right on garter-snapping, jitterbugging,
and playing steel guitars with the Germans at the gates. It is possible to love
America, but it is not possible to respect its brains.

I think that good old Angleterre will hold out and finally outsmart those maniacs, and a lot of other people do, too. Nobody here seems to realize that if they don't hold out we are in the war faster than you could say Lieutenant Commander and Mrs. Wright. The youth of the nation doesn't want to fight, as you have probably heard, hundreds of thousands of them rushing off and marrying girls they probably can't stand in order to escape what they consider a worse fate. You can't expect much more from a nation of jitterbugs, tap-dancers, kettle-drum players, gum-chewers, tree-sitters, marathon-dancers, and the like. The last horrible twenty years of this kind of goings on has rotted the minds of the youth of the nation. In a democracy, everybody can do as he wishes and if they want to sit in a tree for four months or rock back and forth in a rocking chair for 17 days and nights, nobody can stop them. This, of course, brings up before the draft board a lot of feeble-minded grinning young men dragging their weak-minded new wives with them. What do you think Old Hickory and Stonewall would think of them? What do you think of the campaign between Old Slippery Elm Roosevelt and old Weeping Willow Willkie? . . .

I want to know about the magazine and how it is coming along. I get it of course and enjoy it a lot.

We spent one night on the Cape with the Sayres and talked about you two. They are fine.

We would like to see Drax again, and send him our love and kisses
       and the same to you.


Captain Blandish, who, it seems, applied for citizenship papers two years ago up here and has been an American for quite a while, showed up for the registration of aliens and was fingerprinted, etc. This has led to a lot of confusion, charges, and counter-charges, involving both Great Britain and the U.S.

Later: It finally turns out Blandish became an American citizen through a correspondence course, which does not count.


*After eye operations in 1940 and 1941, Thurber was nearly blind. He wrote letters in longhand on yellow paper but couldn't see what he wrote. He stubbornly continued to write a column for the newspaper* PM *and contribute articles to the* Bermudian, *but following the half-dozen unsuccessful operations, he underwent a collapse of nerve and spirit.*

## TO EUGENE SAXTON

*January 8, 1941*

Dear Gene:

I have decided to go over to Harcourt Brace and am signing contracts with them today. Since I am still unable to write or draw, I have to make changes of all kinds in order to keep my mind occupied. I shall probably shift from The New Yorker to Liberty.

In view of my very slow recovery, it doesn't appear that I will have a book of any kind for *any*body, for a long while yet. I should think, at any rate, that ten years of me would be enough for any one firm. I am just learning to dictate, but not learning very rapidly, so that letters of this kind are extremely difficult. I should like to talk to you and hope that you can drop around some afternoon. I leave Harpers with the very best of personal feelings.

We are living at the Grosvenor Hotel, since I have to be in town to see the eye doctors every other day. This is my one and only preoccupation at the moment, although I do come in to The New Yorker to do a little bit of work every few days. I know that I can explain my shift to you in person better than in this way. Anyway, I should like to have a drink with you some afternoon.

Cordially,
Jim

## TO DR. GORDON BRUCE

*The final proposed eye operation, a "capsuledectomy," never did take place.*

*Aug. 1941*

Dear Gordon,

Four weeks ago today I went into a tailspin, crashed, and burst into flames. This is to let you know that I am rapidly getting into shape again. B-2 injections, haliver oil and luminol have helped tremendously. It seems that the nerve exhaustion Russell detected just wasn't being helped enough by Vita-Cape. I have to have more help than that, for I had been hanging on by my fingernails for a hell of a long time. Even through the worst days, I began to gain weight, which I had not done. The Lord, who keeps doing all He can for me, sent in Dr. Ruth Fox, who is a gal with a fine background in neurology, and she pulled me out of it with great skill and understanding.

The things that inhabit the woods I fell into are not nice. I never want to crash there again if I can help it. Helen, my Scotch wife, has been like three nurses rolled into one, and has stood up under it all like the Black Watch.

I paid little attention to the eye during the battle of Chilmark, and strained it in the sun, as Helen told you, I think. Well, we found that uncle Arnold Knapp was up here, so we crashed in on him, knowing you would approve. He was very kind and helpful, suggested scapalomine and compresses, once a day. The eye began to whiten and is almost all white now. I saw him three times. He even made two little jokes, too. We said little about the nerves, as all he would say to that was humph-humph. . . .

I began writing a play in the midst of all the hell. They call me Iron Man Thurber.

We will be here until the 15th, and then to N.Y. for the winter. . . .

Look out for bows and arrows.

As ever,

Jim

## To Harold Ross

*After a fourteen-month absence from the pages of the* New Yorker, *Thurber submitted "The Whip-Poor-Will."*

*[Undated, summer, 1941, from Martha's Vineyard]*

Dear H. W.

Appreciate being the first person to get the new word rate. And I applaud your skill and courage in getting it put in effect. Helen read your nice long letter with the proper inflection.

I had to use a wholly different system on that story. I used to run through a first draft fast and then rewrite several times. This time I had to do the first draft and the rewriting in my head and when I wrote a sentence out it had to stand. The manuscript covers 80 pages and was done in about 10 hours at the rate of a few hundred words an hour. I haven't got the proofs yet, but I will consider McKelway's comment. I think the typescript in the office shows I cut out one refrain such as he suggests and I have asked him to check up on it.

Writing like this is a lot like having sexual intercourse while wearing an open parachute, but I will keep on at it anyway.

Cagney left today for Ottawa to make an airplane picture, but MacNamara, Max Eastman and Arthur Garfield Hays are still here.

Thanks again for your letter and the new word rate. Tell White to write.

Love,

Jim

## TO THE E. B. WHITES

*[Handwritten in semi-legible words, undated,*
*from Chilmark, Martha's Vineyard, Mass.]*

Dear Andy and Katharine:

I keep expecting to write to you any day, or to hear from you. It is easier for you all because you don't have to scribble away in the dark, like this. My new glasses, thick and heavy, bring everything three feet nearer than it was and even enable me to see the pencil more and the faint black track it leaves. (I can't see the words).

Your publisher sent up formal release papers to be signed for the pieces of mine you selected for the book [*A Sub-treasury of American Humor*]. I approve of the choice.

I have just finished the first draft of a fairy tale—it's about 1500 words long and I thought might make a Christmas book, with colorful illus. by some colorful artist . . .

[Remainder of letter missing.]

&ambox; &ambox; &ambox;

*[From Chilmark, Martha's Vineyard]*

Dear Andy & Katharine:

It was swell to get your fine letters. I have been in a tailspin and power dive combined which was awful, but I am pulling out of it with the help of Dr. Ruth Fox, Helen, the Gudes and the Coateses and Sayre, who was here for a few days. I simply cracked wide open and it has been frightful, almost insupportable, but now I'm fighting back. I have had to have hypos of B-1 and luminol, etc., and they are building me up. I think I may have to have help from a psychiatrist, for I got into a complex or two, the kind that frequently results from such things as I have been through . . .

The Coateses are with us now and that helps a lot.

I like the selections of mine you are using in your book, and am very proud to be so lavishly represented. You certainly took on a lot when you started on that venture.

I have a swell idea for a play which I want to get at. I need someone to help me on it, though. I want to do most of the actual writing, but talking it out with someone is important to me, especially now. I may get a girl in to dictate to, and wish I had Margaret Thurlow. She was up here for a day or two. I think the idea has more stuff than The Male Animal and will be funnier.

I wish I could sit around and tell the idea to you. It is a little hard to do it in pencil in a semidarkness . . .

I wrote a fairy tale just before I cracked up, and when it is copied, I want you to see it. I thought it might make a Christmas book, and would like your opinion. The whip-poor-will story was quite an achievement technically, since I wrote it longhand, on some eighty pieces of yellow paper, and since I had to use a new form of composition, doing all the rewriting in my head, before putting the final lines down. We—Helen and I—did a little cutting out later, but no rewriting. I was glad you liked it. Ross wrote me probably his longest known letter about it—some 800 words. He has been very good to me. The new word rate for casuals was partly my work, and the letter told all about that.

We would, of course, love to have a Minnie puppy, and it breaks our hearts that we wouldn't be just right for a dachshund just now. It has long been our dream to have six or eight variegated dogs when we buy our house in the country—a dachshund, a poodle, a water spaniel, etc. There is a wonderful black male poodle up here, name of Hugo. You tell him to get us ice and he bounds out to the kitchen and brings back a pailful—at cocktail time.

I hope you can read this, but I don't see how the hell you can. Althea and Allen [Gilmore, Althea's third husband] will bring Rosemary up here a week from tomorrow . . . I will be big and strong by that time. God knows I have been down in the bowels of terror, but I have climbed out of it with what Dr. Fox thinks is remarkable speed.

I won't go on any further, because this will be task enough for you, the way it is. It's my first finished work of any kind in two weeks. It gives me lift and confidence to get back at my writing table. Helen will go over this and translate the most horribly garbled words. We love to hear from you, about your life and Minnie's and all, so write again before too long.

Love as always,

Jim

There is nothing pathological about me, babies, just nerves. I used to think nervous breakdowns were not so terrible. I know now how wrong I was.

## TO HAROLD ROSS

*October 20, 1941*

Dear Mr. Ross:

After you suggested the other day that I try to do some captions for a sheaf of Petty drawings which seems to have stacked up almost as high as the photostatic copies of rough sketches around the office, I got to thinking that it wouldn't be a bad idea to let me spend, say two afternoons a week in the office not only trying to write captions to pictures, but also having a look at the captions to pictures which have been bought. Since I haven't sent in an idea drawing of my own for a year and a half, my beloved art meeting could hardly say that my criticisms were based on a sheaf of my drawings having just been rejected.

You already have filed away for your autobiography some 50 or 100 blasphemous notes from me on what is the matter with the magazine. Most of these were written, I suppose, just after I got 3 or 4 of my best drawings back. Now we are on a new basis, since I am a blind, gray-haired playwright who still has a great affection for the magazine and is still capable of indignation. It seems to me that something is the matter when the first 3 drawings in the magazine turn out the way they did in the issue of October 18. The parachutist, the man with the little fire extinguisher, and the man painting the sign ("Did he want this on white or rye?") should not have followed one right after the other. These are all definite gag ideas and belong to the rather labored formula type. Most of the great New Yorker captions have not had to depend on some character holding something: a parachute, a fire extinguisher, a cat-o'-nine-tails, or a tomahawk in the scalp. Just to quote a few of the great ones—"I'm the one that should be lying down somewhere," "Yah, and who made 'em the best years?", "I want to report a winking man," "You're so good to me and I'm so tired of it all," "With you I have known peace, Lida, and now you say you're going crazy"—most of the great ones, I repeat, did not have to depend on somebody holding, wrapped up in, or pinned down by, any implement, invention, or piece of apparatus. The really great New Yorker drawings have had to do with people sitting in chairs, lying on the beach, or walking along the street. The easy answer the art meeting always gives to the dearth of ideas like the ones I am trying to describe is that they are hard to get or that nobody sends them in any more. It seems to me that the principal reason for this is that the artists take their cue from the type of drawing which they see constantly published in the magazine. Years ago I wrote a story for The New Yorker in which a woman who tried to put together a cream separator suddenly snarled at those who were looking at her and said, "Why doesn't somebody take this god damned thing away from me?" I want to help to take the cream separators, parachutes, fire extinguishers, paint brushes and tomahawks away from four-fifths of the characters that appear in The New Yorker idea drawings.

There are other things, too. It must have been 6 years ago that you told me drawings about psychoanalysts were terribly out of date. The next week I turned in one in which the analyst says, "A moment ago, Mrs. Ridgway, you said that everybody you looked at seemed to be a rabbit. Now just what did you mean by that?" You are still basically right. Drawings involving analysts have to have something fresh and different in them, such as the one I have just so modestly mentioned. But you can't publish a drawing about an analyst and a woman with the caption, "Your only trouble is, Mrs. Markhan, that you're so horribly normal." This is one of the oldest, tritest, and most often repeated lines in the world. If you will look up a story of mine called "Mr. Higgins' Breakdown," published more than ten years ago, you will find that the first sentence is as follows (I quote from memory), "Gorham P. Higgins, Jr., was so normal that it took the analyst a long time to find out what was the matter with him." Just after that story appeared, the editor of Redbook sent for me and said he wanted me to write something for him because he had been so enchanted by that line. At that time, I have the vanity to believe, it was not old. But the years roll on, Mr. Ross, and turn into decades. So what you probably need is an old blind man sitting in one corner of Mr. Gibb's office and snarling about certain captions which you are too old to remember helped make certain issues of The New Yorker way back before the depression. . . .

If you ever write a comedy for the theatre you will discover that the best laughs invariably follow some simple and natural line which the characters involved would normally say. Thus, one of the best laughs in The Male Animal followed the simple statement, "Yes, you are." To show you what I mean, let's take the specific example of the drawing which appeared in the issue of October 18th in which the salesman says to the lady at the door, "Couldn't we go inside and sit down? I have a rather long sales talk." This is such an extravagant distortion of reality, it is so far removed from what any salesman would ever say, that to be successful it has to be fantastic. But since the situation is not fantastic, it ends up simply as a bad gag. All salesmen that get into drawings in The New Yorker ring the changes on cocksureness, ingenuity, or ignorance. When I was a little boy, in my early 20's, in Columbus, my mother opened the door one afternoon to a tall, sad salesman with a sample case, who said, "I don't suppose you want to buy any of my vanilla. Nobody ever does." There is such a thing as a tired, sad, defeated salesman, but even if there weren't we could use one. I can hear this salesman in the October 18th issue saying, "I just want to say to begin with, madam, that I have been through a great deal to-day." Or, "I simply must talk for a few minutes to some understanding married woman, madam. It's not about my products." I'm just batting these rough ideas out to give you an idea of how a situation and its caption can be explored, as Marc Connelly puts it. In an hour's time I could get 2 or 3 perfect captions for this particular drawing. The best laugh you get in the theatre comes from the women and as the result of hitting a universal and familiar note. The closer you come to what a human being might say, the funnier your caption is going to be. A woman laughs at a line about salesmen because it reminds her of what that funny little Fuller Brush man said to her sister Ella. No salesman ever said to any housewife what you have him saying in the cartoon I am talking about. That is a gag man's idea.

I'll talk this all over with you any time you say. I can't go on any kind of salary basis on account of the State Income Tax, but I am willing to be paid by the caption. You must feel free to reject my ideas if you don't think they are right. I just want somebody to listen to them.

> Love,
> Thurber

# *The*

# CHALLENGING YEARS

## To the Herman Millers

*April 6, 1942*

Dear Herman and Dorothy,

Helen read me Dorothy's note, together with the clipping, which we found very interesting. The Who's Who boys certainly went out in a wholesale manner to get names this year. They had begun to write to me about ten years ago because Dick Connell sent my name in. Dick is a great wag. Their letters finally became threatening, but I still refused to send any facts about myself. Therefore, they looked up my record in old copies of the Ohio State Journal and talked to my deaf Aunt Edith, and sent me a galley proof of the write-up. The gist of this was that Jacob Thurman was born in Toledo, Ohio in 1904; he married Theo Madison in 1920 when he was only 16 and she was 8, apparently. Helen corrected this proof, since she is a stern editor of the old school, and sent it back. . . .

     Jim

*Eugene Saxton suggested to Thurber and White the re-issuing of* Is Sex Necessary? *The fictitious authorities in the book were Dr. Walter Tithridge (White) and Dr. Karl Zaner (Thurber).*

*[Undated, handwritten letter of 1942]*

Dear Andy:

Here is a letter from Gene. Says he has been thinking about sex.

I don't know—I was 34, separated and able to see in 1929. I'm not sure I wouldn't want to do my pieces over or throw them out. I'm neither so lighthearted nor so oblivious of what was going on in the world as I was then. You have to listen sharply to hear the lonesome bell of sex now. Let me hear what you think . . .

As ever,

Jim

≈ ≈ ≈

Dear Tithridge [White]:

The enclosed letter, sent to me by Miss Betty Rew who seems to be a Rew with a difference, is very sad and makes me very sad. Has it only been thirteen years since Zaner and you worked together on that book, or thirteen hundred, in Art Samuels' room? Or was it just eleven years? The chief dreads we had in those days were little dreads indeed: one of mine being the fear that I would have to talk with Filimore Hyde if he came into the office. Think of it.

I am sure that Zaner (whose other letter I know nothing about) has lost his quick light step. His life work was really to no end. He might just as well have devoted it to making deal tables out of sawdust or scrolling names in white ink on little red glasses for visitors to a county fair. The only hope I see is the fact that there are bright strong girls in Sioux City and Lincoln capable of wrapping a thousand bandages a day or shellacking struts on those thousand planes a day as they move by on the assembly line. If you can call that hope, Walter.

In those old days Phillip Wedge worried mainly because of his feeling that the phone bell was ringing as he was half-way down the stairs to the door, or that his canary bird had caught one claw in his little wooden swing and was hanging there, cheeping, head down.

Levick spent his days grousing and muttering about Woollcott, Ross growled because your office and mine were too far from his. Ingersoll spent his days counting the girders that fell from buildings under construction in the downtown business district. Ross wanted to know what Harry Thaw did with himself and how much money Maude Adams really had. Peter Vischer was excited because he had found out about a meeting between Tunney and Lindbergh, Nothing up to that time had yet really happened to Vischer or Lindbergh. Katharine and I worried about whether Ernest and Althea would ever get married to anybody else. Parlous times, great worries that made us pale and thin. The face that haunted our nightmares was not that of Hitler but of Geppert. Ross and Fleischmann did not speak for weeks, Markey and Lippmann did not speak for months. Times of stress and strain.

One wondered a little uneasily not what Mussolini was going to do next but what Margaret Speaks was going to do next.

I was browbeaten into buying a mouse colored belt and was prostrated for days. One was depressed by remarks made by William Rose Benet in the back room at Tony's. Mrs. Parker's chief concern was whether the hotel would put another bottle of gin on the cuff or not. Benchley lay awake at night wondering how to get rid of Betty Starbuck. Ross bought a new gray checked cap to go down the bay and meet Madge Kennedy.

Every time you got on a ship you were afraid not that it would be sunk by a torpedo but that maybe somewhere aboard Vivian Samuels lay in wait, combing out her little dog's hair.

Miss Hokinson woke up one morning to find a Scotty with a big red bow on his neck standing looking at her.

Dey sing, dey bark, dey cry, dey so hoppy.

A tall thin man took off his shirt and spread it over a lot of warm Scotties. A tall dark woman bought eight little bottles of milk to feed to puppies already so gorged with milk they couldn't keep their eyes open.

One did not speculate as to whether Chamberlain would ruin us, the question was would James M. Cain ruin us? The menace was not that Stalin and Hitler would get together, the menace was the probability that Bergman was sleeping with the new office manager he brought in.

The news that depressed a whole city was the news that the morning World had ceased publication. We didn't know how we were going to survive that.

The thing that paled our cheeks when we heard it on the phone was that Aunt Crully was lost in the Grand Central.

What sent Ross home to bed was not tanks and planes in Holland but the sight of two old cuffs and a sock in my outgoing basket.

What in the name of God were we going to do about covering art?

The one ray of hope then was that Ross had found a barber who could cure dandruff and a doctor who could cure piles.

Levick devised a new passing system (White passes to Levick who passed to Ross) which seemed likely to solve all our problems.

Joe and Rosemary were both born with the gift of heaving their stomachs right side up and the correct number of fingers and it seemed that there was nothing else to worry about.

If Estelle agreed to a divorce we could all go back to sleep and sleep till morning.

I could read the fine type in New York, New Haven and Hartford time tables and thought nothing of it.

Ross discovered that you could sleep with a woman without setting her up in a Park Avenue apartment on a five-year lease and was so cheered by it that he spent the Talk Conference hours telling amusing anecdotes about a man named Bogue.

We gave Ingersoll as a hostage to Fortune and there was nothing left to worry about except that White set the office on fire and I was caught playing with dolls.

Woollcott rode out of the office in an old 1903 High Dudgeon, leaving Shouts and Murmurs to die, and we all wondered what in the world would happen, but nothing did.

Johan Bull quit drawing horses and ships and again nothing happened.

Eva Prout Geiger called me on the phone one day and Andy ran into a Miss Burchfield on the street, but again things quieted down.

Margaret Speaks married and Englishman and turned to Christian Science.

Paula got a job . . . and the world quit shaking and turned even on its axis again.

So they came up and so they went away, the old terrors that walked by day, the old perils of the night.

If advancing age hadn't given us a sterner and a calmer viewpoint of things, this war would. The question is what will the both of them together do to us.

I have an idea I will begin to write a cross between Carlyle at his gloomiest and Gerrtrude Stein at her lowest. I speak of the style, not the content. I been reading a few of the old sages, the old sad sages of the Byronic period including Emerson who thought everything was going to be dandy on account of we were all Kings and you could reach out on any side and grab great gobs of God and Nature. He didn't know that when he called on Coleridge in that poet's old age that Coleridge had been taking dope for years. Emerson did not know anybody took dope. He knew that a lot of people were not in tune with Nature and couldn't let themselves go in the Over Soul, but he didn't know anybody really took dope. Coleridge, wearing green spectacles, jumped all over the Unitarian church—since the dope was wearing off—and Emerson said he felt constrained to point out that he was a Unitarian and came from a long line of them. "I thought so," snarled Coleridge.

You shouldn't worry about your mucous membranes or give any thought to any special part of the body, said Carlyle, because "Inquiry is the beginning of Disease."

We will be in New York when you get this letter. I can't carry it aboard, for the war rules say it has to be mailed here.

I am, censors, and so are my friends, a hundred percent non pro-German.

As ever,

Jim

## TO MINNETTE FRITTS PROCTOR

*The book referred to here is Thurber's* My World—and Welcome to It.

*[Undated, 1942]*

Dear Minnette:

I have started a couple letters to you, the hard way, on yellow paper with a pencil. This time I hope to carry through and I hope you can read it. My sight is clearing up slowly and in daylight I can almost make out the words as I write—but this is under an electric lamp, and hard to see. I had to draw on an easel 4 feet by 3 in New York, but now I can see paper half that size, and go back and put in eyes and mouth without trouble. I had five operations in 8 months on my very tricky lone eye. No doctor except my great Gordon Bruce was keen to take on my tough cataract because all hell was pretty sure to happen and it did—adhesions, recurrence of iritis and all the trimmings. I have the prettiest kind of blue and yellow spots to stare at constantly and they were worse when my eye was closed. I was in the hospital 65 days in all. No general anesthetic except the last time. As a result I had a complete nerve crack-up that was a honey—just after Jap left for your coast. I know you will be amused to know that I turned to women doctors finally and got along fine (ah, there, Oscar [Proctor])....

We have taken a house for a year in the lovely old village of Cornwall, Conn, and Helen is taking first aid and also spotting planes. She has become an accomplished eye nurse, too, naturally....

...It would be very nice to see your Alie, or anywhere, as it is hard for me to believe your daughter is old enough for the old sorority. Rosemary (I started late) will be eleven in October. I will have her here next month. Althea is married to her third husband now—a Harvard man eight years her junior, who teaches history at Amherst. Her second was a Yale archeologist. I like the present one better than the one who followed me. So does Rosemary. (and Althea) . . .

Do you plan ever to get to Columbus again? We were there for the World Premier of the Male Animal in the movies and had a hectic time. . . .

Elliott will be back in the fall to appear with Hepburn in the new Phil Barry play. We saw it at New Haven in the Spring and he was superb. One of his lines is "I'm older than I look," and it was loudly applauded. He has a fond following in the East. He is indispensable to me, because of his ever-cheerful nature and I am dedicating my next book to him. It comes out in the Fall—my tenth. I'm going to send you one—after all these years. It isn't my best, but it has some pieces in it I like, including seven or eight I wrote in Europe in 1937 & 1938. We went over to take a last look around.

This has become an impossible scrawl and I'm afraid you will not be able to make out much of it. It isn't a very good letter anyway. As I get into the swing, they will improve.

My best wishes to you & Oscar and the kids, as ever Jim.

## TO HAROLD ROSS

*In the spring of 1942, Ross wrote a letter to the Connecticut governor protesting the state's plan for a park next to Ross's Stamford estate. In it he expressed his fear of noisy revelers from Harlem and the Bronx. The letter was made public, to Ross's embarrassment and Thurber's delight. Dr. Robin Hood was Thurber's proctologist. Thurber's line of parody is of the song "On Moonlight Bay."*

*In January 1943, the Thurbers closed down the rented house in Cornwall, Ct., and took an apartment on East 57th Street in Manhattan to save on rationed heating oil and gasoline.*

*One of the drawings submitted to Ross was captioned: "I think of you as being enormously alive," published in the* New Yorker *March 27, 1943.*

*[Undated, probably spring 1942] Saturday*

Dear Wallace [Ross],

I have finished a casual, which is being copied. You will get it with this or in the same mail. I followed your letter and its sequelae, including Peggy Wood's report to the *Tribune*. I had a towering argument with Ingersoll, who wanted to drive you out of Stamford if you did not behave. This desire of his to run people out of town alarms me. I have seen trippers in action and I know what you mean. I used to write hotheaded letters, but I always held them overnight. (Private wifely notation to H. W. Ross: Not always, eh?) Are they going to let Ingersoll drive the Japs out of Malay, or will he stay here to drive you out of Stamford?

Dr. Bruce, my eye man, has been taken away from that work and assigned to the marines in a capacity any M.D. could handle. This is a stupid waste of a rare talent that does not grow on trees. If he doesn't come back (and the chances are excellent that he won't), I doubt if I would let anyone else operate on me. My viewpoint may seem entirely selfish, but it isn't. He should not be wasted. I can't very well write Washington myself, but I feel it is my duty to do something about it. What would you suggest? Of course, Bruce does not know I plan to do anything about it, and he wouldn't like it. Maybe I'm wrong, and he should not now be taken from his outfit, but I don't think so. I enclose a letter from him, just for your eyes, which you can send back. He writes a neat and vivid sentence.

> Love,
> Jim

P. S. Robin Hood was a medical corps lieutenant in the last war. "Never saw a rectum," he told me sadly. "The heart specialist got rectums. I got hearts." Aw, stick it up your heart, they probably said in those days, or "You have broken her ass, now don't go 'way." Well, the country will never learn.

> J

&ae; &ae; &ae;

February 9, 1943

Dear Ross:

I am sending four pen and ink drawings to the New Yorker art meeting, three of them with new and wonderful captions, and one with the original caption which I and all my admirers feel is perfect.

I want every one of these drawings bought whether or not you approve of the captions. These are four of the last seven Thurber drawings in the world which have never been published. The other three I will turn in next week with appropriate captions and I want them bought too.

It has been as bewildering to me as it has been depressing to have the conference send these priceless drawings back each time I send them in as if they were no more valuable than so many Arnos or Winslow Homers.

I have definitely been persuaded by a little man who lives inside me that I will never again be able to draw in pen and ink. This certainly should give you some idea of the value of these four drawings and the other three to come. There are no more in the world. Hoping I will soon be the same,

J. Thurber

P.S. I think of you as being enormously alive.

## TO DAISE TERRY

*April 3rd [1943]*

Dear Terry,

I am enclosing two more spots. I don't see how you all can fail to be enchanted by that Spring Creature. I don't know exactly what he is. Just a Spring Creature, 1943. I hope you recognize the tall thin man in the other spot, who is trying to touch the floor with his fingers, but is doing no better than the lamp.

I am also enclosing captions for three of my idea drawings which either you or Ross have been holding down there. This first caption is for the drawing, in pen and ink, on white paper, of the women in black hats sitting around the room. Ross has it, together with a caption about Lindbergh, which Andy tried for this picture. My new caption is:

"She's thought up some way of combining the Townsend Plan and Buchman-
ism after the war."

(I still think, and so do Andy and one or two other sound critics, that the original caption, "She claims we can beat Hitler by dreaming true," is perfect and funny for this drawing. Doesn't make a bit of difference whether people know the expression or not.)

Now we come to my second caption, which is for a large, four-by-five-foot yellow paper drawing that Ross has. It shows a man and woman seated, and the caption on it now reads: "If the Japs or Germans captured Connecticut, could they keep me from spotting?" My new caption for this is:

"I don't understand anything that's happened since McKinley was President."

Now comes my caption for the third drawing you have. It's the captionless one on yellow copy paper which I gave you the last time I was in town. It shows a man in a chair, being scowled at by an erect woman. My caption for this is:

"Flagpole sitting has gone forever. Why don't you face it and quit moping around?"

Please have these captions copied and attached to the drawings in question. Then I'd like to have this letter sent on to Mr. Ross for his information and guidance. Thanks, as always, Terry, for your myriad favors.

> Love and kisses,
> J Thurber

*Cornwall. Conn.*

## To the Herman Millers

*1943, May 28*

Dear Herman and Dorothy:

I keep thinking of you sweet people all the time, and so does my wife, Angel Face. What is the color of your life now? What do you write & think as the planet disintegrates? Bring me up to date in a chatty and brilliant letter.

At 48, going on 49, I am getting along as well as might be expected, seeing a trifle better. I draw now with a Zeiss Loop, and look like a welder from Mars.

I'm getting out a Fairy Tale in the fall, with some lovely color work by Louis Slobodkin (no Nipponese, he). It's called "Many Moons" (no relation to the Scarlet Mask play of the same name—1923).

Also a book of drawings, since I haven't had one in eleven years.

Neither had Althea had a baby for eleven years, but on April 16, after several years of trying ending in 2 miscarriages, she gave birth to Linda Adams Gilmore. Nice going.

I want to see you folks & tell you more news and amuzing anecdotes (how in the hell can you read this?). . . .

> Love to you two from
> Jim and Helen

&. &. &.

*1943, June 26*

Dear Herman and Dorothy:

. . . Helen and I were married eight years ago yesterday, and she is prettier & sweeter than ever, like my friendship for you. But you and I should have more intercourse.

(Footnote: Thurber, in the final phase, kept muttering 'intercourse' to himself most of the day, and chuckling.)

My sight is about the same, my nerves better. I make the Best Short Stories of 1943 and also the O. Henry Memorial Collection this year, with "The Catbird Seat" and "The Cane in the Corridor", which maybe you saw.

My brother is starting a new book store on Rich near High. Seems a little out of the way.

Did I tell you Althea had a new daughter. I'm not very productive right now, trying to do a play about the New Yorker. Slow going.

Let us have a word from you.

We send our best love as always.

Jim

## To Eugene Saxton

*Saxton had proposed to Thurber a collection of Thurber's previous work, which Harper & Bros. eventually brought out in 1945 as* The Thurber Carnival. *Thurber's reply is in his semi-legible handwriting.*

*June 11, 1943*

Dear Gene:

I'd like nothing better than an omnibus of the old pieces and pictures, but this seems the worst possible year, since I have two books coming out this fall— a Fairy Tale [*Many Moons*], and a book of drawings [*Men, Women and Dogs*].

I'm afraid a third project would not work out so well, for itself or for the other two.

Let me know what you think.

A week before he died Heywood Broun told me he wanted to see a Thurber anthology, and I began to think about it.

Maybe the fall of 1944 would be all right—if the world goes on. Perhaps we can't hope for another such year as this, but who knows?

I agree in the main with your choice, although you include a couple I am trying to forget, and leave out two or three I still rate high ("Something to Say," "The Greatest Man in the World," "The Black Magic of Barney Haller") But we can thrash this out later . . .

As ever,

Jim Thurber

## TO E. B. WHITE

*May 15, 1943*

Dear Andy:

Six years ago today Helen and I were one day at sea on our way to France with Art Samuels . . .

You will get a chance to see the book which Helen and I will dummy up when we get the drawings. I think a smaller size page and book is a good idea. . . .

For a title I thought of "The More I See of People" if it has not been used.

I have finished Act I of a play for this fall. It takes place in the room at the New Yorker occupied by Terry, who figures largely in it. So does Ross. So does a guy named Jeff Crane, who could be you. Everybody comes out well. Nothing to worry about. Helen and I are pretty excited about the first act, which is very funny. The second act will be funnier. Almost everything that ever happened is in it.

The second act deals with Ross (Walter Bruce) holding in his arms a Scotty with a red ribbon on its neck, as pneumatic drills roar off stage, and saying "God, how I pity me."

I have been working it out in my mind for a year.

Althea has a new daughter, Linda. Pretty good going.

Don't let your gut knot.

    Love,

    Jim

*White had suggested that Thurber's "bravery" in continuing to draw despite his near-blindness be somehow indicated in the introduction of* Men, Women and Dogs.

*Thurber was playing mentor to Mary Mian, a friend of Helen's and Thurber's from the Village days, whose short stories were running in* The New Yorker.

*June 9, 1943*

Dear Andy:

We abandoned that title "The More I See of People" since it sounded too much like a retired lady librarian's sketches about her three spaniels.

I can't very well call my own bravery wonderful. People would say, "There goes proud-ass Thurber—calls himself What-a-Man."

Way it stands now it's "James Thurber's Men, Women, and Dogs." It will be 250 pages—they want to sell the son of a bitch for $3. . . .

Gene S. [Saxton] wants to get out a quote Thurber Sampler unquote—a perfect Harper title. You can just see them winding their watches with a little key as they thought of it, sipping at their madeira.

I hope Katharine & you will stick with me on the Mary Mian pieces. Have you had a look at the two new ones and my idea of how to handle the series? It seems to me this is a new and rare thing which must be cherished.

Jim

## To Peter De Vries

*De Vries, editor of* Poetry *magazine, had published an admiring and insightful essay on Thurber's work and later invited Thurber to speak at a Chicago fundraiser for* Poetry.

*November 19, 1943*

Dear Mr. De Vries:

I am practically moved to accept your invitation not only because of my feeling for the magazine but because of your swell piece about me. It isn't often, as I shoot craps with Merlin below stairs in Axel's Castle, that anyone stops long enough to explore what I am up to. One of my regrets that I brought home from two years in Europe is that I missed meeting [T. S.] Eliot. Some one told me that he was fond of "My Life and Hard Times" which of course pleased me greatly. I think he particularly liked the preface, which he thought was a pretty fair statement of the nature of the artist.

As you probably know, Edmund Wilson comes to this magazine as literary critic the first of the year in place of [Clifton] Fadiman. There will be more fun and confusion in these illiterate halls.

Back to the lecture proposition, it is quite true that I don't go in for that, partly because of my bad vision, partly because of a tendency to shake all over when I face a group of people and partly because I am not sure I really have anything to say. However, I am going to give it my most serious thought and if I can coax Mrs. Thurber we may be able to make it sometime between January and April, since I plan to visit my home town, Columbus, about that time. Another reason for coming out which I omitted is that I would very much like to meet you.

> Cordially,
> James Thurber

*Mr. Peter De Vries, Poetry,*
*232 East Erie Street, Chicago, Ill.*

## TO GUS LOBRANO

*With submarine warfare cutting them off from Bermuda, the Thurbers vacationed in late fall at The Homestead, in Hot Springs, Virginia, where Thurber drafted* The Great Quillow.

*Dec. 1, 1943*

Dear Gus:

A letter from Mary Mian about changes in the Roti piece worries me—and she seems upset.

The changes made in the lead sound appalling to me. Why all the pedestrian itemizing? Is it Ross's old clarity bug?

Mary's prose has a rhythm and color all its own and I think she should be allowed to make her changes.

We are both feeling fine in this tremendous place, and like it a lot. Not many people here now. Good food, amiable service, nice rooms—and it's as big as Grand Central.

I finished my new children's book and am now doing Notes & Comment for Transatlantic, the American mag published in England, a task Andy's refusal dumped in my lap, the dog.

How is he?

Tell Shawn that we lovers of the MARY CELESTE were shocked to see it called the MARIE Celeste in Talk last week.

See you Dec. 6

> as ever,
> Jim

P.S. With propriety, society will say Marie, but it was Mary, Mary, long before the fashions came. . . .

> J

*a. *a. *a.

410 East 57th St., New York 22, N.Y.
March 16, 1944

Mr. Gus Lobrano, The New Yorker
25 West 43rd St., New York, N.Y.

Dear Gus:

I am enclosing, to conform with the ever tightening strictures of the magazine, a little piece with a small special history. I wrote it before I signed the contract by which *The New Yorker* bought the right to see all my pieces before I sent them anywhere else. This story was ordered by a South American magazine called Zap or Yuk or something like that. The idea was to print work by American writers in an effort to bring about Pan-American good will. The lady editor who ordered this story turned it down. I got mad, she got mad, and her agent here, a man named Bunder or Taber or Zap also got mad.

I have this story in mind now for *Madamoiselle* but I want to give you the legal and called-for look.

*The New Yorker*'s demand to see everything we write is of course in one way an effort to form inspiration and to control idiosyncrasy. In this way it can sometimes give itself a lot of unnecessary work.

For instance, some strange impulse has led me to write a piece about "Treadways on Tappets" since I have always wanted to appear in *Popular Mechanics*. I suppose Gibbs will have to read this piece, however. I am also working on a parody of Henry James which will possibly amuse seventeen people in the country.

Another curious problem about *The New Yorker* contract is that a writer often finds he has finished a piece in which he has completely kept *The New Yorker* out of mind. In a word, he doesn't want it to appear there. For instance, when I bowl I always use a bowling alley and I would feel pretty silly bowling at "21". I am sure this will all be very clear to Ross.

Thanks a lot for reading the little poems. You and Maxwell and Andy seem to be agreed. Helen and I thought that perhaps twelve of the poems were really excellent, but we were pretty close to the picture.

As ever,

Jim

## TO PETER DE VRIES

*410 East 57th St., New York 22, N.Y.*
*April 4, 1944*

*Mr. Peter DeVries, 3426 N. Elaine Place,*
*Chicago, Illinois*

Dear Peter:

You put the right color to it when you said Black Saturday. Last night I got to fussing so profoundly about my coming ordeal that I developed a sharp pain in my stomach. Sensing that I was going around in a panicky circle Helen woke up in the middle of the night, got pencil and paper, and wrote down some ideas for me. Her notes together with your letter and some thought of my own have helped me to work out a kind of plan which I think will get me through this.

I want to start off and talk for as long as I can, perhaps fifteen minutes or perhaps half an hour if I get going well, in a kind of preface to the question period. I will say—roughly, and for example—that I am not a speaker because in three months I have not been able to think up a Message and because I am not able to read from my own works and would not if I could. I will then comment on the title I selected for the talk and say that it is likely to get me into trouble. I will recall an experience I had while talking to several hundred English students at Ohio State some six years ago. It was this group that asked me what was my artistic credo, and what did I think of the future of the American theatre and it wasn't until one of them asked me "What is Peter Arno like?" that I could really get going. I will then tell of an experience that Jimmy Sheean had in Bridgeport, I think it was, when *he* actually tried to pull serious questions from his audience but the first person to stand up asked him "What is the Stork Club like?" From there I will go on to state that up until three years ago the question most often asked me at parties or by strangers in hotel lobbies, or by people writing letters or talking on the 'phone was "What is Dorothy Parker like?" Now this question has been displaced by another one. "How old is Elliott Nugent?"

Still sticking to the subject of questions which have been asked me most often during the years I will discuss those that relate to my work. For example, "Is it true that your little daughter really does the drawings for you?", "Where did you get the idea for the Seal in the Bedroom?", and "How did you manage to think up all the crazy things that occur in 'My Life and Hard Times?' " I can then take a few minutes to give to some of these questions the usual answers, some of which ought to be, if I am still able to talk, very amusing.

I will then anticipate questions about the *New Yorker* by giving as humourous an outline of the amusing highlights in its history as I can think up between now and then. There have been some very funny ones and I think this ought to go over.

The only special story outside of this general line of questions in review that I want to tell has a Chicago angle and came to me recently from Lt. Joe Bryan, former editor of the *Saturday Evening Post,* who recently returned from the South Pacific, if I can tell it without seeming to brag too much. It begins a little further back with a story that appeared some months ago in *Harper's* written by Christopher La Farge. LaFarge discovered that a group of American bomber pilots had picked up, as a byword or kind of greeting, an expression from "The Secret Life of Walter Mitty". This was the recurring phrase "Ta pocketa pocketa pocketa." Joe Bryan's story shows that the expression has spread even further and has become in vogue among night fighter pilots in the Bouganville area. A young pilot from Augusta, Ga., cruising around in the night heard over the radio the voice of a strange American pilot dreamily droning "Ta pocketa pocketa pocketa". The Georgian, giving his identification—say "Albatross, 7310," said "Come in, Walter Mitty. Over." The other pilot asked for the Georgian's direction and location and presently showed up alongside in a P-38. The Georgian was a Navy flier, the other man proved to be Lt. Francis Parker of Chicago, an Army pilot. The two men landed their planes and introduced themselves. This is the brief outline of the story which might be added at the end of the question period as an item in conclusion.

I will certainly want you up there on the platform beside me. I also fervently hope that there will be some kind of lectern to kind of hide behind and lean on since this would give me added confidence and help me to stand up for an hour.

I have gone over the questions you sent and I am perfectly willing to take on any of them, although how it will come out I can't promise. The following half dozen seem to me the sort that might give me something to say without too much stumbling around.

1) Is it true that you began drawing just for the hell of it, and that the recog-

nition and critical praise your pictures have received has occasioned some slight surprise on your part?

2) What is the social significance of the *New Yorker*?

3) Have you ever come across a definition of analysis of laughter or humour that you think hits it, or do you have one yourself?

4) What *is* your artistic credo?

5) Do you think an artist should take a specialized or narrowed view of himself and his function in wartime or do you think he should go on Being Himself according to his natural lights?

6) Will you tell us something about your early career, that is, before the *New Yorker* days?

I hate to put on you the tremendous task of handling this question business but however you want to do it will be fine with me. Perhaps the idea of mixing up the questions and picking them out of a hat would work all right. If I get some strange ones or impossible ones I think I'll be able to handle it, and I don't want you to have the slightest fear on that score. I can always turn the questioner off. If I think of any special question I'd like to be asked I'll send it to you airmail or by wire. I don't want you to feel any sense of strain or responsibility about Black Saturday because I think that I now have the thing pretty well in hand and that if it gets going easily and informally it is bound to work out. Best wishes from us both, see you soon.

James Thurber
Per: P. Yowell

❧   ❧   ❧

*410 East 57th St., New York 22, N.Y.*

*May 5, 1944*

Dear Peter:

Thanks very much for your copy of what I like to think of as the speech of the day—not to say the speech of the season. I am afraid you are too late about "The Handsome Heart". I came home from the office to find my colored cook, a Bermudian woman of intelligence and discernment, lost in its pages. She insisted on reading aloud to me from a book which turned out to be yours. She read your remarkable description of hands. If this small passage is any indication, you are wrong as hell about the thing. "The Bugle" hasn't arrived yet but is on the way.

This is really an official communication soliciting in my own name and that of *The New Yorker* whatever pieces you might have on hand or in prospect for us to look at. I have spoken to the editors about you and they asked me to implore you to send something along.

Best to you and Katinka.

As ever,

Jim

❦ ❦ ❦

June 14, 1944

Dear Peter:

By this time you have Ross's dazed and adoring letter. . . . I had handed the whole sheaf of your stuff to Ross who had said, sighing, "I'll read it, but it won't be any good." Half hour later he called me in and said, "Jesus Christ. It is good!"

Thus, in 1944 the advent of P. de Vries. I went over the heads of the art editor and the Talk editor, otherwise your stuff would have been scattered and its shape & impact lost. Hot dog. . . . Now that Ross has taken you over [as your editor], I suggest you send stuff direct to him. Art ideas . . . in letters to me confuse Ross. . . . Casuals, or fiction, as they used to be called, should not go to Ross first, but to me or to Gus Lobrano, a tall, sweet guy you will like.

Ross would take you on as an editor at once, at, say, $12,000 a year, but I am of several minds about that, as follows:

You would like the people and, finally, the work, after you have been allowed to settle down to what you want to do, can do, and like to do. First, however, Ross would decide that you are god, Donald Nelson and Barney Baruch, all in one, a man capable of handling and running everything—from the arrangement of offices to the private life of the contributors. I started out that way. We all did. But he has more sense now, and he also has me to set him straight. I would be around like a mother dog, to snarl and snap in your defense. . . .

It is a considerable thing to recommend so abrupt a change in a friend's life, and I hesitate to do it. But I have confidence in your success whatever you do. . . . I should have introduced Peter [in Chicago] and sat down.

Jim

*While Ronald Williams was on sea duty, his family stayed with Janey's mother and sisters near Geneva, New York. In September 1944, the Thurbers visited them for the christening of Thurber's goddaughter, Dinah Jane Williams. While there Thurber came down with lobar pneumonia and returned home in a weakened condition.*

## To the Palmer Family

*September 21, 1944*

Dear Minna, Janey, Mary, and Cornelia:

Well, here I am again, home safe and unsound. I lay around the Algonquin until train time, while Helen shopped for birthday presents for Rosie and an evening dress for herself to keep up her morale. She tells people that I was sick in the house of my girl, her mother, and sisters. "Well, how nice," say the neighbors primly.

The porter on our train finally showed up after I had dropped the big suitcase in the aisle and Helen had carried it the rest of the way. He was a very old man and asked us to call him at six. Seems he oversleeps.

We were only 20 minutes late, owing to the engineer, who had bella donna in his eyes. The conductor was a pleasant little man who had never made this run before and had the feeling he was going backward.

At Grand Central we could not get a cab till Helen told a redcap I had pneumonia. "Oh, I'll get your father a cab right away," he said, and he did.

The porter woke by himself, I forgot to say. "How are you, George?" he said. "Morning, boss," I said.

*September 22*

A kind of moribundity got me yesterday after so much exercise with a pencil. I feel stronger today—I could easily crack an English walnut.

Yesterday was hot and muggy like a 15-year-old Pekinese, but today is beautiful, clear, sunny, C Major.

This is a plain ordinary bread and butter letter, and it should be a steak and Clos Veugeot letter. We will never be able to express our love and gratitude to the Palmers, so I won't even try. It was the best time a pneumonia patient ever had. . . .

Jim

## TO THE E. B. WHITES

*9/30/44*

Dear Andy & Katharine:

The Navy doctors . . . who knocked out my 105 degree fever in 2 days with sulpha say it is the first time on record a godfather failed to rally after a baptism. . . . I had one 42-minute chill which outdid the earthquake, knocking plates off the plate rail downstairs. . . .

I was up in five days, and am better than ever. . . .

There will soon be enough [penicillin] for us all, and we will live to be 130, they say. In this way we will one day have 13 living ex-presidents. White will live to celebrate the 200th anniversary of the Monroe Doctrine—think of it.

The only thing to worry about is the Mok-Mok—a weapon which will be invented for the next war. Four Mok-Moks will destroy the U.S. Look out for the KM10 also and the horrible ZU58.

To be bumped off in Maine by something that lands in Michigan is not pleasant.

Zeeeeek!

BLONG!

The Zo-Zo 40 is absolutely silent in flight, but has a range of only 2500 miles.

> See you soon
> J. G16 Thurber

## TO E. B. WHITE

*December 1944*

Dear Andy:

If you saw the Huxley piece in Harpers on Varieties of Human Physique, you know you are sitting pretty. I have read Sheldon's book [Sheldon, a social scientist, photographed college students nude for classification under a theory eventually discredited] and it's all about your tough . . . vitality. You are a cerebretonic ectomorph, a man of powerful testicles and firmly rooted hair, capable of orgasms of a pretty high order and equipped with a curious kind of zingless lasting power. You may be dizzy and weak and you may buzz but you will outlast the Lou Gehrigs who run past you up the stairs three at a time.

*Left:* Thurber at the family home in Columbus before leaving for France, about the time his letters begin

*Clockwise, from upper right:*

Elliott Nugent, O.S.U. senior; Eva Prout, in her twenties, when Thurber dated her; Minnette Fritts, 1920 (Courtesy Sally Proctor Luplow)

*Clockwise, from left:*

Thurber, right, visiting his family on Gay Street, circa 1936

In Bermuda, 1936: Thurber and Helen on a late honeymoon, flanked by Ronald and Jane Williams

Thurber, Althea, and Rosemary at the Sandy Hook house, probably the fall of 1931

*Left:* E. B. White and Thurber

*Above:* Helen Thurber, 1941

The West Cornwall, Connecticut, house, purchased in 1945. It was here that many of Thurber's letters were dictated.

Harold W. Ross (Photo by Fabian Bachrach)

*Left*: With Helen, using the Zeiss loop

Thurber and Helen in their apartment on East 57th Street in New York City, circa 1945

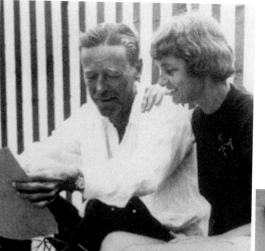

*Above, left*: Dorothy and Herman Miller

*Above, right*: Ann Honeycutt, circa 1950 (Courtesy Joseph Mitchell)

Wolcott and Elinor Gibbs, Fire Island, 1950 (Courtesy Elizabeth Gibbs)

Thurber and Ted Gardiner, 1950s

*Clockwise, from left:*

Joel Sayre, 1950s (Courtesy Nora Sayre);
John O'Hara, 1950s; Peter De Vries at *The New Yorker,* 1964 (Courtesy Jan De Vries);
William Shawn, 1946 (Photo by Hilde Hubbuck)

*Above, left:* John "Jap" Gude, circa 1950 (Courtesy Elizabeth Gude)

*Above, right:* John McNulty in Hollywood, mid-1940s (Courtesy Faith McNulty)

Thurber receiving his honorary degree at Kenyon College, June 1950, something he declined to accept from his alma mater, Ohio State University

*Clockwise, from left:*

Rosemary's wedding in Philadelphia, 1953

At the wedding reception, Rosemary converses with her father while Althea looks on.

Thurber appeared on the NBC morning show, hosted by Dave Garroway, as an expert on the prevention of blindness. Here he is interviewed by Garroway on the set of *A Thurber Carnival,* February 25, 1960. (Photo by Raimondo Borea)

Pale and teetering slightly, you will help carry the coffin of many a meso-morph and endomorph, like Christy Mathewson, Young Stribling, Red Grange, Sayre, and Coates.

Most of the Rudolph Valentino types you know are as good as laid to rest now. Cheer up, man!

Jim

*In late November 1944, while at the Homestead in Hot Springs, Thurber's appendix burst and peritonitis set in. An emergency operation was successful and two weeks later he was back at the Homestead.*

## TO HAROLD ROSS

*December 7, 1944*

*Mr. H. W. Ross, New Yorker Magazine*
*25 West 43rd Street, New York, N. Y.*

Dear Ross:

You will be glad to know that I have written four letters myself today and am now dictating half a dozen. I am gaining strength rapidly and will proba-bly be in good shape when we arrive in town next Monday morning. I will give you a ring then.

I have received two requests: one from Royce Publishers and the other from the World Publishing Company, to reprint stories of mine in these cheap an-thologies. I have written each publisher that the artists and writers of the New Yorker have undertaken a campaign to find out more about the sales and profits, with a view to getting a fairer share of this in the future. One of these anthologies is to be edited by Mr. [Bennett] Cerf. I think you have seen copies of the letters from the publishers. In any case, I will send you copies of my let-ters to them for the files of your campaign.

I cannot help but feel that you are a little bit on the wrong side in asking the Author's League to fight our battle, when all through the years the New Yorker writers have refused to join this organization. It has many times been mentioned at League meetings that the membership of our boys and girls would help put teeth in that worthy organization. As it stands, only Sally Benson and myself belong to the League, and we entered by the back door when we became members of the Dramatists' Guild as the result of our plays on Broadway. . . . If you want to circulate this letter to the writers, it is all right with me.

See you soon.

Love ever,

## TO THE SAYRES AND MCNULTYS

*[Undated, December 1944] Monday*

Dear Sayres and McNultys:

This is my first letter after coming home and I owe it jointly to the two families of pals who kept the letters coming and cheered me up most. So send this on to the McNultys, my dears. I got enough strength for a letter a day. I am feeling great outside of the weakness which decreases fast. Went down to lunch today. I weigh 143 stripped, a loss of about 8 or 9 lbs. I just found out about the ruptured appendix last night and took it with a slight shiver. I imagine old Jake Fisher's appendix busted about 1858 and he just took a stronger physic than usual, and gave it no mind.

. . . The C & O is a great hospital with a fine surgeon, John Morehead Garfield, and a great staff, including the best stomach tube manipulator in the country. Two great nurses—Nettie Jane and Bertha Garfield. . . .

I had a swell time. It was my remarkable wife who took it on the chin, waiting all night in a dreary hotel for the news of general peritonitis.

When I got onto the operating table I told the docs I was in fine shape. When they whisked off the hospital shirt, they must have wondered what it's like when I'm in bad shape. I was picked for a "break-down" of the incision and 2 weeks more in bed, but the chief said my recuperation was "remarkable." He ought to see Mamma and Robert and the Uncle Jake who lost 9/10 of his insides and sold pamphlets about it for 35 years.

I told Dr. Emmett that my great-grandfather could lift a horse, and he said, "The effects of these hypos will wear off in a few days now."

Best line read to me by a nurse: "He is a past Commander of the American Lesion."

I left Garfield Jett [an orderly] an envelope of money . . . Since the others are Lee, Jefferson, and Washington, I asked him if he wasn't a spy. "Yes, suh!" he said. Full name—Garfield Jett, no kin to the propulsion of the same name.

Next day I asked my day orderly, Charley, how come this Garfield. "My name is Garfield, too," said Charley, coolly. The thing began to take on the aspects of "Angel Street" and I suspected one of you guys was behind it. Full name—Charles Garfield Thompson—no kin to Jett. He was born in 1881, the year Garfield was shot. Now when you know that my eye was removed in 1900 at the Garfield Hospital in Washington, you can see how I lay there and brooded. I just call everybody Garfield now and find it restful, Garfield, my boy.

Some reporter called my nurse one morning and said, "Phone me the moment he dies. Don't monkey around the bed—get on the phone!" She hung up on him. Put me in mind of old Red Dolan on the phone badgering secretaries.

Home Sunday or Monday.

> Yours for toujours,
> Jim

P.S. I listened to Hildegard's program one night. Guest star: John Garfield.

## To the Herman Millers

*Dec. 9, 1944, Saturday*

Dearest Herman & Dorothy:

I had a great surgeon, an excellent hospital, and a little help from God & Mother Nature; my appendix was behind my SECUM, and this helped to localize the peritonitis.

Since the Lord wouldn't let me go blind either, I figure he has something in mind for me to do.

Perhaps it is the noble work of prodding that lazy-minded Herman into writing.

Yes, that is it. I feel it. I shall therefore keep after you. At fifty-yesterday—I feel I have just begun to write. These are the best years. I spit on the grave of my awful forties.

My wound still drains after three weeks, but I'm okay and we go back tomorrow to 410 East 57th St., Apt. 8D. . . .

Have you seen the stories about France by Mary Mian in the New Yorker? I urged her to write when she was past forty with three daughters.

You will see pieces soon by Peter DeVries whom I brought on from Chicago where he was editor of Poetry Magazine at $25 a week. Thurber, they say, is always right about talent. Get going.

My new fantasy, or whatever, which runs to 15,000 words is called "The White Deer" and is a new version of the old fairy tale of the deer which, chased by a king and his three sons, is transformed into a princess. Suppose, I said, that it was a real deer which had saved a wizard's life and was given the power of assuming the form of a princess? Most fun I have ever had. I even go in for verse now and then, such as,

> When all is dark within the house,
> Who knows the monster from the mouse?

The Getzloes wired me:

> You would get well quicker
> If you had voted for Dewey & Bricker

I replied:

> The world would be a whole lot sicker,
> If I had voted for Dewey & Bricker.

Let's keep our correspondence going. It's been my fault.
Merry Christmas and Love
from Jim & Helen and thanks for a fine letter.

*In February 1945, a collection of Thurber's best writing and drawing from the previous fifteen years was published as* The Thurber Carnival. *The book's success made Thurber's name a household word, carried throughout the world by the armed services edition. The book remains in print today.*
*McNulty was in Hollywood writing for the movies.*

## To John McNulty

*March 4, 1945*

Dear John:
I will certainly do a preface for your book, eagerly, gladly, and I appreciate your selecting me for the joyful task. I'll wait for publisher's proofs and whatever.

I am also doing prefaces for Mary Petty and Mary Mian. Thrasbie, the preface writer, they call me. I picked the titles for the two girls' books: "This Petty Pace" (Macbeth, Act V) and "My Country-in-Law, France." You are the best titler alive and I won't mess with that.

We are back at Hot Springs at the confluence of the Peritonitis and the Gangrene until March 21, (spring), to rest up from three separate attacks of contract trouble. We finally had to bring in a sixth lawyer. I didn't get the first lawyer in time to handle the Goldwyn deal, so he (Goldwyn) has a 90-day option on Rosemary and my dark blue topcoat. Never sign a Hollywood contract [without] the services of a lawyer. . . . The movies tie up radio, television, comic strip, novelization, lantern slides, ballet, black face, concert, puppet show and guitar rights, if you don't look out. Only lawyers, not agents, can help you.

Watch your publisher's contract, too, and don't sell a cent of movie or stage rights, and don't sign up for two more books. If you empower an agent to close the deal, you are bound by his settlement. Consult me.

Rosemary comes to us for Easter (courtesy of Sam Goldwyn). The New Yorker, Algonquin, etc. buzz with yearning for you. Love
    Jim

      *    *    *

*August 3, 1945*

Dear Johnny, me lad:

I accept your stand as sincere and, as Ross would say, sound, I *guess*, God damn it. The thing is arguable, of course. I would not like to believe you are making a misguidedly generous effort to relieve me of what you conceive to be a chore. It would be a labor of love and pleasure. What makes me incline to agree is that I did a preface for Sayre, just finished one for Mary Petty, and have begun one for Mary Mian. Prefaces by Thrasbie are a drug on the market and I don't want to have the critics say of your book, "It has the customary preface by James Thurber."

## TO MORRIS ERNST

*Thurber's attorney and friend, Morris Ernst, asked permission to include drawings Thurber had given him over the years in a book Ernst was publishing.*

*410 East 57th St., N.Y. 22, N.Y.*

*Feb. 5, 1945*

Dear Morris:

This is to certify, declare, state and assert that I hereby and herewith cause to reside, exist and otherwise be, in you, Morris Ernst, the right, privilege and power to use, reprint and reproduce on the cover of your forthcoming book here and after to be known as The Book, any or all of the alleged drawings said to be of, about or in reference to the party of the first part (herein before not previously identified) but here and after to be referred to as Morris Ernst.

It is understood and hereby set forth that the above mentioned right, privilege and power do not entail any reward, recompense or honorarium, and that they are to be exercised without let, hindrance, suggestion or specification on the part of the party of the first part, herein below, to be set forth as the assignor.

It is further understood that any cracks, gags or drolleries which may be made, delivered, vouchsafed or otherwise said by the party of the first part or the party of the second part in regard to or in connection with the above mentioned right, privilege and power, must be of the first order, class and type.

Nothing herein embodied, implied or hinted at, however, shall be construed as an attempt, effort or move to withdraw, modify, or in any other wise change this simple fact: Dear Morris—sure, go ahead.

Respectfully yours,

Jim

## To Malcolm Cowley

*The Homestead, Hot Springs, VA.,*

*March 12, 1945*

Dear Malcolm,

. . . I want to thank you for your excellent and serious consideration of the book [*The Thurber Carnival*]. A writer lives in dread of criticisms done in dialogue, line, parody or by Kenneth Burke. They also thought your review of Gertrude Stein in the Times was superb. Last summer Mark Van Doren brought Scott Buchanan and Mortimer Adler to our house one evening and Adler was wonderful on the subject of Stein's visit with Hutchins. After 5 hrs. of conversation, mostly by Gertrude, and during which [Alice] Toklas just sat listening, the ladies arose to go and Alice said to Adler: Gertrude has said things tonight it will take her ten years to understand. Best wishes to you and Marylin Robbie.

As ever Jim.

## TO EDWARD ASWELL

*The Homestead. Hot Springs, Virginia*
*March 16, 1945*

*Mr. Edward Aswell, Harper & Brothers*
*49 East 33rd St, New York, N.Y.*

Dear Aswell:

. . . The question was would Ross and I oppose the reprinting of some of my Carnival in Omnibook. I quote here a paragraph from Ross' letter to me on the subject:

"There was a day, and I remember it, by God, when a magazine printed a piece and that was that; there wasn't a whole skyfull of vulture magazines ready to pounce. It has got to a point where the greatest initiative shown in American publishing is in behalf of finding a story to be reprinted. Holy Jesus. Nobody can tell me that these magazines are not the enemies of the magazines that are stodgy and old-fashioned enough to go in for original publication. They sell on the same newsstands, side by side, and that is competition, and also they are very likely to be better in their literary value, issue for issue, for they have a selection of all stuff written for all time, whereas poor bastards getting out a magazine like The New Yorker have to run what's written that week."

I'm a son of a bitch if I don't agree with Ross, by God and by Jesus. I have never believed furthermore in the publisher's right to the 50% they take out of all reprint money. The fact that Harper is not too secure in their feelings about this percentage is shown by two or three contracts of mine in which Harpers omits the clause giving them a share of the reprint rights. This was true of "My Life and Hard Times", which after all had gained a wider circulation in The New Yorker than it got in book form by ten to one. Thus it became known to reprint people chiefly through its publication in the magazine. This seems to me to be true of almost all the stories in almost all my books. Certainly Harcourt, Brace for example cannot claim to have made the publishing world Mitty conscious, and yet my contract apparently gives Harcourt the right not only to dispose of my stories for reprint but to do this without consulting me. In this manner, Bennett Cerf was about to reprint four or five of my stories in a Modern Library Book of short stories for a flat rate of $40 each. This Modern Library Book could have contained and perhaps will contain the cream of The New Yorker humerous pieces at an editorial outlay of a few hundred dollars. Such a book would obviously form competition to The New Yorker Book of Short Stories that has already appeared and any that may appear in the future. Thus not only the reprint magazines but the reprint books form an unfair opposition to The New Yorker and the reward to all concerned, with the exception of the reprint people, is as a rule too inconsiderable to be worth all the fuss and danger.

I have decided to make my stories and drawings unavailable for reprint to any reprint magazine or *book* in the future, except in the case of a personal friendship or the welfare of the community or something as unlikely as that. I have already refused certain reprint permissions to book publishers and in the case of the magazines. I would like to begin by saying "No" to Omnibook. I hope that Harper will see eye to eye with me on this. Surely we are both making enough out of The Carnival to be able to do without the reprint money.

I am sending a copy of this letter to Ross with whom I have joined forces in the reprint battle.

  Cordially,
  Jim Thurber

🙐 🙐 🙐

The Homestead,<br/>Hot Springs, Virginia<br/>March 19, 1945

*Mr. Ed Aswell, Harper & Brothers*
*49 East 33rd Street, New York City*

Dear Ed Aswell:

I would be more than pleased to have The Carnival put into the Overseas Edition.

In connection with the boys in the service, I would like to contribute a couple hundred copies of Carnival to the hospitals, but I don't know how to go about this. Maybe somebody at Harpers would know.

Andy White and I and The New Yorker were considerably upset by the appearance of a story from Is Sex Necessary in a William Penn Anthology for which Arno was paid a large sum to sign a ghost-written preface. The story is wrongly credited to both of us, but it was written by White. Harpers usually consults us in these matters. Perhaps the re-print Company who did the book gave the permission. Just another example of the evils of reprint.

> Cordially,
> James Thurber

## To Lt. James Verdaman

*April 5, 1945*

Dear Lt. Verdaman:

I was more than pleased to hear that one of my books had given you and a few of the other boys a moment of diversion in the midst of all the hell going on around you. Three other books of mine were made into overseas editions some months ago and should be showing up together with a large anthology of my stories and drawings called "The Thurber Carnival," which has also just been published in the same edition.

I hope that all the Jerries you are looking at now have their hands above their heads, where they belong. I just heard tonight the story about Patton, who, when he was told that some of his men were surrounded, said "Hell, that's not surrounded, that's just firing on four sides." True or not, that line seems likely to become a classic.

My very best wishes for a safe and speedy return.

> Sincerely yours,
> James Thurber

*Lt. James M. Verdaman, 92nd Arm'd F.A. Bn.,*
*A.P.O. 252, c/o PM, New York*

## To Harold Ross

*The strain of trying to draw what he could barely see drove Thurber to all but give it up by 1947. Among his final drawings for* The New Yorker *were the "Our New Natural History" series, which ran from March 1945 to January 1946.*

*No other of his drawings attracted such reader participation in the form of suggestions—including that of Ross, who was fascinated by this harvest of Thurber's imagination.*

June 27, 1945

Dear Ross:

Let's clear up this Natural History series. I am attaching two blueprints which were made without my command from originals I do not remember, can not see very well and am not fond of. I have destroyed these originals and suggest that the blueprints and all other matters pertaining thereto be destroyed.

Of all the names suggested to me in letters, notes, memoranda, etc., including the "Crying Shame," there is none that I particularly want to do.

The original drawing you have of four birds on a bough was minus one name, the third bird from the left. I have decided to call him "The Scoutmaster."

There is another series of birds just turned in by me today. This is the last of the bird series and does not make too many, I am sure you will admit.

I have one more group of drawings to mail in and this will probably be the last. This includes "The Thesaurus under a Sacroiliac Tree," and there is also a Peccadillo and one or two other creatures in the panel. This will take care of "The Cedilla" for which I have substituted "The Peccadillo."

After weeks of struggle day and night, I find that I am incapable of doing a title for those butterflies and plants that is not either coy or stilted. I am perfectly willing to call them "A Collection of Butterflies and Plants." If your bright young men can think of any adjective I will approve of, I will approve of it.

There seems to be a disposition to believe that I am not actually an artist so that any of my originals can be hacked to pieces with scissors. I have asked Geraghty to submit to you the Scone and Crumpet drawing which was not only pared down atrociously but has a huge piece of paper pasted to it. You may remember that this drawing was greatly admired by the Curator of the Victoria & Albert Museum, to whom I promised a drawing if it were fit. As the saying around here goes, "There are drawings and those things Thurber does."

Thurber

*410 East 57th St., New York 22, N.Y.*
*April 19, 1945*

Dear Clarence Knapp:

   Thanks very much for your note with its list of creatures. Some of these have popped into my mind in the two years I have spent brooding on the subject. I keep turning the thwart over in my mind, and if I can get something for him to sit in, or someone to fight, I'll try to do some justice to your idea.

   Ross is up to his ankles in some seventy-five birds and beasts I have already done.

   I trust the angels are guarding you.

   Cordially,
   James Thurber

☙ ☙ ☙

*410 East 57th St., New York 22, N.Y.*
*April 19, 1945*

*Mr. James C.G. Conniff*

Dear Mr. Conniff:

   My defense is that the cut made from my drawing was reversed by a man named George Conniff, cut reverser for the New Yorker.

   I knew about the troches and even looked it up to be sure.

   Mercy, I thought you knew I went to Ohio State. Harvard, indeed. All you can think of is Harvard. I may fuss around with those other suggestions of yours. You got much too high grades in school. The most they allowed me was 100%.

   Sincerely yours,
   James Thurber

☙ ☙ ☙

*May 18, 1945*

*Mr. Max Motlay, Miss Geraldine Cogin*

Dear Max Motlay and Geraldine Cogin:

   After several months spent in drawing mythical animals, I have given the practice up forever, partly because I have drawn myself out and partly because The New Yorker, which still has dozens on hand, has reached the saturation point. The surface tension in that place is terrific and there is a constant sound of potassium permanganate colliding with sulphuric acid as the editors discuss the possibility of getting more animal drawings from me.

If I did a picture of Professor Lamb looking for anything, none of you would pass your course. I wish you would draw me a picture of myself looking for a stray idea. Thanks for your letter and all the best to the rest of Physics 204.

Sincerely yours,
James Thurber

*410 East 57th St., New York 22, N.Y.*
*December 31, 1945*

*Mr. John J. Cunningham*

Dear Mr. Cunningham:

Until this summer my wife's mother lived in a little white house within a stone's throw of your Old Mill, and now you will realize what has been hitting the building all these years and leaving those marks. Lakeville is rapidly becoming the most unbelievably interesting town in Connecticut, what with Ralph Ingersoll, Greer Garson and an unidentified man who walked through the town with his eyes right and was never seen again.

I was interested in your list of important creatures, especially the Plimsoll which really should be drawn—only it would simply bewilder Harold Ross, who once had lunch with me at the Lime Rock Inn where he struck up an acquaintance with another man who had ulcers.

The Old Mill has always been one of our favorite landmarks and I suspected that it was really the hideout of the mythical burglars who got away with those engraved plates for the Lincoln book a few years ago. Involved in this thing that never happened was a resident of the community with a wonderful name like Washington Woof, or something.

Best wishes for a Happy New Year.

Sincerely yours,
James Thurber.

## TO HAROLD ROSS

*[Undated, 1945]*

Dear Mr. Ross:

The system of photostating everybody that comes in to The New Yorker office seems to me the most ingenious device since Bill Levick put into effect his famous passing system back in 1930. The office will, of course, be as cluttered up, finally, as the Denver mint was during the Harding administration when secret service men discovered 750,000 bath-towels stacked up there. It occurred to me that to make this new system complete two other departments, or bureaus, are necessary. I dream of the day when everybody who steps off the elevators on the 19th floor is photographed, full face and both profiles, and given a serial number. If this had been in effect earlier, we would have had excellent glossy likenesses of everybody who ever called on Mr. Winney. Furthermore, I think we should have a finger printing room. Since finger prints can now be detected even on pieces of white or yellow paper, you would not only be able to tell through whose hands every manuscript had passed, no matter how they lied about it, but you could also tell whether the manuscript had previously been submitted to any other publication. I suggest a combined photostat and finger print room and I know just the man to take charge of it, a Mr. Jo McElliott, who has just been honorably dismissed from the army because he is an old man of 32. He was formerly chief photographer for the Columbia Broadcasting System and is an expert chemist who has dabbled in finger printing. Any time you want to have a good talk with him, just let me know.

Love,
Thurber

&. &. &.

*The Homestead, Hot Springs, Virginia*
*November 7, 1945*

Dear Ross:

In reference to your note of October 25th, please be reminded that *I* did not enter any kind of complaint about this so-called delay in reviewing my book [*The White Deer*]. As a man who has done reviews for the New Republic and the Saturday Review, I am not only used to, but I approve of leisurely and genteel consideration of works of art. This business of treating the appearance of a book as if it were spot news is so much the property of the minds that control Time that I wonder you would not shed yourself of any share in it.

The enclosed clipping is for your own Who Has Done Most For Whom Department? All I know for sure is that you made Fleischmann what he is today, and wipe that smile off your face.

Yours,
Jim

## To Mrs. Ada McCormick

*November 5, 1945*

*Mrs. Ada P. McCormick*

Dear Mrs. McCormick:

There has not been such traffic in IS SEX NECESSARY since 1929. I was a young man then and now I am a middle aged man, and whereas the early success of the book excited me, I find that its continued popularity is a little embarrassing. It will not be many years before charming ladies point me out and say, "There goes that nasty old man that writes about sex".

Mr. White and I have got several letters from soldiers who were bewildered by the book, since they were only three to eight years old when it appeared first, and have no memory of the peculiar tone and flux of the 1920's which inspired the volume.

All best wishes to you and Letter.

Sincerely yours,
James Thurber

## To E. B. White

*The Homestead, Hot Springs, Virginia*
*November 10, 1945*

Dear Andy:

. . . The day your book arrived with its laconic inscription, both the window shades in our bedroom shot up to the top, ostensibly on their own. There has also been great periodic commotion in the ice pitcher, and somebody has got away with one of my studs. I name no names.

Love,
Jim

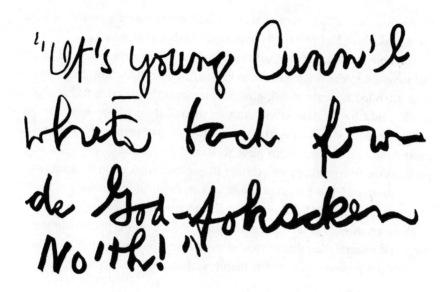

"It's young Cunn'l white fack fum de God-fohsaken No'th!"

## To Henry S. Canby

*410 East 57th Street, New York 22, New York*
*December 26, 1945*

Mr. Henry S. Canby, Secretary,
National Institute of Arts and Letters,
633 West 155th Street, New York 32, N. Y.

Dear Mr. Canby:

I want you to know that I appreciate your letter, but it is only fair to state honestly my inveterate reluctance to join literary organizations. Perhaps this grows out of the fact that I have been for so long associated with Harold Ross' magazine, whose editors and chief contributors are more or less dedicated to staying on the outside of organizations and looking in, or even occasionally tossing something through the window.

I am not at all acquainted with the organization of the National Institute and I do not clearly understand its basis of selections or the work it is engaged in. I feel that one or two writing colleagues of mine, who appear to be outside the Institute, deserve ahead of me the distinction I have been offered. I also find it difficult to see why I should be honored in 1945, in which my principal publication was a collection of things I had written over a period of fifteen years, and which had previously appeared in other volumes.

The only members of the Institute I have talked to appear to be singularly disinterested in the organization, in view of the fact that they claim never to have attended a single meeting of its members. I cannot feel that anyone would profit by my association with an organization whose aims and purposes I could not join in furthering because of two principal facts—my almost continual absence from New York, and my disability of vision which prevents me from taking part in either the general work of an organization or its committees. I was forced to resign as a member of the council of the Authors' League because I was simply unable to attend its meetings.

Once again my thanks to you and your colleagues on the Institute, but I truly and sincerely feel that in view of my ancient disposition in these matters I would not prove to be a worthy member of the National Institute.

        Sincerely yours,
        James Thurber

*Thurber was asked to sit for a portrait by American Portrait Artists, to be used in promoting an unnamed distillery company.*

## To J. Nottingham Zeltzer

*410 East 57th St., New York 22, N.Y.*
*December 31, 1945*

*Mr. J. Nottingham Zeltzer, President,*
*American Portrait Artists*

Dear Mr. Zeltzer:

After a great deal of thought and prayer, together with conferences with my friends and loved ones, I have come to the conclusion—or perhaps I have been pushed to it—that I am scarcely the figure your distinguished company is looking for. This is not only because my face from the eyebrows down has been an insurmountable barrier to both photographers and painters, owing to the fact that I wear a 413 lens on the right eye, and a 45 on the other, but because I have figured that the company in question must either be Rheingold Beer or Calvert Whiskey and I am an inveterate drinker of Pabst's Blue Ribbon and Seagram's V.O.

I appreciate the fact that I was considered for this particular distinction but I feel I could not, in all conscience, impose myself upon the public and upon any painter at this particular period in my life and hard times.

Please accept my sincere best wishes for a Happy New Year.

Sincerely yours,

James Thurber.

*In 1945, Samuel Goldwyn began work on the film "The Secret Life of Walter Mitty," with Danny Kaye as Mitty. Thurber served several weeks as a consultant to screenwriter Ken Englund.*

## To Sam Goldwyn

*December 18, 1945*

Dear Mr. Goldwyn:

I believe we have accomplished what you had in mind, which I am confident is also what I myself wanted to achieve . . .

There is nothing that can be done at this late date about the melodrama, as such, except to blend it more realistically and more humorously with the dreams and with Walter's day to day life with his Mother and his fiancée. The melodrama still remains the spine of our structure, but I feel . . . that it no longer sticks out, but that it has been more ingenuously interlaced with The Dreams and the private life of our Hero . . .

I profoundly believe that the characters in their relations to Walter and to the story are right the way they are now. I should like to have you dismiss those early suggestions of mine as being merely thoughtless ideas, thrown off by a man who was not yet quite familiar with the story and its problems.

I feel that I have learned a great deal in a short time about some of the problems that face a motion picture producer and . . . writer . . .

Sincerely,

James Thurber

*In a December 26, 1945, telegram to Thurber, Goldwyn compliments him on his work and his suggestion for "the courtroom scene" and asks Thurber to develop it further. Thurber worries that the additional work is not covered by his contract.*

## TO KEN ENGLUND

*410 East 57th St., New York 22, N.Y.*
*January 7, 1946*

Dear Ken:

I got a long telegram from Goldwyn some days before your letter came in and he seemed delighted with all the changes. He asked if he could impose on me to write out the courtroom scene, but as I told him in a letter I have just written, I feel you can handle that scene perfectly, and I also mentioned we had all been down with colds here and that I was going to Columbus this week for ten days. Principally, I said that Herndon and my lawyer here would disapprove of me doing any further work on MITTY, by which I meant to indicate they would not let me do it without further remuneration. I was a little puzzled about how to proceed with his request but I think that what I have said above really covers the situation.

He asked me, also, if I thought there should be new villains in the cowboy dream or if the old ones should reappear, and I suggested that new ones would probably be better since Walter has already disposed of the old ones.

One problem still remaining that worries me a great deal now is the baby-talk personality of Gertrude. Both Helen and Nunnally Johnson feel very strongly that this is the wrong type for her, and in a letter I got recently from Nunnally he was actually vehement on the subject and ended his diatribe with "Get her out of there." The only idea I have had as to another type of personality is a girl who during the war has taken over some man's work, possibly as an office manager, or anything else which would make her more forceful and less silly. I did not mention this to Goldwyn but I put it down here for your troubled mind to examine. We had talked about it and I believe you felt that with the mother a forceful woman, we should not duplicate this character. As she stands, she is, of course, the girl from Tarkington's SEVENTEEN, dog and all, and as such she no doubt strikes her critics as being dated. The audience, of course, is likely to wonder how Walter would get tangled up with such a creature and his engagement to her might very likely strike the audience as a proof of his insanity. Maybe this will all wash out in the acting of the part. I mean perhaps the right actress would do the job.

Keep me in constant touch. Best wishes to you and Mabel for a Happy New Year.

> Cordially,
> Jim Thurber

## TO PAT DUGGAN

*The Homestead*
*March 31, 1946*

Dear Duggan,

The scene between Walter and Dr. Ravenscroft is good, but it opens rather flatly. We can get more laughs and make more of a character in just a few lines of dialogue. It's only a little longer and the scene can stand it.

RAVENSCROFT:  Now. Why do you like to play the piano in the dark?
Substitute:
RAVENSCROFT:  Now, just how often do you see this enormous silver fish floating around? (with his hands he makes the shape of a large fish in the air)
WALTER:  (apprehensively) I—I don't see any fish.
RAVENSCROFT:  Hm? Oh, sorry—I was thinking of another patient, a Mr. Ingleby. He's coming along splendidly.
WALTER:  (still apprehensive) He—he sounds fine.

&. &. &.

*April 1, 1946*

The cowboy dreams should be as good as the others, or you have a drop in interest. The last fifty pages should not skimp the dream element. To say that dreams slow up the story is to say the locomotive slows up the cow. The dreams are the best Kaye and the best audience appeal. They are new, unique and universal. . . .

I will personally undertake to thrash anyone who mangles the dreams. They are wonderful.

I will work fast and hard on anything else I can do. I have no idea of *adding* stuff.

> Yours,
> Jim Thurber

*April 10, 1946*

*Mr. Pat Duggan, Samuel Goldwyn*
*Hollywood, California*

Dear Mr. Duggan:

. . . I suppose the boys have already torn through that scene in which Walter turns on his tormentors and puts everybody in his place. As I said in one of my communications, I had an idea for this scene which, as I say, belongs to this last bundle of work I did on the script in Hot Springs. It may be that this has all been changed, but I offer the idea for what it may be worth. . . .

By making Walter overcome Tubby in a comic fashion, we would soften a bit the rather tremendous he-man he suddenly becomes. I don't know how the scene goes from here, but it ought to be easy to get Walter and Rosalind out and in a car. It seems to me now definitely that the final scene of the whole picture should not depict Walter in a ludicrous position on a lame horse, or a stupid donkey. I somehow feel that we should see Walter and his girl go out of this story in a blaze of romantic glory.

This is just an idea and I am sure that Ken has worked it out well. He suggested breaking the cowboy scene, and I suggested Walter saying as he leaves his house forever, "I get to finish a dream."

The idea of completely throwing his mother out seems to me a rather cruel thing, and this is why I suggested above the brief scene in which Rosalind looks after the old lady. The audience can leave convinced that Mrs. Mitty will be welcome when she calls on the couple and will not be left to lead a sad and lonely life. . . .

Walter's scene on Page 20 with the enormous bottle of cologne could be made funnier and just as short, if not even shorter, but a scene which happens to every man who uses a safety razor but which, so far as I know, has not been presented in a movie. I find, on talking to my man friends, that they have all become enormously and comically involved by the following shaving sequences.

A man gets his face all lathered up and his hands all covered with the lather, and then finds he has forgotten to put a blade in the razor. No man, certainly not Walter Mitty, would think of wiping off his face and hands and beginning again. He tries to get the blade in the razor, succeeds only in getting it wet and soapy, and letting it fall into the wash bowl. If you have ever tried to get a wet razor blade out of a wash bowl with soapy fingers, you know what I mean. Finally, what you do is snap the razor out of the bowl and it falls on the tile floor. A wet razor blade sticks to a tile floor like a leech. Using the nail of the index finger to lift up one end, you put your shoe against the other end in the hope that the razor blade will stand up and you can grab it between your fingers. What happens is that the razor now gets stuck to the sole of your left shoe.

I mentioned this process to friends of mine and they had all gone through it in one variation or another. Every man who uses a safety razor will laugh. The Danny Kaye version of this act would be terrifically funny and could be used in place of the bottle of cologne, the gag about the shirt, etc.

Maybe I am trying to make this picture too funny. Anyhow, these are the ideas that I jotted down with the others and if you want them you can have them for the price you have already paid. . . .

I have been working on "The Catbird Seat", and I am convinced that you will all like it and that it will be an excellent picture for Kaye.

Don't think that I fail to realize how difficult it is going to be to follow Walter Mitty with something as good. This is a challenge, however, which I am confident I can meet, and which I feel I already have well in hand.

Best regards to you and all the boys.

Sincerely yours,
James Thurber

*Upon hearing that the firing-squad scene, one of Thurber's favorites, is in trouble, he asks to have "another crack at it."*

Dear Ken:

Arriving in Perth Amboy, [Mitty's] mother remembers she has run out of "toothpaste" and this gives us the chance to have Walter stand against the drug store wall in the rain and go into the Firing Squad Scene. In a Close Shot of his standing erect and brave we hear the footsteps of passersby fall into the tromp, tromp cadence of the approaching firing squad.

Mrs. Mitty's need for "toothpaste" is just a ruse, and we Cut inside the drugstore for a moment to see her and Irmagard [Mitty's future mother-in-law] covertly buying a sedative from The Druggist . . . that will calm "the disturbed Walter."

*Thurber offers a rewrite of "The Cowboy Dream."*

It is a big night at Death Gulch Saloon. We see Gertrude [Mitty's fiancee] dressed in the flashy get-up of a saloon entertainer. At a table sits Calamity Irmagard Griswold, with a holster and gun slung around her waist . . .

*None of Thurber's contributions were used.* Life *magazine's review of the movie* The Secret Life of Walter Mitty *quoted Thurber's dislike of it. Goldwyn's letter to* Life *in response quoted excerpts from Thurber's letters to MGM that expressed approval of certain scenes later deleted from the script. Thurber replied, in his own letter to* Life, *that it was ten months before he had first been shown the movie script, adding:*

During that vital period, my counsel, criticism, and collaboration were never once sought . . .

I was confronted by a set story line appallingly melodramatic for poor Walter . . .

Ken Englund and I worked six hours a day for ten days on an impossible assignment. We could not take out the melodrama but we could attempt to cover it up with additional dream scenes and other devices. . . .

Next to the worry about our new dream scenes, the greatest fear of Mr. Englund and myself was the possibility that this movie might be spoiled by one or more of Mr. [Danny] Kaye's . . . famous, but to me, deplorable scat or git-gat-gittle songs. Mr. Englund . . . and myself had strongly suggested that Mr. Kaye's song in the RAF scene be *Molly Malone*. . . . Mr. Goldwyn lifted the song and substituted what is to me an utterly horrifying, shockingly out-of-taste-and-mood piece of scat.

. . . Another dream scene was written and shot, in which Mr. Kaye did sing *Molly Malone* [but] the scene was cut, along with the courtroom dream and the firing squad dream. My defeat was complete. . . .

Sorry, Walter, sorry for everything.

James Thurber

## TO MICHAEL W. ZEAMER

*410 East 57th St., New York 22, N.Y.*

*January 7, 1946*

*Mr. Michael W. Zeamer, Prince & Co., Inc.*
*5031 Grandy Avenue, Detroit 11, Michigan*

Dear Zeamer:

A correction in the letter I sent you. Benchley said, "funniest caption," not "finest caption."

. . . I have probably made $20,000 from drawings sold to The New Yorker, and another $20,000 from my three books of drawings, THE SEAL IN THE BEDROOM, THE LAST FLOWER and MEN, WOMEN AND DOGS.

Such good drawings as I still possess were caught in London by the war and are still there. Some seven years ago, at the behest of a friend, I sent forty drawings to an art gallery in Hollywood whose director sold ten of them, paid me for five and somehow could never find the remaining thirty to return to me. Since he died this summer, and since this is all true, it would not be libelous to print it. A great many of my drawings, say one hundred, have disappeared one way or another. I used to give them out for reproduction to any well-spoken person who asked me to lend them a drawing for, say, the Art News and in this way I lost forever the drawing of the woman and the house entitled "Home."

Before I knew you could sell originals for as much as $25—this was about 1932—I used to sell mine for five and ten dollars to a Forty-seventh Street art dealer. He told me a client of his sent them out as Christmas cards. One night I told this story to a table in Tony's in which I sat with Robert Benchley, Roland Young and a man whose name I had not caught. He told me quietly that he was the client in question. After he had gone to the men's room (you can make it the bar in your story) I asked Benchley who he was and he said, "That's Jock Whitney."

Among the people who own originals of mine are: Noel Coward, Elmer Davis, Mark Connelly, Dorothy Thompson, Charles Laughton, Franchot Tone, Robert Montgomery, Humphrey Bogart, Robert M. Hutchins, President of Chicago University. The Hutchins drawing is the only thing on the walls of his office except portraits of former presidents of the University. This drawing shows one woman saying to another, in reference to a pontifical looking gent, "He doesn't know anything except facts." Morris Ernst, a close friend of the late President Roosevelt, is married to a lady who wrote a book about the origin of words some eight years ago and I illustrated this book. One of the drawings was an illustration of the word "candidate." Ernst gave the drawing to President Roosevelt some two months before he announced himself as a candidate for a third term. That year I met Roosevelt at Hyde Park, along with some thirty other writers for Roosevelt. Ernst introduced me to him and mentioned I had drawn "the candidate" picture. "I remember it," said the President. "And I didn't say a word, did I?"

Incidentally, Winston Churchill once referred to me as "that insane and depraved artist." Having seen some water colors of Churchill's, I can say that the trouble with him as an artist must be that he is not insane and depraved enough.

People often wonder if it is true that I cannot draw a pretty or stylish woman. It is indeed true, just as it is a fact that I cannot do anything except line drawings. Andy White once came upon me trying to shade in a drawing and said, "Don't do that. If you ever became good, you would be mediocre." . . .

> Yours
> James Thurber

## To E. B. White

*410 East 57th St., New York 22, N.Y.*
*January 9, 1946*

Dear Andy:

A friend of mine from California tells me that one out of every nine persons kills somebody in Los Angeles by knocking him down with an automobile, because the driver is not wearing his glasses, although artificial aid is indicated on the driver's license.

Personally, I believe that we should not let total strangers interfere with our methods of driving. On the other hand, my mother simply walks out into the street, light or no light, raising her right hand.

> Yours,
> James

## To Harvey Smith

*410 E. 57th St., New York, 22, N.Y.*
*January 24, 1946*

*Mr. Harvey Smith, Patterson Fabrics, Inc*
*509 Madison Avenue, New York 22, New York*

Dear Mr. Smith:

. . . Apparently, nothing connected with either textiles or writing or drawing is a simple Yes and No business. There are many angles to your proposition which affect me and I will try to list them.

1) I have been approached by various concerns who wanted textile designs, usually for dresses. I had always firmly stood on the high ground of opposition to a lot of fat women sitting on my dogs in Schrafft's. Two years ago Wragge contacted my publishers for permission to make a dress and a blouse with a design made up of my men and women and dogs. I said no on this, but owing to some confusion on the phone, Wragge went ahead with the product and turned out some fifty dresses. It seemed too much of a problem to oppose this, so I gave in. Out of it I got one dress for my wife, and no money. I was promised that these dresses would appear only in the very first-class shops, in about a dozen cities, but I was the subject of an endless series of jokes when Macy's came out with the same dress. I turned this matter over to my lawyer and learned that remaindering is as common with a man of Wragge's standing as it is with anyone else. The lawyers finally demanded that the roller, or whatever it is, be destroyed, and presumably it was since this embarrassment has now died down. The cost of the whole project to me was a sizable lawyer's fee. I am still unalterably opposed to the use of my designs on dresses or other wearing apparel.

The idea of advertisements in The New Yorker is another one of those things which I would go to some length to avoid. The Wragge dress was reproduced in The New Yorker, and I suppose you would have to be a member of that staff to understand the kidding and the loss of prestige which one has to endure when he lends his name and his work to a commercial enterprise outside his own field.

2) I do not have any sketches around in pen and ink of the kind you mention. An artist is very likely to lose, give away or sell most of this kind of scrap. Because of my deficient vision, I draw with a black grease crayon on large

sheets of yellow tinted paper. I could draw a few sketches on white paper, but I could not use India ink, or any other kind of ink. In order for me to see the line it must be a broad, grease crayon line. It seems to me that this kind of line would reproduce very badly for what you have in mind.

3) Any handicapped writer and artist my age is bound to have more commitments than he can possibly handle, and any outside activity is, therefore, an extra added drudgery. Some drawings of mine in Life [magazine] recently were drawn for an ex-Marine who is a friend of mine, and for no other reason. I have also drawn some seventy-five dogs for men in the service who asked for them. The sheer weight of autographing and answering seventy letters a week on all subjects is simply an added chore. You will begin to see that the tremendous problems you are up against are not too different from those faced by a man in what is usually considered an easy kind of profession.

I guess this just about covers the situation up to now. How do you surmount all this?

> Sincerely yours,
> James Thurber

*In early 1946, when in Columbus for a late celebration of Mame's eightieth birthday, Thurber learned that O.S.U.'s publication* The Sun Dial *had been suspended on obscenity charges and restored as* Scarlet Fever, *a title voted for by the students. As a former editor of the magazine, Thurber made nearly a national issue of the matter. The title,* The Sun Dial, *was restored.*


## To Howard Bevis

*410 East 57th Street, New York City*
*April 24, 1946*

*Mr. Howard L. Bevis, President,*
*The Ohio State University, Columbus, Ohio*

Dear Mr. Bevis:

Early in February I was engaged in correspondence with Mr. Fullen relative to the change in the name of the Sun-Dial when I was stricken by pneumonia, and I am just now able to take up this confusing and disturbing matter again. Mr. Fullen says that he protested against the change in name, but that you and the campus committee on publications believed that the title, the Sun-Dial, "carried unsavory memories". It is difficult for me to believe that the University authorities would not take into consideration the many long years in which the Sun-Dial has had a clean and dignified record. Gardner Rea, myself, and scores of other editors and contributors to the old Sun-Dial, will remain actively indignant on this subject until the cheap title "Scarlet Fever" is abandoned and the traditional name restored. It seems to us that whatever university authorities discarded the old name should take the simple action of authorizing its resumption.

... I can not understand why a simple petition from the editors and contributors would not lead the university authorities to permit the restoration of the name. Surely the title itself was not at fault and the quick and easy abandonment of a university literary tradition seems to me to represent a deterioration in the principles and ideals for which a university should stand.

I do not see why the matter can not be simply arranged without a great deal of protest and petition from persons no longer on the campus. As this affair has dragged on, various rumors of a disturbing nature have arisen, as is bound to be the case when anything so drastic in the way of censorship takes place. It has been suggested to me that an article unfavorable to Mr. Bricker was one cause for the kicking of the magazine off the campus, and what seems even worse the question of social discrimination has also been flatly stated.

All this kind of thing, right or wrong, is bound to creep into the press finally if the matter becomes an issue so large that everybody from Mr. Rea and myself in New York to Elliott Nugent in Hollywood is forced to take a hand in it. We believe that a serious mistake was made in changing the name and that the problem can be simply solved by restoring the name. I should like to know by what process this could be most easily accomplished within the confines of the university. This problem really belongs to the boys and girls who get out the magazine, and it seems to me that their wishes as to the title should be acceded to. I do not believe that a lot of busy middle-aged graduates, who are not in close touch any longer, should be asked to take up the cudgels in what need not be a fight. We are determined, however, on seeing the traditional title restored, and we firmly believe that the University authorities must see this question in the same light that we do. I would be grateful if you would explain the situation more clearly to me and instruct me if I am wrong in my understanding of what has taken place and what should be done.

> Respectfully yours,
> James Thurber

## To Wayne Harsha

*410 East 57th Street, New York, N.Y.*
*April 25, 1946*

*Mr. Wayne Harsha, Department of English,*
*Ohio State University, Columbus, Ohio*

Dear Mr. Harsha:

. . . I am enclosing letters I have just mailed to President Bevis and to Fullen. We are interested right now in the re-establishment of the Sun-Dial. If a simple petition from the boys and girls of "Scarlet Fever" to have the name resumed is not successful, I will be glad to attack the thing from a wide-open angle. There appear to be so many phases of the problem that it is a little difficult to try to handle the thing from so far off. Just how much is involved in the Jewish angle I do not know, and Fullen's references to this were the first I had heard about it. I gather that by "nice kids", he means primarily Gentiles, and this gives the business a whole new dimension. I hope the Jews have not actually been barred from the staff.

. . . I will wait for answers from Bevis and Fullen with great interest and will let you know what happens.

      Sincerely yours,
      James Thurber

## To Dorothy Fiske

*410 East 57th Street, New York, N.Y.*
*February 26, 1946*

*Miss Dorothy Fiske*
*Harper & Brothers*

Dear Miss Fiske:

I am just recovering from a severe attack of pneumonia and one of the things I simply am not strong enough to handle is the recurring headache about who deals with what rights of mine in London. It comes as something of a surprise to me that your London office has ever handled any rights of mine since I have no recollection at all of ever arranging any deal through that office. Curtis Brown usually gets the requests and therefore has usually handled them. It all amounts in the long run to such small change that I feel I am losing by going through so much fuss and using up so much energy on something which sometimes appears to me to be more hopeless than the international situation.

A friend of mine who edits the worthy magazine called "The Land" wants to reprint "The Wood Duck" and I have given him my permission. I think it appeared in a Harper book but as you know in my various contracts with Harper's you shared some of the reprint rights in some cases and in others I controlled the whole business. I feel that if it were not for all the hours I put in on permissions I would get three more books done and live five years longer. At the moment I just don't care what Curtis Brown or anybody else does about anything. I realize that none of this is your fault and that you have done great service in keeping a mixed up situation more straightened out than anybody. I will probably feel better about it in another month . . .

Best wishes to you as always, and don't mind the fussiness of a convalescent.

> Cordially yours,
> James Thurber

## To Robert Yoakum

> 410 East 57th Street, New York, N.Y.
> February 27, 1946

*Mr. Robert H. Yoakum*

Dear Mr. Yoakum:

Rule #1 at the "New Yorker" is that the magazine never prints anything which is concerned with one of its established contributors or staff members. The magazine even reviews books by these people grudgingly. The Lord God Almighty could not have published your piece in the "New Yorker."

Most of the disappointments I know of in people who send things to the magazine result from their ignorance of what type of thing it will print. I don't think your parody quite comes off except in spots. Maybe you should file it away for a while in that file of yours.

I wish you the best of luck in the terrible profession you seem to have chosen.

> Sincerely yours,
> James Thurber

## TO ROSEMARY THURBER

*Thurber's daughter was now fifteen years old.*

410 East 57th Street, New York, N.Y.

*March 1, 1946*

Dear Rosemary:

I drew a few pictures for you this afternoon and you will recognize at least three of the creatures I hope. The other two definitely belong in my new Natural History Series and maybe you can think of names that would fit them. Don't try so hard, however, that you lie awake at night. I hope that by this time your spots have come and gone and that you are practically well.

I went out to get my hair cut today and they gave me a young barber who had just graduated from Barber College. He cut my mustache all wrong because he couldn't shift to the left side and therefore tried to reach the left side by putting his knee in my stomach. At one point he cut my nose a little with the scissors and went "Ouch!" I told him I was the one who was supposed to say "Ouch!" I escaped from him without serious damage.

You owe me a lot of letters now but don't feel that you have to answer every one. Drop me a letter at The Homestead, Hot Springs, Virginia, when you get your strength back. We will leave there on April 1st.

Helen got two books for you today from the Doubleday Bookstore and they have already been mailed to you so they ought to arrive in a day or two.

Love to you and Linnie and your mother and Allen and the poodle and the cats. I hope this covers the household.

> Love,
> Dad

*She questioned his unusual, complimentary close of "Dad" in his last letter. "Muffy" was a classmate and close friend of Rosemary's at the Northampton School for Girls. Rosemary lived in Amherst, Massachusetts, with her mother and stepfather, who taught at Amherst College.*

*March 14, 1946*

Dear Rosabelle:

Throw off that glandular trouble, gal. Ah caint write no poem about it cause ah caint rhyme no word with glandular.

We sure are counting on you and the Muffy but we can't give an exact date right this minute. I got to finish my new Goldwyn movie story and I can't tell just when that'll be, but I'll hop along, sister. We won't have things set to rights so you can come quite as early as last year, but we'll let you know as soon as we possibly can when you-all can see the new house and exhibit the Rosemary quarters.

I've now got so people recognize my face, in spite of my clown's glasses. Fella on the elevator asked me if I was your father, and I said yes. He said he liked my writing but not the drawings. I said I liked his face, but not his manners (no, I didn't).

Kiss everybody for me, write, and I'll answer *same* day.

> Helen and I send love.
> Daddy

That "Dad" was my stenographer's mistake.

&. &. &.

March 30, 1946

Dear Rosabelle:

How is the crutch and bandage situation in Amherst? How are your glands? . . .

I am big and strong now, and weigh a lot.

We are planning to set our house [in Cornwall] to rights in the country as soon as possible. The furniture is all in a pile and we have to get servants since Florence is going to leave, we are pretty sure . . .

"Walter Mitty" is coming along fine and they start shooting soon, with Danny Kaye, Virginia Mayo, Fay Bainter, Boris Karloff, etc. . . .

Gertrude Sayre fell in her bathroom and broke a rib.

Joe White [the Whites' son] went in swimming in Florida, and a crab bit his big toe.

"What's the altitude here?" a visitor asked a native. "Three dollars a pint," the fella said.

> Helen and I send love to all.
> Daddy

*Thurber was extremely generous with his time and thought in helping beginning writers.*

## TO MILDRED HOWARD

*410 East 57th Street, New York City*
*April 19, 1946*

*Miss Mildred Howard*
*Glasgow, Kentucky*

Dear Miss Howard:

Your play arrived when I was in Virginia recovering from pneumonia and I am just now able to get back to work on a long story whose deadline is not far off. . . . It is difficult to interest a producer in a play in which a dog figures so largely, but more serious handicaps than this have been overcome.

In submitting the play you must be sure to have it retyped so that the names of the characters, when they speak, are put in the center of the page and not at the left hand side as you have done. The correct method enables the reader to tell exactly how long the play will run. Typed in this fashion each page should play a minute and the script should be about 120 pages long.

The opening of your play is almost identical with the opening of "I Remember Mama", and I am afraid this device would not appeal to producers.

I can assure you that the use of my drawings would not help in marketing the play, but would only confuse or bewilder the readers . . .

I am sorry I can't be of more help to you, but I send you my sincerest wishes for your success.

      Sincerely yours,
      James Thurber

## TO HAROLD ROSS

*Milton Greenstein handled copyrights for the* New Yorker.

*West Cornwall, Conn.*
*August 27, 1946*

*Mr. H.W. Ross, The New Yorker*
*25 West 43rd Street, New York, 17, N.Y.*

Dear Ross:

In connection with Greenstein's memo on copyright dated August 15th, I need only remind you that because of accident and confusion practically everything is now in public domain. Since no pirate has yet been bold enough to publish all of my books without permission or royalties I intend from now on to taunt the fellows by running the following credit line under all of my drawings, "Copyright by my Aunt Hilda."

If you have any other problems just turn them over to me.

> Yours,
> James Thurber

## To Rosemary Thurber

*October 22, 1946*

Dear Twilter:

. . . A young marine is coming to see me Friday. He sounded fine on the phone. One of my fans.

. . . Are you keeping up in your studies?

That's fine. No wiggle-waggle.

Nancy Nugent lost her purse with $8 in it the other day.

John McNulty who gave you the shorter Oxford Dictionary, says he ought to give you the Taller Oxford Dictionary now.

Nora Sayre is not sick, for once.

Joe White can drive now.

Jan De Vries is tall!

Liz Gude has a sling shot. It is for sparrows. She gets pigeons with a fly-swatter.

> Love & kisses
> Daddikins

## To The Herman Millers

*THE NEW YORKER*
*No. 25 West 43rd Street*
*October 21, 1946*

Dear Herman and Dorothy:

. . . "The Death of the Heart" turned out to be hard to find, but I finally got one through the Holliday Bookshop here. I am glad that you are reading it together because that is exactly what I had in mind. I think it is one of the finest novels of our time and so do my friends who have read it. I bought it in England when we were there eight years ago and still have my copy, I found when

Blind Man's Bluff

( N. Cross )

we unpacked our books and put them up on the shelves of the library of our new house. We spent the summer settling in and falling downstairs. . . . We are going to Hot Springs October 30th for a month, and I will write you again from there since I believe I owe you several letters. . . .

This turned out to be a bad summer for every writer I know including myself, and I think I averaged eight words a day. I have done a short piece probably for The Saturday Review entitled "A Call on Mrs. Forrester." In it I visit the famous lost lady and I will send you a carbon of the piece when it is copied. I hope to get started on something else in Virginia.

I do not know whether you know the other Bowen books, but I think you would like "The House in Paris." . . .

As ever,
Jim

## To Harold Ross

*The Homestead, Hot Springs, Virginia*
*November 6, 1946*

*Mr. H. W. Ross, The New Yorker*
*No. 25 West 43rd Street, New York 18, New York*

Dear Ross:

. . . I worry about Talk of the Town because it was my baby for so many years and Andy and I used to get out a varied and interesting department, we like to think. It seems to me that it has become something of a step-child, largely because of the exalted position the magazine's longer non-fiction pieces have attained to. You said to me something about lack of manpower but you have always said that, and I used to get along with only two reporters. I have been reliably informed that Talk of the Town reporters number around fifteen or twenty now. I presume, of course, that they have all been shunted to the more important non-fiction research work. I am not one who complains that the magazine made a mistake in becoming serious and important about world coverage but I do complain about overemphasis causing Talk of the Town to be struck a glancing blow. I can quote you at least four interviews with movie actors we have had, all very much the same piece. *Time* and even *This Week* seem always to get more entertaining local pieces than we do. See last Sunday's *This Week* for its piece on a coffee taster. We have had tasters but

not as good as this one and not for fifteen years. New York is still the most fabulous city in the world and Talk of the Town used to be the most exciting column. Instead of interviewing, say, Mark Clark, I would rather go to Gunther's
or Revillon Freras and get the latest dope on chinchilla coats and the chinchilla situation generally. I just read a piece in the *Washington Post* for either
November 2nd or November 3rd about a chinchilla farm in Virginia, and it
had some wonderful facts. In all other fur-bearing animals there is only one
hair to a pore but the chinchilla has eighty. It takes years to raise enough animals for one coat which costs $45,000. Silver fox and even mink have only a
fairly long life, from five to fifteen years, but the chinchilla last forever, and
Mary Pickford has one which was made in 1899. In this period of big money,
some New York dame must be ordering a chinchilla for, say, $60,000. There
are about forty farms or ranches in the country.

This kind of stuff is still as interesting as ever to you and me and our
readers. . . .

I thought the enclosed clipping would take you back the way it did me. Just
throw it away. I guess we are no worse off now than we have always been.

> Yours,
> James Thurber

*The Homestead*
*November 19, 1946*

*Mr. H. W. Ross, The New Yorker*
*25 West 43rd Street, New York, New York*

Dear Harold:

What has happened to Talk has many facets. First, none of us is as young
and gay as he used to be and neither is the world. It was much easier to deal
with trivia before Hitler. Second, something happened to the general tone of
the department when we made over for Colin Kelly and the first days of the
war, and later when we devoted the department to the funeral of President
Roosevelt. There are several reasons why I should like to see it get back to, say,
a talk with the Missing Persons Bureau about the number of letters and calls
which still come in about Judge Crater, and things like that. Not only has humor pretty well gone out but Talk of the Town now finds itself wedged in between highly serious and important world reporting and the comment page

of a man who has become the most distinguished political philosopher of the day [E. B. White]. We all read and discuss the heavy subjects but we all spend a great deal of time on the same interesting facts, persons and places that we used to. Anybody, including me, could get up two hundred old-time talk ideas in a week. The thing is to get away from the portentous tone, or whatever it is, and this could be accomplished by a little relaxation of mind and spirit and does not necessitate a tremendous staff. . . .

We will be back about December 11th.

      Yours,

      James Thurber

## To Herman Miller

*The Homestead, Hot Springs, Virginia*

*December 4, 1946*

Dear Herman:

I feel like one of those charred carbon sticks we used to pick up under street lamps in the days when all technics were clumsy and life was fun. I keep wondering what you feel like. Let me know.

Did you like the Death of the Heart as much as I did? Or have you already told me that?

I have not been able to write a God damn thing for eight months (or did I tell you that?)

Which combined with a cold and a gloomy view of man, makes me feel like an empty raspberry basket, frail, stained, and likely to be torn to pieces by a little child.

There is a mysterious sightseeing gentleman here at High Brackets, who Helen assures me is handsome, and who could be an international spy, an F.B.I. man, or a Lotto manufacturer. He contrived an introduction, and we found that he has the romantic name of C. W. Herbet. He won't say what he does. He is of a Teutonic accent. Getting drunk with him I tried what seemed a subtle act in which I hinted, mysteriously, at a sensitive comprehension of certain of the smarter phases of authoritarian government. This to lead him out. He probably *is* a Lotto manufacturor and thinks I am a rich Fascist who knows where Hitler is hiding.

Elliott was here for 4 days and we were braced in the bar by a drunken gent who knew Tom Meek, and who thought Elliott was me. He asked the name of the O.S.U. boy worth a million, who wrote a play with 4 characters. This turned out to be Elliott (me). To add to the confusion the man's name was Furber.

He asked Helen and me to lunch (Elliott being gone) and turned up with the Dowager Mrs. Cornelius Vanderbilt, who told me she had a funny mind, and proved it by urging us all to join hands and make the Russians like us. She then related how she had called, all alone, on the Gromykos to tell them about her dear friends, the late Czar and Czarina, and their nice, charming circle. The ten days that shook Mrs. Vanderbilt.

Love to you and D. from H. and Jim

Mrs. V. also referred to the Russian Revolution as "that time they shot all my nice friends" and said she refused to speak to the Kaiser after 1914 because "he was so deceitful."

## To Rosemary Thurber

*The Homestead, Hot Springs, Virginia*
*November 19, 1946*

Dear Rosie,

You didn't tell me how the other girls found time to learn a speaking part. Well, maybe you can work it in when the next play comes along. There might be a big producer in the audience who would star you opposite Lassie. Let me know how the play comes out, and be sure and do not slip on a rug . . .

Elliott Nugent was down here for a few days and we will be here until December 10th. I suppose that you will want to spend Christmas with Linnie and shall we count on you for New Year's week or something of the sort.

Let me know how you are getting along with those studies as I am counting on you to keep up the Thurber name for high grades. After all, look at the time you have now that you have given up that speaking part.

Helen and I both send you all our love and best wishes. Be sure and write to Grandma Thurber and to us.

Love and kisses,
Daddykins

## TO JOHN G. GUDE

*Cambridge-Beaches, Somerset, Bermuda*
*February 16, 1947*

*Mr. J. G. Gude, 30 Rockefeller Plaza*
*New York 19, New York*

Dear Jap:

I wonder how the script is coming? I do not expect the boys to stick too close to the scene I sent you since it was just batted off. I felt it could be plotted a little more than their version was. Also, it cuts out several things I felt were not right.

Walter would not mention his age even by inference since in the dreamer's mind he is always in his thirties. He should never actually kill anyone, the way they had it, and he should not be equipped with a weapon superior to his enemy's. Walter is the boy who uses fountain pens or nail files to fix complicated machines, and he would use his fists to overcome pistols. I mentioned before that he should not have a Stutz Bearcat, since only the rich and privileged boys had them.

After five summer days down here, it has been both windy and rainy, with a heavy gale blowing now, but the sun comes out from time to time . . . Bermuda, like the French Riviera, is excellent for nerves; and for the first time in several years I have taken no luminal for two weeks. The weather after the middle of March is usually wonderful. If you see a photograph of Charles Jackson and me, the glass on his table contains Coca Cola.

Love to you, Helen, and the children.

As always,
Jim

## TO VIRGINIA BAILEY

*Cambridge-Beaches, Somerset, Bermuda*
*March 3, 1947*

*Miss Virginia Bailey, SPICE,*
*302 Herald Building, Syracuse 2, New York*

Dear Miss Bailey:

In the days when I knew Honey at Columbia it was a habit of mine, like a nervous tic, to do seven or eight hundred drawings for each of my friends. I never realized that these friends passed the drawings on to people I do not know, and the whole thing gives me pause for reflection.

My drawings are published in The New Yorker with very few exceptions, and I do not have any desire to be represented in a magazine with the name SPICE. I do not have the vaguest idea what the drawings you have are about, but I definitely do not want them published at random, or anywhere else.

The next time you see Honey, tell her to quit getting drunk, standing on street corners, and handing things of hers to passing strangers.

   Sincerely yours,
   James Thurber

## To Gus Lobrano

*Cambridge-Beaches, Somerset, Bermuda*
*March 3, 1947*

*Mr. Gus Lobrano, THE NEW YORKER*
*25 West 43rd Street, New York, New York*

Dear Gus:

 . . . Helen and I were greatly disturbed to hear about Wolcott, and we certainly hope that he is out of the hospital by this time. These continual relapses with fever are not good. I can certainly appreciate how a man feels after a month in the hospital, and what a terrible blow it is to plan a vacation and have to be carried back to the corridors again. I think Gibbs is going through a hell of a lot, and I hope that they finally settle his trouble and get it over with once and for all. Please let us know how he is.

 Helen read me Victoria Lincoln's three long stories in "The Wind at My Back." She has developed into one of the best writers we've got, I think, and will no doubt turn up one day with a novel that will be remembered long after the stories of the rest of us have been forgotten. I loved "February Hill", and I am sure it will last forever, but what I had in mind is what Victoria has, too, I think, and that is a work of great seriousness. . . . What our stories amount to is probably notes for stories; but after all, Ross named our type of fiction with great precision when he called it "casual." Malcolm Cowley said of my stories that, "All things being equal, a good long story is better than a good short story." This is true enough, but I feel that it should not have been aimed at me. My casuals have always had, I like to think, a beginning, a middle, and an end.

I have asked God for guidance in avoiding the type of 3,000 word story which begins, "Mrs. Pennyfeather picked up the Begonia", and ends with, "Mrs. Pennyfeather set the Begonia down."

Victoria not only sees it clearly and completely as the result of careful observation, but she knows the words for it. She has the rare fundamental which is the ability to remember exactly how you felt and what you thought when you were very young. This gift belongs to only a handful of persons and is very precious. She can also write about men and do it very well, and if I have a suspicion that she is rather more troubled by dialectic than familiar with it, it is merely because I myself am in the same boat. . . .

Best wishes and love to all.

As ever,

Jim

## To Charles Wiley

*Cambridge-Beaches, Somerset, Bermuda*
*March 3, 1947*

*Mr. Charles W. Wiley, 375 Central Park West,*
*New York, New York*

Dear Mr. Wiley:

. . . I like a lot of the touches and turns of humor in your piece, but it is really only a practice or rehearsal for a funny story. It is too short, it doesn't mean quite enough; and there is absolutely nowhere in the world you could publish it outside of THE ARIZONA KITTY KAT.

Writing humor is fun; writing good humor is hell, and selling it is almost impossible. I should say that after six or seven rejections of things like this you ought to be well on your way. There hasn't been a new humorist since 1930, and it is high time one showed up.

Best wishes to you and all consolations.

Sincerely yours,

James Thurber

*Rosemary, fifteen, now attended the Northampton School for Girls. Thurber's own school records suggest that his claims of high achievement in high school and college are somewhat exaggerated.*

## TO SARAH WHITAKER

*May 13, 1947*

Dear Miss Whitaker:

I appreciate what you and Rosemary's teachers had to say about her and her work in your letter of April 12th. The subject of a young American female is a considerable one, and if I have taken so long to answer your letter, put it down not to a lack of intense interest but to a desire to think the problems out.

As an old teacher's pet myself whose grades at Columbus East High School have been equalled, I was told a few years ago, by only a few students since 1913, and as a college student who for two years was well on his way to Phi Beta Kappa, I naturally hoped that Rosemary might have a greater tendency to study than she seems to show. However, I could say the same thing for almost every girl her age I know, and I have made an effort for many years to talk to these youngsters and try to understand them.

The problem of the American girl in school is as fascinating as it is sometimes disturbing. When I was in grammer grades, high school and the university, I should say that less than four per cent of the girl students showed a genuine interest in English, history, Latin and mathematics. I regret to say that only two girls who could be called pretty and charming belonged to this four per cent. Of course, there is no way of getting around the fact that our girls seem to mature slowly intellectually and that they usually arrive at a desire for knowledge only after they are out of school. The question of outside activities, such as plays, is one in which I take the side of the outside work. I failed myself to become Phi Beta Kappa, but I was editor of my college magazine, one of the editors of the newspaper, a member of the dramatic society, and I believe that I got as much out of these as out of my classroom work.

I am inclined to agree with Morris Bishop who said in a recent lecture that students in this country, as a rule, do not have a great interest in literature or other intellectual subjects. I believe that the tempo of our life, our remarkable technological achievements, our love of gadgets and entertainment, and various other factors militate strongly against a desire for study. I suppose when you come right down to it, a girl is either a natural student or she is not. I believe, as Rosie's teachers do, that she could do honor work if she tried, and I assure you that I have attempted in every way I know how to encourage her to do better in her studies. When she was in grammer grades she got A in both art and English because at that age she was somewhat fascinated by her father's work, and she wanted to be good in the things that he himself did. She tells me that she does not study easily or fast, and I wonder whether the system of roommates is conducive to a chance for application and concentration. I have never been able to study or work with anybody in the room, and I do not see how it can successfully be done. There are also many objections to study hours because of the presence of other persons. With one exception, the members of my fraternity who got the highest grades were the boys who lived at home and not in the fraternity house itself.

From talking to a number of girls in their teens, I have discovered the indisputable fact that world unrest, threats of conflict, radio broadcasts and newspaper stories, have built up a background of apprehension which amounts in some degree to insecurity. In my own day when I was Rosemary's age, the greatest threat to the world was Halley's comet. I don't know how this kind of thing can be combatted, but I have often thought that lectures by staff members or visiting authors on world affairs might do some good. . . .

Rosemary has developed a curious antipathy for college but this does not seem to be based on any influence from other girls, since she assures me that both her roommates want to go to college and intend to go. She seems to think that college will be too hard and she has a certain fear of flunking out. In this regard, I believe that only the passing of the years will be of any avail in changing her mind. I gather from parents of other girls her age that the period from fifteen to sixteen is an especially critical one and that an attitude of apathy seems to develop in most of the girls. A great deal of this, I presume is pose.

I don't think you need to worry about Rosemary's troubled expression since this is definitely familial. I am told that I wear, most of the time, a distressed expression which has been described by one of my friends as "the troubled look of a dog who has forgotten where he has buried his bone." Rosemary's own troubled look may be intensified by worries of her own and heaven knows there are enough to go around in the era we are living in.

If I could be of any help, I wish you would let me know and perhaps you could educate me in the attitude a father should take toward a young lady who can do honor work but doesn't appear to want to. When Rosemary was five, she attended a school for American and English children in Syria. The teacher told her mother that Rosemary was the only child in the class who could not count up to ten. When her mother asked her if this were true, she assured her that she could count up to ten but that she didn't get anything for it.

Sincerely yours,

*Miss Sarah B. Whitaker,*
*Northampton School for Girls, Northampton, Mass.*

## To Jap Gude

*Thurber was researching radio soap opera for his* New Yorker *series, "Soap-land," which began to be published in May 1948.*

THE NEW YORKER
*25 West 43rd Street*
*May 19, 1947*

Dear Jap:

The fact that Rebecca West told Ross that "The Catbird Seat" is my best story revived my interest in the possible sale of the story to both the radio and the movies. Since Studio One at Columbia is doing the dramatization of a Lardner story this week, I thought there might be some chance of them being interested in "The Catbird Seat" which has a definitely unusual plot and might be very effective if it were written properly.

If it were produced by Studio One it is quite possible that it might influence the revival of interest in the story out in Hollywood. . . .

Helen and I are looking forward to having you at Bell Meadow. We found this name on some stationery that had been left in the house. It sounds a little like the name of a successful prostitute and I think I will try to get up a name of my own. The house once belonged to the inventor of the honeycomb automobile radiator and early models of his invention are still occasionally dug up on the place. He was finally killed in an automobile wreck, but whether this was the fault of his invention or not we can't find out. . . .

At Ross' party for Rebecca West the other day someone crashed and fell sprawling across my lap. It turned out to be Michael Arlen. We are all poor windlestraws on the stream of time.

We'll see you soon,

Jim

*In August 1947, the filmed version of "The Secret Life of Walter Mitty" opened. Thurber's public disapproval led Goldwyn to publicize quotes from Thurber's letters to MGM, written while working with its production people. Goldwyn's and Thurber's letters-to-the-editor were published in* Life *magazine.*

  *In 1947, writer Allen Churchill, planning an article on the* New Yorker, *asked Ross for samples of funny or interesting interoffice memos. Ross passed the request on to Gibbs, Thurber and White. None had any.*

## To Harold Ross

West Cornwall, Conn.

August 15, 1947

Dear Ross:

By this time you will have seen the Letters column in *Life* for August 18th. It turns out Goldwyn himself read my letter aloud last night in Hollywood to seven men including members of his staff out there and from New York, and two advertising agency men. I don't think anybody got much out of the reading, which was punctuated by constant laughter from Goldwyn over points of humor which were not clear to his auditors; that is, they couldn't figure why *he* was laughing. His only comment at the end was: "My God, doesn't Thurber get $2 a word?" He couldn't understand, I guess, why such a highly paid man would spend a week on the research and writing of a letter printed for free. . . .

My pieces on soap opera are progressing well in spite of the tremendous research I have had to do and am still doing. My letters and literature on the subject run to half a million words. I expect to do four pieces, each about 5,000 words long. I am even more interested in it all than I was, and the story is amazing and fascinating. *The New Yorker* can put on a soap opera for $104,000 a year, in case you are interested. It could be called "Katharine Takes Over." . . .

In answer to your letter about Allen Churchill who wants to use memoranda of Gibbs and White and me, I'm inclined to sympathize with your realization that, after all, we are always opening up other people's desks and files. I suppose we should be good sports about it. I think the whole mass of memoranda would be the making of your memoirs together, of course, with your own memos which are invariably amusing and penetrating. We have read a great many to delighted groups of cockeyed people.

Somebody once said whereas every word brought out by the old round table group invariably was repeated or printed, nothing ever came out of the *New Yorker* group. We are famous, I was told, for our shyness and modesty. Thus, I was always surprised when anything was printed as coming from *The New Yorker* boys and girls. Most of such anecdotes are either deliberately made up by columnists or are apocryphal in other ways. Gibbs is presumed to have said, beholding the transplanting of a gigantic elm on a Long Island estate at the cost of $200,000, "Shows what God could do if he had money." This is lovely, but Gibbs tells me he didn't say it. His wonderful crack about Max Eastman's book has not been printed anywhere, or at least I haven't seen it. When, in 1929, I felt constrained to advise you where White really was—at the Statler Hotel in Cleveland—because you were going nuts over his disappearance Andy was hurt because I had promised him not to tell. You explained to him that it was a matter of loyalty. "*The New Yorker* is a cesspool of loyalties," Andy said. I have given this and other lines of Gibbs and White currency. I was a bit depressed when something of my own, of which I was fond, was never repeated to me by anyone. Some fifteen years ago, a gentleman representing an exclusive and expensive special editions club came to the office in 45th Street and cornered me in the reception room. "We want you to do new illustrations for a special edition of "Alice in Wonderland." To this I replied, "I tell you what let's do, let's keep the Tenniel drawings and I'll rewrite the book." The man bowed and left, realizing he was defeated. I burst into White's office loudly repeating what had been said, but Andy, engrossed in problems of his own, let it slip from his mind. I happened to recall this some months ago and told it to Pete DeVries. He put the whole thing in the rough notes of a play he hopes to get around to in his sixties.

You once showed me a Woollcott letter in which he said in effect, "two months ago I did a couple of extraordinarily fine things for people in my quiet, anonymous way and it is obvious now that they have not been heard of. I count on you discreetly to tell them around." He then told what they were. I have clippings from various columns of things I have said and twenty-seven of these were news to me. I make no effort to collect these columns but they are sent in. The twenty-eighth is from an old MacIntyre column and, wonder of wonders, it was true. In the old days, you were constantly having partitions removed and then put back and then taken down again. I put up a sign near the elevators reading, "Alterations going on as usual during business." A small thing, but mine own, and the only item in my skimpy file marked "true."

I can't remember any damn memo of mine at all, but I have the distinct impression that almost all of them were written in anger over real or fancied wrongs, and they have more of a fishwife's note than anything else. I have always been willing to reveal all because after twenty-five years of journalism I still hate the uninterviewable person. He is invariably a smug and cocky stuffed shirt.

My chief doubt and uneasiness about a project like Churchill's is the tone that may get into it—"My God don't these boys think they're cute." Anyway, White will give a definite "No" on this and three will get you five that Gibbs will too.

> Keep cool.
> Thurber

*Thurber paid little attention to money until his marriage to Helen, who handled his finances. She steadily encouraged in Thurber the belief that he had been routinely underpaid by the* New Yorker *over the years, and to an arguable extent she was correct.*

*Hawley Truax, a friend of both Ross and Raoul Fleischmann, acted as intermediary between the magazine's editorial and business departments.*

*Baird Leonard was a humorous poetess of the day who published in the* New Yorker.

## To Hawley Truax

*West Cornwall, Conn.*
*August 26, 1947*

Dear Hawley:

Mrs. Thurber's records check with yours on the payments received by me for the various drawings you listed. There is no record of our having paid any of the $500 back by personal check or otherwise, hence I owe you $500.

I wish you would apply to this indebtedness the sum you mention as being due me for cost of living adjustment on "Here Come the Tigers." Also, please apply the sum of $175 which I have so far paid to Miss Jean Hopkins for work in connection with my series on soap opera. . . .

I was more gratified than anything to find the magazine can make mistakes in bookkeeping. And it almost persuades me to turn in an old expense account of mine for the cost of tickets and transportation while covering the tennis in Wimbleton in June 1938. I mislaid my own records of this for several years, and when I came upon them I decided that time had outlawed the account. The total was $92, or almost as much as I got for my story. It has been reprinted in one anthology. . . .

I came to work on the New Yorker in the first week of March 1927 at a salary of $100 a week. In addition to executive work, mainly conferences with Ross on everything from the removing of partitions, the advisability of firing Greta Palmer and the whereabouts of E. B. White, to conferences on the cutting of paper with Ingersoll and Spaulding. In addition I edited all of the departments, did the theatre art captions, many of the blurbs, edited Goings On, and some fifty-five other things. Ross was intent on finding editors, not writers, and he was determined to make an editor out of me at the cost of my giving up writing. It is too bad that Gibbs and Lobrano and Shawn did not show up at that time. The magazine had known me only as a writer of half a dozen casuals it had bought. I assumed it was interested in my writing. When I told Ross that I wanted to write he said, "All right, goddamn it, but it will be considered as editorial work and included in your salary." In other words, I could write if I did it for nothing. The point was, obviously, to crush the writing out of me and nobody, including Mrs. White, did anything in protest. Between March 5th and August 6, 1927 I wrote six casuals, although how I did it is impossible to remember, since in those five months I worked seven days a week at the office including many nights, especially Sunday, up to 11 p.m. I lost ten pounds and my wife made me demand a day off which I finally got. After my piece, "My Trip Abroad," was published August 5th the late Baird Leonard told Ross, "It made me laugh on both sides of my face. Why don't we have more from this man?" "I guess you're a writer goddamn it," said Ross. And from then on I was paid for my writing which everybody on the magazine at that time insists was at all times encouraged. This is not the happiest page of The New Yorker's bright history, and I have always felt that it should have been long since atoned for by payments at my then word rate. You will not find one person at the office who will believe this. They think it is a little joke of mine, like the legend I "made up" about The New Yorker's lack of interest in my drawings. My first drawings appeared in "Is Sex Necessary," published in November 1929. My first New Yorker drawing was published January 31, 1931. This all goes to show that I discovered, encouraged and developed my own writing and drawing. This is not a history for anyone outside the magazine, and I certainly have not told it and would not tell it to the biographers of Ross such as Allen Churchill who, when he comes up here in September, will hear only about the genius, the brilliance and the kindliness of old H.W., which outweigh his flaws at least 1500 to 1.

So much for who owes what to whom.

>Cordially,
>James Thurber

## TO THE RONALD WILLIAMSES

*Oct. 11, 1947*

Dear Ronnie and Janey:

My daughter was 16 October 7, and Eva was 53 October 9. I was in love with Eva in 1904, in Miss Lemmert's 3rd grade. Eva's skirts were as high as her ass in those days. It took her 26 years to learn to love me. Meanwhile she married a swine who left her in Miami, clerking in a book store in the high winds.

Helen, that's my sweet old wife, has been in bed and agony for 3 days with a twisted sacroilliac but is better and will be well in a week.

October's burning on the hills, our maple trees are lighted and there's a soft golden haze on the meadow. It's corn shuck and pumpkin time and the rabbits have got their minks out of storage.

>Love to all
>Jim and Helen

## TO ROSEMARY THURBER

*Sadly, Rosemary was able to find only excerpts from Thurber's marvelous 1947 letters to her. This one follows her having written him that she had been elected president of her dorm at Northampton School for Girls.*

Dear Rosie,

You come by this presidency stuff naturally. Your mother was president of Powder Puff, the girls' musical comedy club at Ohio State, and I was president of the Bryden School Athletic Club . . . which had its headquarters in my grandfather's barn in 1907 and also of the senior class at East High in 1913 to say nothing of my leadership of a gang of ragamuffins at the turn of the century who carried on all sorts of deviltry in the shadow of Holy Cross Cathedral in South Fifth Street, Columbus. When the real toughs from Sullivant

School attacked the Catholic boys my army took the side of the Catholics and that was the beginning of my hatred of racism and other kinds of intolerance . . .

Helen has just gone up the road to buy some pot holders and luncheon sets from a young woman who appears at the edge of the woods on cloudy Saturdays accompanied by a violet-colored dog who shines at night and whose name, unhappily, is Floyd. . . .

Love from Helen and me,
    Daddy

❧  ❧  ❧

*The Homestead, Hot Springs, Virginia*
*November 4, 1947*

Dear Rosie:

. . . . It has been raining since we got here, but it is not cold. I have turned in my first soap opera piece and I am writing the second one. We were glad that the forest fires did not get to Cornwall and I guess the rain has made the trees safe. At 3:00 in the morning, one night at the Algonquin, I woke up and thought I was in the country and I was sure the city lights were the cathedral pines on fire. I thought the autos were everybody in town driving up. I yelled at Helen, "The forest is on fire!" and scared her out of two years growth.

The only play we saw in New York was "The Heiress", which is very fine. We will take you to some plays during Christmas vacation.

Be sure and drop us a note from time to time.

    Love from Helen and me, as ever
    Daddy

## To a "Miss Montgomery"

*The Homestead, Hot Springs, Virginia*
*November 17, 1947*

Dear Miss Montgomery:

"Many Moons" was the first thing I took up after a series of five eye operations which lasted from October, 1940 to April, 1941. I had one of the worst cataracts in history and also one of the most mysterious eyes. I was shot by an arrow when I was six in Falls Church, Virginia, and the sight of my right eye was given up as lost also. Doctors regard it as a miracle that I did not go stone blind when I was six. Of the 30,000 recorded cases in medical history only three of us did not go stone blind. One great doctor said that I saw until the cataract set in in 1940, although I did not have any apparatus of vision. He said I could call it E.S.P. or God. Another man said it was like playing a piano with both hands cut off at the wrist.

The terrible strains of the operations resulted in a severe nervous breakdown which struck me one Sunday night in June, 1941, after I had written the first 300 words of "Many Moons". I began to shake all over but I continued to write. I managed to finish the story that night, which is something of a miracle for me who has often taken eight weeks to write 4,000 words. I used to write on the type-writer and I often did stories over from beginning to end from five to ten times. I had to take up a new system of writing with the loss of 8/10ths of my vision, and starting with "Many Moons" I used a soft black pencil and yellow paper, since black on yellow is the most visible of all color combinations. This is why it is used on all American highways for traffic signs. Since I could not see what I was writing, I used to run my thumb down the page to keep track of where I was, but I often wrote over lines. Now through practice and strong glasses I write over only when I get tired. I write on both sides of the paper and get only 20 words on a side. I use 200 sharpened pencils.

The original draft of "Many Moons" was accidentally left on the kitchen table in the summer house of a friend of mine on Martha's Vineyard, and I did not get it until the following spring. The breakdown had made it impossible for me to write during that summer and winter, anyway. When I had the story copied it ended without the three attempts to conceal the moon. E. B. White, whose criticism has always meant a great deal to me, in both writing and drawing, suggested that the story seemed incomplete the way I had it. The little Princess just went to sleep with the golden moon, and without any problems. I thought up the solution myself, but I gratefully acknowledge the nudge from Mr. White.

The story was condensed in *Reader's Digest* without my consent, since the publisher had all reprint rights at that time. I retain them myself now. It was also done on Radio Reader's Digest. I regard "The Great Quillow", my second fairy tale, as being better than "Many Moons" and it was seven times as hard to write. My final expression in this field, "The White Deer", took me a year and is better than the other two. It was brought out as an adult book. I have no doubt whatever that because of my nervous condition I entered the world of fairy tales partly as an escape. It helped a lot.

I am nearly 6' 2", and I weigh only 155 lbs. I have a thick thatch of hair that is now nearly white. My complexion has been described as "a cranberry in candlelight". I am extremely nervous as a result of not only five eye operations, but of two pneumonias and a ruptured appendix, all within sixteen months. I was given up for lost because of peritonitis, but I had to finish "The White Deer" so I did not have time to die. For further information about my personality write to Mr. White or Joel Sayre at *The New Yorker*, or Miss Ann Honeycutt, an old voice teacher of mine, 22 East 66th Street, New York City. I sing only late at night.

Sincerely yours,

James Thurber

## To Peter De Vries

*Blindness having put an end to Thurber's cartoons, in 1947 De Vries persuaded Ross and the* New Yorker's *art director, Jim Geraghty, to rerun former Thurber drawings with fresh captions. Thurber, hesitant about the arrangement, agreed to it for a time, though opposed to Ross' idea of cutting up the drawings and rearranging their parts.*

*[Undated, 1947]*

Dear Pete:

I thought you might look these over and then discuss them with Ross. I told Ross at lunch more than a month ago that I had talked over new captions for the old drawings with you. This seemed to gratify him, for he said you were the best idea man the magazine ever had. [Helen and I] are sending . . . new captions for four old drawings, and have selected about twenty-six other drawings that would seem to lend themselves well to new captions. Helen has a list of these, numbered from our scrap book which Miss Terry got up, and will send you a copy if you'd like to know the ones we selected as best.

I don't want to jump over Geraghty's head on this, but I know you will be able to handle it with the discretion you are famous for . . .

As ever,

Jim

❧ ❧ ❧

*The Homestead, Hot Springs, Virginia*
*November 25, 1947*

Dear Pete:

Thanks for the book and the Bodenheim poem, which takes me back to the old Penguin book store on West Eighth Street, where he used to sit with his eyes closed, running his iambic hands over the breasts of imaginary women. I have a feeling that the image of death as an idyllic or droll fellow arises only in the healthy mind, that is a mind attached to a healthy body. I have observed for a long time that death seems more awful the closer you approach it and that at a long distance it has something of a romantic air. I will show you later in the year how Paul Nash somehow compromised by prefiguring the flight of the magnolia. Thirty years ago—my God, it was thirty-five—I used to sit around with George Packer and Carson Blair, discussing death in terms of the then extremely popular "Ivory Apes and Peacocks" of old James Huneker. I remember the vision of death as a long room lit only by a single gas jet. Ah, what a dusty answer gets the soul.

I will get four, and maybe five, pieces done down here, including a report on my investigation by Congress and an account of my devious activities in the State Department.

Love from us both to all of you.

As ever,

Jim

*The Congressional House UnAmerican Activities Committee had been holding hearings as to who was, or had been, a Communist. In November 1947, E. B. White, in a* New Yorker *"Comment," stated that the magazine did and would judge contributors to its pages by their submissions, not by their political views. A* New York Herald Tribune *editorial, in response, advocated that employees should declare their political beliefs as a condition of employment. White's letter to the paper in response pointed out that such a requirement would be a violation of the Bill of Rights. The "Trib" ran the letter with an editorial denouncing White's position as quixotic and dangerous. Helen read the exchange to Thurber at The Homestead in Hot Springs, Virginia.*

## TO THE *NEW YORK HERALD TRIBUNE*

*Hot Springs, Va., Dec. 3, 1947*

Your editorial of December 2 entitled "The Party of One" and written in reply to E. B. White's letter in the same issue, could be used as a preface to a book on how to set up a totalitarian state under the bright banner of the security of the nation and the responsibilities of individuals to the Constitution. This is the familiar way in which all such states have been established.

Your editorial clearly suggests Chapter I for the handbook I have mentioned: How to Discredit Liberals as Dangerous Elements Who Imperil the Safety of the Nation and the True Meaning of Its Constitution, and Who Stand in the way of the New Freedom and the Greater Security.

But why should I instruct your editorial writer? He seems to have a natural gift and a peculiar facility for writing the handbook.

James Thurber

## TO ROSEMARY THURBER

*The Homestead, Hot Springs, Virginia*

*December 3, 1947*

Dear Rosikins:

I am glad the roses got there all right and we thank you for the thought you enclosed in your letter that came in today. Pansies have always been one of my favorite flowers and I shall put this one between the pages of the album containing your baby pictures, including the one of you strangling the snake which made us think that you were going to turn out to be the first woman president of the United States.

I forgot to tell you that I spent an afternoon with my old pal Charles MacArthur, the husband of Helen Hayes, and we exchanged anecdotes about our daughters. He told me that last summer he was appalled when Helen Hayes showed the 17 year old girl how to kiss a boy during the rehearsal of a play she was in at a summer theatre. Charley told his wife that their little girl might have to kiss dozens of boys in the next few years on the stage, and what the heck did she think she was teaching her anyway. Helen Hayes said, "You look after her morals, I have to look after her art."

Helen and I will mail you some Christmas money the day we leave here for New York, which will be Wednesday, the 10th. If we send it sooner you would spend it all on Tootsie Fudge Mix or Almond Joy. Even so, getting the money about the 12th, you will have plenty of time to throw a peanut butter spread or something. Save some of the money for your present for Linda.

Helen and I are delighted by the increase of your correspondence and the darn swell letters you write. What are you trying to do, be better than me?

Love and kisses from us both.

Daddy

## To Harold Ross

*Joel Sayre was careless about deadlines, and Ross at times called upon Sayre's friend, Thurber, for help. Elliott Nugent was suffering from periodic mental disorders. "Miss J" is Ebba Jonsson, the magazine's librarian.*

*West Cornwall, Conn.*
*December 18, 1947*

Dear Henry Wallace Rose:

There wasn't anything you could do about the situation of Mr. S. There isn't anything I can do either and, in fact, the only person who can do anything is Mr. S. himself. I hope that Shawn can make something out of what has been turned in, since the failure of this series to reach print would be the final blow. I think it can be whipped into shape and, God knows, I hope so, but I realize that any decision you make will be fair to the magazine first, as it should be.

I can't remember when any situation involving friends has upset me so much, unless you could count the strange interlude of Mr. Nugent. He is, by the way, himself again and seems to show no scars of his recent state. Human beings go through a lot and not many can really take it.

You have said countless times in twenty years that extremely few persons can successfully become free-lance writers. I am more and more impressed by this sound philosophy. What the hell people do about it as they get older I don't know. I have enough to write to last me at least five years and I do not foresee any circumstances that would constitute a block, as they call it. I cannot afford a block and I'm not going to buy one. They cost too much money.

If the State Department piece doesn't hold up don't worry about it. I have a vague memory of having written about my code work, but a month's search has failed to turn it up. In a piece called *An Afternoon in Paris* I discuss the

Herrick-Sharp situation I find, but I haven't been able to locate the code story. Maybe Miss J. could find it or assure me that it was not written. . . .

Helen and I send best wishes for a Merry Christmas to you, Mrs. R. and Patty.

As ever,<br>
James Thurber

## To The Henry Millers

*West Cornwall, Conn.*
*February 25, 1948*

Dear Herman and Dorothy:

. . . I am getting together drawings and stories for a book in the Fall and since one section is 30,000 words on soap opera, it has kept me busy from morning to night. I neglected my daughter who wrote me, "Well, what's the matter—are you still up to your ears in soap?" You will be glad to hear that she is turning out to be quite a writer, according to her English teacher. She is also appearing in "Janie" which her school does in conjunction with a school for boys near by. Rosie says the girls are all a foot taller than the boys. She gave up writing when she was twelve to become an FBI agent on the ground that writing is too hard, but now she seems to like it again. I wrenched away from her an essay she had done on Thoreau. At sixteen, American girls do not like Thoreau and she went to great length to look up criticisms unfavorable to the old boy and built her piece around a basic objection to the validity of his philosophy. On this last point she was supported by the Britannica. She also included a couple of apt quotations from Andy White's piece in "One Man's Meat."

I have rewritten the Henry James thing in order to follow your suggestion and slip into the lead in a more roundabout fashion. I wish you could see "The Heiress," an extremely deft piece of acting and direction. It puts a sharper point on "Washington Square" than the old master did, but it is not too much of a distortion and the best play we have seen in some time.

I will send you pretty soon a piece I have written called "A Call on Mrs. Forrester" in which is a daring middle-aged comparison of Willa Cather's lost lady and Madame de Vionnet.

Helen and I have done a lot of worrying about you but we feel that you are now well out of the woods and hope you can keep your blood where it belongs. The way you and I get through operations at our age is a proof that they grow them tough in central Ohio. My mother started a play when she was eighty and now she wants to learn to bowl. . . .

All of our love to both of you.

As always,

Jim

## TO WILLIAM SHAWN

*Shawn had succeeded St. Clair McKelway as "managing editor," which meant supervising "fact," or everything except fiction, poetry, and art. Thurber's "soap opera" series fell into the "fact" category which led to his first dealings with Shawn as editor. During one discussion of the series with Ross and Shawn, in which Ross remarked, "You would see what we mean if you could see," Thurber exploded in anger.*

*West Cornwall, Conn.*
*March 11, 1948*

Dear Bill:

. . . . My concern was probably exaggerated when I discovered that you and Ross seemed primarily interested in length, and also a little proud of your abilities in estimating wordage by counting pages or hefting the manuscript. I used to estimate Talk to within three words when I made up that department and Whittaker will bear me out on this. I will take on anybody in a word-estimating contest but it seems to be an idle achievement at best.

You and Ross were both cockeyed when you estimated that my original first piece ran to 7,500 words. Miss Ferrell gets about eighteen lines to a page and ten or eleven words to a line. Let's say she gets two hundred words to a page which is putting it high. There were thirty-one pages in my first script and how you can multiply thirty-one by two hundred and get 7,500 is beyond me.

If the idea of length becomes predominant and you and Ross have the idea that this is a series of funny pieces then obviously any cuts you made without my knowledge would be on behalf of funnying-up the pieces by cutting out the necessary facts which make this a survey and give it an importance worthy of my time and your space. The humor in this series is coincidental.

I am willing and eager to consider fairly and respectfully all suggested cuts and changes and omissions you may want to make, but this series is not subject to any editing whatever without my knowledge and consent.

I haven't yet got a carbon of the third piece and I need one before my next rewrite of that.

I am sure this will all work out simply and amicably and I was probably mainly upset by Ross's comment on length without a word about content, coming at the same time that my last casual was treated in typescript and proof as if it had been the work of an unknown beginner. Every now and then a professional and academic purism shows up in the proof reading and this is a menace unmixed, since it operates toward that dreadful "New Yorker style" which we deny and try to avoid. When I write "I had never been there before" the professors suggest "I never had been there before." I had this out with my teachers before the professors were born. Also, in the casual department "without any books" was questioned on the ground that "with no books" is better. Well, my first drawing came back from art meeting with a drawing on it and the words "this is the way a seal's whiskers go." White sent it back with the words "this is the way a Thurber seal's whiskers go." Nobody can do my drawings for me and nobody can write my style.

Love and best wishes,
As always,
James Thurber

*Mr. William Shawn, The New Yorker,*
*25 West 43rd Street, New York, N. Y.*

## TO ROSEMARY THURBER

*West Cornwall, Conn.*
*March 24, 1948*

Dear Rosie:

When I was in high school there wasn't anybody who could lift $15 worth of class rings but that was before inflation. I certainly want you to have a ring and Helen is enclosing a check for it.

Yes, I know what you mean about people taking everything as comic instead of serious. This has plagued all persons with a sense of humor but nobody more than Ed Wynn one night a dozen years ago. He was starring in one of his great musical shows and came up to the footlights at one point to explain seriously to the audience why a certain actress would not appear that night. "I regret to say," he began, "that Miss Parsons will not appear tonight because of an accident." The audience roared. The surprised Mr. Wynn then said, "She suffered a broken ankle this afternoon," and that sent the audience into stitches. He simply had to give up trying to convince them that he was in earnest. But that's what we all get for establishing a reputation for being comical.

I can't blame you girls for being alarmed about the world situation, especially since Mrs. Judd seems to be constantly saying, "Here they come." There are several things to be said though, in explanation of the tenseness of the situation. If the Western democracies were not being touchy and acting firm the Russians would be quietly going ahead grabbing countries and we would not be alarmed at all because they would be smiling and amiable and we would be making no fuss of any kind. The draft and military service should be a move for peace, since Russia would not be likely to attack a country that is prepared. Also, the United States, Great Britain and France have probably saved Italy for democracy by the brilliant diplomatic stroke of asking that Trieste be returned to Italy. The Italians and the other Western countries, as far up as Norway, have united and are taking precautions against a sudden overthrow like the one that happened in Prague. It must be remembered, too, that in spite of all the fuss, our side has always expected Russia to control the countries it has taken over, and Finland as well. The real danger would come if Italy and Norway were seized but Norway is now in a military pact with the rest of Scandinavia. Italy is very close to us and to France and England, and a United States of Europe is well on the way.

Neither Russia nor the United States really wants war and neither one is ready for it. Nobody in his right mind would risk the dropping of atom bombs and we now have enough to destroy Russia, since the new bombs are a hundred times as strong as the old ones. Russia hasn't got any and we can match their weapons. Also remember that Russia lost a hundred thousand towns and villages, and one Russian out of every twenty-two was killed or wounded. Germany lost one out of twenty-five and Japan one out of forty-four, to give you an idea. The Northampton school is a long long way from Russia and most real experts do not believe that any country is actually planning open warfare. By the end of this summer both sides may have solidified their position so that one is as strong as the other and then they would have to come to diplomatic agreements because of the balance of power. There is always a lot of wild talk, especially over here, but a great deal of it is propaganda. The chances are pretty good that you and the other girls will have to go to college after all.

We would like to get some facts about your plans so that we can plan about the New York trip.

> Love and kisses,
> Daddykins

## TO THE THURBER FAMILY

*Mame had dreamed that Thurber and Rosemary had died.*

> *West Cornwall, Conn.*
> *March 24, 1948*

Dear Thurbers:

. . . Rosemary and I are both all right and we would like to have you stop worrying about dreams. If you will make a list of the dreams you've had about people dying who really died you won't find many items. Dreams usually represent an anxiety about something other than the dream itself, and science has also discovered that they are usually about other people than the ones in the dream. Thus Rosemary and I, according to Freud, were surrogates for the persons you were actually worried about . . .

I hope William's toe is all right and that you are all well. Love from us both.

> Jamie

*Mrs. Charles L. Thurber*
*Southern Hotel, Main and High Streets*

## TO KATHARINE WHITE

> *West Cornwall, Conn.*
> *April 24, 1948*

Dear Katharine:

It was nice to get your good and cheerful letter. . . . I can sympathize with you about those intestinal pains. Mine were worse the night they gave me a typhoid shot to run my temperature to 106 in order to combat the iritis. They didn't tell me what this was for—it seems it was discovered by accident during the first World War that one inflammation alleviates another—and I was properly scared to death. One effect of such a high fever is a condition similar to drunkenness and I remember I identified my night nurse as a mindless

Southern girl I had married who was too dumb to know what was the matter. I understand she is no longer in the nursing profession. I called her Honey Chile in my very worst Southern accent.

I got an Easter card this year from another Katharine who is going to enter Radcliffe this fall. When she was a little older than two I sent her an Easter present after reading in the papers that she had spent four days and nights alone in the house with her mother who, like Lucy, had suddenly ceased to be, and oh, the difference to Katharine Wilson. She managed to keep herself alive on crackers and water until she was found. Her note to me after fifteen years is proof of a little girl who has become a charming young woman.

One of our problems in New York was Minnette Fritts Proctor, the wife of Dr. Oscar Speck Dokter Procter, a girl I knew in college who wrote me before my first marriage "Althea Thurber thounds thilly" which under the circumstances was a very daring comment. I took her in to see Andy because she lives in Seattle although right now she is in Belgium, being a flighty woman. Three years ago he met her when she was wearing white overshoes in 21 because of the danger to life and limb in a blackout that no longer existed. In college I mysteriously identified her with one of Henry James's worldly and intelligent women, which gives you some idea of my perspicacity about the opposite sex in those days. She has managed somehow in the intervening years to unhook her own intelligence like a telephone receiver. Her transmitter works but the connection is bad. "Do you mind if I talk about my baby?" she asked Helen who wanted to know how old the child was. "She will be twenty-six in June," said Minnette. Letters I wrote her thirty years ago she has still preserved, it turns out, and they are done up in a packet marked "For Sally," the twenty-six-year-old infant, who is supposed to read them after her mother is dead. This is the kind of thing that happens to me. I would like to see them in a way, but I no longer have the heart, or, I'm afraid, the stomach to tackle the job. I need only tell you that these letters were written several years before I met Althea, to whom, by the way, Minnette introduced me. You will get some idea of the innocent contents when I tell you that before I was engaged to Althea I once presented her in the presence of her mother with a prize I had won for winning the horseshoe pitching contest at a Fourth of July picnic. "You and your mother may have some use for these," I said. "They are a dozen sanitary napkins." I was shocked when her mother clutched at her heart and staggered. I thought the things were for picnics, of course. I was going on twenty-seven at the time.

We are going to Columbus May 2nd for a week but I will be up at the hospital to see you before we leave. I am bringing out a book in the fall containing drawings and stories: the New Natural History series, the Olden Time series, some animals I drew for *The Bermudian*, a series called "The Patient" printed by Night and Day in London after *The New Yorker* rejected them—this was before I became one of New York's leading patients—a dozen miscellaneous drawings, about twelve casuals, the series of five pieces on soap opera, a parody of Henry James, and perhaps a selection of my best Talk pieces to be called "Time Exposures."

The main problem now is a title. Since many of the stories are about animals like the one on the cricket and the one about Jeannie or else have animals in their titles, like "Here Come the Tigers" and "The Beast in the Dingle" we are trying to get a title for the book that will take in all the animals both in drawings and prose. Helen thought of "The Beast in Me" which Doris Schneider at my publisher likes. It would have a subtitle "A new collection of drawings and stories about all kinds of animals including the human being." Other titles I have put down are, Thurber's New Natural History, Of Man and Beast, It's Not a Fit Night, They Are Neither Beast nor Human (a line from Edgar Poe). When I got to This is My Bestiary and The Bestiary Years of My Life I began to fade. Maybe you and Andy would think these over or have an idea of your own.

Helen and I are both cheering for you and we're also cheered by the reports of your fine progress. It will be wonderful for you when you can say you are so tired you feel like sitting down instead of saying you're so tired you feel like standing up. My mother says everything is going to pick up after October 3rd but I am sure you will be happier than ever long before that.

Love and kisses from us both.

As ever,

Jim

*For a number of years* Reader's Digest *paid* The New Yorker *for the right to reprint from its contents. Eventually Ross saw the* Digest *as a newsstand competitor and refused it further reprint rights. Thurber, nonetheless, continued to sell reprint rights to his work to the* Digest.

## TO HAROLD ROSS

*West Cornwall, Conn.*
*August 11, 1948*

Dear Harold:

The problem of the *Digest* reprints depends a lot on the point of view. I think that the phrase "no permission will be given the *Digest*" should be "no permission will be given our authors to reprint in the *Digest.*" In short, any legal language on this point should state clearly what has actually been done.

A dozen years or so ago *The New Yorker* proudly proclaimed that, in fairness to its contributors, it would buy only first serial rights. The editors and the rest of us then discovered that, under the copyright laws, this procedure is impossible. A magazine has to copyright everything and then assign copyright to its authors. Thus, in spite of our noble stand we found that monopoly of rights fell into the hands of the magazine. Under your regime as long as it lasts you will be scrupulously fair but I tremble a little when I think of the future. I began to tremble a few years ago when we gave up the counsel of newspaper men like Ik Shuman and Bernard Bergman for experimentation, first with an engineer and then with a lawyer as chief editorial counsel. There is no lawyer in the whole world who would not be biased in favor of the rights of the corporation as against the rights of the contributor. This is an honest attitude since the corporation hires him and we do not.

Leaving the *Digest* aside, I was worried a little when you said on the phone, "That's right, baby," in reference to my inquiry as to whether the magazine could prevent the publication of books containing material from *The New Yorker*. At three dollars a copy, my new book is a hell of a lot cheaper than the copies of the magazine containing the stuff. You will dismiss this danger as non-existent, and it is under your leadership but I do believe that the fine type on the vouchers of which you and Truax are so proud should be re-written to protect us who no longer have any protection at all. It should contain some such sentence as this: "*The New Yorker* will at all times grant assignments of copyright to its authors on behalf of publication of their material in book form by any reputable publisher of the author's choice."

Quoting excerpts from old letters of authors is quoting matters of mood and moment and only infrequently statements of considered and final judgment. Men and circumstances change. I remember well the remarkable conference on the *Digest* problem attended by you and me, Sally Benson, Bob

Coates, Sid Perelman, and Ogden Nash. I forcefully opposed the use of the major part of the annual *Digest* money for any other purpose than the direct benefit of the authors. The *Digest* was paying for the right to use the creative work of the boys and girls, not for the right to reprint *The New Yorker* itself. Yet the big money was used, you said, for office supplies. In other words the corporation was profiting by money that should have been cut up at least to a larger extent among the reprinted authors. Although you claim now that the *Digest* didn't pay us enough, all you did with the big money was to double the *Digest* payment to us. If I got $100 for a reprint you added the same amount. But do I not find indignant feeling on your part that I should have got four or five times as much? Well, we had the *Digest* money with which you could have made up to us for the bad treatment we received.

Nobody on *The New Yorker* that I know of belongs to any organization whose purpose it is to defend his rights. We are precisely the boys and girls that believe we will be treated rightly by a paternalistic organization. I could cite you a thousand books in the past hundred years which were inspired by the inequities this kind of business setup leads to. None of us is a trade unionist or a communist or a trouble maker. We are exactly the kind of people who might be let down terribly in the future by a magazine which has departed from its original stand and is developing every month a stronger control over the rights of its authors.

Earlier statements of mine are naturally invalid in the face of these changes in control I am writing about and I am afraid of. I didn't see years ago that it would turn out this way. I wanted to allow *The New Yorker* every right it should have in itself, but nothing that jeopardized the rights of its authors and artists.

Yours for free enterprise as long as some of the freedom devolves on me.

> As ever,
> James Thurber

*Mr. Harold Ross, The New Yorker,*
*25 West 43rd Street, New Yorker, N. Y.*

## To Whit Burnett

*Burnett, editor of* Story *magazine, was publishing an anthology of the world's best short stories.*

*West Cornwall, Conn.*
*September 10, 1948*

Dear Mr. Burnett:

   It has been a year since I heard from you about that ambitious anthology and I assumed you had been crushed under its weight and difficulty. After I wrote you, several friends of mine went over your list of authors separately and pointed out a number of astonishing omissions. I can't remember them all but I clearly recall that between Sally Benson and Kay Boyle there was no Elizabeth Bowen, author of "The Death of the Heart," and of some excellent short stories. I hope that in the months that have gone by some of your more glaring omissions were rectified. I wouldn't feel happy in a collection that left out some of my favorites, and I doubt very much that I belong in this book, anyway. There is surely nothing I have done under 3,000 words that belongs even in the collection of Connecticut's best. Even if there were it would take months of searching and word counting. I would feel much more comfortable if you could manage to leave me out.

   Sincerely yours,
   James Thurber

*Mr. Whit Burnett, Story Magazine,*
*116 East 30th Street, New York 16, N. Y.*

## TO ELLIOTT NUGENT

*Thurber's play about* The New Yorker *occupied months of his time but was never finished.*

   *The young people of Cornwall, Connecticut, staged* The Male Animal.

*West Cornwall, Conn.*
*September 13, 1948*

Dear Elliott:

   . . . Before I forget it, the most fascinating mystery of our year is the unique scent of your stationery. It reeks of what has been variously described as creosote, iodoform, ether and ink eradicator. The first of your strangely scented paper arrived last winter and we thought that something had happened but after eight months of it we decided that you were up to some God damn something or other. Have you gone into the sheep dipping business, or what?

The kids put on the best performance of "The Male Animal" we have seen outside the Cort and they were wildly acclaimed at both shows. I saw the James Bells do it and several other companies but the Cornwall people gave it the charm and warmth the thing has to have. Rosie was a triumph as Cleota and was picked as one of the two best by an old gal who played with Sothern and Marlowe. The Joe Ferguson was only sixteen and his eighteen-year-old sister played Ellen with Mark van Doren's twenty-two-year-old son [Charles] as Tommy, but they managed the illusion of maturity. . . .

I realize that the [proposed] play might be called "Tommy Turner on a Magazine" in that the part of the editor-writer is a badgered intellectual up against a Congressman who is a magnified Ed Keller, and that the wife is the same kind of sympathetic woman as Ellen. There are dozens of differences, however, and Tim Norton is involved with two women instead of having his wife involved with two men.

The idea of the girl writing a thesis about Tim Norton is realistic. There is a young man from Columbia going through my scrapbooks at the office right now preparing just such a thesis. We have them around all the time. What I need is to kick this around with someone on behalf of the next move and especially what to hold over for the third act—you will remember our struggle until we hit on the idea of Ellen announcing that she was going to run away with Joe. I want to do even more justice to the Congressman than we did to Ed Keller, since he is a bigger and everpresent menace, but I have to contrive a balance of the shifting holds that the principals have on each other. This needs to be planted more definitely in Act I, since the stealing of a profile is not very much. The girl has dug up a great deal on Tim Norton, innocently, and it might have fallen into the hands of Chadwick. Tim is not me but a composite and he comes out more like Nugent on the *New Yorker* than anything else, but here are a few things about myself she could have found out: I joined the League of American Writers in 1938 without knowing it was a communist front and I never resigned but merely ignored their letters; I am an honorary vice chairman of the Progressive Citizens Committee in Connecticut; and my name appears on a letterhead with Paul Robeson. Helen and I were innocent contributors to the Anti-Fascist League which we thought was merely an anti-fascist league; but most amusing of all, "The Thurber Carnival" was praised in the *New Masses* as the work of a man who was boring from within and doing a lot to hold the middle class up to ridicule. . . .

. . . Once I get the thing plotted the writing is easy enough. I don't want it to get away from a picture of *The New Yorker* which I start out with. There are more ideas but I don't want to clutter you up. What I want is your own thoughts which brought Ed Keller, Wally Meyers, Patricia, Dean Damon and Michael into a play that originally concerned only three people.

Love to you and Norma and all other Nugents.

As ever,

Jim

## To Harold Ross

*Louis Forster was Ross' assistant. A reference in a Thurber piece to the current popular song, "The Java Jive," led Ross to believe it was being confused with a World War I-era song, "Jada, Jada."*

*With Thurber barely able to draw, Ross was running Thurber's formerly-published cartoons with new captions.*

West Cornwall, Conn.
October 28, 1948

Dear H. W.:

I have got about seven more captions which I will send directly to you, but I am vaguely worried about the process of selection and rejection. I feel that since these are drawings with captions they should be submitted to the art meeting just as if they were originals. I hold your own judgment inferior to no man's and your experience wider than any, but a one-person opinion is bound, by the nature of the human being, to be subject to that singularity which grows out of personal taste and private prejudice.

I do not hold a tremendous brief for the two you rejected, but I am interested in the grounds of the rejection. If you don't know that "taut" is a well-known cliche of dramatic criticism the line is lost through no fault of its own. Again, if you are personally opposed to the use of [Westbrook] Pegler's name, it might not be an antipathy shared by Lobrano or [Rea] Irvin. In the case of this "Guru" caption, I was attempting what almost nobody tries for *The New Yorker* except me, and that is captions dealing with the political scene. I have done fifteen or twenty that have been printed and it will interest you to know that "Do you remember, Crosby, when the only thing to fear was fear itself?" has attracted more attention than any drawing in many months. I got two letters from France mentioning it and it will be reprinted in the London *Times*, and *News Chronicle*.

I suggest that you make your own selections but that you get an outside opinion on those which you do not think are suitable.

Helen checks and double checks the new captions with the old drawings by number, and if the dragon picture was set against one of my captions recently it was the fault of someone down there. Her check-back shows that she got the drawings and captions right. Maybe you were thinking of the doctor with the rabbit's head and I agree with you that this one has a uniquity that defies permutations. As a matter of fact, we have found only about twenty-eight old drawings that lend themselves easily to new captions, but this might be brought up to thirty-five or more by the exercise of some remarkable ingenuity. I want to get up my own captions, since an old drawing of mine with somebody else's line would leave me completely out of the picture and could be just as easily done if I were dead. I don't mind your tinkering with captions as long as I have a chance to approve. The one you did fix you made much better.

As for people remembering the drawings, *The New Yorker* printed within a few years of each other drawings with the following captions: 1) "Well, who made the magic go out of our marriage, you or me?" 2) "The magic has gone out of my marriage, has the magic gone out of your marriage?" I was innocent of doing the same line over by intention, and nobody down there caught it. A caption is much more memorable than a drawing as a rule, especially a drawing that is a mere variant of a man and a woman and a lamp and a picture. The only vice we could be guilty of would be the accidental re-using of the same caption.

Several persons have suggested that modern scientists who have done wonders with lighting might contrive a drawing board, a table drawing board, with glass instead of wood to draw on. The proper suffision of light behind the glass and the right quality of paper might make it possible for me to draw with more ease than ever. I just don't know.

I don't know why I suggested back of the book for the new series, since everything I do is major, but it was perhaps because the first of these pieces is definitely one of the least. It won't make much difference what order they appear in, however, except possibly when they are brought together in a book later. I have a couple of great aunts at whose story I have monkeyed for years, and there are many others. Another factor in the self-derogation is unquestionably the present blockage I have had in writing a play. I will have written two million words of casuals by the time I am sixty-eight but they won't seem as important to me as something in three sets or fifteen chapters.

Love to you all.

As ever,

JT

<br>

     🐞   🐞   🐞

*November 24, 1948*

Dear Ross:

Helen, who is a natural born manager, with a unique sense of order, thinks she should have some report, from your end, on those last seven captions. (We were paid for one). She keeps her records up to date. We both insist that you buy the wonderful one that goes "Then what do you expect to do after I'm gone, may I ask—live by your wits?" I stuck the "then" in there and it may help out. I can't force myself to believe that Mr. Forster is the perfect jolly companion for you in passing judgment on my captions.

You better save your strength and don't question me about music. Jada Jada is no more like Java Java than chuffa chuffa is like hubba hubba. I am also an expert on cambric tea, amateur tennis, cipher codes, the game of Boules, the works of Henry James, sexual intercourse, and the libel laws in Ohio.

Happy happy Thanksgiving,

with love

Thurber

<br>

     🐞   🐞   🐞

*West Cornwall, Connecticut*
*November 29, 1948*

*H. W. Ross, The New Yorker*
*25 West 43rd Street, New York, N. Y.*

Dear Ross:

The News Chronicle's revelation of what is going on shows that people will recognize the old drawings, but this makes no difference. If we try to conceal it by avoiding some of the better known, but not the best known drawings, we would cramp our freedom pretty much. It might be better if the audience were frankly let in on the secret and they might even enjoy it more. For example, take the drawing with the caption "What do you want to be inscrutable *for,* Ida?" (You'd better look this up.) Everybody will remember the drawing but there is no reason why the man in it should not be puzzled by the lady for other reasons. I mean it could pop up once a year or every two years, beginning with "But what is *wrong* with compassion, Ida?" I haven't got the girl's name right because the drawing is not before me. I will send this idea along by way of Helen's carefully kept system.

I once said to a man named Ken England, when we were working on a movie, "There are a hundred ways to do everything." Here you are looking for a typewriter to fit a caption, when the caption should be fixed to fit a drawing without a typewriter. This isn't it, but "what's the matter, author, have you lost the old know how?" is the proper line of attack. In the only drawings I know of with typewriters, the man, not the machine, is being talked to and we would have to have something like "He has lost the old know how." This particular caption, however, is not worth too much struggle. I have got a few more but I am going to send in only two at a time after this. If there are six or eight, all good, the human mind cannot master its tendency to select the best, and reject the good. My experience in this matter occupies a chapter in my memoirs. Take it easy

As ever,

🖙 🖙 🖙

*West Cornwall, Connecticut*
*December 2, 1948*

*H. W. Ross, The New Yorker*
*25 West 43rd St., New York, N. Y.*

Dear Ross:

The explanations of those rejections were concise, adequate, and convincing. Any radio listener knows that the Luxing of stockings carries no connotation beyond a symbol of the daintiness of the housewife, but I surrender to the perhaps too sensitive nose of our beloved magazine.

I am keeping an open mind about the pasting up of parts of drawings into a new whole. I see clearly how this device of creating new drawings appeals to editors, but it well may be that you would be tampering with one of the basic principles of artistic integrity. Would you consider pasting new dresses on the woman in Ralph Barton's "The 1930's" and calling them "The 1940's?" If I could have a hand in the permutations myself, which I can't, it might be different. Perhaps both of us are too close to the idea to make a sound and fair judgment. . . .

I would agree with the majority opinion of the following three judges—White, Gibbs, and Mary Petty. I would also consider any choice of yours in place of Mary but I think there should be a female voice outside the office.

The value of running the old drawings just as they are might be lost in using montages. We should stick to one idea or the other. I have no doubt that original compositions would arise from tinkering around but you must realize that the new drawings would represent the comic sense of their arrangers and not of me. It is perhaps different if you merely stick to hunting for men at typewriters and other things to fit new captions of my own. People have made their own drawings out of combining my figures and almost always to my disenchantment.

Maybe the art meeting and I have opposite ideas about a suitable drawing for "Then what do you expect to do after I am gone, may I ask—live by your wits?" This is surely of a piece with "I take it, then, that you regard yourself as omniscient." I want an irate man and an utterly silly woman. Don't look for a vamp or a tough gal or one who looks as if she could live by her wits.

Didn't we have enormous issues just before October 24, 1929?

As ever,

❧   ❧   ❧

*West Cornwall, Connecticut*
*December 27, 1948*

*Mr. H. W. Ross, The New Yorker*
*25 West 43rd St., New York, N. Y.*

Dear Ross:

I keep taking a dimmer view of the project to cut up and rearrange the old drawings. Some future day this operation would hamper and confuse the historian who is bound to write the definitive study of the New Yorker artists under the title "Peter Arno and His Circle", in which I will be briefly discussed in Chapter 12, "Steinberg and The Others." . . .

I have been thinking about the idea of cutting up and rearranging old captions instead of old drawings. We could get effects like this: "All right, have it your way—everybody you look at seems to be a rabbit," and "That isn't my first wife up there—you heard a seal bark." This indicates that the wife on the bookcase is the man's present spouse, and this seems sounder since it is unlikely that a man would still be fond enough of his first wife to have her around the house entirely disrobed.

If you cut captions in two, dropped them in a hat, shook them up, and drew them out at random, you would avoid simple paraphrase. In one breath you tell me that we have used 18,000 captions and that we don't use paraphrases. It is almost impossible to put new lines under old drawings and make them entirely different from the mood of the characters in the original. Take my drawing of the irate husband saying to his wife at a party, "Will you kindly cease calling me Sweetie-pie in public?" I had thought of "Why do you insist on telling everybody we meet that my middle name is Wolfgang?" This is an effort to keep within the tone and character of the couple. You will see at once the awkwardness and incongruity of "Good God, woman, look out for that Packard! Do you want to get yourself killed?" Or "Get these seventeen coach dogs out of here and keep them out of here!"

I have just finished two stories besides "The Notebooks" and Helen is overwhelmed by Christmas work so she hasn't had time to make her careful entry of an old caption of mine she found in a notebook. It is a beauty and there should be a man saying it to a dumb-looking woman. The caption: "You complicated little mechanism, you!" It could fit a four year old drawing now captioned "Where did you get those big brown eyes and that tiny mind?" . . .

Since I am a writer I am not terribly interested in flogging old drawings or whipping up new captions. I also find that I am a little apathetic to the idea of beginning [drawing] again with the aid of General Electric. Under the best circumstances it would still be a strain that Dr. Bruce would not heartily approve.

Maybe we can get out a collection of our letters on this subject.

Happy New Year!

> As ever,
>
> James Thurber

## To Rosemary Thurber

*October 5, 1948*

Dear Rosabelle:

I hope the boxes arrived safely and not squashed, since one of them would be hard to put back together again. I hope this letter arrives on October 7th. It is sent with the happy birthday wishes of Helen and me and the rest of the household including your dog. I can remember when your greatest ambition was to be seventeen, and you've now made it. Nice going.

The poodle cut her right paw while exploring in Litchfield the other day but it is pretty nearly healed up now. She used the old tongue treatment which is more successful than anything Dr. Walker could do. It didn't seem to hurt her because she never squeaked or acted panicky but she did put on a tremendous act showing that she's as great a hambone as the rest of the Thurbers. She could trot along pretty well when she was alone but as soon as she knew she had an audience she put on the biggest limping act in poodle history. You would have thought she had been shot at the Battle of the Bulge or something.

We had her clipped about ten days ago but now that her paw is healing she has developed fleas or mice or something. She bites herself from stem to stern, possibly just to have something more to attract attention. That's what you get for putting her in "The Cherry Orchard"—or maybe it was taking her to rehearsals that did it.

I was going to get a gun to have in the house just in case anybody descended on us out of the radio mysteries or a Bogart picture but Helen has found an ad for a louder and safer device. It's a gadget with a clockwork mechanism that you keep on your bedside table. If you hear anybody at the door after you've gone to bed you just wind it up and let it rip. A siren as loud as the ones they used in London during the war whines for seven minutes, repelling the invaders and waking everybody from Virginia Smith's house to Cream Hill. It costs $12.50 and might be a wonderful thing to try out on your roommate or one of your teachers. . . .

How is the magazine going and what play are you going to do first?

Happy birthday again from all of us. Did you get the book? I sent one to Althea and Allen the other day. It has had several good reviews so far. Don't tease the animals.

Love and kisses from us all.
Daddy

## TO THE RONALD WILLIAMSES

*The Thurbers visited the Williamses at Janey's family home at Long Point, Penn Yan, New York, where Thurber had misbehaved. In Bermuda he had once disembarked from Williams' canoe to wade ashore and embrace a cow. Williams has asked him to help with a* Bermudian *article on the writing of "Anthony Adverse" by Hervey Allen.*

West Cornwall, Conn.
October 30, 1948

Dear Ronnie and Janey:

    . . . We are still wondering why that man [Thurber] got out of the car that night. Helen says it was because he thought Ronnie was driving too fast, but I don't think so. He is a stranger to me, especially when he's drinking, and I understand that he once jumped out of a canoe in Bermuda because Ronnie was paddling too fast. At his age he wants comfort and not speed. Of course, there may have been a cow in the meadow that night. . . .

    Did you ever find out who pulled the mattress off the bed and overturned the chair? If there had been a loaf of bread involved I could put my hand on the culprit.

    I phoned *The New Yorker* this morning to see what they might have down there about Hervey and was delighted to hear that one of our best reporters, Charles Cooke, did a Talk piece about him about 1934 or '35. They are going to send the clipping to me, as well as Cooke's original notes which may contain a lot of stuff Ronnie can use. I think he called on Hervey and other people and the story is about what happened to the manuscript of "Anthony Adverse." I will ship the stuff off to you the moment it arrives but you must be very careful with the Cooke notes because they are the only copy and the magazine wants them back. I still think you should write to Joe [Sayre] for possible anecdotes and other dope. I think you should also mention that Ferdinand the Bull was written in Felicity Hall, since items like this serve to brighten the piece.

    After thinking it over a lot, I can see why Hervey is a little put out by the story of the visitors to Felicity Hall, since it takes the edge off what is really a nice and dignified idea, a pilgrimage to the shrine of a great man. I think you might say that various large offers were made for the sewing chair and the harp gate and mention that Hervey insisted when he left that nothing be disposed of.

    I'm just going to bat this off, but maybe that section should go something like this—if you still insist on using my name.

    "There was never a guest in Felicity Hall, after the Allens left, who was not deeply impressed by the literary history of the old house. The prodigious labors of Hervey Allen over the years left about the place an intangible sense of monumental achievement, and the sensitive visitor could actually feel the ancient hall gradually becoming part of the legend of 'Anthony Adverse.' Not the least impressed was James Thurber, who with his wife spent two weeks as a guest at Felicity. He was pleased that Mr. Allen had done his writing on a simple, rough kitchen table against a wall in the slave quarters, where the light came from an open door on the left and it was with fingers trembling even more than usual that he set about one day what he calls 'plying my tiny trade' with pencil and paper at this very table. During the war he donated a number of his original manuscripts to various war bond drives and across the top of one piece he proudly wrote, 'written on Hervey Allen's table at Felicity Hall.'

"The table represented to Mr. Thurber, he says, Mr. Allen's utter lack of pretentions and of desire for publicity. The author of 'Anthony' never went in for the ostentatious quill pen or the gold typewriter or any of the other marks and flourishes of the booksy man, and if he could have arranged it by the passing of a wand in the air the sewing chair and the harp gate would have remained forever the work of an anonymous craftsman. But in spite of the humility of its famous former resident, Felicity Hall became a shrine and the end of the road for many a literary pilgrim who came to Bermuda from all the continents. During Mr. Thurber's sojourn in the house, he patiently and eagerly showed a hundred visitors around the place, if they turned out to be, in his estimation, serious admirers of Mr. Allen and his book. One afternoon, however, *The New Yorker* author was having some difficulty shaping a sentence to his satisfaction on the old kitchen table. He was suddenly aware of the presence of strange women—Mr. Thurber claims that while he is not always aware of the presence of men he never fails to sense the presence of women. He looked up to behold two aggressive middle-aged ladies from the States, whose accents, when they spoke, betrayed them as Middle Westerners like the writer himself. 'Is this the place where that book was written?' demanded one of the women. Mr. Thurber realized that they were mere sightseers and not genuine devotees of the master. 'What book?' he asked coldly. The woman turned to her companion. 'What did the man say the name of that book was, Clara?' she said. For answer, Clara directed a question to Mr. Thurber. 'Don't you know what the book was?' she asked. At this, Myrtle, for it was she, suddenly cried, 'I got it! "Anthony Allen."' Mr. Thurber sniffed. 'Oh, that,' he said contemptuously. 'You mean the novel by Hervey Adverse. That was nothing.' 'How can you say that?' squealed Myrtle. 'The man said it took five years to write.' The tall, thin author gave this a moment of frowning thought. 'That's because he started from the beginning,' he said. 'I am writing "Anthony Allen" backwards and I expect to finish it in two weeks.' The two women backed slowly away from the open door and then abruptly turned and began to run.

"On another occasion, after Mr. Thurber had shown a Columbia professor and his wife through the house and about the grounds he was relaxing in a chair on the front lawn when a man's voice behind him made him jump. The man had a camera and he said, 'Do you mind if I take a picture of this house? But first, do you mind telling me what it is famous for?' 'This,' said Mr. Thurber solemnly, 'was the ancestral home of Carveth Wells.' The man stared blankly for a moment, and then lowered his camera. 'Thanks,' he said and turned away. 'Not at all,' said Mr. Thurber, 'not at all.' And he sat down again and resumed his reading of 'Anthony Adverse.' "

This way, the story could not offend Hervey, it draws a better picture of me, and there is more point to it. A little faking is an excellent thing.

Helen and I send all of you our love and kisses and our thanks for one of the wonderful times of our lives,

As always,

*Mr. Ronald J. Williams, Long Point,*
*Penn Yan, New York*

## To Dr. Saul Rosenzweig

*In the book* James Thurber: His Life and Times, *the "young man at Columbia," Harrison Kinney, offers his version of Thurber's Freudian discussions. Far from "batting off a kind of indignant reply," Thurber met with Kinney several times for cordial and extended discussions of Freud and other subjects.*

*West Cornwall, Conn.*
*October 30, 1948*

Dear Saul:

I have finished both the items you sent me and will take them up in order. The piece about "A Streetcar Named Desire" and "The Heiress" fascinated me as do all your explorations of the human being in conflict or extremity. It will surely be an article to include permanently in a collection of your things between covers. I am sorry that I can't go all the way with you about the fantasy of the violin. This is one of the toughest of all things to do and I don't think you have brought it off successfully. I know *The New Yorker* would feel the same, and it just happens that Ross and the others are allergic to the animation of the inanimate just as they are to the personification of the animal. I suspect that you hurried this piece a little too much and I can [cite] the damaging evidence of your use of "like" in a way that would disturb Ross and the other purists. Old Joe Conrad liked to use like in this unconventional manner and if he had lived he might have won for it the dignity of common usage. My own experience about stories as difficult as "The Violin" is that a writer has a tendency to hide behind the fabricated belief that he has somehow managed to bring off the job in his very first draft, as by a miracle. When he reads the thing over a few weeks later he is likely to realize that it ought to be run through the wringer at least another time, and then he discovers that it is going to take many rewritings and probably more time than the subject is worth. Ever since Steve Benet began to do variations on the theme of the machine becoming sentient editors have had to deal with a great many stories of talking and walking objects. This type of tale actually put the story of the talking dog and the story of the talking horse in second place.

A young man at Columbia who is doing a thesis about my work turns out to have Professor William York Tyndall as his faculty adviser up there. Hence, the boy has approached my work almost purely from the Freudian viewpoint. He wanted to know, in a letter, if "The Man on the Train" were not an unconscious use of the symbol of the train, and whether I actually had anything to do myself with the drawing of the house turning into a woman. I batted off a kind of indignant reply which I should have rewritten five or six times until I got it right. I have deliberately stayed away from too deep a study of Freud or any of the other boys because hyperconsciousness of the debatable mechanics of the human spirit, whatever that may be, is likely to deprive the writer of such free thought as he would otherwise be capable of and turn him into an apostle rather than an individual creator. I wonder if anyone has suggested that the now famous symbols of the tower and the pond in "The Turn of the Screw" might have been deliberately chosen from the library of symbols that any writer who has studied literature has on his shelves. The male may have originally been identified with the tower like Childe Harold because of the importunate demands of the undermind, but who is to say that later writers did not deliberately select the symbol as the most appropriate among the few shapes the world has to present. I am willing to admit that a man is likely to be called "an old stick" and a woman "an old bag" for the reasons that delight and impress my Columbia student, but try to make a list of the things that neither stand up nor are depressed below that flat level of a geometrical plane. You can't have hills or valleys, trees or poles, mountains or hills, lakes or caves. All you can have is the prairie and the plateau. Regard the starry vault above. Is it not God's great pessary? My best regards to you and Mrs. Rosenzweig.

> Cordially,
>
> J. T.

*Dr. Saul Rosenzweig, Department of Welfare,*
*Western State Psychiatric, Institute and Clinic,*
*O'Hara & DeSoto Sta., Pittsburgh, Pa.*


## To William Shawn

*November 8, 1948*

Dear Bill:

A couple of Talk suggestions:

. . . I went over to Stoeger's Gun Store at 507 5th Avenue this morning with Pete De Vries because I wanted to buy a gun for my house in the country. There is unquestionably a good Talk piece here. The war seems to have knocked the fire arms business into some confusion. You don't seem to be able to get a Colt on the ground that ammunition is hard to find. This famous gun store has no automatic that is not second-hand. Some fifteen years ago I saw a Remington derringer there. This gun, because of the ammunition situation and probably because of discontinuance of many models other than war guns, has now become a museum piece. The man at Stoeger's told me that I might find the derringer at Robert Abels (antiques), 860 Lexington Avenue. Obviously this man Abels would make a good additional source for a Visit piece. . . .

For many years I wanted to take a swing at a "That was Brooklyn" item on a woman named Mollie Fancher. I don't know where the dope could be dug up but I heard a story teller on the radio give the basic facts about five years ago. Mollie, a pretty girl of sixteen during the Civil War, caught her crinoline dress on the rear end of a Brooklyn trolley car and was dragged three blocks. She was unconscious for twenty five years and the story from that point on is really fascinating. She became known to kings and presidents and was one of the medical wonders of her day because of a strange compensation of sight and hearing. Somebody might take a look to see if any substantial data exists.

As ever,

Jim

## TO JANE COOKSON

*West Cornwall, Connecticut*
*November 23, 1948*

*Miss Jane Cookson, 4 Charlesgate East,*
*Boston 15, Mass.*

Dear Miss Cookson:

. . . I wrote Walter Mitty in the fall of 1938 when I was living in Woodbury. I got the idea while sitting in the lobby of the Hotel Elton. It was re-written half a dozen times and took eight weeks to finish. It is more or less the extension of another story called "Mr. Pendley and the Poindexter." This dealt with a man who imagined that he was a great automobile mechanic and the chance to bring in other dreams in a more complete story occurred to me. I have done this several times before, since my book "The Last Flower" grew out of an earlier single drawing with the same title, and the fable called "The Unicorn in the Garden" had a plot that was later expanded into a short story called "The Catbird Seat." "Walter Mitty" has appeared in a dozen anthologies, the Reader's Digest, and in a dozen different languages. The Digest thought the idea was universal enough for translation into all their foreign editions. It is now being translated into Indonesian.

The male daydreamer is common to all parts of America and has often been the subject of stories. The condensation in the Digest introduced it to the American army during the war and the air corps especially adopted Walter as a mascot. Soldiers write me about it from all parts of the world and flyers used to exchange the "tapocketa" while returning from missions.

Many persons regard Walter as their own jealous property and I receive many letters abusing me for selling the story to the movies. A writer always hopes that the movies will do him justice as they did in the case of Hemingway's "The Killers."

The rest of your piece should be your own judgment and conclusions. I hope the above facts will be of some help. If you have further questions let me know.

Sincerely yours,<br>James Thurber

## To Neda Westlake

West Cornwall, Connecticut<br>January 11, 1949

*Mrs. Neda Westlake, 136 E. Herman Street,*
*Philadelphia 44, Pa.*

Dear Mrs. Westlake:

The only time I met Wolfe was in 1935 when he came to a party at my apartment in New York at 6 p.m. and stayed until 7 a.m. Many writers do this and I myself have no superiors in long lingering. I remember him as having been both amusing and witty during the cocktail hour. Later, in common with other writers, he became sad and talked about the reception of his first novel in his home state, always a point of grief with him. About 4 a.m., everybody else having left, except our house guest, who was ill, Wolfe told my wife and me that we didn't know what it was to be a writer. "My husband is a writer," said Mrs. Thurber. "I didn't know that," said Wolfe, "all I see of his is in the New Yorker." He thought of writers only as men who wrote novels. At seven o'clock I suggested he ought to get some sleep. He asked my wife who owned the apartment and she said the Rhinelander estate, and he turned to me and said, "This isn't even your house." Meanwhile he had eaten everything in the refrigerator, and it was an appetite wonderful to watch in action. He left a little after seven, but phoned two hours later to say that he wanted to come back and apologize for having kept us up. I told him he had been perfectly fine and not to bother. I don't think he was as bad that night as many writers I know, but he was probably more egocentric than most authors, since after midnight it was impossible for him to talk or think about anybody but himself. Our house guest had to have a doctor about 5 a.m. and she looked like death. "Touch me," said Wolfe to her. "I'm lucky and it will make you well." The doctor, however, thought she would be better off at the hospital.

The classic story about his late staying involves a cocktail party at the home of Dorothy Parker in Hollywood earlier in 1935. Mrs. Parker finally got everybody out at 5 a.m. and at the door she said to the last stragglers, who included Wolfe, "I want you all to come back at eight o'clock." Three hours later there was a knock on the door. It was, of course, Wolfe.

I don't know that any of this represents a facet of his work, but it may interest your professor. Scott Fitzgerald once wrote about Wolfe, "His secret leaks at every scene. He had practically nothing to say," but I heard him say about 170,000 words that night and much of it was interesting and some of it was humorous. He could tell a story on himself, well and frankly, and his egotism did not obscure his comic sense of himself.

You can quote me, if you want to, since this is known to one and all and has in part been published.

Sincerely yours,
James Thurber

## To Harold Ross

*West Cornwall, Connecticut*
*January 17, 1949*

*H. W. Ross, The New Yorker*
*25 West 43rd Street, New York, N. Y.*

Dear Ross:

Since March 4, 1947 *The New Yorker* has bought twenty-two stories of mine, counting the Soap Opera pieces, which were the hardest. Of these, seventeen have been printed and five are on the bank. I don't believe anybody has tied this record. In addition, you looked at and rejected the Henry James parody which was later published in *Horizon* in England. I also sold a piece to the *Cosmopolitan* and one to *Holiday*. Thus, out of twenty-five pieces, you have seen twenty-three and bought twenty-two. . . .

A magazine that has bought twenty-two pieces in as many months does not seem fair or generous when it objects to two or more sold outside. I strongly favor a new form of contract, specifying that I may if I wish sell two out of every ten pieces anywhere without submission to you. I will always prefer and insist on selling you the eighty percent.

The *Holiday* price was not by any means the only factor in that sale. That magazine could not have bought for any money the other stories. However, a piece of money like that occasionally is necessary in the case of a man who has been a free lancer for fourteen years. White and Gibbs are both on salary, and so is almost everybody else. The successful free lancer, and there are few of us, must be allowed reasonable freedom and not be bound by the same contract that applies to the salaried man. I have written more pieces for you than White and Gibbs put together, and let me be the first to say that I am intensely opposed to the idea of any universal contract that applies to me. I drive a tougher bargain with publishers than any of the other boys or girls. I even get one hundred percent of all reprint rights and sole control of them. I surrender no part of any subsidiary rights. After fourteen years I have taken to making my own contracts. I am in a position to do this. I cannot be swayed by problems of bookkeeping, any universal contract, or a feeling about the inalienable equality of all *New Yorker* writers. When they catch up with me in volume, I might possibly consider this point. I am for the individual and his rights against any corporation. I cannot believe that the threat of a withdrawal of twenty-five percent should ever be used against me.

Incidentally, I think it should be specifically stated in the new Thurber contract that in the event that more than six pieces are submitted in any one year, the extra ones should be applied to the following year. Thus two more pieces would entitle me to a bonus through 1950. This may be the arrangement now. A free lance writer may do twelve in one year and none the next year.

I am willing to keep any contract secret from the youngsters and the slaves. The best of the Photograph Album pieces, "Daguerrotype of a Lady", will be in before I sail for Nassau February 5. There will be at least seven others this year. . . .

> Love and kisses,
> As ever,
> Jim

## To Robert Sherwood

*Sherwood wrote Ross a letter praising Thurber's story "File and Forget."*

*January 24, 1949*

Dear Robert Sherwood:

I was delighted when Harold Ross sent your letter to me, and you will be glad to know that it was delivered to me at the right address. I happened to be staying at the Algonquin on that day. Ross had the letter delivered by hand to be sure that it would not be misdirected and thus become another part of the Great American Confusion which your own experience so beautifully annotates.

Ross and I and the other boys and girls were shocked, but not surprised, to discover that Walter Winchell is the final source, the top of the mountain, when anybody wants to find out how to reach you or, I have no doubt, the President of the United States. Ross and I thought that the New Rochelle Affair would make a lovely Talk of the Town item, but we were constrained about asking your permission in view of the fact that the publication of this remarkable episode would surely influence the Russians in the belief that the United States does not know where anybody is, or how to find him, but has entirely lost track of all Americans since the day they became a year old. . . .

It so happens that I have just signed a contract with Simon and Schuster, in the faint and forlorn hope that this organization might have some vague idea as to what I do and where I might be located. This new relationship got off to a perfect start on the day my piece appeared when I received from Cornwall, Connecticut a letter from S. and S. directed as follows:

> Mr. James Thurber
> Cornwall (Saulisbury) Conn.

Since I could not allow myself to get off to such a start I phoned the firm and was told that their files contained both towns—one of them misspelled—and so they sent the letter the way they did. I had lived only three months in Saulisbury back in the winter of 1940. I told them that the only man I could think of, in an afternoon of thinking, who might properly have been addressed in care of two cities was the late General William T. Sherman whose addresses at one time were Atlanta (Savannah), Georgia.

Thanks again for your letter, and with the deepest appreciation of your existence and residence in this country, wherever it may be.

> Cordially yours,
> James Thurber

## TO ROSEMARY THURBER

*Jim and Anna were the Thurbers' servants. Rosie is trying to settle on a college to attend.*

*West Cornwall, Connecticut*
*January 29, 1949*

Dear Pussabelle:

Jim and Anna pounced on us when we got home and tried to wrench the old Ford away from us so you could crack up in it when it finally goes to pieces at a crossroads. In addition to my reluctance to jeopardize my daughter's life in this eleven year old crate, I have promised my brother and mother that they can have it. This is what is known as "asking for it", but the two of them have lived all told one hundred and thirty-six years, and furthermore they will be safer in the Ford than in their 1931 Studebaker.

Most universities and colleges don't let students have cars and this is a good idea. Have you applied to Michigan yet, or do you need the ten dollars? You must handle this immediately.

Helen and I thought your piece about the Saki story was excellent and a definite proof that you could be a writer if you kept at it. Most women writers are inclined to give up too easily, although more women than men have sold their very first pieces to The New Yorker. I suggest one change in what you wrote. You should not say that people are cruel and ghastly, but only that they can be cruel and ghastly. . . .

Helen and I are sailing on the Mauretania February 5 and driving to New York February 4. Our address will be the British Colonial Hotel, Nassau, The Bahamas, and letters should be sent air mail. We are sailing back March 4, reaching New York March 6, to buy a Cadillac.

Love and kisses from Helen and me, and Jim and Anna, and the poodle.

Daddy

P.S. Somebody got away with several dozen maraschino cherries. The police are baffled.

## To Gus Lobrano

*West Cornwall, Connecticut*
*February 7, 1949*

*Mr. Gus Lobrano, THE NEW YORKER*
*25 West 43rd St., New York, N. Y.*

Dear Gus:

In connection with Daguerrotype of a Lady, herewith some notes for Ross and the checkers.

The use of "old" and "old-fashioned" is deliberately repetitive and it will do no good to call it to my mind.

I am not sure that Dr. Hartman's house was built in 1905, but it was about that time. I have taken many liberties with time in Columbus stories and in one of them I built the Maramor Restaurant five years ahead of its day. Only one person wrote me about it.

The fact about the filling station is correct, or was ten years ago, and if there is a bakery there now, I don't want to hear about it. The same is true of the cobblestones, which were stone paving blocks, cobbles enough for me.

I don't want anything checked with Mr. Blakely, my country pharmacist, because checkers would scare him and I have had several careful talks with him and he knows, and so does the store, that it is for publication.

All the pharmaceutical facts have been checked and rechecked with Blakely and with several doctors. The uses I put down were Mrs. Albright's and are not subject to modernization or quibble. I have used a Daguerrotype style of long sentences deliberately and in the phrase "it was coming summer" I quote her directly as of late May that year. I brought up all these facts out of a period of more than forty years ago, which convicts me of total recall, superior to the sources of the checkers.

Ross will wonder about my utter intimacy with the old house, but to explain this would take a novel. I was farmed out with Mrs. Albright from the age of eight to the age of fourteen, and one reason I have taken so long to get around to this, my favorite story, is that the ancient relationship was at times a sore point with my own mother. It is an odd thing that in this same old frame house my father was raised by Mrs. Albright from the time he was six until he was fourteen. Across the street lived a family named Fisher, whose small daughter became my mother. When I was finally taken to live at my grandfather's fine new house, I could not give up my intense devotion to the frame house on the Alley, and when, at fourteen, I was taken with a high fever, I staggered from my comfortable bed and went back home, collapsing on the very stoop I have mentioned. I was in bed three weeks and nearly died. You will see how deep this all goes, and I hope it is reflected in the story about the greatest individual I have ever known. It was a long way from there to The New Yorker.

As ever,

Jim

## To Jap Gude

*The British Colonial Hotel,*
*Nassau-Bahamas*
*3rd of March, 1949*

*Mr. J. G. Gude, 30 Rockefeller Plaza*
*New York 20, N. Y.*

Dear Jap:

. . . . We have had wonderful weather and a wonderful time here, including a drinking and dinner party at the [J. P.] Marquands along with John Dos Passos, a luncheon on an island here with old James Gerard aged 81 who was our Ambassador to Germany up to the First World War and who is quite a student of Walter Mitty; an afternoon on Treasure Island which is owned by John T. McCutcheon, the old Chicago Tribune cartoonist, and we are having luncheon today with Mr. and Mrs. Norman Armour, also a former ambassador whom we met on the ship going to France twelve years ago and liked immensely. There have been other parties and people including Fritz Dashiell and his wife with whom we have become friends despite a sharp letter from me to him about the soap opera stories which I had planned to sneak into the Reader's Digest. With all this we have managed to get rest and sunshine—it is always bright and in the middle 70's—and I have finished two acts of a play and all but one paragraph of a New Yorker story, about a woman writer of esoteric novels, full of unmeaning and unmethod. At the end after her death, the butler says to me "I was to have been the uncharacter of a nonbutler in one of her books." "Didn't you appear in any of them" I asked "Oh, but, no sir" he corrected me proudly, "I did not appear in *all* of them". This is less than I have not been able to do. Don't miss it, if you can.

Love to you and Helen and the children.

> As ever,
>
> Jim

## To Ann Honeycutt

*West Cornwall, Connecticut*
*March 24, 1949*

*Miss Ann Honeycutt, 22 East 56th Street*
*New York, N. Y.*

Dear Honey:

. . . I am glad to see you showing, for once in your life, about as much business sense as I always show. Jap Gude has been my radio agent for ten years, and you know it, and trying to get to me over his head is like going up to the room without first consulting the madam. He is already handling twelve stories of mine for television and a project about a series for radio. I would never write a radio script for anybody, because I don't know how, and, as Henry James would say, I wonderfully do not want to. I am doing a play and a book. You do not send me Mr. Sherry's address and so you are going to have to communicate with him for me.

We got a lot of sun and liquor in Nassau, and met a lot of nice people who served good drinks. At the Marquands' I heard two different groups of people discussing you. They included Dos Passos, Sarah Murphy, and my wife. I could tell that Helen was beginning to feel her rum when I heard her assuring somebody that you are the only old girl of mine for whom she gives a good Goddamn. This praise of her most dangerous rival is either neurotic or a darned nasty trick. The Marquands asked us for six, but we didn't eat until nine, after at least seventeen cocktails. I remember giving an owlish analysis of American novelists, complete with fuzzy and mythical quotations from their work. The most fun was a luncheon on an island nearby with three former American ambassadors, for whom I recited a long sentence in green code. At the end James Gerard, aged eighty-one, said, "Golux." This was a green code word meaning "Period." Mrs. Norman Armour, the wife of one of the diplomats, is a Russian lady whom you would love and who kept saying to me.

"Don't fuss"—Helen was down in bed and couldn't come that day, and she had to look after me. I was more troublesome than Argentina. . . .

I think Henry Morgan should have Stang recite other poems, especially "Oh Don't you Remember Sweet Alice, Ben Bolt?" The guy is talking to Ben Bolt, but Arnold thinks her name is Alice Ben Bolt, which everybody does. It ends up with something like "She laughed with delight when you gave her a smile, and trembled in fear at your frown." As Stang would say, "What is it with this dame, anyway?—You can't smile or frown without she goes nuts or something." I give you this free of charge.

I join Helen in eternal love for you.

As always,

## To Harold Ross

*The Laughing Lion Society, whose members were former editors of the* Jester, *Columbia University's humor magazine, held a banquet at "21" at which their 1949 Award for Humor was presented to Thurber, Fred Allen, Frank Sullivan, and Ross. Ross agreed to go only if Allen were there, whose radio scripts Ross thought might work out as* New Yorker *material. Allen kept changing his mind and Ross consulted Thurber on the matter.*

*West Cornwall, Connecticut*
*March 25, 1949*

*Mr. H. W. Ross, The New Yorker*
*25 West 43rd Street, New York, N. Y.*

Dear Ross:

I was going to write Fred Allen and ask him to get out from behind that indecision, and let us know if a couple of amateurs like us are going to have, or have not, his support that night. Young Deutsch, as he likes to be called, told me that they might ask Henry Morgan to accept for Allen, but I am sure that Morgan would regard this as similar to Joe Williams accepting for Joe DiMaggio.

Morgan is not a humorist, because he hates people. He hates his sponsors, his audience, and his friends. He wishes everybody were dead, but not in heaven with the angels. I don't think he has mellowed at all. I think he is clucking to the turkey, while he holds an axe behind his back.

The trouble with these youngsters like Morgan and the late Jack Parr is that the lint of the high school magazine sticks to the blue serge of their talent. I used to do things for the East High X-Rays like the following:

. . . Question: My mother-in-law walks in her sleep and comes within six inches of falling off a cliff behind our house. What should I do?

Answer: Move the house six inches nearer the cliff.

This is not really superior to the pranks of the unconscious mind. I once dreamed that a man said to me, "It's as important as the 'r' in shirt". But my brother Robert beat this with, "Many are cold, but few are frozen." Morgan is too near to the snowball and the spitball. Anyway, he didn't give a dime to the Benchley memorial, although I wrote him a charming and irresistible appeal.

I don't want Allen to leave the air without doing the story of Stanley and Livingstone with Orson Welles, the way they did "Les Miserables." Allen plays the lost Livingstone, and as the story opens, everybody is talking about him. Orson, playing Stanley, says, "You see, it's your show," to which Allen replies, "But I'm not even in it yet." And Orson says, "That's because you're lost."

We now see Stanley on his errand of mercy discovering Stanley Falls, Stanley River, Stanley Mountain, and coming upon a herd of strange animals never seen before by white men. "What are those creatures?" his gunbearer asks. "Those," says Welles, "are stanleys."

Now the big pay-off is, of course, the famous meeting of the doctor and the explorer. Welles says the immortal line. "Dr. Livingstone, I presume," and the orchestra bursts into a bright finale of martial music over which Allen has to shout to get attention. "You don't even let me answer," he says. "You don't even let me say that I *am* Dr. Livingstone." Welles says, "We can't distort history, Fred. History records no answer."

This is just a brief outline, but I've dreamed about it for years, and you can send this letter on to Allen. If I addressed him in care of N.B.C. he wouldn't get it for forty days.

Are we going to dress that night, or is it just cocktails? I have a beautiful new dinner jacket, complete, for once in my life, with trousers.

My deepest respects to both you and Mr. Allen.

> As ever,
>
> James Thurber

## TO ANN HONEYCUTT

*West Cornwall, Connecticut*

*April 2, 1949*

*Miss Ann Honeycutt, 22 East 66th Street*
*New York, N. Y.*

Dear Honey:

The other day I wrote a note to Ross which he sent on to Fred Allen, at my request, and in it I did a certain injustice to Henry Morgan. I am writing this note for you to send on to Morgan. In writing to anybody else one simply writes in care of his address, but you have to write radio personalities in care of their friends. Ross tells me that it was extremely hard for him to find out where Allen lives, since his whereabouts are "as devious as Benchley's."

I had been out of fix with Morgan for two reasons: 1) he had said on the air that the thing to do about a ringing in the ears is to answer it, and 2) he had not sent a contribution to the Benchley memorial fund. It now transpires that he did send a generous contribution, after waiting ten weeks for the purpose of drawing me into libel, and I therefore owe him an apology—about the contribution and not about the ringing in the ears.

I had also accused Morgan of not liking people, and then I heard his loving and lovely imitation of a British blow-by-blow prize fight announcer. It served to bring England and the United States closer together, with no holds barred in the infighting.

Some months ago the student and alumni editors of the Columbia Jester decided to give awards to Allen, Ross and me for our distinguished contributions to merriment. Ross, to everybody's amazement, agreed to accept, in person, at the austere ceremonies which will take place at 21. This is the first time that Ross has consented to receive an award in public since the basketball letters were handed out at Aspen High School in 1904. I readily agreed to be present, since I have already received one award, a bronze medal for drawing a double page ad for the Ladies' Home Journal in 1938. Lowell Thomas gave it to me at Rockefeller Plaza on behalf of the American Advertisers' Association. It says only "For distinguished achievement" and I used to show it to the girls, with an owlish wink, and a simple confession "the fellas gave it to me."

My acceptance of the forthcoming honor has been overshadowed by two factors: 1) the miracle of Ross's acquiescence which has the whole city buzzing with comment and speculation, and 2) Allen's somewhat florid modesty, expressed in a variety of doubts and uncertainties. First he won't come, then he can't, then he doesn't think he will, then he is pretty sure he won't. Thus the play has been taken away from me by 1) Ross's astonishing decision to appear and 2) Fred Allen's reluctance to say, for sure, whether he will be there or not. My presence, as a result, is taken as much for granted as the presence of a head waiter.

In the midst of all this, the Columbia students decided to give Allen's medal, or Oscar, to Henry Morgan, in the event that Allen does not show, but there is some doubt as to whether Morgan will be allowed to keep the award for himself or will merely accept it on behalf of Allen. Morgan is a shy fellow and there is now a stubborn rumor circulating that he will ask Jack Parr to accept in his place. Ross has said that if this happens he will send Shawn to accept for him, and thus I may be the only one who accepts in person for himself. This is obviously selfish and I am toying with the idea of sending someone in my place.

I thought you might have some suggestion as to the proper procedure in the event that the Columbia students, because of examinations, are unable to make it themselves. I have the awful feeling that this may not only be the first, but the last award for merriment, in view of the tangled situation. If there is prolonged drinking before the ceremonies, I may accept for Arnold Stang. Would this be all right with Morgan?

Sincerely yours,<br>James Thurber

ક ક ક

West Cornwall, Connecticut<br>April 6, 1949

*Miss Ann Honeycutt, 22 East 66th Street*
*New York, N. Y.*

Dear Nettie:

Henry Morgan has as much right to dislike people as anyone, and I agree with you that his talent, when it becomes demure, loses a certain wham. All I said was that he lacked compassion; that is, it is implicit in what he says that he hopes people do not go to heaven when they die. This lends a note of desperation to his humor and one has the uneasy sense that he proposes to jump off the train when it slows down for a curve. I am really not equipped to criticize Henry Morgan because I have heard his program only three times in the last year. Somebody tells me that he and Allen are now on the Doc Rockwell program and this has cheered me up. My informant tells me that Morgan refused to get mad when Doc Rockwell charged, over most of these stations, that Henry Morgan's father was a phoney eye doctor who made lenses out of mica before he found out that ordinary glass was cheaper. I am naturally somewhat envious of Henry Morgan since I gave away a million dollars worth of bitterness, insult, and savagery, often to my girl friends, before I found out I could sell it.

I have a special reason to maintain cordial relations with you because your attorneys might erroneously suspect that a character in a story I am writing for the Cosmopolitan is, in fact, you. "She was born with a gift of laughter, in magnolia country. I met her at the corner of Bleecker and West Eleventh the year everybody was singing 'Ramona.'" It goes on to tell how this lady blacked me up and dressed me in women's clothes, and the ending is at once comical and sad. You have no way of proving that you are the only girl who fits this picture. My own attorneys feel that you should initial the pages, and I have the gallantry to believe that you are enough of a lady not to demand reinbursement in this matter.

I'll tell you what I am going to do. I am going to send you half a dozen pairs of nylons in hope that this will put you in a state of good humor about the affair. I do not say that I met you in a barn, that I was the finest man you ever knew, or that I gave you entree to a better class of people than you had known when I met you in the barn.

I will send you a carbon of the story and you will initial the pages, or else. Helen says that while it is a vivid picture of you, it is done with such warmth that every reader will think you are a lucky girl.

The Allen-Ross-Henry Morgan-Thurber business has been so confused by my constant letters about it that I very much doubt if the evening will come off without recrimination and bad feeling. My brother writes me that he doesn't think Ross is funny enough to get an award. There are two schools of thought about this.

If you pass this on to Henry Morgan, I want him to know that I did not say Ogden Nash is funnier than he is. I simply said that he is a sounder social critic.

> I am as always, with scarcely any interlude to speak of, devotedly and passionately yours,
> James Thurber

## TO HAROLD ROSS

*West Cornwall, Connecticut*
*April 5, 1949*

H. W. Ross, The New Yorker
25 West 43rd Street, New York, N. Y.

Dear Ross:

I probably should have stayed out of this whole thing, since I have only served to complicate it. Yesterday McNulty phoned me from the Players Club to say that Corey Ford had asked him to call me about getting in touch with Henry Morgan, or something of the sort. The thing is that I don't believe the Columbia boys know that Morgan is aware of the quandary as to whether to make him a direct recipient or a proxy for Allen. Apparently Allen is not going to show up. Morgan is a touchy dog and is likely to sulk if they ask him to accept for Allen, since he now knows there was some idea of selecting him for himself alone. I am responsible for all this confusion. Nobody should let me know about anything ten weeks in advance.

Letting Miss Honeycutt in on this was not too wise, either. When I met her in a barn more than twenty years ago, she only knew three men, a Monty Schuyler, one Dr. Pepper, and Willie Coleman, a young banker. Now, as a middle-aged part of the New York scene, her projected memoirs trouble the sleep of a hundred men of high literary eminence or exalted public office. Her book is to be called, I believe, "They Told Me Everything."

I will see you Monday.

As ever,
James Thurber

## TO SANDRA FELDMAN

*West Cornwall, Connecticut*
*April 2, 1949*

*Miss Sandra Feldman, 176 Via Mariposa*
*San Lorenzo, California*

Dear Miss Feldman:

I am afraid it must be hard to find things about authors in San Lorenzo, unless you have a local library and a newspaper not averse to letting girls browse in its library, looking for clippings which, in my case, may be either thin or non-existent.

I can answer your question about favorite books, not only for myself, but for all authors. The book a writer is working on is too hard to be the favorite, and the ones he has finished he doesn't want to read again. Therefore his favorite book is the one he plans to do some day.

Best wishes,
Sincerely yours,
James Thurber

## To Dorothy Miller

*April 21, 1949*

Dearest Dorothy,

It is hard to write down the day after Herman Miller's death, for it marks the end of my oldest friend, and in so many ways my closest. No matter how long it had been since we saw each other, an old communion was easily and instantly reestablished. There was no other man who knew me so well, and I took pride and comfort in his sensitive understanding. He remembered everything, over thirty-five years, and brought it out with his special humorous soundness. There was more depth and pattern to our friendship than to any other, and I have nothing that can take its place. It was more pleasure to have his laughter and appreciation than anyone else's, because he was the one who completely understood all the references, sources and meanings. I have known nobody else in whom sensibility and intelligence were so perfectly joined.

I tried to make as much of a study of him as he did of me, and since I knew his gentleness as few did, it was a private joy of mine to watch him raise his shield against the dull and ordinary persons whom he kept on the outside. Not many got through to an appreciation of his aristocratic mind, his fine judgment of people and books, and his love of the wonderful, from the comic to the beautiful. For those he loved there was no code or key, though. It was all free and open, generous and devoted. One of the nicest things about him was that genuine shyness which at first couldn't believe that the ones he loved, loved him. His happiness was all the greater when he found out. There was never a moment when he wasn't important to me.

*April 22nd*

I couldn't write any more yesterday, and since then I've been thinking about Herman's good old Henry James awareness, and his fascinated analyses of Joe and Esther Taylor, Billy Graves, Althea-and-me, and others. Helen delighted him like a Christmas gift, because he saw she was made to order for me—and a tough order that is. I keep remembering all our fine days together, the suppers at your home, the party at the Whites in New York, the old chalice in Brooklyn, the time I kept going to the bathroom in the chemistry building, waiting for Minnette, and Herman's magnificent laughter when she rode up in a car and he saw she was going to have to sit on my restless lap all the way to Broad and High. I got more pleasure and satisfaction out of Herman's laughter than any one else's. It was wonderful when his sides actually began to ache and his eyes to stream. I will always remember it. . . .

It is a deep sorrow that I couldn't have seen Herman again, and couldn't have been there with you. I didn't see him often enough, or write to him enough, and I so wanted him to meet Rosemary. But I have long and loving memories of Herman Miller, and I will always have them.

We send you our deepest love, Dorothy. We mourn with you, and we will think of you constantly. God bless you.

> Always,
> Jim


## To Sarah Whitaker

*"Waterville", Paget East, Bermuda.*

*May 15, 1949*

*Miss Sarah B. Whitaker, Principal,*
*Northampton School for Girls,*
*Northampton, Mass., U.S.A.*

Dear Miss Whitaker:

I was very much pleased by the last report of Rosie's school work and to see that she managed to keep both sides of her activities going, in spite of the nuisance of studies. I know that she will regret leaving Northampton School as much as I will to see her go. You have all been of great benefit to her in every possible way, and I feel that she is fitted for the immediate future better than I had thought she could be. She still has that "I can't do it" attitude, but it is really more of a ritual than a reality. The confidence of her schoolmates in her has meant a great deal, also.

One of my closest friends, a former Professor of English, who was one of the best amateur actors I have ever known, deplored, just before his death last month, the fact that Rosie is going to attend a college given over entirely to the teaching of Dramatics. He felt that the best actors and actresses were the product of life and literature, rather than of merely technical study. I have had this in mind also, and one of my graduation presents to Rosie is a list of some twenty books, most of them under 90,000 words, all of them beautifully written, which I thought might help to supply the lack of a general Arts course in college. I have felt that she could write as well as act, but she seems to believe that writing is "too hard". This is definite proof that she knows about writing. I will let the future take care of her career. It is foolish for a father to worry about his daughter, and even more foolish to worry about her career. If he expects a scrap-book full of favourable reviews of her acting or her writing, he is likely to get instead a couple of grand-daughters, this makes him a much luckier man. . . .

Mrs. Thurber and I shall hope to meet you at Commencement time.

Sincerely yours,
James Thurber

ℰ ℰ ℰ

West Cornwall, Connecticut
June 1, 1949

Miss Sarah B. Whitaker, Northampton School
for Girls, Northampton, Massachusetts

Dear Miss Whitaker:

One of Rosie's principal difficulties so far has been her lack of a power of decision and her tendency to let the decision be made by somebody else. I don't believe Mrs. Gilmore is too firmly set in favor of Carnegie Tech, and we would both like to see her select a school out of real volition and interest. Personally, I am opposed to the exercise of pressure by myself or anyone, since I believe every young woman should be able to decide for herself. I have offered suggestions and advice. The question of a woman's college as against a big co-educational university is a very tough one. Just taking into account the young women I have known on newspapers and magazines I feel that the co-eds seemed somehow more well-rounded and perhaps a bit more adjusted to co-educational career than the women's college girls. I base this, of course, on only a handful of examples. Whether a girl should continue, and how long, in a congenial atmosphere in which she has been successful is another big problem. . . .

The list of books I am giving her consists largely of short novels that interested, inspired, or excited me for their story, their style, their originality, or some other quality. They are all easy to read and calculated to prove that worthwhile writing, by Americans and English in this century, can be as absorbing as novels like "Centennial Summer" which Rosie read largely because of the movie. I have long contemplated an article for Harper's on the problem of literature for the young. I was a great reader from the time I was ten, but most of my enthusiasms in high school and college I found outside class. I am a rabid antagonist of the "Silas Marner" kind of required reading. Neither this nor "The Spy", nor "The Talisman", nor "The Return of the Native" stirred my interest as a writer and appreciator as much as the good books I read for myself. I realize that the question of content, especially the sexual, is difficult for teachers everywhere in the case of the adolescent. Rosie, however, will soon be eighteen, at which time my grandmother had two children, and I think that she will discover in reading these books that writing can be fun. In preparation for my article, on which I have much research to do, I have discovered, neither to my dismay nor surprise, that most school girls of seventeen have read the sexy parts of "God's Little Acre" and "Appointment in Samarra", to mention two. They get it out of context and in distortion, exchanging books in which pages are marked, never beginning or ending the books. I was disappointed to see that such a lovely thing as "My Antonia" could become uninteresting to Rosie in prospect merely because it was listed in a reading list. I expect the young girl would come to hate that heroine, but I hope that "A Lost Lady" and "My Mortal Enemy" will restore her belief in Willa Cather. I do not believe they would affect her faith in the American woman, and if she has the creative talent I suspect, she will get more out of the story and the style than she will out of its fictional facts.

Here is the list, copied from the one I sent to my secretary in New York— authors' names were filled in for her guidance, but I'll leave it as it is:

Babbitt
Daisy Miller

Gentle Julia, by Tarkington
Linda Condon, Java Head, Wild Oranges, by Hergesheimer
The Wanderer, by Alain Fournier
The Great Gatsby
The Sun Also Rises
Invitation to the Waltz, by Rosamond Lehman
This Simian World, God and My Father, by Clarence Day
The House in Paris, by Elizabeth Bowen
A Lost Lady, My Mortal Enemy, by Cather
A Handful of Dust, Decline and Fall, by Evelyn Waugh
Heaven's My Destination, The Cabala, by Wilder
February Hill, The Wind at My Back, by Victoria Lincoln
Blue Voyage, by Aiken
The Bitter Tea of General Yen, by G.Z. Stone
Lady into Fox, by Garnett
How to Write Short Stories, by Lardner
The Return of the Soldier, by Rebecca West
Miss Lonely Hearts, by M. West

This is not, needless to say, my selection of the Great Books, it is merely intended as a stimulation to a young lady who, if she ever reads them, may happily discover that writing may be hard, but also desirable, and as exciting as the theater. I will send her other books as she grows older. There are many she has read, including E.B. White's "One Man's Meat", whose perfect writing should be on every reading list.

Many of these books I have not read for fifteen years or longer, but in thinking about short books that affected me as a writer, I arrived at this selection. There are dexterity here, flexibility, color, humor, suspense, and a variety of moods, and a full course in plot and construction. You will note that the woman writers are well represented.

I should be delighted and instructed by any comments you might make on the list, and I would eliminate any items that your experience might find undesirable for reasons that I cannot see as writer and father.

I look forward to seeing you and Miss Bement at graduation.

     Cordially yours,
     James Thurber

## TO JOHN O'HARA

*Thurber tries to cheer up O'Hara who is in a sulk after* The New Yorker's Brendan Gill *panned his novel* A Rage to Live.

**West Cornwall, Connecticut**
October 29, 1949

Dear John and Belle:

When my prize collector's item, an inscribed copy of one of the first six
books off the presses, arrived in Cornwall, there was a tough struggle for possession which was won by Rosemary Adams Thurber, who is younger and
stronger than Helen and me. She had to finish it before she went to Skidmore,
which she did by staying up late. She drove the Cadillac half way to college,
showing that there was no trace of psychic trauma from the accident. The final X-rays prove that the injury healed completely, somewhat to the doctors'
surprise, since they had felt she might not be capable of normal childbirth. A
year ago I sat around in the Algonquin lobby with Charley MacArthur and Jap
Gude, talking about our daughters. Charley was apprehensive about all kinds
of things happening to Mary. At the end I told him nothing would happen to
our daughters and in a year his was dead and mine was nearly killed in a car
wreck. Jap's daughter Liz, a lovely girl of sixteen, was the only one to come
through the year all right.

Everything kind of closed in on me, and we are going to Hot Springs November first for three weeks, carrying in the overnight bag, where we can get
at it, our special copy of "A Rage to Live". We will finish it in the Blue Ridge
Mountains.

We read most of the reviews and the various summaries printed of the
score. It is amazing how the 50–50 ratio kept going. This happened to
"Madame Bovary" in France, to Shaw's first plays in England, and even to
"Alice in Wonderland" which was not even reviewed in Punch the year it came
out. Later a Sir Hobart [Brendan] Gill took a crack at it, referring to the text as
"Those nonsensical legends for the superb Tenniel drawings". The night I was
born, December 8, 1894, Cesar Franck's D-minor symphony had its world
premiere in Paris. Fifty percent of the audience cheered at the end and the
others booed, tore up auditorium seats, and fenced the other side with walking sticks. The piece is now known as "The keystone of modern symphonic
music." At 245 Parsons Avenue that night, the score was 4-1 in favor of me.

I somehow don't believe that Gill's "discursive" was derived from Gibb's "discursive". Gibbs sees very few people outside the office and only grunts to the Gills at the water-cooler, hiding behind his left shoulder. Practically everybody at the place was something more than indignant that Gill had got the book and had written what he must have thought was a witty review. I am told that he is hipped on the subject of novels, and for years has bemoaned the fact that he didn't write one before he was thirty. He still mutters about this in bars and on trains. His only way out is to attack the later novels of men who wrote one before they were thirty. He sings while rewriting Talk of the Town and thus was placed at the far end of the office, where Ross can't hear him.

I am thinking of writing a topical revue, but so far I have only one blackout. We see Lowell Thomas in the mountains of Tibet. He falls and bruises his hip, and many voices cry: "A litter! A litter!" In from the wings left comes Heywood Hale Broun, carrying thirteen collie pups. I have thrown out the scene in which one character says: "Someone shot Donald Culross Peattie", and another character says: "Ah, another Ruskin bit the dust". I feel that Peattie isn't well enough known.

We think it is a wonderful idea to live in Princeton. Helen and I fell in love with the place ten years ago come December when "The Male Animal" opened there. The first act ran sixty-two minutes and the dress rehearsal was so bad that Elliott wanted to put his father in as the trustee and Shumlin thought the dancing incident should be funnied up by lines like: "What do you say we shake a leg." He put glasses on the trustee to make him funnier, but I managed to get them off.

Ann Honeycutt, half way through her book about the American male, was told by Jack Goodman to sex it up, unthink it, and personalize it. I told her that if she personalizes it, she will have to use four photographs of me and one of McKelway, all five of which I will select personally.

Helen and I send you and Belle and Wylie our love and best wishes, congratulations, and personal regards. It's high time we saw you. I will be fifty-five in December and on a street in New York a man recently called to me "Watch it, Pop".

As ever and always,

## To Gus Lobrano

The New Yorker *paid authors by the column inch.*

West Cornwall, Connecticut
July 8, 1949

*Mr. Gus Lobrano, The New Yorker*
*25 West 43rd Street, New York, N.Y.*

Dear Gus:

I am bringing in corrected proof of "The American Literary Scene" and also "The Case of the Laughing Lady." In the first one I think I have satisfied Ross's objections. I also cut out the brief passage he objected to. This brings up a great problem and a sore point with me.

I object strenuously and indignantly to the cut of sixty dollars from "Daguerrotype of a Lady" by the auditing department, and I demand that a check for sixty dollars be sent me. I don't know who is paid to recount corrected proofs, but I think he or she should be fired or sent to Time. I resent the assumption and insinuation that I am trying to get away with something and would turn in stories longer than I intend to make them. This thing may be added to since it is one of my favorites and I have worked on it for months. I have both added to proofs and cut them, and I do not want to be paid for additions or taxed for cuts. Going over a proof takes time and work, and improvement may lie either in shortening or lengthening. In any case, it is hard work. I have added whole paragraphs to stories and taken some out since 1927. Whatever I do to a proof in the future is no business of the overstaffed auditing department. I think it should be investigated before I take it apart some day. The cheap and insulting sixty dollar cut upset me for three days and I ought to charge for this loss of time.

I have made several cuts of from one to seven words in "The Literary Scene." This would amount to $2.85, but nobody should be paid for such recounts.

In the future no reexamination must be made of my proofs by an auditor, after the check has been mailed. Cuts and additions balance out in the end and save you at least one hundred dollars a week on the salary of whoever was hired for this unnecessary and degrading work.

Some fifteen years ago Andy White spent three weeks cutting down a proof, and I believe he was not charged for this extra and devoted work on behalf of improving his story and the magazine. Andy would quit if the auditing department kicked him around, and I will be happy to go over to Cosmopolitan or somewhere if this incredible annoyance is permitted to hang over my head. I would like to know who is responsible for it and to have him or her acquainted with my feelings on the subject. This is a serious situation and The New Yorker's future might well be affected if it persists.

See you Monday.

> Love and kisses,
>
> Jim

## To Rosemary Thurber

*West Cornwall, Connecticut*
*July 13, 1949*

Dear Patient:

The phone has been ringing all the time, even from New York, and everybody is happy that you came out of your [auto] crash so well. As a graduate of three hospitals, and as your old man, I suffer with you since I know about all the annoyances of being tucked away in a bed on your back. I am glad you have your mother's pelvis, which may bend a little but doesn't break. We're all delighted that you got a private room, because the only person I know who likes a ward is your admirer John McNulty. He picks out a ward by preference, so he can have people to talk to. I was put into a ward with fifteen other kids when I was seven, and I still remember the night nurse saying I gave her more trouble than all the others. Wouldn't you know that I would have preceded you into a ward? I have always thought of writing about it, and if you wait as long as I have you will be sixty-six. I remember my mother slipped me chocolates and I trust that yours refrained from this. It wasn't until 1915 that I could stand the sight of one.

I hear that you are a good patient. A good patient hates it but sees it through. We are coming up to see you Friday. I would have been there a few minutes after the ambulance if I hadn't found out you were all right. Everybody was afraid I would dash into the ward, breathing heavily, and stumbling over people, thus leading you to think you were really bad off. We'll have you out of there in no time.

I still say that women are the best drivers. They know they cannot take a curve on two wheels. Everyone I know has had his accident and it's nice to get it over with early.

Helen and I went to see "Detective Story" Monday night, but I didn't like it. Six shots are fired at the end of the play and I was afraid that one of the two guns would not go off. I understand they have prepared for this, and that Ralph Bellamy has practised clutching at his chest and crying, "There goes my heart!"

I came into the room last night when I heard Helen talking to someone, and I hadn't heard anybody come in the house. It turned out she was trying to explain to the poodle what had happened to you. . . .

One of Helen's old beaux took us out last Saturday and insisted on buying champagne. He drank his so fast he got hiccoughs that lasted until four o'clock Monday morning. Then he phoned a doctor out of bed. The doctor told him to hold his breath as long as he could and then hold it twice that long, whereupon he slammed up. It cured the boy anyway.

If you can't get a radio, we will bring you one of ours. Keep a stiff upper lip. I am working on an invention you will like—a hospital bed with a built-in bathroom. The present system of private room with public bath annoyed me for a few days, but you get used to it.

Zabby is tugging at the leash and wants to come up to see you. I like a man who runs out of gas. We all send you our love and kisses and our heartfelt thanks that they can't beat a Thurber by hitting her with a car.

As ever and ever,

Daddy

## To Harvey Breit

*Thurber was asked to review a collection of Robert Benchley essays for the* New York Times Book Review.

*West Cornwall, Connecticut*

*August 26, 1949*

Mr. Harvey Breit, The New York Times
Book Review, Times Square, New York, N. Y.

Dear Mr. Breit:

The tendency of all of us is perhaps to write too intimately about Benchley, and thus the "I" will turn up. I wanted to mention Benchley's first book and his famous Treasurer's Report, and not myself, but I will accept the change with "celebrated" in place of "small".

I have taken out some comparative references to me and I insist on them being left the way I have now fixed them in the proof. It is probably news to you that a well-known American novelist believes, to the point of near legal action, that he invented the modern day dreamer. Most New York writers and Times readers know about this, and thus I went to some length to show Benchley's claim. I have now reinforced it and would like to have it remain the new way.

I have not been accused of "long windup" since the middle Twenties and nobody before you has taken the liberty of throwing out my words and putting in his. When I say "fond preface" I do not mean "affectionate preface". There is an "affection" in the Sullivan quote. I have put back the "fond".

I rarely use the ugly word "grew" and I have changed this back to "was". This is not only good English, it is the way I write, and this is my piece. I cannot refrain from mentioning the loving care for a writer's words which has made Ross the great editor he is.

The Times Book Review appears not to be a place for me. I am too goddam touchy, but I have the vanity to believe it is slightly justified by my intense devotion to English prose. Mr. Lyons was eight days ahead of the Tribune Books in asking me to do this piece. This may have been lucky for him, as a young and highly intelligent editor, but it was unlucky for me, as an old, and perhaps hyper-sensitive writer. I will plague you no further.

> Yours truly,
> James Thurber

## To Charles Saxon

*West Cornwall, Connecticut*
*October 14, 1949*

*Mr. Charles Saxon, Dell Publishing Company, Inc.,*
*261 Fifth Avenue, New York 16, N. Y.*

Dear Mr. Saxon:

As a loyal member of the contributing staff of what you call a magazine of "hidebound tradition", I must say first of all that I could not possibly bring myself to contribute to an out and out rival. I do not believe that you can win over the other boys and girls either, for most of the New Yorker writers and artists are devoted to that magazine.

You don't sell me the idea that "Ballyhoo" has been selected for any other reason than sweet memories of a million sales. You put up such an interesting argument for "Esmeralda" that I wonder you don't use that title instead. I think that your letter shows that what you want to do is to bring back BALLY-HOO without Elmer Zilch and the comic ads, but it seems to me that that magazine died an awful and deserved death and that it cannot be successfully revived, even under the flowery screen of your high and noble dedication. In writing to the New Yorker artists and writers you would have been smart to leave out that crack. It sounds to me as if you would like to take over our boys and girls and have them work for Dell instead of Ross. This won't work and what you need is satirists for the masses, as you say. We have never developed any.

Thanks for the enlightening ride on your dream boat.

> Sincerely yours,
> James Thurber

## TO HAROLD ROSS

*October 10, 1949*

Dear Ross:

I wanted to tell you what a triumph McNulty's ["Back Where I Had Never Been"] was. . . . The surprise comes from the fact that it was not run through our formidable prose machine in a desperate and dedicated Ross-Shawn attempt to make it sound like everybody else. . . . The machine has left almost no differences in tongue or temperament or style . . . since there has to be so much rewriting of most of the authors, this dreadful similarity is hard to avoid.

I understand that McNulty had the usual terrible battle to survive as the magnificent individual he is, but he made it. The curse of our formula editing is that uniformity tends toward desiccation, coldness, and lack of vitality and blood. . . . We are afraid of warmth, as we are afraid of sex and human functions. Our only true boldness lies in the use of "Jesus Christ" to show we're not afraid of the Catholic Church. . . .

> [Thurber]

*The attack on Shawn incensed Ross, for McNulty had become discouraged with the piece and it was Shawn who urged him on, accepted it in pieces, and assembled it into a splendid whole. "You understand as wrong as a man can understand," Ross wrote Thurber heatedly. . . . "Shawn was the obstetrician, the midwife, and the godfather of that piece, and it never would have been done without him."*

*Walden was a staff member whose play about* The New Yorker *was about to open, highlighting a fictitious Ross.*

*"The story of the midget" was Thurber's "You Could Look It Up."*

West Cornwall, Connecticut

October 14, 1949

Mr. H. W. Ross, The New Yorker
25 West 43rd Street, New York, N. Y.

Dear Ross:

I didn't know whether you had seen the enclosed letter from Dell and the prospectus. Here they are with my letter to Dell.

Maybe you will have to have a rally to keep the boys and girls from going to BALLYHOO. It would be interesting to know how many of them got such a letter.

Grantland Rice was once connected with a Saturday morning half hour on the radio which dramatized sports fiction, and they did the story of the midget, who was played by Roy Fant very well. The story appeared in the Post in 1940 or 41. I think it would make a movie, but there isn't a single woman in the story. It wouldn't be too hard to work in Lana Turner. The artist who illustrated the piece hired a midget as a model and the little guy still keeps after him to draw him again. I expected him to call on me, but he never did. You are probably a better agent than Myron Selznick and the movies do a baseball story once a year. The last one dealt with a chemistry prof. who accidentally discovered that a certain solution would make a baseball allergic to wood. He won the pennant for St. Louis.

Keep pitching.

As ever,

James Thurber

P.S. I accept your explanation of the McNulty story, and I'm glad I'm not Shawn. I dreamed the other night that I was Walden.

## TO E. B. WHITE

*West Cornwall, Connecticut*
*October 18, 1949*

Dear Andy:

. . . It was nice to have you and Kay here, but you didn't stay long enough. I didn't even ring my Bermuda carriage bell for you, or get out the 1902 rubber bulb auto horn we found in the house. Fifty years ago the place was owned by a Mr. Livingston, who made a million dollars by inventing the honeycomb radiator, early models of which are still plowed up. He died in a car accident and the last owner died on a ship. I will be killed by a Mrs. Charles L. Schwartz driving the wrong way on a one way street. Mrs. Schwartz will come east in her car from Des Moines, because her sister in Torrington wired her "I am very sick." It will turn out that this is a Western Union garble for "I am very rich."

As ever,
Jim

*Mr. E. B. White, c/o The New Yorker*
*25 West 43rd Street, New York, N. Y.*

## TO ELIZABETH GREEN

*November 18, 1949*

*Miss Elizabeth Green, Director of News Bureau,*
*Mount Holyoke College, South Hadley, Massachusetts*

Dear Miss Green:

I was delighted to learn that Mount Holyoke overwhelmed Harvard 6 to 2 in their gruelling field hockey match. I was confident of the outcome all the time and my fingers were steady as the ticker tape ran through them with the play by play story of an event that was not only a famous moment in history, but also in sex. Please congratulate all the warriors for me and tell them that in 1908 I invented a game to be played in backyards, in which the contestants, armed with sawed off broomsticks, tried to hurl a man's black sock over their opponent's goal, or fence. I was the best.

The drawing of the Mount Holyoke girls defeating Yale in football was drawn nearly eighteen years ago, even though the newspaper account managed to convey the idea that it was fairly new. At 54 I am no longer that bold and skittish.

An undergraduate at Ohio State has written me requesting that I ask the Mount Holyoke girls if they want to wrestle.

Thanks again for your letter.

>Athletically yours,
>James Thurber

## To Harvey Breit

*Breit was preparing an article on Thurber for the* New York Times.

>*West Cornwall, Connecticut*
>*November 22, 1949*

*Mr. Harvey Breit, The Sunday Book Review,*
*New York Times, Times Square, New York, N. Y.*

Dear Breit:

. . . The only piece I ever wrote about the drawings appeared in the New York Times and in my recent book under the title "The Lady on the Bookcase." As I have already told you, I have not done any drawings for two years, but I am still referred to in the New York papers as "the New York playwright and cartoonist." I am not New York. I wrote only one play ten years ago, and I am no longer a cartoonist, but I can't get away from these tags, even though only three of my books are books of drawings and thirteen are books of short pieces.

. . . Some six months after President Franklin D. Roosevelt's death, Mrs. Kermit Roosevelt wrote to the business department of the New Yorker, setting forth a curious request. It seems that during a lull in the Quebec Conference, President Roosevelt, with his tongue in his cheek, told Mrs. Winston Churchill that the Brussels sprout was the great American vegetable, but that the English were not privy to the subtle secrets of its preparation. He said that there were thirty-four interesting ways to cook Brussels sprouts. Mrs. Churchill was dubious, and the President decided on a rather elaborate practical joke. A few months before his death he told Mrs. Kermit Roosevelt that he wanted to get out a privately printed pamphlet called "Thirty-four Ways to Cook Brussels Sprouts", and he outlined most of the mythical recipes in his conversation with Mrs. K. R. He said that he wanted Thurber to do a cover design for the pamphlet and, what is more, he described in full detail how it was to be drawn. I first learned of this posthumous command when a man in the business department of the New Yorker sent for me and explained it. I am no whiz at the composition of drawings, and the President set me a difficult task. What he wanted in the drawing was a long table in the central foreground holding a large glass bowl filled with Brussels sprouts. Converging on the table from behind were to be three separate lines of eager smiling people with forks in their hands, descending on the table. For some reason I don't yet understand, he wanted human faces to appear on the Brussels sprouts in the bowl. When, more than four years ago, I set to work on the project, I gave up the idea of the faces, since I could not get away from a cannibalistic note, and I settled for a series of border designs of rows of sprouts with faces, in addition to the cover.

I spent four afternoons of practice trying to draw a Brussels sprout. They were out of season and I had none to feel, and I couldn't visualize the things. At this point I got the counsel of my friend and neighbor, Armin Landeck, the distinguished painter and etcher and teacher of art at the Brearley School. The New Yorker's business office had sent me a tear sheet of a Brussels sprout from a seed catalogue, but I couldn't see it at all. Landeck would not draw a sprout for me, but simply criticized the ones I tried to draw. "That is an electric light bulb," he would say, or "That is an apple," or "I don't know what that is." After a couple of hours of this, during which I missed the sprout's outlines completely, he went away and in the evening phoned me, saying, "Think of a miniature squeezed baseball, seam and all." The visual picture of a Brussels sprout immediately crossed my mind, and I set to work on the cover. Any artist will tell you that the Roosevelt plan presented a formidable problem in composition, but I had to stick to his exact requirements. I did a dozen covers and finally solved the awkwardness by drawing my dog in front of the table on his hind legs with one paw reaching for the bowl. This broke up the rather grim outlines of the table and people, and I sent it off. The pamphlet was indeed privately printed, for members of the Roosevelt and Churchill families. The artist did not receive a copy. But I understand that a preface by Mrs. Kermit R. told an interesting anecdote about a sequel to the prank some months after the Quebec Conference. It seems that Mrs. Churchill, still meditating on the President's whimsical but vehement defense and praise of the Brussels sprout, spoke to John Winant, then our ambassador to the Court of St. James's during a reception in London. Their talk went something like this. "I under-stand the Brussels sprout is the great American vegetable, Mr. Winant." "Oh, no," said Winant, "It is a dreadful vegetable." "But," exclaimed Mrs. Churchill, "Your President himself told me that it is the great American American veg-etable." It was a tough spot for a diplomat, but he got out of it. "Oh, the Brus-sels sprout!" he cried, "Of course. I guess I was thinking of the parsnip." . . .

If I seemed to run down the human species, it was not altogether uninten-tional. They say that Man is born to the belief that he is superior to the lower animals, and that critical intelligence comes when he realizes that he is more similar than dissimilar. Extending this theory, it has occurred to me that Man's arrogance and aggression arises from a false feeling of transcendency, and that he will not get anywhere until he realizes, in all humility, that he is just another one of God's creatures, less kindly than Dog, possessed of less natural dignity than Swan, and incapable of becoming as magnificent an an-gel as Black Panther. I have grown a little tired of the capitalization of Man, his easy assumption of a dignity more legendary than real, and his faith in a high destiny for which he is not fitted by his long and bloody history. The most frightening study of mankind is Man. I think he has failed to run the world, and that Woman must take over if the species is to survive. Man should be-come a worker with his hands, and no head of a state should be allowed to de-vote his entire time to politics. He should be forced to spend at least a third of it in work, and not in scheming.

I just send this along for what it may be worth, since I feel I didn't give you much to write about.

>Cordially yours,
>James Thurber

## To Whit Burnett

>*West Cornwall, Connecticut*
>*November 29, 1949*

*Mr. Whit Burnett, The STORY PRESS*
*Main Street, Setauket, Long Island, N. Y.*

Dear Whit Burnett:
Since two years have gone by, I thought you had abandoned THE WORLD'S BEST and in my second letter on the subject, I said it seemed to me

and to some of my friends that the list of names from which the final selection was made was somewhat careless and slapdash. Kay Boyle and Sally Benson were listed, but not Elizabeth Bowen, and there were other omissions, especially in poetry. I would like to see a list of the authors to be used. I understand that E. B. White is not among them, and this is to me an impossible omission of one of the great living prose writers. You mention Fadiman, who selected two of White's pieces for his "Reading I've Liked", although one of them was not available. I would feel pretty silly in a book without a piece by him.

MY LIFE AND HARD TIMES was written close to twenty years ago and selections have appeared in seventy-two anthologies. I no longer give permission for these old and worn out stories. I don't think a special value should be placed on a piece because the piece would seem to fit the structure of your collection. The pieces I like the best since 1933 are "A Call on Mrs. Forrester", which took months to write and is White's favorite; "A Final Note on Chanda Bell", which Gibbs, who doesn't like anything, likes; and "The Waters of the Moon", which Maxwell Anderson picked as the New Yorker piece he has liked the best. All of these are written in the way I started to write after MY LIFE AND HARD TIMES and they belong to a group of more than a hundred stories, or about two-thirds of the whole amount. I think you are wrong about THE WHITE DEER, but I long ago realized that there is nothing to do about American critical judgment when it comes to fairy tales.

I still want to reserve permission, and so will the New Yorker, until we can see a list of the contents and find out what system of pay or royalties you have in mind. This is certainly the most ambitious project I ever heard of, and any writer must feel a little squeamish and pretentious in getting into it. Probably a collection of the truly best writing would not sell two thousand copies. I know that there is no Brazilian or Portuguese who can write as well as White, and I would not join in what would amount to a tacit confession that there is. I realize you have put a lot of work on the book. What comes next—those stars which know not Alexander?

     Sincerely yours,
     James Thurber

## To E. B. White

*In 1949 Harper and Brothers wished to re-issue* Is Sex Necessary? *Thurber was reluctant but went along with White's introduction.*

*West Cornwall, Conn.*
*November 20, 1949*

*Mr. E. B. White, The New Yorker*
*25 West 43rd Street, New York, N. Y.*

Dear Andy:

I am glad it was you and not me who took on the task of bringing sex up to date. As far as I can find out, as the father of an eighteen-year-old daughter, the boys spend most of their time arguing about politics, progressive education, Joe DiMaggio, and everything else. "They even argue about their right to argue," Rosie tells me. One school of psychology believes that sex has been split like the atom and an exponent of this school believes that the passionate Pole in "A Streetcar Named Desire" was more in love with his poker playing male companion than with his wife, and destroyed her sister to keep the young man for himself. At any rate, old-fashioned sex rarely makes the theatre, what with two plays about a man and his son, "Edward, My Son" and "Death of a Salesman," and one about a father and his daughter, "The Heiress." A girl barely gets into "Mr. Roberts" and then seems dragged in. Perhaps "Life With Mother" was just too much middle-aged marital love and the audience expected romance among the Day children. On the other hand, romantic sex is aging. In 1918 it was the young Mary Pickford and Douglas Fairbanks, in 1936 the forty-two year old king of England, and today the love life of a vice-president in his seventies and a mayor who is fifty-nine. In the early days of the movies, men like Earle Williams and J. Warren Kerrigen were through at forty, but the aging Bogart, Gary Cooper and Clark Gable still go on.

Honey is writing a book about the American male and is quite an authority on 1949 sex. She recommends a book called "Modern Woman, The Lost Sex," or something like that. I was in a cab with a lady we took home from a party, and she said her psychiatrist would not let her see her fiancé. She was seeing him, however, on the sly. These are the days of bootleg love.

I want to see a copy of your new preface when you get it done. Love to you and Kay from us both.

As ever,

## TO HAROLD ROSS

*O'Hara boycotted* The New Yorker *after it published a negative review of his novel* A Rage to Live. *O'Hara wrongly believed that Gibbs had written the review under Brendan Gill's name, and Gill wrongly believed that Thurber had put the idea in O'Hara's head.*

*West Cornwall, Connecticut*
*November 29, 1949*

*Mr. H. W. Ross, The New Yorker*
*25 West 43rd Street, New York, N. Y.*

Dear Ross:

All we need now is a character named O'Hara in a Sally Benson story. Several years ago, when one of John's casuals ran second in the magazine, he wrote Mrs. White a single line: "My stories run first." So one of them ran second recently. The New Yorker puts no superior value on the first story, but the writers always do. Several persons told O'Hara that Gill said he was going to "get" the O'Hara book before it was published. All I know about Gill is the report that he is hipped on the subject of novel writing and that he has told strangers no writer is any good if he hasn't written a book before he is thirty. The strangers always tell him he is right, since he has the look of a man who will brook no disagreement. O'Hara happens to be the man whose books started the New Yorker type of facetious review. After Fadiman reviewed "Butterfield 8" under the title "Disappointment in O'Hara", some of us felt that he had taken enough and should have been spared "The O'Hara Report". I have nothing against Gill except that, as the talk of the Town writer for eight years, I resent a man who whistles while he rewrites it.

Keep pitching, but not at O'Hara's head. We've had enough violence. I'll see you around the tenth.

As ever,
James Thurber

*Ross wanted Thurber to indicate early in "The Figgerin' of Aunt Wilma" that it took place in Ohio.*

*Thurber was never able to persuade Ross or, later, Shawn to okay a Thurber* New Yorker *article on Houdini.*

*Walden's play,* Metropole, *opened in the fall of 1949. An unsuccessful attempt to satirize Ross and the magazine, it closed after two performances.*

West Cornwall, Conn.
December 10, 1949

*Mr. H. W. Ross, The New Yorker*
*25 West 43rd Street, New York, N. Y.*

Dear Ross:

I will let you peg the Columbus I made famous in the New Yorker, but I think this will have to be done by me, since I don't want the word Ohio to appear in any opening sentence, written by me with a certain rhythm that would be thrown off. Readers who do not flip ahead to find the author's name are not worth bothering about, but as I say, I will put in the state, somewhere.

I have three pieces from the New Yorker of 1925 and 1926 about Houdini, all of them incredibly bad. We had twenty-one months between the time the magazine started and the death of Houdini, but nobody ever wrote about him until Markey did a chocolate epitaph. Here is his final sentence, which you passed: "He will be the character, above many others who now occupy our scene with much of pomp and circumstance, to hold the fancy of some social historian fifty years hence, who sets out to capture again the spirit of the Turbid Twenties".

A letter from O'Hara to me specifically states that what disturbed him was the use of the word "discursive" in the Gibbs letter and the Gill review. There were no other similarities whatsoever. O'Hara believes this is a word rarely used by writers.

I am glad that play closed, and it certainly sounds like a mess from the reviews. In my play there is no mention of the editor's marriage, former marriages, children, girls, or anything else. Such private lives as I touch on are those of an imaginary writer, whose involvements are made up and resemble mine if they resemble anyone's. The magazine has no name and there is no mention of publisher, business department, ulcers, or tearing walls down. The only lines from the Walden play I have read were obviously written by his collaborator [George Kaufman]. Marc Connelly asked if he could see my play, and you can figure what you want out of that. If it is ever written, it will be produced by Shumlin, without Lee Tracy. How could George K. have known you so many years and never got beyond the gestures? The days of the noisy, swiftly-paced comedy are over. I am writing two casuals and will take Houdini in my stride.

As ever,

James Thurber

## TO JAMES BELLENGER

*West Cornwall, Connecticut*
*December 2, 1949*

*Mr. James Bellenger, Matthews 29,*
*Harvard University, Cambridge 38, Mass.*

Dear Mr. Bellenger:

. . . The trouble with the Goldwyn picture [*Walter Mitty*] was that you could see no difference between Walter's dreams and his accomplishments. I doubt if it could be done properly in this country, but the English could do it by spending about a million and a half less money.

No writer chooses his actors, but I would have suggested Roland Young, Robert Benchley, or Charles Butterworth, but when the movies want a character like that they put glasses on Cary Grant or grab a top-flight star like Kaye. I worked two weeks on the picture in New York, taking out stuff that was put back in and putting in stuff that was taken out, although I did put the clock in.

Main incredibility: no man ever dreams of being a milliner.

Sincerely yours,

James Thurber

## TO THE RONALD WILLIAMSES

*January 9, 1950*

*Mr. and Mrs. Ronald J. Williams,*
*The Bermudian Magazine, Hamilton, BERMUDA*

Dear children:

We now regard your problem as not only the least of our worries, but as an example of light and health. A few months ago Helen's mother came down with hardening of the arteries and seven heart conditions, and while Helen was getting her out of the hospital our cook collapsed on the floor, alone with me in the house. She is in the hospital and will be unable to work again, so we have to get new servants. Two days ago the doctors told Helen she has an ovarian cyst and must be operated on early in February, and Rosemary developed something like mumps yesterday, but it may be merely the swelling of a duct.

Happy New Year.

We were shocked by the death of Hervey Allen and I realize that I had considered this monumental man immune to the frailty of mortality. I see that he was born on December 8th, like myself, which is what made him full of calm and repose.

I didn't like my last piece for you very much, but they will improve with the coming of Spring and the ending of our long cycle of disasters. I would bring Helen to Bermuda but we can't very well leave her mother, who is likely to collapse again at any minute. The first thing we will do, when we can, is to get down there. Helen is supposed to be in the hospital three weeks, but she will stay there ten days and the rest of the time at the Algonquin. During the ten days I will have a room at the hospital on a floor given over to husbands of patients.

I have started work again on the play about Bermuda, and I think I solved the problem that bothered me, by putting it in two acts instead of three. It libels nobody, not even the lieutenant in the British Navy, and it places a wreath of roses on the brow of a girl [Janey] not unlike a friend of ours. She is pursued by four men, including an aged millionaire, a painter, a writer (who wins out), and her husband. All very clean and jolly.

God bless you all.

As ever,

Jim

## TO GUS LOBRANO

*West Cornwall, Connecticut*
*January 11, 1950*

*Mr. Gus Lobrano, The New Yorker*
*25 West 43rd Street, New York, N. Y.*

Dear Gus:

In connection with my phone call today, it turns out that I have to budget income this year and, for one thing, I figure that the New Yorker might divide my future checks into two separate ones, twenty-five percent to be sent to the Guaranty Trust Company, and the check for the balance to us in Cornwall. This would not constitute a withholding arrangement, under the law, but would simply amount to a convenience, it seems to me.

As a free lance writer, I have to estimate my income and pay taxes quarterly on the basis of this estimate, which means that the final settlement is payable in January. This year it comes to $13,000 more than we have, and I have to sell bonds, to do which we are coming to town tomorrow.

Our income is from so many sources, most of them unpredictable, that my only way out is to ration my New Yorker work. Last year I simply wrote too many pieces, about ten too many. The income from publishers, "The Male Animal", etc. threw us both into a 60% bracket, and disaster. Since we have settled up in January on our basis of unpredictable income it means that two months from now I pay the first estimate on this year. We should have kept a stricter lookout, but the fault is largely mine, since I got $22,000 from the New Yorker. When the other stuff was added up, my seventeen pieces for you cost me about $8,000. I could blame it, of course, on the other income, but it is not controllable and my New Yorker income is. I will have to check every month against possible income, but it is an imprecise business at best, since a movie sale, or something, might put me in a high bracket unexpectedly. I can't very well turn down movie sales, and cutting my New Yorker output in two is bad enough, since the decline in production of pieces would have the effect of postponing a book for at least a year with its consequent income.

The year always starts badly, since we have always underestimated total income and may continue to do so. Thus, last January, I got an advance from Simon and Schuster to pay the 1948 tax, little knowing there would be $12,000 from Harcourt and $6,000 from Harpers whose most recent book of mine is six years old. After ten years "The Male Animal" brought in the highest amount yet, $4,000 and this amount, while spread over the year, reached its highest payment as late as November. To keep a monthly check on Samuel French, three publishers, and other sources will take a lot of time and trouble.

I see no possibility of estimating in March what I will get from publishers, and the best we can do is to pay too much and get some back. I can't see how old books of mine would bring in more than $8,000 this year, but it might easily jump to $20,000 some way. For instance, one year after the publication of the "Thurber Carnival" the book began to sell a thousand copies a week to the amazement of the publishers and all other experts. This meant an unexpected income of about $3600 in two months. If vice-president Barkley should mention one of my books in a speech on the air it might easily cost me $7500 next January.

I figure that for services alone last year I paid around $600 a month and in view of this I suggested to you the possibility of the New Yorker paying some of the weekly cost of secretarial service, at least for this year, since the vast majority of my work is for the magazine and seventeen casuals in one year is higher than anybody else's rate. We had this arrangement during the year I spent on Soap Opera, but just why working for Shawn is different from working for you I don't know. I think Ross figured there would be research costs, but all research, or most of it, was done from here and by myself on two or three visits to New York. Phone calls and lunches came to less than $100, which I paid myself.

I will have a book out in the fall, but advance royalties take care of the first 12,000 copies. This is perhaps fortunate, since if I have a play on too and it runs a year, the book and play together would put me in the 75% bracket, and I might pay the government as much as $80,000 whether I wrote a piece for the New Yorker or not. The fact that income taxes might necessitate my ceasing to write for the magazine is a truly dreadful thing. But there it is.

Everything is aimed at the free lance writer, who is the greatest victim of taxes. A corporation, making my income, for the past ten years, would have $250,000 profit after taxes. I will have exactly $27,000 in the world when I sell these bonds.

> As ever,
> James Thurber

## To Clinch Calkins

*West Cornwall, Connecticut*
*January 28, 1950*

Dear Clinch Calkins:

I have to answer letters which mention John Mosher, whose death in September 1942, at the appalling age of fifty, was a tremendous loss to all of us. He was the most delightful companion we had ever known. I remember about the time Ross found himself at a trough adjacent to Nosher's in the men's room. "Why don't you write some more pieces?" Ross asked. "Because I've lost the slight fancy that sustained me," John told him. I'm collecting Mosher stories and heard one from a couple we met in Nassau last year. Seems they had driven him home in New York, but had stopped, by accident, two blocks from his house. John got out of the car and wouldn't listen to their protests that they should drive him the two blocks. "Nonsense," said John. "There's a bit of the Daniel Boone in me."

Yes, those were the good old days, and many of us miss your poems. I am glad to find out where you are. Does everybody named M.M. live in Virginia? The Morris Markeys moved there recently. . . .

> Admiringly yours,
> James Thurber

&. &. &.

> *West Cornwall, Connecticut*
> *March 7, 1950*

*Mr. Gus Lobrano, The New Yorker*
*25 West 43rd St., New York, N. Y.*

Dear Gus:

Helen hadn't been able to read "The Interview" in typescript or proof, but she caught an interesting mistake when she read it in the magazine. It was missed by all the twelve people who go over manuscripts and proofs.

Lockhorn says to Price that all the things he names as wonderful can be touched by the hand. This would obviously include "devotion" in "devotion of the dog." Therefore I made Price speculate "on the tactual aspects of devotion." This made a kind of funny point, at least to me. Nobody on the New Yorker seems to have understood what I was after, and it came out "factual aspects of devotion." If this means anything, it means that Price questioned the reality and truth of devotion, thus giving my little man a cynicism not in his character.

Well, we are all fallible, sometimes twelve people at once. If there was some slip in the typing and the word was "factual" in my manuscript, it should nevertheless have been caught by the proof people who are looking for these things.

Eye myself have maid mistakes from tide to tide and I don't thing it is two important. The great curse of the real word gets everybody. If it had been bactual, it would have been easy.

You will have my casual by now. It is only about two thousand words.

I'll see you at the party.

> As always,

## To the John O'Haras

*O'Hara had begun taking violin lessons. He was still in a snit over Gill's review of his book.*

West Cornwall, Conn.
March 17, 1950

Dear John and Belle:

I wonder if you are the same O'Haras I used to know? He was a tall hand-some violinist, and she was a moonlight serenade.

The night Helen went into the hospital, January 31, she tried to call you by phone to say we hadn't forgotten the day and the pinch bottle, but couldn't ship it across the border because the goddam Rebels have such a strong picket line thrown across there. She was in the hospital three weeks, after the excision of a fibroid grapefruit and her appendix, which would have burst in another twenty-four hours. It was quite a do and we are going to Bermuda in April to sun her back to health.

. . . I happen to know that Mr. Wolcott Gibbs was neither in correspon-dence, nor touch of any kind, with Gill from May to September, and no word or sign was passed. The guy [Gibbs] was going to write you to this effect, but halfway through the first paragraph said, "Nuts," even as you and I would do under similar circumstances, believing that to protest friendship is just as silly as to suspect it.

General Hooker has cut down all telephone wires between the Wilderness and Captain Shelby's headquarters on the College Road, and this will be delivered by a Pinkerton man in our next shipment of quinine and ban-dages.

Helen joins me in love and kisses and delayed birthday greetings.

As ever and always,
Jim

## To Rosemary Thurber

*Rosemary, ending her freshman year at Skidmore, had applied to the University of Pennsylvania. The MacLeans and Rose Algrant were Cornwall neighbors. The Swains were the Thurbers' servants who maintained the Cornwall house. Rosemary did join Thurber and Helen in Bermuda.*

*The Ledgelets, Somerset, Bermuda*

*May 2, 1950*

Dear Miss Thucker:

I'm sorry about that carbon and won't do it again. It's like two straws in a soda. I didn't know it was a common practice among the tired business men.

There's a saying that the grass is always greener in the other field and the boys are always grander. I'm glad you had a wonderful time in Canada, but I doubt that those remarkable men could defeat us American boys at every turn. You'll be getting letters from that athletic boy interested in journalism. Don't let him use you for a hockey puck.

We think it would be wonderful for you to come to Bermuda and go back on the ship with us. You would have to take a plane down here and you would have to have your mother's permission, which you better get by phoning her, since you wouldn't write in time. If she says o.k., and she will, if you tell her

"I wasn't worried about my wife when he was just a writer."

that flights to Bermuda are famous for their safety, we will arrange to have Miss Terry get you a reservation on the plane. . . .

We want you to get to Dr. Berman about that tooth as soon as you can, but your elaborate plan of getting there and back is too Thurberesque. Why don't you simply take a train to New York directly, spend one night at the Algonquin, and go directly back? We are enclosing a check for this trip, also we have just received word from Ken MacLean that Rose is moving into Amy Barnes's cottage, wherever that is, and we don't know where she will be. The Swains will be in Cornwall and you could always call them if you wanted to stay at home, but it seems too complicated. Also our plumbing upstairs has gone to hell and you might have to wash in the pool.

This is the first letter ever dictated by Helen and me together. Put it in your museum. The facts are hers and the cracks are mine. We'll rush this off to get the clockwork moving. With love and kisses,

Daddikins and Helen

P.S. Keep after Pennsylvania and satisfy all the requirements, as they say. They couldn't bar Jacob Thucker's daughter.

*Rosemary, now at the University of Pennsylvania, wondered about joining a sorority.*

*[Undated, probably summer of 1950]*

Dear Rosie,

Helen doesn't know any more about sororities than a rabbit but your mother and I were brought up in them and were probably writing Greek letters in our eighth grade textbooks. Girls like Helen who go to Eastern schools for girls never know about outside social activities and get more done than other girls. I went to Ohio State determined to marry a Kappa Rosebud and the first one I met was named Minnette Fritts and she was president of the Kappa chapter. At this time your mother was a little girl of twelve and Minnette remembers her dragging her doll across the room of her house on Indianola Avenue back in 1910. Years went on and in 1920 at a dance my first Kappa introduced me to a girl named Althea Adams. You know the rest of what happened. How your mother followed a hurdy-gurdy all day. Bravely gave up her doll to a Chinese child. Worked for the AP during elections. Handled the downtown Paris office of *The Chicago Tribune,* and so forth.

Next in order at Ohio State and most other places are the Thetas. Both of these sororities contain good looking, attractive, well-dressed girls of moderately good families capable of being aroused when they meet "Mr. Right", capable of straight-arming the boys they don't want and it is a libel when the Ohio State *Sun-Dial* said twenty years ago, 'at midnight the Kappas unsnarl on the porch swing and go to bed.' The Kappas have turned out many happy married women and a lot of successful divorcées. Together with a few girls who became prominent in politics—they can't all turn out well—and I wouldn't be surprised if they have an artist or an actress among their alumnae.

The only Tri Delt I ever met was one so powerfully built she could throw me and during dances when I tried to turn her I sometimes found both my feet off the ground. At that time, thirty years ago, the large girls were spoken of as stylish stouts. (I sort of think maybe that one [Thurber cartoon] that says "Stop me!" is that Tri Delt. I don't know.)

Well, at least they don't serve cocktails at rushing parties. You must have more tea than Lipton. I hope you have a chance in all the flurry to be able to tell one Greek letter from another. You are under no injunction to join your mother's sorority. After all she wouldn't join her mother's church. I have known a lot of Thetas and Tri Delts and after all sorority doesn't change a good girl much. (The more I read that line the more I think about it.) At Ohio State the Kappas ran things and were pretty. The Thetas were pretty and dressed well and the Tri Delts were somewhat more lively. You may remember that Hot Garters Gardiner was thrown out of the Tri Delt house. (Now that was in *The Male Animal,* of course.)

Janey [Williams] wrote us that Ronny had lectured his five year old daughter on good behavior while he was lying in bed in his pajama bottoms. He told her about a prince looking for a good princess and rejecting the bad ones and she said she was going to be a good princess. He was pretty smug until he found out that she had stuck a wad of gum in his navel. They had to get it out with rubbing alcohol. Never torture your father.

Dad

## To the Ted Gardiners

*Gardiner sold or rented theater equipment, including movies.*

*The Ledgelets, Somerset, Bermuda*
*May 29, 1950*

Dear Ted and Julia:

The last time we heard from you was the night you and the Sayres phoned and were having trouble identifying a lot of things, including the wool winder, which you thought was a spool binder, or a rule finder, or something. The Sayres even thought Ted was like Dick Maney. This is like comparing Lillian Gish to Theda Bara.

We wonder if you have begun to crack up or something, since you haven't phoned and are probably in bed by ten o'clock. We have been here two weeks and are coming to Columbus because I have to be at Kenyon Monday, June 11, to get a degree of LLD, believe it or not. We will then be in Columbus until the following Sunday. We aim to see a lot of you if you are up and around.

I met a man down here who has a sister named Lotta in Chicago, and he says you phone her all the time late at night. His first name is Horace, and he says to tell you he has three brothers, Fuller, Oliver, and Richard Evelyn Byrd. He says he is glad his sister Kitty is in heaven and beyond your vulgar reach.

You are not beyond ours, thank goodness, and Helen after her operation is a new woman and joins me in love and kisses.

As always,
Jim

❦   ❦   ❦

*Pennsylvania Railroad, The American*

Dear Mr. Gardiner:

I have had my secretary look into this movie "industry" you are interested in, and I am told it is not on a substantial basis. Those best informed see little hope for commercial success. It seems to be a "novelty" which will pass. They will never be able to conquer the flicker and it is ridiculous to use a sheet on a wall. It will die out like the magic lantern. Stopping every few minutes to change reels is bad. Never heard of Lasky, Griffith and the others you say have approached you. They are doomed to failure.

       Yours,

       J.G. Thurber

## To E. B. White

*West Cornwall, Connecticut*

*June 30, 1950*

Dear Andy:

    This is belated thanks for your letter about "The Thirteen Clocks." The book has undergone changes and is still not finished. I had not realized the similarity of names. Mark has been changed back to my original Zorn and Mock has become Krang. I've also clarified the narrative line here and there. As for a fairy tale princess, she will bear elaborate description, but being the paper doll she is, any actions or speeches of hers indicating that she can live up to her description would destroy her. Like Cinderella and her prince, Saralinda and her prince are Kewpies under their clothes and I have long been in love with the idea that all they ever have is the fact of their preordained meeting which, in itself, covers what it took you and me years and years to understand and develop.

    I am glad you and Katherine have finally gotten away to good old Nova Scotia, home of ship builders and eye men. We were distressed that you have both had such another summer. It doesn't get easier. But every now and then comes a good cycle and I hope yours has started.

    My new preface to THE SEAL IN THE BEDROOM deals lovingly with your part in the complex life that began with a seal on a rock.

    Helen and Rosie and I send you our love and kisses.

       As ever,

## To the E. B. Whites

Time *magazine was preparing a cover story on Thurber.*

    *Bruno Hauptmann used a ladder to kidnap the Lindbergh baby.*

    *Althea's third husband, Allen Gilmore, taught history at Carnegie Tech in Pittsburgh.*

    *Frank Tinney was a former vaudevillian.*

*Evangeline Booth formerly headed the Salvation Army, founded by her father.*

*Morris Markey, a former* New Yorker *staff writer, had died from a discharged rifle.*

West Cornwall, Connecticut
July 19, 1950

Dear Infielders:

A dozen of my friends have been trying to handle those queerly bouncing balls for the past two weeks. My mother and brothers had to deal with a man from the TIME's staff in Washington, D.C., who flew out. "He was born on August 8," she told me later on the phone. They drove him to see all the houses we have lived in, my grandfather's store, and the rifle range where Dr. James E. Snook killed Theora Hix. They hit Honey with "Does he have compassion?" She chose to reply by telling how I had taken her apartment to pieces and lied about my having thrown a box of candy. McNulty said, "I told them everything except how Jimmy held the ladder for Hauptmann," they got twenty pages of notes from Ronnie and Janey Williams, and I haven't heard from Elliott who was cornered in Hollywood. The man they sent to call on Althea acted subdued in Dr. Gilmore's house, since he was the education editor of the Pittsburgh press, as well as the TIME man. He kept swallowing a lot, but Althea phoned me that she came out of it all right but was unable to tell what streets we lived on in Columbus and when I first became interested in dogs, since she wasn't born then. The prize question knocked at me was, "Do you consider yourself complex?"

We all wonder what becomes of TIME men and women after the age of thirty. McNulty said that his man hadn't heard of Frank Tinney, Honey said they couldn't identify anybody before 1928, and Althea reported that her man seemed to regard her as being a contemporary of the late Evangeline Booth. The man who called on me is writing the piece and was six years old when I went to work on the New Yorker. The girl researcher with him was two at that time. They cabled T.S. Eliot after talking to Pete DeVries, said that their dinner with Ross gave them nothing since he can't remember anything, but Lobrano, like the others, found these two smart, friendly and hard working. I tried to keep TIME from tracking you down on vacation, but they love it when it's hard. This cover story originated when we met Tom Matthews at Kenyon and we liked each other and are spending a weekend with him in August. He is a fine man and is responsible, I think, for TIME's mature and unmalicious cover stories, such as the one on Eliot.

I found out a lot about myself in listening to my friends' accounts of what they wouldn't tell. Ross wouldn't tell a remark of Gibbs's that I hadn't known. "He's the nicest guy in the world until five p.m." I passed it on to TIME myself together with Althea's "You're not a bad boy trying to be good, you're a good boy trying to be bad." I told them I had been trying to overcome a stubborn defense mechanism that has operated after five p.m. and was so frank in this regard that they seemed to think I was intent on setting this tone. God knows how the piece will come out, but I hope no one else but me is hit. They have promised to omit the Stanley Walker story of the divorce in the Mirror, which they had dug up along with themes of mine in the 5th Grade. Janey Williams said she never saw me throw anything at a girl and the piece may finally end up as a comparative study of female targets.

When we heard the terrible news about Morris [Markey] I tried to get in touch with Helen [Markey], have written her twice, and called their home in Halifax, Virginia over a period of days, but she is not there. I asked her for details when she feels up to writing them and I told her I am going to write a piece on Morris, probably for the Saturday Review. I feel he should have a memorial, and I can't think of anyone else who will do it.

He was probably killed, certainly accidentally, by the very Remington rifle he once brought to Sandy Hook. The four of us shot a target on a barn and Morris always cocked the gun before handing it to one of us, keeping the muzzle pointed at the ground. It was a sensitive trigger and Althea fired the gun into the ground when it was handed to her. He loved to cock it and to lower the hammer gently against the cartridge. Since he had shot a sick pully, I figure he may have cocked it again and leaned it against a kitchen wall, kicking it when he went out for ice around midnight. He was reckless with firearms and with automobiles, but he denied this with all his vehemence. A man with his gestures and flourishes is dangerous with things that go off or can reach seventy miles an hour. We had heard from Helen six weeks ago and they were all in fine shape. His novel is coming out in the fall, and Sue is marrying a man they liked in October. I must find out if the investigation is still open. I imagine that accidental death has been proved, but if it hasn't, I could certainly testify to its high probability in view of what I knew about that rifle.

Love and kisses from Helen and Rosie and me.

As ever,

Carl Van Doren died in his sleep at five o'clock the other morning from heart and pneumonia a few hours before a letter I had written him arrived. I was always very fond of him and admired his work.

## TO THE RONALD WILLIAMSES

*West Cornwall, Connecticut*
*August 9, 1950*

Dear Ronnie and Janey:

. . . The stuff from the Mid-Ocean man enchanted us, of course, highlighted as it was by delightful indications of how the evening progressed in fluency and lack of restraint, beginning with statements of plain fact, proceeding to lovely magnifications of the subject, and ending in a million dollars worth of libel about the Higginson case, which TIME has promised to omit. Whichever one of you sweet children invented, at two a.m., the word "sloplolly" for Helen, we don't know, but it is now in family use. Janey's sudden emergence as a critic opens my eyes to another phase of her infinite variety and I would settle for her analysis in place of a longer piece. Now that I know that I am "one of the great men of the world" I will not be satisfied with only three pitchers of rum after this.

Captain Blandish was recently rejected in his application to become a major because of three extremely costly mistakes he has made since June. He returned from Africa with his squadron of planes, each of them filled to the wings with flowers. When his commanding officer said, "Where is the uranium?" Blandish replied, "Uranium? I thought you said geraniums." If they ever send him out to bring in the flocks, you know what he will get, and speaking of that this was his second mistake. He was commissioned to collect from one of the debtor countries "payment in kind" and I am trying to get the New Yorker to do a double page spread showing an irate general at the left staring past Blandish at a landscape of 50,000 cows. The caption, Blandish speaking, of course, "I thought you said kine."

. . . Have you thought of Chloe and Jemima for the coming twins?

As ever,

*West Cornwall, Connecticut*
*October 5, 1950*

Dear Janie:

. . . I was loath to tell you about the third adventure of Captain Blandish because it was one of the saddest and most futile of his mistakes. Once again he had got his orders over the telephone, an instrument that has always puzzled him. You will remember the awful dawn when he shot the bugler because he thought his sergeant had said, "The fellow was a burglar." The third incident happened in August, when he was ordered to proceed to Pakistan with a view to "discreetly ascertaining the situation there over a period of six weeks." He was then to report back in person. He did so, of course, and reported that everything in Parkerstown was about what you might imagine it to be in any other place of the same size in New Jersey. He said he had met a lovely couple named Mitchell, that the food in all the hotels was execrable, that he had spent several pleasant evenings with a Miss Ann Honeycutt, but that on the whole he would have enjoyed himself much more at a hotel in New York City. As the result of his report, a lieutenant-colonel named Winterhorn suffered a severe heart attack. . . .

Love and kisses,
As ever,

## To John McNulty

*West Cornwall, Connecticut*
*October 5, 1950*

Dear John:

Honey told me the other day that you are not yet as interested in your baby as you thought you ought to be—this from a woman who lost interest in me in 1928, who doesn't know where her sisters are, and couldn't fill out a form saying whether or not she has any nieces or nephews. I thought you ought to know that the baby is not interested in you either as yet. Rosemary used to glance in my direction with about the same interest she had in a window pane or a passing charwoman. It wasn't until she was two and realized she was stuck with me that she said, during a walk through autumn leaves, "I love you." She will be nineteen October 7, and this I find hard to believe.

One night during the summer she phoned us out of bed at one-thirty a.m. and said, "Have you got any money?" A state cop had picked her up, on the way home from the movies with a Princeton Junior, whose car had no tail-light, windshield wiper, or steering wheel. Rosie got the cop into a friend's home and offered him whiskey and cake. He took the cake and saw my Cadillac which was there and asked her whose it was. "It's mine," she told him and he said, "Well, get in your stinking Cadillac and go home."

The other thing you ought to know about her and me happened last Thanksgiving. She went out with the Princeton boy and a Yale boy, and Helen told me not to lock the front door, but I forgot and locked it. When they brought her home after four in the morning and she couldn't get in, the boys said, "Your father is mad and has locked you out." "Oh, yeah?" she said, coolly, and rang the doorbell. When I turned on the light in the hall and opened the door, she said, "What the hell are you doing up at this ungodly hour?" "I'm sorry," I said. "I won't let it happen again." The two boys are still talking about this confusing dialog and the consensus seems to be, "Jesus, what a father to have."

I remember that boy in Columbus and you will surely get the pony. Rosie had two, Rowdy and Jingle, but she would just stare at them when she was four and say, "The car, please."

Love to you and Faith and John Joseph from Helen and me and Rosie.

As ever,

Jim

## To E. B. White

*Wolcott Gibbs' play,* Season in the Sun, *had opened on Broadway.*

*West Cornwall, Connecticut*
*October 5, 1950*

Dear Andy:

I was happy to hear about the effect of THE SEAL on you and sorry to hear about those Eustachian tubes, but I think this windiness is common and disappears easily, perhaps more easily than the quivering of a muscle in my left groin. This thing about not being able to write is also common with you youngsters and goes away, and all of us will always be broke from now on. I've only known about three people who could sleep.

The TIME piece, as written by a solemn man who was six when I went to work on The New Yorker, who first found out in July that I write and draw, and who for years has been a disciple of Whittaker Chambers, was as great a mess as you would want to see. Of seventy-three facts, only nineteen were right, and all I learned about myself was that I have apparently not got a thickening of the capsule of the lens, but a carapace of glaucoma, or so the piece says. This is a little like finding out that the injury you suffered in the Cornell-Pennsylvania game was actually syphilis.

Matthews had thought of Sayre as well as you—confidentially, a breath after he thought of you—and Joe may take on the piece, since he has got out from under his television stint which he always calls "the garbage." I had told the TIME man so many of the dark things about me that this confession became known at TIME and when I told Matthews I could write the article myself, he said, "We don't want an unfriendly piece." There was also some feeling that, in a later mood, I might sue myself.

The material on me, much of it gleaned from friends between midnight and morning, was so extensive that the writer couldn't find anything he was looking for, and, with data up to his waist, had to guess and make things up. He insisted that the one drawing he liked and the one fable were "the famous ones," which gave me practically nothing to sustain my vanity.

The strain of the Gibbs [play] opening told on me and no one is happier about its obvious success. . . . There were only about three places where I wanted to put in lines or take them out, none of them as inviting as the line in "Daphne Laureola" when a character says, "I knew a man who married a woman old enough to be his great-grandmother." I just wanted to put in, "She was a hundred and two and he was eighteen."

The madame of a whore house and homosexuals barely interest me at all, and Gibbs may have a tiny bit too much of them, but I had to laugh a lot and I would like to see it again and what more can you say than that.

I think it's fine that Joe is at MIT. Rosie seems to be getting along very well at Pennsylvania. She has a roommate named Fifi.

Love and kisses to you and Kay from Helen and me,

    As always,

## TO GUS LOBRANO

*West Cornwall, Connecticut*
*October 10, 1950*

Dear Gus:

Enclosed is the letter from Mary Mian. I wish you would have it copied, send the original back to me and the copy to Bill Maxwell and anyone else you think might enjoy it.

Eudora Welty sent the Mary Mian manuscript last week and we read half of it the other night and it seems excellent to me. We will finish it and get it off to you this week. I don't believe it runs to more than 7500 words.

The story contains two or three phrases in the idiom of Henry James, which I hope Ross will not insist on inverting on behalf of our thirteen-year-old readers, if you take the piece. I mean such things as "It had begun, her dislike, with something he had said." I have felt for a long time that it is a pity that the quality of some of the old boy's manner has gone out of our writing. "Her dislike had begun" is colorless by comparison. The piece is done with only a speck of this and in what seems to me a mature and perfected Mian style, and I was pretty excited to get the thing.

　　　　Yours as ever,

*Mr. Gus Lobrano, The New Yorker*
*25 West 43rd Street, New York, N. Y.*


## TO DALE KRAMER

*Kramer was working on his book,* Ross and The New Yorker, *published in 1951.*

*West Cornwall, Connecticut*
*October 17, 1950*

Dear Kramer:

. . . I remember your saying that some writer was said to have been "ruined by Ross" and I keep wondering how this is managed. I feel that a writer who is ruinable is not really a writer. . . .

This has not been one of White's good years, I guess, or at least he says he hasn't been able to write, but I doubt that he could have been happy doing anything else. As Carl Van Doren said, "It's hard to write, but it's harder not to."

Best wishes,

Cordially yours,

James Thurber

*Mr. Dale Kramer, 32 Bank Street*
*New York, N. Y.*

꙳   ꙳   ꙳

*The Homestead, Hot Springs, Virginia*
*November 2, 1950*

*Dale Kramer, Esq., 79 Washington Place*
*New York 14, New York*

Dear Kramer:

. . . I do not think you can leave Gibbs out of the list of important persons on the magazine in the early days, since he was the best and fastest and most brilliant "writing editor". Not everybody could deal with manuscripts easily and skillfully, and nobody as expertly as he did. I would say Ralph Ingersoll was important, too, since he did amazing and complete work in getting material for "Talk of the Town" and was a hardworking research editor, with a greater knowledge of New York than anybody else.

No, I don't believe any editor actually develops a writer, but Ross did have a way of attracting and holding the people perfectly suited for his magazine, and he was determined to get new people and not depend on old and famous names. No man or woman can add to a writer's skill or talent but they can create a congenial atmosphere and help a great deal by not trying to influence or direct or insist. It was a nice place to work, and we were certainly on our own, and Ross was a great encourager by word of mouth, telegram and letter.

Joe Liebling told me a few years ago that he had carefully compared the magazine in its first ten years with the later magazine and thought it had immensely improved, certainly in a journalistic way. Many of my early stories I did not put in a book, but few of the later ones were left out. You have probably gone over the old issues more carefully than I, but I recognize the fact that some of the oldtimers have a feeling of nostalgia for "the Golden Years" and I suspect this feeling may have magnified the actual differences. . . .

## TO JOEL SAYRE

*Sayre was writing the* Time *cover story on Thurber and had written Thurber that he couldn't seem to avoid occasionally "kicking you in the crotch."*

West Cornwall, Connecticut
December 22, 1950

Dear Joe:

A little crotch-kicking is a good thing, if done in anger. I can't stand guys who are merely piqued by the unforgivable. Good deportment is a minor virtue in a man, but God's own comfort to his friends. The TIME people got all of the dark meat with the white, but you are up against a Matthews who met me in one of my June angelic and extra-sensory moods. . . .

"The White Deer" has been the basis of sermons and Christmas readings in one or two Episcopal churches and I was astonished to find I had done in the last chapter a modern restatement of the Atonement beginning "What you have been you now no longer are."

One of the things I most resent is the idiotic use of the word "genius" for me, and when it came up on Mary Margaret McBride's program the other day I said I was a reporter without enough genius to get off newspapers and make more than forty a week until I was thirty-two. Anybody with the slightest critical ability knows that a genius would not have to slave over his prose so long, or over his drawings so little. The geniuses are O'Hara and Sally Benson and Peter Blume and Hendrik Van Loon. First drafts of my pieces sound twelve years old and only get going on the fourth rewrite. I have never cut off an ear, or stuck my hand in a fire. . . .

. . . I was embarrassed when C. Lester Walker called his piece in the LADIES' HOME JOURNAL "The Fabulous James Thurber," but these apocryphal stories do pop up. There is the one about the case of glass eyes I carry, each of which has a different tone of inflammation, to be used on a long drinking night, and constantly changed in the men's room. The pay off, of course, is one for three o'clock in the morning that has an American flag instead of a pupil. I am also supposed to have had my host arrested at a weekend party in Ridgefield, where I never spent even an hour, when I lost my wallet on Friday night, and I never carried a wallet. I demanded that we all be searched, and the wallet is found in my host's pocket and I had him thrown in jail. Then there is the one about my having gone to someone's house and seen a Picasso drawing on the wall. "I see you have an original Thurber," I said to my host. Who replied sweetly, "No, it is just a Picasso." I traced this one down to an old beau of Helen's, a man whom I later described, at a drinking party, according to a friend of mine who was there, as having "the soul of a secretary." Believe it or not he was secretary to Fiorello LaGuardia.

Please bat us off at least a few lines, filling us in on Gertrude and yourself and Nora, and telling us how things are rolling. The verb is your own.

Janie and Ronnie, and Helen and I send you both our love and kisses. We constantly think of you.

As ever,

ಶ್ಯ   ಶ್ಯ   ಶ್ಯ

West Cornwall, Connecticut<br>December 22, 1950

Dear Joe:

. . . If you are doing the TIME piece you might want to know that people write me about my eye from all parts of the world. Americans suggest watching jumping beans, rubbing my spine, injecting lemon juice, applying hot flatirons to the temple, and using the urine of virgins. A man in Birmingham, England, sent me black paper and an aluminum pencil, and I just got a letter from a doctor named Van Der Merwe suggesting tubercle endotoxoid injections. . . .

It took me a decade to get on to Mark Van Doren's quick temper and occasional tendency to shout. It would not surprise me if Henry James was a secret drinker, or Washington Gladden a preliminary prizefighter, at heart. My poodle thinks I am crazy and cruel, because I step on her, but when she gets stung in the ear she runs to me.

. . . The proof of humor is the ability to put one's self on awkward public record, just as the proof of wit is to do that to others, and while we are going in for profound definitions, the proof of solicitude is not avoidance, and the maddest I get is at people who avoid discussing my eye on the ridiculous ground that it would embarrass me. If the whole piece were about my eye, it would clearly do the job. There is too much talk about the courage or nobility of the afflicted, since I know damn well that the challenge is far greater than the handicap. Remember that one-legged newsboy in Columbus who went on the vaudeville stage and look at the average paraplegic absorbed in learning skills and tricks. I saw an armless woman in a movie short wrapping bundles with her feet, and having more fun than you and I have with our hands. Furthermore, I have been spared the sight of television.

I smoke Philip Morrises, hate all women as the piece on Mrs. Albright proves, attacked football players in "The Male Animal" because I was no good at ping pong or bowling, and like the writing of Henry James because it deals with people who never injure anyone unintentionally. My two great frustrations are my inability to speak French fluently or to play the piano well, but once, in 1910, I blocked a punt by Allen Thurman, wearing my father's shoes at the time and looking pretty silly. The whole story is in this incident and the fact that, at a Methodist church picnic, I threw a ball bat farther than Bugs Shorey and won a bible. . . .

More later, and once again love and kisses and a Merry Christmas.

As ever,

## To the Thurber Family

*Robert and Mame objected to what Thurber was writing about his Grandfather Fisher and his father for* The Thurber Album. *The prolonged arguments resulted in a permanent rift between the brothers.*

> *West Cornwall, Connecticut*
> *December 22, 1950*

Dear Thurbers:

I was glad to get your comments and corrections on "Man With a Rose." I had forgotten the 1884 date because 1878 somehow stuck in my mind; I knew the spelling of Catawba, but missed Daugherty. What you had to read was an uncorrected proof and these would have been caught, except 1884, by our checking department, a group of eight or ten men who keep the New Yorker from making more than a few mistakes a year.

I sent the proof without permission of Ross, for we have found out that people involved in a story have so many objections it takes weeks to iron them out. Subjects of Profiles used to see proofs, but we had to stop it, and "My Life and Hard Times" would have lost the incident of the mice if Mama had got her hands on it. Now nobody in the world believes that I didn't make it up. It is also a fact of human nature that the disinterested reader is not impressed by facts as such and forgets them in a week. Tests have shown that the names of characters and even of the author are forgotten. As for length, it is a quality and a quantity that comes out after many rewritings and consultations with editors, five or six of whom read everything. I made some deletions that they insisted on restoring, and this kind of thing is a matter of personal taste.

Making a man perfect, as those old vanity books did, is to make him colorless and unreal, and readers are suspicious of glossing over a character, as witness Hayes's observation that I saw Columbus people through clear, but "slightly rose-tinted lenses." The danger my book runs is in this direction and not the other. I will emphasize Grandpa's essential work as a farmer during the Civil War and the fact that sending substitutes was common in such cases, but I want to make him tick and to present him in the round, and the perceptive reader, familiar with psychology, would realize that something interesting and actual lay behind his exaggerated love of U.S. Grant and his constant tendency to "make a pass." These are manifestations of one of the simplest of human impulses, known as over-compensation, and in the New Yorker I am writing for a sharp audience. Satisfied by my analysis they would forget about it, but if I left it out they would pick at me. These considerations are the natural result of thirty years in the writing game as writer and editor. The editors and others who have read the piece here, lacking your intimacy, look upon the piece as a tribute to an interesting and living character, and it would not occur to them, for example, that there is too much about the store, but it would to Katherine, who belongs to a branch of the family that has notably not profited from the store.

I think you can trust me completely in dealing with Mama and the others, but I am not going to concern you unnecessarily over a period of months by sending out proofs, which are hard to read, and, as we found out long ago, falsely magnify both length and dull spots. . . .

Merry Christmas and Happy New Year again from us all.

> As ever,
> James

P.S. After reading your letter I have decided to eliminate one of Mama's wittiest remarks—her "Why, Mrs. Miller, it's the business to go into." If I wrote it, the editors and other admirers of Mame Thurber would refuse to leave it out, but I want to stay away from any disturbing factor. Joe Sayre is doing the TIME piece on me, and writes, "It is not easy to get you down on paper without kicking you in the crotch." This is sound, right, and deserved, although you wouldn't guess it—and I have insisted that he do a well-rounded portrait, complete with my yelling at people.

## TO HAROLD ROSS

*West Cornwall, Connecticut*
*December 27, 1950*

Dear Ross:

. . . When Frank does another one of those wonderful inversions of typical news stories I hope he puts in one about an American spy who has been giving secrets to the Russians for years, but is not a "small, mild-mannered, quiet man, respected by his neighbors." The last three such men had been like this. Maybe Frank has done it already, but I don't miss much of his stuff. I send this to you instead of directly to him, because of your well-known nuisance value when it comes to hounding writers and making them work.

I also wonder if he has ever wondered about which of the Harper brothers was the Harper of Harper & Brothers. When one of the Harper brothers, who was not *the* Harper, was asked what Harper he was, did he say, "I am just one of the Harper brothers, and not the Harper of Harper & Brothers?" Maybe he had the money, but if he was merely the egoist of the family, why didn't he use his first name and make it John W. Harper & Brothers.

Happy New Year to you and to Frank Sullivan.

As always,

*Mr. H. W. Ross, The New Yorker*
*25 West 43rd St., New York, N. Y.*

## TO DR. GORDON BRUCE

*West Cornwall, Conn.*
*December 28, 1950*

Dear Gordon:

. . . You may have heard that Oscar [Wilde] was once sent to a house of prostitution in France, by friends who raised the money at a bar one night, and that afterwards, when he was asked what he thought about it, he said, "It was like cold mutton." One of our present day wits is John McNulty, who had this to say about Lillian Ross's Profile of Hemingway: "It was like the Eddie Wakus affair—she loved him so much she shot him." Apparently Miss Ross was bewildered to be told that her piece did Hemingway any damage—and so was Hemingway.

Incidentally, Joel Sayre is now doing the TIME article.

. . . our best wishes for a Happy New Year.

As always,

P.S. Edmund Wilson has referred to Maugham as "the gentleman caterer" and Hemingway said of a colleague's sharp ear, "It's the ear of a writer who asks a croupier to give him a list of the expressions he uses."

## To Saul Rosenzweig

*The Ledgelets, Somerset, Bermuda*
*May 29, 1950*

Dear Saul:

I got started on a new long fairy tale which took me seven weeks to finish, and my correspondence has clogged up. "The Thirteen Clocks" will be published this fall and I will send you a copy. I haven't been able to draw down here, possibly because there is too much light . . .

"What Cocktail Party?" seems to have aroused all sorts of reactions, but it was very favorably received in England, I am told, except perhaps by T.S. Eliot's friend Hayward, who has not replied to an advance tear sheet I sent him. I was trying to put down some of the hundreds of reactions I heard, a number of them through Ann Honeycutt, who declares that "psychiatry is God" and, although she is a writer, subscribes to her psychiatrist's belief that most of the product of creative talent is an excrescence of some unconscious irritation, and that talent should be regarded as what it is, an osis or itis similar to other swellings and inflammations. I was particularly annoyed by a follower of Bergler, whose recent book says that all the thirty-four writers he has treated were test cases and tries to perpetuate the idea of writing being logorhea. The complete treatise on the subject will have to be done by someone who has at least ten years to give to say twenty of the big boys, perhaps from Flaubert to Hemingway. I had a look the other day at Henry James's "The Art of the Novel" and at some of his prefaces, and I am persuaded beyond changing that his was the most conscious and hence selective and rejective method of all the writers. I have reason to believe that he got the idea of a daytime ghost from a whimsical habit he had of peering through windows to titillate old ladies in his family.

Love and kisses as always to all the Rosenzweigs.

>Cordially,

>James Thurber

*Dr. Saul Rosenzweig, 4562 Scott Avenue*
*St. Louis 10, Mo.*

## TO MALCOLM COWLEY

>*West Cornwall, Connecticut*

>*February 3, 1951*

Dear Malcolm:

. . . It turns out that you are . . . suggesting to THE REPORTER that I do a piece about Fitzgerald. It isn't as if I didn't have enough work, but I am now doing the piece.

I would like to get a copy or a tear sheet of the review I did of "The Last Tycoon" in the NEW REPUBLIC—in the winter of 1941–42, I think. Re-reading the book a couple of years ago, I found I hadn't done it justice, in spite of Wilson's note to me saying that it was "one of the few reviews with any critical merit."

I do not believe that Fitzgerald was a worse drinker than most of us, but this is always mystical ground. Hemingway called Scott a rummy, O'Hara says that Eustace Tilley has no right to talk about Hemingway's drinking—obviously a crack at Gibbs and Sally Benson—as if O'Hara could not have held his own with Scott or anybody else, except Benchley and Sinclair Lewis in the days when he went to bed full of Scotch at three a.m. and got up at six a.m. for more Scotch.

I also do not see any validity at all in the theory that Fitzgerald had to be "revived", and I mention half a dozen pieces of evidence on my side, from your own work and Kazin's to "The Portable Fitzgerald", 1945, the CBS "Last Tycoon", 1948, and the latest Gatsby movie, 1949. I also take up the profoundly interesting fact, to me, that the Individual was matched by the Category Man in the Twenties and finally overwhelmed by him around 1930. I describe a party of the time and point out in it the narcissists and voyeurs, the ideology unmaskers, the unimplemented oversimplifiers, the manic depressives, and the products of broken homes, the haters of Lovestoneites, and the admirers, like me, of Sir Tristram—how did I ever get into that?—and dozens of other Group Men. . . .

As ever,

Jim

P.S. I also give my own definitions of rummy, souse, drunk, sot, and the others. The drunk, for instance, is the stranger who annoys your party on the sidewalk as you are leaving 21; the rummy has several suits, but always wears the brown one; and the sot doesn't know where he is, or who you are, and doesn't care; and so on. I suppose a little group of people will yell at me. More fun.

I spent nine hours with Scott one night and could have told Mizener a few interesting notes to add to his rich confusion of facts. It was 1934, and S.F. kept referring to "Tender Is the Night" as "my testament of faith." He wanted me to take him to call on a "good girl" at three a.m., the hour he made famous. Helen and Honey turned us down, but Paula Trueman took us in. Both she and I the next morning had dozens of the catalogues of Zelda's show of paintings which he had kept handing to us.

I am troubled about how much of this to use, since I believe there have been far too many anecdotes like this written about him, without real significance or illumination. I have been a bad behavior boy myself, God knows, but my oldest friend, the late Herman Miller, believed it was not fundamental. It wasn't.

J.T.

## To Dale Kramer

*Kramer had sent Thurber a manuscript draft of his book,* Ross and The New Yorker.

*The Ledgelets, Somerset Bridge, Bermuda*
*April 23, 1951*

*Mr. Dale Kramer, 32 Bank Street*
*New York City 14, New York*

Dear Kramer:

. . . I think you have slighted or blunted one or two of the longer anecdotes, which was natural with so terribly much material to deal with . . .

. . . When I met [Chaplin] at his house in 1939, he said, "You wrote one of the two funniest things in the world." He then described the anecdote that belonged to White and which had been reprinted in Eastman's book, "Involvement of Laughter." I naturally asked the funniest man in the world what was the second funniest thing in the world. His eyes lighted up and he said, "A man is bending over tying his shoe, and a stranger comes up and kicks him in the bottom. 'What did you do that for?' asked the man. 'Well, you were tying your shoe, weren't you?' " This seemed remarkable to me, because it is surely not the second funniest thing in the world, and Chaplin had 6,500 gags that were superior. As a matter of fact, it isn't funny at all. . . .

During the reign of Arthur Samuels as Managing Editor, Ross asked me to see the magazine to bed at the printers, so that I could stand by Samuels and "keep him from doing anything." Samuels got jumpy about a lovely note White had written on page one, in which there was a line about a little dog eating tulips in the graveyard of St. Mark's on the Bouwerie. It was perfectly innocent, and any change would have ruined the note. Nobody can make any change in White's prose without ruining it. Samuels insisted that I get Ross on the phone, and I went out of the composing room and pretended to call him. After a few minutes I came back and said, "Ross says for God's sake, don't touch it, if we are sure that dogs eat tulips." As an old dog man, I said they did, and the line stayed in. After Samuels was gone as Managing Editor, I told Ross about the incident, and four years after that he said to me one day, when we were talking about Samuels, "Dammit, he wanted to take out White's line about the dog eating those lilies."

You have not done justice to Ross and his mother, so that this comes out hasty and flat. She insisted on thinking of Harold as a young man who needed his rest and shouldn't be out after 11:00 p.m. When he got in at 3:00 or 4:00, she was always waiting up for him, and he began to make elaborate excuses. On one occasion, he told her that his host, at 11:00 p.m., when Ross started home, suddenly locked all the doors and said, "No one will leave this house until 3 o'clock in the morning." "Why, I never heard of such a thing in my life," his mother said. The next time he was out late, he told her that he had been attending a men's embroidery class. He said he had got so interested in his embroidery that he didn't notice the hour. She surprised him by asking to see some of his work. During the next week, Ross telephoned my wife and five or six other women friends and said, "Do you know where I could get hold of a doily that looks as though it had been made by a man?" All the women told him there wasn't any such doily.

Like the mothers of almost all of us, Ross's did not think THE NEW YORKER amounted to much. It was only a few years old when she was in New York, it didn't have a national circulation, or many subscribers, and his name did not appear in its pages. She came to the conclusion that he was actually not one of its important figures. To impress her, he took her through the offices, ending up at his own, and explaining that he was the Editor-In-Chief. She made no comment whatever, and that night at dinner, Ross finally said, being a little irked, "Well, mama, what do you think of THE NEW YORKER?" Still thinking it wasn't much, and that he had been overrating his position there, she said, "Well, Harold, all I can say is I hope that some day you become connected with THE SATURDAY EVENING POST." When THE NEW YORKER was eleven years old, Mrs. Thurber and I rented a house for the winter in Litchfield, owned by a woman in her eighties, who, the real-estate agent finally told us, "was dissatisfied with your references. She wants to know if you can give her the name of some institution older and better known than THE NEW YORKER." I gave her Harper & Brothers and HARPER'S MAGAZINE, founded more than a hundred years ago. She was satisfied. When I told this story to Frederick Lewis Allen, Editor of HARPER'S MAGAZINE, he grinned and said, "Do you want to trade?" My mother once heard that I had bought THE NEW YORKER, and was cross with me because I didn't give my two brothers jobs.

I think the best line is missing here. [Henry] Luce sighed, and said to Ross, "There is not a single kind thing about me in this whole profile." And Ross snarled, "That's what you get for being a baby tycoon." When Luce objected to certain references to his wife, Ross took McKelway out of the room—both sides kept going out of the room for conferences—and said, "Was there anything about my wife in the FORTUNE article on THE NEW YORKER?" This proved to us that Ross was telling the truth when he said that he never read a piece about himself. I don't think he ever did.

Ik Shuman deserves a lot more space, since of all the Managing Editors, he lasted far the longest. A crack TIMES reporter and rewrite man, Paul Block's righthand man, head of a news syndicate, and since connected with half a dozen magazines as Editor, he impressed Ross tremendously. In Paris, in 1938, Ross said to me and O'Hara, "If I had had Shuman to begin with, there wouldn't even have been a depression." Shuman arranged for the READER'S DIGEST to pay THE NEW YORKER a large sum, in five figures, for reprints the DIGEST had already used, on the ground that we had not been paid enough. He was responsible for discovering Fleischman's putting nearly a million dollars into STAGE magazine. He got along with the Business Department, from Fleischman down, and once when Ross sent him up there to get a big concession of some sort, Shuman managed it in a few minutes. "How did you go about it?" Ross asked. Shuman said, "I just asked them for it, explained why, and they gave it to me." Ross roared, "Goddammit, you got it the wrong way! I wanted you to beat it out of them!" Shuman was never on an intimate personal basis with Ross, and the secretary who got away with so much of Ross's money counted on this heavily. He would hand Shuman an advance slip, showing that Ross wanted to withdraw $2,000 in expense money, and Shuman would initial the phoney slip without question. Almost any other man might have twitted Ross about gambling or what not, and the stealing would have been out in the open. This young secretary, with the wonderful last name of Winney, once withdrew nearly $1,000 from The Guaranty Trust, on forged checks, in one week. He would take them to a Vice President, or some other official, and tip him the wink, suggesting that the old boy was really living a high life. Winney once gave a champagne party in the Astor for a lot of people with Ross's money. It was on Election night, I think, and Ross remembered later that he had walked past the Astor that night. "I was hit on the head," he said grimly, "by my own champagne corks." In the end, he said of Winney, "He sat out there at his desk and fed me cake." This is a great story to me, since it went on for years. It should have been discovered weeks earlier when Fleischman was disturbed by Ross's apparent desire to draw six month's salary in advance. Fleischman's concern was carried to Ross by three different persons. Ross merely stormed and said, "He's made another damn fool mistake." In Winney's apartment, after he killed himself with gas, letters were found, carefully filed, revealing his correspondence with a real estate agent in Tahiti. The trouble was that the war came along and all passports were withdrawn. The night he killed himself, Winney came to the office, cleared out his desk drawers, left everything very neat and tidy, and went home to die. If he hadn't destroyed all the cancelled checks, Ross might have collected. I don't want to be quoted as the source of this information.

Janet Flanner was both London and Paris correspondent for many years before the war, and later decided to stick to France. She is one of our most brilliant writers, and Ross once said, "You have to have three dictionaries when you edit Flanner's stuff; Webster's, French, and Medical." When he found out that she had got the Legion of Honor from France, he told her, "I have little respect for that decoration. They give it to men who invent stuff to kill potato bugs." The phrase "I have little respect for" is common with Ross, and when I introduced him to my great and famous eye doctor, he said, "I have very little respect for professional men." This includes lawyers, and Ross harps on it.

Daise Terry is an old-timer, whose job is to "hold people's hands," a famous Ross expression. She buys theater tickets, arranges ship, train, and hotel reservations, has actually rented apartments for the old-timers, sends flowers to sick wives and newborn infants, and buys gifts for all occasions. The artists and writers are devoted to her, and she is always visiting one of them.

You give so much space to Hokinson that I think Mary Petty should be given her space, too. This brings up an important item—the artists who use gag men and those who don't. Hokinson mainly used other people's lines, but Petty never used a single one in her life. I was told that 40 per cent of Arno's stuff is contributed, but this would have to be checked. I have used about twenty lines in as many years. I am more often confused with Steig than anybody, and Broun always praised Steig's work when he thought it was mine. My mother told me that Steig is her favorite artist. His "Small Fry" was one of our famous departments.

You mention Markey as being "slight", which puzzles me. He was thin until he reached his twenties, but in 1932, at the Danbury Fair, he weighed 195, and he was six feet tall. I think of him as one of the big men physically I have known. He knocked down McKelway with a right swing at a NEW YORKER party about fifteen years ago, which Stanley Walker made notorious by his famous piece in The Daily News—or was it The Mirror? McKelway is a big man, too, and what made us all sore, since Walker was on the magazine at the time, was this line, "They flew at each other like enraged butterflies." Maybe there is a butterfly tractor.

Since, as I say, I haven't had time, because of my work, to read the manuscript word for word, you may or may not have left out what I consider Ross's most typical line, and the one that I use as the tag of the second act in the play I have been working on for ten years about THE NEW YORKER. He uses it a great deal, or did, never more effectively than the day he found out one writer had disappeared, another was getting married, and another had smashed his hand in a taxi door. "God, how I pity me!" he said. His trying to keep sex out of the office was made into comedy by the fact that, at the height of it, Lois Long married Arno, and Katherine and Andy became engaged. "Sex is an incident," Ross still says. And his greatest contempt is for the man who "makes a career of sex." A sign reading "Leave all sex behind, Ye who enter here" was put on the wall just outside the elevators, and quietly taken down at Ross's order.

These are just suggestions that might add a little to what seems to me a lively, often exciting, extremely amusing history of Ross and his magazine. The more anecdotes, the better. I think that anecdotes helped to make "The Far Side of Paradise" so popular. But, of course, it has a marriage of a man and a woman, and all you have is a man and a magazine. I hope you haven't left out his sad lament, "I came back to this office this afternoon, from the Algonquin, with three writers, who couldn't have got back alone." It was the first time in our lives that White and Gibbs and I had had lunch alone with Ross, and we all must have been in, what he took to be, depressed, desperate, or absentminded moods.

Best Wishes,

James Thurber

P. S. Only one line of yours distressed me, and that is the reference to my first wife as being "large, amiable and firm minded", or something like that. When I married Althea Adams, thirty years ago, she was rated one of the most beautiful girls in the country. We have a 19-year old daughter who also would appreciate one more adjective for the old girl.

J.T.

🙚  🙚  🙚

*West Cornwall, Connecticut*

*June 14, 1951*

Dear Kramer:

I haven't talked to Ross about your book as yet, but I have written Mrs. White asking for her viewpoint, since most of what you say was news to me. I feel I would like to have their opinions and what they base them on.

I don't suppose anyone is really satisfied with a piece about himself, anymore than he accepts as completely true photographs of himself or recordings of his voice. Personally, I never get excited by or deeply involved in anything written about me. I am interested in what a writer thinks, sometimes surprised, but never antagonistic. I seem to remember your saying that I have had "failures" before the New Yorker days and this you must have got from sound sources, so I thought little about it, even though I don't know what the failures were, except that I was getting only forty dollars a week before I joined the magazine. I have always heard that Ross was a first-rate newspaperman. Herbert Asbury once said, "Ross could get it and he could write it." Most newspapermen, including myself and Ross, are proud of their reporting days. Irvin Cobb used to say, "Tell me I can't write a short story or humor, but don't say I wasn't a good reporter." It is hard for me to imagine Ross using hyperbole about being fired from papers on which he is reputed to have had a good record. This is like Gibbs saying, "I have liked more plays than anyone" or McKelway saying, "I have known fewer pretty girls than any man." . . .

. . . I am not a poet and none of my New Yorker verse is much good, but I have no desire whatever to ask you not to use anything I have published. I did the poem and the short, ordinary casual about tootsie rolls while on the Post and had to write them at night. Some of my earliest stuff was more or less a kidding of the New Yorker itself for having rejected some twenty longer casuals that I liked. "I'll give them tootsie rolls and poems, since that's what they seem to want," I once told my first wife. I did not expect them to buy the piece about the man in the revolving door and actually expected a sharp note of rejection. "A Box to Hide In" has a long and involved personal story behind it, much too elaborate to explain in one day. It was, of course, a bold kidding of the return-to-the-womb school of talk going on twenty years ago. The personal, or intimate slant to it will never be revealed. You have my permission to use these things, but I wanted to clear them up a little.

. . . I cannot understand anyone trying to prevent the publication of a book except for outright and intentional libel, obscenity, or defamation of character. I saw absolutely no hint of this in what I read of yours, and your attitude from the beginning has most definitely proved your desire to be fair and accurate and to consult with the chief figures.

When Gibbs wrote, "We have nothing to fear," he must have meant these chief figures, since there is more likelihood of the King of England becoming a circus clown than of Mrs. White and Gibbs ever writing anything together on earth or in heaven. None of us is going to write about the New Yorker, I am pretty sure. Ross had a title for his autobiography; "My Life on a Limb", but this has just been a gag of his.

I must admit I think "Ross and The New Yorker" is better than "Ross of The New Yorker" but I don't really like either one, and kind of hoped for something livelier, with Ross and the New Yorker in the subtitle. . . .

   Cordially yours,
   James Thurber

❧  ❧  ❧

*June 15, 1951*

*Notes and Comment* [To Kramer]:

Don't, for God's sake, change anything about me. I like to be a boy who came up from failure, Ohio lad makes good in big city, etc. . . .

This business about "sophistication" has always annoyed the hell out of some of us. If Ross and White and I are sophisticated, we don't know it. Maybe Gibbs is sophisticated. Alexander King, editor of the defunct magazine "Americana" said, about 1928, quoting Woollcott, "Ross gets out the New Yorker with the aid of two country bumpkins." He meant White and me. I considered myself a hick until I was about thirty and could support this with many facts. I know my way around now, speak a little French, am not afraid of headwaiters, and once slept with a girl with a charming foreign accent, but surely my recent New Yorker series bears no traces of sophistication. E.B. White is the least sophisticated man I have ever known.

J.T.

## To the E. B. Whites

*West Cornwall, Connecticut*
*June 12, 1951*

Dear Andy and Katharine:

We got to New York last Friday to run into all kinds of problems and illnesses. I talked to Ross on the phone and he seemed cheerful, but coughed a lot. We also visited Gertrude [Sayre] at the hospital and she seems wonderfully improved because she has had her teeth out, something that she worried about for six years, and because her heart is actually completely recovered. She spent a weekend in Long Island. Joe takes her food he cooks himself and a chocolate cake of his own making. Elliott got out of the hospital Sunday and we saw him Monday. He is almost completely normal, has his humor and balance back, and shows the fag end of the manic state only in a tendency to talk too much and too fast.

I called my family in Columbus Saturday and my brother Robert answered the phone and began to bawl hell out of me for the piece on my father. He was so nasty that I hung up on him. It turned out that a letter from him was at the Algonquin desk and we got it and read it. It is a savage and relentless attack on almost everything I said and he seems to have persuaded my mother to react in the same way, except not violently. He says the piece should have been called "Hoosier Halfwit," claims I must have had a deep resentment of my father, and categorically denounces almost every paragraph. He said the piece should not have "seen the light of day." "I thought you would refer to his wonderful penmanship," is one sentence. Gus [Lobrano] and I are worried about what they will think of the piece on my mother and Gus has sent a proof together with a letter of praise. I wrote Robert a sharp letter after waiting two days and another note quoting six or eight people who liked it. Joel Sayre has finished the cover story about me for TIME and inserted a sentence saying I had written a fine, affectionate piece about my father. I will put in a paragraph for the book, just to please the family, but it is a rather shocking situation.

Since this was uppermost in my mind when I got home today, I was greatly disturbed by a letter from Dale Kramer indicating that the New Yorker is trying to prevent the publication of his book. Since my family was trying to prevent the publication of my piece, I am probably in no state to face this matter calmly, but I am against the suppression of anything, unless it is libelous or obscene, or defamation of character. I read the Kramer manuscript in part, the section about White and Gibbs and myself, and while I thought the writing was undistinguished, I didn't oppose anything vehemently. I don't see how anybody can force an author to change the title of his book, as Ross apparently wants to. I don't know exactly why Kramer wanted to print my early Villanelle or the casual "A Box to Hide In," since I am not a poet and the casual is not one of my best, but I have no desire whatever to prevent him from printing them. I wish I had time to read the whole book, but I haven't. I answered all his questions, since I feel the New Yorker should take it as well as dish it out. I suppose if we were Woollcott or Luce, we would have got mad about the Profiles on them, and there have been others. Unfortunately I haven't had a chance to talk with you or Ross, or anyone except Russell Lord, about Kramer's book, but Russ did not seem to have been antagonized by it. Perhaps I overlooked passages that would have annoyed me. I don't know.

The letter from Kramer today is a long one, and I don't feel I can answer it properly without getting your viewpoint on the situation. I did ask Kramer to change an unfriendly description of Althea and he agreed to.

We will be here for quite a while, since we're not going to Columbus until the fall. I get my degree at Williams next Sunday.

Love and kisses to you both,

As ever,

## To Frank Sullivan

*The Ledgelets, Somerset Bridge, Bermuda*
*May 7, 1951*

*Mr. Frank Sullivan, The Cornell Club,*
*107 East 48th Street, New York 17, New York*

Dear Frank:

We just finished reading Maggie Harriman's book about the "Round Table," which is freshened by your occasional entrances and comments on life and on the boys and girls. . . .

The fair author of the book did not consult me, and hence missed a couple of items never printed, but not unprintable, about Ross and A.W. [Alexander Woollcott]. I was in Ross's office one day when the phone rang. Ross was wearing his worst mood, defined by his familiar statement, "We have no ingenuity or manpower," and he snarled into the transmitter. It was Woollcott, who wanted to tell Ross the long story of the marriage, the day before, of Charles MacArthur and Helen Hayes. "Go ahead," Ross said, and he then laid the receiver quietly on his desk and walked to the window across the room, jingling his coins, looking out at the street, and insulting Woollcott in a low tone. The desk made a sounding board, but it wasn't quite good enough, so all we heard was a continual chattering. Ross listened to this for half a minute, and said, "The son of a bitch," and then when the receiver shut up, he walked over and picked it up and said, "Jesus, Aleck, I'm sorry, but just after I told you to go ahead, I had to go to the can." We could hear the sharp angry snap as Woollcott slammed up.

After finishing the book, I had a sudden, and possibly ill-advised, idea, and set about writing a brief parody entitled "The Harpers and their Circle," dealing with the famous old Long Table in the old Fifth Avenue Hotel, at which Harper and his brothers used to entertain Dickens, Poe, the Brownings, Charlotte Bronte, Hawthorne, and the others. They never asked Emerson. You may remember the time a strange young lady ran up to Poe, kissed him, and said, "I just simply adore 'The Goldberg'!" Poe gave her his pensive stare. "Madam," he said, "you must be thinking of 'Love Among the Ryans'." There is a great deal more along this same troubling line, and it will probably make Ross more self-conscious than ever. It has occurred to me, however, that I suggested to you that you write something about Harper and his brothers, one of whom wanted to bring out the Dickens novel under the title of "Oliver H. P. Twist" because it sounded smarter that way. Poe's notorious crack that "Emerson looks at life through Rhodes scholared glasses" caused Melville to leave the table forever.

As one of the boys who stood in awe and admiration of the "Round Table," I want to avoid sounding smart-aleck, in the tradition of the vast number of people who pretended to hate the girls and boys and accused them of log rolling and other helpful sins. Maggie must have careless publishers, since they let her get away with "Defarge" instead of Lafarge, but it is her own fault, or gag, that she sent Katherine White to Barnard instead of Bryn Mawr. I also think it was Gerald Brooks, and not Joe, who blackened Broun's eyes, or, at least, Gerald told me it was him. I will always remember the night I was out with Broun, making the rounds, while he talked on the way from place to place. In the bar at our last stop, he asked me not to go through the picket line at 21. Believe it or not, we were sitting in the bar at 21, Broun having walked right through the line, talking and oblivious. When I told him where we were, he said, in the great and lovable Broun tradition, "I think this calls for another drink."

In the event that you are at work on, or plan to be at work on, the history of Harper & Brothers and their circle, I will change my piece to the Little, Brown Brothers and their Jug.

Down here, I am, as Ann Brothers, who attached herself to the group for obvious reasons, once said, "Screw loose and fancy free."

Hope that you are only half that way.

I remain, Your obedient servant,

## TO HAROLD ROSS

*Thurber had submitted to Ross a parody of Margaret Case Harriman's The Vicious Circle. It was never used.*

*The Ledgelets, Somerset Bridge, Bermuda*
*May 9, 1951*

*Mr. H. W. Ross, The New Yorker*
*25 West 43rd St., New York, New York*

Dear Ross:

There are two enclosures here, one of them an important clipping about your second wife's second husband, an ornamental and much decorated fellow. . . . The other little old enclosure is a short casual, of almost forgotten length and type, dealing with a subject that, I hope, will not make you self-conscious . . .

. . . I am getting this story in quickly, just after finishing Maggie's book, because it may run into competition with a parody by Gibbs. If Gibbs does one, I will not be offended if it is taken instead of mine, since he is easily the most gifted parodist in America. I think that all of the gags in this piece are my own, but one can never be sure of this, what with Winchell and David H. Wallace and Raoul Fleischman still getting off their sparkling lines. . . .

The checkers must not attempt to check this casual, since I have deliberately jumbled up dates and some of these men and women were probably dead and most of them never met, and the Brownings were never in America. One true fact is that Carlyle did wear green glasses. On second thought, it was not Carlyle but Coleridge, but I will stick to it anyway. Harper & Brothers was founded more than a hundred years ago.

I have left out the name of Henry George's book, the most famous one, because all I can think of is "Poverty and Prejudice," which is not very close. Have the checkers put it in. If you are too self-conscious about the piece, I will sell it to Luce. I want my sub-title to stand as it is, because I am not taking a crack at the Round Tablers, many of whom I loved, although [Alexander] Woollcott comes out of the book as out of life, probably the one man in the world most difficult to understand. He made everybody's life continually miserable and yet Dorothy Parker almost wept about him on the air, and, at his memorial services, twenty or thirty others did the same thing. I met him only twice and he insulted me once, a batting average of .500. In 1927, you sent me to interview him about the forthcoming theatrical season, which, by the way, he almost completely missed, getting almost everything wrong, and he began by saying "You work for Harold Ross, a man who has the utmost contempt for anything he cannot understand." He once sent me a nice note, consisting of one line: "You are the only artist who should ever be allowed to draw priests."

I have tried to stay fairly close to Maggie's clear and simple style, and to imitate, in some part, her over-use of "pensive" and "sweetly", and her tendency to refer, every time, to a man and his wife by their full names. I spent several days on "Rhodes scholared", and I don't want to be told that Leonard Lyons made it up originally. Once you get started on a thing like this, you annoy your friends for days, and I left out a dozen gags, including what Poe said when he found out that Ann Brothers had married a southern Colonel during the Civil war: "The Colonel's lady is Brothers under the skin."

The latest piece in the Album series will be coming along shortly. It took me eight weeks, and I solved a log jam by cutting out three thousand words and confining it to two men. There are three professors of almost equal prominence, and I could not leave these two out. I am also halfway through a comic casual about a man and his wife, which I will finish while here. We sail June 6, arriving in New York June 8, in the morning. I hear you had your annual visit to the hospital and I hope you are in tiptop shape.

Helen joins me in love and kisses, best wishes, admiration, and wonder.

As always,

Jim

## TO ANTHONY BERTRAM

*The Ledgelets, Somerset Bridge, Bermuda*

*May 4, 1951*

*Mr. Anthony Bertram, Manor House, Bignor,*
*Pulborough, Sussex, England*

Dear Bertram:

I am delighted to write to you about Paul Nash, to whom I was intensely devoted, and I am happy that there is to be a book about him and I know that you will do it well. We did not exchange letters of any consequence, only notes arranging meetings, but he used to send me cablegrams in praise of my drawings, particularly a series called "The Hound and the Bug." I will start at the beginning.

I first met Nash in October 1931. It is easy to remember the date, because my first wife and I gave a cocktail party for him on October 6 that year, the day before the birth of my daughter. Paul had written one or two pieces in the ENGLISH REVIEW, to which he contributed art criticism, pieces that dealt with some American comic artists. There was no one in England, or anywhere else outside the States, who knew our comic art so well, or appreciated it so heartily. I was told that when he came to America in 1931, one of his trunks was nearly filled with American comic strips he had saved, both daily and Sunday. He became interested in my work extraordinarily early, because I began to draw for THE NEW YORKER on January 31, 1931, and had done only twelve or fifteen drawings. But he had also seen "Is Sex Necessary?" written by E. B. White and myself, which came out in October 1929, and bore my first published illustrations.

. . . He was one of three foreign judges picked to select the prize paintings of an annual Pittsburgh gallery show. He was pleased that he was known over here as one of England's most brilliant young painters and critics. When the Pittsburgh gallery had cabled him saying there would be a luncheon in his honor at the dignified old Century Club in New York and asking him whom he would especially like to have present, he amazed and disturbed them by cabling back "Milt Gross, Mrs. Carl Van Vechtin and James Thurber." Mrs. Van Vechtin was Fanny Marinoff, the actress, and I never did find out his special interest in her. I was living in Connecticut at the time and some official in charge of the luncheon phoned me long distance, beseeching me not to fail to show up at the lunch. Even now I do not know much about art, American or otherwise, and then I knew very little, except the names of a few famous painters. At least twenty were on hand when I arrived at the Century Club, and I recognized the names of Jonas Lie, Burchfield, and four or five others. Paul was a little late, and when he did get there, we all lined up to greet him, like the front file of a platoon. He wandered slowly down the line, shaking hands, smiling, and obviously ignorant of most of the names that were mentioned. When he came to me, he embarrassed the hell out of me, stopping to talk, while the other men shifted uneasily and there was a lot of nervous coughing. He insisted that I sit on his right, and I began to get extremely restless and afraid. Across from us sat one of the most formidable figures I ever saw, an enormous man with flashing dark eyes and a great spade beard. Paul looked at him and said, "Do you know how I could get in touch with Milt Gross?" The gentleman, probably the director of a gallery or editor of a recondite art magazine, replied gruffly, "I am sure I wouldn't have the faintest idea." Paul stared at him. "He is one of your great artists," he said, and I kicked him under the table. They had only given us one drink of Scotch, and we decided to hook the bottle on the sideboard, and did. I needed more drinks to get through that amazing lunch. When we finally left, I said to him, "You didn't seem to realize that you were in the midst of the forefront of American art, and that none of those men ever heard of me or Milt Gross." He looked at me and said, "From what I know of their work, they are bringing up the rear of French Modernism." . . .

My wife and I arranged a cocktail party for Nash and asked several of THE NEW YORKER cartoonists he wanted to meet. Twenty minutes before Paul arrived at our hotel apartment, I had started to take a bath, turned on the hot water full force and filled the bathroom with steam. It was too hot there for me to turn off the water, and when Paul arrived—we had left the hall door open—the living room was dense with steam. The hotel engineer had to turn off the water for a while in the whole building. Paul, of course, loved this incident, and especially the fact that, when the fog had cleared there was Otto Soglow sitting on a chair. Soglow is scarcely more than five feet tall, and was one of the men Nash admired for his "Little King" drawings and the rest. But Otto is a man of moods, and he said nothing but monosyllables until Paul rose to go and then suddenly burst into a flow of amusing talk. Again Nash was delighted and sat down for another hour. . . .

In talking about the inability of comic artists to deal with death, he said that the common drawing of a man falling from a building and speaking to someone on the way down did not represent death, since the man was forever poised in the air, and it was Paul who said of my drawing "Touche!" that the man whose head had been cut off was not actually dead, because he could obviously put it back on again. This line has been widely quoted in America, usually without credit. . . .

Nash seemed to know everything about the United States, as he did about the British Isles, and he was eager to meet Harold Ross, the fabulous editor of THE NEW YORKER, especially after I told him that Ross knew nothing about art, or music and, as Alexander Wollcott once said, he had the utmost contempt for anything he didn't understand. I took Nash to his office and introduced him, and Ross began by saying, "Nash, there are only two phoney arts, music and painting." Once more Nash was delighted. I know he must have been capable of anger and temper because he was a fine artist, but they never arose out of anything like that. His utter absorption in the unique and the unusual overcame all other emotions, and he thought Ross was one of the great sights of New York. . . .

Sincerely yours,
James Thurber

ʕ∂ ʕ∂ ʕ∂

*June 21, 1951*

Dear Mr. Bertram:

. . . I left out one amusing incident. In one of Paul's pieces in the review he wrote that "Thurber sometimes starts to scribble idly in the early fashion of Matisse", or words to that effect. I was astounded how this sentence got around, and was distorted in England and over here. It finally came out that Paul Nash had discovered that Matisse was one of my fans, actually.

When I had my show of drawings at the Storran Gallery in London in

1937 one of the Gallery men discovered that Matisse was in London and called the old boy's secretary to arrange a meeting between Matisse and me. I didn't know about this until later. The secretary disappeared from the phone for a moment and returned to say "M. Matisse has never heard of The New Yorker or of Mr. Thurber". I loved it. It still has not put an end to the legend. . . .

Best wishes.

      Cordially yours,

      James Thurber

*Mr. Anthony Bertram, Manor House, Bignor,*
*Pulborough, Sussex, England*

## To the Thurber Family

*West Cornwall, Connecticut*

*July 2, 1951*

Dear Thurbers:

June and July 1951 will be remembered by you as a trying period, but you will have to get through it the best you can, calling on your patience, tolerance, and restraint. As you now know, "Gentleman From Indiana" has been widely hailed as a good piece about a good man and I will fix up the piece for the book. You also know that Mary Thurber will be highly appreciated by a million readers when "Lavender With A Difference" comes out. Your biggest hurdle, however, will probably be the cover story about me in TIME. I don't know whether you will like it or not, and I haven't seen it, but a great many pieces have been written about me and I never worry about them. I expect TIME to do a realistic piece and not a blurb or puff, but the piece will no doubt mention my family and I hope it does not upset you. Remember that a letter to a magazine is privileged, that is, it can be reprinted in whole or in part. I strongly urge you not to write any letters about it, or to show them to someone before you mail them.

The TIME piece is the result of last year's research and was set up in proof a couple of months ago. I had no control over it. I anticipate that it will be a sound and friendly piece, but I cannot anticipate your reactions to it. Take it as calmly as you can, remembering that the piece on Mama, to appear three weeks later [in *The New Yorker*], will be what is remembered.

A book called "Ross of the New Yorker", to be published this fall, says that I was a failure before I got on the New Yorker, and I did not object to this. About seven years ago, a book you didn't see, called "Horse Sense in American Humor" and written by a Chicago University professor, batted me around quite a bit and said I had spent a life of drudgery on newspapers, which was partly true. Far from getting mad and writing the guy, I wrote a piece for the New Yorker called "Memoirs of a Drudge" and openly quoted the man's cracks. "Drudgery stole marches for me, when Lee's brilliance was asleep," wrote U.S. Grant. I should have sent you this book and some other critical pieces, which would have prepared you for the ordeal of 1951. The pieces were soundly thought out and I have never had the desire to be pictured differently from what I am. All in all, the Thurbers will come out better rather than worse, and you must try not to get agonized by criticism or interpretation, and to see the good as well as the unfavorable. Remember that articles do not stick long in anybody's mind, because they are soon outdated and people have too much to think about. The individual concerned in a story magnifies what is said because of his personal interest, but tests have shown that only two percent of people can quote accurately from a piece, even two weeks after it comes out.

I will return Robert's letter which should be destroyed, I think, along with mine, since this is not an exchange worthy of preserving. I would like to know William's address in Columbus since I always send him a check for his vacation. He has always been able to laugh at himself, and this helps a man get through life more easily than most men.

Mrs. Pennington, Maud, and Katherine, were talking about my father and what they would have written about him, rather than about the piece I wrote about him. I suggest that you all try to write about him and let me see the result. I think that an outside opinion is always the best, and these people were close to him personally or related to him. I covered City Hall when Mrs. Pennington was dance inspector and she used to embarrass the newspaperman by her breathtaking reports on the immorality of some dance halls. The true story of Mrs. Pennington would be interesting, but I couldn't write it. I couldn't write about Maud and Katherine either. Could you? Love and kisses,

As ever,

*Leander Thurber was Thurber's paternal grandfather.*

*West Cornwall, Connecticut*
*July 12, 1951*

Dear Mama:

We just got your letter and are glad you like the piece. Joe Sayre had no more to do with the pictures or layout than Eva Prout . . . The brothers were blocked out to focus attention on three of the principal figures. This is up to the make-up man and the editor. They wanted photos of me and Nugent, and me and White. Miss Terry spent three hours finding one of White and me, but it wasn't used. About forty others were thrown out, too.

I keep wondering why none of us has ever known about Leander. He was never mentioned by Belle, or Mrs. Albright, or my father's mother, whom I knew for several years. She looked exactly like Papa. Also there are no photographs, letters, records, or anecdotes. . . . There are probably dozens of grandnieces and grandnephews of Leander standing in the same relation to us as the descendants of Milt, Eddie, and Jake. There is sure to be some record of the old boy in these families. Maybe he was a rascal who got the hell out, leaving his wife stuck with an infant son. I never believed he was thrown from a horse. He may have gone to Texas where there is a town named Thurber. I'm not going to write anything about him, but I'm interested in finding out and astonished that we never showed any curiosity before. It is rare, indeed, when three male adults know nothing whatever about their grandfather. Maybe he didn't even marry Sarah. This would account for the clamming up of everybody. He seems to be the only one of his siblings without any record. There is an A. Edward Thurber, a New York industrialist, who has the best history of the family and I have written to him, without of course suggesting anything strange or mysterious. Best wishes,

> As ever,
> Jamie

& & &

*West Cornwall, Connecticut*
*August 1, 1951*

Dear Mama:

Here are two more letters about your piece, which a lot of people are talking about. . . .

You are wrong about our lack of hospitality up here, but we have more problems about people than Grandpa or Cliff. Of course, Grandpa was, and Cliff is, surrounded by a hundred relatives, but they don't have Charmé and Ray Lee and Fanchon dropping in, or Milt Wilcox and his wife, or dozens of college boys and girls, or sightseers and autograph hunters, or interviewers and photographers, or friends out of work or sick or depressed, or publishers, agents, and advertising men, and they don't have to answer five hundred letters a year from friends, relatives, and strangers, many of whom want and get some kind of help.

What I mean about unnecessary worry is the kind that is concerned with human facts and experiences, which are always interesting, whatever they are, and should not be avoided. A person cannot protect another against life. I remember how little Eva's letter was kept from me—I got this from her twenty years ago—so that I did not have a chance to make a decision about my own life. I would have made the same one, as it happens, but it might have turned everything upside down. Nobody can play God and everybody should simply relax and take everything, including the devil, when it happens. I have learned to believe in all experiences and not to avoid them and there's nothing so destructive to the mind or nervous system as avoidance and silence and bottling things up. This way accounts for the tremendously high neuroticism of our time.

I hope it isn't so hot out there as it is here. I'm trying to finish two books, but I am well and Helen is feeling better, although our servants told us today they are leaving. She doesn't want to work anymore and he has a job near his own house. There are always a hundred things. Love and kisses,

> As ever,

$$\text{\bfseries ⁊} \quad \text{\bfseries ⁊} \quad \text{\bfseries ⁊}$$

> *West Cornwall, Connecticut*
> *August 13, 1951*

Dear Mama:

There's no use worrying about little Eva now, and, as I said, I am not a man to desert a lady at the altar. You are right about her not knowing much, but she left school in the sixth grade, so her mother could be supported by her. Mrs. Prout was the same kind of woman as Mrs. Bierbower. Eva used to say "irregardless" and she had the Central Ohio tendency to cut the "ow" sound out of "flower" and to make all such words rhyme with "are." These people have been called Slurvians and their theme song goes:

"Each little flar,
Down in its bar,
Awaits each are,
The coming shar."

She got over this when she took singing lessons in Chicago and New York. I think Ernest must have left her when she last wrote you. He is a few years younger.

I hope it's not too hot out there.

As ever,

## To Joel Sayre

*Sayre was collecting information for an article on Groucho Marx.*

*West Cornwall, Connecticut*
*July 6, 1951*

Dear Joe:

Ross and I went into the Algonquin dining room a few years ago and Groucho, at another table, stood up menacingly and said loudly, "Ross, you'll join us at this table, if you know what's good for me."

I was amazed at his real appreciation of Henry James, because "The Jolly Corner", a story about a man who has lived in Europe for twenty-five years, returning to the old family mansion on Fifth Avenue and meeting the ghost of the man he would have been, is not for comic book readers. He has a famous way of changing from the sublime to the vulgar, to get people down, and loves to kid filling station attendants in and around Los Angeles, by pretending to be a wealthy New York patron of the arts, and asking them questions about concerts, ballet, and libraries, and then saying, out of the corner of his mouth, "Got any good crap games in this whistle stop?" From there he proceeds to larger vulgarities, as I told you.

He has always been a genial autographer and when two guys waited for three hours in his hotel lobby in New York to get his autograph, Groucho, protected by the desk, but hearing about the boys, dressed and came downstairs. "Make it 'To Bert,'" one of the young men said, and Groucho said he did that only in the case of personal friends. "He don't dedicate," the guy told his friend sadly. Groucho told me later, "I don't dedicate. I keep telling myself, 'I don't dedicate.' Makes me sound as if I belonged to the ages, or something. Important, anyway, and hard to get."

Ross has always said that Groucho, like Frank Adams, is one of the most kindhearted men he knows and is always doing something for people. Like W. C. Fields, he is an expert on comic values and can pretty well figure what will go over and what won't. He was wary of this line in one of the Marx brothers movies, "Either my watch has stopped or this man is dead," and reversed it. He figured it would not be a wow and was right, as he usually is. He was a veterinarian taking a man's pulse.

He came to see "The Male Animal" in its pre-Broadway showing in Los Angeles, and, along with Jed Harris, gave us the soundest criticism. He felt the play was "too funny" and said, "Plays have come to New York with a thousand laughs and folded in a week." We scraped off a lot of gags, revealing the seriousness Groucho was talking about.

When I did caricatures of the three Marx brothers for the defunct Stage magazine in 1936, he wrote and asked for the originals—not for himself, but for a friend. I sent them on.

Only Groucho would have given a dinner party in his house without a hostess, the guests consisting of four men and one woman.

Thanks again for that fine cover story.

As ever,

## To the Ronald Williamses

*West Cornwall, Connecticut*
*July 3, 1951*

Dear kids:

We got back to quite a lot of hell and hot water and have just got straightened around and able to draw a tranquil breath. One of our friends was in an auto crash, banging into a car that had been driven through a red light by a drunken man, whose companion was killed. Our friend, Armin Landeck's son, was unhurt, but for sixteen hours we couldn't find out anything. We saw Gertrude [Sayre], who is better than she has been in six years, and the next day Elliott [Nugent] got out of Hartford. He is also better than usual at the end of the high cycle, but the first week was quite a strain, culminating in a savage letter from my brother Robert, who was all twisted up about the piece I wrote on my father. That was quite a situation and has taken weeks to iron out. . . .

On top of everything, I have had my hands full with work, and Helen has been busy every day. We sat up too late with the Birdsalls the night before landing, putting drinks away, and when we got to our stateroom at three the bilge pumps were raising hell. I set out in my dressing gown to complain, pushed a button under a small light, and the door of an elevator opened. I got in and they closed, and I said, "Take me to the officer in charge of rackets." There was no answer because I was alone in a self-service elevator. I pushed a lighted button, fortunately the right one, and the doors opened again. Helen, meanwhile was on the deck below looking for my body. We came out of it all right, at least I did. Helen will tell her own story.

Love and kisses to all you lovely people.

As ever,

&a  &a  &a

*West Cornwall, Connecticut*
*August 6, 1951*

Dear kids:

. . . I have received a rather stiff letter from Captain Peter Eric David Ashley Blandish, objecting to my "forced libels and smirking calumnies" on his honorable name. He says that his family has had a bright and valiant history since the days of Peter the Fumbling and Eric the Confused. The latter was once ordered to Rome, thought he had been commanded to roam all the rest of his life and was never seen again. The former was told by his physician to drop dominoes and spent his days literally dropping them all around Blandish Castle until the place was ankle-deep in dominoes. Captain Blandish wonders what you two see in my "cruel titterings" and he claims that he was in Parkerstown, New Jersey, only overnight. He does admit that he married Mrs. Blandish by accident, or misunderstanding, when his commanding officer, ordering him out on a mission, told him to "pick up a little baggage." He did, and they were married a week later. Her name was Sarah Elaine Tweazy.

. . . The piece on my mother, one of a tumble of Thurbers, will be reprinted in the Congressional Record at the request of Congressman John Vorys, who was president of the Junior class at East High when I was president of the Senior class. . . .

It was forty-five degrees here last night. Love and kisses from us both.

As always,

## To Rogers Whittaker

West Cornwall, Connecticut
September 7, 1951

Mr. Rogers Whattaker, The New Worker Magazine,
19th Floor, 25 West 43rd St., New York, N. Y.

Dear Miss Briskin:

I just found out that you are in charge of putting "of" into my prose, to make up for some early sorrow of yours growing out of a lack of education in English. We used to have a system there by means of which the ablest checkers had the final say on proofs, but now that there is a Checkerissima with a direct line from the makeup night shift crew to the printers, God only knows what will happen from now on.

I think we'd better start over again and fix it so that your niece cannot come into the office at midnight and change things that Ruth Flint and R.W. and a dozen others have sweated over all week. A pale thin crack has begun to show in the facade of our magazine, and Christ only knows what types, strange book reviewers, and gloomy casuals will seep through it. We've got to get this man Ross back and not tell him what happened while he was away.

Respectively,
James Thurber

## To Harrison Kinney

West Cornwall, Connecticut
July 12, 1951

Dear Harrison:

Since I write five hundred letters a year, I get behind on the tough ones and the good ones. It will probably be better to kick your project around in person. I will be in New York Tuesday and will come over to the office around eleven, or you can phone me at the Algonquin. Everyone is both flattered and frightened, I suppose, at the prospect of a friendly critique, the hardest kind to do. I think Wilson's scheme in "The Wound and the Bow" is the way to do a writer, probably. I don't see myself at fifty-six, taking up a whole book, and the only thing about thirty is that it is usually the gateway to viewpoints, interests, and dedications that often become quite different from those of the earlier years. But thirty varies with individuals. I didn't get anything done until after thirty. The best truth about a man is often left out of a book written by a friend, and this residue should be turned over to a talented enemy, or to someone completely impartial.

I'll see you next week, then, and sorry for the delay in answering your letters.

> As ever,
> Thurber

## To Rudy Vallee

*West Cornwall, Connecticut*
*July 24, 1951*

Dear Mr. Vallee:

The piece in TIME was written by an old friend of mine, with whom I have spent a thousand social evenings since 1920, and he was not referring to any written or planned monologues, but simply meant ad-lib conversation. These things are all gone with the nights and the Scotch. . . . Far and away the best piece about the forties was written a year or so ago by Corey Ford. . . . It shows, among other things, that belts for men's trousers are made much longer than they used to be, and that staircases are built higher. I think it is the best article on middle-age I have read.

. . . I myself am worrying about the approach of sixty. I'm sorry your radio show is off the air, for I listened to it often and I lament the passing of Barrymore, for I remember the night he snarled "What the hell are you laughing at?" I always wondered what the hell the audience was laughing at. Best wishes.

> Sincerely yours,
> James Thurber

*Mr. Rudy Vallee, VALLEE-VIDEO,*
*6611 Santa Monica Blvd., Hollywood 38, California*

## To Rosemary Thurber

*Acting in a campus play, Rosie received favorable notice but the reviewer found the overuse of her hands distracting.*

*The Ledgelets, Somerset Bridge, Bermuda*
*April 2, 1951*

Dear Star:

Helen and I were excited about those reviews of "Light Up the Sky" starring Rosemary Thurber and featuring two or three others. We showed them to all our friends down here and had several copies made, together with copies of the enclosed verse dedicated to you and your errant hands. When I first acted at Ohio State I discovered that I had three hands and only two pockets to put them in. This is a thing that goes away and by the time you are 21 you will have two hands like everybody else. We wish we could have seen the play and that more people had come to it. Maybe they will after this, especially if you put on "Tobacco Road" and let me play the part of Jeeter Lester. You could play the part of Ellie May since the other young girl, Pearl, is a straight part and you don't like that. Ellie May has what was meant to be a hair lip, but Bob Benchley said it looked to him, from where he sat, as if the ailment were more deep seated. . . .

Write and let us know where you are and what you have been doing especially in the classroom. I don't suppose you have cracked a book since rehearsals started, but you better get back at it if you want to get your golden key and a part in the next play.


*TO ROSEMARY*
The critics have made a small sensation
About my daughter's intonation.
They liked her poise and her acting style;
They liked her voice and her pretty smile.
The flaws they found were three small flaws —
One in each of her lovely paws.
See my daughter, where she stands,
Trying to manage her three left hands.
But here is my love, in its loaf and crumbs,
And a kiss for each of her fifteen thumbs.

—James Thurber

*West Cornwall, Connecticut*
*October 2, 1951*

Dear Rosabelle:

We are forwarding a little old note that arrived this morning from Paul ("You know what I mean?") Stewart, and I resisted my evil temptation to steam it open. What does this guy want anyway—my daughter or my mythical fortune? It occurs to me, and did weeks ago, that hard-bitten fellas of the theatre, radio, and movies don't wait forty minutes to say goodbye to all the girls in all the theatres they play. Does it read like this: "Peg has finally agreed to give me a divorce and I hope you remember the promise you made when we killed that fifth of gin on the fire-escape." My memoirs will reveal the discovery I made about daughters. Between the ages of fifteen and eighteen they don't like anybody, but from nineteen to twenty-three they think everybody is wonderful. This leads to an accumulation of the debris of youthful friendships, which has to be swept out, in the middle twenties, with pain, regret, and surprise. Maybe this guy likes the way your mind works. I hear that Falmouth has followed you to Penn, like a poodle dragging a string of sleighbells. Last night I dreamed a paraphrase of "Falmouth is a fine town, with tall ships in the bay." It went "Falmouth is a fine town, with small slips in the hay." Watch it, sister.

It now transpires that you didn't steal my Brooks Brothers shirts, but you can always have the shirt off my back, as you know. Meanwhile, I have hidden that small radio of yours, against the day you come across with the clock that plays "Anchors Aweigh."

Frost the other day turned the maples, maybe for the last time, since this tree has developed a blight of its own. It hasn't hit our own yet, though, Helen said to Frank Calhoun today, "The pine tree doesn't have a blight, does it?" He said, "Sure. Pine blister." Try to get to classes occasionally, and don't high-hat the Kappas just because they have had no experience of the world yet. Bogart and Cagney are personal friends of mine, but I'd be dog if you don't pick out a tough guy I never even met.

Also try to get some sleep, since there is a long winter ahead. Love and kisses from us all, including the poodle, who got scared by something last night and slept downstairs with the Swains.

As always,
D'kins

## To E. B. White

*West Cornwall, Connecticut*
*October 2, 1951*

Dear Andy:

. . . When are you coming to New York? I heard a vague rumor that you had set out to discover the Northwest Passage, but that the trees began to move on you, or something. Remember how [Morris] Markey wrote an intimate account of Baltimore without going there. He got the dope from his friend Logan Clendenning over a few drinks in St. Louis. This was the book in which everybody Markey met, in mines, or factories, or forests, turned out to be Markey himself. He did his best piece, "The Deep South" in a small upstairs front room in Little River, Florida. "There ain't any use wearin' yourself out," he used to say. Who wants to reach Duluth with the smell of Albany still on him?

We are anxious to see you and Katharine, and to hear about Joe and Roger and Evelyn. The new maple blight has not got us yet.

Love and kisses from us both

As always,

Jim

## To John O'Hara

*West Cornwall, Connecticut*
*October 3, 1951*

Dear John:

. . . Your Aunt Lettie and me hope that you are not in the gutter again, or in that terribly smart and expensive Doctors' Hospital. You remind us so much of your grandpaw who gave up hard cider when they told him it was good for him, and started in on it again when they told him it would kill him. There has always been this streak of cussedness on Grandpaw's side, going back to the Devlins and Gilhooleys. They always drunk at home, though, like their friends, and whilst they broke furniture now and then, it was their own. I declare that nowadays the men folks always hit a stranger when they pass out, or break something that don't belong to them.

Aunt Helen and Cousin Jim and us hope to see you in New York soon, at right angles to the floor, if it ain't askin' too much.

Lovingly yours,

Jim

PS. Your Aunt Lettie mixed a martini last night that turned blue. The Dele-
hantys and the Muldoons always had a dry thumb, I told her.

## TO JAMES POLLARD

*West Cornwall, Connecticut*
*October 25, 1951*

*Mr. James E. Pollard, Department of Journalism,*
*Ohio State University, Columbus, Ohio*

Dear Jim:

. . . An indignant Ohio State alumnus and friend of mine has just sent me
most of the clippings about the screening scandal, or patriotic defense movement, as General Dargusch calls it, or just good old plain common sense, as
the governor of Ohio calls it. The questionnaire phase is terribly alarming, together with the fact that such a gag rule, by its very nature, is likely to extend
rather than to decrease in time. I wonder what they will do in the case of the
various men, like myself, who have spoken, without notes, to English and
journalism classes. None of the clips I have does more than mention Dr. Cecil
Hinshaw, and while he is named a Quaker and a pacifist, I find nothing about
his overthrowing the government. I was surprised and pleased to see the
courage of many Ohio State professors and other Columbus people, since
there was a great deal of fear and secrecy during the terrible case of "The Scarlet Fever," a name substituted for "The Sun-Dial," after "the magazine fell into
the hands of a bunch of Cleveland Jews," as a prominent, and even powerful,
Ohio State man wrote me, apparently taking it for granted that any good
alumnus would share his views. I regret that I promised to make no public issue of this if the name of the Sun-Dial was restored. It was restored so fast that
it was hard to believe.

I have always been a vehement anti-communist, a fact that could be proved
in a few hours of research, but I have no doubt that, like almost all writers, I
will one day be named as a Red. Several men and women whom I know to be
anti-communists or non-communists have been named, and even the New
Yorker is mentioned in Counter Attack with this line "Writes for the New
Yorker." We have had three thousand contributors, and they represent all colors of politics, but a good 95% are as anti-communist as the magazine itself.

It is my personal belief that a communist speaker could not possibly sway an Ohio State audience and that in refusing to let communists talk, the university deprives itself of a wonderful chance to heckle and confound such speakers. If we cannot be strong enough Americans to withstand such arguments, if we are in such danger of being politically debauched, then all we really have in the Western Conference is the greatest football area in the world. I have just finished the Denney piece, but I will insert a few sentences about the gag rule. As president of the AAUP he boldly attacked interference by "state legislatures, ecclesiastical bodies, and powerful influence operating through trustees." I wish he were still there pitching and I would like to hear his views on "Gigantic Ohio State," the only piece that ever left out Chic Harley. Leaving out Kettering is all right with me.

> Cordially yours,
> James Thurber

## To Gertrude Sayre

*West Cornwall, Connecticut*
*October 30, 1951*

Dearest Gertrude:

722 sounds a little bit like one of those cruise ships I used to ride on years ago, complete with dancing on the decks and everything. Everything at Medical Center is unlike a hospital and my mother always called it Harkness Hotel. Even the Eye Institute was a nice clean place, with jolly doctors and nurses, but it was definitely a hospital to me, even though I got a rye highball every night.

. . . We will make arrangements when we get to town, and sew you up definitely. We are going down Saturday afternoon, so that I can go on "Invitation to Learning" at 11:30 Sunday morning with Mark Van Doren, to kick Henry James's "The Ambassadors" around for half an hour. It is CBS and maybe you can tune us in. Helen is reading me James's outline for his novel, which runs to three thousand more words than "The White Deer," my longest book in one piece. . . .

It was very sweet of you to say all those nice things about us and to pass on Joe's kind words, too, but we don't feel that we have really done very much. There is still a lot of time, however, something like fifty years for you youngsters, and I won't be ninety myself for quite awhile.

Ross has always said "Life is hard and I don't want to hear about it," and he has always gone on to tell us his own version. He still coughs himself awake a lot and runs an afternoon temperature, but his infection is clearing up. The male lungs are a problem and take time. He has given up smoking, a real miracle, since he used to put away several packs of Camels a day. The only woman in his life seems to be his daughter who is sixteen. He was as difficult around the home as a motorcycle, and I doubt if Ariane could have stood up under this last summer.

We started to read O'Hara's new book last night, "The Farmers Hotel," read Part I, and thought it was fine. It is done like a play, with entrances like this: "A state policeman came in the door across the lobby," all very effective. There is not much description, but you don't notice this since he builds up the hotel with a touch of detail here and there. He does the blizzard so well that when I opened the front door I said, "I thought it was snowing outside." I can't help thinking, confidentially, that his upper class heroines, in everything from sex to liquor, are what O'Hara might be if he were Joanna instead of John. His dialogue is as expert as anybody's and he certainly has a great skill in writing economic speeches and accurate gestures. . . .

We will get in touch with you as soon as we get to town. I am still plugging away at my next book, finishing the next to last piece. We think you are wonderful, and better than ever, and so is your old man. Love and kisses from us both.

As always,

P.S. I'll send you O'Hara's book or, better yet, remind him to send it if he hasn't done so yet. I often get advance books from publishers, even though I don't treat publishers very well.

## To the Ronald Williamses

*West Cornwall, Connecticut*
*November 9, 1951*

Dear Ronnie:

Well, Janey did show up in New York, and I think she had a good time, although she was only with us for one evening, and not all of that. We ended up at Tom Matthew's apartment, where we lost Cornelia, who got mixed up with some military police—George got lost even earlier. Janey wasn't gone more than two hours, having slipped down to a place called "Lover's Lane" in Greenwich Village with a powerfully built young man named Bob Cameron, who says he once took you in straight sets in Singapore or Trinidad. All that Janey said when they came back was, "It was the most fun I've had since that woman bit Ronnie's ear." Or maybe it was a man named Cecil Montague who says he took you in four sets in Rangoon. "All I know about Cecil," Janey said the next morning, "is that he is wonderful on both forehand and backhand." I forgot to say that they slipped away to an all-night indoor tennis court. She also met McKelway, who is writing a play called "The Durable Malloy," but he says he has now changed it to "The Adorable Williams." I don't know why. There were other things that happened, such as me getting tagged by several shots of Baccardi when I said, "Not too dry," meaning "Not too sweet." Tom turned out to be a fine entertainer and a good singer, but I was in B-flat minor most of the early hours. Did I tell you about this man Joe Callahan? Janey says he has one of the cutest apartments she ever saw. It is across from Tom's. Did she bring the etching back with her?

At this writing, Janey is still at Long Point and we will telephone her tonight. I was sorry she didn't get to meet Andy White at whose house the Gudes and Helen and I were singing two nights later. Jap had to leave before Janey showed up and I was sorry about that, for he is a great admirer of yours. Andy said he had met Janey, but he was mixed up on this. One night in 1941 Janey stayed with us just one night—she is always with us just one night—and Andy had the room the following night, when he came down with the galloping jumps and couldn't stay alone. This is the most remarkable tribute to Mrs. Williams I know, since missing her by twenty-four hours gave him the feeling he had met her. . . .

It turns out that our big tax problem is not settled for sure after all, but we have hopes. Some way or other we will manage to get to Bermuda in the spring.

Tell Janey that her coming to see us was the highlight of the year. We wish you had been along and you must make it next time.

Love and kisses from us both to all of you,

    As ever,

    Jim

P.S. A man named David McKenzie just phoned to ask how he could get in touch with "the lady that was with you that night." He thinks she may have picked up a silver cigarette case at his house on 10th Street. Fellow sounded as if he could take you in five sets.

      *   *   *

*November 13, 1951*

Dear Children:

I am sorry about that. I am sorry that the deep tangled wildwood of my premonitions, compulsions, affections, and other curious flora, also happens to be the only place where my clocks strike, my white deer run, and my last flowers grow. I am sorry that only strangers are in no danger of being hurt by my solicitude.

James (I AM SORRY) Thurber

*Mr. and Mrs. R.J. Williams, Seaforth,*
*Somerset Bridge, Bermuda*

## To The Thurber Family

*Robert, angry at Thurber's magazine article about their father, was no longer replying to Thurber's letters. Thurber rewrote the article for* The Thurber Album. *The brothers later effected a grudging reconciliation.*

**West Cornwall, Connecticut**
*December 3, 1951*

Dear Thurbers:

I'm sorry about the check being a little late, but they must have taken a week off November, it went so fast. I tried to call you through the Southern switchboard, but there was no answer and I didn't want to make Mama get up. I called Saturday morning and should have waited until the afternoon. However, when you want calls you will probably put 6761 back, and I will wait, as I told you before, for that.

I have been working very hard on the book which will be called "The Thurber Album." I have rewritten "Gentleman From Indiana," cutting out many things you didn't like, including the line about his finishing at the top of the losers. I said he was beaten by a narrow margin. I put in the name of the commission to recodify federal statutes and said he was its secretary, as he was. I said he was a good rider and first president of the Columbus Bicycle Club, and that governors and others depended on his writing of effective speeches and tactful letters, and handling difficult men. The piece will also contain the enclosed paragraph.

I hope you are all getting along well. William called me one Sunday and it might be a good idea to have him do that every Sunday for awhile. Love and kisses from us all.

As ever,

Jamie

&. &. &.

West Cornwall, Connecticut

December 15, 1951

Dear Thurbers:

I haven't been able to write because of many things, especially the death of Ross which has been a terrible blow to us all. I remember that Mama said about sixteen years ago that he should take care of his lungs. He didn't take care of them in time, for he was not a man to go to doctors for checkups. He suffered no pain and died under the anaesthetic. You will have read White's obituary in the magazine.

William telephoned the other night and I told him we were sending a box for you all, but that we didn't expect anything in return, because we didn't want you to go through any strain this year. You've had enough strain and Christmas is becoming a nuisance as we grow older and we don't want you to feel that you have to send us anything this year. It will be Christmas present enough if you take care of yourselves. The doctors must think Mama is getting along all right or I would have heard from Kissane. William says Mama got down to the lobby a couple of times, and we were glad to hear that.

Ross's funeral showed that he had hundreds of friends and there were hundreds more that couldn't get there. All three of his wives were present and his daughter. She is sixteen and stood the ordeal very well. He had seen her several times recently and his last trip was made to her school. We called on him on his birthday and took him a present. He stayed at the Algonquin and we were there when the news came, and at the office the next day. There have been wonderful editorials about him. Everybody recognized that he was the greatest editor of his time. I had worked for him twenty-four years and I don't know what I would have done without him.

We will send checks for Christmas in addition to the box. This is the way we want to do it and we want you to use your money for yourselves and none of it for us this year. . . .

Merry Christmas and love to you all,

As ever,

## To Howard Bevis

*The New Yorker*
*No. 25 West 43rd Street*
*December 6, 1951*

*President Howard L. Bevis,*
*The Ohio State University, Columbus, Ohio*

Dear President Bevis:

In reply to your letter of November 28th, it is with extreme regret, and after serious consideration, that I find myself unable to accept at this time Ohio State University's offer of the honorary degree of Doctor of Letters. I have faith that Ohio State will restore freedom of speech and freedom of research, but until it does I do not want to seem to approve of its recent action. The acceptance of an honorary degree right now would certainly be construed as such approval, or as indifference to the situation.

I regret that I could not answer your letter more promptly, but it has taken me long hours of thought to arrive at my final decision. I want to thank you for your letter and the committee, the council and the trustees for their offer, and to assure all of you that there is, in my attitude, no personal feeling against any individual, whatever. In conclusion, I wish to express to you my warm personal regards.

> Respectfully yours,
> James Thurber

## To Lester Getzloe

*Thurber enclosed a copy of his letter to President Bevis to Getzloe, a journalism professor at O.S.U.*

*West Cornwall, Connecticut*
*December 8, 1951*

Dear Getz:

My original letter to Bevis was about five hundred words long, but Andy White wisely argued me out of it. I like to see the amelioration of all tyranny and intolerance, even if it comes from a cowardly administration, but freedom cannot be qualified and should not be constantly kicked around and talked about. It should be as natural as breathing and as unobtrusive.

. . . I cannot possibly believe that a candidate for an honorary degree could be forgotten for two years. This is utterly ridiculous and absolutely false. I think I know the answer, Getz. It was that footnote in the TIME article, saying that Ohio State, probably piqued by "The Male Animal," had never given me a degree, and going on to say that Kenyon had in 1950, even before Williams in 1951. Cottrell's statement, of course, makes Ohio State's award 1949. If I am right about this, it is another OSU vulgarity. I am not worth all that fuss, and they know it, or ought to. I doubt that one person out of three thousand at Ohio State has read anything of mine. . . .

Bevis didn't say in so many words that the degree was to be conferred in absentia, but he did not ask me to come out there. The letter seemed to me curt and perfunctory. It was certainly cold and brief compared to the warm intimacy of the letters from Kenyon and Williams. To hell with all those sanitary engineers. Most of my friends here feel that I took the right action.

. . . I don't think any of the trustees read my piece on Joe Taylor, because I used the expression "militant trustees." I don't know if Bricker can read. It was John Vorys, Ohio congressman, who had my piece about my mother read into the Congressional Record.

The New Yorker got an amazing letter yesterday from Ruth McKinney, praising Ross to high heaven, comparing him to Emerson, Tom Paine, Samuel Adams, and others. It contained some small sentences, and sound ones, even though she never met Ross. She also spent part of the letter flagellating herself for her old communism. It was the great Ross, it seems, whose example, learning, courage, and intelligence made her see how little Marx and Lenin were. She says there was only one other editor, William Cullen Bryant. This lady must be losing her buttons. . . .

As ever,

P.S. Ross's death has shocked and grieved us all, and I hate to think about it and can't believe it. Joe and Gertrude had Helen and me up to their house for a steak dinner last night. . . . Joe is writing a five-part Profile on a cop. It will be finished in 1967.

*Mr. Lester Getzloe, Dept. of Journalism,*
*Ohio State University, Columbus, Ohio*

## TO PETER DE VRIES

*De Vries' book,* No But I Saw the Movie, *was about to be published. Thurber had offered to write an introduction.*

Ely's Lodge, Ely's Harbour,
Somerset Bridge, Bermuda
March 31, 1952

*Mr. Peter De Vries,* THE NEW YORKER
*25 West 43rd Street, New York, New York*

Dear Pete:

. . . One thing you over-looked about that preface is that I suggested it quite a while ago when you had published only a few pieces in the magazine, but now everybody knows and talks about your stuff, and I'm thinking of asking you to do a preface to my next book. You don't need any introduction now. We, and everybody else, thought your last piece was one of the best. Under all the circumstances, I humbly take back my offer and apologize for it. I think the title is a good one, and Little, Brown are probably as good as any publishers, which coming from me is little praise, or maybe little brown praise.

One or two people have asked me how good Shawn is in humor, and I realize I don't know. "Does he laugh out loud at Frank Sullivan?" somebody asked me who doesn't like Sullivan as much as I do, I guess. You would have found out about this in the art meeting. I guess humor gets into the fact pieces in a shy way, but I can't remember. I think Shawn is going to do fine and told him so.

. . . I just finished a casual and am getting around to letters and was surprised to find yours was eleven days old. Mencken always answered letters the day they arrived, a wonder to me.

Love to you, Katinka, and the children from us both.

As always,
Jim

P.S. I would be glad to do a review, but how do I get asked? I guess I talk to Harvey Breit or Irita [Van Doren]. After all, I know them both well.

## TO BURGESS MEREDITH

*Ely's Lodge, Somerset Bridge, Bermuda*
*April 19, 1952*

Dear Buzz:

The enclosed clippings will put you up-to-date on [Franchot] Tone, in ac-cordance with your second question the other night. He joined us about 11:30 last Friday and had had a few drinks as we had, but seemed bright and gay on the surface. He didn't seem to listen carefully at all times, and he has a knack of misunderstanding now and then. This comes from being kicked around by both men and women, I guess.

. . . I keep running my play through my head, looking for the right scene sequence and picking up dialog as I go. The great eye doctor finally tells the younger writer to go ahead and have an affair with his wife and get it over with. This is one way to disarm an amorous writer. Nugent had a variant of this theme in his almost successful "By Request," in which the Nugent family starred for six weeks in 1928. George Cohan liked it well enough to produce it. In this one, the Middlewestern wife, Norma Nugent, tells her husband, El-liott Nugent, to have an affair with the New York blonde, Verree Truesdale, saying, "After all, she looks clean and she might be good for you." "You can't call her clean!" cries the husband, indignantly. They were going fine in this second act but lost their way and put the final act on a pullman car, and I don't have to describe that to you, except to say that the comedy died on wheels. You cannot save a comedy by making it ambulant. My doctor is in his early forties and the writer is supposed to be about thirty-eight. The wife is not older than thirty since that is not allowed in American comedy. I think I have a good title, since tennis also figures—"Forty Love."

I'm just giving you one touch of this. I work things up slowly. This one will depend greatly on smart dialog. The woman is not important, as long as she is beautiful, charming, and sexy, and you know how easy it is to find actresses like that!

The guy playing opposite Meredith should be as good as Raymond Massey, but stronger and more physically attractive. I'm not trying to compare this unwritten play with that undying one. I'm just trying to give you an idea of shape and measure. More later.

Helen and I both send our love to you and Kaja.

As ever,

P.S. My daughter Rosie was here, but she didn't fall for Tone. I guess the gal must just be different.

*Mr. Burgess Meredith, 58 West 57th Street,*
*New York, New York*

## To E. B. White

*Ely's Lodge, Somerset Bridge, Bermuda*
*April 25, 1952*

Dear Andy:

. . . I was glad to hear that you had turned in your children's book, and I am anxious to see it. My publishers don't write me anymore, but I hear my book [*The Thurber Album*] is coming out June 12, although they had told me it would be May 28th. I am going to write about imaginary people from now on since real ones take too much out of me.

We all loved your fine description of the great party, but I was sorry to hear that Gluyas Williams couldn't hold more than one, because I am rapidly approaching his age. I have had a neuritis headache for a month, but nobody knows why. The doctor said, "Of course, you know about your own worries, problems, and temperament." I told him that I did in a vague kind of way, vague and voluminous. If the trouble lies somewhere between Eva Prout, with whom I was in love in the third grade, and the fact that my French poodle is nearly thirteen, I could be dead before I figured it out. I've never had anything the doctors didn't suspect might be prostate, since I was fifty, and I can only guess that every symptom is a symptom of that. There is one outstanding one, however, and I haven't got that. One clipping I got of a review of the Kramer book said, "Not only has Ross died, but Cobine and Hokinson were killed, and Thurber is aging and blind." Hell, I am thirty-seven years younger than my Uncle Mahlon Taylor.

Rosie was down here, and we had a fine time with her. She came down on the cuff and went back on a pass, since we didn't have time to buy her ticket down, and she lost her ticket up. We were saved by the courtesy of B.O.A.C.

We send you and Katharine our love and kisses.

As always,

*Mr. E. B. White, The NEW YORKER*
*25 West 43rd St., New York, New York*

## TO CASS CANFIELD

*Ely's Lodge, Somerset Bridge, Bermuda*
*May 28, 1952*

*Mr. Cass Canfield, Harper & Brothers,*
*49 East 33rd Street, New York 16, New York*

Dear Cass:

I wasn't able to answer you sooner because of persistent headaches, an unbelievable volume of mail, and the fact that I am trying to get some rest.

Neither Helen nor I think very much of the front flap stuff for "Fables" which seems flat, uninviting, and written by somebody who didn't really get the point of the book. Harper's used to do this kind of thing for my books until I took to writing the stuff myself. It is probably too late now, and I don't suppose it makes much difference. Ed Murrow could give your writer the right idea of how to do it, and you succeed in quoting on the flap the least interesting of all the morals, the one about the bloodhound. There is a kind of genius in missing things so widely as this, and I respect it. The book has a kind of reputation, and it will probably survive this blurb.

Best wishes to you anyway.
As ever,

## TO THE RONALD WILLIAMSES

*Thurber's hyper-thyroid condition had worsened in Bermuda. It was not properly diagnosed or treated during his three months there, which led to his more cantankerous letters and aggravated his anger over McCarthyism. He was required to give up drinking and smoking. The illness also discouraged him from writing for publication. His July, 1952, essay, "Dark Suspicions: Contemporary Writers Are Handicapped by Current Atmosphere of Distrust," in* The New York Times, *was his last published writing for nearly a year. Only one Thurber piece appeared in 1953 and just three in 1954. His gloom persisted even with the successful return of* The Male Animal *to Broadway.*

*His infatuation with Jane Williams and his impatience with her husband steadily deepened.*

*West Cornwall, Connecticut*
*June 23, 1952*

Dear Janey and Ronnie:

This is our first chance to write, since every day has been crowded and everything has piled up. We had a fine time at the play the night we arrived, although I had to stuff my handkerchief in my mouth every time Robert Preston came on. As I had prefigured, he was the perfect arrested development muscular male and he brought up the comedy to a new level as a powerful tiger who is badgered constantly by two pussycats. We went backstage to meet everybody, and then on to 21 with the Nugents. The Ullmans liked it, too, but said they were mainly delighted by my reaction.

The cocktail party Monday was a strain, and I'm enclosing a clipping about it. One night Janey said, "You go back there and fight!" and the clipping is a play-by-play of the first round. Five or six people called me to "salute you," as Maney put it, and the New York Times has asked me to expand it for their Sunday edition, which I will. I have had no letters, pro or con, since people are no longer much concerned or are afraid to get into it. Nugent's line, "Not in this country! Not yet!" used to get cheers and applause, but met with dead silence that Friday night. People think it has happened in this country, telling people what they can read and write.

Dr. Sullivan in New York diagnosed my condition instantly as a hyperthyroid syndrome, which means a concurrence of symptoms indicating a certain disease. I guess Dr. Curtis had not had much experience with thyroid and he was looking for the wrong factor X. I have always had an Ohio thyroid, but it has never kicked up like this. It is closely connected with the nervous system and can be exacerbated by the constant rantings of noisy sailors. It is nice to know that there is no real stomach or intestinal trouble. I am supposed to take it easy and to be surrounded by quiet and tranquil people like the better half of Seaforth [Jane Williams]. I hope the other half has on this birthday taken up new resolutions. He ran away from domesticity once, and he would like to do it again he says a thousand times, but he can't escape in the salt water and so he escapes into rum, the famous drink of sailors. We have counted a dozen friends of ours with from three to five children, and none of them scream the way he does against their families. I'll always remember Janey's saying, "In the state you're in you couldn't be a fourth officer on a fifth-rate thing." Ronnie's letter to the ship along with the nice flowers actually showed that he thought I was to blame for being on the wagon and unable to take good old-fashioned drunken babbling. If he does not know the truth, it is very sad indeed. I stood a long series of terrible nights for three springs in Bermuda and now my whole nature rebels, and I can't do it again. The highest price I can think of paying for anything is not to see Jane and the children again after a hard winter, but I am afraid that's the way it has to be.

The book [*The Thurber Album*] is doing wonderfully, having outsold "Witness" last week, and the play continues to gross around 20,000. Rosie is here before going into Summer School. I found I couldn't go over to the New Yorker yet on account of the memory of Ross, but I will make it when we go down next time. We naturally hope that Janey will get up here, but we're not building the hope too high because we might get hurt in the crash.

Love to all those who care about such things. Ronnie kept saying that love is nothing more than sexual gratification, so he's not included. How immature, stupid, and pig-headed can you be?

From us all, as ever,

## To Lewis Funke

*West Cornwall, Connecticut*
*June 25, 1952*

*Mr. Lewis Funke, Drama Editor, THE NEW*
*YORK TIMES, Times Square, New York 36, N. Y.*

Dear Mr. Funke:

I will get that piece to you well before July 21, if all goes well, and certainly in time, in any case. I am a good man about making deadlines. . . . I rarely see Ruth [McKenney], but when she was a senior at Ohio State she asked me what chance there was of becoming a successful writer in New York. I told her to forget it, and before long she was outselling me. She wrote a remarkable letter to the New Yorker after Ross's death saying he was responsible for getting her out of far leftism, but Red Channels thinks we are far left. It was the last thing Ross Goddamned and he picked the right monsters. I also advised a young Yale graduate [Vincent Price] to forget about the theatre. In a few months he was playing opposite Helen Hayes as Prince Albert in "Victoria Regina." I now tell all youngsters they can do anything, and many of them can, too.

I'll have my secretary sign this, since I won't be here tomorrow.

Cordially yours,
James Thurber

## TO MRS. GUS PHILLIPS

*West Cornwall, Connecticut*
*July 2, 1952*

Dear Mrs. Phillips:

I still count on the women taking over national and international politics to give it decency, intelligence, and humor, and I will be glad to vote for you for any job. My wife is a Nebraska girl, and she voted for Dewey last time. I voted for Truman. My daughter is for Crosby against Sinatra. I have always called myself an Independent, but I reckon I am really a Democrat, but my record is pretty spotty. I voted for Hoover, a boyhood idol of mine, in 1932, but I had been for good old Al Smith in 1928. The Democrats, however, haven't asked me to contribute anything to anything. I'll send you a copy of "The Thurber Album," which is about my Ohio ancestors, in part, all of whom were staunch Republicans. My father turned Progressive in 1912, and I am the only male in the family who voted for Roosevelt. I will not vote for Taft against anybody, but I will vote for Eisenhower against Truman. I wish we could have Stevenson and Warren on a bi-partisan ticket. If you Republicans lose this time, we've got to stop trying to win by tax tricks, machine tactics, and the old sad G.O.P. guff.

Thanks for what you said about the TIME summary of an explosion of mine. I had been away for three months and was sore about things. The book sells for $3.50 retail, and it has had a bi-partisan sale.

Best wishes

      Sincerely yours,
      James Thurber

*Mrs. Gus Phillips, 2316 Lane St.,*
*Falls City, Nebraska*

## TO ADOLPH WALLER

*On a reader's reaction to* The Thurber Album.

West Cornwall, Connecticut
July 3, 1952

Dear Adolph Waller:

Boy, I didn't get all honeyed words. I went through three years of part hell on this book, including a family break that is just now mended. A guy wrote me that he is glad Kuehner is dead and knows he's in hell. Writing about real people with friends and relatives alive is never milk and honey. Mizener got some brutal letters from the two sisters of Zelda Fitzgerald. I have been bawled out, carped at, insulted, corrected, and Christ knows what else. You Botany boys have all the fun hiding among the petals. Thanks again.

   Cordially yours,
   James Thurber

*Dr. A. E. Waller, Botany Department,*
*Ohio State University, Columbus 10, Ohio*

## TO GUS LOBRANO

West Cornwall, Connecticut
July 3, 1952

Dear Gus:

One of the last things Ross got mad at was one of those magazines which list the political activities of writers. He told me that it sometimes used, in parentheses, "writes for the New Yorker." Do you remember anything about this? He couldn't have read the thing, somebody must have brought it to him. Lewis Funke, drama editor of the *Times,* has asked me to write a piece based on my theory that comedy and humor have been scared out of American writers. I think it's high time we all quit hiding and praying. A great many writers attended one or more Communist meetings before rejecting the whole idea, and they are afraid of subpoenas because they don't want to name who was there. Well, they don't have to, it seems to me. I don't think thousands of writers would be sent to prison for this. It is a problem, of course, because the writer who won't tell all is usually a Communist or a former one. But then, Emmet Lavery, the anti-Communist president of the Movie Writers'

Guild, didn't name anyone on the stand and came off fine. Once a guy says, like Lavery, "I am not a Communist, I have never been a Communist, and I don't propose to become one," the probers are likely to let him alone. But we have gone four years without a Lavery on the stand, as if Congress were trying to identify Communism with literature and the theatre. One of my points is that 95% should demand to be heard.

I am certainly right in believing that Ross never knew the politics of any of us, or at least that he never cared as long as it didn't obtrude into the magazine. He would have been the best witness. I am too nervous, White and Gibbs are too shy, so who have we got?

I hope you read Elmer Davis on Chambers in the Saturday Review, and Stuart Chase's nineteen propositions in the same issue. The last one is this: "The United States faces many dangers in 1952, but Communism is not one of them." He means internally, of course.

> As ever,
> James Thurber

*Mr. Gus Lobrano, The New Yorker,*
*25 West 43rd St., New York, N. Y.*

*Thurber preferred Eisenhower over Taft in the 1952 Republican primaries but later favored Adlai Stevenson, the Democratic Presidential nominee. William Shawn succeeded Ross as editor of* The New Yorker *in early 1952.*

## To E. B. White

> *West Cornwall, Connecticut*
> *July 18, 1952*

Dear Andy:

Yes, I would also like to hear Doc Beall opposing all sides of every convention, and even Jake Fisher throwin' a few delegates. I was interested in the boys who pointed out the merits of over-coverage by television, but while it shows the rascals off guard, a merit, it adds to our unbalance by magnifying and lengthening everything. The Chambers book got more coverage than anything since the fall of Poland, and there were even special editions of magazines dedicated to it. And it was overwritten by a guy who isn't a writer. Maybe we will never get back to the criticism of books written by creative writers. I don't know, because we would rather read the memoirs of Benedict Arnold than the writings of Thoreau. If you missed Joseph Wood Krutch's dialogue between Thoreau and G.B. Shaw in the Saturday Review of May 24, you better get one. . . .

I hope you and Katharine are both up and around, and that your faculties are able to take in all the threats and confusion again. I haven't been able to go back to the New Yorker again yet, because I always looked up Ross first when I came back from Bermuda. They are carrying on his magazine all right, I think, even though everybody I meet seems to suggest that it should now be called "Momentum." I try to explain, making it shorter each time. I'm not going to vote for Eisenhower and Nixon, but I have no data on Shawn. I don't have any on Eisenhower, either, but maybe we'll get some. He is the Great Amateur, and I am not too old to care for amateurs.

Love to you both from both of us.

As ever,

## To the Ronald Williamses

*The "Lincoln letter" is, of course, by Thurber.*

*West Cornwall, Connecticut*
*July 21, 1952*

Dear Janey:

It was wonderful to hear your voice even though it sounded as if you were talking through calico. We had got a note from Ronnie saying you had gone to the Point and adding, with the wistfulness of a shotgun, "She will probably call you up." I knew you would, just as we would phone you after we had been in Hamilton a week and were getting bored. I know you should come down and see the play, and so do you, but the American woman has a way of rationalizing herself out of pleasure, especially when Papa is doing the cooking and the housework at home. I feel helpless against what I now call Williams-Bermuda reasoning, for it is well established, and different, and hard to change.

"The Male Animal" plays every Sunday night, including this coming Sunday, and you would be our guest at the Algonquin and we provide tickets, which cost me nothing in the summer, and a sitter and bed and board in the same way that you have entertained us. Rosie went last Saturday, a performance distinguished by a strange universal laugh from the balcony not shared by the orchestra people and puzzling to Elliott and his daughter who were on stage. It later turned out that the balcony had spotted a mouse on stage. Wildly played this mouse at the foot of the living room stairs. Such an unexplained laugh has an invariable effect on actors: women are sure their pants are falling off, and men are sure their pants are open.

We would be at the Algonquin, too, because Helen's sister is here and wants to see the play. There is always an extra added attraction, it seems, and a few days ago Robert Preston got a nosebleed during one of his yelling scenes with Elliott, who gave him his breast pocket handkerchief and then his hip pocket one. The third act that night was as bloody as the last act of Hamlet. If you go Sunday, one of the thousands of crazy men walking our streets might shoot somebody on stage. More fun.

. . . My great friend Ted Gardiner gave up drinking last November, because his dog died. He was a double-slugger who tried to knock himself off before the last guests had arrived in accordance with the strange masculine desire to take the pleasure and relaxation out of drinking as quickly as possible, to dominate the evening by blabber, and to put on all of his boring rituals for the two thousandth time. Ted wanted to be buried with his dog, a smelly 17-year-old spaniel, but you can't do that in America. Besides Ted wasn't dead. He says the dog was killed by an automobile and he feels it wouldn't have been if he had been sober. His wife took him to Europe to forget aboard the United States on its maiden trip, but he insisted on flying back within a week. His wife Julia is the one who believes that mothers should not wear perfume and who prays every night that God will dream up a less messy way of conceiving children than the present one. They have two daughters and three grandchildren, but one son-in-law got the hell out. I am enclosing a copy of a letter I just wrote to Ted and you don't need to send it back if you promise to send me a letter somebody else sent you.

When the doctor said that he gets metabolism rates of plus 70, my 24 doesn't seem like much. He got one gal down from plus 30 to minus 15. Oops, sorry! I lead the life of a petunia and sometimes don't drink at parties, and never drink at home. It was eight weeks ago today that I smoked my last cigarette. Maybe you'll remember that night, it was quite a do.

It is, of course, risky to avoid meeting old friends who are going on a hundred, no matter how plus they are. I've just dug up a copy of the last letter Lincoln wrote Ann Rutledge, and it points a pertinent moral. He never got to see her again, because he was shot. Either that, or she died of snake bite.

THE WHITE HOUSE

*April*

Dear Miss Rutledge:

It is with exceeding regret that I write to tell you I shall not be able to come to Springfield this year. Mary's mother has decided to sell her house to the Confederate Army, and it is my earnest intention to remove everything that might be of benefit to the enemy. We are at the house as I write this and some faint effort is being made to share the movable property fairly among Mary and her sisters. I am afraid that my wife is not being completely fair, for she walks not with a frou-frou but with the sound of silverware clinking. "To the early bird belong the spoils," she told me this morning.

I shall miss our walks along the river bank with our sack of peppermint candy and your kind attention in listening to my repetition of the talk I made at Gettysburg and the letter I wrote to Mrs. Bixby. No one except you, Ann, will long remember either of these. Needless to say, old Mrs. Todd makes as little sense as usual, and I shall be glad when we return to Washington, even though I have received a threatening letter from some crank named Booth. Within a month we shall go to see a comedy called "Our American Cousin," and I wish you could join us. If by some flaw in the grace of God we shall never meet again, I would appreciate it greatly if you would sometimes recite the speech and the letter to your children. I myself have made nine copies of the address, but they will all fall to dust in years to come. I assure you that my memory of you will endure no such fate.

                Lovingly yours,                                          A. Lincoln

We'll be calling you one of these evenings and working out on you again, if we can get through the calico. . . .

Helen joins me in sighs and regrets.

        As always,
        Jim

## To Carey McWilliams

*West Cornwall, Connecticut*
*July 21, 1952*

Dear Mr. McWilliams:

The first man to ask me to write a piece along the lines of the Harvey Breit interview and the POST explosion was Lewis Funke, drama editor of the

NEW YORK TIMES, and the piece will appear July 28th, or is scheduled for that date. I have spent a lot of intense work on the piece, although it only runs to 1400 words, and I feel that I must get back to my usual kind of writing. There are only a handful of us writing humor and comedy and we are getting old.

I've been brooding about a number of things since I got back from Bermuda, where I spent a hundred days, and one of them is the vast over-coverage of everything, a sort of elephantiasis of exposition. I guess this is a symptom of a country whose dedication to non-fiction, as Ross would have called it, has become a 24-hour-a-day thing. This is a disease of our Era of Fact and Information, and over-seriousness goes along with it, too. This has always been a country of laughter and its loss is dangerous. The great Ross was dismayed when he saw his magazine "becoming grim" twenty years ago, but he also aided and abetted this by building up one of the best foreign news staffs in the country. We still have humor of word and line, but all comedy nowadays has its collar open and is panting for breath. My greatest hatred of Communism was its hatred of humor. "We would make certain concessions in your case," was said to me in some form or other by a dozen non-creative writers I know. I would never name them on the stand, but this situation forms a part of my problem and that of hundreds of my friends which is not generally thought about. In 1933 I exchanged letters with a literary Communist in which he defended and I attacked Communism. I kept no carbons of my letters and I did not keep the originals of his, but he doesn't know this and over-laughs at what I say every time we meet. Since my side knows that no literary person since Tom Paine has had any real authority in this country, we can't be whipped up to any fear of any writer. Hence we would never name any American literary Communist on any witness stand. We will never be subpoenaed, though, because the technical crime of contempt would be up against something too much for it, if writers stood together. They don't, of course, and are the weakest organizational men in the world. . . .

Sincerely yours,
James Thurber

*Mr. Carey McWilliams, THE NATION,*
*20 Vesey Street, New York 7, N.Y.*

West Cornwall, Connecticut

August 13, 1952

Mr. Carey McWilliams, THE NATION,
20 Vesey Street, New York 7, N. Y.

Dear Mr. McWilliams:

. . . As for Schlamm's theory about homesickness and humor, his buttons are twisted. I have done only two out of nineteen books that could be called nostalgic, but some of the outland reviews of "The Thurber Album" point out that I have softened and changed, and one guy in Texas detects a note of farewell in the book. If I quit at 57 my wife and daughter and other dependents would get sore. Fact is, during the three years I was writing the book I wrote twenty-five other pieces, which will appear in a book next spring. This is a great country to pin a guy down on no evidence much. I'd much rather write a piece about "The Cocktail Party" or Sam Spade on the radio, or the sloppy way publishing houses are run than delve into the Columbus past. I had to soften the book a little, because of the people involved, especially my mother and brothers who wanted everything tinted like photographs taken at Buckeye Lake. The emotional debris was terrific, since Columbus is the heart of evasion and fatty degeneration of criticism. Said my mother: "It wouldn't go down very well with the young man of today if you reported that your grandfather sent a substitute to the Civil War." Said a man named Opha Moore out there years ago: "The story of Chic Harley does not point a good moral." (Chic had become a mental case in his senior year.) Said the city attorney of "Jurgen," after thinking a moment: "Why do writers write books that offend people?" There was so much rubble of this sort that the light I threw on the good people got stronger and stronger. "There is an alley between every street in Columbus," wrote one of the town's distinguished columnists, and all you have to do is jog to the right and see the whole scene from the alley. My unfond memories would fill a bucket. Just wanted to clear up this little point.

. . . I remember that David Garnett used to deplore Twain's unimplemented and over-simplified attacks on science, and Garnett was afraid in 1938 that I was in the same danger. Humorists fall into it not because of an inborn anti-intellectualism, but because of the great desire to hit pretentious critics with a fish. This doesn't fit science, but it does fit politics.

I touched on only one phase of the complicated reasons for the state of the theatre. The other reasons are harder and take too much space. One of them is

the fact that a writer is born in a decade and not in a year. "We were all rebel-
lious then," Edmund Wilson said in his NATION piece on Millay, or words
like that. Most of them are dead now, or thin white lines upon the shore, but
the Twenties sure did produce writers, of any shade or temperament. "Writers
are a dime a dozen, Thurber," Ross said to me in 1927, and he spent almost a
year trying to make an editor out of me. Another big factor was the profound
effect of the depression on its young generation, and I used to talk to Journalism and English classes at Ohio State, from 1921 on, and the two chief questions asked me in 1927 and 1928 were: "What is Dorothy Parker like?" and
"How old is Peter Arno?" In 1932 the questions were: "Do you think literature
can survive economic decline?" and "What is the future of American literature?" The kids also talked about credo and dedication, and they didn't laugh.
The hardest factor, of course, is the cyclical nature of national talent. It's like
the curse in women, or the phases of manic depression. There is nobody to
deal with the present scene and it falls flat in the theatre when it is tucked into
corners of old musical comedies. I don't know why "The Green Pastures"
failed, though, which shows how dumb I am. Do you suppose people had
turned away from de Lawd for reasons that only [Whittaker] Chambers could
understand? Then the dead weight of old successful playwrights of the Twenties lies heavy on Broadway. Too many of them are still turned to as play doctors, or directors or producers. Comedy is as old as George Kaufman, and the
average age of the successful comedian is about fifty-five. The biggest factor of
all is the public's love of the actual as against the creative, and who would
cross the street to watch a play if he could sit home and see a gangster's moll
on the witness stand, or a general shaking his fist at Reaction? The musicals
will go on forever, but we may have to wait twenty years for a revival of plays
without music.

   I thought I started out to write a short note.
        Cordially yours,
        James Thurber


## To the E. B. Whites

*West Cornwall, Connecticut*

*August 1, 1952*

My dear Katharine:

   Helen and I are getting envious of you two, because you have more wrong
than we have, in spite of our low RBC, her rash, and my hyperthyroid which

was around plus 60 two months ago, but was down to 24 two weeks ago. Also, I cut my eyeball with a handkerchief and it was a near thing for awhile. I got Bruce out of Englewood on Sunday, in spite of his bursitis, and he doused me with Cortisone. Then you have to turn up with a fancy virus of the liver. Helen and I both hope it is bearable in that hospital and that you won't have to take glucose as long as I did in the railroad hospital in Virginia. Do you remember when all we worried about was love? . . .

We took Helen's sister and Janey Williams to "The Male Animal" Sunday, and it was a lousy performance and a basket supper audience. You could smell the Juicy Fruit and the popcorn. Elliott left out lines and missed an important cue because he was thinking about my piece in the TIMES. I have got two letters about it favorable, and maybe ten favorable comments. People are too preoccupied to bother, but a few professional controversialists will take me apart, and I am told that one named Schlamm already has. Writes in Freedom or New Freedom. A few hysterical and crazy women write me about the stereotype maid in the play or the obvious fact as shown by Harvey Breit's interview that I think dead or mangled soldiers are funny, but 99% of our women go on listening to soap opera and reading movie magazines.

I had lunch with Gus in New York one day, and with Honey the next. Helen says Honey's face has become kindly and this is almost too much for me. I've always dreamed of hitting her with a heavy glass ashtray in my seventies and here she is on her way to becoming sainted. Rosie is in summer school and so is her best beau. She will be twenty-one in nine weeks and rejoices that she can then bypass her mother, who constantly wants to have little talks. . . .

Malcolm Cowley is going to do a piece about me for the REPORTER; we didn't think the Unguentine caption was funny; my book has sold 25,000 copies; the play is only grossing ten thousand, but that's comparatively good and it will pick up.

Helen and I send you all our love and best wishes. Get out of that place and back home.

As ever,

*ба. ба. ба.*

*West Cornwall, Connecticut*
*August 6, 1952*

Dear Andy:

I hope Katharine is back now and that you are doing better than might be expected after hitting your head that way. I'm glad you appreciate my exalted position as a lay authority on the prostate gland. Don't pay too much attention to what a doctor says about consistency, because he fights his way through dark textures and his sense of touch is confused, especially if he keeps his eyes open. As an authority on the problem of tactuality I realize that doctors often think that if you can't see it, you might as well keep your eyes open. This is mistaken, and the quality of touch is often determined or distorted by what the doctor is looking at. To him the firm becomes the hardened, and so on. Eight years ago one of these guys said I was okay, I guess. But I was called smooth and symmetrical by a Bermuda surgeon who had watched erotic movies at the bachelor party of his son-in-law.

A company of rain stimulators started throwing silver iodide yesterday and we are now up to our ankles in rain. Since there were also lightning and thunder, these guys probably think they caused them too. . . .

I have now gone eighty days without smoking and while it doesn't make me feel less nervous, I would have the galloping jumps if I had kept on, since nicotine affects us hyper-thyroids. To me I'm just about the same as I always was. Pity, as my daughter says. Let's all start recuperating now. Love from us all

        As ever,

## TO JEANNETTE TROTTA

*West Cornwall, Connecticut*
*August 14, 1952*

*Miss Jeannette Trotta,*
*New York University, Dept. of Journalism,*
*Washington Square, New York 3, N. Y.*

Dear Miss Trotta:

I never thought I'd live to see the day of the fictionalized interview in which the interviewer takes a phony name and speculates on what the interviewed is thinking about her. Something ought to be done about this. Maybe you ought to go in for short story writing. I don't think you got Shawn in focus, but then you think he is 5 feet 5½, which would make me 6' 11".

I'm not going to be in New York, and so I won't be able to let you imagine what I am thinking about. Why don't you try an imaginary interview, since you are trying to stay away from realistic reporting? I'll help you out.

Alice had always thought of James Thurber as a short fat man, but he turned out to be a tall thin man, mouse-faced, jittery and impatient. "I won-der what she is thinking I am like?" he was thinking. He can't sit still long enough to be interviewed, so Alice and he walked up and down the corridors. He told her the picture was very dark, but she didn't know what picture he meant and she was afraid to ask. He took Journalism at Ohio State thirty-five years ago, when it wasn't fictionalized. He got the daily paper out on Friday night with a staff of twenty-five, only one of whom had brains enough to tie his shoes. He usually put the paper to bed at 3 a.m. Everybody else got it out by midnight. He worked on newspapers in Columbus, Paris, and New York for seven years and finds it hard to believe that girls nowadays take Journalism as a gut course, like comparative religion, or the history of art. He thinks it would be more fun to interview Lillian Ross than Shawn or Thurber. He is willing to answer any question you will write out and send to him, although most of the questions are answered in "The Thurber Album," probably. His favorite flower is the sweet pea, his color white, and he likes girls dressed in yellow.

> Sincerely yours,
> James Thurber

## TO THE RONALD WILLIAMSES

*West Cornwall, Connecticut*
*August 25, 1952*

Dear Janey and Ronnie:

... The Nugents spent Monday night here and the glass I threw left the plaster and lath showing between the doorjamb and the Dufy [painting]. Norma was sitting eight feet away and got all the ice in her lap. We had a fine time, though.

There were some cryptic letters in the TIMES a week after my piece, and I will send you a clipping probably in this envelope, together with a couple of carbons about my condition, carbons of letters to my doctors. I've gained about seven pounds, but I have no energy or elan or joie de vivre, for which the American is not giving a good goddamn. I yelled all my energy away in Bermuda about sea battles I don't care about, books I have never read, Rock-ettes I don't believe in, and so forth and so on. The only thing I've written in six months is the TIMES piece. . . . I can't face the idea of deadline right now, but I hope to get back to Bermudian pieces next year. I have had blocks about writing before, and don't believe the Freudians are right when they connect it with the flow of mother's milk, or something. There is a book called "Writers and Psychoanalysis," or something, which insists this is true, I forget just why.

Rosie arrived the other day and spent 15 bucks phoning her Philadelphia boyfriend, last night, while her Cornwall boyfriend sat downstairs. . . .

I still haven't got to the New Yorker since I came back from Bermuda, and maybe that's it. Ross's appreciation of my writing was the one I wanted most. Writing for it had become a habit. I have no desire to write for the new bunch, although they are all right and I will finally. . . .

Now I know what it's like not to be a writer. What a hell of a dreary life! There is no substitute for the delight of writing, including checking the inventory in a china shop, measuring people for slacks and jackets, hunting for 1930 cuts of frickers under full sail, or even outboxing the compass and shooting the sun. Now that I am in my twelfth week of not smoking I can't betray this unexpected willpower by taking to drink, like stronger but weaker men, or turning to Roxy dancers . . .

The play has picked up greatly and is now making money again and will probably run into the winter if the cast sticks together. The book remains fourth on the Tribune's best seller list, but averages fifth around the country in local reports. My high water mark in the Tribune was thirty-three stores on August 3. This is not absolute accounting, for there is a mystique in it, or guesswork. Also a store is likely to list a book it wishes were selling to stimulate sales.

Well, that being all I can think of saying, I will lay down my pen. The three Thurbers send love to all the Williamses and the new maid. Tell her to tattoo the baby on its hips, not its forearms.

As always,

## To Elliott Nugent

*West Cornwall, Connecticut*
*September 19, 1952*

Dear Elliott:

Those weren't supposed to be real titles I sent you, and I guess I didn't make the point clear. I batted off a few without one second's thought, but you got to spend days getting titles like a few of the five thousand I have done in my time: Afternoon of a Phone, for a Talk of the Town piece; Pussy Wants a Coroner;

and What Say, Let's Be Bodies, for two mystery novels; and Menaces in May, for a little old piece about menaces in May. Notes in May happens to be another title of mine. Nobody ever beat Benchley's title for a Press in Review piece about the Starr Faithful case or something: 8-Point Roman Holiday. The hardest thing I ever had to do in the way of titling was to get the twenty-five morals for my Fables. One of them about the moth and the star took ten days and 173 tries before I got the 174th: Who flies afar from the sphere of our sorrow, is here today and here tomorrow.

Ross was a great man at criticizing and helping title writers. He suggested Soapland, when I had got stuck in a rut of "The World of Soap." He could have saved Gibbs and White and me from putting a ghastly title on each of our early books: No Bed of Neuroses, by Wolcott Gibbs; Quo Vadimus, or The Case for the Bicycle, by E. B. White; and The Middle-Aged Man on the Flying Trapeze, by James Thurber. This last is probably my best collection, but it never sold, and the White and Gibbs books were flops, too. Titles do help, and they should be pertinent. The perfect title for Axelrod's play is, of course, Piece o' Tail, and I weep that we cannot use it. I hope our A Hole in One gets around town, because it will help scratch the itch or stimulate it. I was trying to show in those one-second titles a few directions the thing could take. An author should get his own title, thirty years experience has shown me, but he must sweat blood and ask our Heavenly Father to help him get past the itchy or sticky titles that first enchant him. If he does, and goes on sweating, he may hit on something as wonderful, as perfect, and as simple as "It Happened One Night." Love towards you all

As ever,

## To John Carter

*Carter was the vice-president of "The Raven Society."*

*West Cornwall, Connecticut*
*September 22, 1952*

Dear Mr. Carter:

I got Ik's letter just before yours, but I haven't got the heart to write two rejections of two such nice invitations, so you break the sad news to him for me. I had to give up public appearances of any sort because of my blindness, which doesn't get better and causes a great strain on me and my audience. I like Virginia and its university, and I send you and them my regrets and best wishes for a good winter.

I spoke to a bird that sits on a bust of Pallas just above my chamber door and asked it if I would ever speak again in public. The bird said, "Nevermore," which is all it does say. It comes from a bird sanctuary at Yore, Connecticut.

> Sincerely yours,
> James Thurber

*Mr. John A. Carter, Jr., Vice-President, The Raven Society,*
*1618 Gordon Avenue, Charlottesville, Va.*

## TO ANN HONEYCUTT

*Thurber contributed 32 drawings to* How to Raise a Dog: In the City . . . In the Suburbs, *by Ann Honeycutt and Dr. James R. Kinney, published in 1938. Thurber's running gag was that Honeycutt's text was merely captions for his drawings. Jack Goodman, of Simon & Schuster, planned to re-issue the book in 1953 but wanted it to contain more Thurber drawings.*

> *West Cornwall, Connecticut*
> *September 23, 1952*

Dear Honey:

All publishers are crazy or something, and the idea that your dog book needs more drawings is a further proof. I am for putting in more Honeycutt and taking out a little Kinney. Since the fillum over my eye is twice as thick as it was, I cannot see to draw, and anyway that stuff was done in ink. Jack's assumption, or insinuation, that Thurber is more important to the book than Honeycutt is taking our old gag seriously. If they got out a new Bible at S & S, Christ knows, but nobody else, what kind of illumination they would put in. They would have to have something new, so I suggest a preface by Gov. Stevenson, or Truman Capote, or E. B. White, or James Cagney. (Come to think of it, I seem to remember that White didn't like the book on the ground that girls don't know about dogs. Let's call him up long distance and plague him till hell won't have it.) People not only tell me I look better than I did, they tell me I feel better than I do. Three months without medical care while thyroiding through the sky, has knocked me down and I won't be back to normal until spring, I guess. I feel lousy and limp and have no appetite or high spirits. Some son-of-a-bitch in England has written in the LANCET that giving up cigarettes will cause "an excession of high spirits and a keen appetite." He is a goddamn liar. I have to choke my food down. The cook thinks I don't like her cooking, Helen thinks I'm being stubborn, Rosie thinks I'm showing off, and only the poodle loves it all because I keep feeding her under the table. All these creatures join me in love and kisses and the hope you don't fall and break your neck by using two dollar roller skates. I'll see you in my dreams, or maybe in New York one of these days. Drop in at the hospital and we'll take publishers apart, after I've had my urinalysis.

As always,

P.S. My God, my daughter will be twenty-one years old two weeks from today!

## To Robert Thurber

*West Cornwall, Connecticut*
*September 25, 1952*

Dear Robert:

I got back to writing half a dozen letters every day of the total of 1200 I do every year, and the enclosed will give you an idea of the five hundred I have got about the Album. I haven't answered this because I am trying to spare myself. . . . There is no humor like Thurber humor, Columbus branch, and even that differs in the case of each individual. It is too bad you boys didn't learn to sell it.

The letters are up to the ceiling now, pleas for money, attacks by crazy women, notes from Communist societies, nice letters from sane women, and notes from men who want to sell me their eye for $10,000, ask me the name of my doctor so they can bring their blind child to him, or suggest cures for my blindness, ranging from the injection of lemon juice to sleeping with an Albino woman in the dark of the moon. I have tried them all without success. There are a million other categories, too voluminous to go into. Happy days.

As always,

## To Wolcott Gibbs

*Polly Adler operated a socially chic speakeasy and brothel during Prohibition, patronized by Robert Benchley and others of the Algonquin/New Yorker group.*

West Cornwall, Connecticut
September 29, 1952

Dear Wolcott:

I got a letter today from Polly Adler, who lives and is probably in business, too, out in Burbank. She calls me Jim and "my old friend" and then says she has written a book that will be published by Rinehart & Co. in the spring. It is called "A House Is Not a Home." Maybe you know about this already.

I figure in a mild anecdote about some pictures on the wall of what seems to be the office of a woman prison psychologist. Here appears the fond expression "my old friend Jim Thurber." Polly enclosed a release for me to sign unless I objected to any part of the anecdote, and told me to send it to her lawyer, Gertrude Gottlieb in New York. I wrote Harriet Pilpel at Greenbaum, Wolff and Ernst right away, saying uh-uh, and explaining that my mother is a hundred years old and would drop dead, and that the eyebrows of my daughter, a senior at Penn, have risen high enough because of me.

Maybe we should convince McKelway that he figures as No. 7 in her chapter called "The Ten Best Swordsmen."

Yours,


P.S. I think the wonderful notices of "The Male Animal" in our Goings On Department are what keeps the play going, suh. I saw one fine performance and one awful one—this last one Sunday night. On Sundays there is a basket-lunch audience and they get a basket-lunch performance. It is no night of the week to go to the theatre. Helen and I hope that you and Elinor manage to get through this coming winter somehow. I have not been to the office since February, although I've been to New York several times. It hasn't become a block yet, and maybe I'll be able to get over to that dead place next time.

*Mr. Wolcott Gibbs, The New Yorker,*
*25 West 43rd St., New York, N. Y.*


## TO ROSEMARY THURBER

*[Undated, but meant for her twenty-first*
*birthday, October 7, 1952]*

Dear Rosie,

I'm enclosing a birthday check from Helen and me with our love and best wishes for a coming of age next Tuesday. Have fun from now on because in seven tiny years you will be 28 and then in 12 more you'll be forty and it will be all over. I meant to say you will be all over the place at forty because at that age women set their clocks back an hour, play three sets of tennis instead of two each morning, and are convinced that maturity is better than youth which never did anything for them but trap them with a husband.

The husband contracted in youth is always remembered, even when his picture is turned to the wall, so pick one out with great care and have him tested by doctors, psychiatrists, and old experienced wives. As a matter of fact, I have found out little about marriage after 30 years of it but I think that this might be true. A second wife may get into her husband's things and read letters from the first one, but a second husband is likely to read aloud to his second the letters from the first. Women are nicer than men.

A woman's greatest problem is this: How to make use of her uterus without losing the use of her brain cells. Since God and Nature made woman the creative sex and remind her of it every 28 days, it is natural that talent should be a subsidiary thing in her case. A man has to keep his talent alive even if it kills him. But a woman can let hers die like a rose in a book. It often dies in the shade of a man but she has her children to compensate for this up until the time the oldest boy backs away from a filling station with a gun in one hand and the day's receipts in the other, and the prettiest of the twin girls runs away with a gambler from Memphis. I'm glad to tell you that there is no record of homosexuality in my family as far back as the Thurber Album extends or of insanity before the age of 78 or of any of the major diseases except egotism.

If you are married, never let your husband keep his service revolver in the bedroom because recent news events have proved that if he doesn't shoot you on your way back from the bathroom in the dark, you will shoot him in his sleep because he has begun to get on your nerves and you're pretty sure the babies don't like him. The place for a service revolver is in the nursery because every child knows how to use one and this will keep papa in his place.

When you graduate there will be more and better presents and so you better graduate. I've already bought you a pearl handled submachine gun that once belonged to Al Capone's mother and I'm trying to locate her bullet proof Lincoln town car.

Daddikins

## To Hamilton Basso

*West Cornwall, Connecticut*
*October 13, 1952*

Dear Ham:

I'm proud of your thinking I could do the Ross piece and I keep doing it in my mind ("Get it on paper, Thurber!"), but it will take a long time (goddamn it, you're making me self-conscious). Ross is a terrific subject. In April 1932 Morris Markey asked me, "Who's the most interesting man you ever met?" I told him Ross was and he got up and screamed, "No!" The only other time that professional Virginian ever screamed so loud was when, in playing Categories, I deliberately placed Sherman under the category of hero.

I don't quite know what to tell [Charles] Morton, since several other magazines have approached me, too, but I'll get around to writing him soon.

I've been sick since last March from a thyroid condition that grows worse, or at least doesn't get better, and I am going to Medical Center next week. I can't write anything except letters and I have to sit down to shave. I'm limp and everything has gone temporarily out of me. The trouble with medicine is that it fell into the hands of the doctors, who believe only in the tangible, and who must simply be puzzled by the complicated and mystic nature of metabolism.

What do you mean you don't know any gossip. You can't get along without any gossip, so I'll give you some.

Edna Millay is in love with Arthur Ficke.

Daise Terry was sixty last March 17.

Mrs. White passed the same milestone in September. Her husband has written a book about a pig and a spider.

Gus Lobrano's golf score is in the low nineties, whereas I am running a pulse rate of 110. My record was 124, which Bob Thurber says is a duckpin score. My best duckpin score was 160.

Pete DeVries may soon be arrested for driving his car around town without destination. The motorized cops have their eye on him.

Polly Adler will bring out a book called "A House Is Not a Home" next spring. She referred to me as "my old friend Jim Thurber" and I got that lifted out. I always thought she was awful, but my lawyer, who is also the publisher's, says, "It is a social document." The actual writing seems to have been done by Virginia Faulkner, who bloomed briefly in the literary fields of the early Thirties. She was the author of "Roman Spring," or "Illyrian Summer," or "Fallernum Wine," or "Wind in Lombardy," or something.

More next time.

> Affectionately yours,

P.S. The publishers are Rinehart & Co. The lawyer is Harriet Pilpel, of Greenpel, Wolff & Ernst.

*Mr. Hamilton Basso, R.F.D. #2,*
*Westport, Connecticut*

## To E. B. White

*The book sent Thurber was an early copy of* Charlotte's Web.

> *West Cornwall, Connecticut*
> *October 14, 1952*

Dear Andy:

I'll be down to the city next week to see Dr. William Barclay Parsons, thyroid man, at Medical Center. For seven months I have horsed around, first with a clown who wanted to hunt for Factor X, then a guy who kept taking my blood pressure every ten minutes, to prove his point that it would vary slightly, then a New York surgeon and a Connecticut doctor who caught me between opposing orders: keep on taking three of those pills a day, stop taking them altogether. I was as high as 24, then got down to 3 about five weeks ago. The damage had been done, though, and I have been reduced to nothing. I sit down to shave, can't tie both shoes at the same time, and sometimes have to forego brushing my teeth at night—just don't have the energy. This affects what is known as high spirits and what is known as talent. The best I could do would be to take tickets at a county fair side-show. If you look up metabolism in Webster's you will see that this sum of creation and destruction keeps the world in balance, and sounds as hard as trying to land a Swiss watch on the point of a needle while flying blind.

I went to see Parsons around 1933, after Katharine and you had sent me to old Dr. Chickering, who took a basal and then began screaming for a surgical knife. You remember he had traded in his 1902 Buick Roadster for his metabamobile. I went to Parsons then, who said nonsense about an operation, but I'm an older man now. But then so is he.

We got your book and thanks for putting us on the list. It starts out fine, but I want to wait until my perception has come back before I go on with it. I can't read or write very much and have done no casual this year, the cat one having been finished last year save for its ending. This is the longest period I have gone since the ten months that followed a nightmare in which I saw two Ann Honeycutts at once.

Tell Katharine that Virginia Faulkner has ghosted Polly Adler's biography, "A House Is Not a Home," and see if she can remember who the two ladies are or were. Faulkner died after her first novel, and the other is studying for an AB in California.

We will give you a ring if I have to stay in town. I call on the doctor Wednesday afternoon—a week from tomorrow.

We are anxious to hear about Katharine and about you, too. I have hopes that the blow you got may have straightened out your head, loosened that snatch of "Whistler's dog" that was stuck there, and freed the coil that caused the buzzing. You always hear of people regaining their sight, or giving birth to twins, or walking again after such a bang. About the fox and gosling situation, I don't know. I'd have to look it up and I'm not strong enough to look up anything. I hope that you and the goslings won, but it has been a bad year for my favorites. Love to you all.

As ever,

P.S. Charley Speaks tells me about the fate of one Tart Sapp, the greatest full-back Columbus North ever had (about 1910). He got to talking funny all the time and trying to hide in his own pants pocket or something, and they put him away. Every now and then he is released as cured, goes back home, says after a couple of hours, "Well, I guess we've said all there is to say. Let's go back," and they take him back to the institution. He used to squire Althea around when she was in high school, but he got over that.

## To Peter De Vries

*West Cornwall, Connecticut*
*October 16, 1952*

Dear Pete:

I've been brooding about the kind of change that seems to have darkened the magazine's funny cartoons recently. There is much too much stuff about the man and woman on the raft and the two beachcombers. The first should have ended twelve years ago when the man said, "You look good enough to eat," and I thought I had ended the other one in the Ohio State Sun-Dial in 1917 with:

1st Beachcomber:   "What did you come here to forget?"
2nd       "          "I've forgotten."

I'm beginning to worry a little about Shawn's sense of humor and I hope you will tell me it is simply a case of an old magazine passing through the tail of a comet. I cannot believe the old magazine has begun to cackle, and I don't want to believe that [Rae] Irvin is back. I wish to Christ Ross were. . . .

The best thing the New Yorker has ever done in comic art is the probable or recognizable caption dealing with the actual relationships of people in our middle-class society. All of us have had a fling at fantasy and formula, but they should never predominate. I had hoped to do a few drawings based on captions I have dug out of hell in the past two years, but I think the strain would be too much for me now. Maybe Darrow, who drew the picture for my "When you say you hate your species do you mean everybody?" could do this one about a long married middle-aged couple. The wife is saying, "You're always talking about how dark the future of Man is—well, what do you think I got to look forward to?" This is two years old in my head. I can't do anything now since my humor sounds like that of an assistant embalmer. I hope to God we never get back to the two men on the face of the enormous clock.

The psychiatrists say that there is always as much relief as grief at the passing of any great or beloved figure, and that the relief comes first. Maybe this explains the loose ratchets at the New Yorker, and I have no doubt, and every hope, that time will tighten them.

I'm going to go to Medical Center for a thyroid examination next Wednesday. I have been dealt with rather haphazardly by half a dozen doctors and it is time I saw a specialist. I'm beginning to see a gleam in the surrounding darkness and expect to be in good shape by next Spring. We'll take up the decline of comic art and me when we see you, but I'm not strong enough to cut up any touches or kick the gong around. We send you and all De Vrieses our love and kisses.

As ever,

P.S. How about this? There is a double page spread of cows moving from left to right, and then another double page, and then another single page, all moving from left to right. The right half of the third spread shows the leader of the cows, a defeated biblical king who is presenting the cattle to a victorious biblical king, as reparations after a long war. The defeated king is saying: "Oh, I thought you said payment in kine."

*Mr. Peter De Vries, The New Yorker,*
*25 West 43rd St., N.Y.C.*

## To Harrison Kinney

*Kinney suggested to Thurber rerunning one of his cartoons of a man and woman in a bar, the man saying: "I'm married, yes, but my wife understands me." A contemporary magazine,* Today's Woman, *was running a series of articles by wives of famous men and had just published a piece by Mary Hemingway about her husband.*

*West Cornwall, Connecticut*
*November 10, 1952*

Dear Harrison:

I've been trying to trace my drawing with the caption: "MY wife understands me," but I guess the New Yorker turned it down and I threw it away. This would have been about twenty years ago, when I was closer to your age. I'm afraid every guy plays with that inversion of ideas. In answer to your question why guys think guys understand, there is the old axiom "Oh well, you know how women are," implying that all men understand women.

The stuff about "Woman's Day" is simply not worth bothering about. We so-called humorists seem to be fortunate in marrying women unprone to write cuddly pieces about us. I am puzzled by Hemingway's complacency and his great big cuddly personal notes about preferring life in the North because they had to sleep closer together, or some goddamn thing. I think that unquestionably there can be no humor in the great writer, or so-called great. The point has often been made that the reverse is also true. Anyway, humor has never been greatly respected, but the "serious" writer can get away with any childish behavior without disturbing his stature. The humorist is in-

stantly called crackpot or zany if he gets cuddly, or if he does nothing whatever. . . .

>Cordially yours,
>James Thurber

*Mr. Harrison Kinney,*
*The New Yorker,*
*25 West 43rd St., New York, N. Y.*

## TO FRANCIS BROWN

>*West Cornwall, Connecticut*
>*November 4, 1952*

*Mr. Francis Brown, Editor,*
*The New York Times Book Review,*
*Times Square, New York 36, N. Y.*

Dear Mr. Brown:

You astonish me by intimating that there is at least one book every year a
writer wishes he had written. I cannot agree with this. In the first place, an average writer—take me—has a pretty narrow field and certainly enough humility not to include a translation of the Bible, a collection of great poetry, or
"Sironia" in the wistful range of his aspirations. There have been times when I
wished I could have written Evelyn Waugh's "Decline and Fall," O'Hara's "Appointment in Samarra," Fitzgerald's "The Great Gatsby," and a hundred pieces
by E. B. White, but these are daydreams a man keeps to himself. I think the average writer wishes he had done his own most recent book better than he did.
He rarely has the guts to look at earlier ones.

Perhaps I am circling around a solid major truth: no writer actually wishes,
honest to God, that he had written anybody else's book or books. Maybe it
would be easier to put down one I'm glad I didn't write. I don't know.

>Sincerely yours,
>James Thurber

## TO THE RONALD WILLIAMSES

*West Cornwall, Connecticut*
*October 15, 1952*

Dear children:

. . . Next Wednesday I am going to see a thyroid man at Medical Center, since I have been much worse the past eight weeks. If those clowns down there had discovered my condition, as easy to detect as eight months pregnancy, I could have saved myself this burning out. Six weeks ago I was only plus 3, but the damage had been done. It may take a couple of years to get back the sense of well-being, health, and any trace of energy whatever. The prospect bores me unutterably, and it is hard to make a brave effort in this terrible world. I often wondered what Chloe was like when the man beat his way to her through the smoke and flame and the dismal swamp land. Do you suppose she had taken to saying, "Anyways" and to chewing Juicy Fruit gum? My mouth always tastes like a motorman's glove. I have to sit down to shave and I can do no writing except letters. I have been sleeping fifteen hours and getting up at noon, but in the last few days there has been a gleam of hope. I almost feel alive, can get up at ten, and now and then have a trace of appetite. For three months I had been choking everything down, including coffee. This descent into the sewers of the City of Negation has not even been interesting, and I have been struggling to write a piece, without much success, and would rather have a tooth pulled. . . .

. . . After I have had some competent attention maybe the view will be brighter. Right now I'm an old torn dollar umbrella stuck in a trash bin and it is beginning to rain. . . .

Love and kisses from Helen and me.

As always,

P.S. I used to be deeply interested in myself, but now I can't understand what I saw in me.

&. &. &.

*West Cornwall, Connecticut*
*November 11, 1952*

Dear old Ronnie:

. . . In recent years new drugs have been discovered that are powerful and effective for over-active thyroid, and I'm taking one of these at the rate of four tablets a day. I am supposed to begin to feel human by the end of this month. We will be in Hot Springs from this Friday until November 30. I have to keep taking the pills for from fourteen to eighteen months. After that they are stopped to see if you are cured or slide back. The chances are 50–50, which is good enough odds for me. . . .

I haven't written anything since I did the parody of Shop Hound, but I hope to get back all my urges some time soon. I went a hundred days without smoking, and now I average a cigarette every two weeks. They taste awful, like coffee. I never knew I could stop smoking, though. I wouldn't want to go through very much more of this, and if I don't feel better I'll be operated on.

I wrote a piece called "File and Forget" a few years ago, about the overwhelming inaccuracy of all publishers, who are the dumbest bunnies in the world. You may remember that the week the thing appeared, to the leering delight of all persons who have had books published, I got a letter from my publishers addressed as follows: Mr. James Thurber, Cornwall (Salisbury), Conn. We have been patient with Simon & Schuster, whom I now address as Hleamin & Sttnlan, but that ended when they sent me a letter addressed as follows: Mr. James Thurber, The Heggeletto, Somerset Bridge, Bermuda. It was forwarded to us the other day by the Somerset postmistress.

Now in dealing with S & S, or H & S, we have always typed out the word "Ledgelets," so they must have a transposing room in which type is changed to longhand to slow things down and to add challenge and bite to life. Of course, old Miss Crumble may not know where her glasses are, or maybe old Mr. Flickering may take too much blackberry cordial because of what he saw, or thought he saw, on Hallowe'en. He may also have Miss Crumble's glasses. If you want to, you can use your own version of this in the Crow's Nest, since it is absolutely true. Helen told Jack Goodman on the phone, and he thought it was funny. I don't think anything is funny myself, but it is nice to see one's line of communication with one's publisher gradually being obscured.

I get cockeyed once every ten days or so, but it doesn't do any good. It's a good thing the play is still running, and I've piled up a little money at Shuman & Snooper. I'm also getting "Thurber Country" together for next August, a collection of about twenty-two pieces.

I want you to stop worrying about things, and I'll stop getting so mad. If I hadn't been sick from brains to feet, I would have laughed at you the day you forgot to buy Janey an anniversary present, announced on your third drink that she put everything off, and explained that, as for you, time had crept up on you. I had to get mad when I should have laughed at you, but you got mad in those days, too, often as early as a quarter after seven. We then had seven hours of yelling, which was not good for me at my age. Next time I'll be fine, say around May 1954, which would be the end of the eighteen months period of pill taking. Meanwhile, love and kisses from me and Helen to you, cheers, and jolly times ahead.

     As ever,

## TO ROSEMARY THURBER

*In late November Rosie wrote her father that she wanted to marry a classmate, Fred Sauers, scheduled to put in a couple of years of military service after college.*

Dear Baby,

    As I wrote somebody yesterday my telephone bills are approaching the size of O'Hara's Twenty One bills now that it's June in January. I went over some of the rough spots with your mother last night and the gloomy inter-semester week, the whole damn dental program going down the drain, the awful prospect of camp following [Fred's being drafted], the financial wabbliness and the general lack of communication between Fred and me and my lack of intelligence about his family's viewpoint. The father of the impetuous bridegroom has in two cases I know about persuaded his son to postpone things a bit.

    Joe White was going to marry a girl when all he had was a room in a fraternity house. And Lobrano explained to his son the disadvantages of army marriage. We fathers all belong to another civilization, no doubt about that. When I was a senior at Ohio State, the United States got into the First World War and 80 per cent of the boys in my fraternity chapter put on uniforms to be gone anywhere from a year to two years. Quite a few pinned their fraternity pins on girls but not a single one got married because it had been drilled into us as children that you get married after you get a permanent job. I don't think anybody in the University got married and there were no married people going to classes.

    Times have changed, all right, the way they always do and I'm not trying to change them back. I will back you kids in whatever you finally decide to do but I must keep pointing out the dangers you inherited when the atomic bomb unzipped all the old customs and traditions and disciplines. We had nobody like your friend Betsy Cole to dash from city to city shouting "Get married," like an evangelist. I hope her husband is going to graduate soon. Incidentally, a girl of twelve was married the other day and the school board member who put his foot down and kicked her out was named Thurber.

It is only fair that I should state my own status when I first married. Forty dollars a week on the *Dispatch,* thirty dollars a week for press agent work, and about sixty dollars a month from *The Christian Science Monitor,* and three hundred dollars a season for directing Scarlet Mask. That was thirty years ago when money was worth something and of course your mother married a man seven years older.

      Dad


P.S. We have decided not to have a large invitation list. I don't know why it is that wedding receptions bring together the most awful people in the world out of one's past, making fathers and mothers and brides and bridegrooms wonder what the hell they saw in 60 per cent of the riffraff. "You are the meanest, nastiest man in this city," Elliott Nugent told one of his cherished friends at Nancy's reception. . . .


&#8478; &#8478; &#8478;

*[Undated, November 1952]*

Dear Bride-to-Be,

It was nice of Fred to call me even though we just surveyed the terrain with opera glasses on a misty day. Everybody, including an old girl friend of mine and Carl Van Doren's Barbara, has written about the dreary life of camp-following by young wives. Every piece is bitter and bad. Everyone lives in Dismal Seepage, Ohio. It's like hanging your marriage by the thumbs to see if it can survive. You might take a glance at a fable I wrote called "The Fairly Intelligent Fly". Joe Calhoun, Jack Calhoun's son, has a baby at Harvard Law School, to quote his Uncle Frank. Do you suppose he takes it to classes? I want you to rest up and get rid of stiff necks and headaches (small wonder I had them). You may be the only girl in the world who ever took on senior mid-term exams and marriage in the same fortnight. The dreadful variety of tests that you and Fred are putting marriage to reminds me of the guy that took off his wristwatch in Tony's kitchen and handed it to the drunken Benchley and Dorothy Parker saying proudly, "It's indestructible. Do anything you want with it." They threw it on the floor and stepped on it and Dotty finally whammed it against the stove. When they gave it back to its owner, he said in surprise, "It's stopped." The culprits looked astonished and then Bob said, "You probably wound it too tight."

    Daddikins

## TO JOHN MCNULTY

*West Cornwall, Connecticut*
*Dec. 8, 1952*

Dear John:

    Miss Terry tells me that your son goes around saying, "The wind comes from apples," and if you don't stop this nature faking, I will notify the juvenile authorities. The wind does not come from apples, but from carved pumpkins, when the lid is left off them. This sucks the air through the eye-holes, you can tell Johnny.

    Your son is going to be pretty confused by the time he is six, and you tell him that fig newtons are found at the bottom of holes on battlefields. I thought you were going to name him Twilight Tear. You take good care of him. Like the rest of us you only have one egg in your basket. My daughter, who is twenty-one, although I am not old enough to have a daughter twenty-one, is going to be married next month. If the father of the bride touches one knee to the floor, is he disqualified, or do you know? I have a bad knee, especially if I step forward suddenly. Elliott Nugent has three sons-in-law now, named Gerstad, Glouchevitch, and de Bethancourt. My daughter will become Rosemary Sauers. Well, life breaks us all in the end. Please give my love to yourself, your wife, and your wonderful son. He will probably grow up to be Hans Christian McNulty, if he isn't already. Does he know about the flying saucers yet? I am 58 today, and you won't be that old until next year. In 1952 Frank Sullivan, Katharine White, Miss Terry, and Charmé Speaks became sixty, and it would have been the 60th birthday of Ross and Mosher. Buck Crouse will be 60 in February. Cheers.

        As always,

        Jim

*Mr. John McNulty, The New Yorker,*
*25 West 43rd St., New York, N. Y.*

## To William Ingram

*West Cornwall, Connecticut*
*Dec. 8, 1952*

*Mr. William Ingram, Grinnell College,*
*Grinnell, Iowa*

Dear Mr. Ingram:

About every ten years a college humor magazine tries to get Sid Perelman and Dorothy Parker and the rest to write for it. In 1942 it was the Arizona Kitty Kat. I wrote the Kat, as I write them all, that I admired its courage and deplored its futility. We old-timers have no such things as scraps lying around. We sell everything. I also told the Kat editor that a writer is scared to death of the way his copy is invariably butchered by college periodicals, which do not understand simple proofreading. Twenty years ago I did write a piece for the Ohio State Sun-Dial, because I had been its editor in 1917–18. I told the 1932 editor that I would kill him if he mangled the piece and that he could get his mother or some Botany professor's wife to go over the proofs. In due time he wrote me: "The story you were good enough to send us was so badly garbled by the printers that it makes very little sense and I simply cannot send you a copy of the issue." The next time I went to Columbus, I tried to find the editor so I could kill him, but he had joined the Navy. Maybe Princeton has the right idea.

I never saw anything funny in a college magazine, including my own, but you astonish me when you say that Grinnell humor is "sexless," since college humor has always had sex, if nothing else. It isn't because Grinnell men are not virile and handsome, it must be just because they are clean-minded or innocent.

Merry Christmas and a Happy New Year.

  Cordially yours,
  James Thurber

## To Dinah Williams

*West Cornwall, Connecticut*
*Dec. 9, 1952*

Dear Dinah:

It was nice to get your loving letter, which Helen has read to me twice. It came in spang on my birthday, which is December 8, and not 18, as your mother knows when she puts her mind to it. December 18 is the birthday of Mrs. Charles J. Schwartz, wife of a Des Moines dentist.

You will be glad to know that I am much better now that I have been taking magical pills for six weeks. My hair had begun to look like butcher's twine, but its liveliness has been restored, there is a sparkle in my eyes and I can sit still and listen. Coffee no longer tastes like rain on a hen-house roof, and I can eat cereal without thinking of doll stuffing. Everybody says, "My, he's a hundred percent better than he was, which is a God's blessing for poor Helen." Poor Helen has been wonderful through it all, dodging and hiding, and feeding me pills.

I hope your generation puts a stop to the practice of getting married in college, the way my daughter wants to next month. Imagine being married between semesters in January! Her young man will be taken into the service in June, and they all get married without having any money unless the boy's father does something about it. Andy White stopped his son Joe, who only had $3.25 and a room in a fraternity house. Everybody in college is married nowadays and has at least one baby. Men my age not only support their aged mothers, but their married daughters and sons-in-law. I want you and your generation to do something about this. It is nice to have some place to live and something to live on.

Please give our love to your father, who is as bold as a hawk, and your mother, who is as soft as the dawn, but keep out a lot for yourself and your siblings. Well, almost as soft as the dawn.

Thanks again for your letter, Dinah, and a Merry Christmas to you and yours.

As always,

## To Theodore Rousseau

*In 1939 Thurber drew a similar nudist-camp drawing for display in Dave Chasen's Hollywood restaurant. Chasen also had several copies of it made.*

*Thurber's explanation for this cartoon—one of several on the same subject: "I have long wondered just how even the most sincere and impersonal nudists must react when a terribly well-hung gentleman appears in the colony. Many lady nudists' experiences of gentlemen's physique must be quite limited indeed, and I should imagine that it would be rather difficult to keep one's poise in that first moment of shock and revelation. My drawing shows that first moment as I visualize it, just before everybody settles down to the proper mood of indifference and nonchalance again."*

West Cornwall, Connecticut
December 18, 1952

Dear Theodore Rousseau:

I did that nudist camp drawing solely for Ross about 1933, but he went ahead without authority and had two hundred copies made, which he sent to everybody, even Woollcott, to whom he hated to give anything. Some copies have fallen into the hands of dealers, who sell them for a dollar. . . .

Helen and I hope to get back to France one of these years. I was 58 the other day. We send you all our best wishes for a Merry Christmas and a Happy New Year.

As always,
Thurber

THE NEWCOMER, OR "HELLO, FOLKS!"

## To E. B. White

West Cornwall, Connecticut
December 22, 1952

Dear Andy:

Everybody but me among us old codgers proudly insists that he and his wife were married just like the kids of today, without a blinking cent or the hope of work, and this is simply a lot of whoosh. After you had made the same boast, I sat around figuring that you and Katharine had made, together, a cool $20,800 in 1928, before there were any taxes to speak of. Like me, you would have dropped dead before asking a girl to marry you while you were still in college and had nothing to offer but a room in the Phi Gam House which you shared with brother Kilroy.

Rosie's future father-in-law is Park Commissioner of Chicago, I think, and a Who's Who landscape architect who has been past president of all their organizations. He is a Purdue man, two years older than me. (It's not easy to make Who's Who, since Red Grange couldn't do it and he's one of the ten best known men in America.) What scalds us fathers of the brides is that the fathers of the sons seem to put it all on us, beginning with the wedding reception, at which we buy all the liquor and they don't even set up one round. . . . I never heard of the fathers of Elliott's three sons-in-law, never saw them or heard of them. He used to slip Johnny Gerstad twenty bucks when the lad was first squiring his daughter around the town at night. Now this may all be very friendly and cute, but I find myself unable to warm to it. Love does a lot, of course, so does youth, and they will come out of it fine, and Fred will have a job by 1956, but I don't know whether I will survive that long or not. I'm going to give Rosie a gift piece of some property of mine, which will afford a weekly income during the run of the property.

If I had married Minnette Fritts when I was at Ohio State, we would have had thirty-five cents a day, and the astonishment of it all would have killed my father. I can also see yours, an outstandingly orderly man with a love of the hard-working ballbearing, saying to your mother about 1920, "I have just learned that Andy has married a Kappa Kappa Gamma sophomore at Cornell. Do you know precisely what this means?"

It is the women who love the insecurity before they are thirty. Althea forced me to give up my good paying jobs in Columbus and sail for France. A year later I borrowed $300 from Red Morrison, by collect cable from Villefranche, and six months after that I borrowed a few hundred francs on my return ticket on the Leviathan, hating every part of it. We owed a left bank hotel a couple of hundred francs when I got a check for $90 from "Harper's Lion's Mouth." This made us violently rich and is the most financial fun I ever had, even counting the $3000 I kept out of my check for $40,000 from the Book-of-the-Month Club to buy Helen a mink coat. The other $37,000, with $27,000 added to it, went to the U.S. Treasury. They wanted $17,000 more on this same deal a few years ago, but Helen won a long and adroit battle with the tax court. The poverty-stricken bridegrooms will never get into this, anyway. . . .

. . . Manic depression among young men at college is on the increase. Their brides will see them through, however, just as yours and mine have seen us through. I know that Katharine would slop the pigs for you in a crisis, even if she were wearing an evening dress and silver dancing slippers.

Merry Christmas to you and Katharine and Joe, and all your other loved ones from all of us.

As always,

P.S. When I married Helen I had three pints of rye and no money, and owed $2500. But I had proved I could make money if I put my mind to it and quit sitting around thinking up new ways to kill Ann Honeycutt. She told Helen the other day that she had finally decided I didn't like her. She is right and I have figured out why. Our love never ripened into friendship.

P.S. 2. Even when you got $10,000 for editing the SUN, you didn't plunge into marriage with the Burchfield girl because of what I call economic structure. You reduced yourself to nothing but a homemade banjo and started across country in a homemade car, singing for your supper and for Cush's. You could have had an Alaskan girl when you were cabin boy on the whaler if you had had the modern spirit. Economic structure means cheque books, stocks and bonds, and all that. McKelway told me he was nineteen when he was first married, but he was getting $50 a week and he was out of school and working. This was in 1924. Freddy will give up the $50 a week he's making now when he gets his MA or when the army takes him. Thus their salary comes to an end instead of starting when they leave college! He is in the Wharton School of Finance, but his hobby is the theatre, like Rosie's.

Most of Rosie's married friends are still in college, which gives the wife the curious experience of not having picked her husband because of what he has done or because of his congenial trade. She may have three children before she finds out she has married a funeral director. I guess this adds to the zing of their lives.

Elliott and Norma were making better than $1500 a month in "Dulcy" in 1921 when they were married. I was his best man in a church on Morningside Drive one Saturday morning, after which they went on to the matinee. Their honeymoon consisted of spending fourteen nights at Kew Gardens Inn, thus making theatre life harder by adding the strain of Long Island commuting. A bat got into their room on their wedding night and Elliott fought it until dawn. He was twenty-five when he was married, but you and I and most guys were nearer thirty. Nowadays they are about twenty-one.

If Joe [White] had been Serena, you would share some of my viewpoint in these matters. At least you reasoned with him [when] he wanted to get married at the age of fifteen or so. I have never seen or heard from Fred's father and won't until he drinks my champagne and Scotch at the wedding. All this crap about the father of the girl putting up the money and sometimes bearing the burdens for years is a foolish and incongruous variant of the dowry system, based on the theory, absolutely cross-eyed in this country, that the boys are more valuable than the girls. I'm going to start a move to make the fathers of the bridegrooms stir their stumps and get the lead out, unless the women beat me to it. After all, they control 76% of all the money in America.

Oh, the hell with it, they'll probably be healthier and happier than we were, for we picked at all the flaws during the first year and moaned like hound dogs during the courtship months, while they look for the best. I keep thinking that the greatest forward pass ever thrown in the history of love and marriage was Katharine's famous "Sounds like an old English inn," because it followed the goddamndest line ever spoken by a male fiance: "Let the ivy rest." She saved you just in time. The American idiom, even in those days, was: "To hell with that goddamn ivy," or "Balls towards all potted plants."

Do you realize that the date we made to meet at a certain place is now less than two years distant? I have my dated page of the TIMES tucked away in a small leather dingus with a picture of Eva, aged nine, playing with a dozen yellow chicks, and a rotogravure picture of Minnette Fritts in a blonde wig, playing Dolly Madison in some Seattle pageant, and looking at once constipated and saved.

Merry Christmas to all and to all a good life.

As always,

J.T.

P.S.: Eva was making $70 a week when she was fourteen.

## To Katharine White

West Cornwall, Connecticut
December 30, 1952

Dear Katharine:

Thanks for your letter and for all the jolly things to eat. I hope Andy is back on his feet by now. Gertrude [Sayre] just called and she was in bed with a deep cold for four days at the Jessups—the lady who came to dinner, and Christmas dinner at that. She was back in New York when she phoned and sounded fine.

I exchange letters now and then with Cass Canfield and just the other day found out the unbelievable mess of my Harper contracts. You have to watch all publishers and scrutinize every contract, and I hope you and Andy do this, but I have reason to doubt it. Believe it or not, Andy and I blindly and blithely signed a new contract for "Is Sex Necessary" whereby Harpers gets *50% of our earnings in England.* This is terrible. It simply means that White and I were taken like hicks in our first contract and we have let them screw us again in the same way! I know Andy cares little about such matters, but I am tough with the book men. I recently found out that Harpers had slipped into the contracts of three of my last books a clause giving them 50% of television rights. I explained to Cass that I had verbally told Saxton that I would give up no subsidiary rights whatever and Canfield has agreed to cross out the clause. They probably have White nailed down for the same thing. Harpers gets 15% of English earnings on my other books, I just found out. Harcourt took only 10% and Simon & Schuster get nothing at all, since there is no reason in this world why New York publishers should cut in on London earnings. Established writers owe it to young writers to watch out for things like this and to fight them. I give my publishers nothing except what they make from the sale of books, which is their business. Andy and I should have walked out on Harpers for good the day they told us they did not understand "Sex" and we should have poked stupid Lee Hartman in the jaw when he said of "What Children Should Tell Their Parents" that he didn't know whether it was supposed to be funny or not. I'm afraid to have you look at the contract for "Charlotte's Web."

Since Canfield was willing to drop the 50% television clause, I told him I would stand by the 50% English earnings clause that White and I let them put over on us, but I don't like it. I don't like publishers.

Love and kisses and a Happy New Year.

As always,

## To Henry Sams

West Cornwall, Connecticut
December 22, 1952

Mr. Henry W. Sams, Faculty Exchange,
University of Chicago, Chicago 37, Ill.

Dear Mr. Sams:

. . . I will be glad to give you permission to continue the use of my material in the Goldwyn vs. Thurber bout. I still think it was a great achievement to get Goldwyn's permission, but you must have known the secret: telling him he is the best and you never heard of anybody else. He once wired Ross that he was arriving by plane in New York and wanted to lunch with him. Over the coffee it turned out that Goldwyn wanted a favor, he wanted Ross to let him see advance proofs of all stories that would make great movies. "I'll make it worth your while," he told Ross, who never let anybody see advance proofs. Ross loved to tell this story until his death.

Best holiday greetings to you and yours.

Cordially,
James Thurber

## To Robert Gilkey

West Cornwall, Connecticut
December 30, 1952

Mr. Robert Gilkey, 35 West 75th St.,
New York 23, N. Y.

Dear Mr. Gilkey:

There are so many reasons I can't do the broadcast that I don't know where to begin. Maybe I should begin with the shocking fact that I don't know the work of Mark Twain. I always plan to get into it tomorrow or the day after. I have practically no French at all and could not sustain a conversation in it for thirty seconds, let alone for fifteen minutes. Like the rest of us in Europe twenty-five years ago, I could translate the French press and understand what a public figure was saying, but in speaking it I was strictly a "You resty ici, je returny in a minute" guy. You may remember that Hilaire Belloc always confessed that he was not a linguist, in spite of all the linguists he descended from. It is a gift, pure and simple, like blue eyes or skill in surgery. It is very similar to expert bridge playing, usually the accomplishment of people who know nothing else.

I appreciate your asking me to take part in this program and I am sorry that I have no equipment for it at all.

Sincerely yours,<br>James Thurber

## To Eugene Reynal

*West Cornwall, Connecticut*<br>*January 5, 1953*

Dear Gene:

Helen and I want to thank you for sending us Carl Sandburg's book. He is one of the monuments of America and one of our reassurances that this country will get over its jitters, for it still must have guys like him coming up. I met him for the first time twenty-two years ago and as he left he waved his hand and cried, "Lots of life!" He had already had a bucketful of life and there is a lot more to come, I'm sure. He was up here in Cornwall visiting Van Wyck Brooks a few years ago, and I was able to tell him a new verse of "Casey Jones," which he wrote down on an envelope. It goes:

> Casey Jones he was a son-of-a-bitch,
> He went through Toledo on an open switch,
> Drop-stitch stockin's and low-cut shoes,
> A pack of Fatimas and a bottle of booze.

Happy New Year.

Cordially yours,<br>James Thurber

*Mr. Eugene Reynal, Harcourt, Brace & Co.,*
*383 Madison Avenue, New York, N. Y.*

## TO PETER DE VRIES

*West Cornwall, Connecticut*
*January 16, 1953*

Dear Pete:

Why don't you try neon-Romanticism? You will either end up in jail or cured, if you know Y there is such small difference between the rap and therapy.

I went through my worst attack of your De Sease about forty years ago and was the first to come up with "and sons of habitual drunkards" (1913). My brother Robert still has the ailment and dreamed "Many are cold but few are frozen," and when he was only ten went around the house chanting, "I saw her but a moment." He is the author of this tribute to Bobby Schantz: "Little pitchers have big years." He has what the doctors call a pretty well established pattern, a roundabout expression for "incurable."

I wonder what became of the lawyer who opposed counsellor Elihu Root forty years ago in a court case in which Root represented the Budweiser breweries. Said the other lawyer, "It used to be Hires' root beer, and now it's beer hires Root." And when the Santa Rosa was shrouded in fog off Bermuda twelve years ago, I sang:

> Grace Line, Grace Line, Grace Line boat,
> Grace Line out there hiding.

It took me two years to get over my paraphrase of "And may all your Christmases be white," which was "Edna May Oliver Christmas E. B. White." More complicated than O'Hara's "There's a soft Helen Hayes on the meadow." It's all a matter of sourness of the stomach—I come from Columbus, acidity in Ohio.

Ross hated puns so that I threw one past him after a tirade of his twenty-two years ago, in my tennis column: "I'm tired of watching our tennis hopes carried home from Wimbledon every year on our Wood Shields." Ross later broke Frank Adams' heart by cutting out his "Red Budge of courage." In my "New Natural History" I failed to draw a mother grudge nursing her young, and was chagrined.

People usually worry about this disease when they are younger than you, or about its variants; a phrase that won't leave the mind, the meaninglessness of words like "spool" when repeated all night, and all the Freudian tricks that pop up in nightmares—one of mine was "as important as the 'r' in shirt."

Helen and I thought your piece was wonderful and that you're far and away the most talented of the crazy people. Bob Coates has a similar ailment, as I told you: "Did you shake a tower this morning?" These ailments render a man inert and stupid looking, his eyes glazed and his mouth open. Are you still married?

Love from us both
As always,

P.S. What are you going to do if Katinka answers the doorbell some morning, turns to you and says, "It's the Board of Health. They have come for the body of your work." Vercingetorix writing stuff like this, if he could sell it to the movies. The neighbors are complaining about the body of my work, too.

## To Rosemary Thurber Sauers

*West Cornwall, Connecticut*
*February 19, 1953*

Dear Baby:

. . . I feel as if my daughter had been carried off to the Halls of the Mountain King or Lochinvar Castle, the way fathers of the bride always do, I am told. Nowadays we are foolish enough to be the fathers of only one bride, which leaves us bereft at a single blow, like the sad druggist I found out about in Kerhonkson, New York, years ago. His drugstore stood at the foot of a hill and it was completely destroyed by one blow of a Mack truck. He had just arranged his stock in counters and on shelves and had opened his doors for business. He had gone upstairs to join his wife for a moment in their living quarters when this truck's brakes failed coming down the steep hill. It went right through the front door and destroyed the building and every bottle and every box. The druggist and his wife escaped, but everything they owned upstairs was destroyed. There is a legend that one bottle of Bromo Seltzer survived, but I never believed this. The truck driver was the druggist's first customer. I don't know whether the fellow went back into the same business or not. I am still in the same business as when I last saw you.

It was a wonderful and perfect wedding and everybody still talks about it and of how beautiful you looked in your bridal dress. Everybody also mentions how well Althea looked, and I hope you will tell her this. Also dozens of people have told me how much they liked Fred, and everybody says the whole thing went perfectly from start to sixtieth bottle of champagne. After we went down to our suite, Helen went up to the roof again to find Jay and Bob having a last look around. They came downstairs with six more bottles and joined the Whites and Van Dorens and Rose and Armin and Phil. . . .

If you haven't phoned us by the time you get this, I hope you will give us a ring, just a small one, so I can tell people you sound wonderful, and so I can be sure the poltergeits haven't got you. I have only two instructions for you: be sure to write my mother about that Paisley shawl, and don't forget to give your own mother a call. She was fine, but she will be feeling a little low, I think. This will pass with the both of us in a few days. I will call Althea one of these evenings myself.

It was really a wonderful Valentine's Day, and we send you and Fred our love and blessings again, and again. You will be much better than Hope Williams ever was. She was too damned stylized in a horsey kind of way and never took me by the throat.

    Love and kisses

        As always,

          🙦   🙦   🙦

*Williamsburg Inn, Williamsburg, Virginia*

*March 21, 1953*

Dear Rosie:

I am sorry I got you out of bed that morning, that big morning, but I was beginning to think you had vanished. Anyway brides and leading ladies should be up by ten o'clock on the day of the big show. We are waiting for the reviews and if you or Fred don't send them we will have to fall back on Jay again. I know you were wonderful but I want to hear the other fellows say it too.

We thought the bills for the wedding were reasonable and I would like to do it over again for twice the price. Only the cost of the flowers seemed high to me and I wouldn't worry about that if I weren't counting on a floral horseshoe for my funeral bearing the words "So Long Jim." Now I know it will cost $12,000. Helen has said she will not be photographed standing beside it and I don't suppose you will either. Daughters are funny that way. Ross left a note hoping his daughter might scatter his ashes over Aspen, Colorado from a plane when she is 21. I don't know whether she will or not. I just hope my urn is not left on a bus.

We have deep summer weather here, well over 70 and the most wonderful warblers I have ever heard.

This was just a note to say I won't call you before noon again, so don't worry about it. Gibbs was 51 yesterday and Miss Terry will be 61 tomorrow. I am 83.

Love from us both to you and Fred, as ever

P. S. Actually I feel fine and walk at least a mile every day. I am fat because I am full of frosted chocolates.

*Mrs. Rosemary T. Sauers, 3422 Sansom Street,*
*Philadelphia, Pennsylvania*

&a. &a. &a.

*West Cornwall, Connecticut*
*May 26, 1953*

Dear Rosie and Fred:

Look what's happened to the theatre in your generation (see enclosed). Helen went to the theatre three times a week or more when she got out of college and they always sat in the peanut roost. I began about 1905 in the rafters of the Hartman Theatre in Columbus. That gallery was as steep as a mountain side. We would sometimes arrive two hours early and stand in line so we could get the first row. It only cost a dime. It didn't cost much more than that at the High Street Theatre, where we saw "Custer's Last Fight" and "The Flaming Arrow" ("Moon Dog speak with double tongue"). Also "The Santa Fe Trail" ("Red Wing say spotted pigeons' wing feathers are dusty"). I learned to speak Sweet Sioux before I was 12.

We've got to figure out what to give you for the commencement and you've got to figure out when you are coming up here and going out there, and so forth. Elliott will be out Saturday, Norma told me this morning, and they are going up to Skowhegan after a few days in New York. . . . Jack Mellow, or Melon, who used to teach at Millbrook, had a Kappa here this weekend who came out for MacArthur and against Stevenson at four a.m. A fair-sized brawl resulted. It was the first time liberal Jack had known anything about her above the lips. Rose brought us home and he drove the Kappa around the lake until seven and brought her home in tears, whether of victory or defeat we don't know.

Love and kisses from us both to you all,

As ever,
The Old Man

## To David Foster

*West Cornwall, Connecticut*
*February 24, 1953*

Dear David:

What you really need help on is your incredible spelling of almost every word. I can't understand how your teachers have allowed you to become eleven years old without learning to spell balloon, or laughter, or suggestion, or jewels, or problems. I am not going to help you out about the technical problems you outlined to me, since that is your job and must be worked out by you and your schoolmates. I will say that you don't have to put that strange animal in the play at all. Stage lighting is a special art and you must ask somebody who knows about it. I am not very hopeful that you kids are going to get anywhere, but you must be more inventive and self-reliant than you sound. There are a dozen ways of doing everything and I will be interested to find how you worked out these problems. I wish you good luck.

Sincerely yours,
James Thurber

*David Foster, 100 Albion, Denver, Colo.*

## To Kenneth Maclean

*Williamsburg Inn, Williamsburg, Virginia*
*April 9, 1953*

*Mr. Kenneth Maclean, Victoria College,*
*Toronto, Ontario, Canada*

Dear Ken:

I am not sure I know just what you are trying to find out, but I will take a couple of swings at it. The man who lost or mislaid some thirty of my drawings died about a year afterward and we never did find them. I am told he was a charming chap and a lovely fellow and I forgive him because of an anecdote he wrote me about H. G. Wells. Wells came to see a Toulouse-Lautrec show, hurried from room to room and said on the way out, "Very interesting, very interesting. Local man?" This was in Los Angeles.

It is kind of vulgar to have thirty drawings lost but I was very proud when two of my sketches were stolen at the 1937 show in London—taken right out of a portfolio on a table.

My next collection of stories is the "Thurber Country" and is due next fall. There will be twenty-five pieces, most of them from the New Yorker and several from Cosmopolitan, Holiday, and The Bermudian. The publisher didn't like the title so I suggested "How to Make Love and Money." They hastily decided they would accept mine.

I am mainly working on a fairy tale that will be a kind of satire on the modern American political scene. It is called "The Sleeping Man" and relates the adventures of one C. W. Caldwell, a consulting engineer from Syracuse who finds himself in a fairy tale kingdom but keeps insisting that he's asleep and dreaming it. It has complications too varied to go into. . . .

I don't have the slightest idea what imagination is or the so-called creative urge. It all takes place above the right ear and the writer is often astonished later when he sees it coming out of the typewriter.

I will be in New York from Tuesday, April 14th, until following Monday. Love to you and Sara and the kids from Helen and always

    James Thurber

## TO BURRUS DICKINSON

*Thurber was victimized by a prankster who sent him an official-appearing letter awarding him an honorary degree from Eureka College. Thurber's acceptance led to an embarrassed exchange of letters with the college president. His gullibility was understandable: he had received honorary degrees from Kenyon and Williams, was scheduled to be awarded one at Yale in a few weeks and had been offered degrees from Mt. Holyoke and O.S.U.*

> West Cornwall, Connecticut
> May 29, 1953

*President Burrus Dickinson, Eureka College,*
*Eureka, Illinois*

Dear Mr. Dickinson:

I don't really know the etiquette that should be followed in such a predicament as mine, but I feel that I owe you and Eureka College my sincere apologies. In my college days we played pranks too, but not on aging blind humorists. We selected stuffed shirts. If I had been able to read the letter head I received and to examine the typing and the signature, I don't think I would have been taken in. I was on the point of having my secretary reply signing her name Virginia Creeper, but I do not regard honor or honors as a fitting subject for kidding around. As for the name of the mythical president, it is surely not an unlikely one for the Middle West. An authentic honor was recently extended to me in a letter from an Ohio woman authentically named Mrs. Depew Head. I am a friend of a distinguished Ohioan named H. Morton Bodfish, and I'm a mild authority on a celebrated Bermudian gentleman named H. Outerbridge Horsey. As for my falling for a degree offered on such short notice, I can only report that I was offered one on the identical short notice by a Middle Western State university three years ago. Incidentally, I turned that one down. I am certainly glad that I did not reject the mythical one.

I am afraid I do not regard this hoax as a sign of "appreciation" by a student. If writers my age depended on appreciation from the modern college student, we would probably languish of some kind of malnutrition. I have several times pointed out in recent years that humor is dying in America, a terrifying thing, but not a surprising one in view of the condition of the world, the plight of our species, and the fearful state of the American mind and spirit. I hate to see humor replaced by vulgarity and cruelty, but I'm afraid that's what we're in for.

At least this whole business has given me a chance to find out about Eureka College. I understand that General Omar Bradley is a member of the denomination of the Disciples of Christ and I can't help wondering how in the world he was given that most hedonistic of names, Omar.

You can't blame me for hoping that your prankster student gets thrown out of college. I'm sorry that you have been bothered by all this, and if my apologies should be extended to any other individuals at Eureka, I trust that you will extend them for me.

> Sincerely yours,
> James Thurber

## TO ANN HONEYCUTT

*West Cornwall, Connecticut*
*June 2, 1953*

Dear Nettie:

I told the enclosed lady that you are the unhappy sister of two, and the mother of men, but not of babies. I said that you have only nervous talkers for friends and that the only man you ever married was so goddamned nervous he couldn't get enough breath to talk at all. I saw him a few weeks ago, by the way, and he was in the high phase of his cycle and jabbering like Johnny Parker, without the cigar, and making slightly more sense, but this may be because I always encounter Johnny at Tim's and McKelway at the New Yorker. At Tim's it is hard for me to give anybody my attention. I demand everybody else's, though. I seem to have threatened to get rid of you twenty-five years after our affair ended, which would be this year, I believe. That is, if you could call it an affair.

We ran into Paula [Trueman] in the Algonquin lobby the other day where we were having drinks with some painters and publishers, and where I was getting noisier and noisier. I hate to run into old girls, since my hand shakes so much I can't dial numbers anymore. Numbers with a 0 in them like yours, discourage me easily. Why don't you become a Meridian 1212 operator? I would probably give you a ring then. You can't have many friends left who are sane and un-alcoholic. I don't think they'll ever put you away, but somebody told me that your shoes don't match and that your eyes cross if a man holds your hand. I actually knew a Red Cross girl in Paris thirty-five years ago whose eyes crossed when you held her hand. Her name was Bessie Fisher and she came from Kansas City. I was telling Terry about her one day and it seems that they knew each other in Europe. Terry never held her hand, of course. "Every time I hold a man's hand," Terry said, "I feel like throwing him over my shoulder. My eyes do not cross or my legs uncross for anybody."

Are you uncrossing for anybody these days? I hear you were seen with Durstine, but only having lunch. I ask everybody what you live on, but they won't tell me, or else they don't know. One guy says you still make $2500 a year on my dog book that you did the captions for. How does being a part of the New York scene affect your morale at fifty-one? Dear old John Mosher would have been sixty-one today, June 2. I miss him as much as ever. I do not miss Fitzie or Hannah Josephson. I do not believe Markey is dead. I will be fifty-nine in December, and you said you would make a play for me when I am old. I will be old on December 8. Hoping you are not the same, I remain your obedient servant.

## To the Thurber Family

*West Cornwall, Connecticut*
*June 24, 1953*

Dear Thurbers:

We've been so busy that I have fallen way behind in writing you and I'm sorry. Mrs. Swain has not been well and we have had Rosie and her husband staying with us since we got back from New York. I visited several doctors down there, just for periodical checkup, and I'm in better condition than ever. The allergy man, however, still couldn't find the thing that causes my sneezing. It is probably something unusual, like blue heron's feathers, or the pollen of bishop's ulster. Rosie and Fred were flying a kite when we got up this morning. They just drove Helen to the hairdresser's. Both of them are underweight, but healthy, and are eating like horses. It costs a lot for youngsters to live in these days. He still has his thesis to finish, but it is almost done.

Tomorrow is our wedding anniversary and Helen's birthday is next Sunday. One of our neighbors is giving a birthday party for her. We had full summer for two days and now it is cool again. How are things in Columbus?

We had a wonderful time at Yale and I have heard Helen telling people that I got a greater ovation than Senator Fulbright, which shows that cartoonists rate with liberal statesmen in this neighborhood anyway. I was too dazed to remember much or to hear anything. Senator Fulbright introduced me to Senator Prescott Bush and we talked about Douglas School and Tiny Bradley and Johnny Paxton who Bush said is dead. He got a lot of letters from Douglas School people in response to that interview. We were the guests of the President of Yale Sunday night at dinner and stayed with the Dean of Yale College and his wife over night. We both met and liked Dean Acheson, an extremely attractive man. I am told that Bush is quite handsome still and he seemed very pleasant. At one cocktail party we met Professor Coker and his wife. He taught me Political Science forty years ago and married a coed. They came to Yale in 1923. There must have been eight thousand people present at the ceremonies and we enjoyed every minute of the whole visit. I have got a dozen letters about the citation, everywhere from Ohio State men of my time to people I worked with on newspapers, and there have been some from strangers. I'll call you up on the phone next Sunday, when Helen will be thirty-eight. We all join in sending you our love and best wishes.

As ever,

## To E. B. White

*West Cornwall, Connecticut*
*June 29, 1953*

Dear Andy:

Dwig is an unbelievably ancient comic strip artist, name of Clare Victor Dwiggins, whose Sunday page called "Reg'lar Fellers" had been running for twenty-two years or so when you were born. About July 1926 it was devoted to a guy named Jim and a girl named Althea, who had met the Dwigginses in Nice the year before. Dwig must be seventy-seven now. I visited them at Green Lake, near where Clyde put the pregnant girl away. I hear you're going to spend July in New York. I don't think I could do that anymore and survive myself. We are losing our couple because of the wife's 240 blood pressure, the third couple to be shot out from under us because of the wife's inability to go on. Women outlive us by forty years, but they are through working at fifty, because of their weight, their unbelievably funny shape, and their sore feet. How they live so long nobody can figure out. One old lady up here retired just after

Custer's last fight because of her groin and her pressure, but she is still chipper. Hoping you are the same,

    Agedly yours,

    Jim

              ❧  ❧  ❧

*West Cornwall, Connecticut*

*July 1, 1953*

Dear Andy:

The kites my children fly are called jet kites and do not seem to need any tail. This young married couple would start flying early and come in for supper at twilight with the panting poodle. We do not know yet what they use for money, but I wish I had some, since it seems to conduce to repose. Well, they bicker a lot, usually at table, and so fast I can scarcely follow it. She won't have her grammar corrected by a Wharton School of Finance man and he won't have any woman close in on him. One is about as unneat as the other and they live in a welter. Last night they slept on the floor of their Philadelphia apartment. They had moved their beds to a warehouse or something.

When a couple comes down from Maine in July to spend the month in the hot city, people think the wife has a lover or the husband's prostate has sprung, and is keeping it from the other. That old romance between Katharine and Ordway Tead hasn't flared up again, has it? Most of the people who once loved Katharine or who once loved me are dead and buried, alas, and only their yearbooks and bracelets are left. Did you know that Rosemary Clooney was born in Ohio? So was Johnny Kilbane. He is thirty-seven years younger than she is. Eden is twenty-four years older than his wife. The old woman up here who hasn't worked since Custer's last fight can't bend over or rest her weight on her heels. It's always something. They say that Franklin Pierce was crazy about her, but he married a New York girl who could bend over.

I'll help think up a title for your book if you'll take a look at "The Sleeping Man" when I get it done. It ain't gonna run longer than 8000 words. I like Simon & Schuster because of a girl named Marybob, secretary to Jack Goodman. We what Helen calls clown around when I phone her. I am either Bobbs Merrill or Babs Merrill. The other day I says, "Hello, Marybob, you desirable creature" and a man's voice on some extension said, "I heard that." "We are undone," said Marybob simply. Amy Flashner was never like that.

I like the idea of you putting in a poetry section and some of the timeless comments. It's been too long since you got out a book of stuff. Do you know what a man does standing up, a woman sitting down, and a dog with one leg raised? They shake hands. "Shall I bend you over backward or just shake hands?" I say to my girl friends and they say, "Just shake hands."

Hoping you can still bend over and rest your weight on your heels, I am
Lovingly yours,

## TO PATRICIA BUNKER

*West Cornwall, Connecticut*
*July 13, 1953*

*Miss Patricia Bunker, Lawrence Fertig & Company,*
*Inc., 149 Madison Avenue, New York 16, N. Y.*

Dear Miss Bunker:

If I could be persuaded to drink Scotch or to praise it, your charming and original letter would have won me over, but it is well known that I am an old rye drinker and that my second choice is Bourbon. Also, my forthcoming book would be disconcerting to Bellows, since it is called "Comin' Through the Rye, A Short History of the Bourbons." Moreover, I told the late Harold Ross that no likeness of me would ever appear in the New Yorker's ads, holding a beer or whisky glass, reclining alone or with a gal in the back of a Pontiac, or trying on a hostess gown at Best and Company's. I am sure I have tasted Old Angus and liked it pretty well, but now that I'm fifty-eight all Scotch tastes to me like what I call Burglar's Uncle. I taste Scotch only when I'm in a house where nothing else is served. I'm glad you had me in mind as an old connoisseur and cosmopolite with a sound knowledge of rare drinkin' likker. You have a cute name, and you write a cute letter, and I bet you're cute as a little red wagon.

Cordially yours,
James Thurber

## TO DICK MANEY

*West Cornwall, Connecticut*
*July 13, 1953*

Dear Dick:

I didn't know anything about the American Mercury indictment, but it seems only natural in this ghastly time for an outstanding anti-communist like myself to be called a communist. Puts me right in there with the other Methodists, such as the late James Grover, the well-known radical of Columbus, Ohio, and the city's first librarian. . . . Helen joins me in love and kisses to you, Tuan. Mem Sahib and the old Massa have not seen you for too long a time. Ask Honey about the time I tried to lure her into a suite at the Ambassador, with four champagne bottles and a long-playing record of American folksongs by Jo Stafford. If there ever was a horse's assignation, this was it, entirely because of the way I bungled it. I have promised to seduce that lady before she is seventy, and I got to work fast, Tuan.

     As ever,

*Mr. Richard Maney, 137 West 48th Street,*
*New York, N. Y.*

## To Miss Coburn

*"Miss Coburn" was editor of the* Standard, *Stephens College, Columbia, Missouri.*

                  **West Cornwall, Connecticut**
                        **August 17, 1953**

Dear Miss Coburn:
    Your letter got me when I didn't have a secretary or typewriter, hence the delay. I know about Stephens, of course, like everybody else. I know less about the relationship of the author and his public. What a stuffy theme for you bright youngsters to select! A writer writes to please himself, to pass his wife's scrutiny, to win the praise of half a dozen friends whose critical opinion he values. I have never tried to visualize any public. I get letters from women of ninety, thanking me for this or that, and letters from seven-year-old girls bawling me out. I hear from crazy people and from cranks, and from lovely people and sensitive people. You can't maintain a single relationship with such a jumble. Every writer hopes his books will sell and that readers will like them. This is a wonderful relationship to arrive at, but it can't be planned, it just happens. Best wishes and don't become a writer unless you're terribly tough. We need more tough writers in a world in which they have become a kind of quarry.
      Cordially yours,
      James Thurber

## TO THE RONALD WILLIAMSES

*Jane Williams hoped to have a merry-go-round shipped to Bermuda.*

*October 8, 1953*

Dear Ronnie and Janey:

It was wonderful for Helen to see and for me to hear both you and your spectacular family, as she describes it. We never did seem able to say goodnight, let alone so long, since you were still trying to find out what plane you were going on, at 1 A.M. We don't even know if you landed in Bermuda or ended up in Jamaica. If you did, you can pick up the merry-go-round which seems to have been sent to Jamaica by mistake. This will cost an extra $2800 for reshipment.

. . . As for that wonderful list of missing objects Janey made out, one of the maids found the bedroom slipper, but so far there is no record of Ronnie's red plastic glasses case, the doll's shoe or the gold earring. Helen says Janey was wearing black earrings Saturday night. Was it one of these? She thinks Ronnie must have left his glasses case in the inside coat pocket of the suit he wore to the movies in Geneva. He probably didn't have the glasses Saturday night. I have notified everyone at the hotel and will continue the search when I get back there this afternoon. I feel a little silly about going into a store and asking for one doll's shoe, but anyway they are the same for both feet, if my memory serves. The loss of one shoe, one slipper, and one earring sets a new feminine record, and I am amazed that one glove isn't missing. In the book I am now writing three sox keep showing up and there is a great search for the fourth one. Are you sure you didn't take it with you? Also there is a search all through the book for the thing. Did Ronnie put the thing somewhere? A woman never knows where her husband puts the thing and in my book it is found finally but never identified. If it were identified the book would probably be banned in Boston. . . .

We realize today that you are the first people to call on us who are still all in one piece. Everybody else bumps into things or can't sit down or can't get up without help. I know very few people who can get out of bed in the morning without help and even my doctors complain of being old. I have discovered that women under fifty are a little too energetic for me, now that I can see 60 on a clear day. This is the only thing I can see clearly on any day.

The next time we get to Bermuda to creak around for several weeks, I will probably spend most of my time in an inglenook with Ambrose Gosling and

Ada Trimingham. Remember that if you have another child within three years, Ronnie will be Minna's age when the child is 19. I think he should grow a beard if this happens. He still has time to have a total of seven daughters, something I always wanted with seven different women. My idea was to have seven daughters all the same age, so that I could blame all the faults on each mother if there was any trouble. I can no longer find six women who are interested and I will probably have to go into some other line of fun. Furthermore, after having put one daughter through college, I have decided I could not survive seven. . . .

To all the Williamses, with all the love of all the Thurbers, all the time.

As ever,

P.S. Wednesday, October 17.

We just got Ronnie's letter and are glad he found his razor and his glasses next to the shaving soap. I'll send that slipper to you and let the Customs worry about it. We haven't called Cornelia yet but now we can tell her the news of the hurricane and of your safe arrival. The other lost things haven't shown up yet. The handle that starts the merry-go-round was shipped to Nassau by mistake. Helen is having her hair done this afternoon, after 47 days, a new world's record. There is nothing to worry about, so don't worry about it, whatever it is. All our love to all of you again.

J.T.

## TO THE E. B. WHITES

*West Cornwall, Connecticut*
*October 20, 1953*

Dear Andy and Katharine:

. . . I had heard about your experience with Bachrach from Terry. The only easy photographers are newspapermen, one of whom shot me a few times for the WORLD TELEGRAM taking only about four minutes and not praising my physiognomy the way the others do. Glass said, "The way you put a cigarette in your mouth is most interesting." I do it the same way you do and the same way your dog Freddy did when he loitered in the doorway on cold days for a final puff. The worst was a Latvian, Philippe Halsman, who kept me posed an hour and a half for Simon & Schuster—Glass takes about twenty minutes, Halsman takes about forty shots. Halsman posed me against a brick fireplace because he said I was rugged. He has obviously discovered this is the

American male's favorite adjective. I am just a little more rugged than Mosher was. As I once told Honey, I have a delicate character and I want it caught in photographs. The Latvian also called my hands beautiful and damn near got a right cross for his pains.

I used to have a yen for Magdol myself, but I never got to first base. I was reaching second at the time with a couple of other gals, though, and didn't brood too much. I remember she once said about a guy she knew, "He's twenty-five and he's never had any sex." I can see Ross's tongue drop out if he had been told about her new job. Do you remember the girls who wouldn't sleep with you unless they were drinking and usually got you so sloughed you passed out on their sofa? When you woke up they had gone to work and you went to the corner drugstore for coffee and found it impossible to get the paper off the lump sugar. I use "you" in a general sense. . . . I asked Rosie once what had happened between her and Mark Van Doren's oldest boy who had told me one night recently that he had been in love with her. She said, "He had an intellectual approach to sex and I didn't want that." Dinah Sheean, who has left Jimmy for the second and final time, told me that Jimmy quoted Balzac during their wedding week, to the effect that "a bad woman keeps the lights on, a good woman turns them off." Reach for that light switch, Katharine, and be a good, clean American girl. Most of the girls I love have touchy retinas or bad gall bladders now, and I'm working on a sad ballad entitled "I Would Carry You Back to Old Vagina If It Weren't for My Incision." Ah well, we had our moments and now we have our memories.

As ever,

## TO ANN HONEYCUTT

*West Cornwall, Connecticut*
*November 3, 1953*

Dear Honey:

I called you one night when we were in New York, but you were out with the fellows. . . . I'm enclosing a couple of clips proving that my dog book has got some recent notices. You remember the book you did the captions for. The reviews don't mention you or Dr. Kinney, but then they don't mention McKelway or Althea, either. Once a book becomes timeless, the purely timely folks drop out of it. I venture to predict that you will make a cool twelve dollars out of the new edition. I'm not getting any money, but then you can't eat money. I do get the publicity and Helen says I eat publicity. Who was it said that if I were a violet by a mossy stone I would find a way to make my lapels light up and take the attention away from the tulips?

It seems terribly long since I took any liberties with you. How about a tryst?

As always,

## TO RAYMOND SWING

*Swing had asked Thurber to participate in his radio program, "This I Believe."*

West Cornwall, Connecticut
November 4, 1953

Dear Mr. Swing:

I guess I've dodged that program because I believe that the imponderable is also the ineffable, and that something goes out of it when it is expressed in the well-known offhand conversational undiscipline of radio. I mentioned in a letter to Ed that Mrs. Roosevelt made her faith sound like a jolly Sunday noon dinner before the First World War. This was all very well, for those who are looking for icing or escape, but faith seems to me a sterner thing than that. I'm not so sure it's a time of affirmation, it may be only a time of self-delusion in which people want to be told that the house is not on fire, that the bombs won't go off after all, and that everything is going to be just dandy. I am also troubled by the fact that my belief changes from time to time and might even change during a brief broadcast. This would not reassure anybody. I also feel that networks have done more harm than any other businesses except advertising agencies in the recent years of suspicion and accusation and suppression. Furthermore, I'm not very good at this sort of thing and just don't seem to be able to know where to start. All the foregoing may be simply a defense that I don't understand very well myself. Maybe I am afraid to face myself on the air on this subject. Anyway, I have a Sound Mirror, which works, and if I had a tape I might be able to put something on it some day.

Mrs. Thurber and I are among your great admirers and were two of your most devoted listeners in the dark years when your voice was a great comfort, and she joins me in sending you best wishes for a good life and whatever comes after that.

Sincerely yours,
James Thurber

*Mr. Raymond Swing, "This I Believe," Editorial Office,*
*485 Madison Ave., New York 22, N. Y.*

## To Irwin (Edman, probably)

*December 4, 1953*

Dear Irwin:

Since you read my piece called "File and Forget", I am sure it won't surprise you at all that your very kind note, mailed on October 21st, reached me today, December 3, having taken only 43 days to make the journey. My publishers, of course, sent it to me in Bermuda. Three years ago I stayed for a time at a place there called The Ledgelets, which is spelled "The Hegeletto" by Simon & Schuster. This may be a Freudian attempt to degrade old Hegel. There is no way of knowing about S & S.

Your "forthcoming review" had been out for a month and I have had it read aloud to me several times, to my delight. I'm glad the book [*Thurber Country*] was sent to you. . . .

I have just written a note to Simon & Schuster telling them that they were instrumental in holding up your letter for 43 days. They are always contrite and go right on doing the same sort of thing. Recently they made me sit for some photographs since I hadn't had any taken for more than 20 years. They sent a package to me with a note attached explaining that they liked especially numbers 3 and 12. Need I say that what was enclosed in the package was a dozen photographs of Will Durant?

My respects and affection and all best wishes for a happy holiday season.
            Cordially yours,


## To Fred Sauers

*West Cornwall, Connecticut*
*December 7, 1953*

Dear Fred:

We have a lot in common above the ankles, I guess, but I never had a shoe problem as big as yours. None of my friends ever wore more than an 11, and one guy, Nathan Zatkin, wore a 5 and still does if he's alive. He toppled a little in a high wind and was no good in the backfield and, of course, he had to drink sitting down.

I was telling your beautiful wife, that utterly composed matron who has no anxieties, how I was once tipped fifty cents by a waiter when I was exactly your age. This was in Washington in 1918 when I was a code clerk Grade B (this referred to salary and not ability, I think, or like to think). A guy named George

P. Martin owned the famous Post Cafe in Washington then and when his waiters walked out on him suddenly he asked me if I would stand the midnight to eight watch, all alone, too. He had been kind to me and I actually had a cot in the corridor of his apartment for nothing, since there were no other rooms available—he wouldn't take money for meals either. He had seven straight razors, one marked for each day of the week, in a handsome leather case, and every morning while shaving he would say, "I'll be with you in a minute, Jimmy, and we'll walk down to that den of thieves." One October day as we were walking to the den of thieves—he was sure they were all tapping the till—he stopped, turned pale, and gripped my arm, and said, "Great God, Jimmy, this is my 59th birthday!" I looked at the man who had reached such an obscene age and trembled, but cheered myself up by the thought that I had thirty-five years to go before getting there myself. I will be 59 tomorrow. Well, anyway, I took over the Post Cafe, praying that nobody would show up. The only help I had was a great big wonderful colored male cook, but he was noncommittal. At 1:30 in the morning in came two couples and it turned out that the men were waiters in another restaurant. They kept telling me how to serve and I managed it somehow after explaining that I was actually "an attaché of the State Department." In that innocent day neither the two waiters nor myself realized we were in effect strike breakers. They gave me a fifty cent tip and I proudly rang it up in the cash register. I should have kept it for a pocket piece and passed it on in this letter to my pin boy son-in-law. I used to set up pins myself with my brothers when we were kids in Columbus. I'm quite a bowler, but my father, with a top score of 269, and my brother Bob, who once averaged 200 at duckpins, were better. My best score was 188 with the big pins and 160 with the ducks. I was never beaten by a woman, however, and could spot any colonel's wife forty points, even now. Judy O'Grady might get me though.

We got back from our New York trip Saturday and have to go back tomorrow because I have an ulcerated tooth and a right jaw that was as big as half a football, but 600,000 units of penicillin have got it down together with the pain. I've only got twelve teeth left. George P. Martin lived to be 79. . . .

Just after my jaw swelled up Saturday at 7 p.m. the poodle fell on the linoleum and strained her shoulder, but she will be all right in a few days, the vet says. Mr. Swain carried her to the car and she was indignant. Females do not like to have men carry them around unless they ask for it. Rose [Algrant] was giving me a party tomorrow night, but it will have to be postponed. She was having the Van Dorens, the innocent bystanders who were treated to a stream of my unconscious one Tuesday night, as you will recall. . . .

Helen and the Swains join me in love and every best wish during the holiday season and your whole term of service. President Jackson once asked a British colonel, retired, "What was your period of servitude in the British army?" I guess he got the right word. Keep pitching and try for the corners of the plate. I find that a slow ball with a curve on it is the best. Don't get sore and give them your fast one at the belt.

As always,

   *&* *&* *&*

*West Cornwall, Connecticut*
*December 10, 1953*

Dear Fred:

The late George P. Martin, the man who reached that ghastly age of 59 in 1918, smoked Murads and held them between his middle finger and his next to little finger. Only guy I ever knew who did that. He loved Atlantic City the way most men love Paris and when he was dying he actually thought a trip to Atlantic City would cure him. He took an old familiar room in his favorite hotel but never unpacked. After a look around he said sadly, "It's not the same" and went back to Detroit and died. It was in his Post Cafe that I recognized a guy named Frank Farrington who had played the villain, a villain named Braine, in an ancient movie serial called "The Million Dollar Mystery," full of corn and quandary and Mignon Anderson—or was it Marguerite Snow. Farrington let me take a snapshot of him choking a guy on a park bench. I don't know what my literary executor will make of this one. My brother Robert saved the negative—he saves everything.

My dentist couldn't find any ulceration or cavity, but he found some silver patches on my gums and concluded I had a thing called leucceoplakia, which he rubbed with sulfanilamide paste. . . . There must be a hundred ailments beginning with leucco, which means white. The only one you and I don't need to bother about is Leucceorhea, but the one that interests me is leuccophobia, a pathological fear of anything white. I can understand such a fear of red, or black, or blue, or most of the other colors, all of which are associated with hell, or home, or depression, or politics, or assault and battery, or disease, but white is just the color of virtue and virginity. It is the color of the dresses of little girls singing "Jesus Wants Me for a Sunbeam." I'll look up this phobia and let you know what I find out. . . .

The poodle is all right, but her change of pace is gone for a while. She is in the kennel until Sunday resting her pitching wing. Since she often falls while running up and down the hall linoleum to show how glad she is we're home, we have decided to greet her in the same fashion. I will slide back and forth on the linoleum and Helen will run in and out of the dining room, squeaking. This will astonish the poodle so, she will take it easy. I don't suppose astonishment helps you that way. Don't hit 'em with your fast ball, just back 'em away from the plate, boy. . . .

In my next installment I'll tell you about Jack Bridges, another guy I met in Washington, who made his own tools and built an Hispano Suiza engine with them, whistling "Just a Baby's Prayer at Twilight" as he did so. . . .

As ever,

ða  ða  ða

*West Cornwall, Connecticut*
*January 5, 1954*

Dear old Fred:

. . . It was gloomy in Columbus because, of the two hundred lively people I used to know there, all but six have died or moved away or been put away. My mother's mens is still sano, but her corpus is frail. She sits up for a couple of hours each day but can't walk without help. My brother says that one of his lungs was patched up in 1919 with the thumb of a third baseman's glove. Our family has had all known ailments and all known dangerous remedies, but of twelve grandchildren whose average age is 56.5 only one of us is dead and he had to be shot twice. Reached for a handkerchief in a Columbus bar and grill ten years ago and was shot by the nervous proprietor. This cousin's name was Dale Fisher, who joined the Marines when he was 15, under the name of Robert Madd. I am going to join the Space Cadets under another name. Think of me after this as Roger Merck. . . .

Rosie's experience at the Edwin Long, the Ozark's finest, is typical of all westward journeys by Thurbers, who are no good when they get west of Fort Wayne. That was a goddam unlucky visit for you kids, but it might have been worse. Friend of mine spent the night in a hotel with a girl and she strangled him to death with a handkerchief. Later explained to the judge that she thought he was going to pull a gun on her. I was shot at only once myself, by fraternity brothers during my initiation. Their second shot got a blackbird in a cypress tree, which fell at my feet a fifth of a second before I fell at its. . . .

I've got to get back to work so will close with love from us all.

As ever,

## TO THE THURBERS

*West Cornwall, Connecticut*
*January 5, 1954*

Dear Mama and other Thurbers:

We got on the train all right in spite of the fact that no redcap showed up until after the train got in. Ted [Gardiner] loaded our seven bags on a truck and wheeled them to the gates himself. The station master, a friend of Ted's, kept saying everything would be fine, but he also kept calling me Mr. Gulick. We did get on the train only to find our space had been sold twice, the second time to a Mr. and Mrs. Gulick, who were put out of the compartment shouting and cursing. That's the way everything is run in the Middle West and in the East, too, as far as that goes. The times are falling apart like dunked toast.

We have to go to town Sunday to hear Elliott Nugent in a television version of "The Remarkable Case of Mr. Bruhl." His place has probably been taken by Gulick, but we have to see the dentist and our tax man. Helen will spend all of next Monday with the tax man.

I talked to Rosie on January 2 and Fred had been home for Christmas. She spent a weekend with him in a hotel in the Ozarks and came down with an Ozark virus, but a nice Ozark doctor gave her penicillin and she was all right finally, but it spoiled her visit. Fred will get weekend passes from now on and will probably be sent to a special school because of his intelligence and training.

I made a list of two hundred Columbus people I used to know out there and all but six are dead or moved away or sick abed or in the funny house. I suppose God intends these six to be used as pallbearers. Everything is for the best like I always say.

It was wonderful to see Mama so bright and smart and looking so well and handsome, and we were very much taken with Mrs. Strayer and are glad she is looking after Mama. Everybody joins in sending you love and kisses and all best wishes for a Happy New Year.

As always,

## To the Ronald Williamses

*West Cornwall, Connecticut*
*January 22, 1954*

Dear Ronnie and Janey:

I've been so busy finishing "The Sleeping Man" I haven't had time to write you wide-awake kids or anybody else. Also we keep going to eye men and teeth men and other area men, and to tax experts who have instituted a search for our money. We made the usual enormous amount last year but have nothing to show for it. While on the subject of money, my financial expert Helen is on the trail of "The Woman" which does not seem to have come across with that 50 bucks. . . . Many a woman has cost me $50, but I have usually got something out of it and I don't intend to let "The Woman" get something for nothing. Principle of the thing, you see.

This has been a jumpy winter, although I'm no longer as jumpy as I was. Now that I am almost 60 I feel fine for the first time since I was 25, all dressed up and nowhere to go. We jumped to the doctors, and we jumped out to Columbus for a kind of drab Christmas. My mother is in good spirits at 88, but as blind as I am and much frailer. I turned up with a thing called "plaques of white," a gum infection, and a doctor I met at a party said, "Oh, yes, sometimes leads to cancer." I told my dentist, who said, "What doesn't?" He got rid of the plaques with sulpha and what seemed to be Old Dutch Cleanser.

We jumped down to Princeton last week for a sad occasion, the funeral of Belle [Mrs. John] O'Hara, who died of a heart attack a month after her 41st birthday.

News almost as sad was that announcement that Tom Matthew is going to marry Martha Gellhorn. We met her once with Hemingway while they were married and Helen couldn't stand her guts. . . . I couldn't see her, and since she said nothing I had only an impression of invisible sulkiness. Helen says Tom has always been a little giggly, or boyish, with women in recent years, but had managed to stave them off, till he got thrown by an expert. He's too sweet a guy for this hard baby, and he gets her just as she's about to enter change of life. . . .

The new book runs to 20,000 words and has taken me since last March, except for the month Helen was in the hospital, when I couldn't do anything. She still has double vision—imagine seeing two of me all the time—but she's in fine shape and all the girls say she looks ten to twenty years younger. One of them, Julia Gardiner, our hostess one night in Columbus, told us to go home at 4:30 A.M. "If you want to go, you go," Helen told her, "nobody's holding you." Every night Ted drives her to the animal cemetery where his dog was buried two years ago. This is only five miles east of their home. On icy nights she wishes the son-of-a-bitch were buried nearer their house. . . .

Love and kisses from us all,

## To Louise Mally

*West Cornwall, Connecticut*
*January 7, 1954*

Dear Miss Mally:

Only one other person has written me about my putting Evelyn [Waugh] between the wrong covers. I don't know what possessed me, to use one of my mother's favorite idioms. This wouldn't have happened if the piece had appeared in the New Yorker, but it was one of the Bermudian pieces. The New Yorker has a demon checking department and wouldn't think of writing about the Empire State Building without phoning to see if it is still there. One checker spent a whole afternoon with postal guides and atlases trying to find Weir—Bob Coates, then our book critic, had said that Faulkner actually writes about Weir and not the American South.

I never read enough Joyce to be influenced by him, but I love some of his wonderful wordage and idiomagic; I think my favorite thing of his is "Alfred Lawn Tennison." I wasn't even influenced by Lear, since I was an illiterate when I began to draw and had never even seen Clarence Day's drawings, let alone Lear's. The influence I had to fight off in writing was that of Henry James, and the influence that helped me most was that of E. B. White.

Publishers never get anything completely right, although they have checkers and mysterious people they call "stylists." I don't know what the hell they do. They never helped me.

Thanks for your interesting letter which got the New Year off to a good start.

Cordially yours,
James Thurber

*Miss E. Louise Mally, 210 West 17th St.,*
*New York 11, N. Y.*

## TO LESTER GETZLOE

*West Cornwall, Connecticut*
*January 8, 1954*

Dear Getz:

I was going to say it was fine to see you that day, but I remember I couldn't see you at all, but your voice sounded better than those of most of my elderly friends, most of whom will be 60 this year, like you and me. One of 'em calls it an obscene age, but I remember that Mencken told me he got more done in his sixties than in any other decade. The poor old boy cracked in his seventies, like Emerson, and I was told that he goes to movies wearing a deer stalker's cap, but I hope this isn't true. He had never seen a movie in his life and couldn't be dragged to a play after he got into long pants, on the ground that the stage made everything twenty times as big and unreal as it actually is.

I hope old Russ [Russell Lord, perhaps] has been in to see you, but he probably forgot to tell you the story of his visit a few years ago to an old friend of his on whom he depended for advice and comfort in dark hours. Russ was having a dark hour. His Rock of Gibraltar friend seemed at first glance as familiar and reassuring as ever in a rather dim living room, then Russ realized that he was wearing two hats.

I haven't seen [Joel] Sayre since I got back, but I realize why he is so slow in writing. He has developed a phobia against hospitals since his dreadful experience during Gertrude's ordeal. He used to cook her bacon rolls and other goodies and take them fifty blocks to Bellevue, day after day for months. He and Belle O'Hara sat with me during Helen's first operation and he was in terrible shape, having sat up all night to fortify himself for the ordeal. O'Hara was in the next building at the time, with a possible stomach cancer, and Joe had to call on him, too. O'Hara drew a negative on the big deal and is now out and around and writing a bi-weekly piece for COLLIER'S beginning this month, on every subject from Titus Andronicus to How to Make Love and Money. Pretty soon the first meadow flowers will appear and you'll be able to pitch again. The fellas are counting on you to win the opener from Bexley High.

Love and Happy New Year to you and your wonderful wife from us both.

As ever,

## TO THE JOHN MILLERS

*West Cornwall, Connecticut*
*January 7, 1954*

Dear Millers:

It was lovely of you to send us "Murder in the Cathedral," the pleasant murder of the thousands now surrounding us all. They took the atom apart to make it kill us, now they are taking the cigaret apart to see if they can keep it from killing us. Last year 364 people, mainly guys, died of lung cancer in Connecticut, an increase of 250% over 1952. I keep thinking of a line from Molière's "Imaginary Invalid"—the doctor keeps saying, "It's the lungs." All I seem to get on the air is lethal statistics: last year 20,000 persons were killed in falls, most of them in their own houses. Buster leaves one skate on the next to the top step and it's curtains for Daddy. Baby throws the soap out of the tub and screams for Mummy, who comes running and steps on the soap, and it's lilies for Mummy. I think more mothers are shot by their children than fathers, since more guns are kept in the home than at the office. Three little darlings in Cornwall let Mummy have it, one of them a little girl of six who managed to blow Mummy to hell with a shotgun and, to quote a famous limerick, "They found her vagina in South Carolina, and bits of her anus in Dallas." People used to say, "She worked herself to death for that man and nobody knows what she saw in him." Now they say, "It's so nice her youngest daughter won't remember shooting her because she was only two at the time."

On the brighter side, which is no bigger than a man's hand, there are literally millions of people still alive, and while most of my friends in Columbus are in the funny house or the hospital, enough residents of the city are up and out to fill Ohio Stadium six times every autumn. I have smoked only two cigarets in the past seven days and the best system is to follow a jagged kind of on and off the wagon. This is most un-American, since we either smoke all day or not at all, just as we never take a drink or are always under the table. No wonder we laughed at the moderation and inner check of the neo-humanists. Our kids start in at an early age to go whole hog or nothing. If a girl won't go with you to the Senior High School dance, don't send her a nasty note or cut her dead, mow her down with a Remington rifle while she's having supper. More sweethearts were shot to death in this country last year than in all the other countries put together.

. . . Speaking of death and cathedrals, we were amazed that only one person has tried to kill himself in Notre Dame in eight hundred years. Let's all cheer up. There's so much to be cheerful about, including the fact that most of the people we love are busy preparing a mansion for us au-delà. Love and kisses from us all.

As ever,

Jim

           ℯ   ℯ   ℯ

*April 16, 1954*

Dear Johnnie & Madeline,

. . . Helen and I had a few drinks with Elmer Davis on our last flying visit and we spoke fondly of you. We suffered with him through his TV ordeal on "The Author Meets the Critic" and added this man Fertig to our list of guys not to listen to when you're trying to have a tranquil dinner. Fair play has certainly gone out of the practices of that side and you can scarcely get them to answer one simple question without evasion, half-truth, or deliberate distortion.

The William Buckley family has a big house in Sharon and we lived a hundred yards away from them during the summer of 1940. I was attacked by their four dogs but managed to escape unharmed since I know how to deal with dogs. I just stood still and whistled at them as they snarled around me, which astonished them so much they forgot to take me apart. Two of young Buckley's sisters were members of a little band of girls in their teens who decorated the Sharon Episcopal church that summer by smearing hymn books and other things with a mixture of honey and cornmeal. Quite a family.

I just found out that Bob Montgomery has been the subject of an F.B.I. field investigation and this seems to me the quintessence of super-security. Elliott told me that the agent who called on him asked questions that were very easy to answer. All Elliott had to do was get out a copy of *Who's Who* and there were all the answers. Elliott also told me he hired a secretary for a two weeks' job recently who said that she understood that I was a Red. Elliott tried to set her right about this, but you can't set people right any more. I'll probably see you at a meeting of some subcommittee.

Rosie is living in a trailer at the gates of Camp Leonard Wood and Fred is scheduled to be shipped somewhere just about the time we leave for Bermuda. He stands at the head of his class, having been assigned to the Clerk and Typist School a few weeks ago. Rosie's favorite character in the camp is a

Sergeant who got drunk the other day and tried to find out how to go about resigning from the Army.

Love and kisses to you both from Helen and me.

As ever,

## TO ROBERT BARKER

*March 17, 1954*

Dear Mr. Barker:

Your letter puzzles me, since *Thurber Country* is a collection of 35 pieces and not a novel. If it indicates any basic philosophy I don't know what it is. I wrote the pieces because I am a writer and make a living that way. I think what you want is to find a genuine novelist.

Best wishes.

Sincerely yours,

James Thurber

*Mr. Robert O. Barker, 236 W. Grand River,*
*Michigan State College, E. Lansing, Michigan*

## TO ROSEMARY THURBER

*January 14, 1954*

Dear Rosiekins,

Helen and I just left Leo's chair and he assures me that even if a dentist weren't told that you and I are daughter and father, he would figure it out in about 10 minutes. This goes for our pre-operative lectures, our unfounded and founded apprehensions, and our final show of courage, I am given to understand.

We are driving back at 2:30 this afternoon after a dreadful visit. We had to come down for the dentist and to see our tax man, and shortly after we arrived Mrs. Swain telephoned the following wire from John O'Hara: "Belle died peacefully last night after a heart attack." We went to Princeton for the funeral Tuesday, riding down on the train with Joe Sayre and getting there about noon. We had lunch with the Gibbses and then went to O'Hara's bright, sunny little house on West College Road. The place was full of people, mainly relatives, since he has five brothers and a sister and she has three sisters and two brothers, and their mothers are both alive. John talked to us for a long while in his study and threatened to break only when his eight-year-old daughter came in the room. She apparently looks like her mother and has an identical smile. John was magnificent through the whole ordeal and the services at 2 o'clock in the Episcopal Church were simple and not too agonizing.

Belle had a congenitally bad heart, so mixed up that the doctors at first wanted to keep her from having a child but she got through that alright with a Caesarean. The heart attack occurred a week before her death, last Saturday evening. She had been very cheerful, but when the nurse came back for her supper tray, Belle was dead. As simple and easy as that. She was 41 years old on the 9th of last month. On her 40th birthday she telephoned me and said she was 40 and I said "That's nothing, I was 58 yesterday," and she said "Oh, that's nothing, but 40 is a great milestone in a woman's life."

Happy days and love and kisses,

O.M.T.

᠁ ᠁ ᠁

April 16, 1954

Dear Rosie & Fred,

We were glad to learn that all those things arrived safely and I can tell from your mention of the meat substitute that you got my letter too, you little devils. I've just been telling Terry and the girls about the wonderful Sergeant who wants to exercise his American privilege of resigning, and I am planning to take up with my Congressman or Senator this unfair business of Privates' wives not being allowed PX privileges. After all, I used to play football with Senator Prescott Bush of Connecticut and I am a personal friend of Senator John Vorys, a member of the House Armed Services committee, no less. Senator Bricker and I call each other by our first names, but never ask each other for anything. This would not be interception on behalf of my son-in-law at all. I just want to find out why all the wives are being excluded from this privilege when they are the ones that need it. Senator Vorys, by the way, is the man who had the piece I wrote about my mother read into the Congressional Record.

We anxiously await news of where they are going to send Fred, so that you can quit having nightmares and moist palms. We are delighted but not surprised by the news of his being first in his class. Did I ever tell him about the time an uncle-in-law, Capt. John Amlin, told us Thurber boys that he was the third man up Missionary Ridge during that famous battle, and my brother Robert, then ten, said "Who beat you?"

We were out to dinner with the Nugents night before last, and are driving back to the country today in a fine cold drizzle that seems permanent. It isn't going to freeze under us, though, since the temperature is around 60. Helen read your letter to Leo yesterday. We both had a checkup and sat around with him and Lilly for an hour. He doesn't seem concerned about the bleeding, but pleased by the fact that the old teeth are still properly in place. Most dreams about teeth, as you damn well know, are supposed to have a sexual content and Dr. Thurber thinks that the one about your retainer disappearing illustrates a lack of confidence in contraceptives. You can't just go around talking about your dreams, you know. . . .

We are having lunch with Pete De Vries today. We went to the Van Dorens' for dinner a few nights ago with Rose [Algrant] and the Simonts and spent several hours playing a new word game while Rose slept, since she doesn't know English very well, just teaches it at a boy's school. Her latest wonderful remark is as follows: "Woman's are stronger in the bottom than men." There is no doubt about this, I guess.

I feel I haven't written you kids as often as I should have or have wanted to, but I will make up for that and send further meat substitutes from time to time. Your dog is as wonderful as ever, only hungrier.

Love from us all.

As ever,

## To Jap Gude

*Gude, Thurber's TV agent, had persuaded Thurber to try to adapt his Monroe stories to television.*

*"Waterville," Paget East, Bermuda*
*May 15, 1954*

*Mr. J. G. Gude, c/o Stix & Gude,*
*30 Rockefeller Plaza, New York, New York*

Dear Jap:

Thanks for your report on the general situations, which we read between sunbathing and rum drinking. We are having a good time and pretty good weather for the most part.

Harry Ommerle's criticisms of the scripts were to be expected from most people in the television field, in spite of the daring and the innovations some of them are willing to attempt. Reminds me of what Stanley Kramer said about movie producers: "They are afraid of anything new unless it is familiar." . . .

. . . See what Ommerle thinks of such fresh characters as these: the comic orchestra conductor who drinks too much, or the next-door neighbor who talks too much. If you could get a very short ventriloquist, the dummy could be the size of Edgar Bergen, so that the live character sits on the wooden character's knee. How about a man in a wheelchair who has amnesia and is wrongly accused of murder? Or maybe there could be a servant who keeps calling in the F.B.I. I can't give Mr. Ommerle the character of my brother, William, because I am saving him for something else. William, who has a unique ailment which he calls "being shelled" and who sets trick match boxes on mantels and then absently picks them up himself. Maybe the wife has a dependent great-grandfather who insists on wearing a Southern uniform and hanging out the Confederate flag on the 4th of July. There is always the mother with the weak heart who comes to live with the Monroes without knowing that they have been divorced, so they have to live together again in apparent amity. I got a million of 'em. We could have Ommerle, who keeps saying constantly, "This script is running too short," or "What we need is a permanent sister-in-law."

Love and kisses to you all from Helen and me.

As ever,
James Thurber

## To Gus Lobrano

*Waterville, Paget, East, Bermuda*
*May 15, 1954*

*Mr. Gus Lobrano, The New Yorker,*
*25 West 43rd Street, New York, New York*

Dear Gus:

I have a casual coming up that I'll need some checking for, so you can pass my queries on to the checking boys, if you will? I got the idea the other night when Helen mentioned "THE VOICE OF THE TURTLE" to another woman guest here, who said, "Yes, wasn't she wonderful?" When this same lady said that she had seen the original "MALE ANIMAL" with Gene Tierney, it seemed to me the womanization of the modern theater was complete. (Poor Nugent was sunk without a trace.) . . .

I will also put in a brief reference to the extension of this trend to other fields, a trend made notable by a line that once appeared in The New Yorker: "I'll meet you at the church across from The Tailored Woman." Here even a Saint, old Patrick himself, is shoved out of the way by the women. As old as I am I never heard the name O. H. P. Belmont used, unless it was preceded by Mrs. My over-all conclusion will be that all these items are simply part of a scheme of God and nature to emphasize the female at the expense of the male, so that she will become the dominant sex in everything. The only boys that seem to hold their own are men like Karl Marx, Einstein and Freud, whose wives I have never heard of. Well, I do know that the favorite flower of Mrs. Freud was the cyclamen.

We are having all kinds of weather and rum down here, most of it pretty good. We didn't get together with the New Yorker businessmen, but Helen talked to Russell on the phone a couple of times. His wife got two black eyes and other scars falling off a motorcycle.

I subscribe completely to the opinion expressed in a letter to me by McNulty, who complained about the use of the word "diasyllabically" in Talk. He and I believe that the sentence should have read, "I pronounce his name in two syllables." This return to the stiff collar and the stuffed shirt in my old department is alarming. Pretty soon we will have "umbrageiferous" instead of "shady."

Helen joins me in love and kisses. We are sailing back on June 10.

> As ever,
> James Thurber

## TO MALCOLM COWLEY

*"Waterville," Paget East, Bermuda*
*May 20, 1954*

Mr. Malcolm Cowley
Sherman, Connecticut

Dear Malcolm:

I have no objection to you using that quote. One sentence sounds as if I had argued with [Elliot] Paul recently, but all this was back in the middle Twenties when we both were working on the Chicago Tribune and in Paris with Eugene Jolas, Bill Shirer, and others. Paul had already written about three novels, each of them in three weeks.

Not long ago McNulty expressed surprise at having met a writer who had always wanted to be a writer, and I was surprised that he thought most men drifted into it. I know that Morris Markey was a salesman until he was at least twenty-one, and I see by the papers that William March started out very late.

Dawn Powell once said she lived so near the Lafayette that on a clear day she could see her cheques bounce. And once at Bob Benchley's, when a group of people suddenly fell silent, she broke the silence by saying, "Let's all black up for a minute."

Our best to you all.

As ever,

James Thurber

{🐝 {🐝 {🐝

*"Waterville," Paget East, Bermuda*

*May 21, 1954*

*Mr. Malcolm Cowley*

P. S. Since I dictated the foregoing I have been thinking about your book, which I eagerly await, and about writers, whom I came down here to get away from. Well, I came down to get away from Congress mainly. I got to wondering what writers you have been living with in the manner of Middletown and Margaret Mead. Have you spent any time with the boys who are going through change of life or of religion or of viewpoint? In our neurotic world this late middle age or sunset of the writer is becoming more tangled than the female climacteric. This may be because women give up something they no longer want, whereas men feel everything slipping away. There will be more and more books, I suppose, about once bold and eccentric fellows settling down.

I have always been fascinated by the Hervey Allen legend down here in Bermuda and by his rise and decline, and his present oblivion. Felicity Hall, where he spent at least five years writing "Anthony Adverse," was probably the most visited literary shrine in our hemisphere twenty years ago. Friends of mine lived in his house after he had moved away and for a year or two there was a constant stream of sightseers. They offered fabulous amounts for a harp gate he had built himself, and for a large sewing chair he had made for his wife. And they offered as much as a pound or five dollars for any pencil he had used. His later books didn't seem to do well—I think he had planned an American trilogy and finished at least two of the volumes. I understand that in his final years he claimed to be able to hear his ancestors talking among themselves, which must have made it all too easy for him, and there is something about his having detected a small glittering angel on the handle of his pen from time to time, a divine assistance that has been denied to you and me. I could use it now. As you probably know, he lived on advances during that five-year period and was always strapped, and once reminded a friend of his in a postscript that the man owed him sixty cents in stamps.

The writers most recently associated with Bermuda are Frederic Wakeman and James Ramsey Ullman. After three straight Book Club selections, Ullman is now in India climbing a mountain with one of the men who climbed Everest, for he definitely belongs to the Hemingway school of physical activity on a gigantic scale in between books. Is this rare in the European writer? Do you deal with the other type like D. H. Lawrence, forever looking for The Place? Most former newspapermen can write anywhere, since they learned to write in a crowded and noisy office, and I have never felt the difference between a villa in France and a hotel room in New York. I get as little done one place as another, or as much.

There are two kinds of slow writers, the ones that plod along paragraph by paragraph and the ones, like me, who like to write it all down, or almost all of it, and then go back over it. I always preserve the stuff that should be written fast, but there isn't very much of that as a rule.

Cyril Connolly is always spurring other writers on and then giving reasons why he can't write himself. This led Edmund Wilson to write, "Both peace and fighting keep Cyril from writing."

Somebody told me that Thomas Mann said to a young writer who called on him during these gloomy times, "Are you a frustrated writer?" I gather that many of the writers who called on him couldn't write, and you have probably seen the book by that psychiatrist that deals with writers who have run dry. I heard about it, but didn't read it. I did read an interesting monograph by a psychiatrist named Alexander R. Martin, called "The Dynamics of Insight," tracing the mental process by which writers solve the problems of their second acts or their fifth chapters. I get a lot of help, when I am stuck, by dreams every now and then. In one recently I was in a coupé with an artist I know and two men I didn't know, and the artist said, "This car won't go unless we get rid of these characters." We stopped the car and put them out, and the next day I cut the characters they represented out of my book. According to Erich Fromm, we often get a truer version of certain persons in our dreams than we have of them in real life, and I have found this to be true. One recurring dream tries to help me, but I don't yet know what it's talking about, since it deals with either the chopping away or the falling off or the burning of the limb of a tree. The reason I think it is structural rather than sexual is because there are so many limbs of different kinds in what I'm working on: several women, a mysterious nylon stocking, and the figure of John Silver straight out of "Treasure Island." I also bring in the theme from time to time of Housman's Cherry Tree.

I think the Fromm book, "The Forgotten Language," a study of dreams, myths, and fairy tales, is the best development of dream analysis. He knows that they may rise out of any mental process and he takes apart a few of Freud's and Jung's analyses of their own dreams. I may have written you about this before, but I do so many hundreds of letters I can't always remember. I haven't read his last chapter yet, which is about "The Trial." I think there should be a lot of mystery left, however, since it is definitely a part of creative writing, and a writer could be stymied by too much comprehension of what he is doing.

I keep thinking of how basically inept American writers are in doing much with the political field, and how so many of the boys took a labored swing at it in the Thirties. You were right, of course, in seeing no trace of Marxist tendency in Fitzgerald and he damned near ruined "The Last Tycoon," by wedging that labor leader into it, I thought. Same thing happened to Hemingway toward the end of "To Have and Have Not," as I remember it. This was the same Hemingway who wrote at the end of "Death in the Afternoon" the paragraph that begins, "Let those who want to, save the world. . . ."

The reason I never put genius in quotations is because of Ross, I think. He wanted to surround himself with geniuses and never knew he was one himself. He liked to quote Herbert Spencer, "A genius can do easily what nobody else can do at all." Ross seemed to struggle as if the New Yorker were on the rocks, but the genius part of his mind handled it with ease, although he seemed less like the Editor of "The New Yorker" than anybody in the office when you first knew him. A year or so before he died, I spent the evening with him and [H. L.] Mencken and [George Jean] Nathan at Ross's apartment in

New York. Ross notoriously read nothing except what went into his magazine, unless you can count Spencer, a book on the migration of eels, Dr. Young's medical memoirs, "Life on the Mississippi," and the Britannica, which he took to the bathroom with him. As I told Mencken, Ross had not read a novel since "Black Beauty" and "Beautiful Joe." I said this after a little incident that puzzled Mencken. He and I were talking about Willa Cather and Ross broke in to say, "Willa Cather? Did he write 'The Private Life of Helen of Troy'?" Mencken's admiration for Ross as an Editor was unlimited and it was hard for him to realize that Ross was not a reader. I also remember something Mencken said about Will Durant: "How can an imbecile suddenly become a good writer?" Mencken has been steered to Durant's latest volumes by his old friend Hergesheimer, who did nothing in his last years but read Durant and Toynbee and other voluminous writers. I explained to Ross that it was Will Durant who wrote "The Private Life of Helen of Troy."

If I have written you most of this before, remember that I will be sixty in December. I keep thinking of your review of T. S. Eliot of several years ago in which you said, "He is a young man of sixty."

> Love and kisses, as ever
>
> Jim

## To the Fred Sauerses

*June 18, 1954*

Dear Children:

... I know your old argument that the longer you went without writing the harder it became but that is a lot of nonsense and you know it. All we know or have known since April, is that Mr. Sauers put you on the Burlington for Seattle after you had spent two weeks with them. We kind of wondered what we would have done if I had passed away quietly, or noisily, in Bermuda and we had wanted to get in touch with you for the sake of saying "please omit flowers" or something. Helen is now beginning to believe that your mother's mother had actually been dead three months before your mother found out about it. I don't expect anybody to cross the country or the ocean to attend my final rites and this includes you and Fred. Personally, I believe that each succeeding generation should be allowed to cut loose from the stuffy older one. Charles and Elizabeth Sauers belong to the same cocky generation I belong to and God knows we were the least thoughtful children of any in modern times and thus we raised more hell about our kids than anybody else. Well, that is the way everything turns out. I let my daughter smoke cigarettes when she was fourteen and drink when she was twelve and she turns out to be a non-smoking non-drinking lecturer on abstinence very severe on her husband and on her father, if he were around. Some husbands would rather stay in the army than go back to no cigarettes before breakfast, but I still think you are right about that. After all this you have to be right about something. . . .

We got back from Bermuda on Saturday and are leaving for Cornwall this afternoon. We're having lunch with Joe Sayre and Nora today. She was graduated from Radcliffe yesterday and Andy White got a degree from Harvard. The great sadness around here now is the accidental death of St. Clair McKelway, Jr. while piloting a helicopter near Bordeaux, France. He was 22. You and he sat around stiffly for an hour one afternoon on East 57th Street when you were both 14 or 15. He was a quiet reserved boy with no feeling for fraternities or other junk like that but he had been editor of the Cornell Widow, because he was not only intelligent but he had a quiet sense of humor that came out mainly in writing rather than talking. No one thinks of a helicopter cracking up, but his did, instantly killing him and four other members of the crew.

Helen and I just came back from the dock where we picked up her mink jacket and her pink coat. We had had several drinks at a restaurant in Hamilton before sailing and we got on the ship leaving the coats in the restaurant. Helen has lived in anxiety ever since then but everything is safe now.

This is the last you will hear from me until I hear from you.

Love from us both as always,
Thrasbie

## TO CHARLES SAUERS

*West Cornwall, Connecticut*
*June 21, 1954*

Dear Charles:

. . . Helen and I came back from Bermuda feeling fine, although I developed a gum infection down there which has now been cured by my dentist. We will be here until August when we go to the Vineyard for that month. We enjoyed the clippings, and the one about Columbus is typical. A few years ago a woman out there my age shot a truant officer and calmly said to the cops, "I just pulled the trigger and let 'er go." Then there was a seventy-year-old person who killed his wife with a skillet and explained to the cops, "I had to. Her number came up." He then led them to the kitchen and showed them his wife's number, which turned out to be the serial number on the kitchen range, something like 1683549. The chances of her number coming up were both infinitesimal and inevitable, a condition of life and death common in Columbus. Not long before he died my great friend Herman Miller sent me the clippings about the person and the shooting lady with a single sentence: "Why don't you come back to Ohio, where no news is practically the only good news." At least we get a kind of good news from our children. It isn't much, but I suppose it is something. I told Rosie that I wanted to know where she was so that Helen could let her know when I pass away. I said she might run into somebody some night who would say, "Your father was a good friend of mine" and she would say, "Isn't he still?" and the man would say, "Your father passed away last April."

Love and commiserations to you and Elizabeth from Helen and me

As always

## To the Ronald Williamses

*West Cornwall, Connecticut*
*June 22, 1954*

Dear Children:

Helen made a dozen imaginary trips to Pier 95 for her coats, while lying awake in bed, and each time something awful happened: The coats were lost, or she was arrested for theft, or the coats were loaded with heroin or something, but the day the Queen came in was a lovely June day in New York and we walked onto the pier and she went up the gangplank and got the coats and nobody would have stopped us either way, but she showed her papers on the way out to a Furness official who simply said, "Just take them home," and we took them home. It was dear Vicky Wood who had made Helen park the coats in Pedrolini's anyway, or she wouldn't have forgotten them. It was quite a luncheon and we both got buzzed higher than a kite and quicker. It is always nice to be anaesthetized when we leave you two, anyway. . . .

I still haven't heard from Rosie, but we got a wonderful letter from her father-in-law in reply to Helen's letter to him from Bermuda asking for my daughter's address. I will quote the body of the letter, which goes as follows:

". . . Fritz and Rosie are the most procrastinating pups I ever knew. Moreover Fritz has always treated his parents with the condescension commonly accorded a pair of faithful old family retainers.

"We drove to Leonard Wood and picked up Rosie and the Ford. Rosie was here two weeks and then we put her on the Burlington to Seattle where she has been about a month. Two weeks after she left we finally got a letter which Fred wrote and neglected to post for two weeks. It took them three weeks to return a signed certificate of title on the Ford and which I am trying to sell for them. . . . All of which makes my ass tired in both cheeks and down to my heels." . . .

I wrote Mr. Sauers that his generation and mine hadn't been too wonderful about their own parents and that I don't get as mad as he does. I said I just want to know where Rosie is so that Helen can let her know when I pass on. All this will give you kids some notion of what you still have to go through. . . .

We had only two drinks on the ship, one night with Elaine and young Stewart Outerbridge who was positive that a friend of his in Bermuda had chummed around with Mark Twain in the 1930's. Twain died in 1910, of course, and Outerbridge's friend was probably thinking of Thackeray or Edgar Allan Poe. . . .

As ever,

## To E. B. White

*West Cornwall, Connecticut*
*March 1, 1954*

Dear Andy:

I remember the time Ross found a rough copy of the magazine in a taxi. It was Tuesday, two days ahead of publication, which is two days ahead of actual date. The incident took six years off poor Ross's life. Carbons, of course, are usually all over hell. I have three made now, since I am one of the few living writers who seeks the opinion of various kinds of guys and gals ahead of the proof state. The carbons are mine, of course, and not the magazine's, but this is a technical point. I never used to make carbons and the libretto of a musical comedy I wrote in 1923 was left on a subway train by a young musicker named Haid, one of fifty guys who wrote nice music for Scarlet Mask and who knew absolutely nothing else at all, including his ass from a hole in the ground, or how to button his own pants. That libretto was last heard of between Chambers Street and the Brooklyn Museum stop. It has been read by thousands of subway riders. Guy named George Choos had some idea of producing it and a guy named Bannister was going to supervise the music. He telephoned WJZ while I was in his office and asked if he could come over at three and he took his tie off and they gave him a mike and a piano player and he sang two, three songs. That was radio! One of the songs had been written by Haid and was called "Pretty Mary Ann." Bannister was New York and sophisticated and he knew that wouldn't do. He changed it to "Better Stay Away."

Speaking of publishing, I got a contract now by means of which I don't have to take all the money I make in a year's period. This was arranged by the quiet Lindey, and old Magna Vox [Morris] Ernst. This saves you from giving the government all your money. I once got a check for $40,000 from the Book-of-the-Month and practically made it payable to Uncle Sam and sent it away. Had to give the government $24,000 more that year, too, and Helen spent two years more later on, secretly and ably defending her determination not to give the government another $17,000 for that year. I just got an advance, after a lot of advances, and I got to raise 4,000 bucks by the 15th. Each month starts off with a $1200 outgo, as certain as sunrise, and all of this to stay alive in such a world with such a species! Its greatest talent is destruction and its greatest virtue indestructibility. Keep fit, keep pitching, and love to you both from both of us.

As ever,


## To William Shawn

*West Cornwall, Connecticut*

*July 6, 1954*

Dear Bill:

I gathered from Maxwell that my theatre casual is worrying you people and I can only figure it's because of all the allusions of old-timers to old plays and players. I could cut out one or two small sections if necessary, but I think a better answer would be to use the ingenuity Ross used to talk about and maybe run it under the regular Stage head on some blank week this summer. If necessary, with a sub-head. I realize as well as anyone our consternation at anything not monstrously clear to the fourteen-year-old girl for whom some dog said the magazine is written, and I realize too that even the ancient Ross would have put in a hundred marginal "Who he's." Everything I mentioned was famous in its day, however. I didn't want to spoil the naturalness of dialogue by dull and tedious phrases of identification. If you people don't think the piece is funny, then either Helen or I or you people are slipping. I don't think any of us is. The reference to "The Male Animal" should not bring up the ghost of self-consciousness, since it did not appear in the New Yorker, but I will gladly take out the line about "The Poor Nut." After all, however, New York is the world headquarters of theatre, and the New Yorker is a celebrated magazine of the theatre.

I always have the feeling that half a dozen editors reading one of my pieces is not too good a thing, since when it is sent on from Maxwell to Mrs. Wood to Henderson to Shawn to Mrs. White, each person gets the idea that an unfavorable opinion is somehow expected. I realize you are disabled by the temporary loss of Gus [Lobrano] and I hope he will soon be back. I am in no need of money right now, so that's not a factor. I think HOLIDAY would take this piece because of its Bermuda setting, and there are other places, so I don't worry. I could substitute a name for W. H. Crane, whose "Father and the Boys" was a masculine hit about the year you were born. It doesn't hurt readers to puzzle a little, however, and while the piece may be sophisticated, God save the mark, Jesus knows it isn't recondite.

I've started a series of pieces about Ross, not for the New Yorker, of course, but I would like your opinion on them when they are done and I'll need a lot of checking help. In the first piece I say that you fit Ross's extravagant requirements for his god of the Central Desk better than anyone else ever did, although I give favorable mention also to Ingersoll, Bergman, and Shuman, while showing up Ross's incredible blind spot about Jim Cain and me and some others. The pieces are mainly concerned with Ross and Me, and are not basically a history of the magazine and only in part an attempt at critical appraisal. Best wishes as always, Bill

      Cordially yours,
      James Thurber

*Mr. William Shawn, The New Yorker,*
*25 West 43rd St., New York, N. Y.*

## TO ESTELLE MCKELWAY

*St. Clair McKelway, Jr., died at age twenty-two in a helicopter crash in 1954.*

*West Cornwall, Connecticut*
*July 9, 1954*

Dear Estelle:

There aren't any words I can say to you that would be of great comfort, but I want you to know that I keep thinking about you, as all your friends do, and that we all have the deepest sympathy. How to find consolation is a thing that few of us know anything about. So many of us have only one child, the Sayres, Andy White, John O'Hara, Helen Markey, myself, and many others, and we live in apprehension in a world full of constant dangers. Last winter I wrote a Columbus woman who had lost her son, and all I could think to tell her was a line from a picture called "The Red Danube," based on a novel by an Englishman about my age—60 this December. The line went: "You learn to live with a loss. You may even learn to be proud." I don't know precisely what it means, but I can't escape the feeling that the writer spoke out of a deep sorrow of his own and knew what he was talking about. I think he means partly that you finally manage a strange kind of solace and that you are proud that your grief hasn't overwhelmed you. I heard another line on the radio recently that impressed me: "Grief should not be the final experience." All these things sound easy enough to say, but nobody can teach you how to accept and apply them. I feel that you have the inner strength to know how to do it yourself. I wrote a rather sharp letter recently to an old friend of mine who lost his wife and who had written me that he was "on a heavy bottle routine," kept getting into fights with his employers, and losing one job after another. He felt, he had written me, that he should be dead himself. I told him, among other things, about how courageously John O'Hara had taken the death of Belle, who was only 41. He is left with an eight-year-old daughter, named Wylie. He realized that he would have to keep on writing, going places and doing things, because of the danger, I suppose, of falling into a habit of brooding. It is not easier for a man, because I think women are able to find resources better than men are. "Life must go on, I forget just why," Edna St. Vincent Millay wrote, but she didn't really mean that. After she was left alone she kept on working and was in the midst of a new poem when she died. I remember William Allen White's lovely tribute to his daughter who was killed in a fall from a horse when she was about twenty, I think. His piece showed how courage can come out of imagination and humor. They are hard to employ, but they are the basis of strength and balance. What people can get out of them, or out of religion or work, depends on the individual, but I am convinced that you will find your own way to some sort of serenity, as hard or impossible as it may seem now. I think the pride the Englishman spoke of grows out of the final realization that the good mind stands up under anything and keeps on going. Helen Hayes and Charles MacArthur had to go through this grief, and so many other people I know. Everybody loves a brave person, who takes things with grace and courage, and some kind of philosophy invariably comes to your aid if you face it that way. I was talking to a brain surgeon a few years ago about a woman friend of ours up here who had been terribly beaten when she was only thirty-two, but who has never given up in spite of all the things she has lost, including the hope of marriage because she is no longer able to manage a household. The doctor told me that many brain cases simply give up, but that those that don't invariably show improvement as time goes on. This is a truth I have found out about my increasing blindness, which will finally become total. But my friends worry more about this than I do myself, since the philosophical attitude began to develop quite a few years ago, almost without conscious effort. If you give your spirit and courage a little push, something inside you, something like white corpuscles of the spirit, begins to clear things up, I don't know how. . . .

. . . All we can do is hope for the best and not let the worst destroy us. I remember a proud line from one of George Meredith's novels, which I often quote: "Her heart is not made of the stuff that breaks." I think every heart is made of the stuff that breaks, but the good ones somehow repair themselves, and I know yours will. . . . I tried to see Mac and did manage to talk to him on the phone. I was proud of the way he was holding up and this was also mentioned to me by John O'Hara, whose daughter I called up in Princeton on her eighth birthday, which was June 14. . . .

    With love and best wishes,

P.S. Edna Millay, who had no children, lived all alone in a big house in the country after her husband died. On the day of her own death she had been working on a poem that contained this line: "It has been a lovely day no matter who has died." It stands a little starkly, out of context, but I think it means what I have been trying to say, that there is a lot left in life no matter what sorrow overtakes you, no matter how final it seems.

## To Hudson Hawley

*West Cornwall, Connecticut*
*July 27, 1954*

Dear Hudson Hawley:

. . . I'm afraid Don Skene's old Yale associations are as buried as he is. When I met him on the Paris edition he was covering the Chamber of Deputies and one of my tasks was handling the international financial situation. "What casting!" as Joe Sayre said the other day about this. I had to have Bill Shirer look up the word "moratorium" in his small French-English dictionary. We had thought it had something to do with death or memorials or both. Skene had gone to Europe for the Chicago Tribune to cover the Walker Cup play. He was a sports writer and not a legislative man. I knew less about finance than anybody in the world. I was also assigned to do a series of articles on Poland, including the condition and history of the zloty, this series being mandatory because Poland took advertising in the Tribune. I got my international finance stories by rewriting Le Figaro and one other so-called semi-official newspaper.

I had had three years as City Hall reporter on the Columbus Dispatch and was one of the few trained newspaper men on the Paris desk at the time. I knew how to write headlines, too, and almost always handled the two-column 14-point Cheltenham feature story headlines. Eugene Jolas pounded a typewriter so hard he usually used one up every three weeks—we all had French keyboards, and if you wrote fast enough and fell into the American keyboard style, everything turned out in commas and parentheses and other punctuation marks.

I used to write parody news features mainly for the enjoyment of the other slaves, and one of these accidentally got sent down the chute and was set up, two-column headline and all, by a linotyper who didn't understand English. Dave Darrah found it on the stone and darn near dropped dead, since it involved fifteen or twenty famous international figures in an involved mythical story of robbery, rape, extra-marital relations, Monte Carlo gambling, and running gun fights. Ragner later figured that the Tribune would have had to pay about eight billion dollars worth of libel if the story had appeared. Darrah threw it away, of course, but lectured me only mildly. Some of us still dream about that libel suit that was never filed.

Darrah was always hollering up the tube for short filler items of a sentence or two, and I got away with a dozen or more phonies which were printed. The only one I remember went like this, with a Washington date line: " 'A man who does not pray is not a praying man,' President Coolidge today told the annual convention of the Protestant Churches of America."

Skene got back into sports when he covered the Wills-Lenglen match for the Paris and Chicago editions. The match was held up nearly two weeks by rains, and somebody wrote for the Riviera edition a gossip note saying that the sports writers spent the two weeks staying in bars out of the rain. Skene, who had been on the wagon but fell off, threatened to sue the Riviera edition. . . .

I could tell you a lot more about the old days, including how my first wife acted as society editor of the Riviera paper, and how I made up dozens of items for her, when she ran short, about mythical lords and ladies, commodores, and generals, and villas and yachts. . . .

As always,

## To Peter De Vries

*West Cornwall, Connecticut*
*August 2, 1954*

Dear old Pete:

I don't know how you got to the Cantharides, but the Spanish fly.

As a fellow traveler—I, too have knocked the globe about a bit—I wonder if you have ever visited the Hormones, the Eumenides, and the Valkyries. I may write about my own voyages for HOLIDAY, especially my trip to the West Undies, whose dreadful caste system produced the Unmentionables. It was settled by men of Middlesex, and I believe DiMaggio, the great center feeler, colonized the place in spite of the Monroe Doctrine of hands off.

The Canaries are also known as the Singers. They contain Isle Get By, Isle Be Seeing You, Isle Be Down To Get You. They're not to be confused with the Rollers, also known as the Bull Durham Isles, near Guernsey and Jersey, where hand-made cigarets first appeared. The natives still roll them in the isles. Funny country.

Elia never visited the Sandwich Isles because of all the cannibals and bread-fruit. He once told Mary: "No matter how thin they sliced me, I'd still be lonely."

Were you ever caught in the Inside Straits?

I have thought of a title for Katinka's memoirs: "For the Love of Pete."

What have you thought of? Helen and I will be in the Vineyard all of August. Address: Harborside Inn, Edgartown, Mass. Love to you both from both of us,

As always,

*Mr. Peter De Vries, The New Yorker,*
*25 West 43rd St., New York, N. Y.*


## To Fred Allen

*West Cornwall, Connecticut*
*September 3, 1954*

Dear Fred:

I got a letter from [Edward] Weeks in the same mail with yours in which he threatened to change "The Bee" to "The Flight of the Bumblebee" but I have wired him to lay off. What we don't want is a book by you with additional musical titles by me. At my age I can really screw up a galley proof. At least I didn't change "Love in Bloom" to "Love in Bloomsbury." I am musically illiterate anyway, but I do know that Joe Venuti is the greatest violinist and that Walter Huston was the best vocalist, not counting Bert Williams, or Fred Allen in his rendition of the Titwillow parody.

It's easy enough to say you're only going to write one book, but I hope you'll find yourself doing another one before long. Don Stewart used to say unhappily, "I think I'm going to have another book." He went through change of life, however, in the early thirties, but he had had about eight. You haven't told the whole truth about yourself and there must be something you're holding back, such as a chapter on how to survive Libby Holman. Which reminds me of Howard Dietz's "A day away from Tallulah is like a month in the country."

I've been writing some stuff about Ross, a great character who, as Gibbs says, is hard to make believable. He once said, during a discussion of Willa Cather, "Did he write 'The Private Life of Helen of Troy'?" He shared Sam Goldwyn's belief that Wuthering Heights was something that wuthers. After his daughter was born he said to me, irritably, "I think of a woman as having daughters and a man as having sons." He was scared to death of having too many female hormones. He was pleased when Jack Dempsey turned up with two daughters. . . .

Well, I've just survived another vacation there on the Vineyard, with boats and willow trees flying through the air. During the height of the blow a middle-aged woman said to me, "This is not good for my high blood pleasure." Her husband then complimented me on having written "Showboat" and asked me where I got my ideas. I told him I stole them.

Did I ever tell you how Max Eastman garbled some stuff I told him about you for his book "The Enjoyment of Laughter"? My favorite creatures are still those crows of yours that brought back corn they had stolen two years before. Me, I haven't enough strength left to give back ideas I stole two months ago. Right now I'm doing a piece involving the mythical political courage of the late Will Rogers, based on the prevalent statement "If Rogers were alive today he'd be put in jail." Actually, this bosom friend of senators and congressmen was about as daring as an early Shirley Temple movie. I am, too. Hoping you're the same,

> Affectionately yours,

## To Rosemary Thurber Sauers

> *West Cornwall, Connecticut*
> *October 4, 1954*

Dearest Rosie:

When I was 23 I got mixed up with the Kappas for the first time, and that's something you never get over completely. Eva [Prout] will be 60 on Saturday, or just 37 years older than you lacking two days. Helen and I have sent along a few gifties to mark your anniversary. McNulty keeps track of such things through horse races. "They built the new Neil House the year Black Gold won the Derby" or "My son was born the year Twilight Tear won the Hialeah Handicap."

The poodle talks all the time now just like an old lady and takes my napkin off my lap to hunt for crumbs. She not only sees things that aren't there but has a ringing in her ears, which would have to sound like a doorbell instead of the telephone. She doesn't hear real bells or cars, but is always challenging imaginary ones.

We are all back in the house together for the first time since [Hurricane] Carol and went to Lewis Gannett's 63rd birthday party last night. We had been in New York for two weeks or more and had a quiet night with Armin [Landeck], just back from France, and a noisy night with a lot of disreputable writers, and a fearful night with their wives. Tony Gibbs, aged 19, sophomore at Princeton, asked his mother why his father was so nasty to Tony's friends. "Because your father is a monster," she told him. "You might as well face that."

Rose [Algrant] is finally going to have the doctor look at her infected fingers. She has been dabbing them with toothpaste, and I suppose she brushes her teeth with iodine. Helen says if one of her dogs scratches its paw, Rose has it in Epsom Salts in a minute. Imagine Pepsodent for an open sore. Tobacco Road certainly comes out in her, Turkish tobacco.

Nora Sayre's trip to Europe has been held up a month so that doctors can examine her for cramps next time. What's to examine? All girls at that age seem to be crampy—she was 22 the day Elliott was 58.

Charles Addams is now mixed up with a woman lawyer who bites him and is said to be handy with a knife when she's mad. All I need is a woman with a hot temper and a dagger. We're all scared of the teenagers now and will have to bar our doors and windows now that they have taken to breaking and entering, in Boston and San Francisco, anyway. If it gets worse, we may have to shoot children on sight. What a world! What a species!

We all send you our love and best wishes for a happy birthday, without cramps, and the same to Fred. God knows how often you would write if people still used quill pens, sand and sealing wax. If you didn't get your typewriter, why don't you get some ten-year-old to steal one for you? Boy of eight in Delaware killed his sweetheart aged six. "She was a tramp," he told the police.

>Love and kisses,
>Thrasby

## To Janet Beesley

*West Cornwall, Connecticut*
*November 27, 1954*

Dear Janet:

All girls want to know why about everything. A writer writes what he can write best, so we have everything from authors of Christmas card verses to William Faulkner. I'm glad you think what I do is therapy, but to find out why a man does anything you'd have to interrogate his wife and daughter and doctor and cook and friends. My daughter asked me why I draw pictures when she was only three. She's going to have a baby next year. Do you think I should ask her why?

All best wishes for a Merry Christmas and a happy future.

> Sincerely yours,
> James Thurber

*Miss Janet Beesley, 17 Carden Road,*
*San Anselmo, California*

## To Jap Gude

*Thurber's final sentence in this letter is a play upon* Take Them Up Tenderly, *a popular book at the time.*

> **West Cornwall, Connecticut**
> *December 6, 1954*

*Mr. J. G. Gude, Stix & Gude,*
*30 Rockefeller Plaza, New York, N. Y.*

Dear Jap:

Last week took a lot out of me and although I am rested up now, I realize I will have to take the final years in easier stride. I should really go in for renunciation rather than reconciliation at my age, since endings are easier for oldsters than beginning over. I also find myself worrying and even dreaming about things I may have said in the [Dave] Garroway interview that may have been indiscreet or sounded boastful or took names in vain. When you can't see and are talking to somebody like Garroway you completely forget that you're talking to a million people. In this way radio has compounded anxiety by making the same thing of what you have said and what you are going to say, so that you can spend the interval, or present, worrying about the past and the future at the same time. I had a lovely time with G. and was inclined to babble even more than usual. I would appreciate it if you would check with Mike Zeamer, whom it was also nice to see again, and make a casual check of a couple of things I am going to say and did, to use the idiom of "The Thirteen Clocks." If I talked about Fitzgerald, and I can't remember, since I talked to so many people last week, there may be a reference on the tape to my having been "unhappily married" at the time I saw him and that would be cruel at this season, or any other. Unfortunately, I hadn't planned anything in advance and I suppose I'm foolish to worry about it in retrospect (same as "future") because Garroway always does sensitive and intelligent editing, he being a true artist in conversation and recording. There was so much that it will be cut way down anyway by at least three quarters, I suppose. Everything is improved by cutting, including my peace of mind. An old rewriter like myself invariably goes over and over what he said offhand, improving it in one way and probably spoiling it in another. I am pretty sure I didn't do any injury to good old Ross, but I hope I didn't drop too many names—I seem to remember wedging dogs and me in between a governor and a general, but that's where they were. I'm sure they will let me down tenderly. . . .

> As always,
> James Thurber

## TO THE RONALD WILLIAMSES

*Paris, May 27, 1955*

*Mr. and Mrs. R.J. Williams,*
*The Bermudian, Hamilton, Bermuda*

Dear Children:

We have been too busy since we got here to write any letters until today, but we are both delighted about the arrival of the new baby. I cannot be sorry that it is a girl, because of my well-known affection for girls. By this time you must have found out that people who have four daughters are almost certain to have five. I don't know how you happen to have a son, and it is possible that it does not belong to either one of you.

Please let us know how you all are and what name you will give the latest arrival. It is not easy for me to believe that you will have a daughter two weeks younger than my granddaughter. We have seen a picture of her at the age of one day, and she looks like a baby robin, which is known in French as a rouge-gorge. This baby's name is Sara and her mother says that she has beautiful fingers and shows them to everybody. She does not sleep very much but likes to stay awake all night and is interested in everything that happens after sunset. You can figure out how she inherited this.

Six children is enough for any young couple and I hope that this will be the last one, because my doctors tell me that children born after the mother is 43 years old are likely to cause trouble. I suggest that you learn to play chess or something else to take the place of children from now on.

We send our love and best wishes to all eight of you, if I have counted correctly. We had lunch today with the Millers, who believe that my main interest in a lady resides in her laughter and appreciation. A great deal of it does indeed. You can write us at the Stafford Hotel, St. James's Place, London S.W.1., until June 13.

Bless you all,

As ever,

James Thurber

🐎 🐎 🐎

*Hotel Continental,*
*Rue Castiglione, PARIS. I*
*August 29, 1955*

*Mr. & Mrs. R.J. Williams, Seaforth,*
*Ely's Harbour, Somerset, BERMUDA*

Dearest Ronnie and Janey,

We still don't know the baby's name and can only suppose it is Lavinia. Lavinia is a character in "The Cocktail Party" and also "Titus Andronicus." We keep getting letters from everybody except you, but we keep writing you anyway. I had even thought of writing a letter to us from you and enclosing it, so that you could make changes and return it, but it is still too warm here for that. We have run into a dozen people from Bermuda, all of whom have given us some little piece of news, such as that Janey is back at The Linen Shop, that the baby has no name and will be allowed to choose her own and that you had been drinking with some foxes, the day that Ronnie tried to drive home on the Bias. I used to drink with one or two of my dogs, and once got a flock of chickens drunk in Normandy, but I have only known one fox. He invaded the public library in Columbus, one day, forty years ago, with my grandfather's collie chasing him.

Although the portable tidal wave that engulfed Connecticut flattened shops and other buildings within a few miles of us, carrying away the butchershop as if it were made of cards, nothing happened to our house on its hill except a flooded cellar. The Fire Department came over and drained it and it has been completely cleared up. Our poodle, who wonders what has happened to us and to you, is safe in her kennel. Rose Algrant and Armin Landeck called on the poodle and report that she said: "Kennel ration is all right, but there's nothing like home cooking."

The Swains are coming back to us, at least for the winter and probably longer, even though Rosie and Fred and Sara will be there to look after and, as I said to Helen, it is not going to be easy to look after both Sara and her grandfather. . . .

I found the stuff about Macbeth and I hope Ronnie has looked up the Alsatian dogs. My dog book comes out in the fall and I will send you one of the first copies. A writer named Mark Schorer is writing a biography of Red [Sinclair] Lewis and I put him onto Ronnie. He had written me over here asking for anecdotes and I told him that Ronnie knew Lewis better even than I did, and could probably help him out with a lot of memories. . . .

As ever,

ɕ.   ɕ.   ɕ.

*October 31, 1955*

Dearest Children:

. . . We are delighted that you are moving into your dream house, in spite of its exasperating name, which sounds like an accident during an anagram game played by robots. How anybody could call his yacht the Enchantress and then call his house Socratean, or whatever it is, the good God only knows. I am so glad that you are getting out of Seaforth, where the smell of cat came up so strongly in the living room on damp days that even the Bermuda lilies didn't have a chance against it, where only a hurricane could have opened up that one room properly, and where, if you wanted to go to the bathroom from the dining room without waking the newest baby, you had to go out the front door and around to the side door. This house was designed with all the care of one of my drawings and must have been built on a cloudy day by guys that couldn't see very well under the direction of a cockeyed contractor. It always gave me the leaping willies and since I have suffered also from the heebie jeebies and the screaming meamies as well as the galloping jumps, I could never really lean back there. There may have been a touch of genius in the planning of that house if it was planned, because it had the look of a place that has been struck by a hurricane even in the good summer weather before the hurricane season. One room kind of sprawled into another and the chances of a blind man stepping on a baby became greater and greater as I became blinder and you had more babies.

We were delighted by Ronnie's letter. . . . That letter was obviously written by a man who had bathed comfortably, shaved without cutting himself, and had managed to get his collar on over both the back and front collar buttons. In short, a gentleman not floating in rum at all. The assumption that he was taken into custody because of an oral or vocal transgression is a little strained and it makes me wonder what the cop's version of the exchange was. Probably something like this: "I guess it's just me, a purely personal thing, but I don't like zigzagging cars. My father, who was attached to the homicide squad, had the same feeling about thrown knives. He just couldn't stand their glinting in the air. Maybe my mother was frightened by a snake, I don't know. All I know is I can't stand anything on wheels that has a serpentine motion to it."

What is left of us is returning to Cornwall this afternoon. The Swains have opened up the house for us, our poodle, almost sixteen now but still active and hungry, has been searching for us each day, and my daughter and son-in-law and granddaughter will arrive in about a month.

The first drink we have will be to your happiness in the Dream House and to the health of all of you. Being a constructive critic, I have a suggestion for a name to replace Socratean. How about the Villa Bgudaoglba?

Love and kisses from us both.

      As ever,

## To Duane De Paepe and Oscar Carlson, Jr.

*West Cornwall, Connecticut*
*March 15, 1955*

Dear boys:

I was interested in your daydream compositions, because this is a period of nightmare, and not daydream, to many people. I don't happen to be one of those writers who has a lot of glossy photographs around to send out. Photographs, except those of movie actors and wanted persons, should be sent only to friends and relatives, and lawyers who are trying to prove you are related to the old lady who died and left a million dollars. I get a hundred letters a year from boys and girls your age, and a thousand from older folks, so I am always three months behind in answering them. Some day I'm going to have all my writer friends write to your teacher and ask her for a photograph and a brief story of her life. Not your teacher, come to think of it, but the one who gives her pupils a hundred points if they can get five sentences from any writer in answer to a letter.

Best wishes to your teacher and to all of you.
  Sincerely yours,
  James Thurber

*Duane De Paepe, Oscar Carlson, Jr.,*
*119 North Main St., Cambridge, Illinois*

## To Wolcott Gibbs

*Gibbs, the* New Yorker *theater critic, had reviewed an off-Broadway production of Thurber's "Mr. and Mrs. Monroe" stories of the early Thirties.*

*West Cornwall, Connecticut*
*March 16, 1955*

Dear Wolcott:

We thought you surmounted the Christopher Street ordeal with great skill and humor, at the same time making the best and soundest appraisal of the goings on and off. I sat in at rehearsals a couple of times, nervously sticking a line or a piece of business in here and there, the window shade, the kerosene lamp, etc., in a mild effort to theatricalize the literary stuff. As I told Paula Trueman, who sat next to me, I didn't believe for a moment that the wife's mother had called up, or that she had a sister, or that she had really been in France. It had the effect, for me, of three first acts. I don't think there was much thought or hope of taking them uptown, and the boys had one eye on television, but we like them all immensely and they have a lot of sincerity and maybe a little too much integrity or respect for original writing. I think you were about 26 when I started the Monroe series and I never put any of the pieces in the "Carnival" or any other collections. I think I tried to bury them, but the goo men do lives after them.

I was considerably thrown off, when Jap Gude, who sat on my other side, said, "Morgan is exactly like Morris Markey," and my perspective never rallied after that. I expected him any minute to say to Mrs. Monroe, "If you ain't the dumbest white woman I ever knew, I don't know who is." I still can't believe Markey is dead. There are so many things to which he alone knew the answer. I remember meeting him in "21" after the opening night of "The Eve of St. Marks" and hearing him say to the table at large, "I'll tell you what he's got workin' in there." He told us, but I've forgotten what it was. . . .

I'm going to do you some kind of piece for that May 27 issue. I've just finished my fourth casual in two months for the magazine, with more to do before we sail for Europe on May 4, but I won't forget Fire Island. . . .

Thanks again for your review, which I have had read aloud three times to me, first over the phone by Terry, and love to you and Elinor,

As ever,

P.S. Miss Trueman also threw me a little by saying that a girl friend of hers in the Village, whose apartment was always being robbed, finally had the place burglarized, to keep out the thieves.

## TO MARK SCHORER

*Schorer was writing the biography of Sinclair Lewis.*

*At: The Stafford Hotel,*
*St. James's Place, London, S.W.1.*
*11th. August, 1955.*

Mr. Mark Schorer, 68 Tamalpais Road,
Berkeley 8, California, U.S.A.

Dear Mr. Schorer,

I only met [Sinclair] Lewis twice, but the first time was really a dandy, since he was in his cups most of the time down in Bermuda, and you couldn't always tell at seven in the morning whether he was having his first drink of the day or his last one of the night.

From over here, American writers certainly do loom up as incredible drinking men, and it is small wonder that the average one never reaches sixty-five—and few reach sixty even—while over here there are a hundred well-known writers from seventy to ninety-two years old, all of them still turning out books.

The best story about Lewis in his Bermuda phase deals with his wonderful generosity in paying the expenses for a month in Bermuda of two little old sisters from Vermont who had never before been out of their native state. A man who can tell you this story best, as well as other aspects of Lewis's Bermuda days, is a great friend of mine named Ronald J. Williams, who you can reach c/o The Bermudian, Hamilton, Bermuda. . . .

Lewis had told Williams that he wanted to meet two men, Bronson Cutting and me, one of the whims of his that grew out of Scotch. So, the old boy took the Williamses and us to dinner, and Ronnie can take it from there. Lewis had told his male secretary to bring down to the table a stack of Herald-Tribunes as high as my knee, because he intended to read aloud the Dorothy Thompson column in each one of them. The secretary winked at us and skillfully got Lewis's mind off the subject. He recited before we went downstairs, close enough to word for word, a story I had written for The New Yorker about 1928, called "Mr. Monroe Holds the Fort." It was about an American husband who is afraid to stay alone in his house in the country after dark. "All of us are afraid to be alone in a country house at night, but you are the first one brave enough to admit it in print," he said. He could tell a story, as you know, with fine effect up to his fifteenth or twentieth Scotch.

The only other time I met him was at the Algonquin several years later, when he was having lunch there with Kip [Clifton] Fadiman, who is one of the great sources, I should think, of Lewis anecdotes. The time we met him in Bermuda must have been in 1936. . . .

I think Lewis Gannett once wrote a fine estimate of Lewis's love for America, in refutation of the careless theory that he was a man with a scornful opinion of his native land.

It just occurs to me that Lewis once wrote for Williams' Bermudian, a letter of protest against the coming of motor cars to Bermuda, and he might be able to dig that up for you.

I wish you good luck and jolly times.

  Cordially yours,
  James Thurber


## To Kay Howie

*The New Yorker*
*No. 25 West 43rd Street*
*October 31, 1955*

Mrs. Kay Howie, Librarian,
Greenville Elementary School,
Alexis I. DuPont Special School District,
Kennett Pike, Wilmington, Delaware


Dear Mrs. Howie:

Children write better letters to authors than they get from them and I think the communication should always be in that direction. The younger the child, the shorter the letter, and usually the sharper. "I read 'Many Moons'. It's alright. You can't draw. I can draw. I like the Princess. I guess." I don't know quite what to say to the children, but I am reminded of the seasick man in the deckchair, whose wife, in the chair next to him, was being annoyed by the romping of several children. Finally she said to her husband, "Herbert speak to those children". "Hello children" said Herbert.

> Cordially yours,
> James Thurber

## To Vivien Bennett

> *West Cornwall, Connecticut*
> *November 4, 1955*

*Miss Vivien M. Bennett,*
*Thacker Junior High,*
*1557 Thacker St., Des Plaines, Illinois*

Dear Miss Bennett:

I don't know how in the name of heaven you could put on anything resembling "The White Deer" in a swimming pool full of young girls. I should think "Water Babies" or "Macbeth" would be easier. Right now, unfortunately, all rights to the book are tied up momentarily because of a pending movie production. Otherwise I would take a chance that my story would come out of it all unwaterlogged. There are available my other fairy tales "Many Moons," "The Great Quillow," and "The Thirteen Clocks." I wouldn't know what to charge you, if anything, unless I knew what your profits amount to. If they all go to worthy school projects, you could do any of these books with my compliments. This permission is understood to be confined to this one-time production.

> Sincerely yours,
> James Thurber

## To Gus Lobrano

*The casual under discussion is probably "The Tyranny of Trivia."*

*West Cornwall, Connecticut*
*Nov. 8, 1955*

*Mr. Gus Lobrano, The New Yorker,*
*25 West 43rd St., New York, N.Y.*

Dear Gus:

Here is that word casual, vastly improved, I think. Wallenger has been cut out of it and it has been tightened generally. Should run before Christmas some time, I should think. . . .

The New Yorker is terribly popular in both Paris and London, even though Paris subscribers get their copies from nine to eleven weeks late, since they come by way of the British Isles and are trans-shipped from an Irish port or something. In London they are from a month to six weeks late.

The chief criticism of the magazine, outside of the length of its stories, is its shocking overuse of commas. This surely stemmed from Ross, and I am putting it into my story of him, showing how that magazine would punctuate the title of a famous play: "Alias, Jimmy Valentine" and this familiar line from Wordsworth: "But, she is in her grave, and, oh, the difference, to me."

Would you like to read my copy of "Freedom from Fear," inscribed by the author?

Love and kisses as always,

P.S. A number of professors and writers, both here and abroad, have written me about our flux of commas. They mainly object to commas after moreover and furthermore and otherwise, and other words with the force of but. Also sentences like this: "After dinner, the ladies returned to the drawing room." I realize you've got to be careful about "He saw her but a moment" but here the danger is in a comma after but. I'm all for throwing out commas and even using red white and blue without commas. I simply cannot use quotation marks around every letter mentioned or every word, and maybe a sentence will have to be put in the piece explaining this. Conventional quotes, in the New Yorker fashion, would disfigure the piece, irritate the reader, and adulterate the meaningless.

## TO ROGERS WHITAKER

*February 3, 1956*

Dear Whitaker:

As Ross used to say, the magazine has no manpower or ingenuity, we are surrounded by women and children, and everybody is neurotic. . . . There are lots of other ideas such as "I thought you said peasants." Here we have dead peasants strewn over 20 pages and on page 21 we see this hunter with several brace of pheasants.

Since more than 100 people have asked me to explain The New Yorker's drawings about kings and medieval days, I thought I might give the magazine some ideas for this unbelievable type which would make explanations more fun. A king is eating a pie and we see 23 blackbirds flying about the room. "I ate the other one."

We keep repeating the picture of the king and the populace, with different captions. The most intelligent people in the country asked me to explain this one. Ross used to believe in the reader's being able to tell what character is speaking. In this series it won't make any difference. Here are a few captions.

"Mama don't want no rites no peace no protocol."
"I don't know what happened but Jack and Jill haven't come home."
"And that goes for Peter Townsend too."
"Well, everybody to his taste as the young lady said as she kissed the cowboy."
"Have you bred any good rooks lately?"

That ought to hold us for a while.

In recent years I have constantly heard people around the office saying profoundly, "Length is no object." This refers of course to the books we now publish in various issues, and the short stories running to 24,000 words, in spite of the fact that "We do not publish short stories." I should like to add this slogan to those now current: Length is no objective.

Respectfully yours,
James Thurber

## TO WILLIAM MAXWELL

*West Cornwall, Connecticut*
*February 13, 1956*

Dear old Bill:

The thing to do is just buy the ones you all guess are good, and send the others back to me, without fear or frenzy, and above all things without long delays so depressing to a writer and so characteristic of the now crippled magazine. I don't think you people really know enough about fables to be able to make brief offhand uses of such expressions as "sure of" and "not up to the first twelve." The fable of the frog is a variant of La Fontaine's "The Fox and the Crow." The Latin moral was not to spare the sensitivities of the New Yorker, but a kind of tribute to Phaedrus, one of the few good fable writers from Aesop to La Fontaine (my God, who has there been since! Ah, you're just saying that because it's true). Here and there in my fables there occur rhymes, intentional but unobtrusive, out of an homage to the rhymed fable of tradition. These occasionally start off one of my fables as a substitute for another tradition, the use of the moral as lead. Aristotle, that old conventionalist, believed that fables should concern only birds and beasts and not humans, but the fable should not have foolish restrictions. I don't happen to like the type that deals with speaking flowers or inanimate objects, except those in the shape of animals, like the piggy bank and the cast-iron lawn dog, and weather vanes. The sorriest and most elaborate mistake in the long and honorable history of fable writing was Marianne Moore's rhymed translations of La Fontaine. Don't buy the book, you can borrow my copy. It seems that W. H. Auden, who should have known better, urged Miss Moore to this task, which Ogden Nash could have done perfectly. (Listen to Noel Coward read Nash's rhymes for "The Carnival of Animals.") . . .

La Fontaine, in writing for a temperamental young Dauphin, got into a nursery mood which was part of his charm and also part of his restriction. I do not think that children's attention is better held by animal stories than by those of men, and I do know that they can stand all the human gore you can pour out. The simple truth about the appeal of fables is pointed out in the Preface to my new book which shows that our language is a bestiary, in simile and metaphor, and almost a dialectical natural history. Offhand: "If an old seadog goes home on an owl car in a one-horse town, snake-eyes and the kitty having done him wrong, he may find that his wife has spent the dogwatch pacing the catwalk, mad as a wet hen and fit to have kittens."

You guys quit worrying about what's good of mine and what isn't, and stick to your taste, the main and most troublesome component of editorial criticism. Ours is, of course, the most editor-conscious magazine in the world. You are right that the Duck fable needed one more rewrite—it had only had six. You had told me that they were going to turn down "The Tiger Who Would Be King" and this change of appreciation is mildly puzzling. The fable is bound to be, to a great extent, polemical, and Christ knows the New Yorker is as scared of polemics as it is of physical violence, raised voices, and the fool and her legs who are soon parted. *That* fable, my boy, is up to my best. You gentlemen are just not up to it. The best are still to come, I say, and you will no doubt take most of them. Just send the others without comment. They will not be sold anywhere else, of course, but will appear in my book.

. . . Many of my old fables have been read over the air by Ed Murrow and some time ago a group of English actors read them aloud in London, including M. Redgrave and Sir L. Olivier. I've been asked to recite them for an l.p. record for Caedmon.

I think you should send this to Shawn and to Lobrano, with my love and kisses, and keep plenty for yourself.

As ever,
James Thurber

P.S. The first eighteen fables submitted to the New Yorker had no order of any kind except that of a blind man's pulling numbers out of a hat. It is thus impossible to compare any six against any other six, the chances of this making any sense being infinity to one.

## To John McNulty

*West Cornwall, Connecticut*
*February 16, 1956*

Dear Johnny:

We just heard from Ann Honeycutt, the Louisiana Lily, about your operation, and I have already mailed off to you a copy of "Thurber's Dogs", which belongs in hospital rooms and on trains, and also a little book of old drawings brought out in England a few months ago. Ted Cook's daughter had the same operation as yours twelve years ago and is doing fine. Every time we go to

Tim's [Costello], which was three out of seven one week, we ask and talk about you, and it has been years since we saw you there. Some nights the place is infested by what Tim calls the riff-raff, but many nights bring what he calls the New Yorker crowd, Elinor Gibbs, Dinah Sheean, Johnny Martin, George Oppenheimer, and other assorted characters. I haven't seen Honey there since October 1952, when she told me I had no religion or philosophy. I understand she has white hair and looks like Martha Washington. They come in fascinating packages from Louisiana, and if they get close enough to kiss they may bite your ear off. She used to be a woman of sparkling personality only, for she had put her character in storage somewhere in Oklahoma with the Love brothers, and then she developed this new character, complete with 1952 religion and philosophy. So many interesting things happened when I was riding shotgun on her that I declare I could write a book called "Honey, Honey, Break My Heart," but at 61 I am too old to write about women. Honey is a great friend and we all know that, and a wonderful girl to visit whether you want to live with her or not.

Helen and I were in Europe for six months last year, and may go back again in 1957 if I know who I am by that time. Meanwhile, we join in sending you our love and the greatest hope in the world for your complete and quick recovery.

As ever,

## To H. Allen Smith

*Smith was preparing a book of children's writings.*

*West Cornwall, Connecticut*
*February 24, 1956*

*Mr. H. Allen Smith, R. F. D. 1,*
*Mount Kisco, N. Y.*

Dear Allen Smith:

Sorry I've been unable to answer the letter Jap forwarded to me until now. That title was actually "My Auntie Margery Albright's Garden, 185 South 5th Street, Columbus, Ohio." Why in hell's name I need the paraphrase, I don't know now. Maybe it was in the days when the wolves of investigation were on everybody's traces and I was protecting a lady dead forty years. Anyway, the verses have disappeared. I don't think I have any juvenilia at all, but I bet

Saroyan has, and you know that Edna Millay, E. B. White, and others wrote for the old St. Nicholas as children and appeared in the collected volume of that magazine, I suppose.

The New Yorker's Talk of the Town, of course, has published a thousand brief childish essays, of which quite a lot are very funny, and the magazine might allow you to use half a dozen or so, if you are up to the task of hunting through the files. You may remember that Gibbs's son composed a litany of hate in his bathtub when he was about seven. I think it was reprinted in the New Yorker's Notes and Comment some years ago, and then used in the play "Season in the Sun." If you write Gibbs about this, don't tell him I told you to, just say maybe that you remember the thing. He's a sensitive and difficult man, as you may know, and he may balk anyway. He doesn't think anything much is funny, but his son's chant, faithfully copied down by his father, belongs in the savage category.

When my daughter, now 24 and a mother, was 9 she thought of becoming a writer, perhaps to show her father how it should be done, but at 14 she decided "writing is too hard" and decided to become an actress. Later she decided to get married and have children in the best American tradition of most of our young lady artists. At 9 she could write a line as nice as this: "The swan floated down the river to where the fields ended and the woods began," but my favorite excerpt from her was another nine-year-old piece which began: "Linda Whitney was the youngest F.B.I. agent. She was eighteen."

Good luck and happy days,
James Thurber

## TO WILLIAM MAXWELL

*Maxwell had become Thurber's editor after Lobrano's death, and editor of Thurber's new set of fables.*

*"Windlock," Somerset, Bermuda*
*April 30, 1956*

Mr. William Maxwell, The New Yorker,
25 West 43rd Street, New York 36, New York

Dear Bill:

. . . I am concerned about THE NEW YORKER's rejection of my fables dealing with the history of our time, especially "Ivory, Apes and People" which could be substituted for any two other fables. With the throwing out of the fable of the bears and the one about the "Watchdog," it leaves "The Tiger Who Would Be King" as the only politically polemical fable. I can't quite understand the attitude. Fables are not for children, as I have said, and not merely to amuse our married women writers with comments on husbands and wives and fathers and daughters.

I have done all the fables for this year and this book. I think "Tight Schedule" is just another expression for "Hold! Enough!" The book could be put off until the last week in October. None of my first twenty-eight fables were rejected by Ross, although a few may have been rewritten at his suggestion. He was never a man to disagree with, or oppose, a man's convictions. I can't help but feel in the air a certain developing "corporation" attitude up there, a kind of chairman-of-the-board censorship. I hope I am wrong about this.

Love from us both.

> As always,
> James Thurber

## To Katharine White

> *"Windlock," Somerset, Bermuda*
> *May 7, 1956*

*Mrs. Katharine S. White, The New Yorker,*
*25 West 43rd Street, New York 36, New York*

Dear Katharine:

Thank you for your nice note, and thank Carmin for his good work. I don't care how they use the drawings or what ones and I am sure you are all doing it the best way. Everybody has his own special fables, but I am glad you liked "The Rose, The Fountain, and The Dove." The Nugents don't quite have THE NEW YORKER feeling about "The Truth About Toads" and have their own favorites, and Hamish Hamilton picked five others!

I would prefer THE NEW YORKER to substitute "The Daws on the Dial" for any other fable or two fables, and the same goes for "Ivory, Apes and People," for as I told Bill Maxwell, I do feel THE NEW YORKER should allow me to express just one opinion on world affairs in the fables. This is a tradition of fables, and without it they would seem frail and unimportant. I will consider rewriting the last one if that is the problem. "The Daws" took me since January and about fifteen rewrites. "The Toads" was done without conscious plan, in about fifteen minutes, and not rewritten. It just goes to show there is no way of telling about comics. The piece that Maxwell Anderson liked best of mine was written exactly nine times faster than "The Secret Life of Walter Mitty." "File and Forget" took two afternoons, but "A Call on Mrs. Forrester" took eleven weeks. Did you know that the Reader's Digest paid, for the reprint of "The Night the Ghost Got In" only six hundred dollars less than I got originally for all eight pieces that made up "My Life and Hard Times"?

Don't pay any attention much to me, because I know you have your problems, and we both worry about your working too much and hope you can get out from under. I also worry about Bill Maxwell, but not so much about Shawn, for I regard him as tougher than Harold Ross by three to one. Even when the second Hitkin is elected to the board in the place of an editor, Shawn will be able to hold his own.

The Nugents have been here since Tuesday and we have had a great round of parties, and poor old Helen is giving a cocktail party for sixty people in spite of her bad eye and bad big toe, which she banged against something and knocked the nail off of it. There won't be any more fables coming along at all, at least not for this book, maybe the next one. After all, La Fontaine wrote five books of fables, but almost none of them were his own. I want you and Andy to read Maxwell's wonderful talk which he gave at Smith and is now out in a fifty cent pamphlet. He sent me one at my request. It is called "The Writer as Illusionist" and is truly beautiful and fine. And so are you and Andy.

Love from us both.

As ever,
James Thurber

## TO ELMER DAVIS

*"Windlock," Somerset, Bermuda*
*May 18, 1956*

*Mr. Elmer Davis, 1661 Crescent Place,*
*Washington 9, D.C.*

Dear Elmer:

I should have told you, and I tell you now, that I don't expect answers to my letters to you. I can feel all the way from here the suffering you are going through and the pain and mental anguish. Only a few of us are left in our sixties, and I now wake up each morning earlier than usual, and lie there brooding and trying to be brave and remembering such lines as Conrad's "The best we can hope for is to go out nobly in the end," and Hemingway's "Nothing ever happens to the brave." I don't know whether Lord Jim went out bravely or not, he did it in the gaudy but quick way, and worst of all for the intelligent and sensitive man is not what happens to the heart and the body but to the mind. Nothing will happen to yours and mine. I mean nothing like happened to Emerson or Swift or Pound or a hundred others.

A friend of mine once suggested a book, an unsentimental book, containing not the usual inspirational crap, but some of the strong and truly reassuring things good men and good minds have written, about life and its burdens and death and its whatever-you-call-it. I mean things like William Allen White's piece on the death of his daughter, the factual not the fictional writing, not the elated or the religiously saved or anything else in which man has protected himself by distortion and hiding rather than by coming out and meeting it on the plain. I haven't done much thought about the contents other than their nature. What impels me to this discussion now is the unquestioned success of almost any book about Positive Thinking, the conquest of Fear, usually trash, money-making trash, written by trashy men. Maybe this is true: Nothing ever happens to the trashy. I heard one of the s.o.bs on the air talking about a friend of his who "squirts mental love about a bus every time he boards one." This, in paraphrase, turns up in one of my fables, called "The Bat Who Got the Hell Out." The fables began to run last week in THE NEW YORKER and there are some this week and the third batch will appear May 26. I am now becoming convinced it is my best book and this makes me happier than ever that I picked it for you. . . .

My own case is not anywhere near so bad as you might think, since I went blind over a period of sixteen years gradually and have learned to my astonishment that total blindness is not darkness but light. I had not known before that the totally blind live in a soft light, without shadow or figures or landscape, but light nonetheless. My eye doctor says that many complain about the fact that a totally blacked out room at night is light to them, and some go through panic about this for awhile. It didn't bother me at all, because of its slow approach and because I like light. According to Gordon Bruce, my eye man, only those who have both eyeballs removed would live in darkness. It is the annoyance, as I have often said, and not the disability or the tragedy of blindness that is the hardest to bear, the inability to read a letter that comes in when you are alone or to dial a number on the phone or look one up in the phone book. The loss of visual stimuli is not too important to a man like me who has total recall and can summon up images, familiar or imaginary, without much trouble. Fred Friendly, who works with Ed Murrow, has been planning a piece about eyes and blindness with me as the narrator and central subject and wanted to know what I would like to see and whom I would like to see if I could have my sight again for one day. He seemed astonished that I didn't name Marilyn Monroe or Senator McCarthy or any others upon whom I have never laid eyes. I told him I would like to see what life has done for the faces of the people I have always loved and I would also like to find out, visually, what holds up Jimmy Cagney and Bogart, both of whom must be near sixty. Cagney is a famous hypochondriac and so, he once told me, is Spencer Tracy and they both apparently have a great many ailments, some of them produced by fear, I think. Everybody is afraid except the foolhardy, the foolish, and the crazy, and all of these are escapes from the development of courage, which could not exist unless there were fear, some of it close to unconquerable. I didn't set out to lecture, but here I am. . . .

As always,
James Thurber

## To Janet Flanner

*"Windlock," Somerset, Bermuda*
*May 30, 1956*

*Miss Janet Flanner, Hotel Continental,*
*3 Rue Castiglione, Paris, France*

Dearest Janet:

. . . We have been down here for two months in a big, lovely house jutting out into the ocean. The Williamses are half a mile away and I wish you could see that lovely family of little girls, ranging from one year to fourteen years, and all of them wonderful. Janie is as lovely as ever and Ronnie as great a friend and as difficult a person. They were at the party last night too and everything went fine, in spite of the fact that our hostess described in advance the Japanese food she had prepared and Helen was sure Ronnie would ask if he could have a scrambled egg, since he hates fish, especially shell fish, but it was a truly wonderful dinner and all four of us had second helpings. . . .

Helen got a jolt down here when Mrs. Swain, our great New Hampshire cook, wrote that she and her husband could not return to work for us in Cornwall, but only to help us get settled. So Helen is up to her ears in looking for a couple and spends her time writing letters to agency people and others. I still haven't seen my granddaughter yet, but Rosie and Fred are bringing her to us this summer. We just got a lovely picture of her at the age of nine months—taken five months ago—and Rosie says she is getting pretty now but has a wicked gleam in her eyes and loves to pinch people. Living with her is like living with a honey bee Rosie says. I was a great pincher myself during the Taft administration.

I've got a play about Bermuda half way done, a daring variation on the oldest and tritest of themes, the Enoch Arden story. It was too much of a challenge to resist and I know it is better than Maugham's version, because the idea of the two husbands both trying to get rid of the wife is a gag and won't last three acts. Nor do I believe in the tiptoeing away of either husband, nor the sawing in two of the wife. This has become a fashion in comedy on Broadway, as in a play called "Janus", latest version of the "Design For Living" crap. I want Elliott Nugent to play the second husband and Robert Preston the other one. Unfortunately Elliott will be in his manic state this Fall, and, to our dismay, he has contracted to open in a play in November, when he will probably be at his worst. This always happens. The Nugents were down here for a week and we had a wonderful time, since he is now at his best and should have got into something this last season. I can't bring "The Welcoming Arms" to Broadway until 1957 because of all this. At one point Elliott, as an old professional writer says, "Tragedy can lose its mind, and in many great plays and novels it does, but comedy has to maintain its sanity at all times. This, in any world, at any time, is not easy. Psychiatry gets its key names, like Oedipus, from tragedy, not from comedy."

Later, of course, I realized that the British medical men refer to pathological daydreaming as "a Walter Mitty syndrome." Still, nearly every generalization should have a tiny touch of invalidity in it. I still say I'm basically right and that it is harder to write a comedy character in a drawing-room scene than King Lear in a storm. My also illiterate Grandfather Fisher, in his final ramblings, was far greater than Lear I thought with such lines as "Now here comes old man Ricketts and I can't see him," and "They are playing music far off somewhere and I can't hear it," and "The flies are going to walk up the stairs and eat me up this summer." That long trip of the flies has always stuck in my mind. . . .

As ever,

James Thurber

## TO RICHARD MANEY

*Maney was handling the publicity for* My Fair Lady.

*June 13, 1956*

Mr. Richard Maney, 137 West 48th Street,
New York, New York

Dear Dick:

We came out of "My Fair Lady" on wings last night and our feet still haven't touched the ground. This is the finest union of comedy and music I have ever seen and heard. Everybody has talked about the skill and felicity and ingenuity of the whole thing, but not enough has been said about its great service in restoring comedy to a place of dignity on the American stage. It is reassuring to realize that the most honest and honorable comedy with music, or without, in many years is also the most popular in my memory. I think it will serve to keep the fine art of comedy lifted above the guttersnickery into which it had fallen. Comedy out of Hollywood by Adultery is as dangerous to a country's culture as disrespect for English sentences and plays put together with pipe cleaners and paper clips. The notion that human triangles can be humorously solved by sawing the wife in two keeps waking me up at night. I do not believe that sensibility died before our time with Henry James and I hope that it will open up in further flowers beyond the footlights. . . .

. . . The greatest test of any scene in a play is whether or not it reaches a perfection of artistry that fills the old eyes with tears. In sixty-one years I have probably never walked out of a dozen theatres with my hand or handkerchief shading my eyes. People might wonder about the sanity of a man who cried because something was perfect comedy.

Next time down Helen and I are determined to get together with you and weep in the Scotch about great things, of which "My Fair Lady" is one. It stands so high above almost anything else that it strains your neck to look up at it. Love and kisses.

As always,
James Thurber

P.S. I wish I could make this letter more eloquent and I am sorry I have lost the gift of extravagance, it comes in so handy now and then and is so often and so brutally abused. The place my eyes began misting last night especially, even though I couldn't see the action, was the "Rain in Spain" sequence. There hasn't been anything finer than that in my time and my book.

## To Lewis Gannett

*Gannett, a Cornwall neighbor of Thurber's, reviewed books for the* Herald Tribune.

*West Cornwall, Connecticut*
*June 25, 1956*

Dear old boy:

You are completely right in that Fowler says what you said he had said, mutatis a trifle mutandis, but at the risk of being hit with another smug, I say he is spinach in this particular case and I say the hell with him. The Fowlers were not often wrong, but some of their untenable positions have become notorious at the Grammarians' Club, of which I was once recording secretary. Fowler (we usually make one out of both) was wonderful chiefly because of his non-purist and often anti-purist scholarship, and because of his love of controversy and his amazing OED fund of examples. What nobody who has written on the subject seems to have said about Felicia's awkward line is that its wrongness grows out of her lousiness as a poet and her awkwardness as a writer.

The lady was clearly trying to say, "The boy stood on the burning deck after everybody else had left," and in my time I have done more than fifteen variations of this, none of them fitting the metrical scheme with which she had gyved her small mental wrists. It seems to me the simplest way to say what she was trying to say is this sentence: The boy stood on the burning deck whence all save him had fled.

What causes all the trouble is the fact that the clumsy lady comes up with "but he had fled," which is a fool-the-eye-and-ear because it diverts the mind from the prepositional "but he" to the conjunctive "but he had."

If Fowler was right, then the lady meant to say "The boy stood on the burning deck whence all had fled, but he had not." I think Felicia was a simple "except him" girl, but she got into trouble with her unfortunate use of "whence." She may have been the worst writer of English that ever lived. What mainly keeps the sentence from being poetical, however, is her tone-deaf use of "stood." She did almost everything to make the sentence one of the great ramshackles of our language.

I am surprised that Fowler was behind his time, and Churchill's, in calling "it is me" a blunder. The last of the two brothers, writing through a friend to thank me for my "Our Own Modern English Usage" (circa 1930) particularly liked my holding out for the preservation of "whom," which many people, including Henry Morgan, would like to eliminate. I had said that it was necessary for the purposes of *hauteur* in such expressions as "whom are you anyways?"

I have been planning a piece on personal pronouns and the death of the accusative. Nobody says "I gave it to they," but "me" is almost dead, and I have heard its dying screams from Bermuda to Columbus: "He gave it to Janey and I." (We have to thank Hart, Rodgers, and O'Hara for the lovely attack on this.) My cousin Earl Fisher said to me in Columbus, "Louise and I gave it to he and she last Christmas."

Last night on television a woman announcer said, "It is one of the electrical machines that cools . . ." Since "that" is sometimes forced to do the work of "which," and "which" is said to have the authority of "and it," then "one" would properly be the subject of the sentence. In our wonderful and awkward language anything can be argued, but the lady was wrong as hell is wrong. What it means is "of the electrical machines that cool, it is one." I would have loved to meet, or I would love to have met, the Fowlers—at least we all stood firm against "I would have loved to have met."

The English deplore the New Yorker's commaphilia and speak of "The Century of the Comma Mag." They object especially to such things as this: "In the living room, the argument continued after dinner." This would be necessary only if "room the argument" were a common expression. In "After dinner coffee was served on the terrace" we have a sentence to drive a New Yorker editor crazy. The English know that "moreover" and "furthermore" carry their own commas. Furthermore I don't care what Fowler says about that. Eight years ago I exchanged letters with a punctilious punctuator in England.

The legend that Ross put a comma in "I saw her but a moment" because of the danger that the reader might misconstrue the fourth word, is not true. Love to you and she from Helen and I

As ever,

P.S. See you at Rose's.

## To Peter De Vries

*A play by De Vries was being produced on Broadway.*

*West Cornwall, Connecticut*
*July 2, 1956*

Dear Pete:

The theatre is not reading matter, to quote [William] Maxwell, and, to quote a veteran of two Broadway battles, it is a form of every-man-for-himself in which you die unless you take your own part. You have to say, "Why in the name of hell have you sons-of-bitches left my name out of this list of playwrights?" Don't wait till you're desperate in a corner. Langner can make as many mistakes as anybody. Everybody in the theatre is wrong half the time and some of them most of the time. Langner told Nugent and me in Baltimore that we might get $30,000 for the movie rights of "The Male Animal." We got $150,000. The price he mentioned was being paid for "Peck's Bad Boy" and "The Little Colonel's Knight Comes Riding." (This was upped to $50,000 when the title was changed to "The Little Colonel's Nightgown Comes Off.")

You must insist that you collaborate on the play. Your touch is unique and nobody is going to get it right without your help.

As I told you, I love the family scenes with the father and the magazine, and "Upstairs!" This seems to me what I call recognizable, or better yet, unique and recognizable. I like the theatre laughs that come out of character and situation, and "Upstairs!" would get as many laughs as, or more than, the Nugent-Thurber "Yes, you are" and similar gems of comedic ingenuity. Another was "I felt fine." When I used such stuff in "Brother Endicott", Shawn thought it was "familiar and uncharacteristic."

Delays are theatre. So are changes of title, cast, director, mind, life, to say nothing of five to twenty rewrites of scenes. We cut thirty minutes out of Act I after Princeton, threw out by mutual consent, tacitly, a scene we had fought over for three months. Theatre is also hell. But the best directors and producers will come up with a brilliant suggestion and then ruin something lovely, unless you watch them like a hawk. Take Shumlin's urge to spoil the dancing scene on the ground that it was too charming. So "Let's dance, Ellen" became, till I killed it, "What do you say we shake a leg?" Theatre is vulgar, commercial, sincere and wonderful. It takes a tough spirit and body, and I wish I had yours for my own new play.

This time, after considerable experience, I outlined "The Welcoming Arms" act by act and scene by scene in Bermuda and have written three to six versions of parts of all three acts, putting in new characters and taking out old ones, shifting the viewpoint, as I get to know the people better. I don't believe in sticking too close to a book or a plot or a scene structure. Keep it fluid. I want to have my play make some sense about the predicament of the American writer, while at the same time basically dealing with two men and a woman and two younger men and a younger woman. The man of action against the man of sensibility and thought. I have always been up against this in my own life, not only with Kuehner and then Ross, but with the boy friends of old girls of mine. Ann [Fordice] was going with the ex-middleweight champion of the U.S. Navy when I met her in Westport in 1933. All the girls had at least one athlete in their lives, or sailor, or engineer, except Paula, but I didn't know for three months that her Mr. Delehanty weighed less than me and was one of the few I could have thrown. Minnette had both a farmer and a chest surgeon who could lift tractors out of ditches. I kept ducking Honey's Mr. Duffy before I found out he was a retired tenor who put on his tuxedo every night. Jill had a guy named Hunky who threatened to shoot me, but he was a phony. The writer who takes over from a man of muscle has his work cut out for him. Most of the muscle men believe that the Whiffenpoof song was stolen from Kipling and another composer, not realizing that it was a loving parody and that the music was original. It was written by one Tod Galloway, of Columbus, Ohio, a friend of my father, just as the first and best music for "Sylvia" and "The Road to Mandalay" was written by another Columbus man named Oley Speaks. His niece Margaret, with whom I flirted in 1928, was the wife of one Cooky Cunningham, an All-American right end from Ohio State. The shock of this was not so great as the night a girl named Ruth told me, "I am Walter Winchell's secretary."

When you get it all done, it has to be done over again. I doubt if you can make it before the season of 1957–58. I know I can't. You got plenty of time even to work in a third play.

Don't let your dreams get you even if "Comfort Me With Apples" turns into "Confront Me With Applesauce," for it will change finally to "Comfort Me With Applause." Keep pitching, and try to get the ball between the waist and the heart.

Moral: It is better for a man to have two balls on him than two strikes.
        Love and kisses,
        Jim

## To William Maxwell and William Shawn

July 12, 1956

Dear Bills:

A bloodhound is never known as a police dog. Neither is a German shepherd unless it has undergone police training. The other police dogs are the Dobermans, the Labrador and the German pointer. The English call German shepherds Alsatians, but there is no such breed of course. This was to avoid British antipathy to the word German and to the reputation of the German police dog as brutal and vicious. (The 150 police dogs of Scotland Yard were established in 1946 just after the war, but there were only a handful to begin with.) I may seem to be showing off a little in not wanting to change "police dog" to "German shepherd" and if this really does violence to your inherited obsession about clarity, it could be changed to just "shepherd". The British police dogs had not been written about until I wrote about them for the Daily Mail last summer. I also did a piece about English bloodhounds which are never used by the police of the Commonwealth. English regard them as lacking in courage but as I pointed out to Chief Superintendent John Tickle, my favorite Chief Superintendent and name, they merely lack aggression and possess discretion.

I got a letter two months ago from the present Scotland Yard dog chief, Superintendent Morgan Davies who tells me that the English Alsatians have discovered most of the hidden guns and ammunition on Cyprus. In every news story I have seen the dogs are referred to as bloodhounds. Incidentally, the German pointer boldly known by his own name in London guards the palaces of the royal family because unlike the shepherd, he will accept more than one master and doesn't mind the changing of the guard.

In the New York *Times* of Friday July 6th, I think, there is a story about crime in Central Park. New York loses 42 cops there while London gets along with 2 cops and 2 dogs in Hyde Park. In 1946, before the dogs took over, there were 830 purse snatchings in Hyde Park. In 1954 there were 13. Tickle wrote to the Commissioner of Police here about January 1955 suggesting that he come over or that we send an officer over to London. He never even got an answer to his letter. Every civilized country in the world has sent police to watch the training of the London dogs except the U.S. This reminds me of one of Ross's long marginal ramblings, inspired by the spelling of "shephard".

In "The Daws on the Dial" I think "Dial" is better than "Clock Dial", because the reader will know you're talking about a clock dial and if he doesn't he ought to read some other magazine. We do not say "He lay down upon the supine woman." The word "woman" will suffice. It was Ross's ignorance of such matters that led to our alarming insistence on clarity, once defined as "telling them it's going to happen, tell them it's happening, and tell them it has happened". I don't know what dial you were thinking of unless it was a wrist watch dial.

I am utterly amazed that your Checking Department, the greatest in the world, slipped up on the figuring of centuries in the fable called "The Turtle Who Conquered Time". Since there was no year zero, and we went from 1 B.C. to 1 A.D., a turtle bearing the date 1944 would be only 1999 years old. I left in the word "exactly" just to see what college professor or mathematician on our staff would point out my error in his best old school tie manner. All we have to do is take out the word "exactly" and let the 2000 years stand. When I get drunk at 4 a.m. as I often do and begin bawling out everybody from Cato the Elder to Richard Nixon I will tell the anecdote of the 2000 years along with the one about The New Yorker's calling the Hotel Ruhl in Nice the Hotel Ruhl et des Anglais. . . .

I think you're a keen bunch of fellows and get out a lovely magazine. Also I have had two wives, a daughter and a granddaughter, but I have learned more about women from The New Yorker than from anything else or anyone else. I don't suppose you would be interested in my casual beginning "I was fifteen years old the summer my mother shot my lover. I was twenty-two before I realized that mother was also in love with him and that what he had been doing to me all along was really not ballet lessons at all.

     Love and kisses,

     Jim (James Thurber)

## To William Shawn

*Thurber wrote McNulty's obituary for* The New Yorker. *Shawn, who, as a Talk reporter in the Thirties, had been rewritten by Thurber, now changed Thurber's "as a man and writer" to "man and writer." And Thurber's "darkened the day" to "darkened the world." Asked about it years later, Shawn decided Thurber had been right.*

*West Cornwall, Connecticut*
*July 31, 1956*

Mr. William Shawn, The New Yorker,
25 West 43rd Street, New York, N. Y.

Dear Bill:

Since the New Yorker obits are signed by The Editors and deal with persons we all knew and loved, it is right and fitting that each of us should get in a word of his own, and so I have no complaint about the minor changes in the McNulty piece. I once changed "regret" to "sorrow," in the Dave Lardner obit which I didn't write.

In defense of my own careful writing, however, let me point you a few points: "as a man and writer" is not only intimate and correct, but mcnulty ("A Man Gets Around"); "as man and writer" is painfully correct and utterly reminiscent of the deplorable stuffiness of the Ross funeral oration, still a sorry thing in many of our minds.

"Darkened the day" not only has the literary quality of alliteration, in a piece about a man who loved verbal music, but as a student of the OED I can assure you that "day" refers to something longer than a 24-hour period, when the context clearly supports this extension of time. I didn't object, because "world" would please McNulty's friends and family, but the world is actually a dark place, for one thing, and for another it can scarcely be darkened in a literal sense. Furthermore "darkened the day" has biblical origin, and we speak of a man's day and nation. Again, it is the day that has light, and not the world.

The omission of the word "parlance" made things simpler for our mentally young readers in the great Ross tradition of simple clarity, but McNulty told stories of parlance, as witness any of his titles, such as "She Was a Bostonian, They Call 'Em." Parlance means "a way of speaking, or of language." I am glad that you did not change "people" to "persons," for while McNulty was interested in persons, he always called them people. I put all this down for you editors not so much in defense of my own perfectionism and precision, but as a kind of guide for editors who are likely to be less literary than formalistic, and who occasionally need a lecture about the magnificent use of words as well as their accuracy. I think it turned out fine anyway, and I was glad I could write it for John and for the New Yorker, since I knew him better and longer than any other man and he once said in print that his best friends were Jim Thurber and Tim Costello. Love and kisses to you all

As ever,
James Thurber

P.S. You might be interested in looking up "day" in the OED. It does not come from the Latin, but from the German.

It is a great tribute to the New Yorker that its sometimes cold, grammatical strictures were seldom permitted to bind or confine the special grace and wonder of John McNulty's own personal phrasing. I hope we will never again use "update" or "downgrade."

## To William Faulkner

*President Eisenhower asked Faulkner to help enlist American writers in giving "a true picture of our country" to other people. Thurber was among those Faulkner turned to.*

*October 2, 1956*

*Mr. William Faulkner, c/o Miss Jean Ennis,*
*Random House, Inc., 457 Madison Avenue,*
*New York, New York*

Dear Mr. Faulkner:

The things we say and do at home, not abroad, shape world opinion of America. Foreigners of good will wonder why we seem to admire art and culture as travelers, and hold it in such low esteem as citizens. Friendly French and English people who talked to me in London and Paris last year are alarmed by a nation that takes passports away from its writers and artists. These allies of ours know that nothing the artists and writers could say would do nearly so much damage to our prestige abroad as the denial of their right to say it. No ambassador is more powerful than the facts, more persuasive than the headlines.

It may gratify, and even cheer, our friends in Europe to find out that writers are now being officially used by the administration, not abused by it. One Londoner said to me last summer "Do you actually have probers the way we have point policemen?" The mobile investigatory units of Congress concerned our colleagues abroad and made them sad. The fact that so few voices were raised during the McCarthy era, in defense of free writing and free art, saddened them even more.

I have tried to do my part, through all this dark national weather, to protest against the American assault on its own culture, and I shall continue to do so. It seems to me that a hundred writers, trying to work in concert in any cause, succeed mainly in multiplying glibness by 100. All of them put together could not explain to friends and neutrals around the world why it is an honored tradition of Congress to place such men as Eastland at the head of a committee, simply because of his length of service, and without regard to his power to crush in committee the desires of the President.

My highest personal regards to you.

Very truly yours,

James Thurber

## To William Maxwell

*The New Yorker* wished to publish a version of Thurber's "The Wonderful O" *as edited by Maxwell. Thurber and Helen disagreed with the editing and withdrew the manuscript.*

*West Cornwall, Connecticut*

*October 11, 1956*

Dear Bill:

What Shawn must agree to is my own special omission of quotation marks in such phrases as "leaning against an r" and, in referring to words, "one of them is love." The New Yorker's trained addiction to formal punctuation would make this story a mess of fly specks. It may be an exercise or tour de force, but it was carefully worked out. The magazine once rejected a piece of mine in which I used comin and goin without the apostrophes. Everybody knows the g has been left out.

"Burning like a flame in spars" is what Castor and Pollux actually do, since they are not only the brothers of Helen, sons of Leda and the Swan, and two fixed stars, but also St. Elmo's fire in the rigging of ships. The boys get around. As you know, but others won't, Conrad's Jones is the Mr. Jones of "Victory."

I look forward to your condensed version, and I shall probably adhere in the book to some of your cuts, maybe even all of them, unless any lists are left out, such as the islands. 90% of all the words and proper names came out of memory. "Not, matey, from the regions which are wholly land" will puzzle the boys and girls and bother Poe in Heaven, but not you. I have two other such pieces coming in the future, "The Spoodle" and "The Train Without a Track," both probably nearer the New Yorker kind of thing.

I have been working on titles, such as "The Enchanted O" and many others, and just yesterday thought of "The Man Who Hated O," which may be better for the magazine. I am amazed and delighted that they saw it your way, since I would have bet ten to one against.

Note from Briefly Reviewed column of the New Yorker for August 3, 1863: "Alice in Wonderland," by Lewis Carroll, originally appeared in this magazine in considerably abbreviated form.

"The Heart of Darkness," by Joseph Conrad, was first printed in this magazine in a shorter version under the title "The Aorta of Darkness."

Love and kisses and thanks

As ever,

James Thurber

*Mr. William Maxwell,* The New Yorker,
*25 West 43rd St., New York, N. Y.*

## To William Thurber

*Robert Thurber had lived with his mother all his life, caring for her until her death in December 1955. He was inconsolable for a long time after her passing.*

*Nov. 7, 1956*

Dear Bill,

. . . I didn't intend to be rough on Robert and I know he cannot work, but I was afraid he was sinking into hopelessness. Probably he does go to the library and read the papers and have other activities. Inactivity to me is death or worse; he never writes about his routine and I was alarmed when he said he "Rested more and wrote less". He did some good research for me on the Ryder stuff in 1952, and I had some hope of something else like that. An hour a week or every two weeks, but I take it back.

I promised Mamma to look after him while I lived, and it seemed to me that Cincinnati in the winter would be out of the refrigerator into the snow. . . . I suggest that you go with him to Cincinnati some Sunday and look over the situation and find a place. I want to send him an extra $25.00 each month and am sending it to him for November. His diet must be built up, and I wish he could see a good doctor in Cincinnati. I know he is utterly miserable, and it is miraculous that he can go on. I will be glad to send him to Florida, but he seems not strong enough, and you should both talk to your travel expert about it. The dangers and rackets there are famous for the traveler. Try to explain the situation to him and say I did not intend to hurt his feelings and that we must not get in another period of drawn-out difficulty. I'll write again soon. Love to you both.

# the

# TWILIGHT YEARS

## To George Plimpton

West Cornwall, Connecticut

*West Cornwall, Connecticut*
*January 7, 1957*

*Mr. George Plimpton, THE PARIS REVIEW,*
*2 Columbus Circle, New York 19, N. Y.*

Dear Mr. Plimpton:

Literature today has become in part ad lib conversation transcribed into print, and I'm not very good at it. I would rather not have my interview printed with the others in the Viking book, for that reason, if this letter arrives in time. I was somewhat startled when the ATLANTIC printed a television interview with me, and I don't like this trend, although some of the PARIS REVIEW stuff has been excellent, especially Faulkner's, but not mine. This was my own fault. I also regard talk as such and believe that a man's opinions of writing should be set down by himself when he is alone. If Cowley hasn't got enough of writers already with his book about them and his reviews, this ought to do it. I hope you will understand my position. When I do write, it takes me weeks to get it right. I also think that a whole book of interviews would become tedious in content and form, especially form.

Tex McCrary says interviewing is a science, and he is preceded by three or four technicians before he arrives on the dot to ask the questions you have been prepared for, as by a surgeon's assistants. Just now the biggest television figure is one Mike Wallace, who has made interviewing an hour long business around midnight and asks about everything, from homosexuality in the millinery trade to illegal subsidizing in amateur tennis. We are becoming a vocal species, and writing may soon disappear, but I should like to do my share in fighting against the oral forces in my corner of the barricades. Since the book doesn't come out till fall, there should be plenty of time to keep me out, and my absence will be like the sudden disappearance from a cocktail party of a guy who has been blibbering, as my daughter puts it, not wisely but too much. My highest regards to you and the REVIEW.

        Cordially yours,

        James Thurber


## To Charles Deaton

*West Cornwall, Connecticut*
*April 9, 1957*

*Mr. Charles B. Deaton, 1214 Royal Avenue,*
*Louisville, Kentucky*

Dear Mr. Deaton:

Most of the students who write to me would envy you living in Louisville where there are libraries and source books, for most of the other boys and girls come from Wuffle Point, Minnesota, or Bruised Elbow, Wyoming. One week I got thirteen letters from high school juniors in Bowie, Texas. Most letters simply say "I like everything you have written. What have you written?"

The only new fact I can think of is that I am getting out two new books this year, "The Wonderful O" in May, and a collection of stories and drawings called "Alarms and Diversions" in the fall or winter. Good luck!

        Cordially yours,

        James Thurber


## To the Frederick Sauerses

*The Ledgelets, Somerset Bridge, Bermuda*
*April 24, 1957*

*Mrs. Frederick W. Sauers, Route #1,*
*La Grange, Illinois*

Dear Children:

It's about time I wrote you. Just got back from a night at the Williamses, following a big party at which Canon Sullivan was dancing like mad and sent his dear love to you and said you were a lovely girl. I told him you hadn't forgotten him either. When I called him Canon he asked me to call him Rev. as everybody else does. Rudy Vallee was at the party. I have never met him before, but within three minutes he was telling me all of his conquests, including Hedy Lamarr and Ginger Rogers. I told him then about Lottie Pickford, Julie Marlowe, and my weird experience with Pearl White in the sailboat during the picnic of 1907. He sang the Whiffenpoof song for me. He must be as old as Peter Arno and Fred Astaire, who are 57 this year. He played saxophone in Peter Arno's Yale orchestra as soon ago as 1922.

We just got some sample illustrations for "The Wonderful O" from Marc Simont and they seem wonderful, even better than "The Thirteen Clocks." A man told Helen last night that she has the skin of a sixteen-year old girl. No wonder the barber thinks she is my daughter. I have a very beautiful secretary here. The biggest news is that Janie [Williams] is *not* pregnant. If I can ever get my letters caught up, I'll start fiddling with the play. You'll soon get a copy of the book out May 20. Is the new daughter kicking you in the midrift? Our love to the whole family, including the beagle.

As always,

## To Katharine White

*The Ledgelets, Somerset Bridge, Bermuda*
*May 3, 1957*

*Mrs. Katharine S. White, THE NEW YORKER,*
*25 West 43rd Street, New York 36, New York*

Dear Katharine:
    . . . As you must know, the well-intentioned, but ill-advised, affair of "The Wonderful O" left us all in a bad state. My thyroid had gone to 59 and Dr. Werner was seriously concerned and doubled my dose of Tapazole, so that by the time we arrived here I began to feel better physically and mentally. Actually, I have never felt better and shall continue to do so if I don't have to fret about *The New Yorker*. Like all of you overworked people, I need a long holiday from the magazine and its high pressures. For a year I have been arranging matters toward this end, with the Fables doing well, "The Wonderful O" coming out this month, and "Alarms and Diversions" now in page proof and set for the Fall. The movie sale of "The Catbird Seat" and the five thousand dol-

lars from ALA [the American Library Association] will easily make it possible for me to devote the rest of the year to the play, without any other work. My last piece for anybody this year was the story of the Loch Ness monster, which will appear in *Holiday* this summer and was finished two weeks ago. It had been suggested two years ago by Ted Patrick. It was Roger Angell who, while on *Holiday,* suggested that I do their Paris piece and both of these ideas meant a lot to me. I have long had a hunch that Roger and I, with all deference to the rest of you, would be able to manage any future work of mine there with less stress and strain than I have been through last year.

After this, I don't think any of us should talk about, or brood about, the unfortunate episode of "The Wonderful O". I realize that its mutilation grew out of goodwill and even a loving admiration. The results, however, were little short of complete disaster. This is because I never should have permitted *The New Yorker* to attempt something that could not possibly be managed. Ross and Lobrano must have turned in their graves when a piece of mine was seized with affectionate, but violent, hands and underwent a series of changes in length, motivation, style, and even content and purpose. Wrongly believing that it had originally been intended as a children's book, you people sought to "save" it by performing a miracle of sophistication or something. It should not have been touched, but instead Shawn wanted 4500 words cut out and Maxwell eagerly and lovingly set about the impossible task of what amounted to a destructive collaboration. I should have put a stop to that instantly, but we were all placed in a strange situation by circumstance. Rightly or wrongly, the project of cutting out a third of one of my pieces for a magazine that has a piece this week running to 102 pages, was headed for catastrophe. The story was, as you know, not only cut from beginning to end, sometimes in every other sentence, but also contained a great deal of re-writing completely out of key with my style. You thought it read smoothly, Shawn never could make up his mind about it, Helen and I attempted to save it after it was past saving, and I finally had the good sense to take it away from you all. We all have to face the realistic fact that I have become used to working for Ross through Lobrano, a perfect long-standing arrangement, now no longer possible. But we must find a new system if I am to continue to write things for you. I cannot afford to risk my health and peace of mind with everything I submit, and I think this is a good time to clear up the situation. I can't return to work on the play, I have found out, until I get this settled and I am no longer worried about, or by, *The New Yorker.* My feelings for the magazine and for all of you remain the same, but your letters clearly indicate that you are troubled by a dangerous state of affairs between us.

About two years ago the magazine began using the word "uncharacteristic" about certain pieces of mine and about the kind of stuff I am now dedicated to writing. You all have an unconscious and, I believe, completely wrong concept of this. You would like to have me return to a kind of piece and approach that I used years ago, but I cannot do that. What complicates the whole thing is that you have all become, in a curious inversion of Ross's famous byword "writer-conscious," extremely "editor-conscious." In conversation with writers and in letters of suggestion and rejection you have fallen into the use of such pontifical and often stuffy phrases as "unanimity of opinion," "decision of the majority" and other such evidences of overwrought and over-burdened minds. This has been mentioned to me by a number of writers in the past six or eight months, some of whom may have been, I am afraid, alienated or estranged beyond recall. You have made of the *New Yorker* editorial judgment a rigid thing and you have developed a certain sense of false infallibility, so that Ross's wonderful ability to see the author's side and to ask for outside opinions has been lost. "You will have to accept our judgment," is too often heard up there, with the thoughtlessness of editors undergoing great strain and far too much work. We now come to my main point of concern and sorrow.

The ALA award was given to me for the Simon and Schuster book of fables and, alas, not for those *The New Yorker* printed. This can be clearly established if you will refer to *The New Yorker*'s correspondence with me about the Fables last year at this time. In several letters, including one to Andy, I deplored the obvious intention of the magazine to reject quietly almost all the fables dealing with, as I put it in a letter to Maxwell, national and international affairs and the larger issues and ideals of life, as against the slighter fables about husbands and wives and children. Nevertheless, you rejected the two fables for which the award was, I have been told, principally given, the one against Communism and one against what was once called McCarthyism. These are the only two fables whose morals contain the words freedom and justice. The morals are as follows: "It is better to have the ring of freedom in your ears than in your nose" and "Thou shalt not blindfold justice by pulling the wool over her eyes." Lewis Gannett wanted to mention these omissions in his review, but I requested him not to. The publishers and others wondered vaguely whether *The New Yorker* had developed a policy of retreat from the front lines of the battle for human rights. This had been carried on mainly by Andy in his

Comment and I explained only the pressure of illness, and not editorial pressure, had kept his voice largely silent. I also had to point out that *The New Yorker* apparently felt I should not be the man to deal with serious and large affairs. Of the three other fables devoted to these subjects, only "The Peacelike Mongoose" was accepted without comment. Maxwell actually told me that "The Tiger Who Would Be King" would probably not be used, because it was *too savage!* After "Ivory, Apes and People" had been rejected, I sent it in again with a letter to Shawn, I think it was, saying that I intended to use that title on the book and saying again that I felt the serious fables were an important part of the whole project. This fable was then printed, but for the wrong reason. You may now know that I had no intention of using that title, and it is a source of worry that I had to use lies and devices to put the magazine on the side of outspoken defense of freedom and justice. I deeply regret that I cannot possibly share with *The New Yorker* the ALA award.

. . . Andy wrote me a letter in defense of an editor's rights to his views, however wrong they might be, pointing out that I should be glad such a freedom exists in American publishing. I am now convinced, of course, that all of this was due to haste, overwork, and careless thinking. However, you must surely see the basis of my reluctance to write for the magazine what you lightly call a "Thurber piece."

I must get this play done and possibly another one, without being subjected to the well-known Follow Up and I would appreciate it greatly if you saw to it that the editors do not bother me. I expect to return to the magazine's pages by 1958 which is just around the corner. I shall not violate my contract with *The New Yorker,* and do not want to get any letters from anybody on that point. Not long before Lobrano died he asked me if I knew I was the only writer for the magazine who received full benefit of "the quantity bonus" and the other additional payments whether or not I met the requirements. To this I could only say, "Well, it couldn't happen to a writer who has done more for *The New Yorker* over a longer period." I realize that *The New Yorker* stands somewhat in trepidation of me, and it is this that makes our relationship seem new and distant and difficult. . . .

Just before you left for Florida I explained my dilemma briefly to Andy on the phone, but he was in a bad state then, about which I was thoroughly concerned, and I understood why he said to me about "The Wonderful O" situation, "I'm glad I'm not mixed up in it." This left me nowhere to turn whatever. But it set me to thinking about the new infexibility that Shawn and the rest of

you have established in dealing with old writers as well as new. We either conform, like everybody else, to the famous Unanimity Board up there or we are
left out in the cold. Once again I believe in all of you and I am devoted to you
all and to the magazine, and I expect to write for it again. But I have been in
such a fine state of health and mind after forgetting about the situation that I
want to be allowed to continue on my sabbatical until I feel I can come back
with the old spirit.

    . . . Helen joins me in my convictions and my love and best wishes.

        As always,


## To William Maxwell

*The Ledgelets, Somerset Bridge, Bermuda*
*May 20, 1957*

*Mr. William Maxwell, THE NEW YORKER,*
*25 West 43rd Street, New York 36, New York*


Dear Bill:

    . . . Our time here has gone by like sunlight and I am afraid we shall miss
Janet [Flanner], although I am not sure of her actual departure date. We get
back on June 7, when my second grandchild is expected in Hinsdale.

    Our cottage, called Forbidden Fruit, since it is a honeymoon place, seems a
little out of key for a couple married as long ago as 1935, and I have suggested
adjustable names for the place, depending on the state of the marriage of its
various occupants: The Qualms, Widening Gap, Swords' Point, Evening Falls,
The Rocks, etc. Right now it is Serenity Hall, the name I am using for my
house in the Bermuda play.

    Helen sends her constant love and best wishes along with mine to you and
your family.

        As always,


P.S. K.S.W. recently wrote me, "I thank God every day for Shawn." Well, sir, I
thank God every week or ten days for certain writers. My prayers end in my
own special addition to "Now I lay me down to sleep." I invented it for my
own daughter when she was three or four. "If I should wake before I die, then
let's just call it beddy-bye."

## To Beulah Hagen

*The book under discussion is* Alarms and Diversions.

The Ledgelets, Somerset Bridge, Bermuda
*May 22, 1957*

Mrs. Beulah Hagen, Harper & Brothers,
49 East 33rd Street, New York 16, New York

Dear Mrs. Hagen:

Helen and I have not meant to leave out our genuine delight with the way the book has been organized, in both prose and drawings. It is an excellent arrangement and should come out as a most effective volume.

All of you will probably be shocked and surprised by the great number of small typos, and these must all be changed with great care. If I were a reader for a book club, I am afraid I might have become so bewildered and annoyed by the mistakes that I would have thrown the book aside. I long ago invented the phrase "printer's sense" or "publisher's sense," which takes in those words, phrases, and sentences containing no actual mis-spellings, but the use of a wrong word. There are several bad examples of this in our book, such as "somebody" for "solemnly," and "sacred" for "scared." One little letter of the alphabet completely mucks up "The White Rabbit Caper" in the page proofs. This is the use of the word "bear" for "bead." This brings into a tightly written story about a rabbit, a fox, a frog, an owl, a stork, and two dogs, another animal which doesn't belong there, and completely louses up the meaning. There should always be one proof reader who reads proofs for sense, that is the writer's sense. Page proofs, like galley proofs, should also be carefully read aloud against the original manuscript or tear sheet. The rush to get this book into the hands of the book club was unfortunate. Since some of the more difficult pieces were done perfectly, or nearly so, and others were garbled all the way, there must have been an inexperienced or tired linotyper in the plot somewhere. I have always read galley proofs before and was astonished that Harpers didn't send them along and actually believed I didn't want to read page proof. If the book had come out the way it was in page proof, it would have been a disaster. As I told you, I am used to the perfection of *The New Yorker*. Precision lost a great friend in the death of Harold Ross. "He considered accuracy a personal possession, like his hat or his watch," said the late

Maloney. The fact that you caught my own bad mistake in the lady on the bookcase drawing makes me believe that many of the other mutilations must also have been caught. Tell the boys in the mechanical department that the first "t" in "mustn't" must never be replaced by an apostrophe. The word "often" is pronounced without the "t", but it is not spelled "of'en."

Once again we greatly like the general layout and the handling of the whole project, but please don't let them rush the final corrections. . . .

Cordially yours,
James Thurber

## To the Fred Sauerses

*The Ledgelets, Somerset Bridge, Bermuda*
*May 27, 1957*

*Mrs. Frederick W. Sauers, Route One,*
*La Grange, Illinois*

Dear Rosie, Fred, and Sara:

We keep thinking about all of you and the coming Serena, named after Serenity Hall, the Somerset House in my play, which is stumbling along mostly on all fours at the moment. Janie Williams, the perennial mother of Somerset, is now painting her house, because she says if she can't create a child she has to create something. Her children are all running up like flowers and her husband is holding his own like a weed. I woke up early this morning thinking of this paraphrase:

> Last night, ah, yesternight, betwixt her lips and mine
>   Thy shadow fell, Ida Rapport, the night was thine.

You can see the effects upon my artistic invention brought about by the charm of this "ring on England's finger," as Andy White called Bermuda. He is now in Maine with his hypochondria, having had a dreadful three weeks in Florida. They had a termagant of a landlady and Andy developed a fixation about her—he was sure she had buried her husband in the back yard. Never bury your husband in or around the house. The place to bury your husband is on a heath. Cops never look there, they always look in the woods. Getting him up on the roof to fix the spouting and then pushing him off is not a good idea.

This is much too common and the police suspect the wife at once. Push him off a neighbor's roof and let them suspect the neighbor's wife, or husband.

I was properly horrified by the fourteen-year old boy who shot his mother and twenty-year old sister "on an impulse." We have had compulsion murders and murders of passion, but we are now on our way to whim murders and those originating in passing fancies and moments of jest. Everybody should be allowed to take out a pistol license and shoot their own or the neighbor's children if they so much as reach for a handkerchief or pull open a bureau drawer.

I think you will like this line in my play, spoken by a middle-aged Bermudian colored woman: "We all hoped my youngest sister would not have her baby until after she was married, but God had other plans for her." I am also developing the character of Mark Hilliard's (Elliott Nugent's) daughter, who is a Senior at Penn, or someplace a lot like Penn. She believes in love in the afternoon so that you can get up for cocktails and wine, instead of love at night which ends in scorbic acid, boiled eggs, and sometimes waffles.

My exploration of the nature of the American wife down here has given me a few new facts concerned with a woman's attitude toward her husband when he acts up. The loyal wife is both blind and deaf, a jealous wife sees and hears what's not there, the discontented wife neither looks nor listens. Thus the American wife does not have the vaguest idea of the truth of her husband's behavior or what his friends think about him. A woman cannot swear in court to the truth of what her husband did the night before, but she could describe with absolute accuracy all the details of every gown worn by every woman there.

I have just got a book from England called "The American Woman," written by a sociologist with the wonderful name of Eric John Dingwall. It has a wonderful chapter on dating and courtship. Most people do not realize that America is the only civilized country in the world in which girls start going with boys at the age of thirteen and often shoot their escorts or are shot by them before they are sixteen. The case of the fifteen-year old girl who shot the doctor who was a guest in her father's house presented me with a new criminal charge—carnal mistreatment, or something of the sort. I don't know what this means, but I have made a few random guesses. Now is the season for the so-called "pantie raids" in America, another unique American substitute for love and sex, in which the pants are taken from a bureau drawer instead of off the girl. This is a complete change from the procedure in my own day. Did I ever tell you about Roger Angell, Katharine White's son, now forty and an editor of *The New Yorker*? When he was ten he stole the pants of a ten-year old girl on the way home from school and threw them down the sewer. His teacher told the parents he must be punished and so they made him write the girl a letter of apology. It went like this: "Dear Sara, I am sorry I took your pants off and threw them down the sewer. Love, Roger." He is now married and has two children and it was Roger who suggested to *Holiday*, when he was on its staff, that I write the piece I called "The First Time I Saw Paris." This brought me letters from a sergeant, a private, and a former Lt. Col., now 67 and living in retirement in Florida. He told me about his experiences with the French girls in 1919 in Paris. He got one to bed who was so sleepy that when he asked her if she wanted him to sleep, with her, answered drowsily, "Ça m'est égal." He had better luck the next night with a girl from the chorus of the Casino de Paris, who said, as she took her things off: "Quick, I haven't had any sex since Thursday!" It was then Saturday night. Vive la sport! My two principal girls in Paris forty years ago were Ninette and Ramonde, both of whom would be about sixty now. They married American soldiers and went to live in Chicago and Milwaukee respectively. I presume they buried their husbands long ago with simple ceremonies. My mother was sure if you slept with French girls you got the leaping jitters, and she used to write me this in Paris. So when I came home after nearly two years, I entered the house and greeted her shaking like a leaf, or like the cup and saucer you carried across the stage that time. The French girls know more about sleeping with a man before they are fourteen than the average American woman learns by the time she is forty-four. Science does not understand this problem and has practically given it up. As my cousin, Isabel, once told me when she was eighteen, "They were caught doing what you do when you're married." This is clearly a song cue and may be put in the next O'Hara musical comedy. He is the man who made love a three-letter word, or did he make sex a four-letter word?

I hope you got "The Wonderful O" by now and I am anxious to hear what you think about it when you get time, which ought to be about next August, or three months before my book "Alarms and Diversions" is published. It has the story of the Loch Ness monster, which I finished down here. Love and kisses and all best wishes from Helen and me to all of you!

Forever yours,

P.S. Helen just said, after reading this, that with all the stuff about shooting children, your baby might be born with its hands up.

## TO ALISTAIR COOKE

*West Cornwall, Connecticut*
*August 7, 1957*

Dear Alistair:

I've turned in the first of four or five pieces to the ATLANTIC, called "The Years with Ross," and am working on the others. One of them deals, in part, with the relationship of Ross and Mencken, and I wonder if you ever heard Mencken talk, or ever drew him out, about Ross as an editor. I know H.L. admired the editing of the magazine, but I have no direct quotes. Haven't had a chance yet to read you on Bogart, but am eager to do so. I'm having Charley Morton send me a copy, since I don't subscribe, but expect to when I get around to it. The pieces will start in October. Did you have any encounters with Ross yourself? What do you think of the magazine today. I never get much chance to read it, partly because the stories are too long for Helen's eyes, and my own time and patience are short. Many of the long stories seem deliberately cast in a leisurely mould, and some of them could surely have been done in shorter space and even less literary style. The short piece, or casual, that Ross loved so much seems to be dying, if not dead. He never wanted a literary magazine, but that's what he got. The drawings and captions seem to me to have moved pretty far away from the realistic and recognizable kind of comedy to the elaborate, and sometimes labored, gag, and cousin of the tall tale and shaggy dog genre. My pieces, however, are not critical, in the main, but constitute a narrative of action and dialogue with which I try to throw various lights on Ross, that peculiar genius who was so full of contradictions and God knows what else, wonderful, bad, and indifferent. But the old boy built something noteworthy, and there it stands.

Helen and I greet all the Cookes and send our love in the hope of seeing you in New York where we will spend the last half of September and some of the latter part of October.

Affectionately,

## TO RALPH INGERSOLL

*West Cornwall, Connecticut*
*August 7, 1957*

Dear old boy:

. . . What I would love to get hold of is a copy of the FORTUNE article you wrote about 1934 or 1936. Do you know how that could be arranged?

Would you remember whether Ross fired Hilles, or did you? The story is that Ross just left a note in the man's typewriter. I never met the guy, but most of the staff was cold to me for months because the guy had multiple daughters and I was blamed for ousting him. I think it was Whitaker who got together the big volume containing mistakes I had made as an editor and sent it in to Ross. "Get it out of here and don't tell me what you did with it," he told his secretary, and I never saw the thing. I begged Ross to read it, since I wanted to get fired as an editor, but he wanted to fire Whitaker—I wouldn't let him. I regarded Whitaker as an ally, not an enemy.

Keeping track of all the guys after Hilles is not easy, but I haven't missed many. I support you in your WHO'S WHO contention that you were managing editor from 1925 to 1930, in spite of all the geniuses and central desk Merlins Ross tried out. You don't say what month you started in on the magazine, and I'd like to know that. I say in the first piece I couldn't have survived the early awful months without your patient and sympathetic help.

Love and best wishes to you and yours

As ever,
James Thurber

## TO WOLCOTT GIBBS

*West Cornwall, Connecticut*
*August 15, 1957*

Dear Wolcott:

A wonderful letter and just what I wanted.

We'll be in New York from September 15 until October 1, and I'll be doing the third of my five or six pieces. The tentative sub-titles are: The Walls Came Tumbling Down, The Talk of the Town, The Incident of Sex, The Comings and the Goings, The World Outside.

In the first piece I devote a great deal of space to Ross's theory of and hunt for a Central Desk Miracle Man. This I know well, because I was one of his incredibly miscast hopefuls, the other was Jim Cain, out of 25 or more, including what you call the pinheads. You and White escaped this ordeal. I'll be damned if he didn't even try to bring Ogden Nash in to "run Talk," which I was gunning. I quashed this in one scene and one sentence, as deliberately idiotic as the whole idea: "I couldn't work under an Eastern college man." Three days later Ross scowled into my office with "Goddam it, some of your best friends are Eastern college men." He had been checking. I didn't know what the hell he was talking about, since I was full of Martinis the day he brought Nash in. He didn't know when I was crocked, always thought I had a monthly period, similar to the female one. I went through the strange brief interlude of Thorne Smith, too. I brought my old friend Bergman in to run Talk of the Town, because for two years he had been far and away its best contributor. Ross swore to God he would not steal him from me for Miracle Man, but he did. Bergie is now editor-in-chief of the Philadelphia Daily News. Both Ross and Fleischmann tried separately to get him back in 1934. . . . I was happy to see that your letter is in the very tone and color I am trying for and think maybe I've got. At the end of it all one might easily ask, I suppose, "Who he?"

It will be fine to talk to you and to see any stuff at all that you can dig up. I want to get the taste of Kramer out of people's mouths. Everybody from Shawn down is cooperating. . . .

As ever,

## TO STANLEY WALKER

*West Cornwall, Connecticut*
*August 16, 1957*

Dear Stanley:

What a beautiful job you did for me. The Ross stuff wouldn't stand up without it. I shall not forget the Indian blood theory or Ross's secret love of military systems. Whitaker also subscribes to the military theory, and now so do I. Ross was about as good at devising systems and running the place "like any other business office" as he would have been as a female impersonator. My secretary, who has been through wonderful letters from you and White and Gibbs, with others to come from McKelway, Liebling, and Joe Mitchell, finds it increasingly difficult to believe the magazine ever came out. On the other side of every Ross there was still another Ross. The contradictions are marvellous —he scorned the military as idiots and admired the system, he wanted a perfectly run business office and hated business men, he wanted reporters to take their time, but hired them because they were trained in speed, and in the first few years we put Talk of the Town to bed on Sunday night to shorten as much as possible the gap between bedtime and Thursday morning when the magazine hit the stands. He begged me not to tell anybody that [John] Hersey had spent only two weeks in digging up, writing and rewriting, the Hiroshima stuff. This was clearly not long enough for the first piece ever to occupy the whole book. . . .

Thanks again and my fondest salute to you and your good wife.

As ever,

James Thurber


P.S. I didn't mean to leave out Ed Angly.


## To John Crosby

*Crosby was a* Herald Tribune *columnist.*

*West Cornwall, Connecticut*
*November 20, 1957*

*Mr. John Crosby,*
*NEW YORK HERALD TRIBUNE,*
*230 West 41st St., New York, N.Y.*


Dear John:

Et tu, Crosbe? Last year the AKRON BEACON-JOURNAL practically laid me to rest, reporting that I was not only blind, but "almost entirely bedridden now," and last Friday you said that I am not very active any more.

Now I don't want to brag, but the fact is that three books of mine were published in the past twelve months, the most recent one three days before your piece came out. This is more books than I ever got out before in a similar period. I am halfway through the writing of a book about Harold Ross, and have four other short books in progress, and two plays, one of which should be produced no later than next fall. In my spare time I have written a thousand letters this year, and a little old piece in the front of John McNulty's fine new collection. I did not write [Dick] Maney's book, though. It was done by Tallulah Bankhead. Poor Maney is not very active any more.

My wife says to tell you that if you frequented Tim's instead of Bleeck's, you would have first-hand proof of my activity, but I don't usually get there until after your bedtime. At Tim's I engage in such light pastimes as singing, debating, wine tasting, and chasing girls. A blind man could not catch girls if they didn't squeal, but a chased girl always squeals, and is easy to catch if you are as spry as I am. This keeps me in excellent condition for the daily grind. Say I'm weary, say I'm sad, say I'm growing old but add, I have written 85,000 words in the year now rushing to a close. This in spite of the fact that people keep shoving crutches under my arms and stretchers under my powerful physique. I am happy that the Board of Health has not yet complained about the body of my work and ordered it to be buried, but I suspect every knock on the door and every ring of the phone. Until they do come for me I will keep on going. Right now, though, I must get back to my strenuous inactivity. Love and kisses.

> As ever,
> James Thurber

P.S. I had the crazy notion that George Axelrod had taken over your column. I just never seem to keep in touch any more.

## To "Mary"

*[Last name undetermined]*

*West Cornwall, Connecticut*
*March 18, 1958*

Dear Mary:

First of all, thanks and thanks for the Roquefort book, which we haven't yet had the chance to look at carefully because I do nothing day and night but write about Ross and letters about Ross. I share a little or a lot of every known feeling about Ross, and there are hundreds of different ones. If he said that about constipation to Mrs. Baldridge, it is the most amazing known fact about him, and there are hundreds of amazing known facts. He spelled out the word "sleeping" in front of Helen after he had known her a dozen years. As Russel Crouse said in 1926 and Hobart Weekes in 1938, and forty men in between, Ross turned pale if anyone started a dirty or functional story in front of women. I doubt that he would have used the word "constipation" in front of his last two wives or his mother, even spelled out. . . .

. . . I am writing about the Ross I knew for 25 years myself. I was in Paris in 1918–19, but didn't know him then. Everybody wants to tell me about Ross in the A.E.F. and the S. and S. [Stars and Stripes], from Mel Ryder ("Your friend Ryder is a crook," Woollcott told me) to Guy T. Viskniskki. You left out "The Home Sector," a misguided attempt of the boys to keep the S and S going after the war. Fleischmann put in $40,000 to begin with, and close to a quarter of a million during the next year. According to Jane Grant, Ross did make a lot of money out of "Yank Talk etc." Jane Grant used her maiden name, like Broun's wife and many others, for the S & S boys were surrounded by Lucy Stoners and finally surrendered. Some of them were executed or banished, while others got life imprisonment. Ross was always bothered by hemorrhoids, and that may be what Baldridge means by his taste in ailments. I had the same trouble, like most newspapermen, and Ross and I had the same proctologist, a rectal specialist with the wonderful name of Robin Hood. His choice of professions must have killed his poor mother.

. . . I sometimes wish that of the several attempts to get Ross out of the New Yorker, one of them had succeeded, so that we could have proof of what would have happened without him. The 1933 conspiracy to stab Caesar fell down when almost all of us said we would walk out, too. As early as 1928, and behind Ross's back, Woollcott tried to be named editor in his place. That would have been a national catastrophe. Ross did just as many bad things to him, or more, in the most horrid friendship I have ever known or heard about. It takes up almost a whole chapter in my book. Eight months of writing and research on Harold Ross leave me agreeing with Andy White that "the more light you throw on him, the less clear he becomes." May the good Lord bless and keep you all,

As ever,

P.S. I have facts about Ross, some of them known only to me, which I can't possibly use and I give myself a great deal of leeway at the same time. He could be cruel: "I haven't got time for worms," he said about a young man who left The New Yorker because Ross wouldn't pay him enough money to support his family, and who is now called "the one indispensable man on NEWSWEEK." On the other hand, he was a goddam mother in times of illness and distress to many of us. He did many kind things for people and many coarse ones to them. Here's the worst one, and it fits snugly into the Baldridge picture of him. Cut short by diarrhea at Twenty One, he whipped off his shorts. Next day Winchell printed this line: "The editor of The New Yorker wears no underwear." Ross, who *still* had the underwear, sent it to Winchell by parcel post, told me so himself, gleefully. That was one time he didn't have to ask about what you do for constipation. Winchell printed the most brutal line ever to appear in an American newspaper, the morning after Ross died: "The happiest woman in New York today is Mrs. Harold Ross." This dirty linen outdid Ross's and alienated thousands of people. In their long feud Ross and Winchell often cut their own throats instead of each other's. The six-part Winchell Profile contained some inexcusable stuff. I once asked Sandburg if he had had to leave out any known facts about Lincoln, and he told me several, one of which I myself would have printed. When he was asked why he put his enemy, Stanton, in his Cabinet, Lincoln said, "I would rather have him in the inside pissing out than on the outside pissing in."

What a country! What a species!

## To John O'Hara

*West Cornwall, Connecticut*
*March 19, 1958*

Dear Cousin John:

Most likely we'll never get together again, what with you holed up in Princeton and me going on 64. I look better than ever, I am told, weigh 182, a gain of 40 pounds since 1952, but seem to tire around 5 A.M. after ten hours of drinking. Katharine White will be 66 on September 17, drops things all the time, and falls down. White is just out of Harkness after a brief pneumonia, and Gibbs is out of another hospital after Asiatic, or American, virus pneumonia. At 53 you still have 17 years of writing left ("Thurber calls O'Hara left writer."). Sayre tagged Helen and me for a 1000 fish one night in Tim's at Christmas time and beat it for England and Nora's wedding to a nice guy, Cambridge don, and former war pilot. Not even a card from Joe since. "I had a brainstorm and decided to go to Lapland," he told us, "to write a Letter from Lapland."

I am on my eighth piece for the ATLANTIC—there will be nine there and more in the book to come—and a little tired by it all, as well as disenchanted and disgusted by a long and careful sifting of New Yorker history, Ross's dark side, and the incredible and sickening scandals and slanders that abound from here to 1925, about all of us. I am listing a dozen of them, without naming names, including the one about little old me, which was so wonderfully disproved when my daughter grew up in my veritable image, as Helen Gude once put it, and dismayed and disappointed what I call the New Yorker's scandalmongers and mongresses, the leading ones in the country. Ever fair, I include Ross and me in the first ten. I suppose the mixed doubles champions are Gibbs and Sally Benson. Morris Markey was not only a gossip, but what I call a distorter of untruths, or double-action myth maker. He invented one of the four discrete (but not discreet) versions of the Big Scandal about Ross and his second wife. It's been messy and sticky down where I've been, and increases not my love of my own species.

. . . I want to use, if you don't mind too much, a brief account of the time you wrote Ross saying you wanted either an increase in your word rate or a gold watch. It gave the little boy a lot of infantile fun digging up a watch on 5th Avenue for $16—or was it $8?—and having it inscribed, "To John O'Hara, from The New Yorker, 25 West 43rd Street, Bryant 9-8200." . . .

. . . with love to you and Sister (if I may get fresh) and Wylie, if she's still speaking to me, from Helen and

        Yours truly,

                        *&*   *&*   *&*

*May 6, 1958*

Dear old chap:

. . . We all decided that Ben Hecht was right, for once, when he said in his book about MacArthur that Charley thought he could act the same way in his fifties and sixties as he had in his thirties. Wilson even agreed on this, as he put away his highball and reached for another. I'm older than he is but can keep on going longer. I went on too long Saturday night. I found that whiskey keeps your mind off your problems. I mean my mind off my problems, which are mainly thoughts and feelings of what Tillich of Harvard calls "the ultimate concern". Even if death is 15 years away, it is just around the corner. I heard Tillich on radio one day and he's no help for many reasons, one of which is that he pronounces "faith" and "face" the same way, so you can't tell whether the Chinese are losing face or faith or both.

The goddam book on that crazy man Ross is shaping up, I guess, and I can even see the light at the other end of the tunnel. I am not going to put any further strain on you, about the whole thing, or any part of it, except to send you a carbon of what I am including in one installment or two, from your letter. You can then add or subtract or detract what you want. I have just done this with a carbon I sent to Gibbs today. The touchiest folks are the Whites. I see by the papers that "From The Terrace" will be turned in by you August 1st, the precise date I have given Little Brown for my book, but since it has so many drawings and things it's too big a mechanical job to come out as early as yours. I can't remember just what I had in mind the other night, but I guess it was the short piece Liebling wrote for the back of my book called "End Papers". I gave up my desk job here in 1935 to free lance and so I have written to Stanley Walker and McKelway and Shuman and now Liebling to get their ideas about the editing of the magazine from that year through the war. And it's a mixed up story too. Walker lasted a year and then McKelway took over as fact editor and became managing editor and Shawn took over from him and so on. The story is as mixed up as any New Yorker procedure, filled with "Then he did this" and "No I didn't" and on and on. We had been talking Saturday night about your old love and mine, Alva Johnston, for whom some of those new reporters in the Thirties didn't have as much admiration as we do. I make up for this, however, by running not only what Liebling says about Alva's method in his multiple part profiles, but by running Stanley's great praise of Alva, Ed Angley's "He was the Best", and a lot more, to say nothing of my dedication. What got the boys down was Ross's low pay for everybody (Liebling never got more than $60 a week on drawing account), in spite of his reputation for "standing up for the writers". During the war he put through a $100,000 bonus for contributors and Liebling got $5,000 for his five years of war reporting. The story of Ross and money is really something and I now have it all, having just had lunch with his tax man, and clearing up the whole history of Harold Winney, which is more than something. . . . Trying to make a sound and readable installment out of what all the editors and reporters have told me is quite a task, but it's coming along.

All good luck to you and Sister and "the Terrace". Did you hear about my projected novel based on a return to Columbus, Ohio, three years ago? It is called "The View from Pompous Ass".

>As always,
>Jim Thurber

P.S. I don't know how many people will be speaking to me when the book comes out, but that's what I get for trying to be a biographer and historian. . . .

*Mr. John O'Hara, Linebrook,*
*Pretty Brook Road at Province Line Road,*
*R.D. # 2, Princeton, N.J.*

## TO WOLCOTT GIBBS

*West Cornwall, Connecticut*
*March 24, 1958*

Dear Wolcott:

With a thousand things to read and twenty people to write to, I can't get around to everything, I'm afraid, including your three-part Profile on A. Woollcott. I'm doing a whole piece on the strange Ross-[Alexander] Woollcott friendship, if you could call it that. . . . I was amazed by the childish attitude toward The New Yorker of so many of Woollcott's pals after the Profile came out. I know that [Noel] Coward turned against Ross, and you, and for some reason me. All I ever did to [Woollcott] was to break a dinner date at Wit's End, made one drunken night in Tony's, but Helen and I later dined with him there and saw him in London and in Boston, and in New York after that. All he said about the broken date was, "All you New Yorker people are depraved."

I seem to remember that Woollcott saw and approved all the proofs of the Profile. Then the Lunts stopped their subscription and all hell broke loose. I'll never be able to understand the Woollcott cult, but there it is, like Father Divine's and Oom the Omnipotent's. It's a curious thing that, in their tearful adoration of Woollcott, people mainly come up with stories of his insults, cruelty, and professional rudeness. Maybe his was a circle of masochists.

I think that White and I were at the Round Table only once or twice, and I don't think you were there often, either. Our group was not composed of "tablers," as Margaret Case calls them (she said Katharine was a Barnard girl). We were not a cohesive group, but had social osmosis, or something. Do you remember when Martin and Mino took over the old MacDougall restaurant on 46th St. and set up a "New Yorker Room" on the second floor? Trouble was, none of us, as I remember it, ever went there.

I hope you are back on your feet. I think your reviews have been wonderful.
Love to you all

As ever,

## To Groucho Marx

*April 9, 1958*

Dear Groucho:

I am now working on Ross number 9, a long and, of course, penetrating piece about his friendship, or whatever it was, with the man he called "that glib son-of-abitch" and "that emotionless fish," the late Ross-hater and Marx [Brothers]-lover, A. Woollcott.

What I'm agoin' to do, pardner, is send you a carbon of this piece in its last, or next to last draft, in the hope that it might move you, through some emotion, or all emotions, or none, to write me a few comments on those two crazy and remarkable dead men, or on anything else, even Krasna.

This here, now, total recall memory of mine has brung back, sharp as a dagger, a photograph, torn in four pieces, that the late Morris Markey showed me one day when I could still see photographs, so it had to be before 1941. I think it had been taken by a news photographer in Los Angeles, and it showed Old Vitriol and Violets, a man as fragile as nails and as sweet as death, seated in a big chair and surrounded by the four Marx brothers, all standing. Trouble was, les vêtements de Harpo étaient dérangés, deliberately, and in such impish fashion that his what's-its-name was clearly visible. I thought it was funnier than hell, and a terrible thing to do to Aleck, and I'm damned if that doesn't describe almost everything that happened to him. Do you remember the occasion of this photograph, and is there a copy of one with its fly not open? I won't describe the torn one, at least not directly or by using names.

I would like to have your opinion, and Harpo's if he can still whistle and make signs, on both Ross and Woollcott, singly and together. You come from common stock, but you have a mightily uncommon mind and talent. I toss out these compliments to win your love and devotion. To me Woollcott was such a pompous Grand Marshall of his own daily parade that all men wanted to put banana peels in his path, and all the ladies he praised and insulted in the same sentence wanted to pick him up when he fell. The famous story of the Gibbs Profile is dealt with in my piece, with quotes from Gibbs. He didn't know the Lunts had stopped their subscription to the New Yorker when the

Profile came out, but he did know that [Noel] Coward turned against him and Ross and me, too, because I wore the red rose of Ross and not the white orchid of Woollcott, I guess. Gibbs was also bawled out by Beatrice Kaufman, Edna Ferber, and Neysa McMein.

Me, I don't care who attacked Ross, and I attack him some myself, the way I would any other pageant, or monument, or magician. And if Woollcott couldn't take attack, then nobody could. The letters of the glib son-of-a-bitch definitely prove to me that he loved the clashes and friction and insults in his life, because they gave him a chance to write letters which might just possibly live, like the ones Henry James wrote to H.G. Wells, and those that probably came out of such literary feuds as Dickens versus Thackeray, and Henley versus Stevenson.

Mercy, how I do go on, and the night is falling. Love to you and your ilk, if any . . .

> Affectionately,
> James Thurber

## TO ST. CLAIR MCKELWAY

*West Cornwall, Connecticut*
*April 14, 1958*

Dear Mac:

. . . You're absolutely right about the two kinds of managing editors (how Ross hated to use titles!) and he wouldn't have wanted Ik [Shuman] to edit well, even if he could have, because he was supposed to be executive genius. Ross at first didn't mind the pieces Ik wrote under the name of Clark Sherman, but it finally irked him that "He thinks he can write."

Frances Clark ("Somehow named Frances Clark," as Margaret Case puts it) seems to have been originally called Marie Françoise Elie. Can't you just hear Ross trying to say "Françoise"? He would have made a man's name out of it.

. . . It was about 1933 that Ross, who had his eye on some amiable dame, a lady of what he would call society, said, "Goddam it, if you have an affair with a woman like that, she would expect to be set up in an apartment on Park Avenue." I said if he propositioned her that way, he would probably scare her off, because the thing wouldn't be a careless rapture, but a goddam common law marriage, if he didn't look out. "I know how to play my cards, Thurber," he said.

I had put in piece 8, and then took it out, the story of Ross's finding out about homosexuality in women, from a wartime buddy he met in Grand Central. "He says women like love to go on for hours, and you know how men are—one, two, three, and they're back at the Stork Club."

In dealing with a composite picture of Ross in one future piece, I have Stanley's great study of Ross as an Indian, Maggie Case's "the face of a clown," Ben Hecht's "burglar-faced," Frank Adams' "Well, you know how Ross looks *not* tobogganing," and this morning I woke up with, to me, the authentic notion that Ross was the only visible poltergeist I ever knew. Piece 8 tells how he knocked over two drinks, one after the other, that Paula Trueman was trying to enjoy at Tony's, with me.

"One, two, three to us all," cried Tiny Jim.

Affectionately,

P.S. I'm going to telephone [Peter] Arno to see what Ross said to him about that drawing. I wrote him a letter three months ago, but artists don't write letters. I know what you mean about the drawing exactly. It's what Percy Hammond said about a play based on a real murder. "Just because a thing happened is no reason it's true."

&. &. &.

*West Cornwall, Connecticut*
*April 18, 1958*

Dear Mac:

I certainly could use a few hundred batted off words about the men's doubles that time when you and Ross faced Luce and Ingersoll. The last version I got was from Ingersoll and I did not know about that wonderful line "The inaccuracy is part of the parody." Gibbs has written me how he made up salary figures for TIME, Inc. by hitting the typewriter keys at random.

I can't help thinking of Ross's face if the shoe had been on the other foot (can't you see him stare at that idiom!)

I want to use the gist of that clash in an installment tentatively called "Crises." The theme song for it will be Ross's famous hymn "Nobody knows the trouble *I've* seen, not even Jesus." The crises, so far, are: the Severance half million dollars law suit against us for insulting the Fred F. French Building; the various times that Ross's job seemed in peril, especially after the debacle of STAGE Magazine; the incredible case of Harold Winney who took Ross for $50,000 over a period of years. The amount has been estimated between

$17,000 and $125,000, but I have it from the best source, Ross's tax man; the time the Sherry Netherland threatened to sue because we said the floor maids wore Chanel No. 5; and so on.

. . . The Woollcott Profile crisis comes in another chapter, and so does the time Ross found I was playing with dolls and the time I was playing with actresses. What got him most, in my case, was my buying a .38 at Stoeger's when I was blind. "There's your gun, Jim," said Pete De Vries, who was with me. The man behind the counter was holding it within a foot of my face. I told Ross Helen promptly hid the gun. I still don't know where it is.

"One, two, three, and back to bed," cried Tiny Jim.

As ever,

P.S. I also deal with the time the bank robbers stole White's car. "There's your man, officers," Ross told two cops gleefully. I was with White at the time. White also got into something when his name was forged to checks. I was threatened with suits by Charles Yale Harrison for "The Secret Life of Walter Mitty"; "The Macbeth Murder Mystery"; and something I left out of the soap opera pieces when a Chicago reporter let me down. During that phase Ross kept calling me "defendant." None of these came to anything.

Without using [Richard] Boyer's name, I have to tell the story of his alleged letter to the TIMES and TRIBUNE beginning, "I am an American Communist." I have done no real checking on that yet. Last night I dreamed that you and I were trying to sober up Dylan Thomas in Ross's office before he got there.

## TO THE RONALD WILLIAMSES

*Paris, October 10, 1958*

*Mr. Ronald J. Williams, The Bermudian,*
*Hamilton—Bermuda*

Dear Ronnie and Janey:

. . . It has been a bad year for many of our friends. . . . This year the great shock was the death of Gibbs. Only ten days earlier he had written me a cheerful letter, probably the last one he ever wrote. Bob Coates got drunk at a party and dislocated his thumb, and his wife has arthritis and bursitis and gall bladder. His first wife died two months ago. So it goes.

Helen has been down for a week with a virus and sinus, but is up and herself again. We have had a wonderful time in London and in Paris both, but nevertheless I finished the last six chapters of the Ross book. I mailed them a month ago. I have been four times on Television, and God knows how many interviews we have had with newspaper, magazine and radio people. Four young people, two men and two women, took over our suite here last week, and did an hour long Television film for the Canadian Broadcasting company.

Three weeks ago we had dinner with Adlai Stevenson at the apartment of Johnnie and Madeline Miller, and had a wonderful time with the old boy, who said he wants to visit us in the country, when we get home. He is an old friend of Rosie's father-in-law, who was his State Commissioner of Parks.

We are very anxious to hear from you and to know how everything is going. I implore you both to take wheatgerm pills, and also glutanic acid pills, and live longer. They have kept us going through four months of the hardest work I have done, and with more parties, luncheons, and dinners than we have had in America in ten years.

Is our God-daughter still in love with the same man, or with a Portuguese Trotsky-eyed?

Love and kisses to you all from both of us.

> As ever,
> James Thurber

## To Donald Ogden Stewart

*Paris, October 14, 1958*

*Mr. Donald Ogden Stewart, 103 Frognal,*
*London N.W.3, England*

Dear Don Senior,

Young Don will have a hard enough time on the *New Yorker,* my boy, you can count on that. There are what we call girls all over the place, most of them young graduates of Eastern Colleges for women, as well as Duke, the University of Kansas, and Hardin Simmons. However, the one that works for me when I am there, the Kansas girl, told me that she is a prude and says that is the trend now. In our time, the trend, if I may use so mild a word, was otherwise. You may remember a chap called F. Scott Fitzgerald, who introduced us to love and gin and the way to write "The Great Gatsby". I once wrote a piece about Scott, known to Mencken as "Fitz", for the Reporter. We had stayed up from 10 pm to 9 am, drinking and calling on a girl, a "good girl" for he had asked me, at midnight, if I knew any good girls. Helen, then a spinster, said,

when I phoned her: "You and Fitzgerald both? You must think I am crazy."
And Honeycutt said the same thing, but Paula Trueman took us in. "I sat three
feet from him, and three million miles away," she told me later. "All he wanted
to talk about was Zelda."

I haven't written about Thomas Wolfe, even though he broke Fitzgerald's
record by arriving at our apartment in New York at 6 pm and staying until 9
am. Around 4 in the morning, he said: "Why doesn't somebody get me a
sweetheart?" I explained that in America, north of the Carolinas, the boy is
supposed to do that himself. I understand that he and Scott had a hell of a
night in Paris about 1930, and I can well imagine that it was just that kind of
night. "I am a taker-out, and you are a putter-in," Scott told him, and then
later wrote his daughter: "Wolfe's secret leaks at every seam—he had practically nothing to say." Ross said the same thing about Woollcott, but added
"and he says it all the time."

You have not asked for information about Ohio State University, probably
through an oversight. So here are the facts. O.S.U. has not developed a writer
since Nugent and Thurber, but it has found out how long a bee can live in a
vacuum and how to cure soft foot in swine. They are now working on crabapple scab, but so far have succeeded only in spreading the disease to the cows
and horses in the animal husbandry building. Professor Neff has sued the
University on the ground that he has crabapple scab, too, but his wife says he
always says that. Jesus, Don, I wish that Bob [Benchley] were here to get in on
this. How do we keep on going without that laugh of his?

The other night we went to hear Larry Adler, who was a great success, because he is truly a great musician, and he knows it, too. Various angels must
have turned over in Heaven when he suddenly put in a bar of the "Tennessee
Waltz" when he was playing "St. Louis Blues". I am afraid I shall go to my grave
known as the man who loved the "Tennessee Waltz". Actually, my favorite
song is an old Fraternity one that begins: "When D K E has gone to Hell, and
other frats are there as well".

Let me end with a remarkable true story of Paris life. Ten days ago, we had
dinner with Marc Simont, who illustrates my fairy tales, or whatever they are,
and he introduced us to a man named something like Ivan Dubrowsky-
Williams, whom he had previously described as an underground agent for the
French during the occupation, a man who had been captured and tortured by
the Germans. We expected to see a man broken in spirit and health, but he
was wonderful. The first thing he said to me was "You are a Deke, I believe." I
cleared that up for him, but told him about you and my other great Deke

friend, Jap Gude. Jap was at Brown and the underground agent was at Middlebury, Vermont. You may not know the expression, but in America we often say: "It's a small world." What do *you* often say, as Noel Coward would put it?

Our love to you all,

As ever,

James Thurber

## To Art Buchwald

*Hotel Continental,*
*3 rue de Castiglione, Paris, 1er*
*Paris, October 20, 1958*

*Mr. Art Buchwald, The New York Herald Tribune,*
*21 rue de Berri, Paris, 8°*

My dear General,

The trouble began at the battle of the Antietam, or Sharpsburg, as the Confederates call it. General George B. McClellan, in command of the Federal Forces, should have stayed at Gaines Mill, but his spies, who must have been rebels, told him that Lee had 44 million men. So George got the hell out. "He saw lions in the road," writes Douglas Southold Freeman, in one of the two best accounts of the battle. The other was written by a Major Polofrey, of the army of the Potomac. Mr. Freeman was not born until some years after the battle, at which Major Polofrey was taken prisoner by the Southerners.

The single thrust into the Ruhr is simple, in comparison with what happened, and didn't happen, on September 17–19, 1862. (There will be a lot of inaccuracies in this communiqué, because I have lost my source books.) In the first place, Stonewall Jackson got lost at the battle of White Hollow Oak (or a name something like that) because he made the mistake of asking a Northern farm lad directions. General A.P. Hill, known as Little Ambrose, was 24 hours late in taking over command of the Confederate Right at Sharpsburg, and McClellan could have turned that flank, but somebody told him that Hill was already there, with 280,000 men. Jackson, meanwhile, held the Confederate Left in a cornfield, and this troubled McClellan as much as it would have troubled me. You don't just go banging into cornfields, especially if your spies in the employ of the other side, have told you that 634,000 men are waiting for you there. So General McClellan delayed too long, and the battle has passed into legend as one of the most controversial in history.

Major Polofrey, writing in the 1880's, complained irritably that all Southern writers wrote about the battle romantically, claiming that the Confederate Center was held by six farm hands, a little boy with a 12-gauge shotgun, and a bishop's spunky niece. I would be sore, too, General, if I had been captured by one of that brave band.

Thirteen years after the battle, General McClellan was still writing about it, trying to explain what had not happened, and why. He was writing an article about the Antietam for the *Century Magazine* when he died.

My own contribution to the literature of this famous struggle has been the searching light I have thrown on the number of future presidential candidates who took part in the battle. General McClellan was one of these, and so was a young Captain, in charge of coffee supply, named William McKinley.

Whether Jackson was actually in that cornfield, or not, is still a debatable matter. Don't take the word of people that call you up on the phone about it, or send you unsigned postcards. Be skeptical, General, and deny everything.

You will remember that President Lincoln removed McClellan after the battle. He was replaced by General Burnsides, who was then replaced by General Hooker, who was then replaced by General Meade. It was General Meade who was in command at Gettysburg, and damned near had his center knocked off by General Pickett.

At Appomattox, General Lee met his old West-Point classmate, General Meade, and said to him, "General, I did not remember you as having so many grey hairs." "General, you put them there," said General Meade.

We don't fight wars, or make peace, like that any more, General.

> Respectfully yours,
> James Thurber

⁂

*Hotel Continental,*
*3 rue de Castiglione, Paris, France*
*Paris, October 21, 1958*

*Mr. Art Buchwald, The New York Herald Tribune,*
*21 rue de Berri, Paris*

Dear Art,

After I wrote you the enclosed communiqué, I saw by the papers a reference to controversial battles long ago and far away, specifically the much debated behavior of General Longstreet at Gettysburg. So it goes, and has always gone, from the Civil War to the behavior of General Eisenhower in the Great Invasion.

I have straightened out a great many of these military debates, but nobody listens to me. You may remember that the conduct of the Little Big Horn was investigated by Congress. The big question was then, how come Major Reno and Captain Benteen couldn't find the battlefield, although they kept hearing the shooting.

Some day, you should look up in your history books, and then write about a famous peace time controversy, the Twenty-One Gun Salute, fired in honor of a French President by American war-ships in the harbour of Le Havre, in the late Nineteenth Century. The cannons were not only unfortunately loaded, but were aimed right at the city, with the result that the whole waterfront of Le Havre had the hell blown out of it. The families and descendants of those who were killed were recompensed by our Congress for decades, and they still get money, for all I know.

I don't defend my own record as a General, which led to my Army's pet name for me, Old Bluff and Guess.

Love and kisses,

    As ever,

    James Thurber

## To Eugene King

*December 17, 1958*

*Mr. Eugene King, 108 Manhattan Ave.,*
*Manhattan Beach, California*

Dear Mr. King:

Mark Van Doren showed me your outline for your paper on seasonal cycles when I was at his house recently and I said I would answer you for him and for me. I can't remember just why now, except that the subject of human cycles interests a lot of us. I just read in the papers that peptic ulcer increases in incidence from November to April. I should think the literature of psychiatry might deal with factors in manic depression that would interest you. Many of these cycles seem to reach the manic phase in fall and winter, but I don't know what data there is on this.

Everybody has a cycle of ability, but I know of no literature on this subject.

It may have little to do with seasonal changes, but with unknown factors. I was interested when Mark read your notes because I had recently been thinking about the subject. I think that every writer has a cycle of creativity but it might take the next 50 or 1,000 years to figure out its nature. Maybe surgeons should not be allowed to use surgical instruments during their clumsy phases, whatever that might be, and whatever might cause them. I don't think you could leave out the slang expressions, such as "All my fingers are thumbs today." Maybe it is all a matter of Labor Day from April Fool's Day. Anyway it's a hell of a big subject and if you live to be 100 you might work it out. An aged psychiatrist said to me a few years ago, "We don't know anything about the manic depressive cycle except that there is one. We don't even know much about the commonest of cycles, the menstrual."

All this is just in passing, the passing of a few drinks at the Van Dorens', that is. I was finishing a story at the time and was much too busy to reply.

Best wishes in your researches and a Merry Christmas.

>Sincerely yours,
>James Thurber

## To the Ronald Williamses

*West Cornwall, Connecticut*
*December 19, 1958*

Dear troubled children:

If you're a letter writer you write letters, and you both came through splendidly, at last. We were happy as heaven that R.J., the indefatigable ancient, is on his tennis court feet again, and that Janey sounds as bright and beautiful as ever. But we were depressed by the tidings of Dinah Jane, flusher of women's hats and high-jumper, and Peter Drax, high diver, cliff hanger, and Captain Blandish redivivus. I propose to lecture them a little. After all, as godfather to Dinah, I am entrusted with her spiritual welfare, whose whereabouts are now in jeopardy. It goes to show the Americanization of Bermuda—"Throw that knife at my feet or you're chicken, then jump from that bridge, and then see how far you can drive with your eyes closed." All this is known to psychologists as the Death Wish, a human phenomenon bound to flourish in a generation brought up on permissive education and self-expression. When Sue Markey, aged five, overturned all the chairs in her parents' house, said they were horses, and then, to prove it, filled the parlor with horse namure she had got in the road, her mother was prevented from punishing her because her father said, "Don't interfere with her childish fantasies." That was a generation ago, before the spoiled American child began killing his parents because they refused him the car, or told him to do his homework, or merely said, "Shut up." I figure that 15,000 families will be wiped out by toddlers and teenagers in the next ten years, and it's usually the fault of the goddam parents. What this nation needs for sheer survival, is a sense of responsibility in its children, a getting away from mindlessness and the I-couldn't-care-less attitude. When Mrs. Kermit Roosevelt began a radio talk by saying, "There are eighteen million American children without police records," it could scarcely be called cheery news.

. . . It is shameful, and funny in only a horrible kind of way, that American adults give their toddlers power of attorney over their lives, so that any day now an eight-year-old girl, after her first affair, may say to her parents at dinner, "Lousy lover." I wrote you five years ago that the next war will be the war between adults and children. Everytime a little child comes to our door I am afraid he will say, "Death or treat."

The four teenagers who recently hit a tree at eighty miles an hour are too representative of our childish desire to get nowhere fast. Their interest in life seems to be located south-west of the heart, with all communications severed with the mind.

Dinah, who has long been aware of my adoration of her mother, once said, in a typical Palmer-Williams gush of emotion, "Mother, why didn't you marry Uncle Jim?" In a few years somebody may ask her that about herself. The purely chronological answer is, "Because I didn't meet him until I was sixteen and I was married and pregnant." Falling in love with love is playing the fool, says the song, and a recent survey of 200 girls who quit high school for the "freedom" of marriage, reveals that exactly 100% were disenchanted and wish they had waited. Of course, Dinah has beheld the truly great happiness of her own parents and knows that her mother was married when, in worldly experience, she was about fourteen. But she also must know that premature marriage is about as comfortable and free as waltzing with Long John Silver. The modern American child owes its youth not only to itself, but also to its nation and to the world. The hard-working Russian children have a right to be disdainful about ours. After Dinah, God forbid, has been living for a year in a backstreet in Maracaibo, disenchantment would come a little late. I can see him now, the husband, chewing a broken toothpick, slapping his bare belly, burping, and boasting, "I can open more oysters in one hour than Pedro could open in a month." When everybody else is exploring outer space, this guy is trying to reach the bottom of the ocean. You cannot expect a man to be a good husband or perfect companion when he spends most of his life under water making goo-goo eyes through his goggles at enormous fish. The world is full of wonderful guys, worthy of the girl Dinah Williams could be if she gave herself half a chance.

So much for today's lecture, except to say that Uncle Jim waited 39 years for the right girl, who had waited 32 years for him. She had a chance to marry an oiler and wiper, but she was too proud and sensible, and now she has a man with 23 books and an over-active thyroid. A Merry, Merry Christmas to you all and God bless you.

As ever,

## To Mary Tower

*West Cornwall, Connecticut*
*December 30, 1958*

*Miss Mary S. Tower, 7(½) West 75th Street,*
*New York 23, N.Y.*

Dear Miss Tower:

Well.

If I am right about the typical American girl, you are her in italics, restless, capable, dissatisfied, ambitious, and likely to be among the first to reach the moon. You may have to do stenography up there. I had to show your letter and credentials to Miss Terry at The New Yorker, because she hires girls, always about your age, but not very good spellers, pretty, clean, and soon married. There are not millions, or even dozens, of competent American women stenographers. Most of them are pretty bad, can't even spell "all right," and can type whole sentences that mean nothing. Katzenjammer, Miss Terry calls it. The American girl does not make a very good nurse, either, compared to the Canadian, for instance. She often gets far in the movies before her career is ended by murder or other misfortunes. I don't know what is going to become of her, but I wish her well. I have a 27-year-old American girl daughter, who wanted to be an F.B.I. agent, an actress, a writer, and is now a housewife with two children. Most American girls are happier with their second husband than with their first, until they begin to wish that he were dead and they were in the movies, to quote Jack Roach. I once told an Ohio State girl in Columbus she had little chance of getting anywhere as a writer in New York, and she turned out to be Ruth McKenney. When Vincent Price was 22 I told him he had no chance in the theater or the movies. I don't tell anybody anything any more, except, in your case, stay away from Tasmania. It has endemic goiter, bad for girls' temperaments. Miss Terry says absolutely no. Her pool is full of girls, and The New Yorker shies away from women editors. It has two too many, that is, just two.

A Happy New Year, anyway, and let me hear what happens to you. I wouldn't have the slightest idea where to send you.

Sincerely yours,

James Thurber

## TO WILLIAM SHAWN

*Thurber's submission is of "The Last Clock: A Fable For The Time, Such As It Is, Of Man."*

*West Cornwall, Connecticut*
*January 12, 1959*

*Mr. William Shawn, The New Yorker,*
*25 West 43rd Street, New York, N. Y.*

Bill, old fellow:

Take this one up tenderly, for it's my heart. I worry a little bit, foolishly perhaps, because of my fear that some of your dedicated editors may not so much read this as process it. I have processed it myself, screened it, and rewritten it five times from start to finish. I don't have to tell you, a musician, that the repetitions, a word that is anathema to The New Yorker boys and girls, are not only intentional, but have been worked out with exceeding care. I won't bother your staff by pointing out the indirect influences of Browning's triple rhyme scheme (though I use no actual rhymes), and what Leonard Bernstein might call the architecture of the andante cantabile. The boys and girls will understand this, but someone is sure to point out the use of "so clogged" and "and so" in one sentence. Tell them the hell with it. Some keen mind may even suggest variance for "took the stand" and "took the witness chair." Tell them to forget it. If anybody says this is uncharacteristic and familiar, I shall kill him.

The immediate inspiration occurred to me when I was dozing during the fourth quarter of the last Giants-Browns football game, when the announcer said, "With only 35 seconds left to go, all the Giants have to do is eat up the clock." For further implementation on such phenomena the kids might read "The Dynamics of Insight" by Alexander Reid Martin, or, better yet, not read it. There is nothing in this piece I am unaware of and, for Jesus sake, don't let any of the keen minds point out that there is illogic in the statements of some of the specialists. I don't have to tell you that this is a moving study, moving and a little frightening, too, of what modern mummum has done, and is doing, to muxx up the condition of man. Incidentally, The New Yorker review of "The Human Condition" should easily win the Pulitzer Prize for dullness.

Affectionately,

J. T.

## To Roger Angell

*The rejected short story, "The Other Room," was published in* Harper's Magazine *in 1962.*

*West Cornwall, Connecticut*
*January 21, 1959*

Dear Roger:

I wouldn't worry about that "that." That that "that" should form a serious problem is not conceivable. I know this, that that "that" that we are discussing has long been a concern of mine. I should have written about it when I wrote about the "which" which drives writers, readers, and editors crazy. Have you ever noticed that "that" is one of the small words that resolutely refuses to lend itself to rhythmic repetition? It is a tomtom that doesn't belong in the orchestra.

Now that "The Other Room" is being enlarged and shaped up a bit for another periodical, I have got over some of my incredulous indignation. This morning I discovered that Henry James went through the same thing, on a tremendously magnified scale, when his immortal "The Wings of the Dove" was rejected for serialization by a magazine, probably the NORTH AMERICAN REVIEW, which ran "The Ambassadors" from January through December one year. The following is from James's Preface to "The Wings," written after his 1902 anguish and extremity: "There is fortunately something bracing, ever, in the alpine chill, that of some high icy *arête*, shed by the cold editorial shoulder; sour grapes may at moments fairly intoxicate and the story-teller worth his salt rejoice to feel again how many accomodations he can practise."

I have had many discussions, here and there and over there, about the function of the editor, and I line up always with the writer. I was really saddened when Bill Maxwell said to me two years ago, "I am a dedicated editor." There went a dedicated writer, because you simply cannot be both. The dedicated writer instantly realizes that certain colloquial impurities, and I don't mean those enclosed in the quotes of direct dialogue, are a sacred right of the individual writer, and changes that make them correct can only be regarded as profanation.

Aw, shut up, Thurber, why don't you lecture somewhere?

Regards to you all.

> As ever,
> Jim

*Mr. Roger Angell, The New Yorker,*
*25 West 43rd Street, New York, N. Y.*

## TO THE RONALD WILLIAMSES

> *February 3, 1959*
> *Air Mail*

Dear Ronnie and Janey and all the children
who have not run away to get married:

Will you please let us know what happened about that character from the fringes of Joseph Conrad's lesser and earlier work and your emotional offspring? Here we sit getting no word from you or from anybody in Bermuda because nobody down there can write or will write. It's an island where people go to spend their sunset years in rocking chairs drinking rum straight out of the bottle, or is it?

We have had a crowded life since we got back from France, Helen making over our house so it looks like the House Beautiful and me doing a lot of writing and getting under foot. Do you remember what Dorothy Parker once said about a play "The House Beautiful?" She said " 'The House Beautiful' is the play 'lousy.' " In November my thyroid kicked up but now it's lying flat again like a horse's ear. We just found out that "The Years With Ross" has been taken as a dual selection of the Book-of-the-Month Club for June.

More than 35 pieces like the enclosed woman's are sent to me during the Christmas season and I'm just now getting around to them. This was sent to The New Yorker, and rejected because it's simply not done well enough and because it's not our kind of thing. As one of the editors said, we admire the lady and the America she writes about and the rest of them for their courage but our feeling does not extend to the writing of the piece. You know all about it, Ronnie, so you can tell her in your own charming and sympathetic manner, like a mongoose rejecting a cobra's essay, or vice versa.

Love and kisses and for god's sake write to us.

As ever,
Jim

*Mr. R. J. Williams, The Bermudian,*
*Hamilton, Bermuda*

## TO THE E. B. WHITES

*March 16, 1959*

Dear Katharine and Andy:

To the astonishment, the delighted astonishment, of Doctor Sullivan and Dr. Cameron and the scrub nurse, Helen's cyst, "large grapefruit" category, turned out to be benign. It took five days to learn this, during which, of course, I went crazy. I had a couple of double Old Fashioneds every day at the Algonquin but my main escape was narcosis as the profession calls sleep during battle or tremendous strain or unbearable anguish. My poodle, at my age, also went in for this escape during thunderstorms, wedging her head under a bed and passing out. The danger, I told her, is not nature but Man, to which she replied, "Who do you think is making all that racket up there. Angels?" She feared a man the size of a mountain, but I fear men the size of men. Anyway, the relief was—well, I don't have to tell you people, although I think we should have a parlor game some night matching terrors, real and imaginary. Helen and I have had fourteen operations, the two of us together, since we were married. In 1940 she was whisked to Doctors for galloping anemia and they thought she was a goner but I told them she had a hit on Broadway. This time I felt the Book-of-the-Month would pull her through. She has no record of familial cancer, but neither did my mother's ancestors and both my mother's sisters died of it, one at 24, the age of Milly Theale, alias Minny

Temple (Henry James's beloved cousin) and the other at 64. I was desperately afraid that Sullivan had run a quick test because he was an hour in coming to see me after the operation. I was also afraid the test would be made in an outside laboratory, and the mixing up of specimens in such a case is common— I use one doctor's word for it. Fortunately Doctors [Hospital] has its own laboratory presided over by my favorite pathologist, a Philippino, named, beautifully named, Mr. Trinidad. There was every sign of malignancy, but it didn't mean anything, as you can tell now by Helen's amazing recovery, resilience, and state of mind and body. You can also tell because the doctors, who dodged me for five days, now hang around for half an hour, smoking cigarettes, discussing the dangers of America's appalling and careless use of cortisone, the slow disappearance of phosphorus from the earth, one of the necessary elements in the creation of protoplasm—we won't have to worry for another million years though—and the proud fact that Doctors Hospital does 1700 breast operations a year, or more than any other American hospital, because of its celebrated Dr. Adair.

During all this Nugent was on the loose with his hired Cadillac, with built-in bar containing every known liquor and every known pill according to Jap Gude who had to ride around the park with Elliott to get him off my back one day. He phoned the hospital night before last at 11:30 and was quite a problem. . . . He has made a three and a half hour recording or what he calls a musical comedy. . . . In it a man of 62 had to have a girl. He is played, in Elliott's fantasy, by Fred Astaire, who wants to see how far he can spit and to dance with his shoes off. The heroine is Ingrid Bergman and the babble runs on endlessly, some of it brilliant, almost all of it formless. When I am plus 60 as I was in 1952 I have a lesser formlessness, but it is of the same general pattern. Elliott always says, "I have broken my writing block." I had dreamed last night that I was Elliott's writing block, a broken headstone. If Andy still has his this means he can write on it. Everything is asked backwards.

Your flowers were absolutely beautiful and still are.

. . . Doctors are always saying to us, "How do you account for your recovery?" I always say I was just about to ask them the same question. Except that my grandson's tonsils are as inflamed as Margaret Speaks' used to be in the Village days. Things are straightening out here, including the weather.

Helen and I thank you again for the flowers and for your letter and send you our love.

As ever,

## TO WILLIAM THURBER

*April 9, 1959*

Dear Old Bill:

Helen is recovering very rapidly and we're going back to the country the day after tomorrow. I was glad to hear about your interest in health and physical measurements and also to realize that you have given up the idea of digging for uranium in the snow of Canada. I was afraid you might decide to buy up old Sioux war bonds with counterfeit wampum. You think of more remarkable ideas than a poet or Walter Mitty. Lawn bowling is a purely English pastime and there are only one-half dozen courts or lawns in all the United States, one of them being at Yale. I doubt that the Puerto Ricans or any other West Indians would know what you were talking about, and I don't see how you would work a concession. Anyway, I'd love to listen in when you use your nervous Ohio accent on a West Indian's broken English. How about trying to interest the Eskimos in wood burning sets, or selling Adler elevator shoes to the pygmies? We'll talk about it when you reach New York. I'll be glad to help out on your vacation cost.

Jule Styne has given up "The Wonderful O" but another firm is working on it. The book has not yet been dramatized or the songs written so there's no hurry and I will get you some money in it if it looks good and gets finished. The same for The New Yorker play which I hope to start soon.

Helen joins me in sending love and best wishes.

As Ever,

*Mr. Wm. F. Thurber, 212 E Frambes Ave.,*
*Columbus, Ohio*

## TO ROGER ANGELL

*"The book" is The Years with Ross.*

*West Cornwall, Connecticut*
*July 2, 1959*

Dear Roger:

. . . The book has brought me the oddest experiences of my life, and runs the whole gamut of human expression, for the strangest assortment of reasons, appreciation, jealousy, envy, hatred, and even insanity. Of fifty-five books we sent to those mentioned in the book, about forty-six did not even acknowledge them. Many of my closest friends seem to have clammed up, as if the book were somehow a personal affront, but the men and women who knew Ross longer than I did even are uniformly enthusiastic. So also were Edmund Wilson, McKelway, and Pete De Vries. I can't escape the uneasy conviction, probably absurd, that the word went out from somebody somewhere not to mention it to me in writing or in person. One friend said, "Do you know what the dullest pages in the book are?" Seems they are those "written by Ross." Another friend, a famous writer, said, "Do you realize that your book is autobiographical?" I said any child could tell that from the title. It is utterly amazing to me that, even to minds I have considered intelligent, I have to explain how and why the book was planned. I have to say that I am the only person alive or dead, who started out as Miracle Man, personally on bad terms with Ross, then became a copy editor, a holder of the artists' hands, close friend of Ross, and both writer and cartoonist for his magazine, which surely puts me in the position, to quote McKelway, Nunnally Johnson, and Stanley Walker, of being the ideal one to take on the terrific task. "Both as a literary portrait and a history of journalism it will certainly become a classic," Edmund Wilson wrote me. Bob Sylvester in the Daily News wrote, "It is as dull as The New Yorker—almost, that is." One lady reviewer revealed in herself something dark and fanged and malevolent, coiled in her wit. Antipathy to Ross and The New Yorker is awful when it flashes its fangs, and proves Andy's statement: "Whoever puts pen to paper writes about himself, whether he knows it or not." The death pangs of comedy show up, but only here and there, thank goodness, although many miss the basic planned comedy of the book, I don't see how. There is a lot more to the story of its making, but I'll keep that for my memoirs. It is not my best book, and was not intended to be, since it is entirely expository and in no sense creative. Its popularity is that of magnificent freak, the story of the Great Illiterate of Sophisticated Literature. If the president of U. S. Steel were a midget, if the line coach of the New York Football Giants were a pretty girl, we would have the same freak appeal. I have done the same thing only twice before, in the soap opera series and the story of the Loch Ness monster. Critical estimate at its best often shows up abroad, because of perspective, I guess. Fortunately, most reviewers see at once that it is an affectionate appreciation of Ross and the magazine, a tribute, even a Valentine. Never get into biography, it throws too harsh a light on the prevalence of lunacy.

I have got more letters from "Friends, Romans, Countrymen" than from any other piece I ever wrote, excellent letters, one of which I am enclosing. Send it back when you have time. I now get thirty letters a day and wish I were what Ross once called a "herman," meaning hermit.

All the best to you, Roger,

P.S. Ken Tynan is reviewing the book for The London Observer, Rebecca West for the London Sunday Times.

*Mr. Roger Angell, The New Yorker,*
*25 West 43rd St., New York, N. Y.*


## To Elliott Nugent

*West Cornwall, Connecticut*
*July 7, 1959*

Dear Elliott:

. . . I am an admirer of Meredith Willson's knowledge of, creation of, and dissertations on music, having followed him for years on radio, but I am by no means keen about his ability to write comedy or turn out a book in the key and pitch of our play. If you listened to his dialogue in "The Music Man" as carefully as I did, you will remember that when the music ceased it was all pretty flat stuff, a touch corny and old-fashioned. In such songs as "You've Got Trouble" the weakness was covered over by the music and vitality and the skill of Bob Preston. His dialogue needs seventy trombones to lift it up. I would hate to see "The Male Animal" lose tone and quality the way it did when it was mangled on Playhouse 90. What Danny Kaye might bring to it, except fame and his so-special talents, I don't know, but I'm caught between shudder and high expectation. In places he goddam near ruined "Walter Mitty," with some help from Sam and Sylvia, but in his best scenes his great comic skill and fine mimicry lifted it high. Fabray is so purely television to me, I can't judge her as Ellen, and maybe Eddie Albert could play down the hick in him and play up the football hero and steel executive. I am afraid the seriousness of the play would be largely lost, if we don't look out, as in the ghastly movie musical. Tommy can easily be ruined, and with his part, the whole play, and Griffith showed how this murder can be accomplished in that fearful attempt to bury the social import of the play. It was kicked around like Mussolini's body.

The swift decline of comedy now, emphasized by the loud and the farcical on Broadway, is the result of a panicky attempt to yell down the demons of life and fear, instead of fighting them with angels. In 1951, in the Providence Journal, I predicted that humor would be dead in America in five years, and it did become at least moribund. So I say let's watch our step. Talent can be corrupted by cleverness and a good play can become a tale told by an idiot.

This is the year of Thurber projects for the stage, all of them converging at once. Jimmy Stewart has shown an interest in the Haila Stoddard revue made up from stuff of mine, with Buzz Meredith as director, but this wouldn't reach Broadway this year. I have the Ross play in mind for the winter and might be my own worst competition. Somebody is always threatening to bring "The Thirteen Clocks" to Broadway and "The Wonderful O." Who is this man Thurber, anyway, a corporation?

Love and kisses, and see you soon.

> As ever,

## To Ann Honeycutt

> *West Cornwall, Connecticut*
> *September 21, 1959*

Dear Nettie,

... The year 1947 was one in which I was not in a good temper, partly because of many letters from strange or helpless women, many of them named Virginia or Bailey, or both. During the war, the completely crazy women wrote to me, but since the Ross book came out I've had the most wonderful letters of my life from the warmest women in the world, between the ages of 19 and 90. You're not jealous anymore, but most of them begin "I love you, I love you." The only dissenting voices were raised by Rebecca West in England who was sure she knew Ross better than I did, and one Dusk Powell, in whose wit lies coiled something fanged and malevolent. What's the matter, do you suppose—didn't Ross ever take a flying tackle at her?

We are here until the end of the month and have looked for you twice at Tim's. All my old girls have TEmpleton numbers now. Shades of Chelsea!

Love from us both.

> As ever,
> Old Me

*Miss Ann Honeycutt, 165 East 60 Street,*
*New York, NY*

## TO CHARLES VAN DOREN

*Van Doren, Mark's son, had just testified before a Congressional committee regarding the current dishonesty of quiz shows.*

*West Cornwall, Connecticut*
*November 3, 1959*

Mr. *Charles Van Doren, 399 Bleecker Street,*
*New York, N. Y.*

Dear Charley:

Any time you want to come to my house and sit in the library, just come on in—the latch string is always out. Like the pluperfect subjunctive, it's quiet there and never crowded, except for old dreams and pleasant thoughts and high hopes and, to be sure, regrets. I'll match regrets with you any day and beat you, but, would we through our lives hell forego, quit of scars and tears? For God's sake, No!

Leaving real life out of it, the character who had the hardest time, was poor old John Marcher in Henry James's "The Beast in the Jungle", to whom nothing whatsoever happened. In this week's New Yorker (adv.) I say that "he bore the deep incurable wound of emptiness." On the other hand, everything has happened to you, and don't let anybody tell you you haven't come through it with battle flags flying.

I think the years to come will be even better—maybe a hell of a lot better than they would have been if all hell hadn't broken loose for you.

You had to take the rap too, while a lot of others escaped notice; some of them dressed in women's clothes. I like to think of women in our country as unafraid to come forward and take it. After all, it was Jefferson Davis and Ulysses (Homer's, not America's) who dressed in women's clothes.

In my house, we still have the same old love for Charlie Van Doren as ever, and it seems damned silly to have to say so. We are a nation of actors, and there isn't anything I, myself, wouldn't have done to put the accent on knowledge and learning in order to attract the so-called human eye away from the sadism of westerns and cop programs.

Keep pitching, and as old Ross used to say: Take it in your stride. Don't give it a second thought. Let the dead past bury its dead, to coin a phrase. Full speed ahead and damn the torpedoes. And God bless you.

As always,
James Thurber

## TO BURGESS MEREDITH

*Meredith was directing the revue,* A Thurber Carnival.

*West Cornwall, Connecticut*
*November 4, 1959*

*Mr. Burgess Meredith*
*Spring Valley, New York*

Dear Buzz:

That was a very productive afternoon we had with you boys, and we cleared up a lot of points, but managed to get off on the wrong foot about the way to put over the fables, I think.

I am absolutely sure that each fable we use must be presented as clearly as possible by direct reading with a background of music, not jazzed up. It must be the temper of the times that has caused our musicals on Broadway to get 140 trombones into the act, all playing so loudly you can't hear anything. The quality of the fables is lyrical, and we saw what happens when they are drama-tized on Camera Three, which put so much music into the fable of "The Cricket and the Wren" that the rhythm of the fable was shattered like a dropped glass, and the effect was lost. Each solo, both vocal and instrumental was well done, but diluted the story and obscured the moral.

I would have "The Truth About Toads" read aloud slowly, not fast, with a background of muted music that segues from "Bye Bye Blackbird" into "we are poor little lambs that have lost our way" from the Whiffenpoof Song. And then back again to "Bye Bye Blackbird".

If you have the orchestra leader coming in with "squawked the macaw" you break the lyric in two, and confuse the listener. Furthermore, none of the fables is done with any sense of jazz tempo in mind. You might as well try to jazz up "sunset and evening star".

The only way to prove this is to try it out.

Just a thought for today. Love from us both.

As ever,
James Thurber

## TO MR. CANTOR

*[First name undetermined]*

*West Cornwall, Connecticut*
*March 10, 1960*

Dear Mr. Cantor:

Ours is a country of rumor and report, as we all know, and not of record and research. I have never in my life said, written, or even heard of anything about Will Rogers and anti-Semitism. I am sorry you didn't see the piece in the New York Sunday Times of November or December 1958. Mort Sahl and Steve Allen and I and several others wrote about the state of humor, and I remember nothing whatever about anti-Semitism by any of us.

The point I have kept making about Mr. Rogers is this. He was not a genuine political satirist or a sound philosopher and the record of his writings stands there to prove it. Read his book called "Letters of a Self-Made Diplomat to His President," which ran serially in the SATURDAY EVENING POST in the middle Twenties. He kidded around with the awful Mussolini and wrote this: "Dictator kind of government is the best kind of government there is, if you have the right dictator, and these people have sure got him." That is from memory and may be slightly inexact in a word or two. Will Rogers was a kidder, not a philosopher or a satirist. He was a great friend of presidents and vice-presidents, and senators and congressmen, and it doesn't take courage to kid your friends. I have nothing against him as an entertainer, and a loyal American, but I am afraid that we have come to depend too much on the aw shucks philosopher in this country.

Thanks for your kind words about the "Carnival."

Sincerely yours,
James Thurber

## TO RICHARD GETTELL

*In January, Thurber, as script doctor, accompanied* The Thurber Carnival, *a revue composed of his prose and drawings, on a tryout tour of six cities.*

West Cornwall, Connecticut
March 29, 1960

President Richard Glenn Gettell,
Mount Holyoke College,
South Hadley, Massachusetts

Dear President Gettell:

Your letter of March 18th found me down in bed with a severe attack of what might be called, I suppose, Carnivalitis, or I should have replied promptly, thanking you and Mount Holyoke for your decision to honor me with a degree of Doctor of Letters. Mount Holyoke happens to be, as of course you know, the most important of American colleges for women to me. I shall have been married twenty-five years to the former Helen Wismer this June, and could scarcely have got through that stretch of years without her help. Your letter served as a spur to my recovery, and today for the first time I am able to deal with my correspondence after a month of enforced idleness. Nothing could please me more than to be able to accept the degree in person, but long ago Helen and I made arrangements to sail for England in May, and various commitments there, including the London production of our play, prevent me from changing my plans. I should understand it thoroughly if this unfortunate arrangement impels you to withhold the degree until another year. Since I am sixty-five and blind, I cannot count with certainty on being able to meet future engagements. In any case, the offer of the degree has lighted my heart and I shall always cherish it. Helen and I both send you and Mount Holyoke our love and best wishes. Through her I have met many other Mount Holyoke graduates and each of them has increased my affection and admiration for the college. I understand why Gertrude Stein said it was her favorite of all American colleges for women.

Please forgive me for the delay, which I am sure you will understand. Helen and I survived, somehow, an extremely arduous road tour lasting eight weeks and taking us to six Middle Western cities. The success of the Carnival in New York is owing, in no small part, to a Mount Holyoke girl who was, as every member of the company has repeatedly said, a fountain of strength on our long pre-Broadway trip. Once again, then, my profound thanks and sincere good wishes.

Cordially yours,
James Thurber

## TO KENNETH TYNAN

*Columbus, Ohio*
*April 5, 1960*

*Mr. Kenneth Tynan, The New Yorker,*
*25 West 43rd St., New York 36, N.Y.*

Dear Ken:

We came out here by train last Wednesday night and, oh, wonder unmixed, we are going back to New York alive tonight. It was a series of ordeals this time all in one day, a luncheon at the faculty club at which I sat on the right of President Novice Fawcett (shake hands with Wragford Novice), and then the dedication of Denney Hall, the new Arts and Science Building, named in honor of one of the truly first-rate scholars, teachers and gentlemen of his time, which was my time in the university too. Nugent and I had him in mind when we wrote the part of the Dean in "The Male Animal." Having been sick in bed for a month, I didn't have time to finish my speech and learn it too, so Helen stepped into the breach and read it for me, in a very moving performance; the day was hers. Then came the reception and for some reason there wasn't a dry palm in the damn line of 70 women I shook hands with. My daughter tells me that all girls have moist hands nowadays on account of everything.

Not long after I talked with you on the phone, somebody connected with that Madison Square Garden affair phoned me and asked if "The Last Flower" could be read that night and I said I was sure arrangements could be made with the producers of the play, and I believe they have been made. I suggested Elliott Nugent, who read it so beautifully on television last year, but if Lauren Bacall wants to do it, that is all right with me. I will leave it up to the Committee to decide.

Your perfect picture and description of Truman Capote was properly chilling. Instant Woollcott is exactly what he is. . . .

As always,
James Thurber

## TO THE RONALD WILLIAMSES

*West Cornwall, Connecticut*

*April 29, 1960*

Dearest Children,

It was just two months ago to the day, February 29, that we wired Janey happy birthday, and said we would write you about our "smash hit." The play [*A Thurber Carnival*] had opened on February 26 and it is still truly a smash hit, since all reviews except one in The Nation were highly favorable. The day after Janey's birthday I came down with the flu, followed by a general let-down after eight hard weeks on the snowy road, working day and night to get the play in shape in Columbus, Detroit, Cleveland, St. Louis, Cincinnati and Pittsburgh. Then Helen came down with the flu and exhaustion too and we are just now pulling out of the shadows. At least five hundred letters have piled up, Helen answers seven phone calls a day, or seventeen, and life is now three times as crowded as it was. It is not easy for a man who will be eighty in a little more than fourteen years. I can just hear Ronnie wailing, "He doesn't know anything about age. I'm fifty-three years old!" Well, it's all a matter of genes and diet, my boy and girl, as I learn by following the radio programs of Dr. Carlton Fredericks. It now seems that my black lock indicates that I have slowed down the aging process. You do this with a heavy intake of the Vitamin B complex, which stimulates the pituitary gland. That happened to me nineteen years ago with heavy injections of B complex, but the continuance of the black lock indicates I am still holding my own better than most. This is tricky, because it can give you the illusion of being as young as you were in 1936 or thereabouts. Remember that far away year?

I hope "The Battle of the Sexes," the Peter Sellers film based on "The Catbird Seat," gets to Bermuda, for it's just one of several things that have happened all together. Another is a long playing record of "A Thurber Carnival" which is selling well, and we are going to send you one as soon as we can. But first of all we want to find out how you all are and we also want you to come up and see the play, but not in May, because we are going to spend that month in Cornwall lying down, and practically hiding from the world. We have been here in New York for the past month and we've got to slow down, black lock or no black lock. I am in close touch with the lunatic fringe too, for everybody on that wide margin calls up writers and playwrights, or writes them asking for something. We think of you all the time and hope you are all well and as happy as anyone can be in this troubled world. . . .

With all my love.

As ever,

*West Cornwall, Connecticut*
*June 16, 1960*

Dear Middle-Agers:

New York City has 144 fires every day, so Helen and I have escaped being in darn near a million since we first came to the awful city. We got out of this one by the grace of God and the skin of our teeth, and though it was no fault of ours we have paid the woman $2500 to replace her living room furniture and to get her out of our hair and off our backs. Right now we never want to see New York again and we shall never go to strange apartments with strange people. She had come up to us at Maria's, our favorite restaurant. We had met her husband, Lee Berker, at The Ledgelets, and she said Arthur Kober lived in her apartment building. He came to the party with his 18-year-old daughter, and there were eight of us in all, but Helen and I were the last two. Helen had gone to the kitchen to help the woman clean up and had stepped into the maid's bathroom there when I discovered a chair was on fire in the living room. When Helen came out smoke and flame separated us and the woman, after turning in an alarm, went down eleven floors and left us there. Why she didn't get us out, God only knows, but she didn't panic, and I had been through fires before, but Helen hadn't. What scared us to death was the fear of each of us that the other was lost and dead. This is all confidential, as we never want to mention it again.

Well, the young ensign sounds better than the google fisherman, and it's a blessing Dinah didn't marry at fourteen. The Ladies' Home Journal recently ran a story called "Guess What, Mom—I'm Married!" They are all doing it, but Jap Gude's youngster, Johnny, another godchild of mine, phoned long distance to say the same thing and ask for money, but then his girl beat it. What a species! Early marriage and almost continuous pregnancy have now become escapes like liquor and cigarettes and Rock-'n-roll. But *toujours gai,* what the hell! We wish the young couple a long and happy life and we hope to be there for the wedding, to see you all, and we send you beaucoup love and kisses and messing around. (A new song says, "Don't knock rock-'n-roll, it's a rockin' good way to mess around and fall in love.") It was wonderful to hear from Janey and nice to know that Ronnie has got religion, given up drinking and smoking, and hopes to spell Canon Sullivan in the pulpit. That ever-lovin' Ronnie is a born parson, and we should all have known it. Amen.

As ever and ever,

## To Cass Canfield

West Cornwall, Connecticut
May 2, 1960

*Mr. Cass Canfield, Harper & Bros.,*
*49 East 33rd Street, New York, New York*

Dear Cass:

I agree with you that one publisher from now on is the best thing, and it still leaves me with a total of four. Others keep calling up, too. I think maybe we should proceed one book at a time, though, and I don't know which I will finish first, "The Nightinghoul" or a new collection of stories and essays, tentatively called "Lanterns and Lances". I have about fifteen pieces finished for it and should finish five more this spring and early summer. That ought to bring it above sixty thousand words.

Planned publisherhood is not the easiest thing in the world, as you know. It's like planned parenthood—you can never tell what's going to happen between covers.

Our best to you and all the rest.

As ever,
Jim Thurber

## To Cyrus Durgin

West Cornwall, Connecticut
May 18, 1960

*Mr. Cyrus W. Durgin, Music and Drama Editor,*
*The Boston Globe, Boston 7, Massachusetts*

Dear Mr. Durgin:

Various persons in recent years have come to me with ideas for a Thurber revue, but Haila Stoddard's was the best basic outline of suggested material. She spent two years on my work and can tell me more about it than I want to know. The credit for arrangement, or routining, and the idea of Don Elliott's music belongs largely to [Burgess] Meredith, but he and Haila and I, especially he and I, did a great deal of changing, putting in and taking out, for eight weeks on the road. I dramatized two stories of mine which were later abandoned on the road, "Am Not I Your Rosalind" and "The Departure of Emma Inch," and a couple of fables were taken out and two were written by me, but not used at all. I wrote "Gentlemen Shoppers" four years ago for a revue and put it in this one, and also insisted on dramatizing "Walter Mitty." On the road we tried out the drawings of "The War Between Men and Women" with somewhat longer captions, and all of us loved it, but audiences did not get it, so out it went. I did a great deal of rewriting, and there were wonderful suggestions from Meredith and Haila and many of the cast. It was Paul Ford's brilliant idea to start the second scene of "Mr. Preble" with "Let's go down in the cellar," the biggest laugh in the show. I had that line in, but it was preceded by two others. The playwright has to see instantly: when suggestions are sound, or great, or bad. The title "Word Dance" was my own, like the lines used in it, but credit for arrangement goes also to Meredith, Elliott, and Starbuck, the choreographer. On the road I also wrote three new skits, one of them "Take Her Up Tenderly," the last thing to go in the play, in Pittsburgh. Two long ones, "Cocktails with the Captain" and "A Song of Love" were original skits written with the whole cast in mind, but not completed in time to rehearse them for New York. Thus I have a basis for a new Carnival some day. I would say that this Carnival is definitely a collaboration of minds and theater know-how working well together. Some things, like "Casuals of the Keys," were rewritten four or five times. I am not a writer, but a rewriter, usually rewriting slowly, but in the theater you've got to work fast. I learned to write for the theater twenty years ago with "The Male Animal" and 35 to 40 years ago with one-act plays and four musical comedy librettos at Ohio State University. It gave me the hang of what goes and what doesn't go, and the profound difference between the printed page and the speaking stage. Many of my stories were written with playable dialogue in mind. I always dictate dialogue to get it right. Adapting it for the stage is thus made easier than is the case of purely literary conversation.

The figure in the carpet of my kind of comedy is a varied study of human confusion, American style, and everything in the Carnival reveals this figure —confusion about sex, love, marriage, history, geography, education, language, and literature, with special jibes at our carelessness of observation (as in "The Pet Department"), our drinking, hasty judgments, and haziness about the values of life in all fields. The point is to do all this as hilariously as possible and, indeed, no critic has actually detected the serious figure running through it all. My serious viewpoint of life, in fact, is often lost sight of, for the devices of laughter are deceptive. Comedy should always overlay the message, and not vice-versa.

Comedy must have something to say, both basic and recognizable, about what we call the human predicament. The trouble with humor and comedy in recent years has been its descent into farce, a generally over-strident effort to entertain mindlessly. In these skits and fables, as in "The Last Flower," and "The Male Animal," I have striven to combine humor and seriousness. It is, as Churchill would say, a considerable undertaking.

I see no merit whatever in vulgarity or dirt, and have always believed that the writer who fails to see the humor inherent in love, sex, and marriage misses half of what they mean. A loss of comedy, as in many modern dramas, leaves a residue of brutality and obscenity. In reaching for shock, both form and content are lost or confused. Comedy with a message is the hardest thing to write there is. If you lose the recognizable and the real you end up with the lugubrious. If Lauren Bacall ran into my arms (ah, unlikely dream!) crying, "I am the late Jake Kilrain!"—well, maybe we ought to have a national playwrights' competition to see who could handle that combination of the physical and the metaphysical of desirable woman and reincarnated prizefighter. It is the kind of fancy that my own imagination rejects.

Much of the writing of today seems to me without the form and content that grow out of thought, contemplation, and loving care. We are in an Oral Culture now, a period of babble in which the mind turns too easily to reminiscence, and the tongue outruns the mind. All writing must reflect the state of culture, civilization, and society, and their main faults now are emptiness, decline, and sickness.

What seems to me to be mainly wrong with the writing end of the theater now is a compulsion toward the kicks of climax and culmination, rather than a writer's proper concern with the slowly developing processes of fulfillment and completion. We have become jet-propelled Mary Celestes, and seem to have abandoned the old necessary disciplines. It is all a reflection of an era of fear and hysteria moving too fast toward no goal in particular.

As for women, I believe and hope that they will take over civilization, unless they wait too long. It couldn't happen to a nicer or a saner sex. All best wishes to you, and I hope this answers most of your questions.

Cordially yours,
James Thurber

## TO JAMES POLLARD

*West Cornwall, Connecticut*
*June 2, 1960*

*Mr. James Pollard,*
*The Ohio State University,*
*School of Journalism, Columbus 10, Ohio*

Dear Jim:

First, here are my efforts to answer your questions in order.

1) I try to make as perceptive and helpful comment on the human predicament as I can, in fables, fairy tales, stories and essays. I am surprised that so few people see the figure of seriousness in the carpet of my humor and comedy. My favorite recent book is "Further Fables for our Time," which strives to say things sharply, but entertainingly about men and women, Man and Woman, politicians and people. I am proud that it won the award given in 1957 by the Fund for the Republic of the Ford Foundation for the work in the entire field of imaginative literature that had done the most for the cause of liberty and justice. It was selected by a committee that included two professors, a poet, and a librarian, and represented the country at large.

2) I have no idea what things of mine, if any, will be remembered after I am dead, and I don't give it much thought. You can get any kind of opinion you want about the drawings. On the whole, my work, as writer and cartoonist, has been as well received in England as here, whatever that may indicate.

3) I let other people pick my best single work, and never speculate about it. "Further Fables for our Time" is the best from a social conscious viewpoint, I guess, but I should also include my original book, "Fables for our Time." I have often said, "My best book is the one I'm working on."

4) As Thornton Wilder has said, we are all influenced by other writers to begin with, but must throw off that influence as we mature. I had to throw off the influence of Henry James and Joseph Hergesheimer, and the tendency to write such a Jamesian sentence as this: "First of all, it occurred to me, there was one thing, to begin with, to do," and such a Hergesheimerism as this: "He remembered a girl in a boat, on a river, when it was summer, and afternoon."

5) When I went to the New Yorker in 1927, after ten years of newspaper

writing, I learned a lot from E. B. White's fine clarity and pure declarative sentences. The way I write now, however, is absolutely my own, I think. . . .

Good luck and best wishes, Jim. It was nice to see you again.

As ever,

Jim

## To Roger Angell

*West Cornwall, Connecticut*

*July 1, 1960*

Dear Roger:

I don't anticipate any quarrel over this piece, which has taken me a long time to write and rewrite. It is timely, in its way, because of the dolphin story. If anyone down there says that the dolphin and the porpoise are identical, tell him to go eat a grampus. Such a person would identify the wombat and the bandicoot with the American badger.

Did you know that most of the animals of Tasmania, and even the toys manufactured there, have goiters? So do many mammals and even fish in and around the Great Lakes. Our thyroid glands need iodine because, before our species came ashore, we played around with a spongy creature full of iodine. I myself didn't, though, since I have insufficient iodine, having probably said to her, "Ah, shut up, you're full of iodine."

As ever,

Th

*Mr. Roger Angell, The New Yorker Magazine,*
*25 West 43rd Street, New York, N. Y.*

## To the Mark Van Dorens

*West Cornwall, Connecticut*

*August 25, 1960*

Dear Mark and Dorothy:

. . . After taking the show to nine great American cities, I have come home from Denver feeling that la chute, as Camus calls it, is well under way. (I see now why he translated "The Last Flower" into French.)

As I may have told you, the ATLANTIC has taken a piece of mine called

"The Case for Comedy, or The Defense Rests, but It Can't Sleep," one of half a dozen pieces I have written about the decline of humor and comedy. Today I sent to the Sunday TIMES "The State of Humor in the States" which will appear a week from Sunday in the drama section. It reports my encounter at a Denver garden party with a charming young lady named Cynthia, who said to me, "Edgar Allan Poe and Hemingway are intellectual. I *can't understand them!*" (Please help yourself to my italics.) When I got up off the floor, I asked her what writer was non-intellectual and understandable. "Why, W. Somerset Maugham," she said through the smoke and fumes. To this I could only murmur, "Jack go stumble, Jack go slow, Jack jump over the afterglow." The intellectual Mother Goose is becoming as hard to understand as a Child's Garden of Verses. At dawn this morning I thought that a species living under the threat of obliteration is bound to produce obliterature. Of course, my present sense of terminality may be a passing phase of gloom. Andy White once rebuffed H. G. Wells in the New Yorker for saying in his last years that he had a terminal feeling about the world. White, who has had a terminal feeling since 1912, alleged that Wells's depression was caused by a sense of personal termination. But as long ago as 1933, when I interviewed Wells in New York, he said, "Get out of this city. It will be the worst place of all to be when the collapse of civilization comes." I saw him for the last time in 1937 in London, but all he talked about was his physical symptoms and the incompetence of medical men who "can't even stop pain." In that year we saw him at various restaurants with this or that charming young woman. The English writer (cf. Bertrand Russell) believes, rightly, that the propinquity of young ladies arrests the aging process. But it doesn't stop pain.

In recent years, two or three writers have timidly mentioned to me the need for a book about death in a nation now massively depressed by the thought of it, but disinclined to discuss what that German theologian at Harvard called the Ultimate Concern. . . . What brings this up right now is that poem you read me by the valiant Beverly Bowie, and the recitation in "Sunrise at Campobello" of Henley's Invictus. The book shouldn't be called "The Terror of the Shade" or even, I suppose, Henley's other line, "The Ruffian on the Stair," though it is a favorite of mine. Maybe "The Tenant of the Room."

I learn that readers avoid Gunther's "Death Be Not Proud," Mrs. Wertenbaker's "Death of a Man," and a book by a woman cancer victim called "I Die Daily." People just don't want to contemplate death through prose. A psychiatrist recently reported that almost no dying person will face objectively the idea of death. Conrad's line in Lord Jim, "The best that a man can hope for is to go out nobly in the end," lacks the curious comfort that any poetic line carries, such as "finds and shall find me unafraid."

I don't think it is wolves that plague me, but ghouls, and the fool's gold is a necessary part of my peculiar measure and balance.

The ghoul's fold, and the fool's gold turns once again to lead.

I'll be seeing you. Love from us all

As ever,

## To Charles Bidwell

*West Cornwall, Connecticut*
*August 26, 1960*

*Mr. Charles E. Bidwell, Department of Social*
*Relations, Emerson Hall, Harvard University,*
*Cambridge 38, Mass.*

Dear Mr. Bidwell:

I find myself in strong disagreement with the particular phase of your project that concerns my fables. My old professor, Joseph Russell Taylor, Ohio State English Department, once said: "Intellect is the conventional part of imagination." However that may be, I regard intellect as exploratory and analytical, but in no true sense creative. At least, it has nothing whatever to do with the creative process that produces imaginative work. My chief antipathy to your plan is aroused by your assumption that the humorous, the moralistic, and the sad are separate values. I have devoted a lifetime to trying to show that humor covers morals, just as, by definition, it is part and parcel of pathos, or sadness, if you will. Sid Perelman's favorite moral is my "Youth will be served, frequently stuffed with chestnuts." You don't have to ponder that very long to see that it combines your falsely disintegrated values. I have never written a fable that was nonsense, and I take it that you regard humor as just that. I have written four or five articles recently for the ATLANTIC, the New York TIMES, and other publications, sharply mourning and attacking the decline of humor and comedy in a nation that never had much of either, basically. I bewail the forces of thoughtlessness that would create a fragmentation of tragicomedy, for this trend shows up in the state of our theatre and of television and of the novel. Recently, a youngster of eleven, who shows evidences of a wild and misaimed tendency to combine intellect and creativity, took apart a fable of mine called "The Princess and the Tin Box." He objected to my invention of "aluminum silicate," for his intellect was fighting his less well developed creative sense. I told him there was also a thing called cranium penetrate, but that it is becoming rare in America.

. . . I cannot believe that any educational purpose would be served by taking my fables apart and rebuilding them in the way you suggest. I shall not, of course, withhold my permission for you to make the attempt, but I will insist that you let me know the results. . . .

Smashing a sorry, or starry, scheme of things and rebuilding it nearer to academic desire seems to me indeed a questionable undertaking. Several softheaded American women have taken to rewriting certain poems to make them *more cheerful!* One victim of this vandalism was "Villanelle of Horatio Street, Manhattan," which I wrote for the New Yorker in 1927. Wrote one of the softheads to me: "Where you put rusty bedsprings in the street, I have substituted lovely flowers."

Why not see if your students can write fables of their own, or even try to discover, first of all, whether they know what the fables I have written are about. I regret to report, after taking "A Thurber Carnival" to nine American cities, that only New York critics perceived serious intent in my humor and comedy. To most critics elsewhere I am a Pixy or a zany, so it is comforting to have the stuff understood by certain persons in New York, England, and other places on the continent. We are said to have 250,000 intelligent readers of books in America, but I regard that as an extravagant figure, in a country that buys 900,000 cigarettes a minute, uses 65,000,000 prescriptions for tranquilizers every year, and consumes eight times as much vodka now as it did ten years ago.

Any exercise of the human mind whatever, even though misapplied, is an advance of a sort, I suppose. Maybe your students should try rewriting "The Waste Land" to get some cheer and zing into it. Good luck, anyway.

Sincerely yours,
James Thurber

## TO THE PETER DE VRIESES

*The De Vrieses had just lost a 10-year-old daughter to leukemia.*

> *Algonquin Hotel,*
> *59 West 44th Street, New York 36, N.Y.*
> *September 21, 1960*

Dearest Katinka and Pete:

There aren't any words of comfort that don't sound tiny and trivial. Pete told me on the phone once that infinity isn't out there, but in our pocket, and I knew that was true and kept thinking about it. Strength comes finally from God knows where, but it always does for a woman and a man like you two.

You have to know that Helen and I have been in despair and hopelessness with you. There has not been a day or night that this wasn't true. I know that calling you would be nothing more than a reminder. I have known what the valley and the shade are since the day the doctors thought Helen would die, a year ago last March.

I know that the despair and hopelessness seem too deep to get out of, but I also know that great people get out of it. There is and will be no day or hour of our life that you cannot call on us for anything whenever you feel that you want to. You are precious and important to Helen and me. I know that the four of us belong to those that stick through everything. You have our everlasting love.

> Jim

## TO MALCOLM MERMORSTEIN

> *Algonquin Hotel,*
> *59 West 44th Street, New York 36, N. Y.*
> *December 5, 1960*

Dear Mal:

I am afraid neither Helen nor I was impressed by your play, and I always come out with exactly what I think. I decided on that method more than thirty years ago when manuscripts were first sent to me for my opinion. Insincere praise or hopeful talking around the subject does no good. It is not easy for a writer to get help from another writer, because the only sound criticism is self-criticism, and you must learn that the hard way. . . .

A friend of mine recently sent us his first novel to read. He knows Hollywood studios and Hollywood parties the way you know backstage, and what he gives us is authentic, dreary, and dull. At one long Hollywood dinner party we are told that the Andy Johnsons had decided to skip the party and so far they are the only two people in the book I like. It was the kind of party I liked to skip in Hollywood. I would also like to skip overhearing a scene backstage between any man and woman having an affair, she calling it a ball, and the whole business of career and children coming up.

I have written a series of pieces in recent years about the theatre, comedy, and so on, deploring the present tendency of almost every writer to find the immoral person, the uncourageous person, the person who raises his voice and yells, interesting. This tendency has given us some of the dreariest plays and novels of the century, during the 1950's. I cannot find myself caring what happens to your people and there should be in every play and novel characters one likes and is interested in. Maybe it is because of my own personal life and principles that I lose interest in the man or woman who gives up easily. For God's sake, let us have, now and then, characters of "gay strength and bright courage," even in this crapulating era. I said in the November ATLANTIC that Tennessee Williams and his colleagues are not so much expressers of their time as expressions of it.

It is the tendency of a writer who has not been at the game too long, or rather long enough, to use expressions like "Pansy!" and "Son-of-a-bitch!" and to hurl "Jesus!" and "Christ!" around as if yelling and anger and expletive were the secret of the dramatic. An old sage I used to know, who knew as much about writing as any man, said, "You can't get expression into a story with exclamation points." Volume of sound is not passion, either, any more than italics are. I think one fault of yours is basic: the belief that in writing about the theatre, backstage and on stage, you are writing about what you know best. But it is the people in themselves and not the setting that count. Harold Ross of The New Yorker used to say, quite rightly, that every newspaperman wanted to write about the city room, and every writer wanted to write about a writer's life, and that they almost invariably turned out to be dull.

This, then, is exactly what I feel about "Matinee Day." If the lady at Columbia is giving you help on the play and knows what she is about, you still should consult your own self primarily, and nobody else at all. I often throw out things of mine that I have worked on for as long as two years, because, after putting them aside, I now really know the good, and the bad, and the indifferent. Writing is a headache any way you look at it.

Helen joins me in affection and best wishes.

As ever,

James Thurber

P.S. One of the most striking arguments I ever heard in real life between a man and his wife became wonderful and theatrical, in the best sense, when the husband resolutely refused to yell back at her, and she finally screamed, "Don't you dare keep your voice down to me!"

*Mr. Malcolm Mermorstein, 443 Prospect Street,*
*Nutley 10, New Jersey*

## TO PEGGY WOOD

*West Cornwall, Connecticut*
*December 8, 1960*

Dear Peggy:

I didn't know anything about the Franklin Simon deal, except that I was against it, but it was arranged by my lawyer. I would not have permitted the use of advertising captions. They are selling, or have on sale, books of mine at the store, and I thought this was not a bad idea for a nation steeped in morbid plays and "Deer Park" and wife stabbing and decadence in general.

I have fought off the commercialization of this town for many years, and I could have made a million dollars on the side or under the counter. I am the only person in the world, I think, that ever went on the Jack Paar Show and refused to take money for it. I once returned a $10,000 check to Sam Goldwyn because my agent out there had slipped one over on the old boy, and I could have kept the check technically. Louella Parsons printed this story.

Once you get into the theatre, now the second most venal area, next to television, of our rigged and meretricious civilization, the so-called tie-ups run into the thousands. My wife and I turn down hundreds, but we can't handle everything. I wanted to go into my play for nothing, but Equity wouldn't let me. I doubt that I shall ever get back into the theatre again.

You can tell people that they are using an old drawing of mine of a little girl saying to her parents, "I was elected the biggest heel in school." Tell them that the new caption is now, "Guess who I saw at Franklin Simon's today. I'll kiss your ass if it wasn't Santa Claus." For this I will get $850,000, or enough to live on in London and Paris the rest of my life. I am, as you can see, sick and fed up.

As ever,

*Miss Peggy Wood, 277 Park Avenue,*
*New York 17, N. Y.*


*Had Thurber's last year been 1960, he would have ended life on a high note. In that year, his were the featured remarks at the dedication of Denney Hall, a triumphant farewell to O.S.U. That September he realized his dream of a lifetime by appearing on the Broadway stage in his revue, which earned him the Tony Award. His twenty-fourth book was at the publisher's and two of his final casuals appeared in the* New Yorker. *The new year, however, became one of disappointment, anger, and anxiety for Thurber. Four months in England spent trying to produce* A Thurber Carnival *ended in frustration. It was assumed that this disappointment was contributing to the eccentricities and paranoia increasingly evident in Thurber's actions and letters. Nobody realized that a brain condition that would lead to a fatal, massive stroke had been affecting his behavior for several months.*


## To Elliott Nugent

*West Cornwall, Conn.*
*January 3, 1961*

Dear Elliott,

Helen and I, who keep thinking of you, as always, were house-bound and even bedridden for more than two weeks when we came up here after the CARNIVAL closed. I realize that eighty-eight straight performances, the last thirty-two with a throat virus, were considerably harder on me than my two appearances with you and Bertha Holtkamp in that Arnold Bennett one-act play in which I played your uncle. "It's my infernal generosity!" was one of my lines. . . .

Thanks for sending me the Housman poem. He never wrote a line that wasn't moving or tinged with sorrow and I remember how we put him in "The Male Animal" along with Hodgson's "The Bell" and the lines you got from whoever wrote "And Love Has Turned to Kindliness." . . .

We like to think of you up there safe from the highways of the air and the highways of earth, which are taking lives with a fly swatter. I have had to pull out of my deepest depression, real *Angst,* at least the worst since 1941 when I went into a combination tailspin and nosedive after my fifth eye operation in eight months. Old Psychic Trauma dogged my step for months but I fought my way out of it, to the amazement of several psychologists who admired the way I got over, or around, a castration complex without help from anybody except myself. We all have to keep pitching for the angels against the demons.

> Our heaven lies so near our hell
> That almost any night
> The angels singing there look down
> And watch the demons fight.

I now have a new line to take the place of "It's later than you think." I have changed it to "It is lighter than you think." . . .

As ever,

Jim

*West Cornwall, Conn.*
*January 19, 1961*

Dear Elliott,

We are leaving for England tomorrow and taking your novel along with us to read on the way over. In the last few days we have been busy every minute getting ready for the trip. I will have to rewrite some of the sketches to make them suitable for English audiences, but this will not be too hard. I want an Englishman to play the part of the Englishman in "Macbeth" and also the inhabitant of the lovely island in "Casuals of the Keys" and, naturally, Mr. Pritchard-Mitford, the doctor flown over from London in "Walter Mitty."

I have great expectations for "Of Cheat and Charmer" but I shall probably be severe about four-letter words and what publishers call "frankly sexual scenes." I belong to the unhappy, diminishing company of writers who deplores the fact that we have made love a four-letter word in this country. The decline of the drama and the novel into the lower corridors of bestiality is a sign of our depleted culture and we ought to all help to pull literature and the arts out of the muck and mire. Everybody knows about sex now and it does have, believe it or not, romantic aspects. I am planning a play or novel to be called "The Last Romantic" but I hope I do not become the only survivor of a lost lyrical world. And let us remember what Percy Hammond said, "Just because a thing happened is no reason it's true."

. . . you have our love and best wishes to count on, as always.

Jim

*Mr. Elliott Nugent, Box 2070,*
*Hartford 2, Connecticut*

## To Ernest Hemingway

*News of Hemingway's failing grip on health and sanity led Thurber to write a letter intended to cheer him up. Helen persuaded him not to send it.*

*January 11, 1961*

Dear Ernest:

This is what the gals call a chatty letter intended to cheer, and not to be answered until you and I meet at Tim Costello's—one, ten or twenty years from now, and the sooner the better. . . .

This has been the damnest November and December for friends of mine, and for me, too, in my memory. Everyone of us, though, began to pick up again during the first week of January. I have been doing some research about the cycle of ailments and moods in the human being, and have found out that the medical men, as well as psychiatrists have become aware of seasonal phases of the body and the mind. It is now known that stomach ulcers increase greatly in November and, as for the mind, "the winter of our discontent" just scratches the melancholy surface. I believe that all of us, especially the men, are manic-depressives, but only a small percentage are malignant ones. My friend, Elliott Nugent, was hard hit by his cycle this November, but he is putting up a good fight. He used to get hit worse in March, which rates second among the bad months.

A few years ago I wrote Ross's Boston doctor, Sarah Jordan, about the cyclical nature of Man and said that I believed that it also affected ability and skill, but that each person had his own time-table. I suggested that there are periods when surgeons should not be allowed to operate. She wrote back that the psychiatrists agreed with me, but the surgeons did not. I never write like an angel, but I have recurrent phases when I write like a charwoman. . . .

In 1951 I had a medical examination for insurance at the New Yorker. A few days later I met my insurance agent on the street. He approached me shaking his head and said "you have sugar in your urine and a murmur in your heart." "That's not a diagnosis", I said, "that's a song cue." . . .

. . . Let's have some drinks together on New Year's Eve, 1980. Your luck, she is always with you, and I know you are not jealous that I share her with you.

One final anecdote about the docs. My appendix ruptured at six A M in November, 1944 and I wasn't operated on until nine o'clock that night. . . . When after three weeks, I got out of bed and dressed and went home, old Dr. Bennett said "We thought you were gone. How do you account your putting on your clothes and leaving here?" "I always dress before I go out into the street," I told him, "I am romantic".

The other night I dreamed that you and I were walking toward a sunset and suddenly the sun began to rise. Reminds me of a favorite book of mine. But, then I had the same dream about two other men, when they were down, Carl Sandburg and Robert Frost. Carl was eighty-three on January 6 and Frost is even older. God bless you and keep you. I'll see you in 1980.

As always,
James Thurber

## To Hugh Wheldon

*1st February, 1961*

*Hugh Wheldon Esq., Editor, MONITOR*
*Programme, The British Broadcasting Corporation,*
*Television Studios, Lime Grove, London, W.12.*

Dear Mr. Wheldon,

In my first five days in London I was interviewed thirteen times, by Television, Radio and the Press, and I no longer have the strength or time for further interviews or appearances.

I begin casting and redrafting my play for London tomorrow, and it will take all my time for the next six weeks or two months. Moreover, there is no such thing any more as exclusivity. I am writing an article about what Television and Radio have done to the old-fashioned hour and minute. Five minutes of one's time now means half-an-hour, and half-an-hour means all afternoon. Three years ago, Alistair Cooke came to interview me one afternoon for OMNIBUS at my home in Connecticut, and he and his crew stayed for three days. One or two of them may still be around the house somewhere. They are all charming men, but almost completely undetachable.

Thanks for asking me anyway.

Sincerely yours,

James Thurber

## TO GERALD McKNIGHT

*At: The Stafford Hotel,*
*St. James's Place, London, S.W.1.*
*13th February, 1961*

*Gerald McKnight Esq., Sunday Dispatch,*
*Editorial Department,*
*Northcliffe House, London, E.C.4.*

Dear Mr. McKnight,

I was wrongly quoted by that part of the Press which reported, upon my arrival in England, that I was seeking to escape from the rat race in New York. It is not a rat race, but a man race, both in New York and in London. Rats are not aggressively competitive, like human beings, and the only time they race is when they abandon a sinking ship, operated by men.

I wrote an article not long ago called "The Trouble with Man is Man," in which I pointed out that we blame too much on the so-called lower animals, calling one another chicken-livered and pig-headed, attributing aerial combat to canines, in the phrase "dog fight", and saying that a man has gone to the dogs when he has actually gone to a place where there are no dogs. I regret that the French poodle and the porpoise are not able to write a treatise on Man revealing our faults and failures in the human terms they deserve. To return to those rats for a moment, it was Conrad's Lord Jim who abandoned the famous ship that later sailed safely into harbour with all the rats still aboard.

I shall forever cherish the warm reception that I am lucky enough to receive every time I visit England, and it is the fault of no individual person that I am so overwhelmed by interviews that I have had no time at all for my own writing. But all this will quiet down in time, and I shall be able to enjoy, once again, the song of the blackbird in Green Park, the sound of band music in the Summertime, and the chimes and bells now temporarily drowned out by the voices of people.

I keep pointing out that we have gone into an oral culture, and that the very existence of the printed word is threatened, for in all the babble and bedlam the printed word now lives at the corner of Dread and Jeopardy, near Vicious Circle. It seems to me that too many people now carry sound recorders around with them as they used to carry books. The human voice and the spoken word have their great merit and value, but these do not lie in the ad lib, the offhand, the unstudied phrase. A few playwrights now actually dictate dialogue directly to the actors on stage, without the benefit of pen or paper, thought or contemplation. We also have the New Comedians, who make up their lines on stage as they go along, so that the gracious quality of form is being lost in a flounder of length and repetition. I should hate to live long enough to see the babble box and the psychiatrist's couch replace the typewriter and the author's study chair. The human tongue is now so often ahead of thought, that the mind must be surprised by the words that issue from the lips.

Nearly a quarter of a century ago in London, Alexander Korda, who had wanted me to write dialogue for some American characters in a proposed motion picture, asked me, "If I turned to you on the set and asked you for a new line, how long would it take you to give it to me?"

"Anywhere from three hours to three days," I told him, "depending on how long it took me to select the words and shape the sentence to my satisfaction."

Nothing ever came of that projected cinema. Mr. Korda and I, I am happy to say, ended in complete agreement about the nature of composition in a world of babble, bicker, and backfire. . . .

      Cordially yours,
      James Thurber

## TO CHARLES MCDOWELL

*In Thurber's "Bateman Comes Home" he writes: "He was . . . watching the moon come up lazily out of the old cemetery in which nine of his daughters were lying, only two of whom were dead." An English professor wondered if the sentence could be made funnier by dropping the "only."*

*At: The Stafford Hotel,*
*St. James's Place, London, S.W.1.*
*17th February, 1961*

Mr. Charles McDowell Jr.,
Richmond Times-Dispatch,
Richmond, VIRGINIA, U.S.A.

Dear Mr. McDowell,

I think your English professor should get his mind off that "only," and I could suggest a great many other things, of no importance whatever for him to worry about, such as the famous rhyming of "pearl" and "alcohol," and Housman's "Fifty years is little room."

I am working on a piece that will take up, among other trivia, Henley's line "one or two women, God bless them, have loved me," to show how it would have worried Harold Ross. Should it not be "one or two women, God bless her and them, has and have loved me"?

Not long ago the New Yorker objected to my leaving out the word "that" in some such sentence as, "He told her he loved her." I am now engaged on a series of 25 rules of my own for writing, called "The Theory and Practice of Criticising the Editing of New Yorker Articles." In it I say this, "I woke up this morning and decided that that 'that' that worries us so much should be forgotten."

Your professor friend not only believes in ball-bat impact in humor, but would sacrifice rhythm to obtain it. I would rather lose my right hand than take "only" out of that line. Let us suppose, Professor, that a neighbor has said to old Nate Birge, "You got nine daughters lyin' out there dead, ain't you, Nate?"

Nate (angrily), "Only two of 'em are dead, goddam it, only two of 'em are dead."

I have not tried to write the above dialogue precisely as it should be written. . . .

I hope your professor friend would not take a single word out of the great Southern phrase "little bitty" or "those little old boys."

All best wishes,

Cordially yours,

James Thurber

P.S. If I had all year, or even all day, I would go into this even more deeply for the good professor, dealing with the differences between the written and the spoken word, the printed page and the speaking stage, and on and on. If I were, for instance, to tell the story of Nate Birge and his daughters to an audience of listeners, not of readers, I should certainly say, "He watched the moon rise over the cemetery in which nine of his daughters were lying . . . two of whom were dead."

By golly, the University of California in its "extension area" at San Diego has just started a course in Thurber, numbered X144E. Hot dog! Maybe our professor, whom I shall always think of as "the only one," might go out there and engage in wordicuffs with whoever is teaching that course.

## To Goodridge MacDonald

*At: The Stafford Hotel,*
*St. James's Place, London, S.W.1.*
*20th February, 1961*

*Mr. Goodridge MacDonald, 17 Marloes Road,*
*London, W.8.*

Dear Mr. MacDonald,

Not long ago I announced (I don't mean proclaimed, but just said) that a writer should participate actively in the life of his time, but I now believe that the author cannot exist outside an ivory tower, because journalists, televisionists, and radiotics will not give him a moment's peace if he appears in public. As John Hersey recently said, "It is not what a writer says but what he writes that counts," and long ago Hemingway said "It is the job of the writer to write."

I say all this to the scores of interviewers who plague me, and they invariably answer that it is their job to interview authors. I have been able to accomplish nothing at all in London for nearly a month, because of the ringing telephone, the knock on the door, the lurking and prowling stranger with the babble box, or sound recorder. I have been an interviewer myself since 1913, and for eleven months, in the Nineteen Twenties, I ran a half-page in the Columbus Ohio Sunday Dispatch, much of it dealing with books and authors. I reviewed the books but did not plague the authors. I have interviewed General Pershing, Jack Johnson, the Negro pugilist, Eddie Rickenbacker, famous ace of the First World War, Huey Long, Thomas Elva Edison, Henry Ford, and a hundred others, but I did avoid the literary people. In 1927, however, The New York Evening Post sent me out to interview Ford Madox Ford. All I remember is that he had never heard of Scott Fitzgerald and was shocked by the high divorce rate in the United States.

Mrs. Thurber and I are fleeing from London to hide in the country for two weeks, and not even Sherlock Holmes could find us.

Sincerely yours,
James Thurber

## To Jap Gude

*At: The Stafford Hotel,*
*St. James's Place, London, S.W.1.*
*25th February 1961*

*J.G. Gude Esq., Messrs. Stix & Gude,*
*30 Rockefeller Plaza, New York City, U.S.A.*

Dear Jap,

I am not going to go into the Situation at length, because it makes about as much sense as my brother William did the day my grandfather asked him to bring him a blank, and William brought him a blanket. After a couple of meaningless auditions, things just came to a dead stop. Then Meredith and I had an all-afternoon session in my hotel room with Albery and Ann Jenkins. This went around in circles, but everybody was pleasant about it, and there were no angry words, only confusion. It was a little like a summit conference in Wonderland, and I expected the March Hare and the Mad Hatter to show up any minute. (The Sane Hatter, by the way, is Harry Truman. I wish he had been here.)

Meredith is out of it for good, to name one of the few facts that emerged, and he went back to New York by way of Ireland, where he visited John

Huston for a few days. We got a rather stiff letter from Haila the other day, just another document in the Confusion. Albery says the play cannot be cast until May, but none of us knew that in advance, but everybody said that everybody else knew everything in advance. The way I feel about it now is simple, and I share this opinion with Meredith. We believe that we have put all the time we can on "Carnival". As you know, art is long and time is fleeting, and I have many things to do. If the play does get on here, with English cast and director, I will help out to the best of my ability, but not at the cost of my health or of all my spare time, and I do not believe it would be advisable for me to go into the show in London. After all, aging blind men have their limits of endurance.

For the first time in my life I have begun taking Miltown, three a day, and I feel comparatively calm most of the time. We are both pretty well worn down, however, and so we are going to rest up for two or three weeks at an inn in the country, where my secretary will come in as she does here in London. Our mail will be forwarded by the Stafford.

I have had eighteen interviews, and two final ones last Friday, one of them with a blind Australian newspaper reporter who appeared with his secretary, and the other with a C.B.S. representative with a recorder. As we say in the theatre, I have been over-exposed.

I cannot see that Helen and I have been at fault in this whole business in any way. We have merely been puzzled and confused and considerably harried by it all. As I said during the conference here, I understand most writers, some editors, and a few publishers, but I have never had the vaguest idea what anybody in the theatre is trying to say. I speak English, American, and some French, but I cannot talk Theatre or understand it. They managed to put on "Carnival" in Sweden without any help from Meredith or from me, and, as you know, it is a big success there, the last we heard.

Last night we relaxed a little by going to dinner at the Nunnally Johnsons with Melvin Frank and his wife. Nunnally thinks this is a good time to cast a play in London. Nobody thinks the same thing about anything in the theatre. If you ever find out what it's all about, I wish you would let us know.

There is one parallel in ancient history. When Caesar crossed the Rubicon he said "The die is cast." When this got back to Rome, his wife said, to a reporter, "All I know is that he is shooting dice with a woman named Ruby Kahn." She didn't hear very well, anyway, and it is my opinion that she always thought Hannibal was a girl named Annabel. But then, as someone said to me at the conference, "Why do you have a Japanese agent in New York?"

"Because he is a Gude man," I replied.

Albery, by the way, pronounces Haila's name as if it were Hyla.

Well, that brings it up to date, old boy. We both send our love to you and Helen and the others.

As ever,

Jim

## TO ROGER ANGELL

*At: The Stafford Hotel,*
*St. James's Place, London, S.W.1.*
*29th February, 1961*

*Mr. Roger Angell, The New Yorker,*
*25 West 43rd Street, New York City 36, U.S.A.*

Dear Roger,

We just heard this morning from Jap Gude about your mother, and it upset both of us terribly. Jap is scarcely a medical authority, and we must know, privately and confidentially, of course, just what the condition is. . . .

I was greatly concerned about Katharine the last time I talked to her on the phone, because she suddenly began talking about "The Years With Ross" in a strange, and, it seemed to me, almost obsessive way. I keep remembering, with my damned total recall, one thing she said: "We like the old Thurber but not the new Thurber who wrote the Ross book, because you put so many things into it we didn't like. I think maybe we should all get together about it."

As you must know, we have been all over this ground, beginning as long ago as early 1957, when I first wrote the Whites that I was going to write pieces about Ross. Since then there have been letters from both of them, several phone talks, and one or two actual brief meetings, but in all of this Andy had been much the least agreeable. I think of that book as gathering dust on the shelf of my mind, and it dismayed me to realise that your mother was still so terribly upset. When Helen got home, after Katharine's phone call to me, she found me pacing the floor and then she wrote Katharine a letter that she now regrets. I had told Shawn, just before leaving New York, that I was worried about Katharine and Andy, and felt that they had had too much of The New Yorker for their own good. I think Helen had a fine idea, a kind of therapy, when she suggested in her letter that they should write their own memoirs of Ross and The New Yorker. As you know, this is often catharsis, and I have been recently writing about my own mind for the same purpose, for I have been desperately depressed, even despondent, at intervals during the past two years. I began taking Miltown three weeks ago, the first tranquilizers of my life. . . .

I think maybe [Clifton] Fadiman has the right idea. He never holds one job more than ten years. The Whites and I have been with The New Yorker more than thirty-four years, and that is much too long: makes one stir crazy in a curious way. He becomes lonely in a group of new people in an office, and begins seeing ghosts, imagining things, and building up complexes in his mind.

I go into this at length, Roger, because I feel I must, just for you. Five years ago in New York and then in London, Katharine suddenly began crying, first when having lunch with Andy and me at the Algonquin, and then when the four of us were having dinner at the Hotel Stafford here in London. Andy asked her, in astonishment, at the Stafford, what was the matter. At the Algonquin she had suddenly said to me, after I had been interviewed by Gibney for the Newsweek anniversary tribute to The New Yorker, "You see, Gus Lobrano is one of Andy's oldest friends." I didn't know then, and still don't know for sure, what she meant, but I think it was perhaps the beginning of her deep brooding about all of us, especially the three of us who began working on The New Yorker such a long, long time ago. I came to London this time to break away from a pattern of despair and from a deep feeling that we were all in a dangerous rut of thinking and worrying. But I was more worried about Andy and the Ross book than anybody else, and two things he said in letters distressed me terribly. One of them was, "I drifted away from your pieces in The Atlantic when you got into sex and money." The other was, "From reports I hear of explosions high above 43rd Street, I don't think I'm going to like your piece on editing either." Then there had been the incident, at the Algonquin, when Helen started to read him a piece I felt sure he would enjoy, the one I called "Mencken and Nathan and Ross." I told the absolutely true incident about Ross's and Mencken's conversation about Willa Cather. Andy suddenly stood up and said, "I hope it's true." That truly disturbed me greatly, because Andy knows my memory for detail, my total recall of conversation, and I almost sent him a sentence that Fadiman wrote about me a few months ago in Holiday, "In more than thirty years of writing he has never written a hasty or dishonest sentence." I had been waking up at nights for a long time, worrying about this whole complex that involves the three of us about Ross.

I have figured out that one of the basic problems, and causes, was the unfortunate fact that before Andy and Katharine were married, I was the confidante of both of them and of Ernest [Angell] too, having once sat up almost all night with him discussing the situation. Then Katharine moved into the front room of my apartment on 11th Street, when Andy lived on 12th Street, and they would meet in her half of the apartment, which I had divided into two, both of us managing to share the same bathroom without embarrassment. But I had to meet my own girl outside my own home, you might say, and the agonies of all of us were considerable. Andy, as you may or may not know, kept blowing hot and cold, and running away and coming back, and running away again and then coming back once more. I went with them several times to Sneedon's Landing and thus tried to juggle three persons at the same time in a genuinely sincere effort to straighten out a deep emotional tangle. At one time, before the marriage, I stayed two weeks alone at Sneedon's with Josephine, the cook, a female Scottie of mine, and her seven pups. During this interlude I once heard Ross say over the phone in his office, "All I know is that Thurber is living with Mrs. Angell at Sneedon's Landing." I was sharp and gruff in straightening him out about that, but made the mistake, I see now, of telling Katharine about it, and I think it worried her and still does. . . .

The New Yorker people have always been, as I told Andy, too secretive about everything, and he has especially stored up a lot inside himself that he ought to bring out. I now think that his fear of eating clams, his occasional certainty that there are clams in something he ate which never contained clams, might be a kind of mental symbolism. . . .

Persons who have been thrown too closely together over a long period of time are inclined to cover up, to bury deeply, things they should discuss freely, and I happen to know that symptoms like Katharine's are occasionally the result of this kind of interior conflict. I kept telling Andy and Katharine in letters that I did not intend to give up my love for them or our friendship, which more and more seemed threatened. Right now, I feel mentally immobilised about it all and scarcely know what to write them, if anything, at the moment. I determined long ago not to let the past invade and occupy the present, and I have had to go sometimes to heroic measures in order to pull out of what might have been grave psycho-somatic problems of my own. That is the main reason I decided to go into "A Thurber Carnival" and it operated to restore a very shaky balance. You once said to me on the phone, "All of us are tortured," and that is one reason I feel free, and obligated, to write all this to you. I know you will understand it, and know you ought to be aware of it. Please advise me what you think I can do.

I firmly believe that the breaking up of friendships, like the breaking up of marriages, is a growing and darkening phenomenon of the awful times we live in, whose effects are shown in almost every morbid play that comes to the stage in New York and in London. In the rather long piece I now keep working at, tentatively called "Autobiography of a Mind," I discussed, briefly, the awful but unmistakable tendency of writers to break off friendships in anger and despond. Among the famous pairs who were thus smashed up are Dickens and Thackeray, Stephenson and Henley, Henry James and H.G. Wells, Lord Bertrand Russell and D.H. Lawrence, Gilbert and Sullivan, Kaufman and Connelly (off and on), Ross and Woollcott, O'Hara and myself (to name just one of O'Hara's breaks), Robert Coates and me, Bill Maxwell and me, Benchley and Don Stewart (again off and on), and any number of others. One of Henley's poems begins, "What is it ends with friends?" . . .

> As ever,
> James Thurber

&a. &a. &a.

> *At: The Stafford Hotel,*
> *St. James's Place, London, S.W.1.*
> *13th March, 1961*

*Mr. Roger Angell, The New Yorker,*
*No. 25 West 43rd Street, New York, U.S.A.*

Dear Roger,

Ever since Ross and Gus died, the magazine has become more and more like a university English department, run by lecturers and instructors, rather than a publication conducted by editors. This is natural enough, I suppose, since Ross and Gus were editors and not writers, and you boys are writers, novelists, and even critics. . . .

The New New Yorker Frontier began disturbing me long ago, or what seems long ago, although it was only a few years. As you may know, two-thirds of what I send you is rejected, whereas a rejection in the old days was rare, and once, when I got two manuscripts back at the same time—both of them stuffed in my pigeonhole mailbox at the office—I broke into the Art meeting, then going on, and bawled the holy bejesus out of Ross, your mother, and the Magazine in general. In my calmer years (helped along by two Miltowns a day) I have given up storming at editors, critics, or even writers. . . .

. . . Only a lecturer or instructor, which I do not need at my age, would dissect that small piece I sent you in the way in which you boys have dissected it. It amounts, in fact, to your challenging my experience, my understanding, and my viewpoint as developed over a period of many years of writing. . . .

I shall still send an occasional piece to The New Yorker, even though one of us has outgrown the other, but my experiences since 1957 have warned me that there is not much chance of acceptance of anything of mine that is unusual or different, for to quote Shawn, The New Yorker looks for the "characteristic" in what I write, and what I intend to write in the years that are left is not going to be characteristic of what I have written in the past. I will not be set back in a pigeonhole of the past on behalf of any frame or policy of sameness and conformity. A nightmare is, by its very nature, exclusive of all the shadings of light and dark on any given subject. You have a perfect right to maintain the magazine as you see fit, but I shall never attempt to adjust myself to what I think is wrong. . . .

By the way, here are a couple of palindromes, and—as you and I know, Roger—they are not subject to change.

Diaper deliverer rereviled, repaid.

"The noon sex alert relaxes no one." H-T.

I suppose, in the first case, the stork had brought the seventh child to a house, but I doubt that the Herald-Tribune ever printed the other quote, or ever will.

> Cordially, as always,
> James Thurber

*West Cornwall, Connecticut*
*July 3, 1961*

Dear Roger:

Your copy tinkerers left out a wood-burning set, a chafing dish, an electrical coffee pot, and a Waring mixer.

It would not harm The New Yorker editors to read a piece I wrote for the Sunday TIMES in February of last year called "The Quality of Mirth," which dealt with the Fourth Strike or the delusion that nine objects are three times as funny as three. In the past, which seems more and more glorious, The New Yorker never touched a word of mine without consulting me, but I expect anything down there nowadays.

Here are several retroactive suggestions.

"All right, have it your way—you heard a seal, a St. Bernard, and a porpoise bark."

"I seem to have these six rabbits and a guinea pig."

"My wife had me arrested three times last month."

"My wife wants to spend Hallowe'en, Thanksgiving, Christmas, New Year's Eve, and Lincoln's birthday with her first husband."

I am afraid you are all now compulsive collaborators and that only psychiatry could cure it. Sad. Well, keep your chin, upper lip, and head high.

As ever, always, eternally,

James Thurber

*Mr. Roger Angell, The New Yorker,*
*25 West 43rd St., New York 36, N. Y.*


## To J. B. Boothroyd

*3rd March, 1961*

*J.B. Boothroyd Esq., Punch,*
*10 Bouverie Street, London, E.C.4.*


Dear Mr. Boothroyd,

Away back in 1938, John O'Hara, the American authority on instant sex, and I, were lucky enough to be guests of the Savage Club, but not at one of their Saturday night do's.

I regret very much that present plans will prevent me from attending the one you have been kind enough to invite me to have fun at, and I know it would be fun. Being only fifteen years younger than God, approximately, I've had to get away from the London pressures, and pleasures, and Providence seems to approve of this because of the excellent weather that has suddenly been shipped to us. I understand that the flowers are growing in Helsinki, and that little children are singing in the Congo. God may not be in His Heaven, and all is certainly not right with the world, but my friends, the hounds of Spring, have come to my rescue this March. Last March and the March before that were two of the worst months in my life, for one reason and another, and I am thinking of appealing to President Kennedy to eliminate the month altogether from the American calendar (and to remove November too).

One phrase in your kind and interesting letter brought vividly to my mind something Harold Ross said one day many years ago when he and I were asked to be guests of honour at Columbia University, and to receive a small dingbat called a Laughing Lion. This phrase was, "No speeches" and here's the way Ross put it to the man who rang him up, "I won't come if I have to speak, and Thurber won't come unless he can." This tendency of mine to speak at gatherings of congenial men is a by-product of Scotch and good companions. Last year I attended a pipe night at the Players' Club in New York and was called upon late in the evening, or early in the morning rather, as the last speaker. I followed a man only three years older than me, who said, in a bittersweet tone, "Well, at least at our age, most of us are over the hump." This struck me in a tender, or perhaps I should say in a tough spot, and I gave, in part, a brief set lecture on the short sex life of the American male as compared with that of the British male. I re-told a story that Clifton Fadiman had told me, after he had interviewed Lord Bertrand Russell one day when that great man was, I think, eighty-two years old. Fadiman had asked him what was his greatest pleasure in life at that age, and he looked astonished and said, quite simply but forcefully, "Screwing." When I told this story a few weeks ago to an Englishman in London, he said, "Why, Bertie knows how to say that word in seventeen different languages."

I also quoted, at the Players', a sentence written for the old American Mercury many years ago by Frank Harris, in a piece he had written for that magazine about Ruskin. His concluding line was, "Without the pleasures of love, life is but a poor inheritance." Incidentally, when I worked on the Riviera edition of the old Paris Tribune, in the Winter of 1925–26, I met old Harris many times and he told me that one of his secrets of longevity was that one hour after eating dinner every night, he cleared out his stomach with a stomach pump. He was certain, he told me, that he would live to be a hundred, and he might indeed have made it if he had given up that pump. I visited his home in Nice one evening, and he showed me the photographs, on one wall, of what he called "the three greatest American writers of all time." On the right was

Mark Twain, on the left Walt Whitman, and in the centre, somewhat elevated above the others, Frank Harris. . . .

I recently rejoined the Players' Club after having dropped my membership about twenty-five years ago, because I almost never got down there, and when I did, I became known as the unknown member. When I tried to buy a drink at the bar, for example, for other members, the bartender invariably said, "You'll have to let one of the members of the Club buy the drinks, sir." I told him that was fine with me, but the other members spoke up and insisted that I belonged to the Club too.

My favourite story about the Players', by the way, deals with a remark made years ago in the Billiard Room there by the late and wonderful Franklyn P. Adams. A man with whom he was playing billiards was not only drunk but profane and obscene, and Frank finally said to him, "This is a gentleman's club, sir, and he may be here any minute." The only other Club story I like as well as that goes back to what Groucho Marx said when he was asked to join a certain club in Hollywood, and rejected the invitation: "I wouldn't join a club that would have me for a member." . . .

My compliments and best wishes to all of you,
>Cordially yours,
>James Thurber

## To Mary Balliett

*20th March, 1961*

Dear Mary,

You can tell your class and Mr. McFarland that your letter is the kind that has worried American writers since the war, and still does worry us. . . .

What worries the most is a kind of spreading apathy among the school children today. I get some fifty to a hundred letters like this every year and they all sound the same. They all say "I know you are a busy man but—", and most of them show a complete lack of self-reliance, industry, enterprise and mental curiosity and no talent at all for research. The great majority of letters might be summed up in this composite question: "Will you please write for me what I think about your work?" . . .

In place of researchers and reporters and writers your generation seems to be producing collectors of autographs and photographs, and your children, I am afraid, may even ask authors for overcoat buttons or pencils they have used. So many letters tell me that if I send a photograph or answer them in any way whatever, the writers will get an "A." I don't believe that a collector of autographs and photographs should get an "A" in literature because of his or her skill in collecting. Please ask Mr. McFarland if it is true that there is a national conspiracy among teachers to keep us writers from getting anything else written, by having the school children of America take up all our time. If you were not the sister of a man you call "writer" I would not say all this, but just throw your letter away. I get between 2,000 and 3,000 letters a year, and every single person seems to believe I hear from nobody else but from him or her.

Good luck and best wishes.

Sincerely yours

James Thurber

*Miss Mary Balliett, 5161 Highview Drive,*
*Cincinnati 38, Ohio*


## TO MICHAEL FREEDLAND

*13th April, 1961*

Dear Mr. Freedland,

. . . A real writer does not decide to become a writer, any more than an unborn baby decides what its sex will be. You can call it God or nature or both, but there it is, and it is baffling the many psychologists now interested in isolating and examining the so called creative process. The happy man, in his profession, does what he was designed to do. Could you imagine becoming a dentist unless you were a born dentist? Have you ever met a writer who you think could ever learn to take out an appendix? I don't even know a writer that I would let take something out of my eye, I mean my artificial one. This is a big subject, too big for any individual person. I began writing when I was six and I expect to continue up to the last.

I have discovered one fact in my lifetime, it is that most people want to believe rather than to know, to take for granted rather than to find out. Thus the human being knows very little about Man and seems to have given up the subject in order to explore outer space, but he does not seem to be able to do that without the aid of the so-called lower animals. Now that man has got into outer space, he should be a bit dashed by the fact that the dog and even the mouse have beaten him to it.

Blindness doesn't increase the powers of the other senses, but simply focuses them in the same way that a music lover closes his eyes at a concert in order not to be disturbed by the flashing of the instruments in a symphony orchestra or by the strange looks of one of the players, or the gestures of the conductor.

My study of voices in a room, and I can tell a great deal from inflection and tone, isn't qualified or disturbed by expressions of the face or eyes, which are often deceptive. "A man may smile and smile and be a villain still," but he can't fool me because I can hear the villainy in his voice without seeing the smile on his lips.

The question I am most often asked is, "How did you happen to create a character like Walter Mitty?" I have been asked this question 934 times in the past ten years. I did not create Walter Mitty, he created himself. It is like asking me how I happened to think up my own species, masculine sex, and what in the world made me create the modern middle-aged male American . . .

There were Walter Mittys, under other names, in the writings of dozens of men ahead of my time, including Shakespeare. My own Walter Mitty, coming to life as he did at the very start of the decade of *Angst,* has often been quoted or alluded to as a symbol of our time. It was some fifteen years ago that the English medical journal, The Lancet, first began using the expression "Walter Mitty" syndrome. . . . All normal men are Walter Mittys, some of the time, but it is only in such psychopathic cases that their condition is alarming. All psychologists know that the normal man is possessed of more than one personality.

The unread books I would like to read are now stacked as high as my heart, and those I don't want to read form a pile higher than my head. I never list my favourite writers, because it would be too long a list. The American literary critic Clifton Fadiman recently got out a book called "A Lifelong Reading Plan," in which he lists books and authors of the West through modern times. In his preface he says, "Reading these books makes the interior life more meaningful and interesting, the way a love affair does." No writer should be too greatly influenced by other writers . . .

I believe that the administration of President Kennedy is having a salubrious effect upon thinking people of the world, and that Mr. Kennedy and the men around him are valuable to the world because they are not provincial, but internationally minded. The English and the Americans have always had an outstanding tendency to be only vaguely interested in each other's history and politics, even in each other's language. . . .

In conclusion, I am a pantheist, that is, a believer in Coleridge's line, "He prayeth best who loveth best all things both great and small." Man, the most self-destructive of all species, has always rated himself too high among God's other creatures. The birds can fly better than we can, the fish can swim better, the penguins and the polar bears have adjusted more easily to the climate, the kangaroo is funnier, the French poodle more amusing, and recent investigations have proved the bottle-nosed dolphin has a brain as complex as ours and maybe even more intelligent. That would not be such a feat, after all.

A standard French poodle I once owned had two litters of eleven pups each, the second one on the very day that the Dionne quintuplets were born. I swear that when she heard us discussing this human miracle she looked up from where she was lying in front of the fireplace with a gaze of surprise and disbelief. She thought we had said, not five, but fifteen. I straightened this out for her, and she sighed happily and went back to sleep.

Sincerely yours,
James Thurber

*Michael R. Freedland, Esq., 549 Kenton Road,*
*Kenton, Middlesex*

## TO THE RONALD WILLIAMSES

*At: The Stafford Hotel,*
*St. James's Place, London, S.W.1.*
*20th April, 1961*

*Mr. and Mrs. R. J. Williams, Socatean Ledges,*
*Somerset, Bermuda*

Dear Ronnie and Janey:

What has happened since that wild night when Ronnie phoned us to say that he was running away with Mary Trentham—or was it Ellerie Fricker, wife of Fricker, first frucker on the famous French fruit frigate?

We got a letter today from Mary, saying the usual cheerful but undetailed things, namely how much she depends on both of you and how well you both look, and how Ronnie is still playing his usual game of tennis, "making his balls dance on the very edge of the chalk line."

Ellerie, who is here in London, as you well know, has dropped us a note, but we haven't seen her yet. I remember that, at Felicity Hall, she seemed a bit spooky—but who isn't spooky now? Do you think that she would like a job haunting a yacht? London is haunted by a lot of spooks, but also by quite a few lively people whom we like, but we wish you were over here. The Gudes are arriving next month as part of a European trip. They are now in France, trying to avoid the bombs in men's rooms and other places. One of the papers here said that children are now making bombs out of weed-killer, the way we used to fly kites when we were young.

I was glad to hear that Trentham is not tottery, but it is pretty hard to tell whether one is or not in such a tottery century.

I have a new book of pieces coming out in a few days, and you will receive one. We miss all the Williamses, and certainly hope to see you before I begin to totter, which I have not yet done. It has been a long time since we all danced at the Bermudiana, fifty or sixty years ago. I now know only twelve people of my own generation who are still up and doing. The Stafford Hotel is a quiet and restful place, compared with the Algonquin, and we have concerts all day by a blackbird and by a male pigeon, whose viola needs tuning and at least one more string. Still, he does his best.

Love from us both to all of you,

As always,

Jim

## To the Jap Gudes

*At: The Hotel Stafford,*
*St. James's Place, London, S.W.1.*
*24th April, 1961*

Dear Gudes and dear God,

It must be better on some other planet! We are worried about you, and want to hear from you as soon as possible, assuring us that you are all right.

Three years ago, in Paris, when the home-made bomb first became popular, I used to walk out of the Hotel Continental with both hands held above my head, saying in French, "I am an American." The only time I was shot at was when somebody thought I had said, "I am a Moroccan."

We have gone through seven stages of hell here, the latest being acute homesickness, and we want to get the hell out of hell. There isn't going to be any Thurber Carnival, since we have not heard a word about auditions. The crazy man calls us once in a while and tells us to see a certain actor in a certain horrible farce. [Burgess] Meredith is now in Venus, and Haila [Stoddard] is on Mars, I suppose.

We want to sail back to New York in May, if possible. But we don't know whether you are going by ship or plane. Please let us know. I shall not go by plane until the day I set out for Canopus.

Angst has so deepened in the Western world that everybody I know has the acute glooms, including even Helen and me from time to time. Nunnally [Johnson] came over the other afternoon just to talk, not to drink more than one drink, because he was down too. A whole year without progress, he says of his own coming to a dead start here.

We are going out tomorrow night, to break the gloom, with a young Yale professor and his wife, the Beecher-Hogans. He is a friend of Dwight Macdonald. Everything happens to me!

Give my love to Lyons, the old birthplace of Henri Cochet, the ball boy of Lyons.

Love, love and love: and help, help, help.

As ever, or however long, whatever it is, lasts.
JAMES THURBER.


## To Milton Greenstein

*At: The Stafford Hotel,*
*St. James's Place, London, S.W.1.*
*26th April, 1961.*

*Mr. Milton Greenstein, The New Yorker,*
*25 West 43rd Street, New York City, U.S.A.*

Dear Milt,

I can only conclude from nearly a month's silence since I wrote Shawn, Angell, and Mr. and Mrs. White, that *The New Yorker* has finally decided, in the tradition begun by Ross, when he would disappear and let somebody else fire a man, that I am being shown the door. This does not depress me at all, for I share Gibbs's feeling during his last years that the Office had become so dreary and humorless that hell wouldn't have it. . . .

"The House in West 113th Street" is shaping up as one of my best pieces in recent years, and because of the background I have outlined here, I have the sense and integrity to realise that I should offer it first to the *New Yorker,* which I shall do, unless you advise me that they do not care to have it submitted. . . .

Since it has become obvious, although both of us have genuinely tried, that the *New Yorker* and I can no longer see eye to eye on anything at all, I have quite reasonably decided that this will be, if taken, the last piece I shall submit. At my age, I no longer have the strength of mind or body to engage in controversy and misunderstanding and recrimination and long silences with editors with whom I seem to share an almost chemical disagreement. They think that I am unreasonable and too outspoken, especially in my criticism of the magazine, inside and outside the Office, and I think that *they* are, in the great and sad tradition of *New Yorker* secrecy, anonymity, and easily hurt feelings.

My old relationship really died with Ross and Lobrano, with whom I worked perfectly, as you must know. But the end finally came with the publication of "The Years With Ross" and with Mrs. White's incurable antipathy to that book, an antipathy that White shares completely. I would not have changed a single word in that, or in anything else I write, to please a mouse or a pussycat or a human being. We all have our credos, and that is mine. I want you to know that I spent a great many hours and even days thinking this out, and I know it is the thing to do. Angell has tried to do his best about me, but there is that profound disparity of nature, viewpoint, and belief, and, moreover, he is, after all, Mrs. White's son, and she has said, on the phone, that I no longer regard myself as "a member of the family." The 34-year-old truth is that I never was a member of the family, because everything in me rebelled against our exclusivity and snobbishness and aloofness. Ross, God bless him, was able to take this, in spite of our 24 years of fighting, and Lobrano was wonderful as our go-between when we needed one. I have the ineradicable feeling that I am really not wanted any more, and patronised, whether intentionally or not, and the things I have submitted in recent years have sometimes been treated flippantly or coldly and, in my estimation, without humour.

You must also know that my stuff has often been slashed, changed, and even misunderstood, and the young editors have taken it upon themselves, whatever their intentions may have been, to criticize my knowledge, information, and understanding of life and people in the modern world.

These things happen in any life, and in any career, in one place that has lasted too long, and I am perfectly adjusted and resigned to the inevitable end. In view of all this, Milt, I anticipate with something like distaste any obituary about me that might eventually appear in the *New Yorker,* and I suggest to you that the best, and most honest tribute, when that day comes, would simply be the reprinting of "The Secret Life of Walter Mitty," with a brief note saying that I had requested it in my will. This would, of course, involve a radical breaking of precedent in a magazine that has taken on a rigorous form, but I suggest it anyway.

I shall always want to see you, Miss Terry, Miss Jonnson [New Yorker librarian], Pete de Vries, and McKelway, and a few others. I shall never write another piece about the *New Yorker,* the editors will be glad to know, but I shall always answer, honestly and fully, any questions about the *New Yorker* when I am asked . . . Ross once wrote me, "Your contribution to this magazine has been enormous," and it was things like that that kept my spirits up; but those men are gone for ever, the ones I could love, fight with, and make up with.

Anyway, my last years will be devoted mainly to books and plays.

We are sailing back soon, because the play is not going to get anywhere over here, and I have been left alone by both Meredith and Haila Stoddard and could not manage that way. We have been in London exactly three months today, and they have been, in large part, a period of hell and depression equalled only by the months of my five eye operations in 1940 and 1941.

I manage, though, to keep on going.

Helen and I send you our love and best wishes, as always. . . .

> Cordially yours,
> James Thurber

## TO BURGESS MEREDITH

*Donald Albury was a British play producer.*
*Kaja, Meredith's wife, was in Florida.*

> *At: The Stafford Hotel,*
> *St. James's Place, London, S.W.1.*
> *10th May, 1961*

Dear old Buzz,

Aren't you the chap that was on tour with the Thurber or Benchley play last year in the West? I have become a bit tottery during the years we have spent here, still going round and round the Albury bush. . . .

I am glad that Kaja got away to Florida for a rest, and I certainly do remember Hollywood down there. When I was there nearly thirty years ago, there was a bear cage with a mother bear and several cubs, and you could buy them a bottle of milk with a nipple and watch them drink it. One man slipped mama a pint of whisky when the management wasn't looking, and she got plenty crocked. "Bear with me," she kept saying, because she was beginning to see her mate, who had been gone for several months, to Hollywood, California, I think.

We are sailing back home on the Liberte on May 19th, just nine days from now, with the Gudes, who will arrive from France in a few days. We will be at the Algonquin on the night of May 25th, but go up to Cornwall the next day. I am glad to say that my new book has got some good reviews, and seems to be doing pretty well. . . .

Peter Ustinov dropped in for a drink one evening. At forty he is busy doing two plays, but so could I when I was forty, but I didn't want to show off that way. Let us know where you are, and if you are all alone too. We hope not. Love and salutes from us both to all of you.

As always,

## To the Peter De Vrieses

*At: The Stafford Hotel,*
*St. James's Place, London, S.W.1.*
*11th May, 1961*

*Mr. and Mrs. Peter De Vries, 170 Cross Highway,*
*Westport, Connecticut, U.S.A.*

Dear Katinka and Pete:

Having had enough trouble over here, without getting anywhere so far with the play, we are sailing for New York on the Liberte on May 19th, with Jap and Helen Gude.

It seems now that the play will not be put on in London until Autumn, because of casting problems. They are now trying to get Paul Ford, which puts us back where we were many months ago. I am anxious to get on to new work and not spend the rest of my life in that play.

We have both had bad recurring attacks of angst, the new world plague, which everybody seems to catch from the despondent zeitgeist. Almost every other letter we get from anywhere reveals a new victim of anxiety of the 1961 variety, which spreads like a virus. I have a theory of my own that it is spread by mass mental telepathy, and that this is what affects the stage and literature and everything else. My only solution is a high heart and a brave spirit, however hard these flags may be to flaunt in the stormy weather of today. I truly believe that a new mass frame of mind is the only answer. . . .

> As ever,

## TO THE NUNNALLY JOHNSONS

*West Cornwall, Connecticut*
*June 6, 1961*

Dear Nunnally & Dorris,

There ought to be a law against this city. It is far noisier than Hell, and has 144 fire alarms every day, which Hell doesn't have. We are at the Algonquin for a few days seeing doctors, some of them in pretty bad shape. This morning at 8 o'clock, all New York broke loose outside our window, with about twenty engines and drills going at once. Nobody knows what they are taking apart and there are those of us who believe it is being done under the direction of Charley MacArthur. The death of George Kaufman is another one of those reminders that only about one tenth of my generation is left in literature, entertainment and the arts. He wrote me several good letters while I was doing the Ross book and I was always promising myself to call on him but never did. . . .

The best story current here comes from Joe Krutch, author of "HUMAN NATURE AND THE HUMAN CONDITION" by way of Mark Van Doren. A young married couple have been trying to have a baby for a long time without any luck and went to see their doctor finally. He asked about their system and the husband said, "Every Wednesday and Saturday." The doctor told them to get away from that routine and simply follow impulse whenever and wherever. A year later the doctor met them on the street pushing a baby carriage. "I see you were finally successful," he said. The wife smiled and sighed and said, "Yes, but they'll never let us in Schrafft's again."

We miss both of you for as you damn well know, you were our mainstays in London. Why don't you come over to America and be our mainstays here? Lots of love and best wishes to both of you from both of us.

> As ever,

## To Mike Taylor

*West Cornwall, Connecticut*
*June 8, 1961*

Dear Mike Taylor,

I appreciate your remembering me in prayers, and my selection as a member of your Gallery. The trouble with footprints in the sands of time is that they are likely to disappear, and I believe that autographs in books or at the end of letters are likely to fade and the best a man can hope for, if he is a writer, is that some character he has created may outlive him. If Walter Mitty outlasts me, it wouldn't surprise me, and I hope he does.

You all have my blessings and best wishes and Walter's too.

        Cordially yours,
        James Thurber

*Mr. Mike Taylor, President, Associated Students,*
*Gonzaga Preparatory School,*
*1224 East Euclid Ave., Spokane 21, Washington*

## To E. B. White

*West Cornwall, Connecticut*
*June 19, 1961*

Dear Andy:

I get the darndest mail, and today there came a letter from a man in England who has a problem completely divorced from politics, nuclear worries, Kennedy's back, and the exchange of man for machines. He is worried because his son's rabbits do not like carrots! I can deal, a little, with the other problems listed above, but I have no idea what to do about rabbits that won't eat carrots. I also don't know what to do about a phoebe outside my window who keeps calling "Mabel!" instead of "Phoebe!" I hope that what is the matter with all of us human beings, in diet and in sex, is not spreading to the animal world.

It was good talking to both of you the other day. I am pulling out of the deepest Angst I have had since the summer of 1941, when I cracked up after my fifth eye operation. We had one hell of a time in London, but at least there was a blackbird singing outside my window every morning. I am sure he was singing to another blackbird, a female, and that he can still eat what he is supposed to eat.

We spent ten days at a country inn in England where a Cockney waiter said to me one morning, "I couldn't sleep last night because of howls 'ooting."

I wonder if the sex life of the bivalve has changed since Benchley died. Love and kisses to you and Katharine

As ever,

P.S. . . . If the United States had had you and G.B. Shaw working together, would the country have had the E.B.G.B's? If so, it would have been good for us.

## TO TED GARDINER

*West Cornwall, Connecticut*
*June 22, 1961*

Dear old Ted:

Try saying Barbara Corcoran backward, to get the Rover Boys off your mind, but don't start shouting it aloud around the house, because it sounds like a dog fight. I have been having a bad case of Angst, which Andy White used to call the colly wobbles, but is better described as the mumbling sagbadlies. . . .

. . . And if you need a line for a Western saloon gun fight, which I am sure you must, try this: "Ward, draw now!" Ward won draw.

. . . We had a lousy four months waiting for nothing to happen in London, and nothing did happen. The play could not be cast, said the producer, a man with a game leg who calls me "chum." What could I do but call him sport? We were pleased that some people, Americans and English, that we love, now live there or visit there. I thought of wiring you, "Having lousy time. Wish you were here."

Now that the movies have laid everybody to rest except Cagney, Hollywood is a ghost town. I know six guys my own age who are still alive, but a third of them are spooky. One guy, ten years younger, gives cocktail parties for ten imaginary people, with martinis or highballs beside as many chairs. One girl, who actually showed up, and, from the next room, saw him talking to all ten people in turn, turned and fled. She isn't too mentally sound, either, since she thinks she is married to Maurice Costello.

I have been named by the Birch Society in an anonymous thing they got out, and also in a Hollywood pamphlet, along with *Eddie Cantor, Gregory Peck,* and *Douglas Fairbanks!* (Help yourself to my italics.) I'm glad to say that several California papers rushed to my defense, one heading its editorial "Poor Jim." Did I tell you my favorite story, heard on the Jack Paar program? He reads a letter from a listener and answers it, like this.

Letter

My daughter leaps out at strangers from behind bushes and trees and cries, "Boo!" She will be 43 next Wednesday. What can I say to her?

Answer: Happy Birthday.

A woman ran into a psychiatrist's office, crying, "I think I'm a piece of pie!" "Then don't come to me," said the doctor. "I think I'm a fork."

Are there any Columbus people besides you and your family who are still sane? Helen and I love you all and wish we could see you all the time.

Old Me

## To Robert Coates

*West Cornwall, Connecticut*

*July 3, 1961*

Dear Bob:

Our generation is melting away like snow in the sun.

We did get a copy of "The View From Here" and it is smack on top of the 26 books we found waiting for us when we got to Cornwall. We seem to be pretty well dug in here for the summer and doubt if we can get away, but I hope we can see you both in New York later on.

After Ham Basso wrote "The View from Pompey's Head" I decided to write a novel about my return to Columbus and call it "The View from Pompous Ass."

Helen and I send our love and best wishes to you and Boo.

As ever,

## To Irene Cole

*West Cornwall, Connecticut*

*July 3, 1961*

Dear Miss Cole:

I swear I cannot see the faintest resemblance between your Mr. Buttered Wallet and my Walter Mitty. The Walter Mittys do not share their daydreams with anyone, and I wonder how you know about his.

Would you believe it—I get seven letters a day from women with some desperate problem. Along with yours came one from a Lady Clementine who has to have a drawing of my dog, and one from a New Jersey woman who wants me to bring my dachshund to call on her sister-in-law who has a slipped disk.

Your project about "a book" including only the "Secret Life of Walter Mitty" is a very dangerous venture and might ruin me. Even if you get out only one copy, which is all The New Yorker, my publishers, my agent, and lawyer would allow, unless it carried the exactly right copyright and credit line, which I could not give you from here, it would cause the story to fall into public domain and anybody could print it in a book without my permission or without any remuneration to me.

I would have to take this up with my lawyer at The New Yorker, and I haven't got time for that right now, since I am working hard and have 113 letters from other American women in a variety of predicaments. . . .

> Sincerely yours,
> James Thurber

*Miss Irene P. Cole, 107 Beach Lane,*
*Forest Brook Glen, Wilmington 4, Del.*


## To Laurette Pizer

> **West Cornwall, Connecticut**
> **July 18, 1961**

*Miss Laurette Pizer, 21 East 62nd Street,*
*New York 21, N. Y.*

Dear Miss Pizer:

I do not have any uncommitted book, because at my age I cannot go flapping around like a loose parrot that can't find its cage. Good luck and look out for the space capsules.

> Sincerely yours,
> James Thurber

## TO JANE WILLIAMS

*West Cornwall, Connecticut*
*August 26, 1961*

Dear Janey:

It was wonderful to hear your voice the other night, and next afternoon, because in spite of the tears, it was still you, one of the soundest and strongest human beings left on earth, in spite of all the children you have to deal with, including R.J.

We are planning to come down to Bermuda in October or November, to get a closeup view of the situation and see if we can do anything to restore the ruins of Brother Williams. Surely something must be done, at any cost, to get an able assistant for him, qualified to take over if Ronnie should be bitten by a snake or run away with some disturbed American dipsomaniac with a million dollars and a 1 to 10 chance of reaching Jamaica before she blows her top completely.

As time goes on in this disturbed hemisphere (the psychiatrists say disturbed when they mean unhinged) I get madder and madder at the childishness of the Americans and of those whose habits we have Americanized, like the once self-disciplined Lt. Williams of the Royal Canadian Navy. We not only never stop to think, we don't even think to stop, which is why 37,000 Americans are killed on the highways every year, and 19,000,000 accidents occur in homes annually, including the births of about 2,000,000 unwanted babies. It is quite common up here in these crazy years for a tall teenage boy to say to me, "Shake hands with my bride," and for her to say when I extend my hand, "Don't bweak my didie doll." . . .

More than thirty years ago Hendrik van Loon said to me, "You Americans always have to have from two to three pleasures going at once. You are the only people I know who mix sex and alcohol and then have to have a cigarette, and ask some people in for the rest of the night, or go to a movie and eat popcorn."

Why will we never learn that Euphoria is a mirage, and that the only way out of it is the Lonesome Road that leads through Jeopardy and ends up in the Wilderness of Despair.

Inner resources do not mean cocktails or brandy or highballs. A person has to face the fact that what has usually happened to him was himself. In what Fadiman calls the somnolent decades the chafing dish was regarded as more dangerous than the bottle (Welsh rarebit gave you bad dreams,) there was more fudgemaking than fuck, and tea was actually served at tea parties. A woman could go to the ladies' room without being thrown on her way out, by a strange, lurking obstetrician or major-general or waiter or little boy. . . .

. . . Why do we no longer get older and wiser, but only odder and wider?

As I write this I have not had a drink or a cigarette in two days, even though I have been through, and so has Helen, for more than seven months, the terror of the shade, the valley of the shadow, and the encircling gloom. That last phrase comes from the old hymn, "Lead, Kindly Light." We have replaced that with the new hymn, "Keep 'em Comin'."

Let us then be up and drinking, with a heart for any fight, still pursuing our old grudges, learn to hit, and scratch and bite.

We can never replace, and get anywhere by so doing, a famous old political battle cry, with "Now is the time for all goofy men to come to the aid of their country."

We are coming down in October, but not to drink and stay up all night. I want to get a play finished. Do not rise above the battle, but do rise above the bottle.

With love and kisses from us both

As ever,

Old Me

## To Fred Allen

*One of Thurber's favorite radio programs was Fred Allen's Sunday evening Town Hall Tonight. When Allen's widow, Portland, was collecting his letters for publication Thurber used the occasion to write a late farewell to Allen. In a few weeks Thurber's own life and letters would be suddenly stopped like—to use a Thurber phrase—"a clock in a thunderstorm."*

*August 20, 1961*

To Fred in Heaven:

I have just sent Portland the letters that you and I, old boy, exchanged a few years ago, years that seem to me in some ways yesterday, because the memory of you is still so vivid in my heart, and in some ways a hundred years ago, since any time at all without the sound of your voice or the sight of your words on paper is bound to seem a century in length. This will, of course, be called sentimental, and it is, but there is a sincerity of friendship between men that must have a touch of sentimentality to be true.

In 1957 I brought out a book called "Further Fables for Our Time," during the writing of which there you stood, one afternoon, silently reminding me of many things, including those unforgettable crows of yours who were scared so badly by the scarecrow that they brought back corn they had stolen two years before. . . .

Another of my favorite lines of yours that keeps coming back to me was when you said to the bald bass fiddler in the orchestra, "How much would you charge to haunt a house?" You still haunt my house, Fred, a benign, cheerful, happy, and inspiring ghost, and you always will until the day that I join you, Bob Benchley, Bill Fields, Fanny Brice, and the others whose humor and comedy helped to keep me going and still do. Humor and comedy are no longer what they used to be, Fred, when you were on earth with those others.

Make reservations for me up yonder, heah? God bless you

As ever,

# INDEX